HOW TO GROW NATIVE PLANTS
OF TEXAS AND THE SOUTHWEST

HOW TO GROW

Native Plants

OF TEXAS AND THE SOUTHWEST

REVISED AND UPDATED EDITION

BY

Jill Nokes

ILLUSTRATIONS BY

Kathryn Miller Brown

UNIVERSITY OF TEXAS PRESS

AUSTIN

Printed in the United States of America
First edition, 2001

Requests for permission to reproduce material from this work should be sent to Permissions, University of Texas Press, P.O. Box 7819, Austin, TX 78713-7819.

∞ The paper used in this book meets the minimum requirements of ANSI/NISO Z39.48-1992 (R1997) (Permanence of Paper).

LIBRARY OF CONGRESS CATALOGING-IN-PUBLICATION DATA

Nokes, Jill, 1951–
How to grow native plants of Texas and the Southwest / Jill Nokes ; illustrations by Kathryn Miller Brown.—New ed., 1st ed.
p. cm.
Includes bibliographical references (p.) and index.
ISBN 0-292-75574-0 (cloth : alk. paper)—ISBN 0-292-75573-2 (pbk. : alk. paper)
1. Native plant gardening—Texas. 2. Native plant gardening—Southwestern States. 3. Native plants for cultivation—Texas. 4. Native plants for cultivation—Southwestern States. I. Title.
SB439.24 .N65 2001
635.9'5176—dc21 00-044352

Dedicated to the Most Beautiful Women in the World

WREN *and* **CLAIRE NOKES**

Contents

List of Genera and Species *ix*

Preface to the New Edition *xxi*

Acknowledgments *xxvii*

Map of Texas *xxxiv*

I. *Introduction* *1*

II. *Gathering and Storing Seeds* *4*
Seed Provenance ~ When and Where to Collect ~ Guidelines for Judging Ripeness ~ Stock Plants ~ Collection Tools and Materials ~ Cleaning ~ Storage

III. *Seed Germination* *15*
The Germination Process ~ Seed Dormancy ~ Types of Dormancy and Pretreatment Methods ~ Hard Seed Coats and Scarification ~ General Guidelines for Acid Scarification ~ Sodium Hypochlorite Treatment ~ Hot Water Seed Scarification ~ Active Yeast Method ~ Early Collection of Hard-Seeded Species ~ Plants with Apparently Hard Seed Coats ~ Seed Coats with Chemical Inhibitors ~ Physiological Dormancy of the Inner Seed ~ Stratification ~ Length of Stratification Period ~ "Pulsing" ~ Double Dormancy and After-Ripening

IV. *Planting* *28*
Late Winter Planting in a Greenhouse ~ Outdoor Fall Planting ~ Spring Planting ~ Aeration Procedure for Seed

Germination ∾ Pregermination on Moist Paper ∾ Fall Planting in a Greenhouse or Cold Frame ∾ Cold Frames ∾ Containers ∾ Benefits of Air Pruning Roots ∾ Soil Mixes ∾ Beneficial Soil Microorganisms ∾ Indoor Sowing ∾ Seedling Diseases ∾ Field Sowing ∾ Transplanting Seedlings

V. *Vegetative Propagation* 37

Advantages of Cutting Propagation ∾ Some Drawbacks to Vegetative Propagation ∾ The Rooting Process ∾ How New Roots Are Produced ∾ Inherent Ability to Root ∾ Age of the Cutting: The Juvenility Factor ∾ Location of the Cut ∾ When to Take Cuttings ∾ Types of Cuttings ∾ Hardwood Stem Cuttings ∾ Rooting Deciduous Hardwood Cuttings ∾ Rooting Cuttings of Narrow-Leaved Evergreens ∾ Root Cuttings ∾ Semihardwood (or Greenwood) Cuttings ∾ Softwood Cuttings ∾ Selecting a Plant to Propagate from Cuttings ∾ Wounding ∾ Rooting Hormones ∾ Willow Rooting Substance ∾ Application of Rooting Hormones ∾ Preparing Quick-Dip Solutions ∾ The Proper Environment for Rooting a Cutting ∾ Containers ∾ Rooting Media ∾ Fungicides ∾ Controlling Water Loss ∾ Intermittent Misting Systems ∾ Hardening Off ∾ Transplanting the Cutting

VI. *Transplanting* 59

Time of Year ∾ Choosing the Plant ∾ Transplanting Tools and Procedures ∾ Preparing the Site

VII. *Propagation of Individual Species* 71

Plants listed alphabetically according to botanical name. Consult List of Genera and Species for page numbers of individual species.

Glossary 523

Bibliography 531

Index 537

List of Genera and Species

1. ***Acacia*** — **Acacia** *73*
  - *A. berlandieri* — Guajillo *76*
  - *A. constricta* — Whitethorn Acacia, Largancillo, Mescat Acacia *76*
  - *A. farnesiana* — Huisache *76*
  - *A. greggii* — Catclaw Acacia, Uña de Gato *77*
  - *A. hirta* — Fern Acacia *77*
  - *A. rigidula* — Black-brush Acacia, Chaparro Prieto *77*
  - *A. roemeriana* — Romer Acacia, Catclaw Acacia, Gatuño *77*
  - *A. schaffneri var. bravoensis* — Twisted Acacia, Huisachillo *77*
  - *A. wrightii* — Wright's Acacia, Catclaw, Uña de Gato *78*
2. ***Acer*** — **Maple** *79*
  - *A. barbatum* — Southern Sugar Maple *85*
  - *A. grandidentatum* — Big-toothed Maple *85*
  - *A. leucoderme* — Chalk Maple *86*
  - *A. rubrum var. drummondii* — Drummond Red Maple *86*
  - *A. rubrum var. trilobum* — Trident Red Maple *86*
  - *A. saccharum* — Sugar Maple *86*
3. ***Adelia vaseyi*** — **Vasey's Adelia** *88*
4. ***Aesculus*** — **Buckeye** *90*
  - *A. glabra var. arguta* — Texas Buckeye *93*
  - *A. pavia var. flavescens* — Scarlet Buckeye *93*
  - *A. pavia var. pavia* — Red Buckeye *93*
5. ***Agave*** — **Agave, Maguey** *94*
  - *A. americana* — Century Plant, Maguey *96*
  - *A. americana var. protoamericana* — Maguey *96*
  - *A. havardiana* — Havard Maguey *97*
  - *A. lechuguilla* — Lechuguilla *97*
  - *A. lophantha* — Big Lechuguilla *98*

A. scabra — Rough Maguey, Maguey Cenizo *98*

6. ***Alnus serrulata*** — **Smooth Alder** *99*

7. ***Aloysia*** — **Bee-brush** *101*

A. gratissima — Bee-brush, Jazminillo, White Brush *102*

A. macrostachya — Vara Dulce, Sweetbrush *103*

A. wrightii — Oreganillo *103*

8. ***Amelanchier*** — **Service-berry** *104*

A. arborea — Service-berry *105*

A. denticulata — Big Bend Service-berry *106*

A. utahensis — Utah Service-berry *106*

9. ***Amorpha*** — **False Indigo** *107*

A. fruticosa — False Indigo *108*

A. fruticosa var. angustifolia — False Indigo *109*

A. paniculata — Panicled Amorpha *109*

A. roemeriana — Texas Indigo Bush *109*

10. ***Ampelopsis*** — **Pepper-vine** *110*

A. arborea — Pepper-vine *111*

A. cordata — Heart-leaf Pepper-vine *111*

11. ***Amyris*** — **Torchwood, Limonaria** *112*

A. madrensis — Sierra Madre Torchwood, Limonaria *114*

A. texana — Texas Torchwood, Lantrisco, Chapotillo *114*

12. ***Anisacanthus*** — **Anisacanthus** *115*

A. linearis — Dwarf Anisacanthus *117*

A. puberulus — Pink Anisacanthus *117*

A. quadrifidus var. wrightii — Flame Acanthus, Orange Hummingbird-bush *117*

13. ***Aralia spinosa*** — **Devil's Walking-stick** *118*

14. ***Arbutus xalapensis*** — **Madrone** *120*

15. ***Asimina triloba*** — **Paw-paw** *124*

A. triloba — Paw-paw *126*

16. ***Atriplex*** — **Saltbush** *127*

A. acanthocarpa — Tubercled Saltbush *129*

A. canescens — Four-winged Saltbush *129*

A. confertifolia — Spiny Saltbush, Shadscale *129*

A. ovata — Oval-leaf Saltbush *130*

17. ***Baccharis neglecta*** — **False-willow** *131*

18. ***Bauhinia lunaroides*** — **Orchid-tree, Pata de Vaca, Pata de Cabra** *133*

19. ***Berberis*** — **Barberry, Mahonia** *136*
B. haematocarpa — Red Barberry *139*
B. repens — Creeping Barberry *139*
B. swayseii — Texas Mahonia *139*
B. trifoliolata — Agarita *139*
20. ***Betula nigra*** — **River Birch** *140*
21. ***Bignonia capreolata*** — **Cross-vine, Cola de Iguana** *142*
22. ***Bouchea*** — **Bouchea** *144*
B. linifolia — Groovestem Bouchea *145*
B. spathulata — Spoon-leaf Bouchea *145*
23. ***Buddleia*** — **Butterfly-bush** *146*
B. marrubifolia — Woolly Butterfly-bush *148*
B. racemosa — Wand Butterfly-bush *148*
B. scordioides — Escobilla Butterfly-bush *148*
B. sessilflora — Tepozán *148*
24. ***Bumelia lanuginosa*** — **Gum-elastic Tree** *149*
25. ***Caesalpinia mexicana*** — **Mexican Caesalpinia, Tabachín del Monte** *151*
26. ***Calliandra eriophylla*** — **Fairy Duster, False Mesquite** *153*
27. ***Callicarpa americana*** — American Beauty-berry *155*
28. ***Campsis radicans*** — **Trumpet-creeper, Monapesto** *158*
29. ***Capsicum annum*** — **Chile Pequín** *160*
30. ***Carpinus caroliniana*** — **Hornbeam, Lechillo** *162*
31. ***Carya*** — **Hickory, Pecan, Nogal, Nueces** *164*
C. aquatica — Water Hickory *166*
C. cordiformis — Bitternut Hickory *166*
C. illinoinensis — Pecan, Nogal, Nueces *166*
C. ovata — Shagbark Hickory *166*
C. tomentosa — Mockernut Hickory *166*
32. ***Cassia wislizenii*** — **Wislizeni Senna, Cassia, Palo Prieto, Pinacate** *167*
C. greggii — Gregg Senna *169*
C. lindheimeriana — Lindheimer's Senna *169*
C. roemeriana — Romer's Senna *169*
33. ***Castanea*** — **Chinquapin** *170*
C. alnifolia — Downy Chinquapin *171*
C. pumila — Chinquapin *171*
34. ***Castela erecta*** — **Chaparro Amargoso, Goatbush, Bisbirinda** *172*
35. ***Catalpa speciosa*** — **Catalpa** *174*
36. ***Ceanothus*** — **Ceanothus, Jersey-tea** *176*

C. americanus — Jersey-tea *178*
C. greggii — Desert Ceanothus *178*
C. herbaceus — Redroot *178*
C. fendleri — Fendler Ceanothus *178*
37. ***Celatrus scandens*** — **American Bittersweet** *179*
38. ***Celtis*** — **Sugarberry, Hackberry** *181*
C. laevigata — Sugarberry, Hackberry *182*
C. occidentalis — Hackberry *182*
C. pallida — Granjeno *183*
C. reticulata — Netleaf Hackberry, Palo Blanco *183*
C. tenuifolia — Dwarf Hackberry *183*
39. ***Cephalanthus occidentalis*** — **Button-bush** *184*
40. ***Ceratoides lanata*** — **Winterfat** *186*
41. ***Cercidium texanum*** — **Palo Verde, Retama China** *189*
42. ***Cercis*** — **Redbud** *192*
C. canadensis var. canadensis — Eastern Redbud *195*
C. canadensis var. mexicana — Mexican Redbud *195*
C. canadensis var. texensis — Texas Redbud *196*
43. ***Cercocarpus montanus var. argenteus*** — **Silver-leaf Mountain Mahogany** *197*
44. ***Chilopsis linearis*** — **Desert Willow, Flor de Mimbre** *200*
45. ***Chionanthus virginica*** — **Fringe-tree** *204*
46. ***Choisya dumosa*** — **Mexican Star-leaf Orange, Zorillo** *206*
47. ***Chrysactinia mexicana*** — **Damianita** *208*
48. ***Citharexylum berlandieri*** — **Fiddlewood, Negrito** *210*
49. ***Clematis*** — **Clematis, Virgin-bower** *212*
C. drummondii — Virgin-bower, Barba de Viejo *213*
C. pitcheri — Pitcher Clematis *213*
C. texensis — Scarlet or Texas Clematis *214*
50. ***Clethra alnifolia*** — **White Alder, Sweet Pepper-bush** *215*
51. ***Colubrina texensis*** — **Hog-plum, Guajalote** *217*
52. ***Condalia hookeri*** — **Brasil, Bluewood Condalia** *219*
53. ***Cordia boisseri*** — **Wild Olive, Anacahuita** *221*
54. ***Cornus*** — **Dogwood** *224*
C. drummondii — Rough-leaf Dogwood *227*
C. florida — Flowering Dogwood *227*
C. racemosa — Gray Dogwood *227*
55. ***Cotinus obovatus*** — **Smoke Tree** *228*
56. ***Coursetia axillaris*** — **Baby Bonnets, Coursetia** *232*
57. ***Cowania ericaefolia*** — **Heath Cliff-rose** *234*

58. ***Crataegus*** **Hawthorn** *236*
C. brachyacantha Blueberry Hawthorn *238*
C. crus-galli Cockspur Hawthorn *238*
C. marshallii Parsley Hawthorn *238*
C. opaca Mayhaw *238*
C. reverchonii Reverchon's Hawthorn *239*
C. spathulata Little-hip Hawthorn *239*
C. tracyi Mountain Hawthorn *239*
C. viburnifolia Viburnum Hawthorn *239*
59. ***Cupressus arizonica var. arizonica*** **Arizona Cypress** *240*
60. ***Cyrilla racemiflora*** **Leatherwood** *243*
61. ***Dalea*** **Dalea** *245*
D. bicolor var. argyraea Silver Dalea, Escobilla Cenizo *246*
D. formosa Feather Dalea, Limoncillo *247*
D. frutescens Black Dalea *247*
D. greggii Gregg's Dalea *247*
D. scoparia Broom Dalea *247*
62. ***Dasylirion*** **Sotol, Desert Spoon** *248*
D. leiophyllum Sotol *250*
D. texanum Texas Sotol *250*
D. wheeleri Desert Spoon *250*
63. ***Diospyros*** **Persimmon** *251*
D. texana Mexican Persimmon, Chapote Prieto *254*
D. virginiana Eastern Persimmon *254*
64. ***Ehretia anacua*** **Sand-paper Tree, Anacua, Knock-away Tree** *255*
65. ***Erythrina herbaceae*** **Coral-bean, Colorín** *258*
66. ***Esenbeckia runyonii*** **Limoncillo** *260*
67. ***Euonymus americanus*** **Strawberry Bush** *262*
68. ***Eupatorium havanense*** **Fragrant Mist Flower** *264*
69. ***Eysenhardtia texana*** **Texas Kidney-wood** *267*
70. ***Fagus grandiflora*** **American Beech** *270*
71. ***Fallugia paradoxa*** **Apache Plume** *272*
72. ***Fendlera rupicola*** **Cliff Fendler-bush** *275*
73. ***Forestiera*** **Desert Olive, Panalero** *277*
F. acuminata Swamp Privet, Texas Adelia *278*
F. angustifolia Narrow-leaf Forestiera, Panalero *279*
F. pubescens Texas Elbow-bush *279*
F. neomexicana New Mexican Forestiera *279*
F. reticulata Netleaf Forestiera *279*

74. ***Fouquiera splendens*** **Ocotillo** *280*
75. ***Fraxinus*** **Ash, Fresno** *282*
F. americana White Ash *283*
F. berlandieriana Mexican Ash, Fresno, Plumero *284*
F. caroliniana Water Ash, Carolina Ash *284*
F. cuspidata Fragrant Ash, Flowering Ash *284*
F. greggii Little-leaf Ash, Escobilla, Barreta de Cochino *285*
F. pensylvanica Green Ash *285*
F. texensis Texas Ash *285*
F. veluntina Velvet Ash, Fresno *285*
76. ***Garrya ovata* subsp. *lindheimeri*** **Mexican Silk-tassel** *286*
77. ***Gochnatia hypoleuca*** **Chomonque** *290*
78. ***Guaiacum angustifolium*** **Guayacan, Soap-bush** *292*
79. ***Halesia diptera*** **Two-winged Silverbell** *295*
80. ***Hamamelis virginiana*** **Witch-hazel** *297*
81. ***Hesperaloe parviflora*** **Coral Yucca** *300*
82. ***Hibiscus*** **Hibiscus** *302*
H. aculeatus Pineland Hibiscus *304*
H. cardiophyllus Heart-leaf Hibiscus, Tulipán del Monte *304*
H. coulteri Desert Rose Mallow *304*
H. dasycalyx Neches River Rose Mallow *305*
H. laevis Halberd-leaf Hibiscus *305*
83. ***Hypericum*** **St. John's Wort** *306*
H. densiflorum Dense St. John's Wort *307*
H. fasciculatum Sand-weed *307*
H. frondosum Golden St. John's Wort *308*
H. nudiflorum Naked St. John's Wort *308*
84. ***Ilex*** **Holly** *309*
I. ambigua Carolina Holly, Sand Holly *311*
I. coriaceae Bay-gall Bush, Ink-berry Holly *311*
I. decidua Possum-haw Holly *311*
I. opaca American Holly *312*
I. verticillata Common Winterberry *312*
I. vomitoria Yaupon Holly *312*
85. ***Itea virginica*** **Virginia Sweet-spire** *313*
86. ***Juglans*** **Walnut, Nogal** *315*
J. major Arizona Walnut, Nogal *316*
J. microcarpa Little-leaf Walnut *316*

J. nigra	Black Walnut *317*
87. ***Juniperus***	**Juniper** *318*
J. ashei	Ashe Juniper *320*
J. deppeana	Alligator Juniper *320*
J. flaccida	Weeping Juniper *321*
J. monosperma	One-seeded Juniper *321*
J. pinchotii	Red-berried Juniper *321*
J. silicicola	Southern Red-coat Juniper *321*
J. virginiana	Eastern Red Cedar *321*
88. ***Koeberlinia spinosa***	**Allthorn, Corona de Cristo Junco** *322*
89. ***Lantana horrida***	**Texas Lantana** *324*
90. ***Larrea tridentata***	**Creosote Bush, Gobernadora** *327*
91. ***Leitneria floridana***	**Corkwood** *330*
92. ***Leucaena retusa***	**Goldenball Leadtree, Guaje** *332*
93. ***Leucophyllum***	**Cenizo, Purple Sage** *335*
L. candidum	Violet Silver-leaf *339*
L. frutescens	Cenizo, Purple Sage, Texas Ranger *339*
L. minus	Big-Bend Silver-leaf *340*
94. ***Leucothoe racemosa***	**Sweetbells, Fetter-bush** *341*
95. ***Lindera benzoin***	**Spicebush** *343*
96. ***Liquidambar styraciflua***	**Sweetgum, Balsamo, Copalme** *345*
97. ***Liriodendron tulipfera***	**Tulip-tree** *347*
98. ***Lonicera***	**Honeysuckle** *349*
L. albiflora var. albiflora	White Bush Honeysuckle *350*
L. sempervirens	Coral or Evergreen Honeysuckle *351*
99. ***Lycium***	**Wolfberry, Desert-thorn, Cilindrillo** *352*
L. berlandieri var. berlandieri	Berlander Wolfberry, Tomatillo, Cilindrillo *353*
L. carolinianum var. quadrifidium	Carolina Wolfberry *353*
L. pallidum var. pallidum	Pallid Wolfberry *353*
100. ***Lyonia***	**Huckleberry** *354*
L. ligustrina	He-huckleberry *355*
L. mariana	Stagger-bush *355*
101. ***Magnolia***	**Magnolia** *356*
M. grandiflora	Southern Magnolia *358*
M. pyramidata	Pyramid Magnolia, Cucumber Tree *359*
M. virginiana	Sweetbay Magnolia *359*
102. ***Malpighia glabra***	**Barbados-cherry, Cereza, Huacacote** *360*

103. ***Malvaviscus arboreus var. drummondii*** **Turk's Cap, Manzanilla** *362*
104. ***Melochia tomentosa*** **Woolly Pyramid Bush** *365*
105. ***Mimosa*** **Mimosa, Uña de Gato, Cat's Claw** *367*
M. biuncifera Cat's Claw, Uña de Gato *368*
M. borealis Fragrant Mimosa *369*
M. dysocarpa Velvet-pod Mimosa, Gatuño *369*
M. emoryana Emory Mimosa *369*
M. pigra Zarza, Coatante *369*
106. ***Morus*** **Morus, Mora** *370*
M. microphylla Mountain Mulberry *371*
M. rubra Red Mulberry *371*
107. ***Myrica cerifera*** **Wax-myrtle, Southern Bay-berry, Árbol de la Sierra** *372*
M. pusilla Dwarf Wax-myrtle *374*
108. ***Nolina*** **Beargrass, Sacahuiste** *375*
N. erumpens Basketgrass *376*
N. lindheimeriana Devil's Shoestring *376*
N. micrantha Beargrass *377*
N. texana Texas Sacahuiste *377*
109. ***Nyssa*** **Tupelo, Sour-gum** *378*
N. aquatica Water Tupelo *379*
N. sylvatica var. sylvatica Blackgum, Black Tupelo *379*
110. ***Ostrya virginiana*** **American Hop-hornbeam** *380*
111. ***Parkinsonia aculeata*** **Retama, Mexican Palo Verde** *382*
112. ***Parthenium argentatum*** **Guayule, Afinador** *385*
113. ***Parthenocissus quinquefolia*** **Virginia Creeper, Guaco** *388*
P. heptaphylla Seven-leaf creeper *389*
114. ***Pavonia lasiopetala*** **Rose-mallow Pavonia, Rock-rose** *390*
115. ***Persea borbonia var. borbonia*** **Sweetbay, Red Bay** *392*
116. ***Philadelphus*** **Mock-orange** *394*
P. ernestii Canyon Mock-orange *396*
P. microphyllus Little-leaf Mock-orange *396*
P. texensis Texas Mock-orange *396*
117. ***Pinus*** **Pine, Pino, Pinyon** *397*
P. cembroides Mexican Pinyon *399*
P. cembroides var. remota Remote Pinyon, Papershell Pinyon *399*
P. echinata Shortleaf Pine *399*
P. edulis New Mexico Pinyon *399*
P. palustris Longleaf Pine *400*
P. ponderosa Ponderosa Pine *400*

P. strobiformis	Southwestern White Pine, Pino Enano *400*
P. taeda	Loblolly Pine *400*
118. ***Pistacia texana***	**Texas Pistachio** *401*
119. ***Pithecellobium flexicaule***	**Texas Ebony, Ébano** *404*
120. ***Platanus occidentalis***	**Sycamore Plane Tree** *407*
121. ***Populus***	**Cottonwood, Alamo** *409*
P. deltoides var. deltoides	Eastern Cottonwood *411*
P. deltoides var. occidentalis	Plains Cottonwood *411*
P. fremontii var. wislizenii	Rio Grande Cottonwood *411*
122. ***Prosopis***	**Mesquite** *412*
P. glandulosa var. glandulosa	Honey Mesquite *414*
P. glandulosa var. torreyana	Western Mesquite *414*
P. pubescens	Screwbean Mesquite, Tornillo *414*
P. reptans	Creeping Mesquite, Dwarf Screwbean Mesquite *414*
123. ***Prunus***	**Plum, Cherry** *415*
P. angustifolia	Chickasaw Plum, Sandhill Plum *417*
P. caroliniana	Cherry Laurel *417*
P. havardii	Havard Plum *418*
P. mexicana	Mexican Plum *418*
P. minutiflora	Texas Almond, Peach-brush *418*
P. rivularis	Creek Plum *418*
P. serotina var. serotina	Choke-cherry *418*
P. serotina var. eximia	Escarpment Choke-cherry *419*
P. serotina var. rufula	Southwestern Black Cherry *419*
P. texana	Sand Plum *419*
P. umbellata	Flatwoods Plum *419*
124. ***Ptelea trifoliolata***	**Wafer-ash, Hop-tree, Cola de Zorillo** *420*
125. ***Pyrus ioensis***	**Blanco Crabapple** *422*
P. angustifolia	Southern Crabapple *423*
P. arbutifolia	Red Chokeberry *423*
126. ***Quercus***	**Oak, Encino** *424*
Q. alba	White Oak *429*
Q. buckleyi	Texas or Spanish Red Oak *429*
Q. emoryi	Emory Oak *429*
Q. falcata	Southern Red Oak *430*
Q. fusiformis	Escarpment Live Oak, Encino Chaparro *430*
Q. gambelii	Gambel Oak *430*

Q. glaucoides Lacey Oak *430*
Q. graciliformis Graceful Oak *431*
Q. gravesii Chisos Red Oak, Encino Colorado *431*
Q. grisea Gray Oak, Encino Prieto *431*
Q. hinckleyi Hinckley Oak *431*
Q. hypoleucoides Silverleaf Oak *431*
Q. incana Sandjack Oak, Bluejack Oak *431*
Q. intricata Coahuila Scrub Oak *432*
Q. laurifolia Laurel Oak *432*
Q. macrocarpa Bur Oak *432*
Q. marilandica Blackjack Oak *432*
Q. michauxii Swamp Chestnut Oak *432*
Q. mohriana Mohr Oak *432*
Q. muehlenbergii Chinquapin Oak *432*
Q. nigra Water Oak *433*
Q. oblongifolia Mexican Blue Oak *433*
Q. phellos Willow Oak *433*
Q. polymorpha Mexican White Oak *433*
Q. pungens var. vaseyana Vasey Oak *434*
Q. rugosa Netleaf Oak *434*
Q. shumardii Shumard Red Oak *434*
Q. sinuata var. breviloba Bigelow Oak, Shin Oak *435*
Q. stellata Post Oak *435*
Q. velutina Black Oak *435*
Q. virginiana Coastal Live Oak *436*
127. ***Rhamnis caroliniana*** **Carolina Buckthorn** *437*
128. ***Rhododendron*** **Azalea, Wild Honeysuckle** *440*
R. canescens Hoary Azalea *441*
R. coryi Azalea *441*
R. oblongifolium Texas Azalea *441*
R. prinophyllum Texas Honeysuckle, Early Azalea *442*
129. ***Rhus*** **Sumac** *443*
R. aromatica Fragrant Sumac *446*
R. coppalina Shining Sumac *446*
R. glabra Smooth Sumac *447*
R. lanceolata Prairie Flame-leaf Sumac *447*
R. microphylla Little-leaf or Desert Sumac *448*
R. trilobata var. pilosissima Squaw Bush, Polecat Bush *448*
R. virens Evergreen Sumac *448*
130. ***Sabal*** **Sabal, Soyate, Palmetto** *450*

S. minor	Dwarf Palmetto *451*
S. mexicana	Texas Palmetto, Palma Micharros *451*
131. ***Salix nigra***	**Black Willow, Sauz** *454*
132. ***Salvia***	**Salvia** *456*
S. ballotaeflora	Blue Shrub Sage, Mejorana *458*
S. greggii	Cherry Sage, Autumn Sage *458*
S. regla	Mountain Sage *459*
133. ***Sambucus canadensis***	**Elderberry** *460*
134. ***Sapindus saponaria var. drummondii***	**Soapberry or Jaboncillo** *463*
135. ***Sassafras albidum***	**Sassafras** *466*
136. ***Schaefferia cuneifolia***	**Desert Yaupon, Panalero, Capul** *469*
137. ***Smilax***	**Cat-briar** *471*
S. glauca	Saw-briar *472*
S. laurifolia	Bamboo-vine *472*
S. pumila	Sarsaparilla-vine *472*
S. rotundifolia	Green-briar *472*
138. ***Sophora secundiflora***	**Texas Mountain Laurel** *473*
139. ***Stewartia malacodendron***	**Silky Camellia** *476*
140. ***Styrax***	**Snowbell** *478*
S. americana	American Snowbell *480*
S. platanifolia	Sycamore-leaf Snowbell *480*
S. texana	Texas Snowbell *480*
141. ***Symphoricarpos orbiculatus***	**Indian Currant, Snowberry** *481*
S. guadalupensis	Guadalupe Snowberry *482*
S. longiflorus	Fragrant Snowberry *482*
142. ***Taxodium distichum var. distichum***	**Bald Cypress, Sabino, Ahuehuete** *483*
143. ***Tecoma stans var. angustata***	**Esperanza, Yellow-bells** *486*
144. ***Tilia caroliniana***	**Carolina Basswood** *488*
145. ***Tiquilia greggii***	**Plume Tiquilia** *490*
146. ***Ulmus***	**Elm, Olmo** *492*
U. alata	Winged Elm *493*
U. americana	American Elm *493*
U. crassifolia	Cedar Elm *494*
U. rubra	Slippery Elm *494*
147. ***Ungnadia speciosa***	**Mexican Buckeye, Mona, Monilla** *495*
148. ***Vaccinium***	**Blueberry, Farkleberry** *497*
V. arboreum	Farkleberry *498*
V. arkansanum	Highbush Blueberry *498*
V. virgatum	Rabbit-eye Blueberry *499*

149. ***Vauquelinia angustifolia*** **Chisos Rosewood, Palo Prieto** *500*
150. ***Viburnum*** **Viburnum, Arrow-wood** *502*
V. acerifolium Maple-leaf Viburnum *504*
V. dentatum Southern Arrow-wood *505*
V. nudum Possum-haw Viburnum *505*
V. rufidulum Rusty Black-haw Viburnum *505*
151. ***Viguiera stenoloba*** **Skelton-leaf Goldeneye Daisy** *506*
152. ***Vitis*** **Grape, Uva** *509*
V. acerifolia Panhandle Grape *511*
V. aestivalis Pigeon Grape *511*
V. arizonica Canyon Grape *511*
V. berlandiera Spanish Grape *511*
V. cinerea Sweet Grape *511*
V. cordifolia Frost Grape *511*
V. monticola Sweet Mountain Grape *511*
V. mustangensis Mustang Grape *511*
V. palmata Missouri Grape *511*
V. riparia Riverbank Grape *511*
V. rotundifolia Muscadine Grape *512*
V. vulpina Fox Grape *512*
153. ***Yucca*** **Yucca, Spanish-Bayonet** *513*
Y. angustifolia Narrow-leaf Yucca *515*
Y. arkansana Arkansas Yucca *515*
Y. baccata Datil Yucca, Banana Yucca *515*
Y. constricta Buckley Yucca *516*
Y. elata Soaptree Yucca *516*
Y. faxoniana Giant Dagger *516*
Y. pallida Pale-leaf Yucca *517*
Y. rostrata Beaked Yucca *517*
Y. rupicola Twisted-leaf Yucca *517*
Y. treculeana Torrey Yucca *518*
154. ***Zanthoxylum fagara*** **Lime Prickly-ash, Colima** *519*
155. ***Zexmenia hispidia*** **Wedelia or Zexmenia Daisy** *521*

Preface to the New Edition

Around 1973, I went with my friend Lynn Lowrey and a retired Texas Forest Service Ranger named Oza Hall to look at some Silky Camellias that Oza had discovered on timber company property while roaming back roads in Newton County. We traveled down a sandy logging road and across a sloping wooded field to find a small cluster growing near the afternoon shade of Swamp White Oaks, hickories, maples, and gum trees. The camellias were lovely and unassuming, their delicate flowers waiting like a gift to be opened at an unexpected moment. When I went back to visit next spring, Lynn had talked the timber company into setting a corral around the plants to protect them. A year or two later, the entire hillside had been clear-cut and the corral bulldozed. The soil had eroded and congealed into the spring creek below the camellias that had fed the roots of the protecting hardwoods. Across the rutted field, fast-growing pine seedlings were laid out in straight rows. Sumacs, Sassafras, and False Willow had also invaded the roughed up ground to take their turn in the sun. The camellias were gone.

This story in many ways reflects much of what has happened in the native plant movement in the fifteen years since I wrote the first edition of this book. There is more appreciation of our native plants; there is wider agreement that certain rare and endangered species ought to be protected; and yet there is ongoing destruction of the natural places where these species are at home.

In the first edition, I emphasized the positive contributions native plants make to the landscape. I believed that simply extolling the beauty and uniqueness of our native plants would be sufficient to persuade all but those most reluctant to leave their spans of emerald green lawns and join the trend toward naturalistic landscaping. But now I see the challenge as much more complex. By primarily promoting individual outstanding native species, we have not acknowledged the deeper patterns of the way

Americans relate to their landscape, and this has caused the native plant movement to be misunderstood and in some cases ignored.

Over the past ten years, a harsh series of droughts, water rationing, and unusual freezes have certainly emphasized the virtue of using native plants. Indigenous species have adapted over the millennia to the extreme demands of our climate and still beautifully thrive. Nonetheless, for many people, the appeal of using native plants is similar to the one attached to eating brussels sprouts: it's not your top food choice, but it's good for you and you ought to do it.

The notion that native plants are somehow fundamentally shabby, ill behaved, or second-rate when compared to flashy plants with gaudy blooms found in magazines persists in the minds of many people. This perception may be partially based on our increased dissociation from the natural world.

In his book *Landscape and Memory*, Simon Schama asserts that "one of our most powerful yearnings [is] the craving to find in nature a consolation for our own mortality" (15). Yet it would seem that most of us are not in tune with our heart's desire; our disconnection from the natural world is unexamined and unmourned. Children no longer roam the remnant agricultural fields at the edges of their neighborhoods. They don't build forts made from discarded Christmas trees along creek sides and undeveloped lots. They seldom have time to daydream while watching ants or lizards. Their opportunity to explore, to stare at clouds, to waste time, is limited by safety concerns, the expectations of organized play, and the velocity of modern life. Separation from the natural world is not the issue; more and more children are never connected in the first place. Successive generations are growing up unfamiliar with the experience of simply being outside watching things grow and change.

At the same time, our natural landscapes are more threatened than ever by fragmentation of habitat and increasingly intensive land use. Fifteen years ago few of us imagined how much the once remote edges of our cities would change as widespread prosperity drives a huge building boom. Too often, the look of the urban landscape is determined by developers (usually from out of town), who fundamentally shape the kind of living experience people will have when they go home from work every night. When the developers do not value the native landscape, except to determine if there is a view or water nearby that could be factored in as a selling feature, then we see the contractors scraping the lots with bulldozers before setting the foundation of a new home. Soil that was originally on site is hauled off, and inferior weed-infested subsoil is brought back to replace it. Each home is then assigned a formulaic combination of plants to "green up" the site before the sale sign goes up. Later when those plants struggle and die, replacing them is the problem of the purchaser. Since the indigenous mosaic of plants has been obliterated, what clues remain for the homeowner, perhaps also new to the area, to interpret what the natural association of plants should look like? The natural aspects of the original property have long been forgotten. How can he tell and why should he care that a Mexican Plum, in the long run, offers many advantages over a fast-growing Bradford Pear?

In this age of the machine, we have become a nation of specialists. Construction technology is now so complex that each professional is forced to confine himself to his own area of expertise instead of assuming responsibility for planning in a more comprehensive way. Too often what happens outside the building is considered an "extra" to be resolved by someone else after the project is completed, which usually coincides with the exhaustion of the budget. At this point, a "landscaper" is employed to cover up the construction damage with inexpensive, fast-growing plants.

How much better would our homes and building projects be if architects, engineers, landscape architects, designers, and contractors developed a team approach to site planning and management? Many buildings could be well on their way to having a mature landscape around them at the end of construction by first protecting the remnant vegetation instead of waiting until the end to plug smaller plants in the compacted earth. In our haste to build, we lose much of our understanding of the local plant communities as they become further fragmented and pushed to the edge, out of reach and out of sight.

In the nursery industry, the national trend is toward consolidation: huge multistate conglomerate growers are geared toward the giant discount store market. These kinds of operations must have plants that they can sell in huge volumes over a wide geographical area. The "one size fits all" sales promotion of plants ignores the subtle suggestion that what might thrive in Houston may not work so well in El Paso. From advertising campaigns and glossy pictures of gardens from other areas, the consumer has come to expect that all plants should be compact, similar in form, and covered with eye-catching flowers all season long. Most native plants, especially western species, do not measure up to the rigid uniformity of the exotic landscape plants. Often their true beauty is revealed later, when they are established in the landscape, blooming and taking shape in a way that only gets better over time, while less adapted plants struggle and eventually die. But it is hard for the new gardener to know this if he has not seen those native plants in landscape situations.

Even native plant advocates must shoulder responsibility for contributing to the public's reluctance to embrace indigenous plants as the foundation of a garden. A garden doesn't have to be a bleak "zero-scape" or scientifically accurate restored habitat to be acceptable. Gardens are for people, as the designer Thomas Church declared so well. We should never insist that only plants found in the immediate area since pre-Columbian times are appropriate. To do so is to ignore a fundamental truth of human nature. People have always gathered plants that they found beautiful or useful. Part of what it means to garden is to collect the plants and objects that have a personal appeal to you or that have an associated memory. This can be the reminder of one's homeland, a loved one (represented by a lily or rose dug from a grandmother's garden), or a souvenir from travel. To judge this very fundamental impulse of the gardener as wrong only encourages people to turn a deaf ear to the many positive reasons for emphasizing the use of native plants. Instead, I believe it is our responsibility to inspire the gardener to first love her land and those plants that give it a unique quality. When people are encouraged to preserve and protect as many of the plants on their property as possible (not just the specimen shade trees), and these indigenous plants form the foundations of their gardens, the inclusion of certain adapted species can be achieved in delicate harmony.

In naturalistic gardening style, plants are free to assume their true qualities instead of being sheared into contorted green balls. It is only when we try to reproduce the form and display of other regions that our attempts at gardening seem shabby, second-rate, and ultimately unsatisfying. At the same time, the less formal and more "natural" the garden, the stronger the basic design should be or the layout can quickly slip into chaos. With a controlled design that takes into account all the kinds of human activity which may occur in the garden, the gardener can learn to take pleasure in cyclical rhythms, including the buff and amber colors of seed heads, drying leaves, and the pause in the long growing season caused by drought's summer dormancy. If a garden is well designed and sensitively maintained, our cultural desire for perpetual greenness will gradually shift to an acceptance of the subtle variations in texture that predominate during the dry cycles as much as the exuberant colors of spring and fall.

When people experience success in their gardening, that satisfaction will inevitably result in their deeper connection to the larger natural world and a greater desire to protect it. There are signs that more people are beginning to accept the privilege and challenges of land stewardship, whatever the size of their property. When I wrote the first edition of this book, there were few resources to guide people. Now the shelves bulge with field guides, books on butterfly gardening, gardening for wildlife, and naturalistic garden design. Groups such as the Native Plant Society, the Prairie Association, and the Master Gardener Program are establishing their informed constituencies that are then sent out to educate their communities. The TV and the Internet are likewise rich in information, but we still need more public environments where people can directly experience a naturalistic garden. We need more parks, arboretums, and botanical gardens for people to casually and spontaneously attend and learn more about these plants. All public buildings offer opportunities for smaller display gardens showcasing native plants. We should support city ordinances that favor the planting of native plants over exotic species. But these places must not be plant museums; we must never forget to provide a bench, a comfortable path, and some shade for people to pause in the midst of the garden to rest and observe.

Where does the native plant movement go from here? The challenges are daunting, but despite a very mobile population, I believe native plants have established themselves as a resource to be valued. In a very basic sense, we have come full circle to the place Benny Simpson began thirty years ago. To explain what motivated his then very unfashionable interest in studying native plants, he declared, "It's getting to be important that we save as much water as we can and grow the kind of plants that can survive on very little water." Incorporating native plants in landscape design is a major part of an integrated management strategy to address our dwindling water supplies. For many parts of Texas, current projections predict that by 2030, our demand for water will exceed our supplies. This will affect not only the homeowner but also the nursery operator, because agriculture and agriculture-related industries will be allocated less water when surface and ground water supplies become strained as our population increases.

The native plant movement will be a success when a garden that does not use native plants to form the framework looks odd and out of place to us, when the pressure on our water resources eliminates poorly adapted species from consideration, and when we have articulated to ourselves and our children that the earth needs us and we need the earth.

Acknowledgments

In the winter of 1998, I called the warehouse of my then-publisher to order some books to take to a workshop where I was to speak. A bored and underpaid stock clerk told me, "Oh, we run outta that book." It took several phone calls to determine that yes, I had been dropped from the list and all the books were gone. Where were they? In a burn pile? On remainders tables in Minnesota? I barely had a few extra copies around the house saved for my children.

It has been a long time since the book was first published. Occasionally I had entertained thoughts of updating it, but these were the same kinds of considerations I would give to, say, taking tango lessons or getting another degree. Nice to think about being that productive and creative, but not likely to happen. I was busy with my landscape design and construction company and I could not imagine taking on such a project in "my free time."

But when the book went out of print and the University of Texas Press kindly showed an interest in publishing a revised edition, I could procrastinate no more. We have learned so much more about these plants. There are many plants I should have included earlier, but was unfamiliar with. As long as the first edition existed gospel-like in its handsome packaging, I believed it could stand there as the focus for discussion about propagation of native plants and their use. With it gone, my main vehicle for bringing attention to the challenges and importance of growing these plants went with it.

The most daunting part about beginning this project was to fully realize that all of the people who had helped and guided me with the first edition are gone. Principally, Benny Simpson, research scientist at Texas A&M at Dallas, and Lynn Lowrey, horticulturist and nurseryman of Houston and Carrizo Springs. These two men believed in me and in the value of recording what was then known about these plants even when my own sense of self and purpose was vague and unsure. After them came Dr. Barton Warnock of Sul Ross University, who drove me around the Trans-Pecos, Dr. Jimmy Tipton, who had gone to graduate school with me and eventually on to Arizona and who shared so much of his research with me, and finally Dr. J. C. Raulston, who was a new enthusiastic professor at Texas A&M when I showed up as a bewildered graduate student in 1973. All gone.

There wasn't a day that went by when I didn't miss their presence, or wished to call them on the phone and report what I had discovered or ask a question. But slowly I began to realize something else: that I was the bridge from those founders of the native Texas plants movement to a new generation of horticulturalists who had built on the experience of these elders and taken that understanding and knowledge to a higher level. Talking with these horticulturists was like meeting long-lost relatives at a family reunion. We found ourselves connected through the kinship of having been influenced by Benny, Lynn, and the others, and we shared a passion for plants. I could not have revised this new edition in such a short time without their help. It never failed to amaze me how generous people were with their time and knowledge. I talked with very few people who were reluctant to share "trade secrets." Most of these people have forsaken worldly goods and fame to pursue their passion for plants and to have as their life's work a desire to increase the beauty of this world. I am so indebted to them.

First I must thank my compadre Scott Ogden, who accompanied me on a trip way down into the Rio Grande Valley, then later to east Texas. I realize now how important it was to give myself a little time initially to look at the natural landscape in general and to visit various people in a somewhat random manner. Before setting down to the task of collecting research, it was very helpful first to get a sense of what the horticultural world was like outside of my own local sphere. But to travel with Scott was a revelation. How many people can say they drove down the highway discussing geologic events of 200 million years ago, or Pringle's plant explorations in northern Mexico in the early 1900s, or stopped to collect giant ball moss from live oak mottes on remnant caliche cuestas? Later, Scott would teach me to use a little rock hammer to dislodge fossilized seashells from soft green rock in east Texas. Scott convinced me that rewriting this book could be a great adventure.

Chris Best, plant ecologist with the U.S. Fish and Wildlife Service at the Lower Rio Grande National Wildlife Refuge, became a good friend and inspiration. He freely turned over information he has been gathering for nine years in the revegetation project at the Lower Rio Grande Valley National Wildlife Refuge. From Chris I learned so much about many subtropical species I had ignored the first time around. Chris showed me what was involved in making large restoration projects successful. He is a pioneer in this field, and I hope he gets more attention for the work he has so faithfully been doing.

Dr. Mike Arnold, professor of horticulture at Texas A&M, Dr. David Creech of Stephen F. Austin University, Dr. Wayne Mackay, plant scientist at Texas A&M Research and Extension Center in Dallas, and Skip Richter, Travis County Extension horticulturist, were all very helpful in keeping me aware of what was happening on the academic side. It is with their encouragement that I hope this information leads to more discussion among growers, researchers, and students.

So many nursery owners and horticulturists shared time and information with me. The words on these pages are an attempt to record their experiences, their observations of the natural world, and their independence. A special thanks to Pat McNeal, who patiently sat through marathon interviews with me as I downloaded his considerable plant knowledge onto these pages. His generosity and patience amazed me.

I am listing the names and addresses of my "collaborators" below to recognize them and to encourage further discussion. A deep heartfelt thanks to each and every one of you, and for the precious time you gave to me.

Dr. Michael A. Arnold
Professor of Horticulture
Department of Horticultural Sciences
Texas A&M University
College Station, Texas 77843-2133
e-mail: ma-arnold@tamu.edu

Conrad Bering, Horticulturist/Owner
Bernadine Bering, Horticulturist/Owner
Barton Springs Nursery
3601 Bee Caves Road
Austin, Texas 78746
(512) 328-6655

Chris Best, Plant Ecologist
Lower Rio Grande Valley National Wildlife Refuge
U.S. Fish and Wildlife Service
Route 2, Box 202a
Alamo, Texas 78516
(956) 787-3079 ext. 124
email: chris_best@fws.gov

Mark Bronstad, Horticulturist and Propagator
Doremus Wholesale Nursery
Route 2, Box 750
Warren, Texas 77664
(409) 547-3536
email: edoremus3@aol.com

Paul Cox, Assistant Director
San Antonio Botanical Gardens
555 Funston Place
San Antonio, Texas 78209
(210) 207-3264

Dr. David Creech, Director
Stephen F. Austin Mast Arboreum
P.O. Box 13000
Stephen F. Austin University
Nacogdoches, Texas 75962
(409) 468-3705
email: dcreech@sfasu.edu

Ron Gass, Horticulturist/Owner
Mountain States Wholesale Nursery
P.O. Box 2500
Litchfield Park, Arizona 85340-2500
1-800-840-8509

Daniel Goodspeed, Horticulturist
Mountain States Wholesale Nursery
P.O. Box 2500
Litchfield Park, Arizona 85340-2500
1-800-840-8509

Dan Hosage, Horticulturist/Owner
Madrone Nursery
2318 Hilliard Road
San Marcos, Texas 78666
(512) 353-3944

Chuck Janzow, Horticulturist/Owner
Green Cloud Nursery
Boerne, Texas
(830) 249-3844

Patrick Kirwin, Horticulturist
1131 Martin Luther King Drive
San Marcos, Texas 78666

Dr. Wayne Mackay, Plant Scientist, Horticulturist
Texas Research and Extension Service
Texas A&M University
17360 Coit Road
Dallas, Texas 75252-6599
(972) 952-9251

Patty Manning, Environmental Science Technician
Department of Biology
P.O. Box C 64
Sul Ross State University
Alpine, Texas 79832
(915) 837-8242

Pat McNeal, Horticulturist/Owner
McNeal Growers
P.O. Box 371
Manchaca, Texas 78652
(512) 280-2233
email: limmrick@i.o.com

Scott Ogden, Horticulturist, Garden Designer, Author
1111 W. Oltorf
Austin, Texas 78704

William A. Pfeiffer, Horticulturist
2327 Copper Ash
San Antonio, Texas 78232
(210) 490-5249

Mary Sonier, Landscape Designer
Box 609
Capitan, New Mexico 88316
(505) 354-2794

Sue Tracy
Medina, Texas 78055-1434
email: tracy@hctc.net

Robbi Daves Will, Horticulturist/Owner
Gottlieb Gardens Nursery
8263 Huber Road
Seguin, Texas 78155
(830) 629-9876

Grateful thoughts are also extended to my colleagues Marla Smith, Krista Whitson, and John Davis. Not only did their talents and support raise the professional level of my landscape design business, but also they kept the shop open while I took a lengthy pause to write this book. I'm so lucky to have them in my life. Thanks also to Amon Burton for his friendship and guidance on launching this new edition. I find I have come to rely on his relentless curiosity to keep me actively wondering about things. I have also saved a special thanks for a special friend: Rob Lallier, who ran the last lap of writing with me when I was very tired. I hope you know how much I appreciated your help with this manuscript just at that time, Rob.

Following the time-honored tradition of saving the best for last, I must thank my family. My in-laws, George and Virginia Nokes, always loving and supportive, really outdid themselves this time. Thank you for encouraging me in this effort. My husband Jack hung in there through the absences of long days and nights. It was a comfort to me to know he was there, waiting for me to return to my real life. My daughters were three and five when I wrote this book the first time. Now they are grown and have been the joy of my life. This book has become for me a marker of how fast time passes and how rich the unexpected opportunities and blessings are all along the way. To my family: thanks for making this work possible.

JILL NOKES
AUTUMN 1999

HOW TO GROW NATIVE PLANTS
OF TEXAS AND THE SOUTHWEST

Vegetational Areas of Texas

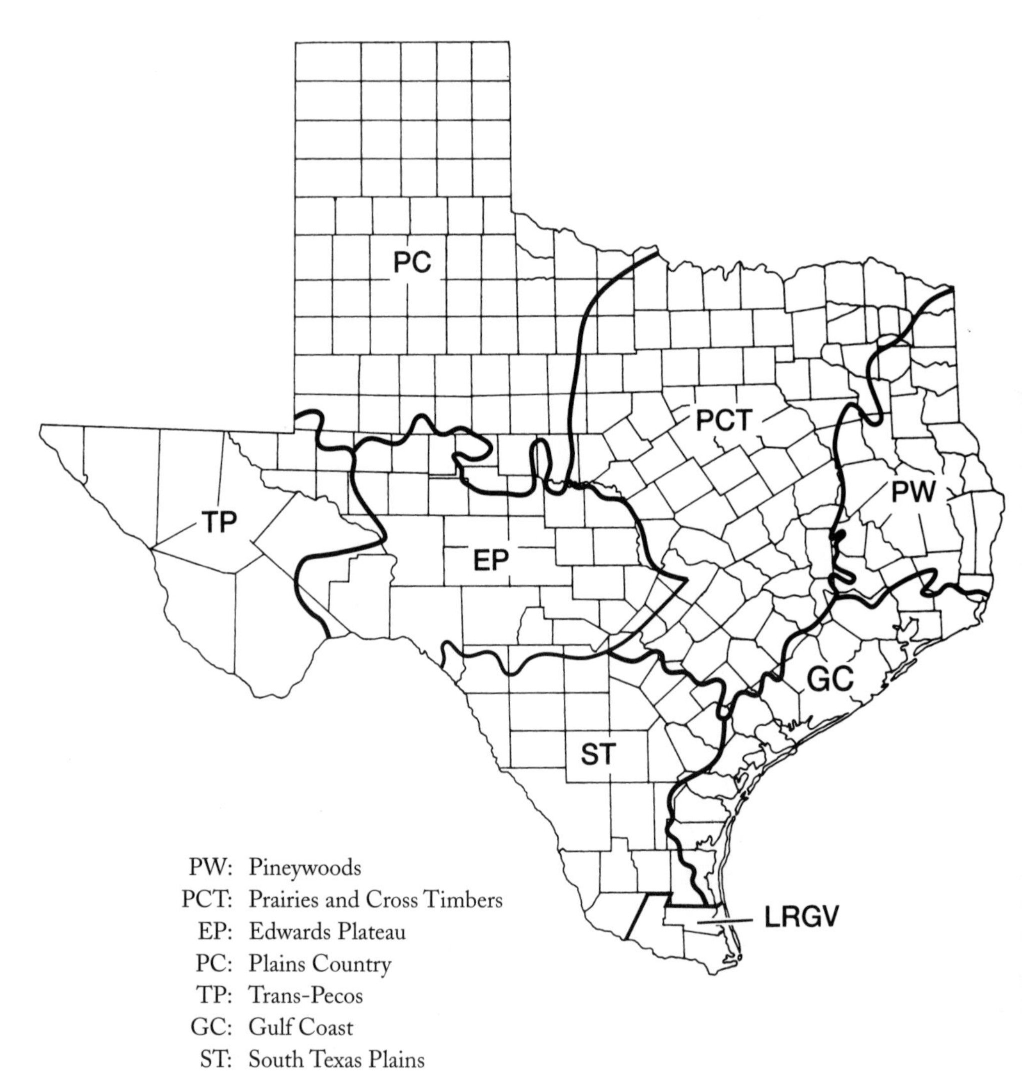

PW: Pineywoods
PCT: Prairies and Cross Timbers
EP: Edwards Plateau
PC: Plains Country
TP: Trans-Pecos
GC: Gulf Coast
ST: South Texas Plains
LRGV: Lower Rio Grande Valley

Source: Modified from a map by Frank W. Gould in "Texas Plants: A Checklist and Ecological Summary" (1969). Texas Agricultural Experiment Station, Texas A&M University, College Station, Texas. MP-581 Revised. Used by permission.

I ~ *Introduction*

Advances in technology, especially in the areas of genetic engineering and tissue culture, are rapidly changing the field of horticulture and certain expectations of nursery production. Continuing research will be able to provide exact techniques for propagation of certain species that, until now, we have only been able to guess at. Yet there remains a mystical and unexplainable quality about growing plants.

Why, for example, do agave seeds planted in trays left outdoors suddenly germinate all at once after a rainstorm? Why do so many plants seem to be stimulated to germinate in the presence of other germinating seeds? Seeds sown in communal trays often behave this way, while germination for the same seeds planted in individual containers are sporadic and prolonged. What is it exactly that causes a stunted Goldenball Leadtree to suddenly grow rapidly after being planted in the ground after lingering as a wimpy seedling in a container for 3 years? Why can you root *Fraxinus greggii*, but not other members of the ash family?

I believe it is this bit of mystery and the sense of being on the frontier of understanding about our overlooked native plants that makes this field so interesting and attracts people who could easily make a lot more money in another line of work.

The commercial production of native species will become more feasible as growers in the Southwest move away from strict adherence to the model of nursery production offered by east coast or California growers, and instead adapt to the unique situations of their climate and product. As I talked with growers throughout the region for the new edition of this book, I learned of new or revised concepts and methods being experimented by nurser-

ies that I believe will improve the ways we have been growing native plants. These techniques will affect a nursery's ability to grow those species once considered too difficult or unreliable to be profitable.

For example, we know that many southern strains of woody plants require much less cold chilling of seeds to break dormancy than their more northern and eastern counterparts. Likewise, our long hot growing season has a dormant period in the middle, which means germination and rootability is often impaired during the summer months. However, as compensation, production can be extended in the early fall by using a "wet-wall" greenhouse that lowers temperatures in August just enough to flush new growth or encourage sprouting. Spring production may be jump-started by using bottom heat to encourage early sprouting before hot temperatures.

We know that many of our western species have adapted to erratic and infrequent rainfall patterns by developing fast-growing nonbranched taproots. This is important for survival in their native habitat, but not helpful when the grower is trying to get the plant to thrive in a container with a typical pine-bark-based soil medium. More growers are experimenting with different kinds of containers for seedlings, cuttings, and larger plants that encourage air pruning of roots and development of lateral or interior branching. Pots with interior surfaces treated with copper have been developed to "burn" root tips and thus stimulate lateral and interior branching in much the same way as air pruning does.

Many plants native to arid soils do not have defenses against the increased bacterial activity found in potting soil with a rich organic component. Seedlings may die because of damping-off fungi, while others wait until they are moved up to larger containers to crash and die. But now we are seeing the introduction of beneficial microorganisms used to inoculate the soil and form symbiotic relationships with the plant helps protect them by promoting a more vigorous and densely branched root system. More growers are also experimenting with different soil blends, adjusting the standard "recipes" to more accurately reflect an individual plant's real need of fertility and soil structure.

The demand for dwindling water supplies will mean more opportunities for the niche grower of native plants. There will be a need for reliable supplies of liners for the growing number of revegetation or restoration projects. Knowledgeable and efficient growers tuned to a special market may be successful even though the trend is toward the consolidation of huge corporate nurseries geared toward the discount chain stores.

Consumers, tired of replacing unsuitable mass-marketed plants that die on schedule each August, will find their craving for something new satisfied by the introduction of hardy and beautiful native cultivars. Before, we focused just on trying to figure out how to grow the darn things. Now the refinement and selection of superior forms can really begin. The selection of ornamental cultivars of our native species has only barely been explored.

In *The Reference Manual of Woody Plant Propagation,* Michael Dirr writes, "[The] senior author has watched many seed experiments ruined by diseases, insects, chipmunks, and fate" (Dirr and Heuser 1987:17). No other industry that I can think of links chipmunks and fate in the same sentence, but he's right. There are many unpredictable hazards in the nursery business. Perhaps our best chance is to adopt all the known practices, common sense, scientific innovations, and experience that apply to our situation while at the same time never forgetting to follow nature's clues as the ultimate model for procedure. I heard from many growers that as a general rule of thumb, they simply try to expose the seeds to what Mother Nature would give them. Our willingness to credit "unscientific" methods (like soaking seeds in active yeast to pretreat them), if they are effective, may mean that many more species previously considered impossible to grow can now be offered to the public. And until many more native plants are available in the nursery trade, we will never see significant change in how our domestic landscapes look or how we heal the hard-used places.

II ~ *Gathering and Storing Seeds*

Seed collection is often the most difficult part of propagating native plants. One reason more native plants are not commercially produced in large numbers is that harvesting seeds can be an erratic and tedious enterprise. Often a grower does not know where or when to begin collection or how to determine if the fruit is ripe or if the seeds inside are of good quality.

SEED PROVENANCE

Following the guidelines below will help to set reasonable goals for seed collection and make collection more productive. Proper planning begins by emphasizing the importance of provenance or geographic source of the seed. Provenance is important because seeds of the same species will grow differently under cultivation (see Bald Cypress, *T. distichum*, or Shumard Red Oak, *Quercus shumardii*). When gathering seed from plants already in cultivation as opposed to the field it is important to make the distinction between indigenous and introduced plants. A plant may be well adapted to local conditions and therefore worth selecting, but at the same time, one cannot always assume that the plant will demonstrate the same inherent longevity under long-term climatic pressures as might be said of indigenous populations. This is especially true of isolated trees in the cultivated landscape. Find out where the original genetic material came from and then base your collection on this understanding. Proper labeling of the collections will not only help identify superior populations of certain plants based on observations after the seed has germinated, but can also be used when marketing the plant. It's easy to let all the seed get in a jumble and later lose the valuable information of dates, location, climatic pressures (dry or wet year), and so on, that one thinks one will remember but by the next year does not.

WHEN AND WHERE TO COLLECT

Productive harvesting requires knowledge of seed ripening, methods of dispersal, and the influence of seasonal weather trends on the timing of collection. First, collectors must familiarize themselves with flowering and fruiting dates and then be able to recognize a mature fruit or seed. It is important to seek this background information in field guides written for the general geographic area where collection will take place. Although many of the plants native to Texas are also found growing elsewhere in the United States, flowering and fruiting dates may vary widely. Seed collection for many species in Texas begins in early to mid-summer and continues through fall, while other species can be collected at other times throughout the year. An early spring and dry summer may cause very early seed ripening and dispersal. A high wind or rainstorm may result in the loss of an entire crop of mature seeds on some plants. Some plants do not produce good seed crops every year (see Bur Oak, *Quercus macrocarpa*). There is also no substitute for simply regularly exploring the roadsides and fields where one has access throughout the year, to identify collecting sites and to monitor the quality and ripening of the crop.

Many factors affect seed production, and seed quality can vary from year to year as well as from location to location. Collection should begin as soon as the fruit and seeds are mature. A delay of a few days may make the difference between success or failure in collecting a good crop, especially of those species having seeds that are dispersed by wind or forcibly ejected from capsules, or that dry out rapidly or may be attractive to birds and other animals.

Before harvest time, collectors should find several different stands of the plant they wish to propagate. Choose healthy thriving trees or shrubs of good form that have average or superior growth rates. It is best to harvest only from mature plants that have proven their ability to thrive on a given site. Isolated plants that may not have had adequate cross-pollination should be avoided. In addition to hardiness, selection of trees or shrubs may also be based on particularly outstanding qualities of flowering, fruiting, and form.

Collectors need to obtain permission from the landowner before gathering from private fields or woods. Trees or shrubs that are considered rare, endangered, or threatened should not be completely stripped, transplanted, or damaged during collection. A conscientious propagator will leave some seeds behind to give these plants an opportunity to increase at their natural site. Rare plants successfully reproduced under cultivation may sometimes be successfully reintroduced into their native habitats.

Many plants set seeds at sporadic or intermittent intervals following periods of intermittent blooming. This is especially true of western species like Cenizo (*Leucophyllum spp.*) or Plume Tiquilia (*Tiquilia greggii*), which may have a main blooming period but also flower several times during a season following rainfall or periods of high humidity. Seeds may therefore be on the plant along with later blooms, and collection may be accomplished throughout the season. It is most practical for the collector to gather seeds from a large population of the species he seeks. An individual plant may not have many seeds, but gathering from an entire colony may make the trip worthwhile. Seeds or fruits may mature at different rates among individual trees or shrubs and even on different parts of the same plant. Collection can be delayed a few days to insure the gathering of more mature fruits, or selective gathering may be done.

GUIDELINES FOR JUDGING RIPENESS

Before collecting large numbers of fruit, one should examine the seeds inside to determine their quality. In general, seeds are ripe when there is no increase in fresh (or dry) weight. Knowing the mature size and time of maturity of the seeds is the only way to judge ripeness. Mature seeds are usually somewhat dark in color, filled out and firm, and should be free from insect damage or mold. The collector should avoid harvesting fruit with markedly immature seeds because they may be incapable of surviving and often produce weak and deformed seedlings. However, seeds of certain species benefit from early collection and immediate planting (see Carolina Buckthorn, *Rhamnus caroliniana*, or Texas Pistachio, *Pistacia texana*). Overdrying of the seed can contribute to dormancy and a delay in germination.

Some genera, like Hickory (*Carya*), Oak (*Quercus*), and Walnut (*Juglans*) produce good seed crops only every 3–5 years. Members of the Black Oak group, which includes the red oaks like Texas Red Oak (*Quercus buckleyi*), bear acorns only every other year. Still other plants (e.g., Smoke-tree, *Cotinus obovatus*, and Redbud, *Cercis canadensis*), may set fruit each year, but much of the crop may be self-sterile, aborted, or otherwise empty. To obtain an adequate harvest from plants that typically produce a poor seed crop, it may be necessary to gather especially large numbers of seeds from several separate stands.

Various Fruit Shapes

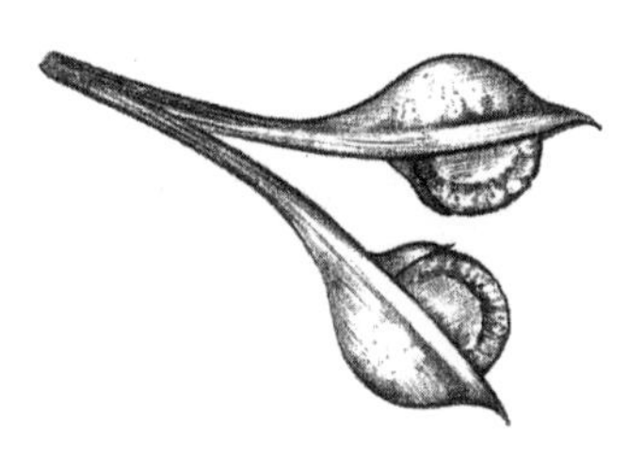

a. capsule (Flame Acanthus)

b. aggregate of achenes (clematis)

c. acorn/nut (Bur Oak)

d. pome (crabapple)

e. drupelets in a cluster (dewberry)

f. berry (grape)

Various Seed Shapes

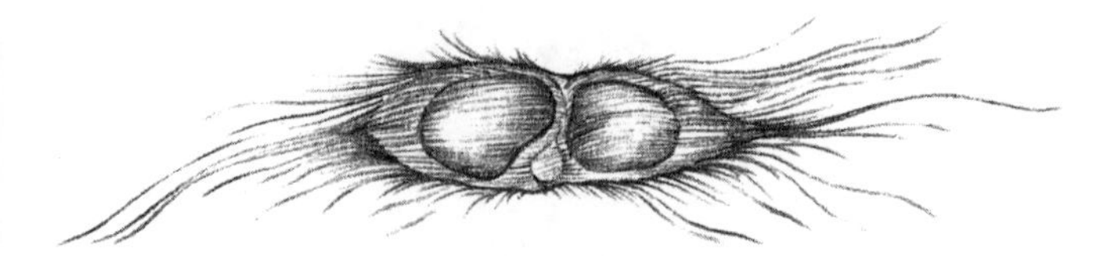

a. Desert Willow (*Chilopsis linearis*)

d. Bald Cypress *(Taxodium distichum)*

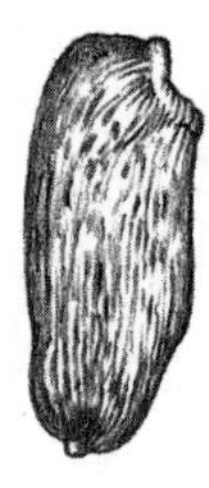

b. Osage-orange *(Maclura pomifera)*

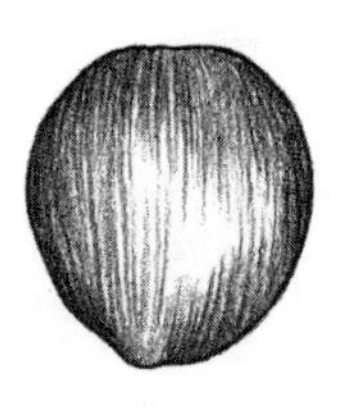

e. Mexican Plum *(Prunus mexicana)*

c. Skelton-leaf Goldeneye Daisy
(Viguiera stenoloba)

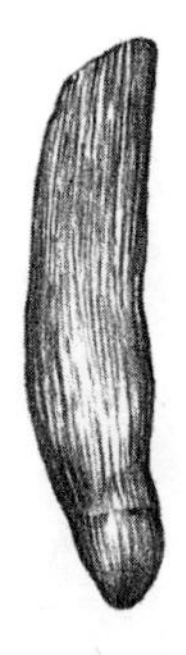

f. Longleaf Pine *(Pinus palustris)*

Various Seed Shapes (continued)

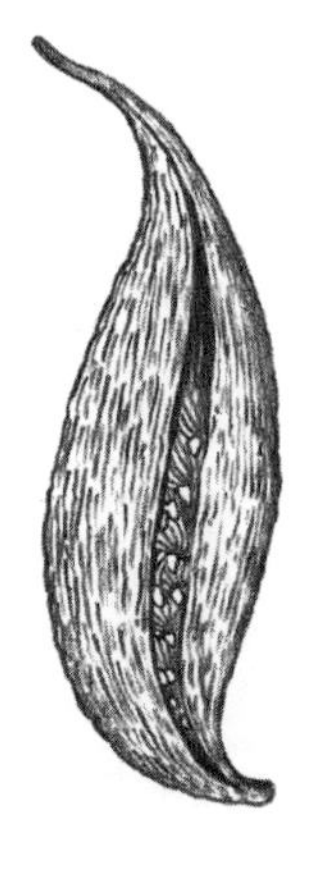

a. follicle (Butterfly Weed)

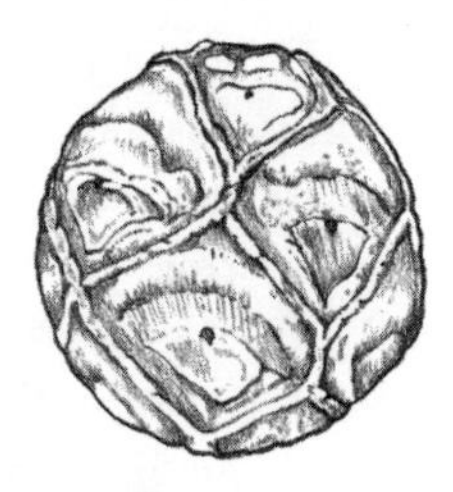

b. cone (Bald Cypress)

c. ament (Hop-hornbeam)

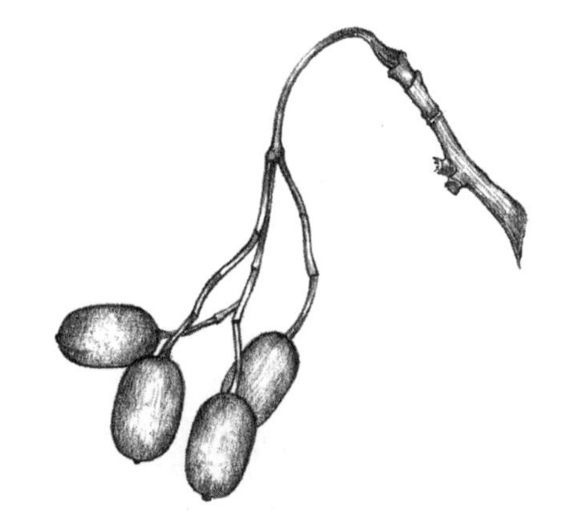

d. drupe (Rusty Black-haw Viburnum)

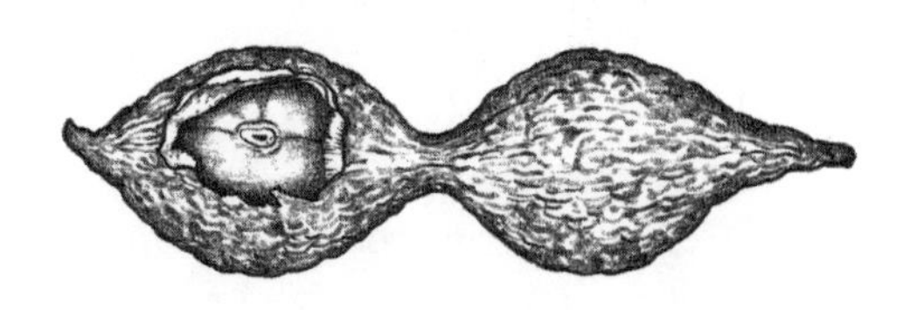

e. legume (Texas Mountain Laurel)

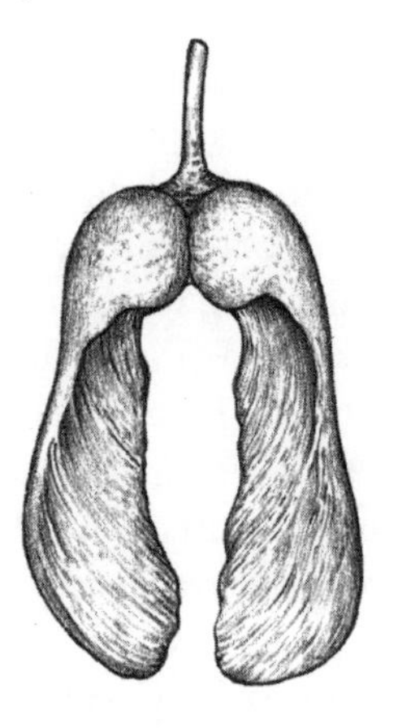

f. samara (maple)

Such seeds as acorns, nuts, and fleshy fruits like plums or berries are gathered and eaten by many forms of wildlife, so collection may be a competitive enterprise. Certain growers enthusiastically report that gathering seeds such as Mexican Persimmon (*Diospyros texana*) or Flame-leaf Sumac (*Rhus lanceolata*) from animal scat is a good way to acquire precleaned seed. Whatever the source, carefully examine the fruits or seeds for insect damage before mixing in bags with the harvest from other plants to avoid contaminating any sound seeds.

The flesh of such pulpy fruits as drupes (plums, *Prunus*), pomes (crabapples, *Pyrus*), berries (Agarita, *Berberis*), or aggregate fruits like American Beauty-berry (*Callicarpa americana*) become soft and juicy and change from green or yellowish to reddish or blue-purple when ripe. Some plants, like Carolina Buckthorn (*Rhamnus caroliniana*), first turn reddish and then blue-purple when ripe. Often the seeds are mature a week or more before the fleshy fruits turn color and fall from the plant. Seed maturity can be determined by cutting open the fruit and examining the seeds for firmness, fullness, and dark color.

Seeds in a legume (pod), achene, or other dry covering should be collected just before or as the fruit turns brown and dries. Often a mature pod will twist and split open to drop the seeds. Other dry fruits forcibly eject their seeds, making collection from the ground difficult. Delayed harvesting of species with persistent pods, or pods that remain attached, such as redbud (*Cercis*) or Huisache (*Acacia farnesiana*), often results in weevil-infested seeds. Even if hard-seeded species show no sign of infestation, it is a good idea to fumigate the crop in a tightly closed container with a pest strip (2.2 dichlorovinyl dimethyl phosphate 18.6%) or dust with a powder insecticide before mixing with other seeds in storage.

Nonpulpy but moist, meaty fruits such as acorns, buckeyes (*Aesculus* species), and walnuts should be collected from the tree as soon as they appear ripe. Acorns will usually turn from green to brown and the husks on walnuts and Texas buckeyes will begin to dry, become wrinkled, and split apart. Collect these kinds of fruits from the tree by hand or by shaking or flailing the fruits onto drop cloths. Gather the fruits from the ground only if they have very recently dropped. Fruits or seeds that have fallen in leaf mold, become wet, or been on the ground for some time should be rejected because they probably will have begun to decay or become infested with insects. They could ruin the rest of the harvest if combined with other seeds during storage.

Seeds with a high moisture content such as walnuts, acorns, and Texas buckeyes must be kept moist to maintain their viability during long transportation and storage periods. If allowed to dry out, they will either germinate prematurely or not at all. This type of seed should be planted immediately or mixed with moist sand/sphagnum moss or a peat/perlite mixture. Often large fleshy seeds will begin to germinate in moist storage. If the radicle (primary root) emerges from the seed during storage, the seedling must be removed and planted immediately. Acorns and walnuts do not have to be cleaned before storing or sowing, but the cap or husk can be removed to reduce bulk.

Some seeds, like those of Witch-hazel (*Hamamelis virginiana*) and Flame Acanthus (*Anisacanthus quadrifidus var. wrightii*), are held in capsules that either forcibly eject the seeds some distance as they dry or open and drop the small seed on the ground, where they are hard to find. Collect these fruits when the capsules are beginning to ripen and have turned yellow-brown. Keep in paper bags in a warm, dry place and let them dry and open there where they can be separated later.

STOCK PLANTS

Some nurseries find it advantageous to establish stands of certain plants on nursery property in order to have a convenient source of seeds and cutting wood. Only proven superior plants should be used for this purpose. The gene pool should be varied enough to maintain vigorous offspring, and the stand of plants should be refreshed with the introduction of new plantings from time to time.

COLLECTION TOOLS AND MATERIALS

Every seed collector gradually assembles his or her favorite tools and equipment for gathering seeds. Among the tools generally used are gloves, pruning shears, drop cloths, boots, flailing sticks, long pruning poles, hooks, and ladders. Many plants may be stripped by hand, or the seeds may be beaten onto drop cloths. Clusters of fruit like sumacs (*Rhus* species) are most easily clipped off into bags or boxes. Large commercial operations use machines like vacuum strippers, mechanical harvesters, and tractor-drawn seed strippers to gather large quantities of seeds (U.S. Department of Agriculture [USDA] 1974).

Boxes, baskets, or paper bags are best for holding seeds and fleshy fruits during the collection process. Use plastic trash bags only for short periods of time because they tend to keep the fruit too moist and encourage overheating.

All fleshy fruits should be cleaned immediately after collection by removing the pulp. Nonpulpy seeds, if they are not to be planted immediately, should be spread in thin layers on tables or screens in a protected dry place to thoroughly air dry before storage.

CLEANING

After collecting the seeds, it is important to clean them to protect from mold, insects, or overheating caused by fermentation of the pulp of fleshy fruits. Cleaning methods vary with seed types.

Cleaning such dry fruits as legumes (Mesquite, *Prosopis glandulosa*), woody capsules (Mexican Buckeye, *Ungnadia speciosa*), or achenes (Silverleaf Mountain Mahogany, *Cercocarpus montanus var. argenteus*) is best accomplished by collecting the fruits before they completely dry and split open to reveal the seeds. The seeds or beans then should be dried in single layers thinly spread on canvas cloth, screens, or trays off the ground. Air drying takes 1–3 days, depending on humidity levels. Once the pods are dried, the extraction of the seeds from the pod or husk may be accomplished by beating, treading, or rubbing between boards. A mechanical thresher is sometimes employed for cleaning dry seeds in large commercial operations. After beating or threshing, the seeds can be separated from the pod or chaff and fumigated or dusted with an insecticide to prevent insect damage, before being stored in sealed containers in a cool dry place.

The cones of some species of conifers, like pines or Bald Cypress (*Taxodium distichum*), will open if they are first dried in raised racks in open air at low humidity for 2–12 weeks. The cones can then be shaken to loosen the seeds.

Seed types such as samaras (maples, *Acer spp.*, or ashes, *Fraxinus spp.*) have appendages or wings that can be removed to reduce bulk in storage. Removal of these outer parts usually does not affect germination or viability in storage. Clean seeds of this type by either beating them in a sack or rubbing them between your hands or two boards. For large seed lots, a commercial machine is available that has been designed to dewing the seed. For smaller amounts, no cleaning other than thorough drying is necessary.

Fleshy fruits with pulp or meat—grapes (*Vitis*), plums (*Prunus*), crabapples (*Pyrus*)—must be cleaned immediately after collection to avoid mold and fermentation. Pulpy fruits like plums with large seeds may be cleaned in small quantities by rubbing the fruit on a screen under running water or macerating it with a rolling pin or fruit press. Sometimes it is necessary to briefly soak the fruit to soften it. Crush the fruit and then wash under running water into a large container. The debris and pulp will float to the top, and the sound seeds will sink. Strain the seeds through a fine mesh screen and plant them immediately or dry them before storage. Don't soak the seeds for very long during the cleaning process because it may cause them to imbibe water and then rot during storage. Fleshy fruits with hard-coated seeds such as dogwoods (*Cornus spp.*) are easily cleaned. Other types of seeds, like those of *Magnolia*, are softer and easily crushed during the cleaning process. Some growers have modified a blender by placing rubber tubing over the blades, or by wrapping the blades in thick layers of tape to clean soft-seeded fleshy fruits. The blender is filled with equal amounts of seed and water, and the motor pulsed on and off in short bursts to separate the flesh from the seed. Then the seeds are strained through a sieve before air drying and storage.

Heating crabapples (*Pyrus spp.*), persimmons (*Diospyros spp.*), or other hard fruits to soften the pulp is not recommended because high temperatures may kill the seed embryo. It may be necessary to cut these fruits and remove the seeds by hand.

Some species of junipers, like Red-berried Juniper, have a conelike resinous fruit that must first be soaked overnight in a lye solution (1 teaspoon per gallon of water) to dissolve the oily coating. After cleaning, the cones will break apart and release the seeds. Other junipers, like Alligator Juniper (*J. deppeana*), which have simple, berrylike fruits, may also be cleaned by soaking the fruits in a lye solution, by rubbing them on a screen, or macerating them in a blender.

There are several machines designed to process large quantities of fleshy fruits. These include feed grinders, customized cement mixers, hammermills, and macerators, and small leaf shredders (USDA 1974).

Seeds of species with thin fleshy coverings like sumacs and Mexican Silk-tassel (*Garrya ovata* subsp. *lindheimeri*) can be dried, stored, and planted with the skin intact. Or they may be cleaned by rubbing on a screen under running water as described above.

STORAGE

Many factors influence the longevity of seeds in storage. Mature seeds will remain viable longer than immature seeds. Seeds that have been nicked, soaked in water for extended periods, or otherwise damaged during cleaning will lose viability rapidly during storage. The inherent potential for longevity of each different species combined with conditions of temperature and moisture are most important in affecting seed viability. Some seeds are short-lived and must be sown immediately. Spring-ripened seeds, such as elms (*Ulmus* species), willows (*Salix* species), and some maples (*Acer spp.*) belong in this category. Put these types of seed in cold moist storage immediately after collection or sow as soon as possible.

Many species will lose viability if their moisture content is reduced, but for other species, just the opposite is true. Follow the guidelines on individual species.

Seeds with large cotyledons—acorns, walnuts, pecans, and buckeyes—are short-lived if allowed to dry out. The best results are gained by simply planting the seeds immediately after collection. Be sure to provide good drainage and ventilation to prevent rotting and mold. The seeds will begin to germinate by taking up moisture and extending their radicles (initial roots) during the fall and winter. Warm temperatures of spring will trigger shoot initiation.

Seeds such as legumes with hard seed coats are inherently long-lived because they are impermeable to water. These types of seeds should be carefully dried and then stored in sealed, moisture-resistant containers. Fumigation is also recommended to prevent insect damage. These seeds will remain viable for several years if held at low temperatures (35–41° F) and low humidity.

Small seeds such as maples (*Acer*) and snowbells (*Styrax*) that must not dry out should be mixed with sphagnum moss or a peat/perlite/vermiculite combination and kept in the refrigerator immediately after collection. This cold moist storage can also provide the stratification period necessary to break dormancy for certain seeds (see Types of Dormancy and Required Pretreatment Methods section in Chapter III; see also *Acer*). Check the containers periodically during storage to make sure the medium remains moist but not soggy and to determine that mold is not present. Misting the container with a dilute solution of fungicide will help minimize mold problems.

The best temperature range for storage is 32–50° F, with 41° F being ideal. Fluctuations in seed moisture and temperature will reduce seed longevity. When in doubt about the optimum conditions for storage of a certain species, place the clean, air-dried seeds in containers in the refrigerator and plant within a year. Useful containers for storing seeds include bags or sacks, coffee cans, and jars with lids. For storage in the refrigerator, polyethylene bags may also be used, especially when you are combining seeds with moist soil media. Seed that is not sufficiently air dried prior to storage may mold in the refrigerator.

III ~ *Seed Germination*

In order to produce significant numbers of seedlings, the grower must have a basic understanding of the germination process. By recognizing certain seed characteristics, one can determine the treatment necessary to germinate those species for which little or no information on germination is available.

THE GERMINATION PROCESS

A seed consists of an embryo and its stored food supply surrounded by a protective covering, or seed coat. Three factors must be present before germination will take place. First, the seed must be viable. Second, the internal conditions of the seed must be active and ready to germinate. And finally, the seed must be exposed to a favorable environment. The latter includes appropriate levels of moisture, temperature, oxygen, and, for some species, light.

The germination process takes place in three stages. The first is absorption, or imbibition, of water. The seed soaks up water and swells, and the seed coat may crack. In the second stage, the metabolic processes are activated, and the reserve food within the seed is digested and transferred to the growing parts of the seed to make leaves, shoots, and roots. The final stage is the emergence of the seedling radicle followed by the appearance of the shoot and the growth of the entire seedling.

SEED DORMANCY

A seed is said to be dormant if any stage of germination is blocked. Dormancy is a mechanism within the seed or part of the seed struc-

Stages of Seed Germination

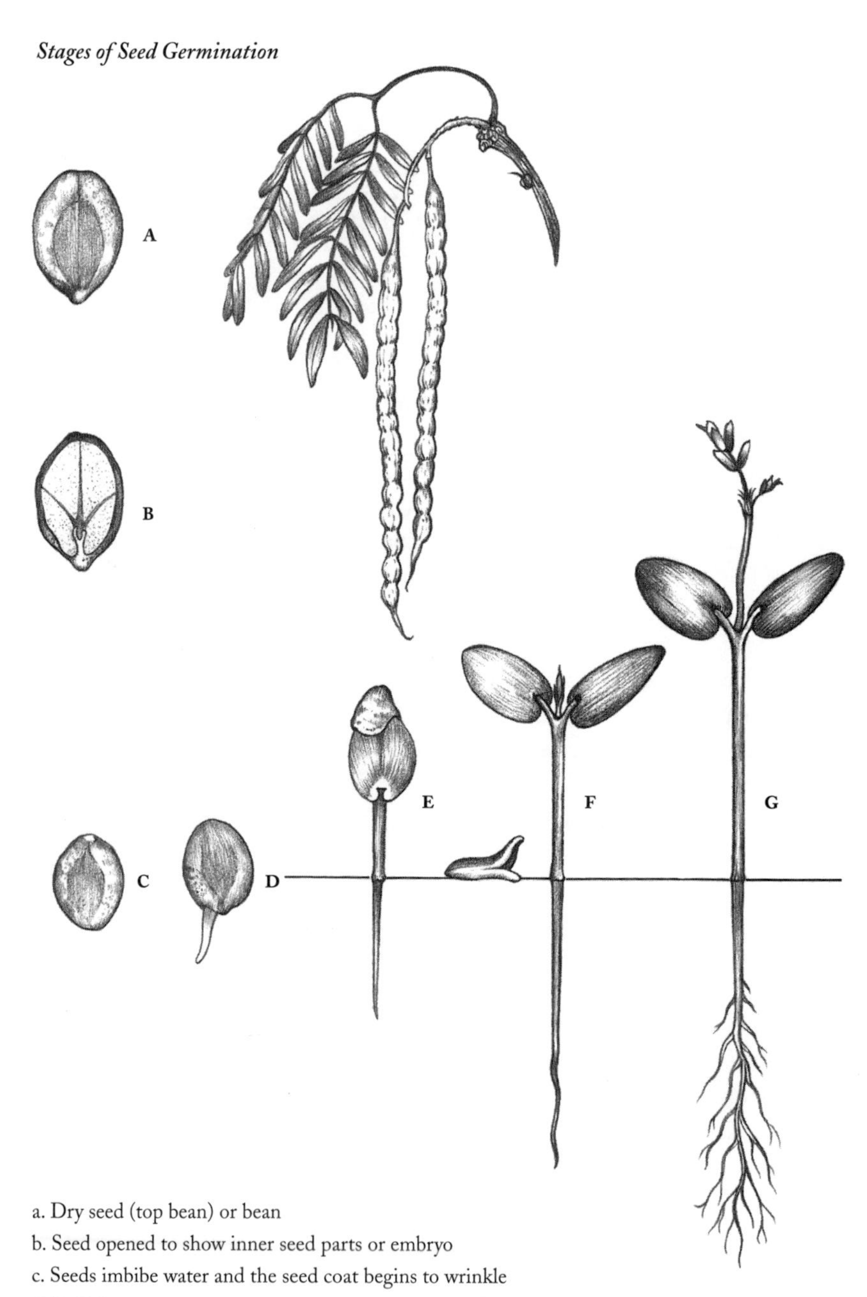

a. Dry seed (top bean) or bean

b. Seed opened to show inner seed parts or embryo

c. Seeds imbibe water and the seed coat begins to wrinkle

d. Radicle emerges

e. Seedling pushes up through the soil

f. Primary leaves or cotyledons unfold

g. Stem elongates and true pinnate leaves appear

ture that delays germination until environmental conditions are most favorable to seedling survival.

Approximately two-thirds of North American tree species exhibit some form of seed dormancy (USDA 1974). Dormancy may last only a few days during harvesting and drying, or it may be prolonged and involve lengthy treatments before germination will proceed. In addition, a seed may have more than one kind of dormancy.

TYPES OF DORMANCY AND PRETREATMENT METHODS

Dormancy may be caused by either the internal mechanisms of the seed or the seed's physical characteristics, such as a hard seed coat. Some species exhibit a combination of both kinds of dormancy. Under natural conditions the changes causing dormancy take place gradually under different combinations of aeration, moisture, temperature, and light. These natural environmental conditions can be carefully reproduced by the grower to meet the dormancy requirements of a plant and speed up its germination.

HARD SEED COATS AND SCARIFICATION

A hard seed coat is the most common external factor inhibiting germination. The first stage of germination, imbibition, is delayed because the hard seed coat will not permit the absorption of water. For some species, such as Guayule (*Parthenium argentatum*), the seed coat limits gas exchange. If respiration is inhibited, germination will not proceed because the metabolic processes involved in germination are fueled by oxygen and produce carbon dioxide. Therefore seed coats that limit either water intake or gas exchange must be nicked, thinned, or slightly reduced before germination will proceed.

Hard-seededness is characteristic of certain families such as the western legumes. A hard seed coat insures that the seed will not germinate until the seed coat has been reduced or cracked by exposure to sun, rain, heat, and cold. After several seasons of weathering, the seed may be buried in leaf litter or soil, which provides a more protected situation for germination than exposed soil. Seed coat thickness may vary among seed lots or among various populations, and even with different seasons. This delay mechanism permits a small percentage of seeds to germinate each time it rains, sometimes over a period of many years. This is an adaptation to a climate characterized by erratic and unpredictable rainfall.

Species with hard seed coats must be pretreated prior to sowing by *scarification*, a process whereby the seed coat is reduced or penetrated by either mechanical or chemical means. Treatment depends on the type and quantity of seeds. Small seed lots may be nicked by a knife, filed, or sanded by hand. With all types of seeds, it is very important that only the outer seed coat, which is usually dark in color, be nicked or reduced, while the inner seed coat remains untouched. Large quantities of seeds may be scarified in a mechanical tumbler or gem polisher or, more commonly, soaked in technical grade (93%) concentrated sulfuric acid.

GENERAL GUIDELINES FOR ACID SCARIFICATION

Used properly, acid scarification reduces or "thins" the seed coat without overheating or killing the seed embryo. Use sulfuric acid with *extreme caution* because it is very caustic and reacts with water. Gloves, goggles, long-sleeved shirts, and pants should be worn when you are handling sulfuric acid, and splashing or agitation of the acid should be avoided. If acid is spilled on your skin, wash immediately. Use large glass vessels or polyethylene buckets for soaking the seed. The process of acid scarification should be done outdoors on a caliche pad. This minimizes exposure to sulfuric acid vapors and makes emergency cleaning of spills more feasible. Caliche is composed mainly of carbonates of calcium and magnesium which will react with spilled acid to generate calcium carbonate and calcium sulfate, a fertilizer. The neutralization of any spills or acid water waste minimizes contamination of the ground. Acid scarification is not recommended or practical for the noncommercial grower. Instead, use the boiling water or mechanical scarification technique (see below).

The traditional method of acid scarification calls for the seeds to be very carefully dried and then set in the beaker alone before the acid is added. Pour about twice the volume of acid to seeds into the beaker. Leave the seed soaking in the acid for the required length of time, depending on the species. Stir gently with a glass rod at frequent intervals during the treatment. The treatment time may vary from a few seconds to 6 hours or more. If no guidelines are given, small amounts of the seed should be soaked in increasing intervals beginning with a few minutes. Check each test lot for imbibition. Most kinds of seeds will have a velvety iridescence when properly scarified. Overtreatment will result in cracked or peeling seed coat, which exposes the soft internal tissues to the acid. Seed coat thickness often varies from year to year for the same species, and so some testing within known parameters of treatment may be necessary each season to determine the optimum length of treatment for each particular lot. It is better to underscarify seeds than to overscarify. Seeds that are allowed to soak too long in acid may be weakened or even destroyed. In general, seeds should be scarified immediately before planting or stratification. However, Chris Best found that acid scarifying large amounts of seed prior to cold storage enabled him to consolidate the messy and tedious procedure rather than having to repeatedly set up and handle the acid for smaller seed lots. The seeds (primarily those of legumes) do not lose viability during subsequent cold storage and are ready for immediate aeration and germination as needed by the nursery (Best 1999).

When you are finished with all your acid scarification, pour off the acid over a screen and into a safe receptacle for recycled use on another batch of seed or for proper disposal. Wash the seed carefully for 5–10 minutes. Spread the seeds on paper, making sure they are not stuck together. Allow to dry at room temperature for 8 hours before storage.

The drawback with using sulfuric acid this way is that with each batch of seeds (especially seed like that of sumacs, which can be scarified with the pulp still on), the acid carbonizes and leaches substances out of the seed coats. These substances quickly build up in the acid and begin to solidify, turning it into a dark, sticky goo. "Dirty" acid is useless for seed treatment, even though it is still highly acid. Disposal of used acid can become a serious problem, and requires that greater amounts of new acid be purchased to treat new batches of seeds.

Chris Best developed a "one-minute" method for acid scarification that minimizes acid use without reducing its effectiveness. Before treating the seeds, he prepares a 3 × 4 × 2 foot "neutralizing bin" containing agricultural lime (one 50-pound sack for about 10 gallons of seed treated) and crushed limestone gravel. Over this bin are placed screens for catching the seeds as the neutralizing water is poured off. Seeds are first carefully dried and set to one side. Next, a portion of acid is poured into polyethylene buckets. Unlike galvanized buckets, the plastic buckets are resistant to acid. The seed are then added and thoroughly but gently stirred with the acid in the buckets for 1 minute, after which the acid is strained off into a separate glass container or bucket for use on another batch of seed. Meanwhile, the acid-covered seeds are left unrinsed in the buckets until they are ready for washing and neutralizing. The recommended length of treatment remains the same as with the continuous soak method. The bulk of the used acid turns black, but does not leach enough organic substances to solidify. The acid can be reused again and again, until it has been physically used up. If only dry seeds are mixed with the acid in each batch, then the acid does not lose much strength, even after many seeds have been treated. After the recommended treatment time has passed, the bucket containing the unrinsed acid-soaked seeds is filled two-thirds full with water, and the seeds are gently stirred to make sure they are not lumped together. The rinse water contains sulfuric acid, carbon, and an unknown mixture of burned organic compounds leached from the seed coat. This acid water is poured off the seeds through a screen into the neutralizing bin. A total of three rinsings is recommended. The acid foams as it reacts with the lime in the neutralizer. Any acid water not completely neutralized as it passes through the neutralizing bin will be neutralized as it leeches onto the caliche pad. After the three rinsings, four heaping trowels of lime are added to the wet seeds and stirred thoroughly. The wet lime will produce a lot of foam. When the foaming subsides, fill the bucket one-half full with water again and add two more scoops of lime. Let this react for 5–10 minutes and stir occasionally. Then pour the lime water through the screen into the neutralizing bin. The acid should be sufficiently neutralized by this time. If necessary, more rinsing with lime and water can be repeated until no foam is noticed. Pour the seeds onto a drying screen and wash with a hose. Rub the seeds on the screen while washing to further remove any adhering lime and carbon. Finally, spread the seeds on a drying screen to air dry. Seeds to be stored should be dried quickly. All drops and surface water should disappear within 30 minutes. Then leave seeds out an additional 8 hours to finish drying before storing. Seed to be sown does not have to be dried. The material in the neutralizing bin is then recycled at intervals as caliche road base for trails and paths (Best, personal communication, 1999).

SODIUM HYPOCHLORITE TREATMENT

For some species, like Guayule (*Parthenium argentatum*), acid scarification is too severe and sodium hypochlorite is recommended to thin or reduce the seed coat. Household bleach mixed in a 1:10 ratio with water is an effective source of this chemical. Seeds soaked in the sodium hypochlorite solution must then be rinsed under running water for 2 hours to avoid damaging the seeds (see *Parthenium*).

HOT WATER SEED SCARIFICATION

Other growers have found that a brief exposure to heat or very hot water effectively scarifies the seed coat without the danger or hassle of acid. Water is boiled while the seeds are placed in a wire mesh bag. Do not put too many seeds in the bucket, or they will cause the boiling water to cool too rapidly. The seeds are then immersed for the prescribed length of time. When the time is up, the bag of seeds is removed and then immediately immersed in cold water until the seeds are no longer hot to the touch. If the seeds are to be stored or planted at another time, spread them out in a single layer on drying screens to dry as quickly as possible to insure that no imbibition occurs (Best, personal communication, 1999). Some growers "steep" the seeds of certain species (e.g., Coral Bean, *Erythrina herbaceae*; Texas Mountain Laurel, *Sophora secundiflora*; and sumac, *Rhus spp.*) in boiling water (190° F) that is allowed to cool for 6–24 hours, until imbibition occurs, and then they plant the seeds immediately (Bering, personal communication, 1999).

ACTIVE YEAST METHOD

Chuck Janzow (personal communication, 1999) developed a method for treating species with pulpy fruit and somewhat hard pericarps (e.g., *Garrya* and *Prunus*). The seeds are cleaned by rubbing the pulp off on a screen and then they are aerated (see below) for 2 weeks in a solution of warm water to which active yeast and a teaspoon of sugar has been added. He found that the bacteria in the yeast broke down the remaining bits of pulp stuck to the seed, as well as reducing the seed coat itself. Acid scarification or hot water treatment is sometimes too harsh for these species. It is important, however, that the seed be aerated during the soaking period, or they will rot.

EARLY COLLECTION OF HARD-SEEDED SPECIES

Early harvest of seeds that are mature but have not completely hardened their seed coats is one way of avoiding scarification altogether. However, it does require that harvest be well timed. The seeds should be firm, filled out, and approximately of mature size, but at the stage when the seed coats are just beginning to turn a darker color. Gently scratching the surface of the seed with a thumbnail should reveal the difference in color between the inner and outer seed coats. Seeds planted precisely at this stage will often germinate promptly without treatment. But seeds collected early will often continue to harden their seed coats during the drying process prior to storage and may require scarification later.

Caution is advised in regard to planting partially mature seeds. Seeds that are too immature will produce weak and spindly seedlings or fail to germinate altogether. Many growers have experienced this problem when planting Texas Mountain Laurel (*Sophora secundiflora*) seeds that are a pink color and that have not hardened or turned the deep red of mature seeds. The advantage of planting soft-coated immature seeds may be outweighed by the inevitable production of weak offspring. Other growers report no difference in the vigor of young seedlings raised this way. Early-collected seeds should not be acid scarified.

PLANTS WITH APPARENTLY HARD SEED COATS

Some seemingly hard-seeded species like Mexican Buckeye (*Ungnadia speciosa*), Texas Buckeye (*Aesculus spp.*), and Goldenball Lead-tree (*Leucaena retusa*) germinate promptly without scarification. Scarification may hasten and unify germination, but it is not imperative. In some cases scarification will kill the seed or produce a weakened or deformed seedling. Germination of these species usually occurs within 3 weeks. Pregermination (see below) of the seeds overnight or for a few days and checking for swelling will determine if scarification is necessary.

Such species as walnuts or those with stony pits like olives and some fruits are slow to germinate because their hard seed coverings do not allow expansion of the seed embryo. However, scarification sometimes is not necessary, since the delay is usually not a prolonged obstacle to germination.

SEED COATS WITH CHEMICAL INHIBITORS

Some seed coverings have chemical inhibitors that delay germination. This occurs in resinous fruits like junipers or in the juices of certain fleshy fruits. These inhibitors are usually removed during the cleaning process. Especially sticky fruits may require soaking in a 1% lye solution to dissolve the coating (see Cleaning section in Chapter II). Chemical inhibitors are often found on the seeds of desert species where germination is influenced by the competition among plants for limited water resources. In nature the inhibitors are removed over time by leaching by rainfall or absorption in the soil. This insures that the seeds will germinate during infrequent wet periods of heavy thundershowers.

PHYSIOLOGICAL DORMANCY OF THE INNER SEED

The second general cause of seed dormancy is the internal physiological conditions within the seed. Internal or embryo dormancy may be exhibited as a short delay in germination lasting only a few days or a prolonged dormancy requiring long periods of moist chilling before the seed will sprout. Sometimes an embryo requires a period of *after-ripening*, which is usually fulfilled by a period of storage or *stratification*. During stratification seeds are undergoing chemical changes that will eventually allow germination. There are several conditions that must be provided for during stratification. The seed must have imbibed water (therefore any hard seed coats must be removed). The imbibition of water triggers certain internal enzymes that mobilize stored compounds and carbohydrates to various sites within the seed. After imbibition, the seed has to have adequate oxygen, proper temperature, and proper length of time exposed to certain temperatures. Embryo dormancy protects the seed from premature germination during the same season it ripens even if environmental conditions of temperature and moisture are right. The embryo dormancy of some species can be broken by exposing the seed to a period of cold moist storage or *cold stratification*. Other types of seed must be exposed to a period of warm moist temperatures to complete the development of the seed embryo before being exposed to cold temperatures. This condition, along with hard seed coats, contributes to *double dormancy*.

STRATIFICATION

Cold dormancy requirements protect fall-ripening species from germinating during the warm days of autumn only to be killed by frost later. Natural germination for most of these species is delayed until spring.

During the stratification process it is important that the cold period be combined with moist conditions so that the first stage of germination, imbibition, can occur. Embryo dormancy arrests germination at the second stage involving the initiation of metabolic activity within the seed. The growth of the seed embryo cannot proceed unless the seed has soaked up water. Therefore, dry cold storage alone is insufficient.

Seeds exhibiting a dormant embryo may be pretreated or stratified in a number of different ways. The easiest method to satisfy dormancy is to sow the seeds in prepared beds outdoors after harvest and cleaning in the fall. Eastern temperate forest species thrive best in best in well-tilled beds with a fair amount of sandy loam and organic matter to provide sufficient drainage. It should be kept moist but not soggy. For coarse-rooted western species, the most important element is drainage and enough space for the full extension of the initial root. Several growers have had very good results using caliche road base (see *Garrya*) or mineral sand mixed with a small amount of decomposed bark. For these types of plants, heavier rich soils should be avoided. A light mulch is often beneficial, but it should be

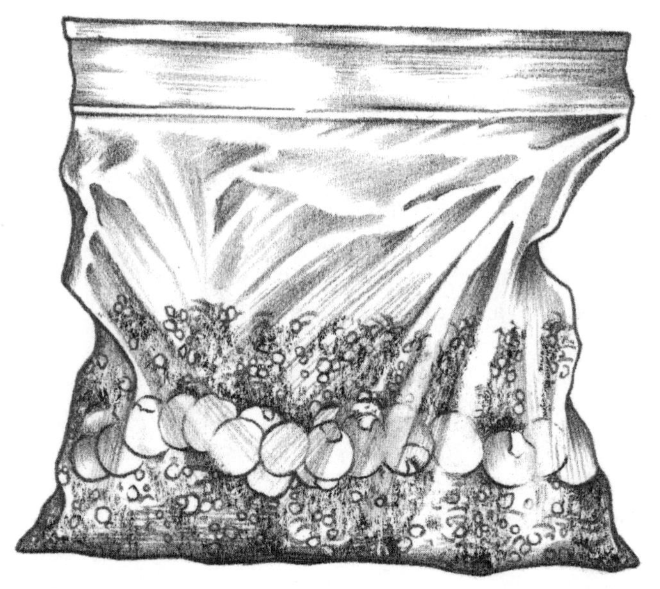

Cold Storage of Seeds

Seeds are stratified or held in cold moist storage in a plastic bag with alternate layers of a moist peat/perlite mixture. Layering the seeds allows them to be easily separated for planting later.

removed once germination begins. It may be necessary to cover the seedbed with wire or screen to keep out squirrels and other rodents. Early germinating seedlings may need protection from the dangers of a late killing frost, which can be accomplished by keeping the seedbed moist and covering it with plastic or a portable cold-frame structure.

Seeds with a cold dormancy requirement can also be pretreated indoors and later sown in flats or containers outside or in a greenhouse in early spring. Indoor treatment is often more effective than outdoor stratification because a refrigerator provides consistently low temperatures, while outdoor conditions may fluctuate. In Texas, winters are sometimes so mild that seed sown outdoors is not exposed to enough cold temperatures to break dormancy. Also, outdoor seedbeds require a lot of space for seeds whose viability and vigor cannot be guaranteed. Cold indoor storage can sometimes offer more control over germination than outdoor sowing. Cold stratification may be accomplished by stratifying the seeds in moist sand, sphagnum moss, or a peat/perlite mixture in a ventilated jar or plastic bag that is then placed in the refrigerator.

The seeds should be evenly combined with the media and kept moist. Mixing the seeds in alternating layers with the media makes them easy to separate later for sowing. Stratifying in perlite alone is another way to observe the seed. Optimum temperatures for cold stratification are 32–41° F (USDA 1974). The media should be misted periodically during the storage period to prevent drying.

LENGTH OF STRATIFICATION PERIOD

The stratification period varies for each species. It may be as short as a week or as long as 4 months. In general, southern strains of most species require a shorter period of stratification than their northern counterparts. Some southern strains require no pretreatment at all (Best, personal communication, 1999). Seed source and cleaning methods affect the duration of cold moist storage. Stratification periods for the same species may also vary slightly from year to year. In many cases, a short, 30-day cold stratification was sufficient to initiate and unify the germination period. Untreated seeds tend to have seedlings emerge at more staggered rates.

Check the containers regularly during cold stratification to insure that the seeds are not too far advanced in the germination process. If the radicle or initial root has begun to show, the emerging seedlings should be gently lifted out and placed in individual containers in a greenhouse. The stratification process should be planned so that the seeds may be removed from cold storage in early spring before the onset of hot temperatures. The mistake many growers make is to delay stratification after harvest and cleaning so that the seeds are still in cold storage in early spring when they should have fulfilled their dormancy requirements and been ready for sowing. Many species do not germinate well in hot temperatures. For early production, time the removal of the seeds from cold storage to begin in late January or February, and plant the seeds in a greenhouse. Although many growers in our part of the country typically don't utilize bottom heat, it has been shown to be effective in improving germination of certain seeds as they are removed from cold stratification. The air temperatures in the greenhouse are still cool, which can help reduce disease, yet the bottom heat stimulates the seed to germinate faster and stronger (Bering, personal communication, 1999).

If the dormancy requirements for a particular lot of seeds is unknown, stratify part of the seeds for 30 days, remove, plant, and then wait 3–4 weeks for germination results. Next remove a second lot that has remained in cold moist storage for 60 days, plant, and compare germination rates with the first lot. If germination rates are low even under optimum growing conditions, continue testing seed lots until the final group has been stratified for 120 days or, rarely in our climate, for as long as 180 days. Stratification periods should begin in the fall so that germination is not adversely affected by high temperatures in late spring. It is also recommended that a certain amount of seed be planted outdoors soon after collection as a control group for comparison. Many growers report that simply following nature's timetable and exposing the seeds to outdoor conditions is as good as any intervention or manipulation (Gass, personal communication, 1999).

"PULSING"

One grower developed a technique he calls "pulsing" for enhancing the germination of certain species (e.g., *Viburnum*, *Acer*) that have dormant embryos and that tend to germinate in staggered numbers over a long period after removal from cold stratification. He found that he can condense the length of cold storage into a shorter period by removing the bags of seeds (mixed with perlite or sphagnum moss) from cold storage at 2-week intervals, beginning about 6 weeks before they are scheduled to be removed for sowing. Let the bags warm up (no higher than 75° F) for 6–24 hours. Open up the bags briefly to provide air and moisture exchange, then reseal and put in the refrigerator for another 2 weeks. In nature, these seeds are typically subjected to warming and cooling periods. "Pulsing" provides for more uniform and sharper alternating temperatures and promotes earlier germination. Sometimes the seed will begin to sprout in the bag (Janzow, personal communication, 1999).

DOUBLE DORMANCY AND AFTER-RIPENING

Some seeds, like Rusty Black-haw Viburnum (*Viburnum rufidulum*) and American Holly (*Ilex opaca*), require a period of *after-ripening* or warm moist stratification prior to a period of cold moist storage. Warm stratification promotes the growth of the primary root and seedling stem within the seed. Seeds that naturally ripen in late summer or early fall are exposed to 1–2 months of relatively mild warm weather before frost hits and the cold begins. One reason some seeds require this period of warm stratification is because the seed embryos are immature at the time of harvest and must be allowed time to completely develop before they will germinate. Warm temperatures provide this period for embryo growth.

Other seeds, such as Rough-leaf Dogwood (*Cornus drummondii*) and Fragrant Sumac (*Rhus aromatica*), exhibit a combination of both hard-seededness and embryo dormancy. As mentioned above, the seed must imbibe water before the germination process will proceed. Seeds with both kinds of dormancy must first be scarified before stratification. Scarification or stratification alone is ineffective. Procedures for double-dormant seeds are the same as those described above for after-ripening.

IV ~ *Planting*

LATE WINTER PLANTING IN A GREENHOUSE

Once the seeds have been collected, cleaned, stored, and, if necessary, pretreated, the next step is to provide the proper environment for germination. Sound seeds are ready to germinate if given the proper levels of temperature and moisture. Seed-sowing guidelines that are too general can be misleading; conditions in the forest belt east and north to the Atlantic or the western states at higher elevations are quite different from those in Texas. In Texas, the spring is so short that planting in late January or at least no later than March in a cold frame or greenhouse is recommended because temperatures quickly become too warm for optimum germination and seedling survival. Optimum germination temperature for temperate forest species is 50–62° F. Propagation in a greenhouse in Texas should begin as early as January for some species and be planned so that all seedlings are ready to be removed to individual containers outdoors no later than the first of May. This procedure will provide sturdier seedlings able to withstand the heat stress of summer and also will encourage higher germination rates.

OUTDOOR FALL PLANTING

Seeds to be sown outdoors should be cleaned and placed in prepared beds as soon as is feasible after collection, to simulate what the seed would undergo on its own in nature.

SPRING PLANTING

Many hardwood species having seeds that require varying amounts of moist chilling will not germinate after treatment until the soil becomes warm. This is also true of shrubby perennials in the mallow family, Pavonia (*Pavonia lasiopetala*), for example. Optimum germination temperatures for these seeds are 68–86° F. Seeds of these species do not germinate in the cool fall season but instead emerge in late spring. They may be planted in late fall for spring emergence. Or they may be held in cool dry storage over winter and then planted in very early spring in a greenhouse or cold frame, or outdoors after all danger of frost is past.

AERATION PROCEDURE FOR SEED GERMINATION

Aerating seeds in water for one or more days can enhance uniform germination for two reasons. First, seeds left to imbibe water without aeration begin to respire and rapidly consume all available dissolved oxygen. The seed will then suffocate if left too long in water. Aerating the water allows seeds to be left for a long period in water without danger of suffocation. Second, the seed coat may still have inhibitory substances, even after cleaning, drying, and washing, which can be leached from the seed. The aeration method is very simple: seeds are placed in jars or buckets and covered with enough water to give them room to swirl around. Generally, 2–3 volumes of water for each volume of seeds is sufficient. Add enough water to take into account that seed swelling will soon occur. The bucket or beaker is supplied with air through flexible hoses connected by gang valves to aquarium pumps. The hose is connected with a scintillated glass aerator (air stone) that is set at the bottom of the container. Proper aeration requires only a slight air flow. Too much pressure may disconnect the hose from the aerator or bubble the seeds out of the beaker. Strain and replace the water every 12 hours. Many species produce large volumes of foam after a few hours of aeration, which can cause the seed to float off, so water volume and quality should be monitored regularly. The majority of seeds do not need more than 1 or 2 days of aeration. Do not let the seeds germinate in the water. When the aeration period is finished, rinse the seeds again and sow directly in containers, or lay them in germination trays on moist paper towels (see below). The aerators will develop a bacterial slime after several uses that can clog the pores. Gently scrub the air stones with a dish-scrubbing pad and detergent after every few uses. Rinse the detergent thoroughly before reuse. Aeration has been very effective in germination of species such as *Pithecellobium flexicaule* (Texas Ebony), *Coursetia axillaris*, and *Forestiera* (Best 1999).

PREGERMINATION ON MOIST PAPER

Some species can be efficiently propagated by pregerminating their seeds on moist newspaper or paper towels on trays in the greenhouse or cold frame. The paper must be *moist*, not wet. There should never be droplets of water surrounding the seeds. Excess water or too many layers of paper encourages bacterial rot and can suffocate the seeds. This method allows the grower to carefully regulate temperature, light, and moisture in order to maximize germination rates. Once germination begins, the germinated seeds can be removed and individually planted in separate containers. The tray is kept moist until all the good seeds have germinated. In this way, space and containers are not taken up by "duds." One end of the tray should be elevated about 2 inches, to drain off any excess water and also to encourage tap roots to grow down the incline. Keep trays in a shaded, warm, but not hot, location. Pregerminated seeds can often be planted in containers almost as fast as direct seeding untreated seeds. This method is especially useful for species which germinate over a long period of time, such as Sabal Palm (*Sabal mexicana*), Anacahuita (*Cordia boisseri*), and Texas Persimmon (*Diospyros texana*). It is also useful for those species (e.g., oaks, Sierra Madre Torchwood [*Amyris madrensis*]) which produce a long taproot before shoot emergence. Tap-rooted seedlings are unsuitable for sowing in seed flats because their roots get tangled and contorted in a short flat, yet uncertain germination rates mean that many more containers must be filled with potting soil than will actually hold plants when the germination process is complete.

FALL PLANTING IN A GREENHOUSE OR COLD FRAME

Some growers have found it helpful to begin fall germination of certain species in a "wet-wall" greenhouse. This is a simple greenhouse with one end fitted entirely with evaporative cooling pads and the other side with fans which can lower the high temperatures of late August by as little as 10° to make germination and seedling survival possible. The young seedlings are then held over the winter in cold frames that keep temperatures no lower than 41° F. This allows the grower to collect the heat during sunny days in winter to maintain minimal temperatures to protect young plants. Bottom heat is also used to promote root growth. After the last frost, the plants are ready to be hardened off and moved outside. The result is that a larger plant is ready earlier in the season and can be moved into larger containers. Over-wintered plants are often stronger and better able to withstand high seasonal temperatures (Pfeiffer, personal communication, 1999).

If sowing must be delayed until April or later, better results are often obtained if the seeds are sown in flats or containers outdoors and given some shade and wind protection.

COLD FRAMES

In a climate with moderate winters, a simple cold frame generally provides adequate protection and warmth for planting seeds in early February. The cold frame may be a permanent structure or a portable frame to place over outside containers or seedbeds. The cold frame should be ventilated during warm spells in spring to remove condensation and avoid fungi and overheating. A cold frame is less expensive than a greenhouse to build and operate and usually provides sufficient protection for germinating seedlings. However, during exceptionally cold weather, it may be necessary to move the flats indoors or install a portable heater. Raising seedlings in the lower temperatures of a cold frame encourages them to harden off and adapt more quickly to outside temperatures.

CONTAINERS

Seeds may be sown in flats, boxes, or separate pots or containers. Seeds with large taproots, like acorns, buckeyes, and pecans, do best if planted in containers that allow enough room for the initial taproot. Recent studies have shown that coarse-rooted western species develop better root systems and, in some cases, stem growth, when planted in containers that promote root pruning. This can be accomplished in several ways. For liners, the seeds can be planted in individual "conetainers" or paper "Plant Bands." These containers are long paper or plastic cylinders held in special racks that provide plenty of room for the long initial taproot yet require a minimum of potting soil. Holes at the bottom of the tubes air prune the root and encourage development of secondary roots. The narrow planting tubes are set in cases on top of mesh tables. As the long root extends to the holes of the tube, the air "burns" it and retards growth. Interior or secondary roots are then developed. By the time the seedling is transplanted, there is a dense mat of roots instead of one woody girdled taproot. Big improvements in seedling survival both in the field and when transplanted into larger containers have been observed.

BENEFITS OF AIR PRUNING ROOTS

Most growers of coarse-rooted western species are familiar with the problem of managing the long taproots these plants develop, which quickly seek the drainage holes in the bottom of the containers to root themselves into the soil. As the container is lifted from the ground, the root is often broken, causing the whip-like stem to wilt immediately. In addition, many of these species (e.g., Desert Willow, *Chilopsis linearis*) have a tendency to send out one main root that easily becomes root girdled in the pot. A strong taproot is a necessary adaptive mechanism for plants that need to become established quickly in xeric situations, but it is a drawback in container production. Recent studies have explored the benefits of growing woody ornamental plants in copper-treated containers. Cupric hydroxide applied to the interior surfaces or embedded in the plastic material of the pot itself inhibits root growth through low-level toxicity. The root tips are "burned" when they come in contact with the copper compound. This results in a change in the root system's morphology: a greater number of secondary and interior roots are produced, increasing the root system density. Greater root mass enables plants to use water and nutrients more efficiently and better survive transplant shock or dryness. These changes in root density and distribution may contribute to larger and faster stem growth (Struve et al. 1994). Copper-treated containers have proven beneficial in production of Wright's Acacia (*Acacia wrightii*), Flame-leaf Sumac (*Rhus lanceolata*), Desert Willow (*Chilopsis linearis*), Eve's Necklace (*Sophora affinis*), Live Oak (*Quercus virginiana*), and Bald Cypress (*Taxodium distichum*) (Arnold, personal communication, 1999).

In addition to the copper-treated pots, several other types of containers with air-root pruning design have been developed which provide more air holes to inhibit root tips, encourage lateral branching of roots, and minimize girdling. These pots have a series of holes tiered or spiraled around the pot in addition to the drainage holes at the bottom. One grower reported up to 30% more stem growth and greater root mass in Texas Redbuds grown in 15-gallon "Whitcomb Root-maker" pots when compared to a standard container (Will, personal communication, 1999). Whatever the method, properly air pruned seedlings and young trees have greater rates of survival and growth in the field (Best 1999).

Young seedlings are placed on wire benches to promote air pruning of new roots.

SOIL MIXES

There are many different soil media components and combinations that can be used for container propagation. Whatever the materials, all soil mixtures must have certain characteristics. They should be sufficiently firm and dense to hold seedlings in place, without being too heavy. They should have a constant volume, whether wet or dry. They should not be too difficult to rewet; avoid straight peat or clay. They should be able to hold moisture adequately and not get too dry, yet be sufficiently well drained to encourage fibrous root development and never become soggy. Soggy soil limits the supply of oxygen and may inhibit germination. Soil mixes should also be free from weeds, fungus, and insects.

Every grower eventually develops his or her own recipe for a soil mix. These are usually based on available local materials, modified in their proportions to meet the criteria listed above. Many western species do not thrive in the typical pine-bark-based container medium used in nurseries in the east. Several growers report that they have had good growth in pure limestone gravel for some species like Mexican Silk-tassel (*Garrya ovata* subsp. *lindheimeri*) and Evergreen Sumac (*Rhus virens*). The disadvantage to this cheap substrate is that the containers are almost too heavy to lift. Drainage, not fertility, is the most important consideration in container growing of these more xeric plants.

A standard soil mix commonly used to germinate seeds in containers is peat moss and perlite combined either in equal parts or one part peat to two parts perlite for a well-drained mix. Vermiculite may be substituted for perlite. Milled sphagnum moss and worm castings are also good media components when combined with perlite or vermiculite. Commercially bagged and sterilized potting soil is excellent for seed germination, although it may be necessary to add more perlite or vermiculite to insure good drainage.

BENEFICIAL SOIL MICROORGANISMS

Most species of higher plants form mycorrhizal associations. Mycorrhizal fungi help plants compete in nature because they increase the surface area of the roots and thus enhance the plant's ability to take up water, phosphates, and other nutrients from the soil. They may also help protect the plant against soil-borne plant pathogens. In turn, the plant provides carbohydrates gathered from sunlight through photosynthesis to the mycorrhizae. A group of bacteria called rhizobium are associated with many legumes. These bacteria form nodules on the roots that fix atmospheric nitrogen and thus improve soil fertility. However, the legumes must supply the bacteria with large amounts of chemical energy (adenosine triphosphate). Recent experience of several growers indicates that production and survival of many slow-growing plants, especially those species that form sparse or single taproots, often without lateral branching, can be improved by either incorporating native soil into the potting soil mix or inoculating a sterile soil blend with these beneficial microorganisms. Initial use of these inoculant products has resulted in greater survival of plants as they are moved up to bigger containers and planted in the field, and in some cases has improved stem growth as well (Gass, personal communication, 1999).

INDOOR SOWING

The seed flat or container should be premoistened before the seeds are planted. Heavy watering after sowing may wash away or bury the seeds too deeply, especially if they are small. Most small seeds should be pressed into the soil instead of buried. Some small seeds require only a light sprinkling of fine sand. Burying fine seeds too deeply may delay or hinder germination. In contrast, if larger seeds are planted too shallowly, they may dry out in the upper surface of the soil. Depth of planting varies with the type and size of the seeds and the environment in which they are planted. A basic guideline is to plant the seeds two to four times as deep as the diameter of the seeds.

SEEDLING DISEASES

Many seeds are susceptible to a seedling disease caused by damping-off fungi, primarily *Pythium ultimum* and *Rhizoctonia solani*. Slow-growing or weak seeds are especially vulnerable. To prevent or minimize damping off, the soil media should be drenched with an appropriate fungicide prior to sowing. Follow this initial drenching with periodic applications of the fungicide when watering. Damping off can also be effectively prevented by following simple cultural practices of sanitation and maintenance. Damping off and powdery mildew fungi thrive in conditions that include overwatering, poor drainage, lack of ventilation, and high relative humidity. Damping-off fungi also thrive in concentrations of soluble salts, often present in the water supply, that are high enough to weaken seedlings. Providing a well-drained medium and avoiding overwatering will help to prevent serious damage by this disease. Sphagnum moss inhibits damping-off fungi and is therefore a good germination medium. Fungi thrive in a temperature range of 69° to 86° F and are not as active at higher and lower temperatures. Improperly ventilated greenhouses provide the warm moist conditions that are ideal for the proliferation of damping-off fungi, powdery mildew, and other diseases. Once these diseases take over, they are very difficult to control.

FIELD SOWING

If the seeds are to be field sown, till the beds at least 6–8 inches and provide a soil mixture that is well drained and does not pack down or crust over. Ideal seedbeds have a mix of organic material like composted manure and bark to improve the soil structure and fertility. This is best when combined with a mineral soil such as decomposed granite or "Orange," "Poteet," or some other type of washed sand. Avoid using clay or peat moss. Fall-sown seedbeds should be covered with a light mulch that is removed in early spring as soon as germination begins. It is important to keep the seedbed moist but not soggy throughout the winter, especially for such species as Texas Buckeye (*Aesculus spp.*), which extend their roots immediately after fall planting. A dry seedbed may kill the growing seedling and also make the plant more vulnerable to freeze damage.

It may be necessary to place a screen or wire mesh over an outdoor seedbed to prevent predation by rodents or birds. Seeds that are fall sown in flats outdoors should also be covered with screen and placed in blocks or racks off the ground.

TRANSPLANTING SEEDLINGS

Transplant seedlings from the flat after the second set of leaves has appeared and when the plants are large enough to handle. Seeds should not be sown too densely, or separation during transplanting will be difficult to achieve without breaking the roots. Crowding also results in poor stem formation and overall growth retardation. Plants have greater chances of survival if the roots are not exposed to air and if a little dirt is allowed to remain around the roots. Seedlings should be planted without delay, before they become root bound. Containers or flats with screen mesh bottoms placed on raised slat tables will stimulate the formation of branch roots by air pruning the main root as it extends past the screen. Later pruning should take place when the liner flat is transplanted by removing the roots that protrude from the pot by about an inch. Another technique that has proven critical to seedling survival minimizes exposure of the roots to air during transplanting. Young seedlings are soaked in a solution of root stimulator and water before they are repotted in a one-gallon container. Plants are then watered immediately after potting and kept moist but not soggy for the first week to avoid shock (see *Garrya*). Losses during transplanting are reduced substantially with this technique (Janzow, personal communication, 1999).

V ~ *Vegetative Propagation*

ADVANTAGES OF CUTTING PROPAGATION

When plants are grown from cuttings, the unique characteristics of any single plant are duplicated in the clone. A clone is a group of plants reproduced vegetatively from a single plant. Cutting propagation allows commercial nurseries to grow plants more quickly and often in greater numbers than from seed. Besides the perpetuation of certain outstanding characteristics of the parent plant, vegetative propagation is often less expensive and more predictable than seed propagation. The grower does not have to rely on a good seed crop to provide propagating material. Good seed crops do not occur every year, and even in good years, an abundant harvest of viable seeds depends on prompt collection and proper storage. Some seeds, even if viable, require complex and lengthy pretreatments before they will germinate. In contrast, most cuttings can be taken over a long growing season and some species may be grown year round from cuttings.

Cuttings are used to duplicate specific characteristics or special qualities such as showy flowers, fruits, leaf shapes, or such unusual forms as dwarfness or "weeping" branches. The potential for selection of showy cultivars among native plants has been largely overlooked. Yet the success of some recent native plant selections (e.g., 'Greencloud' Cenizo, *Leucophyllum frutescens*) indicates that vegetative production should not be considered more difficult for native plants than the more familiar mass-produced exotic cultivars. Selections of superior forms are typically made after many years of collecting individual wild specimens or choosing seedling plants that have exhibited superior flower or leaf color

and form. A test block of plants is established in the nursery to monitor performance of the plant over several seasons. Next, cuttings of the strongest specimens with the best characteristics are taken and grown to mature size. Finally, the plant is evaluated for its suitability as a stock plant from which many cuttings could be made and then the selections are released as cultivars to the public. Cultivars are registered with a name given by the nursery that has invested in the research and selection of these superior forms. Some nurseries apply trademark names on these plants as well. Trademark and patent laws for plants are part of a controversial and flawed system that is better left for another discussion. Most professional nursery owners agree that all growers should share in the expense and time of developing new cultivars and that unfair raiding and renaming of plant selections one nursery has worked hard to introduce is unethical and damaging to the whole profession.

SOME DRAWBACKS TO VEGETATIVE PROPAGATION

Some propagators believe a cutting will make a larger plant sooner than one raised from seed. Others maintain that a healthy seedling quickly makes up for the initial advantage in size achieved by a rooted cutting, and eventually may exceed a cutting in vigorous growth or superior form (Simpson, personal communication, 1986). Certain shrubby perennials like the salvias, Turk's Cap (*Malvaviscus arboreus var. drummondii*), Rose-mallow Pavonia (*Pavonia lasiopetala*), and certain woody vines like honeysuckle (*Lonicera* species) and Virginia Creeper (*Parthenocissus quinquefolia*) root much more quickly and economically than they can be grown from seeds. Other species such as ash (*Fraxinus spp.*) and Madrone (*Arbutus xalapensis*) are difficult or impossible to root and therefore can be profitably increased only by seeds.

A plant reproduced vegetatively over a long period may be at a disadvantage if a change in the environment or a sudden insect or disease attack occurs because it has had no opportunity to evolve adapted forms. All members of a clone will be equally affected and perhaps even destroyed. An ornamental landscape composed of mass plantings of the same clone is also vulnerable to these kinds of changes (see *Salvia*).

THE ROOTING PROCESS

The process of rooting requires several general steps. First, a plant is selected for vegetative propagation. This selection requires knowledge of the right time of year to gather the cutting wood and the proper methods necessary for different species. Cuttings may be selected from nursery-grown stock plants or from plants gathered from the field. Then, the stem or root is cut or otherwise wounded to trigger the beginning of root development. Next, a callus or swollen mass of cells develops around wounded plant tissues on the basal part of stem cutting. Callusing is an important step preceding real root development in most stem cuttings. Then adventitious roots or new growing points emerge from the base of stem cuttings. In root cuttings, stems begin to form as well as additional roots. Finally, an independent plant is transplanted to a separate container.

HOW NEW ROOTS ARE PRODUCED

Within the stem exist groups of meristematic cells or undeveloped embryonic cells that are able to differentiate into adventitious roots and eventually into fully developed roots. The initiation of new roots from these specialized embryonic cells is first stimulated by some type of wounding, such as cutting the stem. When root cuttings are cut, adventitious buds eventually form new shoots. Production of adventitious roots on stem cuttings depends on five main factors: the inherent ability of the plant (dependent on its type and age) to develop new roots, the presence or application of root-promoting substances, the location on the stem where the wound or cut was taken, the time of year the cutting was made and therefore the type of wood used, and proper environmental conditions. Different types of wood even on the same plant root may result in different levels of success. The time required to develop new roots after cuttings are placed in the rooting bed varies widely. Some herbaceous plants like the carnation root within 5 days, while some woody species, especially narrow-leaf evergreens, may take 6 weeks to several months to root.

INHERENT ABILITY TO ROOT

Such easily rooted species as Willow (*Salix*) and Cottonwood (*Populus spp.*) have adventitious roots already present in the stem before the cuttings are taken. These are generally dormant until the stems are made into cuttings and placed in a rooting bed under favorable conditions. Other hard-to-root species may have the capacity for generating adventitious roots but require more time and careful treatment in order to complete development.

Stages of Rooting

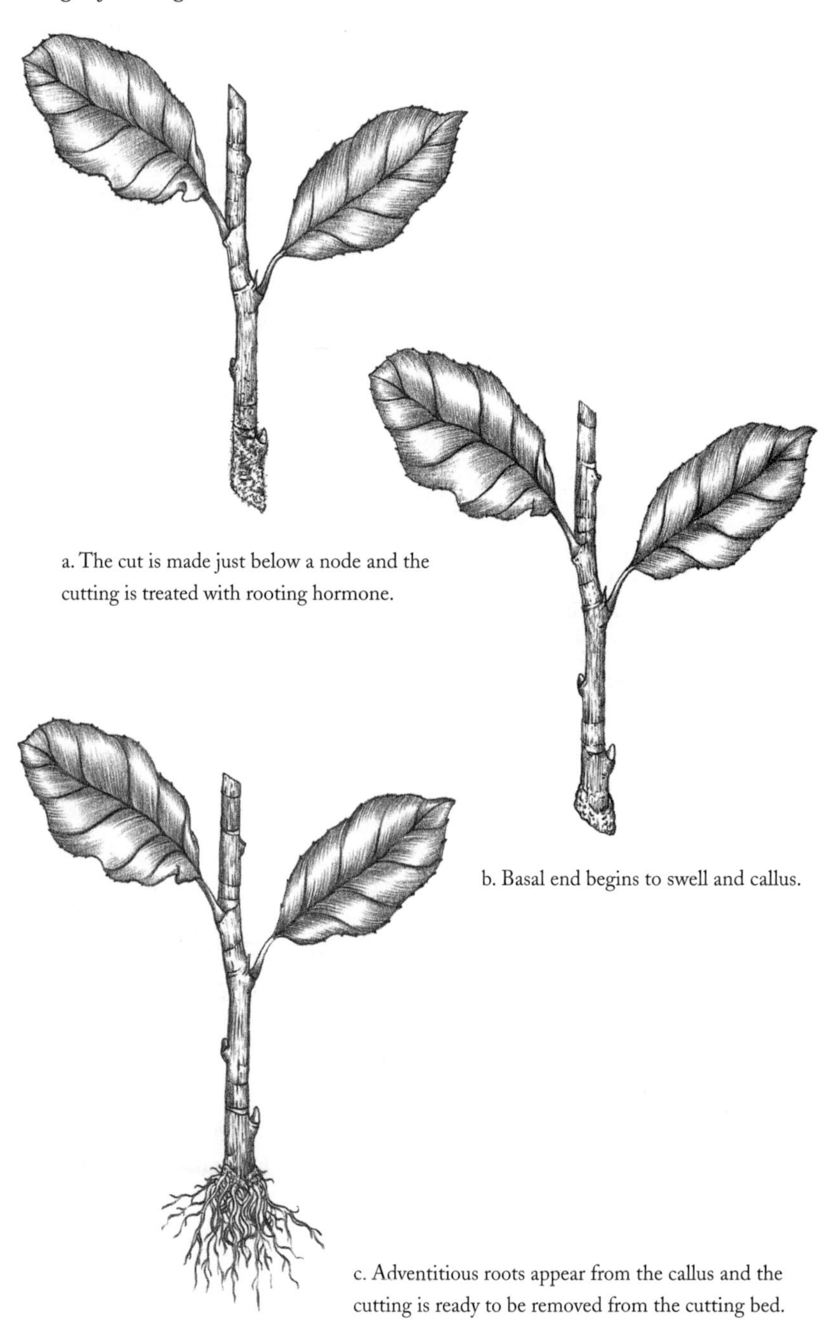

a. The cut is made just below a node and the cutting is treated with rooting hormone.

b. Basal end begins to swell and callus.

c. Adventitious roots appear from the callus and the cutting is ready to be removed from the cutting bed.

Types of Cuttings

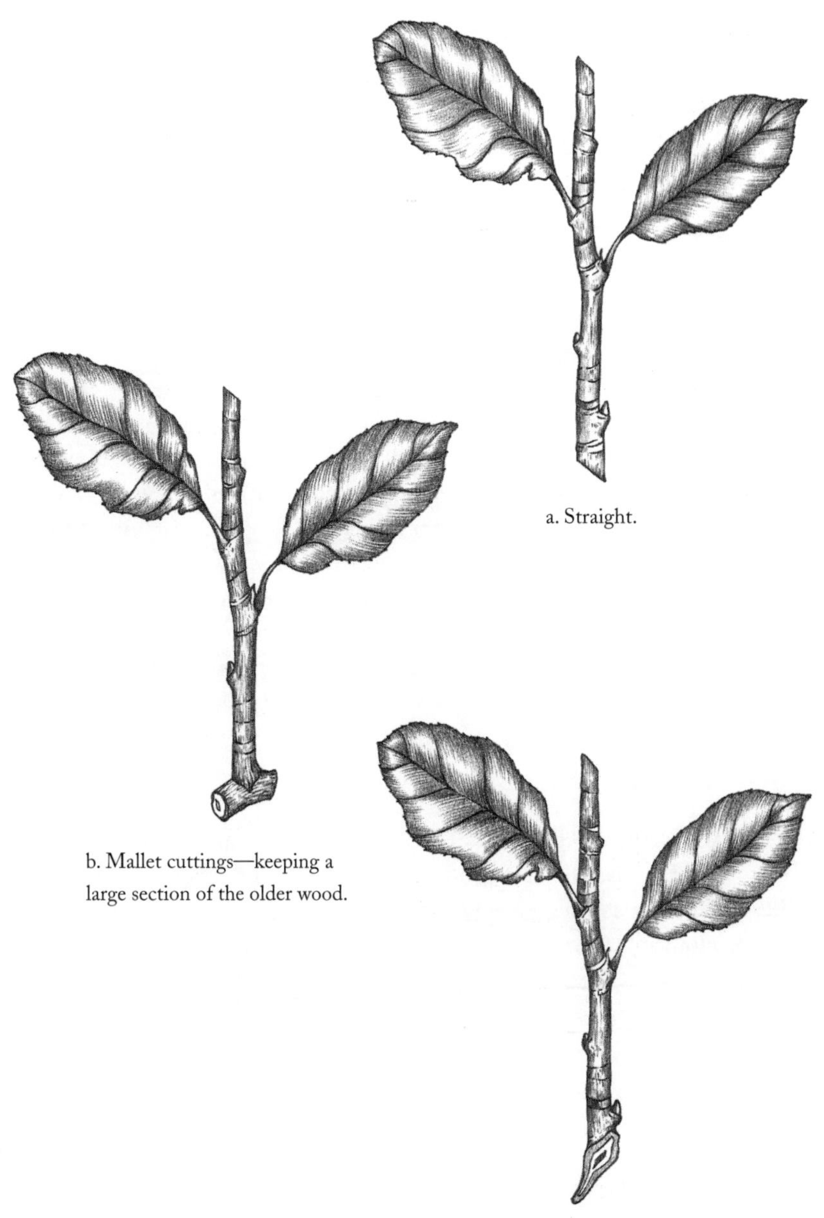

a. Straight.

b. Mallet cuttings—keeping a large section of the older wood.

c. Heel cutting—only a small piece or sliver of the older wood is retained as part of the cutting.

AGE OF THE CUTTING: THE JUVENILITY FACTOR

One-year-old seedlings and other young plants often root in larger percentages than older plants because of some little-understood factors related to the juvenile growth stage. As a plant grows older it may produce growth inhibitors. Since these are not often present in young plants, the juvenile wood of trees and shrubs, especially for hard-to-root species, is often selected for cutting material. The juvenile stage of a plant is usually described as the period of vigorous growth preceding flowering and fruiting. The juvenile form may differ from the mature plant by having different leaf shapes, excessive thorniness, or a distinct overall shape. Cuttings taken from young cutting-produced or seedling plants are much more amenable to rooting than cuttings from older plants (Dirr and Heuser 1987). Many growers maintain certain stock plants at the nursery as a continuous source of juvenile cutting wood. The juvenile phase, in its duration and characteristics, is different for every species/cultivar. The only way to determine the best type of wood for cuttings is to experiment with different aged stock.

Seedling stock plants under 1 or 2 years old are also a good source of juvenile wood. Juvenile wood of some species may also be obtained from the base of older plants that are kept severely cut back or are coppiced every winter (see *Quercus*).

LOCATION OF THE CUT

Leaves and buds also stimulate rooting in cuttings taken from nondormant wood because they are producers of growth-influencing hormones. These auxins appear in greatest concentrations directly below a bud or leaf and therefore adventitious roots are most likely to develop at this location. Unless otherwise recommended, it is important to make the bottom cut just below a leaf node or bud.

WHEN TO TAKE CUTTINGS

The time of year the cutting is taken is not as important as the physiology of the wood. Some plants (e.g., *Forestiera* and *Lonicera*) can be rooted from cuttings taken year round; with others, success is limited to specific types of wood produced only at certain times. The methods for taking stem cuttings of woody species are generally prescribed by the type of wood used and the time of year the cuttings are gathered. If you are collecting wood from plants in the wild, it is important to remember that often the rootability of cuttings is affected by climatic cycles. During a dry year, the plant will generate less new growth, making suitable cutting material difficult to gather. Production levels could vary from year to year unless stock plants are kept fertilized and watered at the nursery, forcing the plant to flush out new growth despite the weather patterns. Keeping good records for each season is the only way to refine the techniques that include all the variables required for good rooting.

TYPES OF CUTTINGS

Hardwood cuttings are taken during the dormant (late fall and winter) season from wood of the previous season's growth. Rooting some plants from hardwood cuttings taken in winter can be the easiest and least expensive way to produce new plants because a minimum of equipment and facilities is required. However, rooting from dormant wood is typically very slow and may take from several months to a year to achieve. Species that are generally hard to root will not root from hardwood cuttings. *Semihardwood* cuttings are taken during the growing season from new wood that has finished its first flush of growth; the wood is reasonably hard, not flexible, especially toward the base, and the leaves are mature. Semihardwood cuttings are not as sensitive to drying as softwood cuttings. They are also generally easier to handle and stick. *Softwood* cuttings are taken from the emerging tender shoots and growing tips of the current season's growth. The wood is easily bent or bruised and the new leaves small and undeveloped from the bud. Softwood cuttings are the most delicate type of wood. Their shoots are easily bent and they quickly wilt after being collected from the parent plant.

HARDWOOD STEM CUTTINGS

Several factors are key to rooting success with hardwood cuttings. Wood with the highest rooting potential is of moderate size and in good condition, with carbohydrate reserves stored from the growing season to support it during the long rooting process. Tip cuttings are usually not selected. Hormone treatments of 2,000 to 5,000 ppm is beneficial. Careful water regimes and a well-drained rooting bed are necessary to avoid rotting during the many cool months it may require to generate new roots. Keeping the tops cool inhibits bud break on the stems that could cause the cutting to dry out before new roots are formed. Hardwood cuttings of deciduous species are generally taken in the dormant season (late fall through mid-winter) from wood of the previous season's growth. Select cuttings from healthy plants growing in full sun. Take the cuttings in the winter well before the buds have begun to swell and develop or the cuttings may quickly leaf out and die before new roots are formed. Avoid taking cuttings from spindly growth. The central and basal portions of the stem make the best cuttings because they have a higher concentration of stored carbohydrates that sustain the shoot and new roots until the cutting is fully developed.

The length of hardwood cuttings varies from 6 to 20 inches, depending on the species and the intended use of the cuttings. Cuttings as long as 30 inches are used as rootstocks for fruit trees. This length allows room later for varietal grafting. Cuttings of the same species should be uniform in length and tied together in small bundles; make sure all the basal ends (the ends cut closest to the main trunks of the parent trees) are together. Without leaves it may be hard to tell the top from the bottom of the cutting. Therefore it is best to cut all the basal ends at a slant to avoid confusion. Each cutting should have at least two nodes or buds. The basal cut should be taken just below a node and the top cut ½ inch or 1 inch above a node. The diameter of hardwood cuttings may range from ¼ inch to 1 or 2 inches, depending on the species. Some species root better if a "heel" is taken at the basal end. A heeled cutting is one that includes a short section of older wood (see illustration). "Mallet" cuttings are also used to propagate some species. A mallet cutting is similar to a heel, except the section of older wood is larger and the cutting has a T shape at the base (see illustration). Cuttings are treated with a rooting hormone and either stuck directly in the field (late fall or winter) or rooted in a greenhouse and planted out.

ROOTING DECIDUOUS HARDWOOD CUTTINGS

Cuttings of deciduous plants taken in winter and tied together in small bundles as described above should then be buried upside down outdoors in well-drained boxes containing sandy soil, sand, sawdust, or a peat/perlite mixture. The basal ends must be near the surface because the warmer temperatures on top will stimulate root initiation. The colder temperatures deeper in the box will inhibit development on the top or proximal end of the cutting. Keep the rooting media moist but well drained to prevent either extreme of desiccation or rotting during the winter. Periodically check the cuttings for drying and signs of bud development. Cuttings that have started to leaf out should be removed immediately and planted in a greenhouse or cold frame. Otherwise, the bundles are removed all at the same time in the spring and planted right side up.

Some dormant cuttings of easily rooted species are taken in winter, wrapped in moist sphagnum or peat moss, and stored indoors at 32–42° F to promote callusing. In the spring they are directly planted in containers or in the field.

In areas with relatively mild winters, cuttings of some species may be taken in the fall, treated with rooting hormone, and planted immediately in prepared outdoor beds. The beds are mulched and kept damp throughout the winter and rooting occurs in the spring.

Difficult-to-root species may often be successfully propagated by using bottom heat to promote callusing. In this method the cuttings are taken in the fall, treated with high concentrations of a root-promoting substance, usually IBA, and then placed upright in boxes containing damp sawdust, sand, or perlite and equipped with a special apparatus to maintain bottom-heat temperatures of 65–70° F. Keep the boxes outdoors or in unheated sheds or cold frames. The warm bottom heat encourages root development, while the colder outdoor temperatures inhibit shoot or bud development. Protect the rooting boxes from high winds, rains, and rodent damage. Cuttings should be transplanted as soon as the roots emerge and before the shoots or buds begin to grow. If conditions are not right for immediate field or container planting, the cuttings may be kept damp in the rooting box with the heat shut off.

ROOTING CUTTINGS OF NARROW-LEAVED EVERGREENS

Narrow-leaved evergreen species like pines and junipers are best propagated from cuttings taken from late fall through the winter. Cuttings of this type require fine misting and a controlled environment to prevent drying because they may take 3 months to a year to root. Cuttings made from juvenile wood of young seedling plants generally root better than those taken from mature plants. The standard hardwood cutting is taken from mature tip growth 4–8 inches long of the previous season's growth. Some growers prefer smaller tip cuttings of 2–3 inches placed very close together in a rooting flat. Applications of high concentrations of IBA are usually necessary. Cuttings should be prepared and then stuck in the rooting bed immediately after they are gathered. Dormant cuttings of narrow-leaved evergreen species root best in a greenhouse under conditions of high light intensity and light intermittent misting. Bottom-heat temperatures of 75–80° F are recommended to promote faster rooting.

ROOT CUTTINGS

Root cuttings may develop adventitious shoots as well as additional roots to produce an independent plant. Best results are achieved if root cuttings are taken from young stock plants in late winter or early spring when the roots have plenty of stored foods, but before new growth begins. In commercial operations, root cuttings are often taken from field-grown plants that are being dug and prepared for shipping. Digging root cuttings from plants in the wild is often too time-consuming to be profitable.

It is important to keep the same ends of the root cuttings together to avoid planting them upside down. This can be accomplished by cutting all the distal ends (bottom ends farthest from the crown) at a slant. The proximal ends (nearest the crown) may be cut straight across. In contrast to hardwood stem cuttings, the proximal ends should always be planted up. If planting in a prepared outdoor bed, the cuttings may be inserted vertically so that the top ends are near the soil level. Other kinds of root cuttings started in outdoor boxes may be placed either vertically or horizontally 1–2 inches deep (Hartmann and Kester 1975).

Plants with small delicate roots should be started in moist sand or finely screened soil in flats that are placed in a greenhouse or cold frame. Small lengths of 1–2 inches are best. Lay these horizontally on the soil and cover with ½ inch of fine soil or sand. Keep the box or flat from drying out until new stems appear. After the plants have achieved noticeable growth, transplant them to other containers or place in outdoor beds.

Plants with fleshy roots may be cut into slightly larger sections 2–3 inches long and planted vertically with the distal ends down.

Plants with very large woody roots may be planted outdoors in boxes containing damp sand, sawdust, or peat moss. These types of cuttings are 2–6 inches long and tied together with the same ends carefully placed together. Some species root best if plastic or a pane of glass is placed over the box to provide some protection and hold in moisture. Other species may be planted directly in the field after being held in the boxes for 3–4 weeks at an average temperature of 40° F. They should be planted with their tops level with or just below the soil surface. Shoot development will begin when spring temperatures rise and the soil begins to warm.

SEMIHARDWOOD (OR GREENWOOD) CUTTINGS

Semihardwood cuttings are taken from late spring through summer and early fall from new shoots that have partially matured and are woody at the base. The harvesting of cutting wood is impacted by the climate. In hot climates, semihardwood cuttings for many species are taken in April through early June, with a hiatus during the hot weather as the plants go into summer dormancy or heat stress. With the return of cooler weather and fall rains, plants often put on a second flush of growth which can be utilized for taking another round of semihardwood cuttings in late summer or fall. Rooting success for cuttings taken late in the season can be improved if the mist bench is in a greenhouse with a "wet wall" or other kind of cooling system. Lowering the temperature even slightly helps keep the cuttings in good shape instead of melting in heat and high humidity before new roots can be initiated (Pfeiffer, personal communication, 1999). Some growers have found that certain species root best from semihardwood cuttings taken in late summer to early fall because the wood has had more time to mature and store carbohydrates, which enables it to survive until new roots are produced. In some cases, the use of bottom heat later in the fall has been shown to be helpful in speeding root development before the onset of winter. Fall-rooted cuttings need to be protected over the winter in cold frames. Semihardwood cuttings are usually 3–6 inches long with the leaves removed from the bottom half. If the remaining top leaves are large, they should be trimmed to reduce transpiration and to allow placement of the cuttings closer together in the beds.

The best cutting wood usually comes from the growing tips of the stems, although basal ends of the stems on easily rooted species may also be used. Make the bottom cut just below a node. Application of a root-promoting hormone is beneficial and even imperative to achieve the rooting of certain species. The leaves of the cuttings as well as the rooting bed should be kept shaded and damp throughout the rooting process.

SOFTWOOD CUTTINGS

Softwood cuttings are prepared from the soft, succulent new spring growth of deciduous or evergreen species. These cuttings tend to root more readily than do hardwood cuttings made in winter. Softwood cuttings are taken from shoot tips of side branches after a flush of growth has been completed, and when the wood is partially mature but before it is thoroughly woody. The wood should be flexible but sufficiently mature so that it will snap if bent. For some species, rooting will take place only during a very short period in the spring. This is related to the physiological condition of the plant rather than the season when the cuttings are made. Rapidly developing buds in the spring often promote root formation. The difference

Softwood tip cuttings are gathered for propagation.

Small softwood cuttings of Dalea greggii *are stuck in individual plant cells to root.*

between semihardwood and softwood cuttings is slight. Softwood cuttings are generally only taken during a few weeks early in the growing season from tender wood; semihardwood cuttings can be taken during an extended period from early summer through fall.

Broad-leaved evergreens, like magnolias and some hollies, usually root best from cuttings taken after a flush of growth has been completed and the wood is partially matured; generally from spring to late fall. Narrow-leaved evergreens, like junipers, do not root well from softwood or semihardwood cuttings.

When collecting wood for softwood cuttings, avoid extremely tender, spindly, weak, or interior growth. Periodic trimming back of stock plants will often force the growth of more lateral shoots from which good cutting wood may be taken.

Softwood and semihardwood cuttings often root more easily and quickly than hardwood cuttings. But because they are taken in an active growing phase, they are susceptible to drying out. They must be handled very carefully and often require climate-controlled facilities that add to the cost of their production. Ideal temperatures for softwood cuttings are 75–80° F at the base and 70° F at the leaves. An intermittent misting system minimizes water loss for large numbers of cuttings. Many softwood cuttings root in 2–4 weeks and respond well to applications of root-promoting substances, usually IBA. The cuttings are generally 2–5 inches long with two or more nodes. The basal cut must be right below a node. Remove the leaves from the bottom half of the cuttings, and, if necessary, trim back the top leaves to limit transpiration and water loss. Remove all flower buds and place the cuttings in the rooting bed as soon as possible after they have been cut from the parent plant. Soaking the cuttings in water is not recommended.

SELECTING A PLANT TO PROPAGATE FROM CUTTINGS

When gathering cuttings from the field, select material from full-grown plants that have proven their ability to thrive and produce an outstanding characteristic such as flowers, fruit, form, or drought tolerance. Individual plants should be examined for genetic disorders or symptoms of disease.

The best time to take stem cuttings is early in the day when they are still fresh and firm rather than wilted or desiccated by the hot afternoon sun. Cutting wood gathered from the field at some distance from the propagation area should be taken in large lengths, held in plastic bags containing wet newspapers, and misted periodically. Keep the bags out of direct sunlight and do not store in a warm vehicle for longer than is absolutely

Stock plants are kept on site at the nursery as a convenient source of seeds and cuttings.

necessary. If the cuttings must be held for a period of time before they are treated and placed in the rooting bed, keep them in plastic bags in a cooler with ice to prevent wilting. This is especially true of hard-to-root species taken during the warm growing season. For best results, gather only the amount of cutting material that can be effectively processed immediately after collecting. It is less expensive to produce fewer well-rooted cuttings than to process with poor results many cuttings that have been kept in storage too long. Cutting the wood into short lengths at the gathering site may result in excessive desiccation and therefore affect rooting. The proper cutting and treatment of the cuttings should be performed just before placing them in a rooting medium. Soaking the cuttings in water for a long period of time is not recommended because it does not encourage root formation and may cause the wood to rot.

WOUNDING

Some species have better root development if they are wounded before hormone treatment and placement in the rooting bed. This can be accomplished by slightly breaking or hitting the basal end of the cutting with a hammer. Wounding seems to stimulate the production of greater amounts of callus cells as well as allowing more water and root-promoting substances to be absorbed. For most species, merely cutting the wood at the proper location provides enough wounding stimulus to encourage callus and root development.

ROOTING HORMONES

All plants produce certain growth-promoting substances that influence rooting. They may be present in high or low levels within the plant. Certain hormones, or auxins, are the substances that have the most effect on the production of new roots on stems: indole-3-acetic acid (IAA), indolebutyric acid (IBA), and naphthalene-acetic acid (NAA). Without these hormones, many plants will not complete the process of developing roots, or the process will be so slow that the cutting dies before new roots emerge and enable it to take up water and nutrients. IBA and NAA and their derivatives are most commonly used by growers to hasten or improve rooting and are synthetically reproduced in a pure chemical concentrate or talc form. IBA is the best auxin-type growth regulator because it has been proven to be a requirement for root formation. When applied as a synthetic chemical, it is nontoxic over a wide concentration range and is effective in promoting the rooting of a large number of plant species.

WILLOW ROOTING SUBSTANCE

A natural substance found in willows ("Willow Rooting Substance," or WRS) has been shown to improve the rooting of certain plants, especially when used in conjunction with IBA. WRS is produced by gathering the current year's stems, removing the leaves, cutting the stems into small pieces, packing them in a container, and covering them with water. Allow this mixture to steep for 24 hours and then drain off, saving the liquid to treat cuttings. Place the WRS in a beaker and soak the cuttings standing up for 24 hours. The extract can be made from most willow (*Salix*) species (Dirr and Heuser 1987).

APPLICATION OF ROOTING HORMONES

Cuttings should be freshly cut and slightly damp just before hormones are applied. Many growers use the concentrated "quick-dip" method. Cuttings are dipped for about five seconds into a solution of the acid form of IBA or NAA dissolved in an organic solvent. IBA is soluble in ethanol, while NAA is soluble at the ratio of 1 to 30 parts alcohol (3.3%). The standard solvent is usually a 50% alcohol/water mixture, but any concentration is acceptable as long as the pure chemical dissolves (Dirr and Heuser 1987). The "quick-dip" method has been proven to be superior to talc treatment for the majority of plants. The IBA solutions are more uniformly applied and absorbed by the stem. For most plants, soaking the cuttings for a longer period can result in decreased rooting, overcallusing, or burning of the plant. The acid forms of IBA and NAA are also available as potassium or sodium salts. These are more expensive, but since they are freely soluble in water, some growers find them easier to use. However, they are not as easily absorbed by the plant as the alcohol solvent. Some plants, such as Fringe-tree (*Chionanthus virginicus*), are sensitive to alcohol, so the talc or salt form of IBA is more suitable.

PREPARING QUICK-DIP SOLUTIONS

To prepare 10,000 ppm (1.0% IBA, NAA) hormone, dissolve 5 grams of hormone in 1 pint (16 ounces) of isopropyl alcohol (70%). For 5,000 ppm IBA, mix one part hormone to one part isopropyl alcohol; 2,500 ppm is one part hormone to three parts isopropyl alcohol. For treatments combining IBA and NAA, mix the separate solutions of each together. NAA is typically one-third to one-half the concentration of IBA because it is more toxic. IBA/NAA dips are often used for hard-to-root species, or with plants for which the window of time to collect suitable wood is very narrow. Ideal auxin concentration treatments vary among species, and also during the year for the same plant, as the physiology of the wood changes in response to climate and season. Easy-to-root species like Lantana (*Lantana spp.*) can be rooted with levels as low as 1,250 ppm IBA. Semihardwood cuttings for deciduous species are typically treated with 3,000–5,000 ppm IBA. Hardwood cuttings may require as much as 10,000 ppm to promote rooting. To determine the "ideal" rate for a particular plant, use a range of concentrations from 2,500, to 5,000, 10,000, and 20,000 IBA. Leave one set of cuttings untreated as a control (Dirr and Heuser 1987). One grower experienced success with several slow-rooting species (Rusty Black-haw

Viburnum, *Viburnum rufidulum*) using a "double-dip" method. Semihardwood cuttings were first dipped in a relatively low concentration (1,250 ppm) of IBA solution and then immediately dipped again in talc (3,000–5000 ppm IBA). The solution seemed to shock or stimulate root initiation without promoting the rapid overdevelopment of a thick callus that tends to block the emergence of the new root initials. The more slowly absorbed talc formulation promoted the complete development of the new roots (Pfeiffer, personal communication, 1999).

Prepared stock of the concentrated solution should be kept well covered and out of the sunlight to prevent evaporation of the alcohol, which would affect the concentration of the solution. Insert the cuttings into the rooting medium immediately after they are dipped in the solution. For a thorough discussion of commercial root-promoting formulations, their comparative effectiveness, and their toxicity, see Dirr and Heuser (1987). As with any chemical, these rooting hormones should be used with respect and caution.

For the noncommercial grower, the talc form of IBA is more practical. Rooting-hormone powders or talcs are readily available in premixed concentrations. For best results, take out only the amount of talc necessary to treat the cuttings on hand to avoid contaminating or affecting the potency of the main container. After the cutting has been dipped, it should be gently tapped to remove excess powder and then inserted immediately into the rooting bed. The rooting medium should then be firmed around the cutting.

THE PROPER ENVIRONMENT FOR ROOTING A CUTTING

After the cuttings have been taken from the stock or field plant, cut into appropriate lengths, and treated with root-promoting hormones, the next step is to provide them with the proper environment for stem survival and root development. These conditions include an optimum temperature range of 70–80° F for softwood and semihardwood cuttings. Water loss by leaves or stems should be limited by an intermittent mist system or a high-humidity case and moist rooting media. Cuttings must have ample but not too intense light. The soil media used for rooting must be clean, moist, well drained, and well aerated.

CONTAINERS

Semihardwood and softwood cuttings may be rooted in boxes, flats, or individual containers. Rooting in individual containers initially requires

Trays of cuttings are set on wire-mesh tables in the mist house.

more labor and potting soil, but each cutting is then able to develop unrestricted roots that do not break or tangle with other cuttings at transplanting time. All containers or boxes should provide adequate drainage. Some flats have wire mesh bottoms and are placed on raised tables, which provide good drainage and allow the roots to be air pruned once they extend beyond the bottom of the flat. This encourages the development of more secondary and lateral roots.

ROOTING MEDIA

Cuttings will usually root in a variety of rooting media as long as they are well drained and firm enough to support the cutting. Yet the size and quality of the roots as well as the prolonged survival of the cutting during rooting often depend on the soil media. Clean, sharp masonry sand has been traditionally used in a rooting bed, especially in the propagation of evergreen species. Very coarse rocky sand or very fine sugar sand used alone should be avoided because it does not retain enough moisture. Some species rooted in coarse sand produce long, brittle, unbranched roots. Peat moss alone makes a poor rooting medium because it is not well drained, and, if allowed to dry, is hard to rewet. However, peat is an excellent media component when combined with perlite, vermiculite, or sand in ratios of one to two or one to three. Either perlite or vermiculite alone is a good rooting medium for some species.

There is evidence that the pH of the rooting medium can influence the type of callus produced, which in turn can affect the emergence of newly formed adventitious roots. Some species produce large callus cells and root better in a slightly acid pH (0.60). The peat moss helps to acidify the rooting medium and therefore lowers the pH.

It is important to thoroughly wet the rooting bed before inserting the cuttings. This avoids knocking over the cuttings with a spray of water when soaking the bed or washing off the root-promoting powder or substance that may have been applied to the cutting. Rooting flats that have not been carefully soaked may have dry pockets that will affect rooting.

FUNGICIDES

Drenching the flat or container with fungicide before inserting the cuttings is also recommended to prevent attacks from various fungi, especially for those plants that are slow to root. Some rooting hormones in talc form also contain fungicides. Disease problems can be kept to a minimum by providing adequate drainage and good ventilation. Many growers also periodically mist the rooting bed with fungicide during the rooting process.

CONTROLLING WATER LOSS

One of the most critical requirements in propagation of softwood or semihardwood cuttings is to provide an environment that prevents excessive water loss from the leaves. Until a cutting produces new roots that enable it to take up moisture and nutrients, the cutting must not be allowed to dry out. Normal transpiration rates from the leaves must be kept to a minimum. For the noncommercial grower, a wooden box half-filled with the rooting medium and covered with a pane of glass or a sheet of polyethylene plastic will provide a terrarium-type atmosphere of high humidity and low water loss. The danger of this setup is that the box may get too hot or too soggy. It is important to keep the box in light shade and mist it regularly. Plastic sheets may also be draped in a tentlike fashion over the boxes with one end of the tent left open to provide ventilation. The containers or flats should be raised off the ground on bricks or platforms to allow adequate drainage.

INTERMITTENT MISTING SYSTEMS

Intermittent misting systems increase rooting percentages because they project periodic fine sprays of water over the rooting bed and thus minimize water loss. With misting systems, rooting percentages are more predictable because the automatic timer insures that moisture levels remain more or less constant and that all areas receive the same amount of spray. Water quality, important to all stages of plant propagation, is critical in a mist house. Water with high salts or calcium is detrimental to the plant and can also clog up the emitters, reducing the fine spray to uneven droplets which leave deposits on the plants and in the rooting bed. Rainwater collection and recycling systems with filters can sometimes make the difference between a successful or marginal nursery operation.

Misting systems may be installed in a greenhouse, cold frame, or outdoors. Some commercial operators have set up their vegetative propagation on large gravel beds with mist nozzles positioned on pipes 2 or 3 feet high. The cuttings are treated and placed in separate containers, which in turn are set in boxes to make them easy to carry. The gravel allows good drainage from the boxes and also produces a cooling effect as the moisture on the rocks evaporates. Ventilation is not a problem since the rooting is occurring outdoors, and the grower does not have the expense of constructing, maintaining, and cooling a greenhouse. A lath structure over the gravel yard keeps the leaves from getting sunburned and also reduces temperatures.

HARDENING OFF

It is very important to leave the cuttings undisturbed in the rooting bed or container until rooting is completed. Lifting the cuttings frequently to check their progress may break their newly emerging roots. The cuttings should not be disturbed for at least 2 weeks, and then a sample cutting may be gently lifted using a knife or other small tool. If a callus has developed or is emerging, the misting intervals should be gradually reduced to en-

Newly rooted cuttings are hardened off under shade cloth.

Simple shade structures promote new growth on newly potted plants.

courage the plant to harden off and to reduce the risk of rotting the cutting with too much moisture and a lack of oxygen. Even after the cuttings are lifted out of the misting bed and potted up into individual containers, it is a good idea to provide light shade until significant new growth is produced, or, in some cases, for the first season.

TRANSPLANTING THE CUTTING

Once the cutting has developed a healthy bundle of roots, carefully lift it out of the rooting bed and plant it in a larger container with a fertile and well-drained potting soil (see the Soil Mixes section in Chapter IV). Some plants, like Texas Pistachio (*Pistacia texana*) and Mexican Silk-tassel (*Garrya ovata* subsp. *lindheimeri*), will callus and produce roots under the right conditions, but they often fail to thrive as independent plants after transplanting. Plants like this may require a period of careful watering and frequent applications of diluted fertilizers until they are well established. Some hard-to-root species require extra maintenance because they take so long to root and the reserve food sources in the stem are completely used up by the time new roots begin to develop.

After transplanting newly rooted cuttings, provide them with light shade and careful watering for the first growing season. Cuttings made in the summer are especially susceptible to desiccation. Cuttings taken in the fall usually require protection in a cold frame during periods of freezing temperatures because their root system is not mature or hardened off.

VI ~ *Transplanting*

Once a plant has been carefully propagated and has achieved a sturdy size, the final step to establish it in the landscape is proper transplanting. In addition, many native specimen plants may be "rescued" from the wild and placed in cultivation if they are properly selected, dug, and replanted. Successful transplanting may be achieved by following a few commonsense guidelines.

TIME OF YEAR

The dormant season from late November through February is the best time for moving plants because the roots will have a chance to become established before the plant leafs out and active growth begins. If the plant must be moved during the growing season, it is important to provide frequent watering and, if possible, some shade.

CHOOSING THE PLANT

Many plants may be successfully transplanted from the field. Select plants that are abundant in nature, and preserve those species that are rare, endangered, or threatened unless their natural habitat is facing imminent destruction or disturbance.

When collecting from the wild, the size of the plant one is able to move usually depends on the time of year it is dug and the equipment available to move it. Plants under 5 feet are the easiest to transplant by hand. Large plants, especially those with deep taproots, require special commercial plant-moving equipment. Emphasis should be placed on the survival of the plants rather

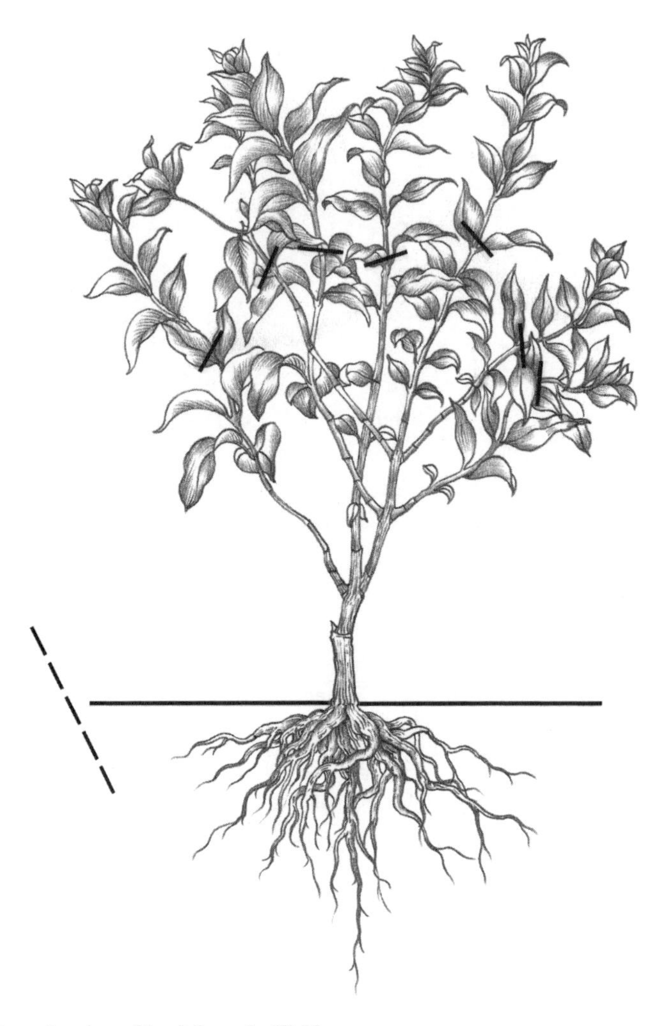

Transplanting a Shrub from the Field

Marks show where to prune back the top to prevent die-back and encourage a bushy form. Shovel line indicates where to start digging in order to obtain most of the roots.

Transplanting a Tree (facing page)

a. Unpruned tree growing in a field
b. Same tree pruned, leaving leader shoot and main branches; tree correctly placed at new site
c. Balled and burlapped tree; root ball large enough to support a tree which has been previously root-pruned in the field
d. Tree supported by guys or stakes; hole slightly saucer shaped to hold water

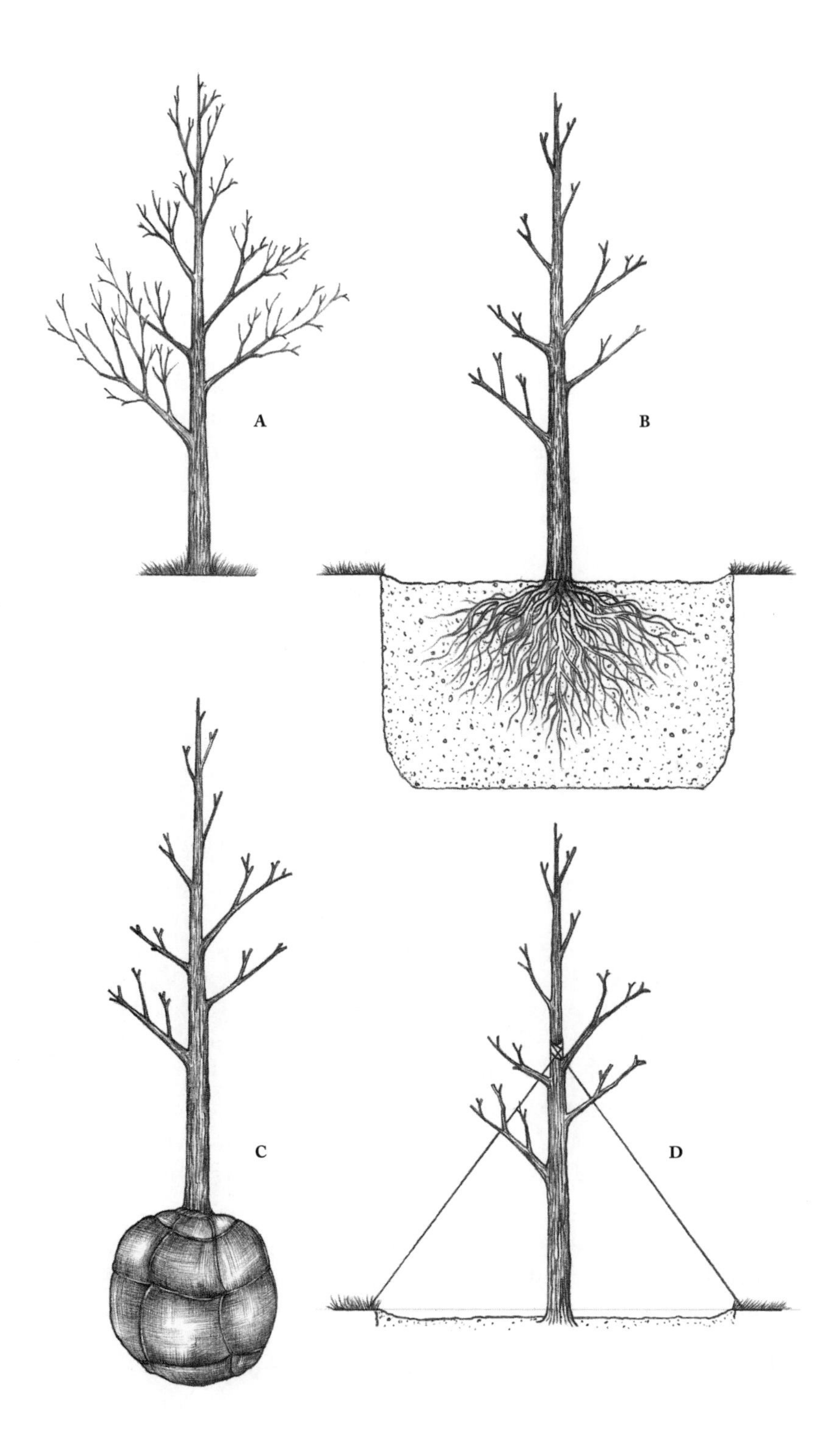

A
B
C
D

than their quantity or size. Many people are unsuccessful at transplanting because they choose a plant that is too large, or they dig on a rocky site where obtaining a root ball is impossible, or they inadequately prepare the new site. In most cases, smaller plants properly dug with most of their roots intact will overcome transplant shock more quickly and begin active growth sooner than large plants. Large plants dug by hand die back and are slow to produce new growth. It is better, therefore, to select a plant smaller than initially desired and then carefully maintain it so that it quickly resumes active growth.

When selecting a plant to transplant from the field, consider the site in terms both of ease of digging and obtaining all the roots and of its similarity to the new site where it will be planted. Is it in the sun or shade? Is it on a rocky exposed slope with well-drained soil, or is it in a moist river bottom or near a seep or spring? Many western species will adapt to a soil and site richer and loamier than their native habitat, as long as it is well drained. But shade-loving plants native to bogs or swampy low places will seldom thrive if moved to a poor, rocky site, even if provided with additional irrigation.

Plants growing in the open in deep sandy soil are more easily dug than those growing in a dense thicket where their roots may be intertwined with those of other plants or those on rocky sites where the root system may be sparse and hard to dig without breaking. On poor sites, small plants should be selected. Field-grown nursery plants are often periodically root pruned to encourage the development of a more compact and fibrous root system.

TRANSPLANTING TOOLS AND PROCEDURES

A sharp-shooter shovel is the best tool for hand digging a plant from the field. Have a large container in which to place the plant, preserving as much of the dirt around the roots as possible. The root ball may also be placed on a piece of burlap cloth and tied securely.

Root and top drying is a major cause of death in transplanted plants. Bare-rooted trees and shrubs should be covered with wet burlap as soon as they are dug. Broken and extra-long roots need to be cut clean. The plants can be put in plastic bags with damp but not excessively soggy sphagnum or peat moss. If plants are to be kept several days in the plastic bags, air holes should be cut in them to prevent mold and rotting. All plants to be held before being transplanted should be kept in the shade. A better method of holding bare-rooted plants for a few days before transplanting is to heel them into the ground or a prepared and shaded raised bed containing moist sand or sawdust.

When balling plants, it is important to get a solid ball and handle it so that it will not break. Plants should be carried by the ball and not by the stem or trunk. Pinning burlap tightly around the ball with nails lessens the danger of breaking the ball. If the ball is larger than easy handling will allow, it is more likely to fall apart. If it is too small, not enough roots will be left to support the plant.

To judge the distance from the plant to begin digging, measure the crown, or the spread of the branches, which is usually approximately the same size as the spread of the roots. Desert plants and those growing in thin rocky soil or among boulders generally will have deep-growing woody taproots instead of a far-ranging fibrous root system. It is best to move only small plants of this type and to obtain as much of the main root as possible without breaking it. Then cut back the plant to minimize transplant shock, which can be aggravated by a lack of secondary roots. Evergreens are always more successfully moved with a ball of dirt around the roots, while many deciduous plants may be easily moved with bare roots during winter. If the plants are bushy, tie or bale them before digging begins. This minimizes the danger of breaking the limbs.

It is important to obtain as much of the root as possible, and that task is made easier if a plant is dug from a site with adequate soil rather than a site where the main root may be entwined among the crevices of rocks. If the root is broken or if transplanting occurs during the growing season, it is best to cut back the top part of the plant by a third to a half, which will reduce the stress on the remaining roots supporting the plant.

During the growing season, transplant in the morning while the plant is still firm and unwilted by mid-day heat. Avoid digging in either extremely soggy or hard arid soil.

After transplanting, it is important to prune the plant carefully to compensate for root loss by reducing the leaf area and limiting transpiration (see illustration). At least one-third of the plant should be cut back if transplanting occurs during the dormant season. Plants moved during the spring or summer should be cut back by at least half or as much as two-thirds. The more care and water the plant receives after transplanting, the less it needs to be cut back. In addition, the older canes, intersecting branches, and part of the crown should be removed from transplanted shrubs. Plants with a poor root system or roots that have dried out should be radically pruned before transplanting. Sometimes placing a temporary shade tent over the plant in its new location helps minimize transplant shock. The leader stem of trees should never be cut unless the tree is excessively spindly. Top pruning of shade trees usually spoils their shape and development. Instead, the lateral branches of small trees should be pruned, leaving most of the small twigs and buds near the center of the crown. Severe pruning, which leaves only the buds at the branch tips, makes it difficult for the tree to provide nourishment for these ends and reduces necessary shade for the bark, thus exposing it to sun scald and borers. A good time to prune evergreen species is after growth has started; any dead, broken, or intertwining branches can be removed and the buds can be pinched back to encourage more compact growth.

PREPARING THE SITE

Most experienced arborists agree that when planning the installation of a new landscape, one should allot about three-quarters of the budget to site preparation (tilling, bringing in new soil, fertilizing, and so on) and about a quarter of the budget to the purchase of new plant materials. Inadequate soil preparation is more frequently responsible for the loss of transplanted trees than any other single cause. If a large number of plants is to be moved or if the plants are big specimens, it is best to have the site prepared before the arrival of the plants. This minimizes the length of time the plants are out of the soil.

The planting holes should be large enough for the roots to be spread out in a natural arrangement without cramping or twisting. There should be 6 inches to several feet of clearance on all sides of the roots, depending on the quality of the site and the amount of fill soil to be added. The diameter of the hole is generally one-and-a-half times larger than the root ball. The plant should be placed at the same level as it was in its natural site or container, which is indicated by a discolored ring on the bark. For many plants, the application of root stimulators containing indolebutyric acid promotes a quick adjustment to a new site. For large specimen plants, do not fill in the hole with soil blends rich in organic material. Backfill with the excavated soil, mixing in 15% compost. Too much organic material or peat moss will cause the hole to "sink" as the material is absorbed, and will delay the plant's adaptation to its surroundings. Some trees even get "pot bound" in a rocky hole if it is filled with high-grade soil blend. Press the soil firmly around the roots to eliminate air pockets and to avoid extreme sinking later. Creating a slight depression or saucer around the tree will help hold water for slow soaking, especially during the summer (see illustration). The plants should not be fertilized at planting time. It is best to fertilize after new growth starts in the spring. Cover the root ball and adjacent soil with 3 inches of organic mulch. Do not pile the mulch against the trunk. Adding compost under the canopy line in early spring is usually sufficient fertilization. Some western plants thrive better in gravel or existing soils that are unamended.

It is important to provide adequate drainage at the transplanted site, especially for western or desert species. To check the soil's internal drainage, fill the hole with water before placing the plant in it. If the water doesn't seep out in 24 hours, the roots could suffer from lack of oxygen and rotting may result. Drainage in large pits dug for shade trees may be improved by digging a trench away from the bottom of the hole and filling two-thirds of it with gravel.

If the site is too acid for the species being transplanted, it may be "sweetened" or made more alkaline by the addition of lime, wood ashes, dolomitic limestone, or calcium nitrate. If it is too alkaline, the soil may be made more acid by adding peat moss, well-cured compost, or such soil acidifiers as sulfur or ammonium sulfate. A pH range of 5.5–7.0 is best for most plants.

Large plants may need staking to support them in the proper position until the roots are established. The trunks of plants moved late in the season may require wrapping to protect them from sun scald, drying winds, and borer attacks.

Drip or soaker hose irrigation is the best way to maintain newly transplanted stock. Plants should be thoroughly soaked whenever the soil becomes moderately dry. Keep the plants damp but not soggy, especially in winter. Periodic deep soakings are more beneficial than frequent light surface waterings. Most native plants placed in the appropriate locations will require extra watering the first season to get established. After that, infrequent periodic deep soakings during dry weather are generally adequate to keep them healthy, as long as they are not in a compacted or high-traffic area. For a good general guide on the transplanting, care, and pruning of western trees and shrubs, see Johnson (1997). Detailed information on methods for transplanting certain species is included in the following chapter. Where specific information was not available for either transplanting or survival rates, I recommend that the reader cautiously follow the techniques outlined in the present chapter.

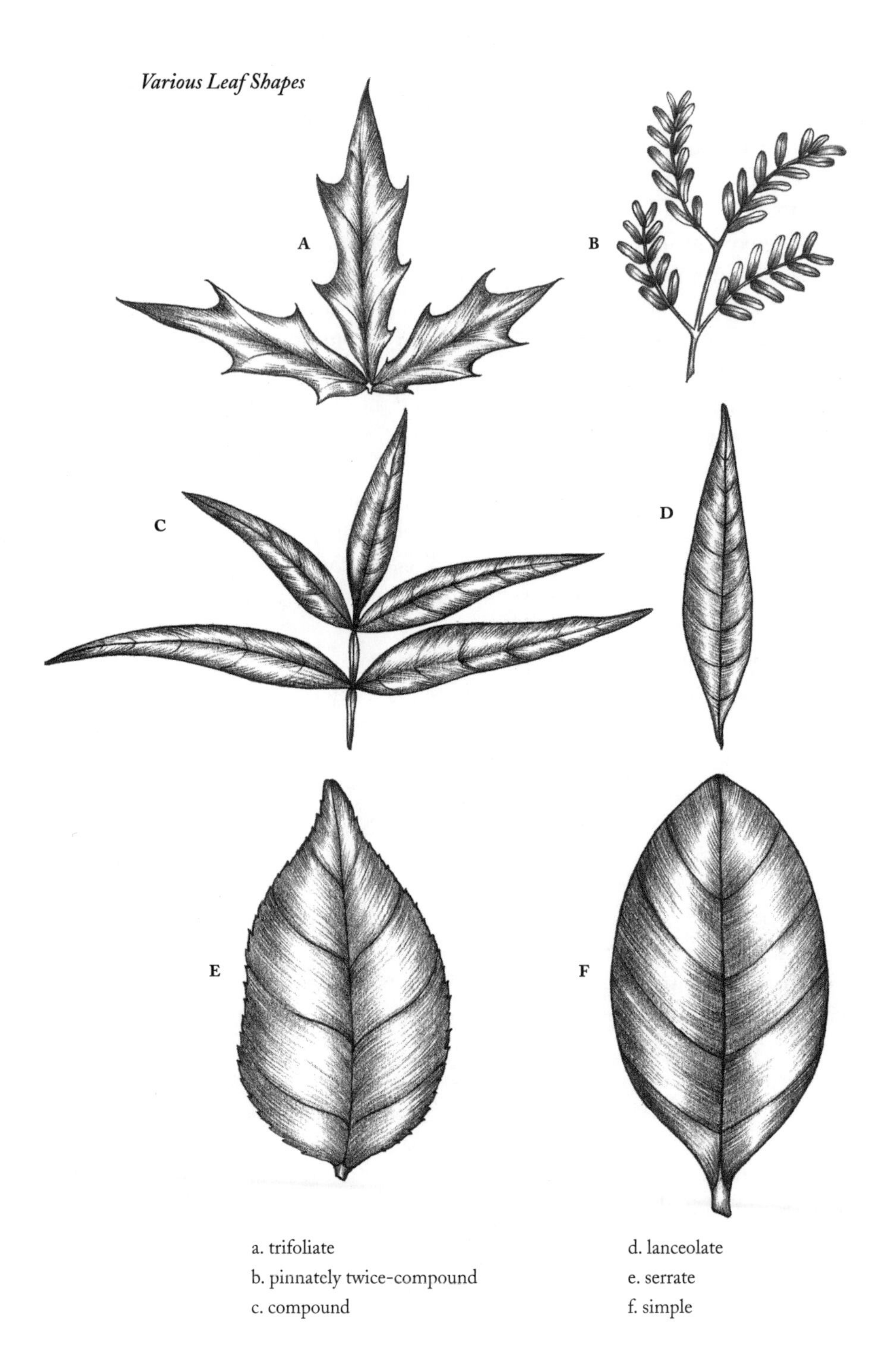

Various Leaf Shapes

a. trifoliate
b. pinnately twice-compound
c. compound
d. lanceolate
e. serrate
f. simple

Various Leaf Shapes (continued)

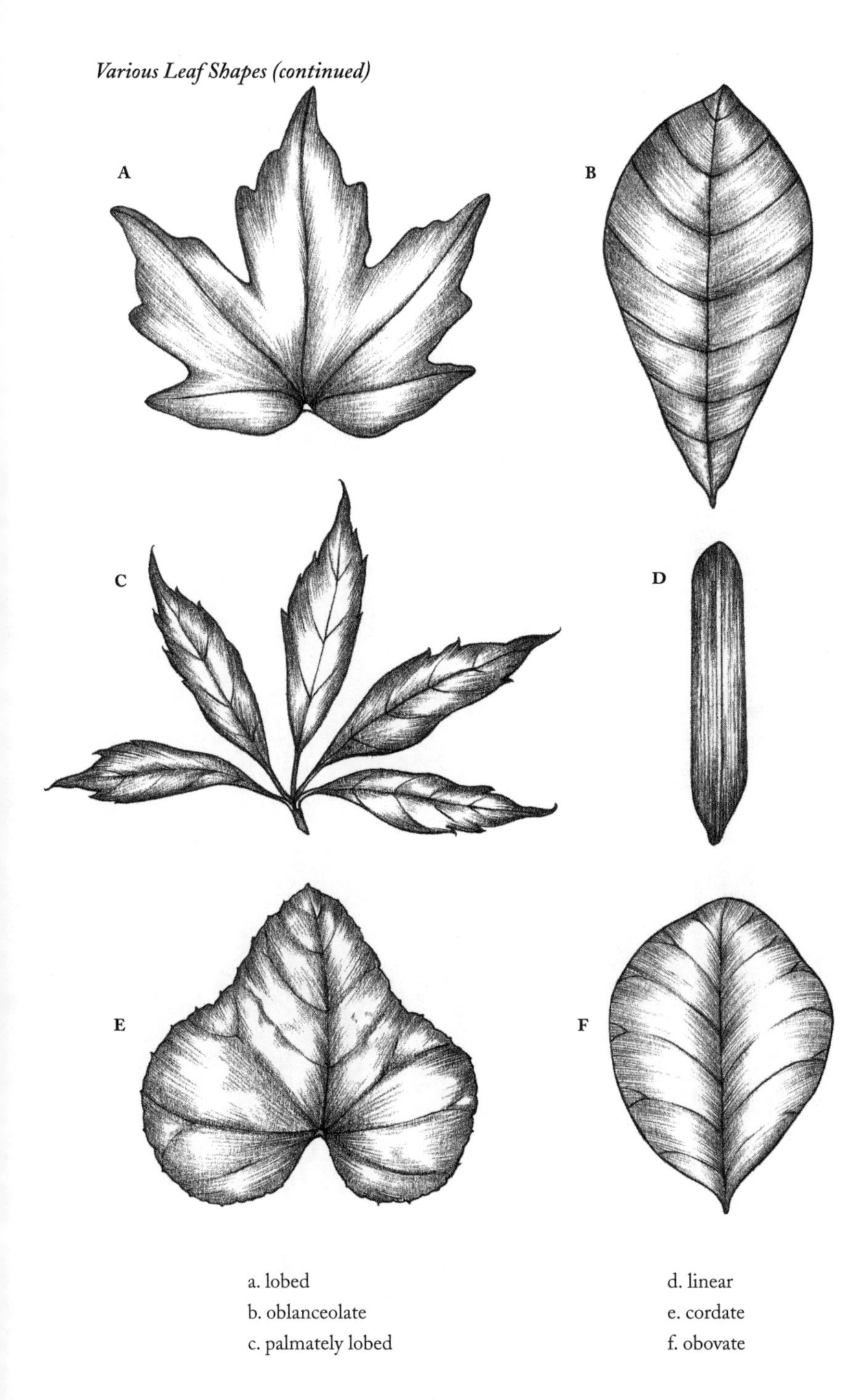

a. lobed
b. oblanceolate
c. palmately lobed
d. linear
e. cordate
f. obovate

Various Floral Arrangements

a. raceme

b. panicle

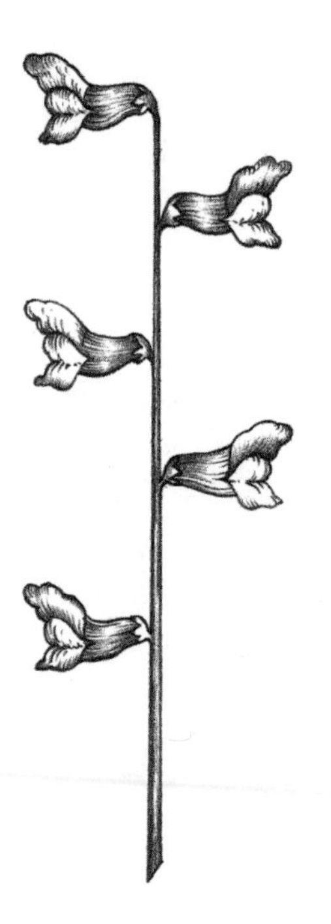

c. spike

d. cyme

Various Floral Arrangements (continued)

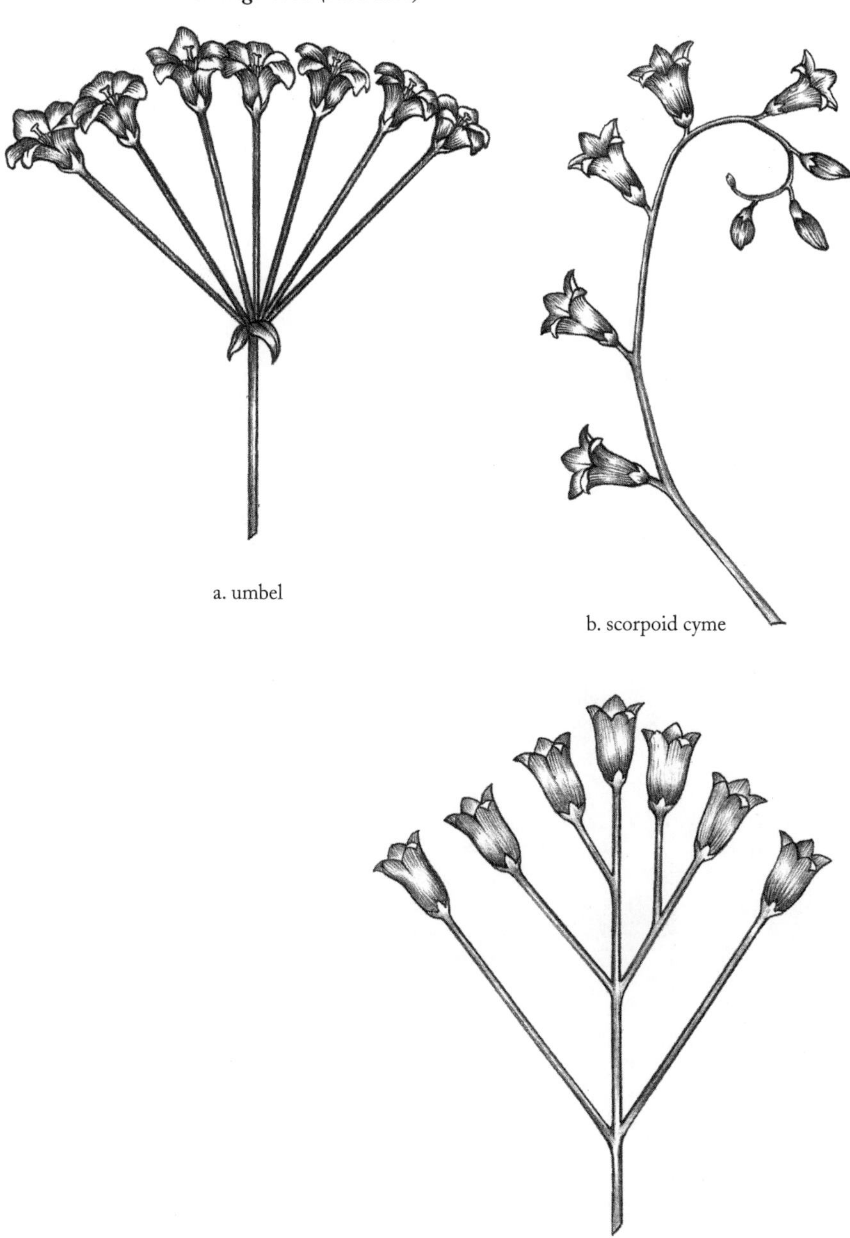

VII ~ *Propagation of Individual Species*

Acacia

Acacia

FABACEAE (LEGUME FAMILY)

GENERAL DESCRIPTION

Acacias are spreading deciduous shrubs or small trees with delicate bipinnate leaves. Acacias are often armed with small thorns or in some species, fierce spines at the leaf nodes.

FLOWERS AND FRUIT

Individual flowers are tiny but gathered together in fragrant round heads or elongated clusters. They are typically yellow or white and their extended stamens give them a powder-puff appearance. Spring is the main flowering season for acacias, though flowers will also appear in lesser numbers after rains through the fall. Fruit is a woody legume containing one or more seeds.

NATURAL HABITAT, RANGE, AND PREFERRED SITE

Acacias grow in sunny, well-drained sites primarily in the southern parts of the Trans-Pecos and in south and south central Texas, northern Mexico, and southern southwest United States. See Species Descriptions for individual distribution and habitat. Acacias are generally drought tolerant and grow well in full sun on poor, sandy, or gravelly soil. Acacias are typical members of the mattoral (shrub land) plant community in southwest Texas and are among the earliest invaders of disturbed sites, such as overgrazed pastures, fallow fields, or construction sites.

COLLECTION AND STORAGE

Collect the pods in summer to early fall as soon as the seeds are firm, filled out, and dark brown. It's a good idea to collect a large amount of pods because often they are empty or only half-filled with seeds, or the seeds are damaged by weevils. Fumigate seeds with pest strips before storage. *A. wrightii*, *A. roemeriana*, and *A. greggii* all have soft, papery pods that are easy to split once they are dried. This group of acacias tends to form the more treelike group. Although their roots grow fast, stem growth is slower. *A. farnesiana*, *A. rigidula*, *A. schaffneri var. bravoensis*, and *A. neovernicosa* are more shrubby in their growth habit and have harder, rounder pods which must be crushed or decayed somehow before they can be opened to extract the seed. Some growers deal with these kinds of pods in large numbers by tossing them in layers with compost in the fall after collection to decay the pods. By spring, the pods are softened and easier to open. The hard seed coat has typically not been impacted by decay during this period (McNeal, personal communication, 1999). Seeds of *A. schaffneri*, *A. rigidula*, and *A. constricta* have been effectively cleaned by first drying them and then shredding them in a chipper-shredder that has been fitted with a modified screen (Best 1999). *Acacia* seeds will remain viable for several years if first fumigated and then stored in sealed containers in the refrigerator.

PROPAGATION

Seeds

Acacias are easily propagated from seeds. However, germination for many species is often delayed by an impermeable seed coat, and mechanical or acid scarification for 20 to 60 minutes, depending on species, is usually necessary (see Species Descriptions for individual guidelines). Seed coat thickness may vary with the crop from year to year. For large quantities of seed, test each season's seed lot by soaking seeds in concentrated sulfuric acid for different time intervals, beginning with 10 or 15 minutes, increasing by 5 minutes until imbibition by a certain group is observed after 24 hours. A 30-minute soak in concentrated sulfuric acid is generally the standard treatment for most acacias (McNeal, personal communication, 1999). After scarification, seeds will germinate in 7 to 12 days under the proper conditions, including warm soil temperatures (80–86° F). Aeration of treated seeds has also improved germination (Best 1999). Without scarification, germination for some species may be delayed a month or longer.

Acacia seeds are not light sensitive, and seedlings emerge best when the seeds are planted at a depth of ¾ to 1 inch, depending on soil type. Seedlings must be grown under strong sunlight or they will become spindly and weak. Seeds started indoors in a greenhouse or cold frame in the fall can be put outdoors in pots in March after all danger of frost is past. With regular but light fertilization, they will be ready for a five-gallon pot by that same fall. Or, seed can be stored and planted outdoors in the spring. The strongest, most vigorous plants are produced when seeds are sown in individual containers at least 8 inches deep that also promote root pruning and the development of secondary roots. Seeds sown in a flat tend to have cramped, contorted roots that are subject to breaking when transplanted.

Acacias are rapid growing. Most species planted in spring will be tall enough for a one- or three-gallon container by fall. Acacias should not be allowed to become root bound in the container. You will also notice that the roots of most *Acacia* seedlings will quickly find the holes in the container and rapidly root themselves through the pot to the ground if left too long in one spot. When moving acacias up to larger containers, use containers that promote air pruning to promote a bushy root mass instead of a single taproot, which can make transplanting more difficult.

Cuttings

Some species of *Acacia* may be rooted from softwood or semihardwood cuttings taken in late spring or early summer. They should be 3 to 4 inches long with a heel. Insert them into a well-drained rooting bed and place under mist. The application of root-inducing hormones is recommended. More research needs to be made on clonal propagation of certain selections of acacias. There is much opportunity for developing qualities such as thornlessness, cold-hardiness, and superior flowers of some acacias (Arnold, personal communication, 1999).

Transplanting

The long woody taproots of many acacias enable them to withstand periods of drought, but they also make transplanting difficult, especially from the hard, rocky sites where they often grow. Small plants in reasonably deep soil may be moved in winter if cut back severely and given adequate watering and shade.

NOTES

The delicate, fernlike foliage, aromatic flowers in early spring, and exceptional drought tolerance all contribute to the worthiness of this genus as an ornamental plant. Many acacias are attractive when planted in a group as tall background plants or alone as fast-growing specimen plants in harsh open areas or dry rocky slopes that receive little supplemental irrigation. On many ranches acacias are valued as firewood and used to make fence posts. They are also important sources of pollen and nectar for honey production in south Texas. Acacias provide cover for many forms of wildlife. Cattle and deer occasionally browse the leaves and pods. For a thorough and fascinating discussion of the many ways acacias have been used for tools, medicine, perfume, browse fodder, and other purposes, see volume 1 of Cheatham and Johnston (1995).

SPECIES DESCRIPTIONS

Acacia berlandieri **(Guajillo)**

Spreading shrub usually 5–15 feet with many stems rising from the base. Leaves are large, light green, and fernlike. The flowers appear as round white fuzzy balls in early spring. Guajillo is abundant in the Rio Grande Plains westward and adapted as far north as Austin. It is not hardy below 10° F. The foliage and growth habit makes a beautiful contrast when planted below Mountain Laurel (*Sophora secundiflora*) and Cenizo (*Leucophyllum frutescens*) (Ogden, personal communication, 1999). Guajillo produces lots of pods, but often they don't contain many seeds. An abundant seed crop is produced every 3–4 years. One method suggests aerating the untreated mature seed for one day and then planting immediately. Seeds germinate within 7–10 days (Best 1999). Other growers scarify the seed for up to 30 minutes before planting (McNeal, personal communication, 1999). Light tip pruning when the plant is a seedling encourages stronger branching. Without pruning, Guajillo tends to form a single long gangly cane until planted in the landscape, where it will sucker to form a spreading colony (Will, personal communication, 1999).

Acacia constricta **(Whitethorn Acacia, Largancillo, Mescat Acacia)**

A graceful, spreading shrub with delicate foliage and conspicuously large (½-inch) spines. Its mature size can be as large as 10 × 15 feet. Round yellow fragrant flowers are attached at the leaf axils. Blooming occurs in the summer and early fall, especially after rains. Pods are about 4 inches long, constricted like pop-beads between the seeds. Occurs in various desert habitats from Arizona to western Texas. Reported to hybridize with Viscid Acacia (*A. neovernicosa*).

Acacia farnesiana **(Huisache)**

Huisache is the most fragrant of all the acacias. In spring the tree is covered with rich yellow puff-ball flowers. Huisache is typically a multi-trunked tree or shrub to 7–20 feet, with small dark green compound leaves. The branches are armed with needle-like spines. Smooth, black, rounded pods are 1–3 inches long and tapered at the ends. Huisache is common throughout Mexico and is cold hardy as far north as Austin, Texas, though in hard winters it may freeze to the ground and is also vulnerable to having the flower buds burned in a late frost. Huisache is very invasive in the disturbed soils, and in some parts of southeast Texas has, along with the Chinese Tallow Tree, absolutely taken over old fields and pastures. Despite this aggressive behavior, Huisache is one of the showiest and most attractive members of this genus. Its flowers have been used for several hundred years in Europe in the manufacture of fine perfumes (Cheatham and Johnston 1995). It is a fast-growing specimen shade tree, especially suited for very hot and dry locations. Acid scarify the seed for 20–45 minutes (depending on seed lot) or nick with a knife to prepare for germination.

Acacia greggii **(Catclaw Acacia, Uña de Gato)**
Most often a spreading shrub 3–7 feet tall with straight stems, but occasionally seen as a reasonably tall tree in the southern part of its range. Flowers are creamy white, the pods flat, thin, and contorted. Catclaw Acacia is abundant in dry, gravelly, sandy soils in the Rio Grande Plains and Trans-Pecos. Catclaw Acacia does not tend to have as strong a leader shoot as some of the other acacias. Instead, it is more often seen as a sprawling, spreading shrub. Germination techniques are the same as for *A. wrightii.*

Acacia hirta **(Fern Acacia)**
Rounded subshrub to 2–4 feet, often forming colonies by means of woody rhizomes. Stems graceful and wandlike. White flowers are clustered in balls and followed by flat, thin pods 2 inches long. Good deciduous ground cover. Common throughout the eastern two-thirds of Texas and also in Oklahoma, but rare in the Trans-Pecos and the High Plains.

Acacia rigidula **(Black-brush Acacia, Chaparro Prieto)**
Tall shrub 3–10 feet with straight thorns. Prolific, fragrant creamy yellow flowers held in spikes about ½ inch thick and 3 inches long. Common in west and southwest Texas as far north as Travis County. Slow growing but vigorous. Pruning encourages dense branching and more flowers. Good honey plant. Seed germinates after 20–25 minutes of acid scarification. Hot water treatments have not proved as effective (Best 1999). Slow growing and must have full sun.

Acacia roemeriana **(Romer Acacia, Catclaw Acacia, Gatuño)**
Small tree or shrub 3–7 feet with spreading branches. Greenish yellow flowers. Romer Acacia grows in a variety of brushy vegetation, usually on limestone soils in the Trans-Pecos, south and east to the Edwards Plateau. Good honey plant.

Acacia schaffneri. var. bravoensis **(Twisted Acacia, Huisachillo)**
Low-growing, spiny, multi-trunked spreading shrub usually under 8 feet, with a spread of two to three times its height. It is almost identical in appearance to Huisache (*A. farnesiana*), except that it is usually smaller and is distinguished by its long (up to 5-inch) velvety pods. Huisachillo is

abundant in the Rio Grande Plains and Trans-Pecos. Good ornamental plant for situations demanding a low-branching shrub or tree. It will bloom when only 2 feet high. Adapted to Houston and will grow in Dallas if given south wall protection.

Acacia wrightii **(Wright's Acacia, Catclaw, Uña de Gato)**
Medium-sized tree that may reach 30 feet in moist locations in the Lower Rio Grande Valley. Wright's Acacia has semi-evergreen foliage and white flowers. It has a more sturdy and upright growth habit than many of the other acacias. The trunk is dark brown and attractively grooved, and even in winter the branches cast attractive lacy shadows on a wall or pavement. Pruning of the sometimes spindly lower branches improves it appearance. It is native to dry, well-drained calcareous soils in the Rio Grande Plains, Edwards Plateau, and Rolling Plains. Wright's Acacia is the most cold hardy of all native acacias. It is generally a taller plant than *A. greggii.* Plants at the Lower Rio Grande Valley National Wildlife Refuge reached almost 11 feet tall and over 3 feet wide after 4 years. These trees were not irrigated or fertilized at any time, nor did they receive any weed control (Best 1999). In another nursery, seeds were successfully germinated after a 20-minute soak in concentrated sulfuric acid. These were planted in the fall in a cold frame in liners placed on wire-mesh tables that provided plenty of air circulation and air-root pruning. Seedlings were transplanted in May in a soil mix that had a native soil component instead of the standard pine bark mix. Light tip pruning while the plant was in a one-gallon container promoted better branching structure and overall form (Will, personal communication, 1999).

Acer

Maple

ACERACEAE (MAPLE FAMILY)

GENERAL DESCRIPTION

There are approximately 200 species of maples in temperate forests throughout the world, with seven species occurring in Texas. Maples are a taxonomically complex and controversial group. Most are large to medium trees with sharply lobed deciduous leaves turning colors in the fall. (See Species Descriptions.)

FLOWERS AND FRUIT

Flowers are both perfect and imperfect, small and regular, and generally inconspicuous, except for Red Maple (*A. rubrum var. rubrum*), which has showy reddish pink male flowers. All species except Red Maple ripen in late summer to early fall. Red Maple ripens in early summer, soon after flowering. Fruit is the familiar two-winged samara. Samaras turn from pink to yellowish or reddish brown when ripe and are dispersed by wind or sometimes by water. Most maples bear seeds at an early age and produce annually, though the quality and quantity of the crop vary greatly from year to year.

NATURAL HABITAT, RANGE, AND PREFERRED SITE

Members of this genus generally are found in river bottoms, moist canyons, or along creeks in fairly rich soil. Big-toothed Maples, *A. grandidentatum*, can tolerate lower summer rainfall rates than their eastern relatives, though they are generally not found on drier upland sites. See Species Descriptions for individual range and habitat.

COLLECTION AND STORAGE

Collect the seeds from early summer to fall, depending on species. The key to successful production of maples is gathering the seed at the right moment of ripeness. There is often a very narrow window of time when the seeds are at their peak, and a delay of even a week can impair germination rates because the seeds dry out very quickly (Will, personal communication, 1999). Watch the maturing crop carefully and begin harvesting as soon as the samaras turn yellowish or reddish brown and the seeds inside are firm, filled out, and dark brown. Collect seed from several populations, as seed quality can vary significantly among trees. Sometimes a tree will appear to be full of samaras, but closer inspection reveals that the fruit is empty. Cut open about 10 fruits to see if at least 20–30% of them have seeds before wasting time collecting more fruit. Different branches of the same tree can bear different amounts of good seed. It is best to gather the seeds by hand from the tree because seeds that have already dropped lose viability quickly and are easily infested by insects. Also, seed collected before they have fully ripened often show less internal dormancy and are therefore easier to germinate (McNeal, personal communication, 1999). Studies conducted in Utah of the Big-toothed Maple indicated that an average of 30% of the seeds produced each year are aborted, empty, or infested with the eucalyptus larvae or a moth larvae (Barker 1975).

Seed collection of Big-toothed Maple should begin by late August or the first of September. Nutlets need not be extracted or de-winged prior to storage or planting. Seed production and viability vary from year to year depending on climatic conditions. Number of seeds per pound also varies among the species. Fruit yield for Big-toothed Maple is frequently low. Fumigate the seeds and immediately stratify them or, if absolutely necessary, keep in cold moist storage at 36–40° F. Seeds kept in dry storage seldom germinate well.

PROPAGATION

Seeds

Maples are most often propagated by seeds, though high germination rates are difficult to achieve because of embryo dormancy and a slow rate of growth, which makes them vulnerable to fungi and changing environmental conditions that could harm seedlings. One exception is the spring-ripening Drummond Red Maple (*Acer rubrum var. drummondii*), which germinates immediately without pretreatment. Red Maple seeds are collected in March and sown immediately in individual "bullet" containers. Red Maples are fast growing and often produce a finished one-gallon container in 3 months (Bronstad, personal communication, 1999). Fall-ripening species exhibit internal dormancy and germinate the spring following seed fall.

The internal dormancy of fall-ripening species may be broken by stratification in moist sphagnum moss (although some growers prefer perlite or other material) at 41° F for 30 to 160 days, depending on species and where the seeds were collected.

Seeds of Big-toothed Maple from high elevations generally require longer periods of cold stratification than do maple seeds from east Texas (Simpson, personal communication, 1986).

Most southern strains of Sugar Maple, *A. saccharum*, do not exhibit the same lengthy dormancy period as do the northern strains (Lowrey, personal communication, 1986).

Germination of maple seeds usually begins while the seeds are still in stratification. Complete germination for the entire seed lot is staggered over a period of time as long as 40 days after the emergence of the radicle or primary root in a few seeds to heavy or complete germination of the majority of the seed lot. The seeds should be frequently checked as the period for breaking dormancy nears fulfillment. Germination may be enhanced and unified by using the "pulsing" method (see Chapter III). As soon as the roots appear on a few seeds, remove the entire lot from cold moist storage and plant in individual plant cells in a cold frame or greenhouse where germination for the remainder of the seeds may proceed. If seeds are left too long in cold moist storage after sprouting, they will be difficult to transplant or may even die. Germination can occur over a long period of time, with about 20% emerging immediately following stratification. These will be the most vigorous, followed by another 20% with less vigorous germination. The most tardy or last 20% of seedlings to sprout will be the runts and only reluctantly demonstrate an inclination to thrive as seedlings or after transplanting. Therefore, some growers select only the first 20–30% of young seedlings as being worth cultivating because they have the most vigor (McNeal, personal communication, 1999).

Benny Simpson, plant scientist at the Texas A&M Research and Extension Service Center at Dallas, studied maples and developed the following guidelines to determine the length of the stratification period for several native species. These were held at 40° F in a peat/perlite mixture.

A. barbatum (from Rusk in northeast Texas): 84–89 days.

A. grandidentatum (from Guadalupe Mountains): 138–162 days.

A. grandidentatum (from the Sabinal River canyons): 98–122 days. Other growers have varied this timetable by placing the seed in bags of moistened peat moss in December for 85 days. Seeds are then removed by March and planted in individual containers. They are put outdoors under shade when they are about 4 inches tall. By the following fall, they are 2 feet tall. They can grow up to 7 feet tall by the second year (Janzow, personal communication, 1999).

A. grandidentatum (from Wichita Mountains in Oklahoma): 113–152 days.

A. leucoderme (from Sabine National Forest in east Texas): 81–84 days. Mark Bronstad from Doremus Nursery collects Chalk Maple seed in October/November, depending on how dry or wet the season has been. He stratifies the seed for 120 days and has noticed that radicles often begin to emerge by 90–100 days. Seeds are individually removed and planted in bullet tubes. Chalk Maple requires a year to make a finished one-gallon container plant about 18 inches tall. From a gallon pot, the maples are shifted into four-gallon containers that promote better drainage. Once they are in the four-gallon pots, they grow rapidly. It is essential to use a lighter soil blend in the container and to provide slow-release fertilizer, micro-nutrients, and lime. If Chalk Maples are kept too wet, their growth stagnates and they eventually die.

A. saccharum: 80–120 days.

Different populations may show a shorter or longer stratification time. In another study, germination of Big-toothed Maple was improved when the samaras were submerged in water immediately after collection for 2 to 3 weeks and kept in the refrigerator. This period of cold soaking was followed by cold stratification in moist sphagnum moss. Under this treatment, germination averaged 20% (Tipton, personal communication, 1986).

Maple seedlings are difficult to transplant from flats and survive better if planted in individual containers such as plant band liners or bullet tubes set on raised wire-mesh beds or raised seedbeds about 18 inches deep, also with wire bottoms set on cinder blocks. Eastern maples are often raised as bare-root liners in bedded rows in the field. Seeds should be sown ¾ to 1 inch deep. Young maple seedlings are sensitive to both damping-off fungi and desiccation. Establishment of a program of fungicide drenching and inoculation with beneficial microorganisms is recommended beginning with the seed flat stage to larger container sizes.

Maple seedlings have poor germination and seedling survival rates at hot temperatures. Therefore it is very important to plan the stratification treatment so that the seeds are removed from cold moist storage by late winter or no later than the first of March. Seedlings may be moved out of a greenhouse or cold frame as soon as all danger of frost is past and will benefit from light shade during the first growing season. However, if shade is too dense, seedlings will be spindly.

Big-toothed Maple seedlings are heavy feeders when producing their first and second flush of growth as they come out of dormancy in the spring. Supplement the slow-release fertilizer in the soil mix with a 20-20-20 foliar feed. Use fertilizer judiciously; too much feeding will cause burning (Will, personal communication, 1999).

Any loss of the leader such as desiccation or bruising of the apical meristem during transplanting in the seedling stage will typically cause the plant to die, so the plants must be handled gently when they are being moved up to larger containers (Pfeiffer, personal communication, 1999).

For outdoor planting, plant the seeds immediately after collection in prepared beds in the fall. The beds should contain a good amount of loose organic matter and be mulched lightly. Keep the beds moist but not soggy, and remove the mulch as soon as germination is well progressed. Portable cold-frame protection may be necessary for young seedlings during extremely cold weather.

In a study conducted in Idaho, Big-toothed Maple seedlings were transplanted into one-gallon plastic containers when 6 weeks of age and later moved into half- or one-gallon metal containers at the beginning of the second growing season. The soil medium in the containers was a mixture of equal volumes of sand, peat moss, and fine sandy loam. Seedlings were fertilized weekly with a water-soluble 20-20-20 fertilizer. The seedlings averaged 9–33 inches after the second growing season (Barker 1975).

Big-toothed Maples seem to devote the first two growing seasons to developing roots instead of stem growth. This is a growth mechanism that helps them survive on the typically thin soil and rocky sites of their native habitat.

In Texas, Big-toothed Maples showed a sensitivity to both ammonium nitrate and ammonium sulfate. Young foliage is easily burned by heavy fertilization and by salts in the irrigation water. Peat moss and pine bark are not recommended as soil mix components of Texas Big-toothed Maples. Though Big-toothed Maples are slow growing, they need to be carefully watched to avoid root girdling. They make take up to 5 years to reach the 15-gallon size, at which point they should be lightly tip pruned to promote full branching (Kirwin, personal communication, 1999).

Big-toothed Maples of all sizes benefit from 30% shade in the afternoon. In nature, they are an understory tree and thrive best if eventually planted in locations that offer protection from direct afternoon sun.

Cuttings

Vegetative propagation of *Acer* can be complicated. Some species root better than others. The season and amount of stored carbohydrates in the stem may determine the survival of the cutting (see Chapter V). Best results for many species seem to occur when semihardwood cuttings are taken from late May to mid-June. Another problem with rooting maples from cuttings is that the rooted new plants tend to remain shrubby instead of developing a single stem. Eventually, one of the stems may pull ahead of the others and form a leader trunk, but this may take a while. Maples have determinate buds on the stems that may become dormant when the cutting is taken, and often the stem will stop growing and consequently rot in the rooting bed before new roots can form (McNeal, personal communication, 1999). Concentrations of IBA under 10,000 ppm seem to have little effect.

Cuttings must be kept under intermittent mist in a shaded mist house. Over-wintering the rooted cuttings is sometimes a problem, but can be achieved if the cuttings are vigorously rooted. Rooted cuttings survive best if potted in separate containers and kept in a cold frame until spring. Rooting can take up to 3 months to complete. Survival of the rooted maple cuttings often depends on periodic supplemental feeding and careful watering until the plant is well established and begins new growth.

Preliminary attempts to root Big-toothed Maple indicated that application of high levels of root-promoting hormones did not improve callusing or rooting (Simpson, personal communication, 1986). Information on grafting or budding the Big-toothed Maple is lacking.

Studies of vegetative propagation of Red Maple showed that softwood cuttings taken from the lower half of the crown rooted better than those taken from the upper half and that cuttings taken from trees with a light fruit crop rooted better than those bearing a heavy fruit crop.

Transplanting

Small trees of Drummond Red Maple, *A. rubrum var. drummondii*, and Sugar Maple (*A. saccharum*), have been successfully transplanted bare-root in the winter (Lowrey, personal communication, 1986). Field-grown maple seedlings should be root pruned prior to transplanting.

NOTES

The horticultural qualities of Texas maples are impressive. Maples are long-lived shade trees offering a wide range of reliable fall colors and forms. In the spring the male flowers, ripening samaras, and expanding leaves are an attractive pink color. Once mature, most maples have few serious disease or insect problems. As a group, maples do not generally thrive on arid upland sites, although the Big-toothed Maple is best able to tolerate long dry spells (see Species Descriptions).

There are species of maples appropriate to nearly every area of the state. All maples cast dense shade and have rather shallow, far-ranging root systems. Grass will not grow to the base of most mature maples.

For a complete discussion of maple sugar production and other uses of maples, see Cheatham and Johnston (1995).

SPECIES DESCRIPTIONS

Acer barbatum **(Southern Sugar Maple)**
Tree to 64 feet. Leaves with three to five coarsely toothed lobes, resembling the smaller western species. Native to moist rich soil along streams and flood plains in southeast Texas, especially Cherokee, Rusk, and nearby counties; also east to Florida and north to Virginia. Often mistaken for a small specimen of its close relative, Sugar Maple. *A. barbatum* is often planted in the southern states as a medium-sized shade tree. Lynn Lowrey considered Southern Sugar Maple to have the most reliable fall color of all the maples for our state. It will also grow in calcareous soils. The 'Caddo' was chosen for its tolerance of cold and drought, and is available from nurseries in north-central Texas.

Acer grandidentatum **(Big-toothed Maple)**
Tree to 48 feet, with dark brown scaly bark and thickish leaves having three to five lobes. Leaves turn from gold to crimson in late October and early November if conditions are right. Big-toothed Maple is native to canyons in Edwards Plateau and Trans-Pecos. It has adapted to heat and dry spells but is seldom found growing on exposed rocky hillsides. The population at Fort Hood, near Killeen, Texas, grows in more exposed and dry conditions than populations further west, where they seem to be confined to moist canyons or north- and east-facing bottoms of hills where dry conditions are mitigated by accumulation of leaves and other organic material, and/or a presence of seeps or springs. Deer relentlessly browse young maple seedlings, which is why small plants are seldom seen in the Hill Country. At Fort Hood, where there is a more rigorous game management plan in place than at the state parks, nearly waist high seedlings of Big-toothed Maple can be found (McNeal, personal communication, 1999). Big-toothed Maples are very susceptible to fire damage. Big-toothed Maple has been used successfully as a landscape plant in well-drained alkaline soils in Dallas. It is often slow growing, and young trees under 1½-inch caliper are vulnerable when planted in "tough love" situations such as parks or commercial landscapes. Larger trees (2½-caliper) adapt to the new site more quickly and grow more rapidly in those situations.

This maple looks best if planted in somewhat protected locations with deeper soils and shade in the hot afternoons. Its moderate scale, its outstanding fall colors, and overall form make it hard to understand why the Big-toothed Maple is not the number one street tree in the Texas Hill Country.

Acer leucoderme **(Chalk Maple)**
Small, sometimes shrublike or multi-trunked graceful tree to 25 feet, rarely to 40 feet, with distinctive white bark when mature. Leaves turn golden or red in autumn. Rare in Texas, found only occasionally in moist soil along riverbanks and streams in southeast Texas. More widespread but not abundant in Louisiana across the south to Florida. Has been in cultivation since 1900. It prefers light shade to full morning sun and acid loamy soils. Chalk Maple is a lovely specimen understory plant, or a plant designated at the edge of woods.

Acer rubrum var. drummondii **(Drummond Red Maple)**
In Texas, red maple is most likely seen only in two varietal forms: *drummondii* and *trilobum*. Drummond Red Maple is a tall tree up to 100 feet with flowers appearing in early spring with or before the new leaves. Red stamens cover the tree in a wispy red cloud, later replaced by attractive rosy pink samaras that ripen by early summer. Native to alluvial forests and moist rich soil in partial sun in east Texas. It is cold hardy only to USDA zone 7 or 8 (Arnold 1999).

Acer rubrum var. trilobum **(Trident Red Maple)**
Differs from *var. drummondii* in having only three-lobed leaves and turning bright yellow instead of red in the fall. Found in slightly drier sites than Drummond Red Maple in northeast Texas near Rusk. Red maples are easy to germinate but the most difficult of all native maples to raise in cultivation because they require acid or neutral sand and continuous moisture in order to thrive. In nature seedlings frequently germinate and grow in standing water. Red maples cannot stand dry conditions or soil with a clay hardpan, and this restricts their natural range to the deep sand of the Pineywoods. See Species Descriptions for *A. rubrum*.

Acer saccharum **(Sugar Maple)**
Large tree to 128 feet with wide spreading branches and a pointed crown. Leaves have three to five lobes, turning red or orange-yellow in the fall. Wooded hillsides, slopes in northeast Texas, across the south to Mississippi and north to Canada. Cuttings of Sugar Maple root best when taken in late spring after the first stage of shoot elongation has ended. For this

species, thick cuttings, 4 to 6 inches, taken from terminal or lateral twigs in the summer, root best. In east Texas, fall color of Sugar Maples is usually restricted to yellow. It has been recommended as a superior shade tree for the drier alkaline blackland and rocky soils of northeast Texas (Wasowski 1988). It is not drought or salt tolerant and suffers in high temperatures. Sugar Maple is also sensitive to reflected heat and compacted soils (Arnold 1999).

Adelia vaseyi

Vasey's Adelia

EUPHORBIACEAE (SPURGE FAMILY)

GENERAL DESCRIPTION

Vasey's Adelia is a multi-trunked shrub up to 9 feet tall with a unique growth form. Slender stems all with the same diameter rise together from the base like a candelabra. Narrow leaves in small clusters are closely attached here and there along the smooth grayish stems.

FLOWERS AND FRUIT

Male and female flowers appear January through June on separate plants. Seeds are usually available around April or May. Fruit is a three-seeded capsule that dehisces shortly after it matures. The seed is dark brown to black when ripe.

NATURAL HABITAT, RANGE, AND PREFERRED SITE

The southern Rio Grande Delta (Cameron and Hidalgo counties) is at the northern limit of this plant's range. Vasey's Adelia is very characteristic of humid subtropical forest and mattoral (shrub land), although it is sometimes found in drier locations in loamy soils (Best, personal communication, 1999).

COLLECTION AND STORAGE

Closely monitor this plant in late spring in order to time collection before the capsule has split open and dropped all the seed. Seeds are hard to come by because the plant is rare, seed are not always viable, and the capsule quickly shatters. Flotation tests for viability are misleading because even viable seeds float initially. Seeds stored in a paper sack at room temperature still germinated the spring following collection (Best 1999).

PROPAGATION

Seeds

Germination of Vasey's Adelia is enhanced by light mechanical scarification with sandpaper. Seeds lightly scarified in this manner and aerated for 1 day germinated 100% in 3 days while untreated seeds in the same lot germinated at rates of 63% in 12 days. Acid scarification has not yet been tested. Seedling growth is moderate (Best 1999).

Cuttings

Information is lacking on vegetative propagation of Vasey's Adelia.

NOTES

This rare plant of south Texas could be protected by introducing it into cultivation. Further study is needed to determine cold hardiness and predictable nursery production methods. Its interesting, spare form could be an asset as a specimen plant in a dry garden.

Aesculus

Buckeye

HIPPOCASTANACEAE (BUCKEYE FAMILY)

GENERAL DESCRIPTION

Buckeyes are small trees or tall shrubs with deciduous palmately compound leaves composed of five to seven glossy leaflets. Buckeyes are often multi-trunked with open, spreading crowns.

FLOWERS AND FRUIT

Perfect and unisexual flowers occur on the same plant, held in large showy panicles just before or at the same time the leaves emerge. Each flower is tubular or bell-shaped, almost an inch long, and either red or yellow or a combination of red and yellow, depending on species. Fruit is a leathery capsule usually containing three large, smooth, light brown seeds. Ripening begins by late August through early fall, depending on climatic conditions and location.

NATURAL HABITAT, RANGE, AND PREFERRED SITE

The range of buckeyes depends on species. They most often grow as an understory plant in deeper soils and are seldom found on arid upland sites. Western buckeyes can survive dry periods, although they almost always defoliate completely by August. All buckeyes grow best if protected from direct afternoon sun and watered during prolonged dry spells. Under cultivation, buckeyes may keep their leaves longer if given extra water. See Species Descriptions for individual distribution and habitat.

COLLECTION AND STORAGE

Collect the seeds from the tree as soon as the leathery capsule turns brown and begins to peel back from the smooth, firm, golden brown seeds. Avoid collecting green or soft seeds or seeds off the ground unless they have only very recently dropped.

Buckeye seeds must be planted immediately after collection because they have high contents of fats and lipids and degenerate quickly after collection. They will lose viability rapidly if allowed to dry out. They will also rot if kept for more than a few days in plastic bags or if they have been buried beneath leaves or laid on damp ground. If sowing must be delayed a few days following collection, storing the seeds in trays or loose paper bags in a refrigerator will help to preserve viability. Seeds kept in dry storage over winter seldom germinate well the next spring.

PROPAGATION

Seeds

Buckeyes germinate promptly from fresh untreated seeds. Often the roots will emerge from seeds while still in storage. Do not scarify the seeds. Seeds should be planted outdoors or in a cold frame immediately after collection. An appropriate seedbed contains an even mixture of loose, well-aerated sandy loam and organic matter. It must retain moisture but be well drained. Protect from squirrels and other rodents. It is very important to provide enough room in the seedbed or container to accommodate the long, fleshy, and brittle initial root, which is easily broken when the seedling is transplanted from a cramped container or seed flat. The best containers are those that are 18 inches deep with either a wire bottom or with copper-treated interior surfaces, which encourages root pruning (see Chapter IV). Plant the seeds an inch deep and 4 inches apart. Germination of all seeds in a lot may be staggered; some seeds will germinate within 3 days, and others may require up to a month to emerge. Overwatering during the germination period may cause seed to rot. Buckeyes spend the first season following germination developing their root systems, waiting until spring to exhibit much shoot growth. A light frost will usually not damage the emerging stem, but mulching or cold-frame protection is recommended for severe weather. Often buckeye seeds sown outdoors with shoots that have been frozen back will sprout new stems the next spring. Once the stems have broken growth, fertilize the plant heavily to encourage as much top growth as possible. Root-pruned buckeyes that receive supplemental fertilization will be large enough for a five-gallon container by the second fall (McNeal, personal communication, 1999).

Seedlings are susceptible to spider mites and powdery mildew. Sanitation and good horticultural practices will reduce these problems.

Cuttings

In one study, cuttings of *A. parviflora* were taken in early April in Illinois from sucker growth under a mature plant. They were treated with 1,000 ppm IBA solution and stuck in a peat/perlite mixture, where they rooted at rates of 70–80% in 4 weeks. Cuttings collected later required higher rates of IBA for best rooting results (Dirr and Heuser 1987). Root cuttings taken February to March also rooted at rates of 50–60%. Some species of buckeyes may be reproduced from root cuttings taken in late winter before new growth begins. Root cuttings should be 2 to 3 inches long and tied in bundles of 8 to 10, making sure that all the top or proximal ends are together. The cuttings should then be packed in boxes of damp sand, sawdust, or peat moss and held for about 3 weeks at a constant temperature of 40° F. After this period of cold moist storage they should be planted 2 to 3 inches apart in well-prepared seedbeds with the tops of the cuttings level with or just below the surface of the soil. Keep the rooting bed slightly moist but not soggy (Hartmann and Kester 1975).

Transplanting

Small buckeyes under 5 feet can be moved in winter if lifted with the root ball intact. Larger specimens have a lower survival rate.

NOTES

The large showy flowers of early spring and the glossy widespread leaves make buckeye an outstanding specimen as a small tree or large shrub, especially when planted in groups or as an understory. In the winter the light brown crooked branches with their large leaf buds add an interesting sculptural form to an otherwise quiet landscape. Buckeyes enjoy the dappled light they receive when they are growing at the edge of woodlands. If not protected from western sun, the leaves may become scorched. In areas such as the Edwards Plateau, where populations of various species overlap, buckeyes will hybridize, and variations of yellow, red, even tangerine, can be observed (Pfeiffer, personal communication, 1999).

Some companion plants to grow below buckeyes include Turk's Cap (*Malvaviscus arboreus var. drummondii*), Pigeon Berry (*Rivinia humilis*), Bear grass (*Nolina spp.*), and Chile Pequín (*Capsicum annum*). Deer do not browse Buckeye. The one disadvantage of buckeyes is that they tend to defoliate as early as the end of August, leading many people to assume that they are dead instead of dormant. Periodic watering during dry spells in summer will help prolong their foliage. *Aesculus* is susceptible to leaf-spot disease (*Septoria hippocastani*), leaf blotch (*Guignardia aesculi*), and anthracnose (*Glomerella sp.*), all of which can cause defoliation. Avoid overhead watering. Buckeyes are also intolerant of foliar-applied salts. Buckeyes tend to put on a single flush of leaves and then go into semidormancy. *Aesculus* leaves and fruits are known to have a toxic effect on humans and livestock

(Cheatham and Johnston 1995). The toxic seeds and roots were used by Native Americans to stun fish in shallow pools, making them easier to capture.

SPECIES DESCRIPTIONS

Aesculus glabra var. arguta **(Texas Buckeye)**
Large shrub or small tree to 23 feet, often multi-trunked with creamy yellow flowers and 7 to 11 pointed leaflets. Native sandy or limestone soil in woods or along streams from Kansas south to Llano, Gillespie, and Burnet counties in central Texas. Good specimen tree for a small space. Texas Buckeye is possibly the most drought tolerant of all the Texas species.

Aesculus pavia var. flavescens **(Scarlet Buckeye)**
Typically a large shrub or small tree 7–10 feet tall. Leaves have five or sometimes seven leaflets. Bright yellow flowers. Range confined to about six counties in the western part of the Edwards Plateau. Where their ranges overlap, it may hybridize with Red Buckeye (*A. pavia var. pavia*), resulting in yellow flowers tinged with red or with a red throat.

Aesculus pavia var. pavia **(Red Buckeye)**
Most often seen as a shrub 7–10 feet tall. Flowers typically elongated, narrow, and red. Locally abundant in east Texas and canyons in the eastern edge of the Edwards Plateau, east to Florida, North Carolina, and Missouri. It prefers wooded areas near seeps or springs in sandy or loose alkaline soils.

Agave

Agave, Century Plant, Maguey

AMARYLLIDACEAE (AMARYLLIS FAMILY)

GENERAL DESCRIPTION

A genus of about 250 species, with 9 species native to Texas. Plants easily recognized by their rosettes of thick linear to lanceolate spine-tipped leaves at ground level.

FLOWERS AND FRUIT

A single leafless flower stalk rises from the center of the rosette high above the leaves. Each agave concludes its life span by devoting all its energies to produce one single beautiful bloom stalk. It has been estimated that 60% of the water used for flowering is sapped from the leaves, which causes the parent plant to shrivel and die 2–5 months after the plant sets blooms (Cheatham and Johnson 1995). Flowers are held on stocky lateral branches on the upper half of the stem. Each flower has three petals and three sepals about the same size, constricted into a slender neck with six yellow stamens that extend out twice as long as the petal size. Some species are deliciously fragrant.

The flowers of most species are yellow, but can vary to purple or brick red (see Species Descriptions). Usually before flowering, the parent plant produces suckers or small rosettes ("pups" or "hijos") around its base to take its place. In the garden, these can be transplanted to another location.

Because some agaves have the common name "Century Plant," many people believe that agaves bloom once every 100 years. However, it is not possible to accurately predict the length of time needed to produce a flower stalk. Generally, the larger agave species will send up a flower stalk in 8–10 years.

Seed is a late-maturing capsule which splits sideways to release the seeds. Fruit and seeds are usually produced from July through November.

NATURAL HABITAT, RANGE, AND PREFERRED SITE

Agaves are found in the southern and western parts of the state in dry, well-drained, and rocky soils. Agaves from Mexico have also escaped cultivation and become naturalized, especially in the Rio Grande Plains.

COLLECTION AND STORAGE

Collect the seeds from the capsules as soon as they begin to dry out and turn brown but before they split and disperse the seeds (late summer through fall). Seeds are easily removed by crushing the capsules. Seeds may be effectively stored for one year in ventilated containers in the refrigerator.

PROPAGATION

Seeds

Freshly gathered seeds germinate promptly without treatment. One-fourth cup of seed will yield about 3,000 plants (McNeal, personal communication, 1999). Remove the seeds from the pods as soon as they are ripe, and plant in a flat immediately. The seedbed should contain well-drained media. Do not plant the seeds too deeply (less than ½ inch of soil is usually sufficient). Many of the seeds will germinate within 3 weeks, while the remainder will germinate at staggered intervals over the next year. Keep moist but not soggy (McNeal, personal communication, 1999). Another method is to press the seed on top of seed flats containing perlite, and then place the seed flats in the mist house. Germination occurs in 3–7 weeks. Carefully remove the individual seedlings with tweezers after they have extended their primary root, and put them into 4-inch pots. If regularly fertilized, they will grow to a liner size in one year and salable one-gallon pot in 1–2 years (Hosage, personal communication, 1999). By the third year, they will be ready for a five-gallon container (McNeal, personal communication, 1999). Young agaves are easiest to transplant into one-gallon containers if first sown in segregated plant cells (about 200 seedlings per tray) or in individual pots. Germination of agaves is also improved when the seed are planted outdoors after collection to take advantage of fall rains (Gass, personal communication, 1999). Move plants up to five-gallon or larger containers before they produce offshoots. Agaves respond well to light fertilization and standard greenhouse practices. Young agaves benefit from light shade (30%) until the leaves harden off. Unshaded plants often get sun scald (Manning, personal communication, 1999).

Transplanting

After blooming, the older plant dies and young plants grow around the base of the rosette of leaves. These new plants may be separated and transplanted to a new site in late winter and early spring.

NOTES

It is no exaggeration to state that whole cultures depended on the *Agave*. Agaves have been used in a multitude of ways—as food (for both humans and livestock), as nutritional and alcoholic beverages, and as a source of fiber for weaving mats, making clothing, fashioning tools and utensils, and building shelter. For a thorough and fascinating account of the history and uses of *Agave*, see Cheatham and Johnson (1995).

SPECIES DESCRIPTIONS

Agave americana (Century Plant, Maguey)

Native in Texas only on gravelly hills in extreme south Texas, but naturalized elsewhere in the state and in warm regions throughout the world. The wild species, *Agave americana spp. protoamericana*, is native in the eastern Sierras from near Monterrey south into the state of San Luis Potosi. There are similar plants near Zapata, Texas (Ogden, personal communication, 1999). Century Plant is the largest of our native agaves; its leaves are pale gray to glaucous green, up to 40 inches long and 6 inches wide. The blade may be bent downward or twisted like the letter "S," with spines usually less than ½ inch long on its margins. The flower stalk can extend as high as 23 feet with 18–30 wide-spreading branches each bearing at its tip a tight cluster of yellow flowers. This species appears in many forms and special horticultural selections, and has been widely used in cultivation. Some selections include *var. marginata*, which has leaves with yellow or white edges; *var. variegata*, with twisted yellow and green banded leaves; *var. striata*, with variously lined leaves, and *var. medio-picta*, with a broad yellow center stripe. The variety *medio-picta* is one of the most beautiful and striking of all variegated plants. Both it and Marginata are only marginally cold hardy north of San Antonio. All are descended from plants that were domesticated in pre-Columbian times (Ogden, personal communication, 1999). *Agave americana* has played an important role in revegetation work in arid regions. The ferocious cluster of basal leaves protects grasses from browsing animals, and when the plant dies after flowering, it returns valuable organic matter to infertile soils. The waxy coating on the leaves also supplies saponins to the soil, which act as wetting agents by lessening the surface tension of the water; this in turn allows more water to soak into the ground rather than running off (Cheatham and Johnson 1995).

In ornamental landscapes, it's important to allow ample room for this dramatic and powerful plant to spread its pointed leaves. Agaves can be planted in dappled shade, but they will lean and stretch their flower stalks to catch the sun instead of holding them upright high above the leaves.

Agave havardiana **(Havard Maguey)**

Havard Maguey has glaucous gray to pale green leaves 12–24 inches long and 6–8 inches wide with a broad base and reflexed spines on the leaf margins. They form a distinctively symmetrical rosette with the leaves clasped upward like a perfect basket made from thick scales. In May and June, Havard Maguey sends up a magnificent stout flower stalk 6–13 feet tall with 12–20 side branches, each bearing a dense cluster of fragrant yellow flowers. Havard Maguey grows in the southern part of the Trans-Pecos, south to northern Mexico. The large agaves in the Davis and Glass mountains were formerly identified as *A. neomexicana*, but are now named as *A. havardiana* (Gentry 1982). *A. neomexicana* (Apache Mescal, New Mexico Agave) is found on rocky mountain slopes of southern New Mexico and south to the Guadalupe Mountains. The gray green leaves are slightly longer than *A. havardiana* with fewer and more widely spread teeth on the leaf margin. They form a very attractive tight pineapple-shaped rosette of overlapping leaves from which rises a 10–13 foot flower stalk with yellow or reddish flowers. Collect the seed in late summer and fall. Some growers collect the seed while the pods are still green and before they have split; others wait until the pod turns brown. Seed require no pretreatment in order to germinate. Plant in the fall or early spring. Havard Magueys will begin to form a small rosette within a year. In two years, they will grow to a 6–8 inch wide rosette and the leaves will have begun to stiffen and harden off (Manning, personal communication, 1999).

Agave lechuguilla **(Lechuguilla)**

Lechuguilla is one of the indicator plants that characterize the Chihuahuan Desert. It is extremely common on rocky limestone hills below 7,500 feet. It has a stiff, slightly cupped narrow yellow green leaf 12–20 inches long, with down-flexed spines on the margins. The parent plant sets offshoots or "hijos" which eventually form clumps 8 feet across or larger. The tender rhizome-like offshoots are browsed by javelina and deer. Lechuguilla has a slender flower stalk 8–13 feet tall with short branches bearing a tight cluster of three or four yellow, green, brown, or brick red flowers. Flowers appear early in the summer after rains and are pollinated by nectivorous bats, hummingbirds, butterflies, hawk moths, and small bees. Lechuguilla usually produces a bloom after 3–4 years. In cultivation, Lechuguilla has potential as a ground cover, especially in remnant margins of naturalized areas or where a barrier is needed. Plant starter rosettes of Lechuguilla 6 feet from a path and 10 feet from long-lived shrubs (Mielke 1993). Lechuguilla is also a useful plant for erosion control, especially on dry, rocky slopes that receive no supplemental irrigation. In Texas, Lechuguilla has been planted as far north as Brady, Texas. *A. lophantha* (Big Lechuguilla, Thorn-crested Agave) is very similar to *A. lechuguilla*, but its native range is restricted to rocky soils in the Rio Grande Plains. Numerous stands of *A. lophantha* have also naturalized in central Texas. The distinguishing feature of *A. lechuguilla* is that the leaf margin of Big Lechuguilla is more firmly attached. *A. lophantha* flowers are pale green to yellowish green.

***Agave scabra* (Rough Maguey, Maguey Cenizo)**
This plant is common in Mexico, but in Texas is only found in a few counties in extreme south Texas and in an isolated population south of San Antonio (Cheatham and Johnston 1995). It has a very gray concave or gutter-shaped leaf 24–44 inches long and 5–6.5 inches wide with a rough, sandpapery texture. The flower stalk is stout, rising 13–20 feet with a dense terminal flower cluster bearing yellow tubular flowers. This is another large *Agave* with terrific potential as a landscape plant (McNeal, personal communication, 1999).

Alnus serrulata

Smooth Alder, Hazel Alder

BETULACEAE (BIRCH FAMILY)

GENERAL DESCRIPTION

Smooth Alder is a tall, regularly branched shrub or small tree no taller than 20 feet. Dark green glossy leaves are 2–4 inches long with distinctly serrated edges, turning yellow in the fall.

FLOWERS AND FRUIT

Male and female flowers occur separately on the same plant in late winter or early spring. Male flowers are showy yellow catkins 4 inches long. Female flowers develop into persistent conelike fruits, called strobiles, by the following fall. Each strobile contains two to four compressed winged nutlets, ⅛ inch long.

NATURAL HABITAT, RANGE, AND PREFERRED SITE

Smooth Alder is native to creek banks, swamps, and other low wet places with frequent standing water in east Texas. Occasionally found farther west in suitable wet situations; also east to Florida, Oklahoma, Missouri, Indiana, and Ohio. Prefers shady places and poorly drained soil. Smooth Alder prefers wet or flooded places in full sun.

COLLECTION AND STORAGE

Gather strobiles in early fall before they completely dry and disperse the nutlets or drop from the plants. Seeds should be thoroughly air dried before storage. Storage in sealed containers in a dry place is adequate for over winter. For longer storage, refrigeration is recommended. Smooth Alder seeds held in sealed containers at 34–38° F have been known to retain their viability for as long as 10 years.

PROPAGATION

Seeds

Alnus seeds require 1–2 months of cold stratification before germination will proceed. Seeds may be sown outdoors in well-prepared seedbeds in late fall. Gently press the seeds into the soil and cover lightly with washed sand or a light soil mix. The seedbed should be mulched over winter, and the mulch later removed as germination begins.

Seeds sown indoors or in spring must first be stratified for 60–90 days at 30–40° F. Stratification should be planned so the seeds are ready for planting by late February or early March. Seed germination and seedling survival during hot weather is poor. Do not allow the seedbed or container to dry out.

Cuttings

Take cuttings in late spring or early summer. Treat with 8,000 ppm IBA talc, stick in vermiculite, and keep under mist. In one study, cuttings rooted 52%. Cuttings taken in early spring and treated the same way only rooted 30% (Dirr and Heuser 1987).

NOTES

The bright yellow male catkins, golden fall color, and female winter fruits all contribute to Smooth Alder's appeal. It must have consistent moisture, and prefers full sun. Because Smooth Alder tends to form thickets by suckering from the roots, it is useful in preventing erosion along stream banks. Its roots also have a relationship with nitrogen-fixing actinomycetes, which are important in soil stabilization and improvement. Smooth Alder is a good understory plant for shady, poorly drained places.

The seeds are eaten by a number of small birds. The bark reportedly yields a tannic acid and an astringent. It was used in traditional folk medicine to treat fever.

Aloysia

Bee-brush, White Brush, Jazminillo

VERBENACEAE (VERBENA FAMILY)

GENERAL DESCRIPTION

Aloysia spp. are small deciduous aromatic shrubs with opposite, simple leaves. Many brittle and slender branches with yellow inner wood rise from a woody base.

FLOWERS AND FRUIT

Flowers are held in delicate long spikes at the ends of branches. Individual flowers are small, tubular shaped, and colored white to pinkish lavender. The narrow clusters of flowers at the ends of branches are very fragrant. *Aloysia* will bloom in the spring and again at intervals in the summer after rains. Fruit is a small dry schizocarp containing two seeds.

NATURAL HABITAT, RANGE, AND PREFERRED SITE

Members of this genus are native to south and west Texas, Mexico, and southwest United States. See Species Descriptions for individual range and habitat. All species prefer full sun and are able to thrive in poor, rocky soil but in cultivation may adapt to light shade and more fertile soil. Bee-brush is often an early invader of disturbed sites.

COLLECTION AND STORAGE

Collect seeds throughout summer when the schizocarps are brown and beginning to dry. Prompt collecting is important because once the fruit is completely dry, the schizocarp splits and quickly drops the seeds. The fruit may be slightly crushed and the seeds removed by hand, or the seed can be dried in the fruit (Best 1999). Seeds should be thoroughly air dried before storage. Seeds placed in sealed containers in a cool dry place will remain viable at least over winter.

PROPAGATION

Seeds

Aloysia will germinate without pretreatment from freshly gathered seeds. Germination proceeds best at temperatures ranging from 70° to 85°F. Seedlings sprouting in the fall should be held in a cold frame or greenhouse over winter. Sow the seeds thinly, just pressing on top of the flat or containers. Do not bury. Soil must be well drained.

Cuttings

Softwood tip cuttings that are slightly woody toward the base, taken in spring or early summer, root the best. Take the bottom cut just below a node. Taking a heel may also improve rooting. Insert the cuttings gently in flats or boxes containing a well-drained soil mixture and then place under mist. Rooting usually occurs within 18 days and is improved by application of IBA (1,500 ppm) and bottom heat (McNeal, personal communication, 1999). Prune plants, whether grown from seed or cutting, while still young (under 12 inches in height), and prune often. Unpruned seedlings tend to develop a single, long, gangly woody stem with fewer branches and hence fewer blooms (Will, personal communication, 1999).

Transplanting

Aloysia is easy to transplant if sheared heavily and given extra water until it is established. Field plants coppice freely even when cut to the base. Some growers believe that seedlings show more vigor than cuttings (Bering, personal communication, 1999).

NOTES

Aloysia is a valuable honey plant and also provides browse material for wildlife and livestock. It is a good background or screen plant for rocky hillsides and poor soil. Previously called *Lippia*, this genus contains several ornamental cultivated members. Bee-brush will grow in shade but blooms better in full sun. It should be cut back periodically to promote more flowers and more compact growth.

SPECIES DESCRIPTIONS

Aloysia gratissima **(Bee-brush, White Brush, Hierba de la Princesa, Jazminillo)**
Slender shrub to 10 feet. White or violet-tinged flowers have a strong vanilla odor. Native to rocky outcrops, desert grasslands, bluffs, and woods throughout Texas except the High Plains; also New Mexico and Mexico. Ranchers often consider this aggressive plant a pest because it is quick to

take over abandoned fields or overgrazed pastures. Once established, it is very hard to eradicate. It often grows in association with Prickly Pear Cactus (*Nolina lindheimeri*), Mexican Persimmon (*Diospyros texana*), and Tasajillo (*Opuntia leptocaulis*).

Aloysia macrostachya **(Vara Dulce, Cabradora, Sweetbrush)**
Perhaps the showiest of the aloysias, this plant is a tall shrub (up to 12 feet in the Lower Rio Grande Valley), with many wandlike stems rising from the base bearing larger, fuzzy leaves. Vara Dulce is covered with fragrant purple flowers from April to October. In one out of five winters in Austin, it will freeze to the ground, but will return from the root. From San Antonio south, Vara Dulce is semi-evergreen (McNeal, personal communication, 1999).

Aloysia wrightii **(Oreganillo)**
Shrub to 5 feet with small scalloped oval leaves embossed with a waffle pattern, and white flowers in dense spikes. The leaves release a very pungent smell when crushed or rubbed, thus giving the Spanish name "Oreganillo." Oreganillo grows on limestone hills and canyon walls in the Trans-Pecos, west to New Mexico, Arizona, and southeast California. In low elevations, it is most common on rocky, north-facing slopes, and at higher elevations where frost is frequent, Oreganillo prefers a protected niche in warm, dry, south-facing slopes (Bower 1993). After reaching its mature height, Oreganillo, like many desert shrubs, grows slowly, living perhaps as long as 75 years (Bowers 1993).

Amelanchier

Service-berry, Shadbush, Juneberry

ROSACEAE (ROSE FAMILY)

GENERAL DESCRIPTION

Small trees or shrubs with simple, deciduous leaves and unarmed branches.

FLOWERS AND FRUIT

Showy clusters of white flowers bloom early in spring as the new leaves appear. Each flower has five white petals and numerous showy stamens. Fruit is a berrylike pome containing 4 to 10 seeds.

NATURAL HABITAT, RANGE, AND PREFERRED SITE

Amelanchier is represented by species native to both far west and deep east Texas. See Species Descriptions for individual range and habitat.

COLLECTION AND STORAGE

To minimize loss due to birds and other wildlife, collect the fruits as soon as they ripen. Fruits may be hand picked or beaten from the bush onto blankets or stripped onto a mechanical hopper. It is usually necessary to collect large amounts of fruit because the seeds are often infertile or insect infested. Clean seeds immediately to prevent fermentation. Seeds that have been carefully cleaned, air dried, and stored in sealed containers in the refrigerator can remain viable up to 5 years (USDA 1974).

PROPAGATION

Seeds

Germination of *Amelanchier* is delayed by one or more of the following factors: an immature embryo, a cold dormancy requirement, and a hard seed coat. Germination may be achieved for some species of *Amelanchier* by planting the seeds outdoors immediately after collection in fertile, well-prepared beds. The mild temperatures of autumn encourage complete development of the embryo. Gradually the colder winter temperatures will provide the cold moist chilling necessary to break dormancy. Keep the beds mulched until germination occurs.

For indoor or spring planting, first stratify the seeds for 60–180 days at 41° F. *Amelanchier* germinates best in cool temperatures, so the stratification period should be completed by late February. Germination of the entire lot may be staggered over several months.

Hard-seeded species must be scarified in acid for up to 30 minutes before the stratification period or they will not germinate. See Species Descriptions for individual recommendations.

Amelanchier seeds are very susceptible to soil-borne fungi, and seedlings will damp off or rot in heavy clay soils. New plants should be very carefully watered. Do not let them dry out or become too soggy.

Eastern forest species of Amelanchier prefer well-drained, moderately deep, and slightly acid soil. Seedlings will need partial shade until they are well established. Western species prefer well-drained alkaline soil and full sun.

Cuttings

Amelanchier roots best from semihardwood cuttings. These should be 3–6 inches long, treated with IBA (50 mg/l for 24 hours), and placed under mist. Cuttings generally root in low numbers and are slow growing after rooting.

Amelanchier may also be increased by root cuttings, layering, or rooting of suckers taken in the spring.

NOTES

Amelanchier spp. are attractive spring-flowering shrubs. The fruit of many species may be eaten raw or cooked. Members of this genus provide important browse and food plant for many species of birds and other wildlife. Western species of *Amelanchier* tend to become disease prone when planted farther east and at lower elevations in more hot and humid environments (Simpson, personal communication, 1986).

SPECIES DESCRIPTIONS

Amelanchier arborea (Service-berry)

Shrub or slender tree to 64 feet, usually smaller, with oval leaves, white flowers, and bright red fruit ripening in May. Native to rich woodlands along streams and in thickets in east Texas, Oklahoma, east to Florida. Stratify for 90–120 days at 41° F prior to sowing.

***Amelanchier denticulata* (Big Bend Service-berry)**
Shrub 3–10 feet with persistent, glossy, toothed leaves. Whitish pink flowers, about 2½ inches wide. Fruit consisting of large "rosehips," borne in clusters of two to four, turning purplish black when ripe in August to October. Native to talus slopes and canyon rimrocks at high elevations in the southern Trans-Pecos. Big Bend Service-berry prefers well-drained limey soils. Seeds exhibit a double dormancy and are difficult to germinate. Scarification prior to cold stratification may improve germination. Early fall sowing of untreated seeds is also sometimes effective. Seedlings may begin to emerge during cold stratification and have to be removed individually at staggered intervals (Simpson, personal communication, 1986). Big Bend Service-berry can be rooted from semihardwood cuttings, but not easily. Keep rooted cuttings in a one-gallon container in the shade for 1–2 years. Keep the roots cool (McNeal, personal communication, 1999).

***Amelanchier utahensis* (Utah Service-berry)**
Shrub or small tree to 16 feet with small oval leaves, racemes of white flowers, and small dark purple fruit. Limestone soil on canyon slopes in the Guadalupe Mountains of west Texas, also New Mexico, north and west to California and Oregon. Stratify seeds at 40°F for 2–6 months. Forty percent of the seeds will germinate within 60 days (Vories 1981). Seeds are often infertile or infested. Semihardwood cuttings have been known to root at rates of 40–50% (McNeal, personal communication, 1999). This species would make a good landscape plant for the high desert or the area north of Abilene in Texas.

Amorpha

False Indigo, Indigo bush

FABACEAE (LEGUME FAMILY)

GENERAL DESCRIPTION

False Indigos are thornless, weak-stemmed shrubs with deciduous compound leaves. The leaves are often dotted with tiny translucent glands.

FLOWERS AND FRUIT

Flowers appear in late spring, forming dense elongated spike clusters. Flower size varies with species (see Species Descriptions). Fruit is a small pod containing one or two seeds.

NATURAL HABITAT, RANGE, AND PREFERRED SITE

See Species Descriptions.

COLLECTION AND STORAGE

Collect the seeds in late summer or early fall when the pod turns yellowish brown and begins to dry. Since the seeds are tiny, it is not necessary for them to be removed entirely from the pods before sowing or storage. Seeds (in or out of their pod) stored in sealed containers at 41° F may retain viability for 3 to 5 years (USDA 1974).

PROPAGATION

Seeds

Production of False Indigo is affected by limited seed production and viability, variability from year to year in seed coat thickness, and a seedling that tends to be slow growing (Will, personal communication, 1999). General guidelines for seed propagation call for crushing the small pods open and soaking them with the seeds in warm water. Viable seeds will imbibe water in less than 24 hours. Strain off the seeds from the pods and plant immediately following imbibition (McNeal, personal communication, 1999).

Another method for growing *A. fruticosa* recommends sowing several freshly gathered seeds in each "bullet" tube. Seedling will grow from a "bullet tube" to a finished one-gallon container in 4–5 months. Seedlings tend to be fast growing and are hard to maintain in a pot because they get leggy and spreading very quickly (Bronstad, personal communication, 1999).

Seeds sown outdoors in the fall should be protected from hard freezes. In nature, germination usually occurs in the spring following seed maturity. Germination rates are best when the soil is warm. Another method for growing central Texas species of *Amorpha* recommends scarifying the seed for up to 15 minutes in concentrated sulfuric acid before sowing (Hosage, personal communication, 1999).

Plant *Amorpha* in individual containers at least 6 inches deep to accommodate the relatively long initial root. Fall-planted seeds kept in a cold frame over winter will require a year to a year and a half to make a one-gallon plant (Pfeiffer, personal communication, 1999).

Cuttings

False Indigo may be propagated from softwood cuttings taken in late spring through summer and treated with 1,500 ppm IBA (Pfeiffer, personal communication, 1999). Spring-rooted cuttings will make a one-gallon plant by the following fall. In one study, untreated cuttings of *A. fruticosa* taken in July with the basal cut made at a node rooted 100% in sand (Doran 1957). Hardwood cuttings may also be taken in the fall, placed in a cold frame, and transplanted the following summer.

New plants of *Amorpha* are also produced by transplanting suckers from large clumps of mature plants. Some growers regularly shear stock plants to encourage coppicing, which provides a renewable source of cutting material. In one study of *A. canescens*, cuttings taken in the summer and treated with 3,000–8,000 ppm IBA talc plus thiram rooted 80 and 90% when placed in a sand/perlite mix and kept under mist (Dirr and Heuser 1987).

NOTES

Amorpha is widely distributed in North America, with six species found in Texas. *Amorpha* is toxic to livestock, but has many traditional uses in Native American medicine (see Cheatham and Johnston 1995).

SPECIES DESCRIPTIONS

***Amorpha fruticosa* (False Indigo, Indigo-bush Amorpha)**

A much-branched shrub to 6 feet tall, with many weak or wandlike stems rising from the base. The leaflets are dark green and slightly fuzzy on the undersurface. Flowers deep purple with orange anthers, hanging in showy racemes 6 to 8 inches long at the ends of branches in April. Fruit is a dark, gland-dotted persistent pod. False Indigo prefers moist, slightly alkaline soils along stream banks or bar ditches. False Indigo has been cultivated since 1724. It is an attractive ornamental plant and has been used in erosion control and in wetland mitigation (Bronstad, personal communication, 1999). An especially showy cultivar of the variety *angustifolia*, 'Dark Lance,' was developed by Benny Simpson of the Texas A&M Research and Extension Service Center at Dallas. The name "Dark Lance" refers to its prolific, dark purple-brown flower spikes. It is a profuse bloomer and will grow in partial shade but flowers best in full sun and in soils between a pH of 7.0 and 8.5. It is rarely attacked by insects or disease, and it is not browsed by livestock. 'Dark Lance' is recommended as a tall background or border shrub, especially for low wet places, such as near drainage ditches or beside ponds. Under periods of extended drought, False Indigo may defoliate, but watering enough for an average lawn will keep it green. In spring a mature stand of this plant will form a dense thicket of fragrant purple flowers. Despite its many qualities, the 'Dark Lance' selection has not gained much favor in the nursery trade.

Germination of False Indigo can be hastened by soaking the seed in hot water for 10 minutes or soaking in sulfuric acid for 5–8 minutes. Scarified seed will germinate in high percentages in less than 15 days if sown when the weather is warm.

***Amorpha paniculata* (Panicled Amorpha)**

Densely fuzzy leaflets with conspicuous raised veins on the lower surface identify this species of *Amorpha*. As with *A. roemeriana*, the purple flowers are held in narrow, wandlike racemes above the branches. Panicled Amorpha is native to wooded and wet areas in the far eastern margin of northeast Texas. Lynn Lowrey considered Panicled Amorpha to be the best-suited *Amorpha* for moist, shady locations in the eastern half of the state.

***Amorpha roemeriana* (Texas Indigo Bush)**

Endemic to the Edwards Plateau of Texas, where it prefers moist limestone soils in canyons or beside creeks, Texas Indigo Bush is a shrub 3–10 feet tall with loose, spreading branches. Unlike *A. fruticosa*, Texas Indigo Bush is not fuzzy. The flowers are purple, held in slender but crowded racemes above the leaves. These flower clusters are longer and perhaps showier than most other *Amorpha* species. Pat McNeal suggests using Texas Indigo Bush as a substitute for Butterfly Bush (*Buddleia davidii*) in the landscape.

Ampelopsis

Pepper-vine

VITACEAE (GRAPE FAMILY)

GENERAL DESCRIPTION

Pepper-vines are climbing or erect shrubs that attach by means of tendrils. The leaves are thin, shiny, deciduous, and 1 to 6 inches long. New leaves and tendrils are a shiny reddish maroon. Young stems are green to reddish, and older stems are tan to reddish brown.

FLOWERS AND FRUIT

Small, individually inconspicuous greenish flowers are borne in a dichotomous cyme. Fruit is a several-seeded berry turning purple-black when ripe in late summer or early fall. The fruits, though messy over a sidewalk, are showier than the flowers. Bees work the flowers for nectar and produce a thin, reddish honey (Cheatham and Johnston 1995).

NATURAL HABITAT, RANGE, AND PREFERRED SITE

The two species of *Ampelopsis* native to Texas are generally found in thickets, along roadsides, streams, or rivers mostly in the eastern half of Texas, east to Florida, north to Illinois, Oklahoma, and northern Mexico (see Species Descriptions). They are adapted to a wide range of soils and sites, except extremely arid situations, and will grow in sun or shade.

COLLECTION AND STORAGE

Collect the seeds when the fruit turns dark blue-black. Clean the seeds from the pulp and thoroughly air dry on screens before storing. Sealed containers in the refrigerator provide the best type of storage.

PROPAGATION

Seeds

Seeds may be sown outdoors in the fall or stratified for 30–60 days at 41° F and then sown in February to March.

Cuttings

Ampelopsis will root easily from mature semihardwood cuttings of the current season's growth. Select a section of stem with at least 2–3 nodes, and make the cut one-half the distance between nodes. Remove the leaves from the lower half of the cutting. Insert the cuttings in well-drained soil media and keep under mist. Rooting occurs within 30 days. *Ampelopsis* may also be increased by root cuttings.

Transplanting

Small plants or rooted sections of larger plants are easily transplanted if cut back to the second or third leaf node and kept well watered.

NOTES

Pepper-vines like to climb up other shrubs or trees and take over a bed. However, this ability to adapt to different soil types makes it a good plant for such open, isolated sites as median strips, along roadways, in parking lots, or on eroded hillsides on the edges of property.

SPECIES DESCRIPTIONS

Ampelopsis arborea (Pepper-vine)

Vine with glossy bi- or tripinnately compound leaves, inconspicuous flowers, and showy clusters of blue-black fruit. Native to edges of forests and along streams and fencerows from Florida to central Texas, north to Oklahoma and Illinois. Will adapt to many different sites.

Ampelopsis cordata (Heart-leaf Pepper-vine)

Smooth vine with triangular-ovate leaves. Flowers held in loose greenish cymes followed by bluish green or reddish berries. Rich woodlands and bottomlands along rivers from Florida to the eastern third of Texas, north to Ohio. Heart-leaf Pepper-vine is susceptible to powdery mildew attacks on the upper side of the leaf. Birds are very fond of the fruit of both species. It is very easy to root from semihardwood cuttings taken in May/June with 2–3 nodes. Make the cut halfway between the final nodes and root under mist in well-drained media (McNeal, personal communication, 1999).

Amyris

Torchwood, Chapotillo, Lantrisco, Limonaria

RUTACEAE (CITRUS FAMILY)

GENERAL DESCRIPTION

Torchwoods are densely branched shrubs or trees, with dark green pinnately compound leaves. The leaves have aromatic oils that produce a pleasant citrus smell when crushed.

FLOWERS AND FRUIT

Inconspicuous flowers are held in clusters at the ends of branches from spring through fall. The fruit is a round, juicy black drupe with one seed.

NATURAL HABITAT, RANGE, AND PREFERRED SITE

Native to well drained sandy, loamy, or clay soils in extreme south Texas and Northern Mexico (see Species Descriptions). Torchwoods are extremely heat and drought tolerant.

COLLECTION AND STORAGE

Collect the seeds when the fruits turn from green to blackish brown. Because the seed is soft, depulp the fruit gently. For best results, plant the seed immediately. Stored seed of *A. texana* will not germinate. *A. madrensis* can be stored longer. In storage, the seeds give off moisture, so rotting becomes a problem. Use ventilated containers even for short-term storage. Seeds lose viability rapidly when kept at room temperature (Best 1999).

PROPAGATION

Seeds

A. texana will germinate only from fresh seed. Even seed stored only a few months will fail to germinate. The seeds of *A. texana* are soft, so they must be depulped gently. Immediately aerate them for 1–2 days, before they have a chance to dry after cleaning. Seeds planted in September to November right after collection usually germinate in 2–3 weeks (Best 1999).

A. madrensis may be grown from untreated seed collected the previous season and then planted outdoors in the spring after all danger of frost is past, or earlier in the greenhouse. The soil must be warm before germination will proceed. To achieve reasonable germination rates from *A. madrensis*, it is first necessary to remove the outer seed coat or testa (Best 1999). The seeds imbibe water but can't break through the testa unless it is removed. After the fruit has been gently cleaned and allowed to dry slightly, the testa becomes parchment-like. A tedious but effective method of opening the testa is to pierce each seed with a needle. In one study, untreated seed germinated at .06%, while seed germinated at 85% after being depulped and the testa removed. In another test, 60% of a small sample of seeds collected from raccoon scat germinated (Best 1999). Even short periods of acid scarification proved ineffective in preliminary trials.

A. madrensis is remarkably slow growing. It is very susceptible to damping-off fungi during the seedling stage. In the nursery, it benefits from applications of chelated iron every 2 months although once planted in the field, it does not seem to require it. After 1 year, *A. madrensis* may reach only 12–18 inches. Other reports indicate that *A. madrensis* will respond to fertilization and may make a small but sturdy one-gallon plant in 8–10 months (Hosage, personal communication, 1999).

Cuttings

A. madrensis roots readily from softwood cuttings that are slightly woody toward the base. These should be inserted in a well-drained rooting bed under constant mist. Application of IBA improves rooting. Information on exact techniques is lacking.

Transplanting

A. madrensis plants under 3 feet tall are easily transplanted if shaded and well watered until they are established. Fall or winter transplants are most successful (Lowrey, personal communication, 1986).

NOTES

Both species of torchwood are beginning to be valued as landscape plants in south Texas. Their dark green, aromatic foliage and the scent of their small white flowers make them a welcome addition to a drought-stressed garden. They are outstanding specimen plants for locations that require a smaller tree or evergreen shrub. Birds are very fond of the fruit of both species (Cheatham and Johnston 1995). *A. madrensis* will only thrive on full-sun sites, while *A. texana* often occurs as an understory plant.

SPECIES DESCRIPTIONS

***Amyris madrensis* (Sierra Madre Torchwood, Limonaria)**

Sierra Madre Torchwood is a spineless shrub or small tree 9–18 feet tall with smooth gray bark and an umbrella-shaped form. The leaves are composed of 5–11 gland-dotted leaflets that have a strong citrusy smell when crushed. Sierra Madre Torchwood is an uncommon or rare species of undisturbed shrub lands. It is an indicator of high-quality habitat. It is found only in a few sites in the extreme part of the Rio Grande Delta (Cameron, Hidalgo, and Willacy counties), where it grows in full sun. The fruits of Sierra Madre Torchwood are larger than those of *A. texana*. Overall, it is a more showy plant.

***Amyris texana* (Texas Torchwood, Lantrisco, Chapotillo)**

Subtropical, compact, densely branched, rounded shrub usually no taller than 3–6 feet, occasionally larger. Leaves smooth, shiny, trifoliate, and mostly evergreen. Texas Torchwood is native to northeastern Mexico and south Texas, extending along the Rio Grande Plains and up the coast as far as Jackson County in Texas (Cheatham and Johnson 1995).

Anisacanthus

Anisacanthus

ACANTHACEAE (ACANTHUS FAMILY)

GENERAL DESCRIPTION

Anisacanthus spp. are slender spreading shrubs usually less than 6 feet tall with brittle stems and broadly lanceolate to linear light green leaves (see Species Descriptions).

FLOWERS AND FRUIT

Showy tubular-shaped flowers vary in color among species from red, orange, yellowish, or pinkish (see Species Descriptions). Seed is a club-shaped capsule containing flat, black, heart-shaped seeds. When the capsule is dry, it splits open and sometimes forcibly ejects the seed at a distance, thus introducing new plants in the garden where you may not have intended them. Blooming begins with the onset of hot weather in mid-summer and continues intermittently until the first frost. Heaviest blooming period is from August through September.

NATURAL HABITAT, RANGE, AND PREFERRED SITE

Anisacanthus spp. are native to rocky banks and flood plains of streams, roadsides, and open woodlands of the Edwards Plateau, the Trans-Pecos, and northern Mexico. *Anisacanthus* is very drought tolerant and prefers full sun. In shade it will produce fewer blooms.

COLLECTION AND STORAGE

Collect the seeds as soon as the capsules begin to dry and turn brown but before they split open. Because *Anisacanthus* blooms intermittently, it may be necessary to collect seeds over several blooming periods. Air dry seeds before storage. Dried capsules are also easier to separate from the seeds. Storage in ventilated containers in a cool dry place is adequate for at least one season. Light dusting of the seeds with an insecticide is recommended to prevent insect damage.

PROPAGATION

Seeds

Anisacanthus germinates promptly from fresh untreated seeds planted in a greenhouse or outdoors in spring after the soil has warmed and all danger of frost is past. Sowing in early spring in a greenhouse produces a larger seedling that is better able to withstand heat stress. Seeds should be planted no deeper than ½ to ⅓ inch deep in a well-drained soil mix. Keep the seed flat moist but not soggy. Germination occurs in 2 to 3 weeks. Seedlings sprouted in early spring will often be large enough for a three-gallon container by fall.

Cuttings

Anisacanthus is easily propagated from cuttings. *A. puberulus* grows from juvenile wood, and *A. linearis* and *A. quadrifidus var. wrightii* are best produced from softwood cuttings (McNeal, personal communication, 1999). Take cuttings in early summer and again in the fall right after a flush of growth has begun to harden off at the base. Make the cut just below a node, 4–6 inches long, with the leaves removed from the bottom half. Application of IBA (1,500 ppm) improves rooting but is not imperative. Often the cutting will develop aerial roots on woody stems (Will, personal communication, 1999). Insert cuttings at least 3 inches apart in a flat or in separate 3-inch pots to allow enough space for formation of bushy roots and easy transplanting. Cuttings root best when placed under intermittent mist. Rooting is usually completed within 3 weeks. A 4-inch pot can be produced in 1 month and a salable one-gallon plant in 3 months (Bering, personal communication, 1999).

Transplanting

Anisacanthus is easily transplanted if the site is not too rocky. Transplants should be cut back by at least one-third and kept moist, especially in warm months. *Anisacanthus* freely self-seeds in situations with adequate topsoil, and often many young plants may be transplanted from around the parent.

NOTES

As a group, *Anisacanthus* is tolerant of dry weather and will grow in a variety of soil types. Hummingbirds and migrating butterflies are very fond of the late summer and early fall flowers. *Anisacanthus* responds well to shearing, and some people like to form it into a low clipped hedge. Seasonal shearing will produce a bushier plant with more blooms, although it is not necessary to clip it into an unnatural shape. In a mixed native shrub border or perennial garden, *Anisacanthus* is a good companion plant to Lantana (*L. horrida*), Blue Shrub Sage (*Salvia ballotaeflora*), Lindheimer's Senna (*Cassia lindheimeriana*), and Agarita (*Berberis trifoliolata*).

SPECIES DESCRIPTIONS

Anisacanthus linearis (Dwarf Anisacanthus)

A shrub usually less than 10 feet tall, found only in the Chihuahuan Desert. This is the most common anisacanthus in the Trans-Pecos. It grows in dry creek beds, canyons, and arroyos. The leaves are narrow, almost needle-like, and the flowers are red, orange-red, or yellowish. Dwarf Anisacanthus seed often has insect damage. Take cuttings in May from the first flush of growth. Rooting is not as successful when wood has hardened off. Treat with 1,000 ppm IBA talc or "Dip and Grow" (Manning, personal communication, 1999). Do not shear Dwarf Anisacanthus as much as you might the other species. It should be allowed to get as big as it wants. Moderate irrigation if you want to control growth (Manning, personal communication, 1999).

Anisacanthus puberulus (Pinky Anisacanthus)

Taller shrub generally 3–4 feet with many branches rising from the base. Broad lance-shaped leaves and pink flowers. Native to but not commonly found in the Chinati mountains in the Trans-Pecos and adjacent northern Mexico. A larger plant than other members of this genus, with larger leaves. In its native habitat, it blooms early in spring, often before the plant puts on leaves. In central Texas it blooms late (end of October) and blooms are not particularly impressive.

Anisacanthus quadrifidus var. wrightii (Flame Acanthus, Orange Hummingbird-bush)

Spreading, deciduous shrub up to 4 feet tall and 5 feet wide. Flame Acanthus has broadly lanceolate lower leaves and orange to reddish orange flowers. The stems are light colored and somewhat brittle. Native to southwestern Texas, Flame Acanthus is shoot hardy to USDA zone 8 (marginally in 7), and root hardy to USDA zone 7 (Arnold 1999). Flowers appear from April to October after rains. It is very adaptable to other parts of the state, including Houston. The long-lasting prolific orange blooms and drooping, spreading branches of light green leaves make Flame Acanthus a desirable ornamental, especially for sunny, exposed sites and poor soil. Cutting the plant back severely in winter will provide more blooms and encourage a bushy, compact form.

Aralia spinosa

Devil's Walking-stick

ARALIACEAE (GINSENG FAMILY)

GENERAL DESCRIPTION

Devil's Walking-stick is a treelike shrub with an umbrella-shaped crown formed by large leaves and stout, prickly stems. It is easily recognized by its large compound leaves, which are 3–4 feet long and 2–4 feet wide. The bark is dark brown with a shallow groove, armed with ferocious large orange prickles.

FLOWERS AND FRUIT

Immense flat white clusters of tiny white flowers appear on the plant from July through August. Fruit is a small black drupe containing a single seed ⅙ inch long.

NATURAL HABITAT, RANGE, AND PREFERRED SITE

Devil's Walking-stick grows in rich moist soil along streams and woods in east Texas, across the southern United States, north to New Jersey and the Midwest. It will grow in full or partial shade.

COLLECTION AND STORAGE

The seed is mature when the endocarp (outer covering) of the nutlet is hard and brittle. This may or may not coincide with the darkening of the fruit pulp to blue-black. Fruit is generally ripe from September/October. Clean the seeds immediately to avoid fermentation. Seed quality varies from year to year. Do not allow the seed to dry out during storage. For best results, plant the seed immediately (Wyman 1972).

PROPAGATION

Seeds

Germination is delayed by a dormant embryo. Seed can either be sown outdoors in the fall or stratified for 60–90 days. Pretreated seed will germinate at approximately 55% (Dirr and Heuser 1987).

Cuttings

Devil's Walking-stick suckers freely off the parent plant, and these shoots can be transplanted to form separate plants. It also reproduces vegetatively best from root cuttings. Dig and store roots in fall (⅓–⅖ inches wide, 4–4½ inches long are best). Place vertically in damp sand in a cool but protected place until spring, then plant outdoors in prepared beds with the tops of the cuttings barely covered with sand (Doran 1957). A 6–8 inch plant can be produced the first season (Dirr and Heuser 1987).

Transplanting

Devil's Walking-stick is easily transplanted and thrives in moist soil.

NOTES

Devil's Walking-stick has been cultivated as an ornamental shrub since 1688. The seeds are favored by birds, and the leaves browsed by deer (Vines 1970).

Arbutus xalapensis

Madrone, Madrona, Naked Indian's Leg

ERICACEAE (HEATH OR AZALEA FAMILY)

GENERAL DESCRIPTION

Madrone is a small irregularly shaped evergreen tree or multi-trunked shrub sometimes growing as tall as 40 feet, though usually smaller. Its distinctive feature is the shredding reddish brown bark that peels off in sheets to reveal the beautiful smooth underbark. This bark may vary in color from coppery red to orange-tan or ivory-white. New leaves are reddish, maturing into dark glossy green with red tinges on the undersides and edges.

FLOWERS AND FRUIT

Creamy white to pale pink flowers are urn shaped and held in fuzzy panicles from February through April. Fruit is a dark red or sometimes golden fleshy berry when ripe, containing 1–10 seeds. Fruit usually matures in late October but may remain on the tree as late as January.

NATURAL HABITAT, RANGE, AND PREFERRED SITE

Madrone is widespread but nowhere abundant on rocky limestone, igneous soil in canyons, and occasionally open plains in the Edwards Plateau and mountains of the Trans-Pecos; also southeastern New Mexico, and Mexico south to Guatemala.

COLLECTION AND STORAGE

In some years, collection of fruits may begin as early as September, but more often the berries are fully ripe in October and November. They should be filled out, soft, and a red or reddish orange color. Seed collectors often compete with birds for the best fruit. The largest berries usually have the heaviest and most fertile seeds. Seeds do not store well and should be cleaned by hand and the pulp removed by floating. Or they may be cleaned in a blender fitted with rubber blades. Seeds not planted immediately should be air dried and held in cold moist storage (35–40° F). Germination rates decline rapidly from 80% when harvested to 40% after 6 months of dry cold storage to only 4% after 30 months of storage (Simpson and Hipp 1985a).

PROPAGATION

Seeds

If seeds are gathered in November to December, they often exhibit no embryo dormancy. Seeds collected earlier may require 30 days of cold stratification in order to germinate uniformly. Plant Madrone seedlings no deeper than ¼ inch in well-drained media such as perlite or vermiculite. Germination is usually complete within 4 weeks.

Seedlings are extremely sensitive to water stress levels and also damping-off fungi. They must be kept very damp at the initial establishment and early growth stages. As the seedling grows, gradually lessen the watering to prevent damping off. Avoid overhead watering of young seedlings. In one report, seedlings survived best when a half-strength solution of a fungicide was applied with every watering until the seedling had three or four true leaves. In addition to the fungicide, the seedlings were fertilized at every watering with a 15-16-17 soluble fertilizer (220 ppm nitrogen) until they were planted in the landscape (Tipton, personal communication, 1986). Proper fertilizing is an important component in the production of container-grown Madrones. Weekly irrigation with a fertilizer solution containing 100 ppm nitrogen has also been recommended (Hipp and Simpson 1985a). If nitrogen is not a limiting factor, growth of Madrone seedlings has proven to be much better in a mixture of equal amounts of peat and perlite than in either a perlite and vermiculite or soil and perlite mixture (Simpson and Hipp 1985a).

Madrones planted in a container or in a landscape situation should be kept moist because their root system, which, like those of the blueberry and other members of the heath family, is lacking in root hairs (Simpson and Hipp 1985a). To minimize transplant shock, many growers plant seeds directly into "Jiffy" pots, black polybags, peat pots, milk containers, or other biodegradable containers that provide good drainage. Later the container can be placed in a bigger pot or planting bed without removing the seedling and disturbing the roots.

Once planted in the landscape, Madrones grow best in well-drained soil and under drip irrigation. Young seedlings benefit from partial shade the first growing season. Stake the trees to protect from wind, and cage out deer.

Madrones begin new growth in March and, with proper care and the right conditions, may grow as much as 18 inches in a year (Tipton, personal communication, 1986).

Germination of Madrone seedlings is not the real barrier to nursery production of this plant. Like most members of the Heath family or Ericaceae, the Madrone probably depends on a symbiotic relationship with mycorrhizal fungi, which enables the plant's rudimentary root system to absorb nutrients and water from the soil. However, the specific mycorrhizal association has not been identified for Texas Madrone as it has for other members of this genus, such as the Pacific Madrone (*A. menziesii*) (Zak 1974). Without the aid of these beneficial microorganisms, both the grower and the consumer can expect consistent and heavy losses of this plant as they move it into larger containers, as well as its eventual planting in the landscape. Madrone demands a very careful water regime; it cannot get either too wet or too dry, which is hard to manage while using standard greenhouse irrigation systems and pine-bark-based soil medium.

Some growers inoculate their potting soil with native soil dug from under Ashe Juniper (*J. ashei*) trees or the parent tree. Anecdotal reports suggest that this is the cure for the cultivation problems, but there is not enough evidence to adamantly recommend it. Another concern is that the consumer, not understanding the temperamental nature of this incredible plant, may put it near a sprinkler head or in compacted soil and eventually kill it, making him unhappy with the nursery where it was purchased.

Therefore, my recommendation is that the Texas Madrone be cherished and fiercely protected where it grows in nature, and that even scrawny trees be given protection from browsing, bulldozers, trampling, and crowding.

Cuttings

Vegetative propagation of Madrone is complex. Preliminary studies indicate that juvenile wood from 6-month-old seedlings treated with 4 mg/g (4 milligrams per gram) NAA powder or 5,000 mg/l IBA concentrate may be rooted in high-humidity chambers. In these studies, rooting was accomplished in 31 days. The timing of gathering cutting wood is critical. A few weeks difference in taking the cuttings can greatly influence rooting success. Cuttings taken from 6-month-old seedlings rooted best, while wood taken from a 6-year-old plant was not successful. The overall difficulty and expense of propagating the Madrone from cuttings does not encourage its immediate commercial feasibility.

Transplanting

Madrones do not transplant well from the thin, rocky soil of their native habitat. Their root system does not afford them the opportunity to survive transplant shock.

NOTES

The angular and interesting shape of the tree with its peeling and smooth bark, white flowers, glossy leaves, and red berries makes the Madrone one of our most beautiful native trees. It is considered by some to be a remnant tree from earlier geologic ages, when there was less browsing, more biomass, more rainfall, and deeper soils than there is today in their native habitat. Limits to its feasibility as a nursery crop mean that their dwindling numbers should be protected. Deer are very fond of browsing the young plants and foliage.

Asimina triloba

Paw-paw, Custard Apple

ANNONANACEAE (CUSTARD APPLE FAMILY)

GENERAL DESCRIPTION

Paw-paw is a small tree or large shrub 10–30 feet tall. Young shoots and new leaves are covered with a rusty down, later becoming smooth. The leaves of Paw-paw are up to 6 inches wide and 12 inches long, among the largest of any tree in America. They turn a rich butter yellow in autumn. In the winter, the Paw-paw reveals its delicate sculptural branching structure.

FLOWERS AND FRUIT

The drooping flowers are 2 inches across and brownish to maroon red, appearing before the new leaves in spring. The unusual fruit is a banana- or mango-shaped berry, thick and green when young, brown or black when mature, with a sweet yellow or white edible pulp. Each fruit contains several seeds.

NATURAL HABITAT, RANGE, AND PREFERRED SITE

Paw-paw grows in rich bottomland soils near streams in northeast Texas, east to Florida, north to Ontario, and northwest to Nebraska. Paw-paws will adapt to sites outside their range if placed in rich loamy soil and kept fairly moist. Paw-paw used to occur in large drifts and thickets, but today is mostly limited to isolated understory trees or small groves (Simpson 1988). Paw-paw prefers partial shade but will grow in stronger sunlight if moisture is adequate.

COLLECTION AND STORAGE

Fruit ripens in early fall but often drops from the tree while still hard, green, and sour tasting. It may be collected when still green as long as it is firm and filled out. Animals really like this fruit, so collection may be very competitive. Store greener fruit in single layers on trays until the pulp begins to soften. Seeds should be removed from the pulp and air dried a few days prior to storage.

PROPAGATION

Seeds

Germination of Paw-paw is often delayed by a hard seed coat and a dormant embryo. Seeds may be sown outdoors in the fall after collection, but germination may be slow and irregular. More uniform germination rates may be achieved by first scarifying the seeds and following that with stratification for 90–120 days at 41° F. Seeds rarely germinate while still in cold moist storage. Remove seeds from the refrigerator and sow individually in bullet tubes.

Germination typically does not begin until late March, and seedlings are slow growing. Allow the seedlings to develop a good root system before shifting into one-gallon containers.

Seedlings do best if kept in the one-gallon containers the fall after they germinate in unheated greenhouses or cold frames. Paw-paws require a solid 12 months to grow into a finished one-gallon container. The second spring, if the young plants are well rooted, they may be shifted into three-gallon containers, and later into a four-gallon the end of second season. Seedlings like to be moist but not too wet. Trying to "hurry" growth on this plant by moving it up prematurely into a five-gallon container is usually unsuccessful. Smaller containers are better as the plant develops a root system because they are not as likely to maintain a layer of wet soil at the bottom of the pot (Bronstad, personal communication, 1999).

For outdoor sowing, the seedbed should consist of loose sandy loam combined with organic matter. Plant the seeds 1½ inches deep. Light shade is beneficial to young seedlings.

Cuttings

Paw-paw can also be grown by layering and root cuttings (Bailey and Bailey 1947). Specific information on exact techniques is lacking.

Transplanting

Transplanting trees up to 12 feet may be achieved successfully in the winter when the trees are dormant and if the tops are severely cut back and the roots pruned before digging to make a good root ball (Lowrey, personal communication, 1986). Long taproots make moving large Paw-paws difficult.

NOTES

The fruits of Paw-paw are sweet and smooth, similar to some tropical fruits. The size and taste vary from tree to tree. Like the persimmon, the fruit of the Paw-paw must be kept in cool storage (or if outdoors, exposed to frost), until fully soft and ripe; otherwise it will be hard and sour tasting.

The interesting fruit and flowers as well as the large, smooth leaves make the Paw-paw a good small specimen tree for the moist acid soils of eastern Texas. Paw-paw was one of Lynn Lowrey's favorite trees, and he felt it was underappreciated. Paw-paw will grow in areas that are periodically flooded, and it is moderately salt tolerant (Arnold 1999). Several selections have been made for enhanced fruit production, and are typically sold as grafted plants.

A related species, *Asimina parviflora* (Dwarf Paw-paw) is a small shrub 2–6½ feet tall with thick leaves. Flowers and fruit are smaller than that of *A. triloba*. Native to dry piney woods, thickets, and oak woods in southeast Texas, east to northern Florida.

Atriplex

Saltbush, Chamiso, Costilla de Vaca

CHENOPODIACEAE (GOOSEFOOT FAMILY)

GENERAL DESCRIPTION

There are nearly 60 species of saltbushes occurring in the United States. They are annual or perennial herbs or shrubs up to 3 feet tall, usually with scale-covered stems. Leaves alternate or opposite, of variable shape (see Species Descriptions).

FLOWERS AND FRUIT

Small male and female flowers are borne on the same or separate plants. Fruit is a capsule compressed by two or more winged leafy bracts ripening in late summer and fall. The wings, formed from the flower bracts, are designed for wind dispersal. The prolific fruit is more ornamental than the flowers.

NATURAL HABITAT, RANGE, AND PREFERRED SITE

Found mostly in alkaline soil and dry roadsides in west Texas, New Mexico, Arizona, south to Mexico. See Species Descriptions for individual range and habitat. As a group, *Atriplex* prefers full sun and is very drought resistant.

COLLECTION AND STORAGE

Atriplex produces many seeds, which are usually gathered by hand when ripe in late summer or fall. Often the seeds remain on the plants until the following spring. Cleaning or de-winging the seeds before storage is not necessary. For large lots of seeds, cleaning in a hammermill will reduce the bulk of chaff and other debris without affecting germination. De-winged seeds average between 13,000 and 148,000 per pound (USDA 1974). Seeds with the moisture content reduced to 6–8% of the fresh weight can be stored in cloth or paper bags in a cool place for 6 or 7 years with little loss in viability (USDA 1974).

PROPAGATION

Seeds

Seeds of most *Atriplex* species must undergo a period of after-ripening following harvest before they will germinate. This period varies with the species and quality of the seeds. Four-winged Saltbush (*A. canescens*) requires 10 months of after-ripening. Stratification, scarification, soaking, and other chemical pretreatments have all been unsuccessful in improving germination rates (USDA 1974). The best way to improve germination is to keep the seeds in dry storage over winter to allow them time to completely mature.

Atriplex germinates best at relatively low temperatures (55–75° F). Seedling emergence and survival are reduced by high soil temperatures. In one report, 22% of the seeds germinated within 20 days. Natural germination is erratic, depending on adequate moisture and proper timing of precipitation.

Broadcast sowing in early spring yields dense stands of plants for nursery production (USDA 1974). Cover the seeds with ⅛ to ¼ inch of soil, never more than 1 inch.

The best seedbed is one containing a fine soil texture and an alkaline pH. Mulching improves establishment of seedlings in warm weather but must be removed if the soil remains too damp. Four- to six-week-old seedlings have been successfully field planted. Seedlings are also very frost tender.

Seedlings are susceptible to damping-off fungi and must be planted in extremely well drained soil, carefully watered, and treated periodically with appropriate fungicides.

Cuttings

Atriplex may be rooted from softwood cuttings taken from late summer through early fall. Cultivated or forced plants in a greenhouse provide more new growth or juvenile wood, which is easiest to root. Rooting takes place in 18 to 30 days, depending on species (Simpson, personal communication, 1986). The cuttings should be treated with IBA and placed in an extremely well drained soil medium under intermittent mist. Frequency of misting should be reduced as the cuttings begin to develop roots. Cuttings require careful maintenance after rooting to insure survival. Protect fall-rooted cuttings in a cold frame over winter.

NOTES

Atriplex is useful as a soil stabilizer along canals, ditch banks, and other disturbed and easily eroded sites. It is drought resistant and will thrive on an average annual rainfall of 6–10 inches. Certain species make interesting specimen plants because of their various forms, silvery foliage, and attractive winged seeds. They are used as hedges or background plants and are planted in pastures to provide browse material for game and livestock. Part of this plant's success as an arid zone plant is its adaptability. Four-winged Saltbush exhibits considerable ecotypic differentiation. It has evolved many different forms to suit different habitats and climates. Plant breeders have even developed a variety that will survive on the toxic soils of mine wastes (Bowers 1993).

Many species of *Atriplex* provide valuable browse for both domesticated and wild animals. The seeds are eaten by several kinds of birds and small animals. The branches also provide shade and shelter in the open plains.

SPECIES DESCRIPTIONS

Atriplex acanthocarpa (Tubercled Saltbush)

Shrub to 2 or 3 feet with persistent silver-gray toothed leaves. Male flowers in dense panicles. Alkaline soil in west Texas and southern New Mexico. Planted as an ornamental and roadside shrub.

Atriplex canescens (Four-winged Saltbush)

Perennial woody herb 1–8 feet with closely attached linear leaves. Fruit conspicuously four-winged. Dry mesas and alkaline valleys and hillsides in west Texas, Arizona, Mexico, and California. Most widely distributed species. It is highly valued by the Navahos, who use it as forage for their cattle, sheep, and goats, especially in winter and early spring when grazing plants are scarce. The leaves and young shoots are used as greens or added to soups.

In well-watered areas, Four-winged Saltbush can become invasive. It can be used as a fast-growing background plant for a screen or barrier, especially when used in combination with Texas Mountain Laurel (*Sophora secundiflora*), Arizona Cypress (*Cupressus arizonica*), Texas Pistachio (*Pistacia texana*), and Cenizo (*Leucophyllum frutescens*). It is adaptable to a wide range of soils, and is extremely salt tolerant. Four-winged Saltbush can become leggy if given too much water. Its form can be controlled somewhat by shearing. On overirrigated sites, it can become invasive.

Atriplex confertifolia (Spiny Saltbush, Shadscale)

A rounded, 1–2 foot tall shrub. The leaves vary in shape from nearly circular to elliptic or oblong. During the winter, the plants are typically leafless. Winter rains and snows stimulate spring leafing and flowering. The fruits are clustered near the branch tips. The two leaf-sized bracts surrounding the seed often turn red or pink as they mature, becoming much showier than the inconspicuous flowers. Native to extreme west Texas and the Panhandle, also northern Arizona and the Great Basin desert. Shadscale is a good plant for the High Plains. Shadscale can survive extreme temperatures in fine textured, somewhat salty and very dry soils that are often inhospitable to other plants.

***Atriplex ovata* (Oval-leaf Saltbush)**
Considered by some to be the most ornamental of the saltbushes. Perennial rounded shrub 1–1½ feet, woody at the base, and covered with silver-gray fuzzy leaves. Leaves persistent. Native to alkaline soil from Colorado south to west Texas, southern New Mexico, and Mexico.

Baccharis neglecta

False-willow, Seep-willow, Roosevelt or New Deal Weed

ASTERACEAE (SUNFLOWER FAMILY)

GENERAL DESCRIPTION

False-willow is a tall, multi-stemmed spreading shrub, 5½–9 feet tall with semi-evergreen leaves covering the stems. Each leaf is narrowly elliptic in shape, similar to the willow (hence its common name).

FLOWERS AND FRUIT

Male and female flowers borne on separate plants. Female plants produce a profusion of dense, fuzzy white flower heads in late summer. Fruit is a flattened and ribbed achene, borne in clusters on the plant from October through December.

NATURAL HABITAT, RANGE, AND PREFERRED SITE

Roadsides in sandy or calcareous soil throughout the state, except the forests of east Texas and the high elevations of the plains from North Carolina to Arizona. False-willow adapts itself to almost any location in full sun with well-drained soil. It is one of the first species to invade disturbed areas. False-willow is also cold hardy.

COLLECTION AND STORAGE

The light, feathery seeds are dispersed by wind and should be collected by hand beginning in October when they are no longer green but before they completely dry out and blow away. Spread the achenes on a screen or table to air dry a few days before storage. Seeds may be stored for at least 2 years in sealed containers held at 35–40° F. If held at an average temperature of 70° F, length of viability is reduced to 1 year (Vories 1981).

PROPAGATION

Seeds

Seeds may be sown immediately after collection in a greenhouse or cold frame or stored over winter and planted outdoors in the spring after all danger of frost is past. The seed flat must contain light, well-drained soil, and the seeds should be covered lightly. Fresh seeds will germinate in 7–15 days.

Cuttings

Some species of *Baccharis* can be increased by taking cuttings from the current season's growth and placing them under mist. Detailed information is lacking.

Transplanting

Older False-willow plants are difficult to transplant because they have long, woody, and brittle taproots that are hard to remove intact from the rocky sites where they frequently grow. Smaller plants, 4 feet and under, may be moved if cut back and kept well watered.

NOTES

False-willow is a good plant for seashore plantings because it is tolerant of high salt levels in the soil and water. Although considered by most to be an ugly invasive weed, False-willow does have some potential as a screen and background plant or specimen plant in really harsh and neglected sites, such as along roadsides, median strips, and parking lots. As an early succession plant, False-willow's contribution is limited to providing cover and shade to abandoned pastures and fields. Typically, False-willow phases out after 4 or 5 years, as other species, especially grasses, get a foothold. The genus *Baccharis* contains the largest members of the sunflower family.

Bauhinia lunaroides

Orchid-tree, Pata de Vaca, Pata de Cabra

FABACEAE (LEGUME FAMILY)

GENERAL DESCRIPTION

Orchid-tree is a multi-trunked shrub or small tree typically under 8 feet tall in its native habitat. Under cultivation, however, it may become the size of a small redbud tree (12–15 feet). It has distinctive light green deciduous leaves divided at the base into two leaflets, yet appearing as one broad, deeply cleft, hoof-shaped leaf.

FLOWERS AND FRUIT

Flowers are showy, borne in tight clusters among the leafy twigs from March through April, with intermittent blooming occurring in late summer to early fall after rains. Flower color ranges from white to pinkish with five petals and 9 or 10 long extended stamens. Flower color of plants in their natural habitat tends to be predominantly pink. Because many Orchid-trees in cultivation have been grown from a limited seed source, they are most often seen in the white form. Fruit is a flattened, several-seeded legume 1–3 inches long and containing one to four oblong, smooth, flattened brown seeds. When ripe, the pods dry and twist open, quickly dropping the seeds.

NATURAL HABITAT, RANGE, AND PREFERRED SITE

Bauhinia is uncommon in Texas, known only in canyons and arroyos in the limestone hills of the Anacacho Mountains in Kinney County and from an isolated site along the Devil's River in Val Verde County, both in west Texas. Increasingly found in cultivation, Orchid-tree will tolerate temperatures as low as 10° F and will adapt to well-drained sites in Houston and Austin. It can be grown as far north as Dallas if given south-wall protection but will suffer heavy limb damage during severe winters.

COLLECTION AND STORAGE

Collect the pods in early July to August when they have turned brown and are slightly dried out but before they dehisce. The pods may be collected earlier as long as the seeds inside are firm, filled out, and brown. Air dry the pods a few days in paper bags to make them easier to split open. Seeds should be fumigated before storage to prevent infestation by weevils. Viability may be preserved for up to 2 years if stored in sealed containers in a cool dry place.

PROPAGATION

Seeds

The seed coat of Orchid-tree is not equally thick on all sides. The "seam" is typically denser than the flat side, and for this reason, acid scarification can be hard to calculate. One method is to pour boiling water on the seeds and let them cool in the same water as they imbibe. One grower had more vigorous germination when a product called "Superthrive" was added to the cooling water (2–4 drops per cup of water) (Will, personal communication, 1999). Seeds can also be acid scarified. The length of time for scarification depends on the seed lot. Test small amounts of seed beginning with 10 minutes, increasing by 5-minute intervals until imbibition occurs. Length of acid scarification can be as long as 30 minutes (Hosage, personal communication, 1999). It is not known if aeration would further promote strong germination, but it is worth trying.

Plant the seeds in the fall in a cold frame, or store and sow in early spring. Seeds should be planted ½ inch beneath the soil in containers at least 6 inches deep to accommodate the relatively long initial root. Seedlings grow most vigorously and are more successfully moved into larger containers if planted in bottomless containers which root prune the initial taproot and encourage secondary branching. The soil media should be well drained, and application of fungicide to prevent damping off is recommended.

Compared to other shrub species in the legume family, Orchid-tree is slow growing, taking 2 years to achieve a strong five-gallon size plant, although the growth rate accelerates the second year (Gass, personal communication, 1999). However, even small plants of 1 year will produce flowers. Information is lacking on the effects of rhizobium inoculation on seedling vigor. Because Orchid-trees like to form several trunks from the base, they can appear weak and badly formed in a container. Root girdling can be a problem. A strong web of roots will help anchor the spindly branches and support a stronger trunk or stem.

In the garden, Orchid-trees require well-drained, slightly alkaline soil and will respond to fertilizers applied periodically during the growing season. However, once planted, Orchid-tree does not require supplemental feeding, and, in fact, fertilizing may cause the plant to produce fewer blooms and more spindly, brittle growth.

Cuttings

Stem cuttings of Orchid-tree root with difficulty. Some tropical members of this genus have been noted to root from suckers (Bailey and Bailey 1947). Clonal production would exploit this plant's potential as a weeping form as well as its potential for a stronger, single trunk (Kirwin, personal communication, 1999). Selection could also be made for darker pink flower color.

NOTES

The interesting foliage and prolific orchid-like flowers make Orchid-tree an outstanding specimen plant for rocky locations in full sun. It may be pruned to make a more compact tall shrub or trimmed to form a small single-trunked tree. Orchid-tree does best when planted on the south side of a building, protected from winter winds. Orchid-tree makes a nice contrast to stronger formed plants such as agaves, yuccas, nopal (*Opuntia spp.*), and cenizo (*Leucophyllum frutescens*).

Berberis

Agarita, Mahonia, Barberry

BERBERIDACEAE (BARBERRY FAMILY)

GENERAL DESCRIPTION

Members of this genus are evergreen shrubs with sharp trifoliate or pinnately compound leaves. They are typically densely branched, compact, and irregularly shaped. Interior wood is bright yellow.

FLOWERS AND FRUIT

Small yellow flowers are held in clusters from February through April and make a nice contrast to the dark green foliage. Fruit is a round fleshy drupe containing several seeds. See Species Descriptions.

NATURAL HABITAT, RANGE, AND PREFERRED SITE

Species listed here are most often found in caliche or shallow clay topsoil with underlying limestone. See Species Descriptions for individual distribution and habitat.

COLLECTION AND STORAGE

Collect the fruit when it has turned deep red, amber, or purple. One way of collecting the fruit from these sharp-pointed plants is to spread a cloth beneath the bush and beat the branches with a stick. The ripe fruit will fall onto the cloth and can be separated later from sticks, bugs, and other debris. Remove the seeds from the pulp and air dry before storage.

One method for cleaning large quantities of seed for all the *Berberis* species listed below involves fitting a paint mixer with rubber blades or paddles onto a drill bit. The drill is used to stir a bucket filled with seeds and a little warm water until the contents of the bucket resemble a *Berberis* smoothie. Strain the pulp and seed mixture through cheesecloth at least three times, washing as much of the pulp and debris off the seeds as possible. It is important to flush the seed three times because high levels of pectin in the fruit will cause the whole mixture to set up in a thick gelatinous mass, making it very difficult to separate the seed later. Cleaned seeds are then mixed with sand and stored in the refrigerator (McNeal, personal communication, 1999).

Another method suggests cleaning small amounts of seed in a blender fitted with rubber blades (Hosage, personal communication, 1999). Wash and strain the seeds as noted above. Fruit can also be softened briefly in water and then rubbed on a screen to separate the seed. Many washings and strainings are needed with this method as well.

Seed can be stored dry in the refrigerator or immediately stratified in perlite. *Berberis* seeds do not remain viable for long. Best results are achieved when seeds are planted the same year they are collected.

PROPAGATION

Seeds

Germination of *Berberis* is delayed by embryo dormancy. Stratification for 30–60 days at 41° F is usually sufficient pretreatment to overcome dormancy for Agarita (*B. trifoliolata*) and Texas Mahonia (*B. swayseii*). One method mixes cleaned seed with sand (see above), cold stratifies them over the summer, and then sows several seeds per plug tray in cold frames in the fall. Germination usually begins in November or December (McNeal, personal communication, 1999).

Another technique is to stratify the seed for 30 days in September and then sow in October in a cold frame. These will grow as liners inside all winter, and can be transplanted in the early spring (Pfeiffer, personal communication, 1999). Do not bury the seed deeply. Instead, press them into the soil and cover with a light dusting of sand or sifted perlite. Germination is slow and erratic even for pretreated seed. Some seedlings will emerge within 30 days following planting, while others will sprout on and off over several months. Germination is best when temperatures are cool (under 70° F) (Hosage, personal communication, 1999).

It is important that the seeds be planted in a well-drained soil medium that has been drenched with a fungicide to prevent damping-off fungi. *Berberis* seedlings do poorly when conditions are too hot, too wet, or too dry. They are sensitive to fluctuations outside a very narrow moisture regime. Once they are hardened out of the liner phase, they become somewhat more tolerant.

Some growers prefer to keep the slow-growing seedlings in plug trays for a year before moving them into a one-gallon container (McNeal, personal communication, 1999). Individual containers or biodegradable plant plugs are recommended because seedlings tend to develop delicate but extensive fibrous root systems even while top growth remains small, and are difficult to transplant.

Most barberries require a minimum of 3 years to make an acceptable five-gallon plant. Often they will have irregular shoot growth; a single stem will grow long and straggly, while the remainder of the plant stays low in the pot. To encourage more branching, pinch back these longer stems halfway back once or twice during the season as the plant is flushing new growth. Reduce watering intervals after the plant has been pruned (Will, personal communication, 1999). Young *Berberis* plants respond well to fertilization. We have observed that once even a small plant is placed in the landscape, its growth rate speeds up considerably after the first year.

Creeping Barberry (*B. repens*) requires successive cold, warm, and cold stratification before germination will proceed. Moist chill at 34° F for 30 days, followed by warm moist storage at 68° F for 30 more days, and finally stratify at 34° F for up to 196 days (Vories 1981).

Berberis seeds may also be sown outdoors in prepared seedbeds in early fall. Natural germination occurs the spring following seed dispersal.

Cuttings

Leafy cuttings of Creeping Barberry (*B. repens*) taken in the spring can be rooted under intermittent mist. Dormant hardwood cuttings of Agarita (*B. trifoliolata*) and Red Barberry (*B. haematocarpa*) taken in the winter from the previous year's growth rooted at rates of 60% for one grower. These were 5–6 inches long and treated with 8,000 ppm IBA talc. They were kept under mist and by the next summer grew to a salable one-gallon plant (Manning, personal communication, 1999).

Softwood and semihardwood cuttings have also been reported to root, though success is uneven. Take cuttings in late summer and fall of the current season's growth. Make the basal cut between nodes, treat with high concentrations of IBA (5,000–10,000 ppm), and place in a sand/peat or peat/perlite mixture under intermittent mist. Carefully monitor the watering regime: too much water is very detrimental.

Grafting, layering, and rooting suckers of some members of this genus have also been practiced.

Agarita (*Berberis trifoliolata*) has been successfully reproduced from tissue culture (Molinar et al. 1996). Because Agarita is often difficult to root, micropropagation may allow rapid and large-scale multiplication of superior clones if the other problems in nursery production of this plant can be solved as well. Both Agarita and Texas Mahonia are extremely variable in their form, leaf color, fruit size, and amount of flowering.

NOTES

Many people mistake *Berberis* for a holly because of its evergreen sharp-pointed leaves and red fruit. Several species make excellent hedges and boundary plants as well as providing wildlife cover. Creeping Barberry

(*B. repens*) is a good ground cover for shadier locations. Agarita (*B. trifoliolata*) and Texas Mahonia (*B. swayseii*) will grow under light shade or on the edges of woods, but form larger and more well-shaped plants in full sun. The fruit is eaten by a number of birds and other wildlife. Fruit of *Berberis* can be made into a delicious jelly or wine, and the wood yields a bright yellow dye.

SPECIES DESCRIPTIONS

***Berberis haematocarpa* (Red Barberry)**
Evergreen shrub to 5 feet high by 5 feet wide with erect branches with grayish blue-green leaves. This plant is distinguished by its large, juicy red berries. Native to the mountains of central Trans-Pecos and the higher desert grasslands and canyons, west to Arizona. In low desert areas, Red Barberry will benefit from supplemental watering in the summer (Mielke 1993).

***Berberis repens* (Creeping Barberry)**
Dwarf or prostrate shrub less than 10 inches tall with five to seven leaflets. Fruit showy, round, and purple. Native to walls of wooded canyons and in pine forests of Guadalupe Mountains in west Texas, also New Mexico, Arizona, and California. Does not thrive on arid sites. Prefers partial shade. The fruit ripens from June through September.

***Berberis swayseii* (Texas Mahonia, Texas Barberry)**
Shrub to 5 feet with spreading branches and five to nine leaflets. Fruit amber-red when ripe. Endemic to the Edwards Plateau in central Texas. Full sun in limestone soil.

The flowers, fruit, and leaves of this species are larger than those of the more common Agarita and offer more potential for selection of superior cultivars. *B. swayseii* and *B. trifoliolata* are among the earliest woody plants to bloom in the spring (March).

***Berberis trifoliolata* (Agarita, Paisano Bush)**
Shrub to 6½ feet with trifoliate leaves. Fruit red when ripe. Abundant in rocky limestone soil in pastures and thickets from coastal south Texas north to central and west Texas, also southern Arizona, New Mexico, and Mexico. Prefers full sun, but will grow in dappled light on the edge of woods. It is tolerant of most soil situations, as long as they are well drained. Like other members of the genus, it can be susceptible to rust diseases of the stem. It is tolerant of Texas cotton root rot (Arnold 1999). Agaritas growing west of Kerrville often have an attractive blue-green cast to their leaves.

Betula nigra

River Birch

BETULACEAE (BIRCH FAMILY)

GENERAL DESCRIPTION

River Birch is a specimen shade tree sometimes growing 100 feet tall with a conical to pyramidal form when young, later becoming more rounded. Bark is pale creamy brown, becoming darker and scaly with age. The leaves are deciduous, rhombic-ovate in shape, and sometimes providing good fall color.

FLOWERS AND FRUIT

Flowers form in the fall and bloom in early spring before or with the appearance of new leaves. Male and female flowers are in separate catkins that develop into woody strobiles containing tiny compressed winged nutlets ⅛ inch long, ripening from April through June.

NATURAL HABITAT, RANGE, AND PREFERRED SITE

River Birch grows along creeks, bottomlands, or in wet areas from Florida to east Texas, north to Ohio. Birches prefer moist sandy or loamy soil and occasionally grow in standing water in bogs.

COLLECTION AND STORAGE

Collect River Birch seeds as soon as the cones are full grown and beginning to turn brown but before they dry completely and open to disperse the seeds, from April through June. The strobiles can be collected when still slightly green by picking or stripping the tree and then can be spread out to air dry until they have opened. Seed quality varies from year to year and from location to location. Sow seeds immediately or store in sealed containers at temperatures slightly above freezing (USDA 1974).

PROPAGATION

Seeds

Seeds may be sown in the fall after collection or stored and stratified for spring sowing. Seeds gathered when mature and sown immediately in well-prepared beds of sandy loam often germinate in the highest percentages.

Press the seeds firmly into the soil and cover lightly with fine sand. Do not bury seeds. The best seedbed contains moist sandy loam with a liberal amount of organic matter. Keep the seedbed continuously moist and provide light shade during the first growing season.

For spring or indoor sowing, stratify the seeds 30–60 days at 41° F, remove in early spring, and plant as recommended above.

Cuttings

River Birch will root from cuttings made all year, although those made in spring root fastest. Treat the cuttings with 1,500 ppm IBA quick-dip solution or soak overnight in a bucket containing willow water (see Chapter V). Cuttings take 30–45 days to root. After rooting, harden off for 30 days before potting up into individual containers outside (Bronstad, personal communication, 1999). Rooting percentages for other species are reported to occur at less than 50%.

Another species, Gray Birch (*B. populifolia*), was taken with only 1–2 inches of leaf surfaces remaining and the terminal bud removed. The cutting was soaked in a solution of IBA (50 mg/l) for 6 hours and eventually demonstrated 30% rooting.

NOTES

River Birch has been cultivated since 1736 (Vines 1970). It is fast growing with strong wood, a graceful form, and splendid yellow fall foliage. The bark peels gradually, revealing the interesting texture and color of the underbark. River Birch is relatively long lived and has been recommended as a good substitute for American Elm. Because of its distribution in the south, local ecotypes are more tolerant of heat, dryness, and oxygen-poor soil than those found in more northern regions.

River Birch typically becomes chlorotic on soils with a high pH. It is heat but not drought tolerant, and will grow in full sun to partial shade. River Birches' main enemies in the landscape are borers, Japanese beetle, and leaf scorch on hot sites (Arnold 1999).

Bignonia capreolata

Cross-Vine, Cola de Iguana

BIGNONIACEAE (TRUMPET-CREEPER FAMILY)

GENERAL DESCRIPTION

Cross-vine is a high-climbing woody vine reaching 65 feet. Leaves are evergreen compound with two wide, long, pointed leaflets. Cross-vine climbs by means of tendrils with flattened disklike appendages on the tips.

FLOWERS AND FRUIT

Showy bell-shaped flowers, 2–3 inches long, bloom in two to five hanging clusters from April to June. Flower color can be from all yellow to brick red, with everything in between. Fruit is a large woody capsule containing numerous leathery, flattened, and winged seeds ⅜ to ½ inch long.

NATURAL HABITAT, RANGE, AND PREFERRED SITE

Cross-vine is typically seen on the edges of rich moist woods and swamps from east Texas to Florida, north to Virginia and Illinois. Cross-vine takes a few years to become limestone tolerant. Generally in less fertile soils it will take two or three seasons to become established before rapidly showing shoot growth. Cross-vine will grow in full sun if given extra water and soil containing generous amounts of organic material.

COLLECTION AND STORAGE

Collect the capsules from late summer through the fall when they are light brown and beginning to dry but before they split open. The seeds are dispersed by wind. Seeds will remain viable for up to 1 year if kept in sealed containers in the refrigerator.

PROPAGATION

Seeds

Cross-vine is easily grown from fresh seeds sown soon after collection in a greenhouse. Seeds may also be stored over winter and sown outdoors after all danger of frost is past. Sow the seeds in a well-drained soil mixture no deeper than ½ inch. Germination usually occurs within 2 to 4 weeks. Seedlings may be transplanted from the flat into one-gallon containers when they have four to six true leaves.

Cuttings

Cross-vine can be propagated from both root and softwood cuttings, although it is slow to root and roots in low percentages (McNeal, personal communication, 1999). The best stem cuttings are made from firm, stout, short-jointed lateral stems of the current season's growth gathered in late spring through the summer. Removal of at least one-third of the leaves is recommended. Treat the cuttings with hormones (3,000–5,000 ppm) and place under intermittent mist. Rooting usually takes place in 4 to 8 weeks.

Transplanting

Small Cross-vine plants have been successfully transplanted in warm weather if cut back, kept well watered, and given light shade. Larger plants may be moved in winter if the site is suitable for digging and the vine is subsequently cut back.

NOTES

Cross-vine is an attractive vine for a fence or arbor. Its persistent glossy leaves and large showy flowers make it very ornamental. It is a good vine for partially shady locations. Hummingbirds are fond of the flowers (Vines 1970). Cross-vine will cling to brick, stone, or wood. The vines should be trained so as to avoid crowding the stems and to allow free circulation of air among the branches. This aids in the formation of flowering shoots.

To encourage full, lush growth and lots of flowers, trim back the plant somewhat in the winter or after the main flowering period (Bailey and Bailey 1947). A cultivar of Cross-vine, 'Tangerine Beauty,' has been popular in the nursery trade. It is a very floriferous selection, with deep orange flowers. After a heavy bloom period in late spring, flowers may again appear in smaller quantities until mid-summer.

Bouchea

Bouchea

VERBENACEAE (VERBENA FAMILY)

GENERAL DESCRIPTION

Low shrubs, woody at the base, less than 3 feet high with closely attached opposite leaves (see Species Descriptions).

FLOWERS AND FRUIT

Flowers are large, showy, tubular shaped, and varying in color from lavender to purplish. Fruit is a dry, linear berry, separating into two parts.

NATURAL HABITAT, RANGE, AND PREFERRED SITE

Both species of *Bouchea* listed here are native to desert limestone habitats in the Trans-Pecos and western Edwards Plateau (see Species Descriptions).

COLLECTION AND STORAGE

Collect seed throughout the summer and fall. Seed is very fine and is produced intermittently over a long blooming period. Seed of *B. linifolia* kept in dry storage 8 years still germinated at rates of 20% (Manning, personal communication, 1999).

PROPAGATION

Seeds
Seed of *B. linifolia* germinated without pretreatment when sown in the greenhouse in early spring. Damping off was a minor problem (Manning, personal communication, 1999).

Cuttings
Bouchea may be grown from semihardwood cuttings taken from April to June, treated with 1,000 ppm IBA talc and placed under mist. Gradually reduce watering intervals as cutting begins to develop roots (Will, personal communication, 1999). *B. linifolia* is reportedly easier to grow than *B. spathulata* (McNeal, personal communication, 1999).

Transplanting
Because of the rocky sites where *Bouchea spp.* frequently grow, they can be difficult to transplant. Small plants in winter are easiest to move.

NOTES

Bouchea spp. are a lovely, long-blooming perennial for dry gardens. They must be planted in full sun in well-drained mineral soils. Do not mulch these plants, except with gravel, and do not plant them in soils that have been heavily amended with organic material. Cut back the spent flower clusters to encourage more blooming. It is a lovely companion plant on the edge of planting with Snake Herb (*Dychoriste linearis*), Skelton-leaf Goldeneye Daisy (*Viguiera stenoloba*), Yellow-bells (*Tecoma stans*), and Dalea (*Dalea spp.*).

SPECIES DESCRIPTIONS

Bouchea linifolia **(Groovestem Bouchea)**
Low and shrubby with numerous branches, Groovestem Bouchea is less than 3 feet high with narrow flaxlike leaves. Large lavender flowers are held in slender clusters. Native to dry limestone hillsides and shrub-covered valleys in the Trans-Pecos, west to New Mexico, east to Uvalde County, and south to Mexico.

Bouchea spathulata **(Spoon-leaf Bouchea)**
Spoon-leaf Bouchea is distinguished from *B. linifolia* by its crowded, spatulate leaves. It is normally 2–3 feet tall. Flowers are large and rose-pink, and bloom from May to August. This species is rare in Texas, confined to limestone soils in the Dead Horse Mountains in Brewster County at elevations of 2,200–3,800 feet.

Buddleia

Woolly Butterfly-bush, Escobilla Butterfly-bush, Azafran

LOGANIACEAE (LOGANIA FAMILY)

GENERAL DESCRIPTION

Butterfly-bushes are deciduous or semi-evergreen shrubs often covered with woolly hairs. The leaf margins have sharp or rounded teeth (see Species Descriptions).

FLOWERS AND FRUIT

Flowers are typically showy, crowded in clusters or racemes at the ends of branches. Each flower is tubular- or bell-shaped, appearing in various colors (see Species Descriptions). Fruit is a capsule containing many small seeds.

NATURAL HABITAT, RANGE, AND PREFERRED SITE

Species listed here are native to central, extreme southern, and west Texas. All *Buddleia* species prefer full sun and are tolerant of drought and heat.

COLLECTION AND STORAGE

Collect the seeds by hand from mid- to late summer. Gather the spent flower heads in paper bags. Shake the bags to crush the flower heads and release the seeds. To separate the tiny seeds from the chaff, rub the contents of the paper collecting bag through a series of graduated sieves (Manning, personal communication, 1999). Air dry and store in ventilated containers over winter. Information on viability during extended storage is lacking.

PROPAGATION

Seeds

Buddleia is easily grown from first-year seeds. No pretreatment is necessary. Sow seeds in late spring after all danger of frost is past or earlier in a greenhouse or cold frame. *Buddleia* germinates best in warm but not overly hot soil temperatures. Seed flats should contain a well-drained soil mix.

Sow seeds thinly, press into soil, and cover lightly with sifted sand or a fine potting soil. Some recommend covering the seed flat with white paper until germination (Bailey and Bailey 1947).

Seedlings are very sensitive to overwatering and damping-off fungi. Seeds of *B. marrubifolia* were sown in April in the greenhouse in separate containers set in trays and were watered from the bottom until they germinated. As germination began, the containers were watered carefully with a gentle mist. Seedlings were slow growing initially but by September had made a salable one-gallon container. Seedlings tend to make a prettier, shrubbier plant than those generated from cuttings (Manning, personal communication, 1999).

Cuttings

Buddleia roots easily from softwood cuttings taken from April to June. Cuttings should be 3 inches long with a slight heel. Application of IBA (5,000 ppm) speeds the rooting process. Place cuttings under intermittent mist for best results. As soon as the cuttings have callused and begun to develop roots, reduce the frequency of misting to harden off the cuttings. This reduces the chance of stem rot and helps the cutting survive when it is removed from the cutting bed.

With all cuttings and young seedlings, pinch back the tips periodically to encourage bushy growth. Softwood cuttings of *B. marrubifolia* taken in the summer rooted promptly when treated with 3,000 IBA talc and kept under mist (Manning, personal communication, 1999).

Some species of *Buddleia* will also root from hardwood cuttings taken in the winter from firm wood of the current season's growth, 6 to 8 inches long, with or without a heel. Line the cuttings out in a field or seedbed until they are well rooted in the spring (Sheats 1953).

Transplanting

Buddleia spp. under 4 feet can be moved in winter if cut back by one-half the overall size and kept damp.

NOTES

Buddleia spp. make attractive landscape specimen plants, especially in a dry shrub border combined with *Salvia*, *Lantana*, and Zexmenia daisies (*Zexmenia hispida*), and in combination with stronger evergreen plants such as Mountain Laurel (*Sophora secundiflora*), Skelton-leaf Goldeneye Daisy (*Viguiera stenoloba*), and Cenizo (*Leucophyllum frutescens*). They thrive in poor soils and are drought tolerant. To encourage bushier growth, cut back the plant in the winter or early spring. As their name suggests, butterfly-bushes are attractive to butterflies and other nectar-feeding insects. They also provide browse for wildlife.

SPECIES DESCRIPTIONS

***Buddleia marrubifolia* (Woolly Butterfly-bush, Azafran)**
Deciduous or semi-evergreen shrub up to 3 feet with many brittle stems rising from a single base. All parts of the plant are densely covered with brown fuzz and the leaves are aromatic. Solitary round heads of golden yellow to orange-red aromatic flowers bloom throughout hot weather. Woolly Butterfly-bush is native to sunny well-drained sites in southern and western Texas and northern Mexico. In Mexico, an infusion of the flowers is used to color butter. It is a showy bloomer for full sun and poor soil. It does poorly in any kind of shade and is typically not cold hardy north of Austin.

***Buddleia racemosa* (Wand Butterfly-bush)**
Low-growing, loosely branched shrub 3 feet tall or less with yellow-white flowers borne on graceful drooping racemes. Wand Butterfly-bush is endemic to the southwestern edge of the Edwards Plateau of Texas along the Devil's River, where it is found growing on rocky banks and in crevices of limestone ledges. It is a good specimen shrub for dry shade.

***Buddleia scordioides* (Escobilla Butterfly-bush)**
Aromatic shrub usually under 6 feet tall with more narrow leaves than *B. marrubifolia*, and yellow round balls of flowers strung on the stem at the ascending stem apexes. Plants are reported to be a good browse for livestock, and a tea made from the leaves is used to treat indigestion. Escobilla Butterfly-bush has good potential as a landscape plant because it is compact (typically 2 feet by 2 feet), evergreen, and bears interesting flower clusters (McNeal, personal communication, 1999). It is widespread in various dry habitats including both limestone and igneous soils at elevations of 2,200 to 6,500 feet. Also grows in New Mexico and northern Mexico.

***Buddleia sessilflora* (Tepozán)**
An uncommon species native to sandbars and palm groves in Cameron and Hidalgo counties in the extreme southern Rio Grande Plains, also southern Arizona and south to Oaxaca. Tepozán is an open, irregularly branched shrub usually less than 6 feet tall with typically fuzzy young stems and leaves and dense clusters of fragrant, greenish yellow flowers crowded at the leaf axils.

Bumelia lanuginosa

Gum-elastic Tree, La Coma, Chittamwood

SAPOTACEAE (SAPODILLA FAMILY)

GENERAL DESCRIPTION

Gum-elastic Tree is a multi-trunked tall shrub or medium-sized tree to 48 feet tall or more. Leaves are semi-evergreen, leathery, bright shiny green above, paler and fuzzy white below. The stems and branches are often thorny, especially on the ends of smaller branchlets.

FLOWERS AND FRUIT

Small, whitish yellow flowers are borne together in small groups on short stems from the base of the leaf clusters. Fruit is a fleshy blue-black drupe containing a solitary seed ¼–⅓ inch long, ripening from September through October.

NATURAL HABITAT, RANGE, AND PREFERRED SITE

Gum-elastic Tree grows in a wide range of soil types, most often on the edges of sunny fields, along streams, or in open thickets from Florida west to Texas and southern Arizona, northern Mexico, and north to Missouri.

COLLECTION AND STORAGE

Gather fruits in early fall when they are filled out, soft, and blue-black in color. Seeds can be either cleaned or air dried with the pulp on before storing. Storage in sealed containers at 41° F is adequate for 1 year.

PROPAGATION

Seeds

Germination of Gum-elastic Tree is inhibited by a hard impermeable seed coat and a dormant embryo. To hasten germination, scarify the seeds in concentrated sulfuric acid for 20 minutes followed immediately by stratification for 30–60 days at 41° F. Scarified seeds can also be sown directly into seed flats or beds outdoors in the fall. Germination rates for pretreated seeds have been reported to average between 21% and 44% (USDA 1974).

Cuttings

Gum-elastic Tree may be rooted from softwood cuttings (Bailey and Bailey 1947). Semihardwood cuttings of La Coma, *B. celastrina*, rooted when treated with 5,000 ppm IBA talc and kept under mist (Cox, personal communication, 1999).

NOTES

Gum-elastic Tree is relatively slow growing with a deep taproot that enables it to withstand long periods of drought. This survival characteristic, combined with the tough semi-evergreen foliage, makes this plant appropriate for situations too small or harsh for live oaks or other tall evergreen specimen plants. Under favorable conditions, Gum-elastic Tree may be thicket forming. However, the tendency for Gum-elastic Tree to sucker from the base and the spiny nature of its small branches detract from this plant's desirability as an ornamental landscape plant. Perhaps the greatest value of Gum-elastic Tree is as a wildlife plant; the fruit is eaten by birds, and white-tailed deer browse the leaves and fruit. Although small, the flowers are very fragrant and provide early season nourishment for honey bees (Everitt and Drawe 1993). Gum-elastic Tree is evergreen in south Texas. It is resistant to root rot and cold hardy to 16° F.

A related species, La Coma (*B. celastrina*), is worth mentioning. Smaller than Gum-elastic Tree, La Coma is a spiny shrub or small tree up to 25 feet with dark green leaves and very fragrant greenish white flowers from May to November. The fruit is a juicy one-seeded blue-black drupe. Fruits are sweet and edible. La Coma grows on gravelly hills, resacas, thickets, and salt marshes of the Rio Grande Plains. This is another one of the rugged brush country plants that keep their leaves on during the hottest, most brutal weather. They provide valuable cover and food for wildlife, and their flowers, though inconspicuous, produce a fragrance that is noticeable long before the plant itself is seen (Cox, personal communication, 1999).

Caesalpinia mexicana

Mexican Caesalpinia, Tabachín del Monte

FABACEAE (PEA FAMILY)

GENERAL DESCRIPTION

Mexican Caesalpinia is a small thornless tree, typically 10–15 feet tall, though sometimes taller, with compound leaves and light green oval leaflets.

FLOWERS AND FRUIT

Flowers are bright yellow and showy, sometimes with red markings, appearing from February through July. They are held in clusters of 10–30 flowers. Fruit is a brown pod about 3 inches long. Seed pods are poisonous.

NATURAL HABITAT, RANGE, AND PREFERRED SITE

Mexican Caesalpinia grows in brushy thickets in extreme south Texas (Cameron and Hidalgo counties). It has been widely grown in cultivation elsewhere, but is not cold hardy much further north than Corpus Christi, Texas.

COLLECTION AND STORAGE

Gather the seeds throughout the growing season when the seeds have filled out and the pods are brown, but before they split to spill the seeds. Remove the seeds from the pods and fumigate before storing.

PROPAGATION

Seeds

Mexican Caesalpinia can be easily grown from untreated seed (McNeal, personal communication, 1999). One method recommends pouring boiling water over the seed. Add "Superthrive" to the cooling water to enhance germination (Will, personal communication, 1999).

Germination is stronger in hot weather. Start the seed in March and April rather than in a cold frame the previous fall. In 1 year following germination, this plant will make a large one-gallon plant. In less than 2 years it will reach five-gallon plant size.

Cuttings

Mexican Caesalpinia is so easy to grow from seed that most growers have not been motivated to develop vegetative propagation methods.

NOTES

Mexican Caesalpinia is a fast-growing tree or large shrub that produces flowers from spring to frost, or year round in the tropics. The emerging leaves have a pink-olive color, and the mature leaves are a dark green, providing a lush, tropical look even in the arid climate of their natural habitat. In San Antonio and Houston, or anyplace where the winter temperatures fall below 40° F, Mexican Caesalpinia will freeze back to the ground, returning with warm spring temperatures as an 8–10 foot multi-trunked shrub. Some people regard this plant as messy because of its tendency to drop pods, branches, and spent flowers continuously. Periodic pruning can remove weak or dead stems and select the stronger trunks.

Calliandra eriophylla

Fairy Duster, False Mesquite, Charrasquillo

FABACEAE (LEGUME FAMILY)

GENERAL DESCRIPTION

Fairy Duster is a small shrub typically 2 feet high with slender upright rigid branches covered with dark green leaflets. During periods of extended drought the leaves may drop as a response to stress. Under favorable landscape conditions Fairy Duster may achieve a rounded form of 3 feet high and 4 feet wide with semi-evergreen foliage.

FLOWERS AND FRUIT

From February to May, Fairy Duster is covered with delicate pink to deep rose feathery flowers consisting of fuzzy thread-like stamens crowded together, creating a showy, fluffy ball about 1 inch in diameter. The fruit is a small, elastically dehiscent flat legume.

NATURAL HABITAT, RANGE, AND PREFERRED SITE

Fairy Duster is native to dry gravelly limestone and caliche washes, slopes, and mesas between 1,000 and 5,000 feet in elevation. It occurs from southeastern California through southern Arizona and New Mexico to western Texas, and as far south as Jalisco, Mexico. As demonstrated by its broad geographic distribution, Fairy Duster will grow under a wide range of conditions. It is hardy to 15° F (Mielke 1993). It prefers gravelly well-drained soils and full sun but will tolerate dappled shade, although the foliage and flowers will be less abundant.

COLLECTION AND STORAGE

Collect the seeds as soon as the pods have turned brown, but before they completely dry and release the seed. Intermittent blooming periods result in uneven ripening times for the pods. Both pods and flowers may appear on the plant at the same time. Place the pods on a screen out of the wind and weather to dry, and fumigate with insecticide to reduce damage by weevils, or store with a pest strip. Dry storage at room temperature is sufficient.

PROPAGATION

Seeds

Fairy Duster will typically germinate without pretreatment. However, gently nicking the seeds may hasten and unify germination. Seedlings are relatively fast growing and are easily moved up into larger container sizes. Seedlings will produce a five-gallon plant in 1 year (Gass, personal communication, 1999).

Cuttings

Information is lacking on exact techniques for rooting this plant.

NOTES

The abundant, showy, feathery pink blooms of Fairy Duster make it an outstanding specimen plant for the desert garden. It has a light, open texture and form, and is an effective accent when combined with heavier and stronger plants like the agaves and Purple Sages (*Leucophyllum* species). Heavy shearing ruins its natural open form. In its habitat, Fairy Duster often has a stunted, gnarled form due to heavy browsing by deer, sheep, and goats. It can take dappled light, but reaches its fullest form in full sun.

Callicarpa americana

American Beauty-berry, Filigrana

VERBENACAE (VERBENA FAMILY)

GENERAL DESCRIPTION

American Beauty-berry is a mounding multi-trunked shrub 4–6 feet tall with long, arching branches. It has large, light green leaves that sometimes turn yellow in the fall.

FLOWERS AND FRUIT

Tight clusters of small greenish yellow flowers are borne in the leaf axils, later developing into showy bright purple berries forming a ball around the stem. The berry clusters often remain on the stem into the winter after the leaves have dropped. Each berry contains four small seeds.

NATURAL HABITAT, RANGE, AND PREFERRED SITE

American Beauty-berry grows in woods and thickets and in open prairies, as well as shady locations in the Coastal Prairies, inland to parts of the Edwards Plateau. Its range extends north to Arkansas, and in woodlands east to the Atlantic. American Beauty-berry is adapted to a wide range of soils. Though fairly drought tolerant, American Beauty-berry will not thrive on hot, dry, rocky hills and may temporarily defoliate during periods of prolonged drought.

COLLECTION AND STORAGE

Collect the seeds in late summer or early fall after they have filled out and turned a deep purple. The seeds may be cleaned or the fruits spread out on screens and dried with the pulp on before storage. Store in sealed containers at low temperatures (32–40° F).

Another method is to gently smash the fruits to release the seed, letting them dry, then mixing the seed with perlite. The perlite/seed mixture can then be sprinkled directly on the seed flat or containers when it is time to plant (McNeal, personal communication, 1999).

PROPAGATION

Seeds

American Beauty-berry can be produced by sowing the cleaned seeds lightly in a greenhouse kept just above 40° in November. They will germinate in January and February, and are ready to plant outside under shade by April (McNeal, personal communication, 1999).

Another method recommends soaking cleaned seed in a mixture of sugar water and active yeast. The yeast breaks down the pulp and slightly reduces the seed coat, thus making the seed ready for immediate germination. Spread the seed thinly on top of flats in a mist tent in late February (Janzow, personal communication, 1999). Simple cold stratification for 1 month produced adequate germination for one grower (Pfeiffer, personal communication, 1999).

American Beauty-berry will make a salable one-gallon container in 4 months. Seedlings require partial shade to thrive. In full sun, they become susceptible to spider mites.

Cuttings

American Beauty-berry roots easily from softwood or hardwood cuttings. Take softwood cuttings from early May through June, just after the first flush of growth but before the plant has flowered. These should be 4–5 inches long and treated with 5,000 ppm IBA. Remove all leaves from the bottom half of the cutting. Tip cuttings tend to root better than wood taken from the base of the stem. Root initiation usually begins in 7–14 days (Pfeiffer, personal communication, 1999).

Hardwood cuttings can also be rooted. These should be 5–8 inches long. Treat with 10,000 IBA and place under intermittent mist. American Beauty-berry may also be increased from root cuttings or by separating large clumps of mature plants in the winter.

Transplanting

American Beauty-berry is easily transplanted even in warm weather if cut back by at least two-thirds and kept shaded and well watered (Lowrey, personal communication, 1986).

NOTES

American Beauty-berry is useful as a screen in either dry shade or poorly drained soil. It makes a good tall background or specimen shrub in partially sunny locations, such as under pecan or mesquite trees. American Beauty-berry will grow in full sun if kept watered. It should be cut back by half of its overall height each winter to encourage more compact growth, flowers, and fruit.

White American Beauty-berry, *C. americana var. lactea*, is another desirable variety for garden use. It does come true to type from seed. It produces abundant creamy white berries instead of the more common purple form. It will grow in the same situations as American Beauty-berry. Birds, especially mockingbirds, love the fruit. Good companion plants for American Beauty-berry include River Fern (*Dryopteris spp.*), Coral-berry (*Symphoricarpos orbiculatus*), Pigeon berry (*Rivinia humilis*), and Texas Betony (*Stachys coccinea*).

Campsis radicans

Trumpet-creeper, Monapesto

BIGNONIACEAE (TRUMPET-CREEPER FAMILY)

GENERAL DESCRIPTION

Trumpet-creeper is a vigorous woody vine climbing 32 feet or more by aerial rootlets. Leaves deciduous, compound, composed of 9 to 11 leaflets.

FLOWERS AND FRUIT

Throughout the hot summer, this vine is covered with trumpet-shaped flowers with bright orange waxy petals. Fruit is a stout woody capsule containing many feathery seeds ripening in late summer to early fall.

NATURAL HABITAT, RANGE, AND PREFERRED SITE

Trumpet-creeper is commonly found climbing trees or telephone poles in moist woods or growing along fencerows and in old fields from Florida west to Texas and north to Ohio. It is adapted to soils as far west as central and south Texas and is also found in cultivation. Trumpet-creeper is fairly drought tolerant and in favorable conditions may become an aggressive grower, quickly taking over a bed by means of root sprouts and self-layering.

COLLECTION AND STORAGE

Gather the ripe capsules when they turn grayish brown but before they completely dry and split open. Remove the seeds from the pods and spread them to air dry in a shed or garage. Store in sealed containers at 41° F.

PROPAGATION

Seeds

Seeds may be sown outdoors in the fall immediately after collection or stored and sown the next spring. Stored seeds germinate better after stratification from 30 to 60 days at 41–50° F (USDA 1974). Do not bury the seeds too deeply, and use a light, well-drained soil mix.

Cuttings

Trumpet-creeper will readily grow from semihardwood cuttings taken May through October. Hormone treatment is not necessary. Take stem cuttings from shoots of the new growth, 3–4 inches long and firm toward the base. Insert the cuttings fairly close together in a rooting bed or flat containing well-drained soil media, such as a 1:2 ratio of peat and perlite. Cuttings root best under intermittent mist.

Trumpet-creeper will also root from root cuttings. Choose the strongest or most developed sections of the current season's growth. These roots should be cut to 2 inches and packed in a box of milled sphagnum moss. The moss should be kept moist but not soggy. Leave the roots in the sphagnum for 3 days and then place in rooting pots containing a well-drained mixture. Lay the root cuttings horizontally in the pots on top of the soil and cover with ¼ inch of sand followed by a thin layer of sifted compost or premoistened peat moss. Firm down and water the pots lightly. Cover the pots with dark paper and keep damp until shoot growth begins. Do not disturb the cuttings until rooting and shoot growth is well advanced (Sheats 1953).

Transplanting

Trumpet creeper can be transplanted if the long canes are cut back to the second or third leaf node. Rooted stems can also be cut from the parent plant and moved.

NOTES

To keep Trumpet-creeper blooming and lush during prolonged drought, give it periodic deep soakings; otherwise it will survive on little watering, flushing out with new growth once rains arrive. To encourage the most attractive growth, fertilize in the spring with superphosphate. In the winter cut back the branches to two buds to promote bushier growth and more blooms. Trumpet-creeper will bloom more if planted in full sun.

Hummingbirds are fond of trumpet-creeper flowers. This vine provides a hardy and ornamental vine to cover telephone poles, chainlink fences, or alleyways where it will receive little maintenance. It is not recommended for planting around old historic stone or stucco structures because the rootlets can damage loose mortar between stones. Although Trumpet-creeper is typically disease resistant, it does frequently suffer from leaf miners.

Capsicum annum

Chile Pequín, Bush-pepper

SOLANACEAE (NIGHTSHADE FAMILY)

GENERAL DESCRIPTION

Chile Pequín is a small deciduous shrub growing from a woody base that may reach as high as 4 feet in its southern range. It has small, simple, dark green leaves, held on slender green stems.

FLOWERS AND FRUIT

Flowers occur year round in south Texas. They are small and white, and produce an orange or red berry with many seeds. Chile Pequín is very attractive when covered with red berries.

NATURAL HABITAT, RANGE, AND PREFERRED SITE

Chile Pequín is an extremely variable species whose range extends from southern Arizona, New Mexico, south Texas, and south all the way to South America. In Texas it grows along rivers, in thickets and groves along arroyos in the Edwards Plateau, the Rio Grande Plains, and the southern Coastal Prairie. It is drought tolerant, but will wilt and slightly defoliate during extreme dry spells. North of Laredo it will freeze back to the ground every winter.

COLLECTION AND STORAGE

Fruit can be collected beginning in mid to late summer, and continues to frost in some areas. Fruit is red when ripe. Spread the fruit on fine screens and let dry on the seeds. Then rub the fruits to break up the dried cluster of seeds.

You can also clean the seeds in a blender with water. Then strain repeatedly on fine screens to separate seed from pulp. Dry thoroughly and store in a paper bag until ready to plant.

PROPAGATION

Seeds

Chile Pequín is easy to grow from seed, but temperatures must be warm before they will sprout. Store seed over winter and plant in April, or plant in September and keep in a greenhouse over winter (Will, personal communication, 1999). High germination rates were achieved by aerating the seeds 2–3 days in a solution of water mixed with potassium nitrate (1 tablespoon per gallon) before sowing. Seeds will germinate in 10–20 days (Best, personal communication, 1999).

As with many native plants, germination is also stimulated by rainwater. Pretreated seeds planted outdoors and exposed to rainfall germinate all at once (Best 1999). Plant in individual 4-inch pots after seedlings have put on the third set of leaves; transfer to a one-gallon pot by summer.

Cuttings

Chile Pequín roots readily from softwood cuttings slightly hardened off toward the base. Apply IBA (3,000 ppm) and keep under mist.

Transplanting

Younger Chile Pequín plants are easily transplanted. Cut back by one-half to avoid wilting and keep damp until the plant is over transplant shock.

NOTES

Chile Pequín is an excellent understory plant for dry shade. It makes a good companion to Turk's Cap (*Malvaviscus arboreus var. drummondii*), Tropical Sage (*Salvia coccinea*), Manfreda (*Manfreda variegata*), Cedar Sage (*Salvia roemeriana*), and Cedar Sedge (*Carex texensis*). The fruit is eaten by many species of birds, including the Rio Grande turkey, and is also used in cooking as a spicy seasoning.

Carpinus caroliniana

Hornbeam, Blue-beech, Lechillo, Mora de la Sierra

BETULACEAE (BIRCH FAMILY)

GENERAL DESCRIPTION

Hornbeam is a small, crooked deciduous tree growing to 30 feet with a slender trunk covered with gray raised ridges. Graceful drooping branches give an overall antlered shape. Deciduous leaves are bluish green and smooth above, paler and sometimes pubescent on the underside.

FLOWERS AND FRUIT

Male and female flowers grow on different trees in late spring through early summer. Fruit is a ribbed nutlet held in loose pendant clusters, each containing a small seed that ripens from late August to October.

NATURAL HABITAT, RANGE, AND PREFERRED SITE

Hornbeam is found mainly on rich moist soil in bottomlands and along streams from east Texas to Florida, north to Illinois. Hornbeam prefers partial shade. It is relatively slow growing and will adapt to sites drier than its natural habitat (Bailey and Bailey 1947).

COLLECTION AND STORAGE

Collect the fruits by hand in late summer or early fall. The bracts will turn a pale greenish brown color when ripe. If still green, spread the fruits in thin layers on racks or screens to dry, and then beat them inside a bag to separate the seeds from the involucre or chaff. Fresh seeds placed immediately in cold storage will remain viable up to 2 years (USDA 1974).

PROPAGATION

Seeds

Seeds collected in the summer while still slightly green and not fully dried often germinate promptly. Dried seeds (either on the tree or in storage) usually exhibit dormancy and must be stratified for 2–3 months at 41° F before they will germinate. Fresh seeds may first be air dried and then held in cold moist storage over winter. Stratified seeds germinate best if sown outdoors or in a cold frame in early spring.

Fresh seeds may be sown outdoors directly following harvest in the fall. Natural germination occurs during the following May to June. The best seedbed contains continuously moist, rich, loamy soil. Cover the seeds with ¼ inch of firm soil. Keep the seedbed mulched until seeds emerge in spring, then remove.

Hornbeam often has irregular germination rates (Bailey and Bailey 1947). Partial shade is recommended for young seedlings.

Cuttings

Members of the birch family are not easy to root from cuttings. Some cultivars of European Hornbeam (*C. betulus*) were rooted when cuttings were selected during a very narrow window of time which occurred during the period when the last leaf reached mature size and the last bud had not fully developed. These were treated with very high levels of hormone (2% IBA or 20,000 ppm). The cuttings were stuck in a peat/perlite mixture. After rooting, the cuttings required a dormancy period during which they were held at 32° F for several months. In early spring, the rooted cuttings were transplanted to containers (Dirr and Heuser 1987). No study has been reported for rooting our native species, but success with its European relative could suggest some beginning parameters. The showy female fruits and male flowers of this tree are two aspects worth horticultural selection.

NOTES

Hornbeam seeds are eaten by several species of birds, and the plant provides cover for other wildlife. The wood is used for tool handles, levers, and wedges. Hornbeam has been in cultivation since 1912 (Bailey and Bailey 1947). It is a good understory tree for low, shady places. The hanging papery fruit and overall branching make an interesting contrast to other plants. The leaves are occasionally attacked by black mold (*Dimerosporum pulchrum*).

Carya

Hickory, Pecan, Nogal, Nueces

JUGLANDACEAE (WALNUT FAMILY)

GENERAL DESCRIPTION

Members of this genus are slow-growing, long-lived trees with hard durable wood. Leaves are deciduous and compound with five to nine leaflets.

FLOWERS AND FRUIT

Male and female flowers are borne separately on the same tree. Male flowers bloom in drooping catkins, and the female flowers are held in crowded clusters with or just before the emergence of the leaves in the spring. Fruit is a large hard-shelled nut ripening from September to November.

NATURAL HABITAT, RANGE, AND PREFERRED SITE

These trees are most often found in low, wet woods, valleys, and river bottoms in eastern and central Texas and in cultivation throughout the United States. See Species Descriptions for individual range and habitat.

COLLECTION AND STORAGE

Collect the nuts from the ground or shake from the branches from September to November. Persistent husks can be removed by a corn sheller (USDA 1974). The husks of pecans will usually dry and split open by themselves when the nuts are mature. Good crops of all species are produced at intervals of 1–3 years.

Seeds germinate best when planted the same year they fall, but nuts have been successfully stored for up to 5 years in sealed containers held at 41° F and 90% relative humidity. Do not let nuts dry out during storage over winter.

PROPAGATION

Seeds

Carya species are most easily grown from fresh seeds. Sow the seeds immediately after collection in outdoor beds, or stratify for at least 30–60 days at 41° F and sow outdoors in the spring or late winter in a cold frame. Containers should be at least 8 inches deep to accommodate the long initial root. *Carya* roots do not seem to be completely controlled by containers with copper-treated interior surfaces (Struve et al. 1994). Typically roots will emerge over winter and stem growth is initiated by warmer temperatures in spring.

The best seedbeds contain a well-tilled, loose, sandy loam. Protect containers and seedbeds from squirrels and other rodents with wire mesh. Most species benefit from light shade the first season.

For field production of nursery liners, sow seeds in rows 8–12 inches apart with six to eight nuts per linear foot. Plant seeds ½–¾ inch deep. Mulch the beds until the seedlings completely emerge.

Cuttings

Hardwood cuttings ½ inch in diameter taken in April from the previous season's growth of certain varieties of pecan have been rooted. These were allowed to callus in moist sphagnum held at 68–78° F for about 3 weeks. After callusing, the basal ends were soaked in IBA (100 mg/l) for 24 hours. Next the cuttings were set in a rooting bed containing sand and given bottom heat (70° F). Using these methods, rooting averaged 63%. Smaller cuttings did not root as well. Untreated cuttings of all sizes formed no roots (Doran 1957).

Transplanting

Pecans and hickories are often transplanted bare-root from the field in winter. Best results are achieved when the tree has been periodically root pruned prior to digging and a solid ball of loam is maintained around the roots.

NOTES

Hickories and Pecans have been in cultivation for several centuries. A large selection of research and information on the selection, breeding, and propagation of pecans and hickories is available. For more information, consult the Texas A&M web site: http://extension-horticulture.tamu.edu/carya/species/index.htm. Another excellent source is the Northern Nut Growers Association, Inc. This organization brings together people interested in growing nut trees. For more information, contact tuckerh@mail.microserve.net.

The National Clonal Germplasm Repository (NCGR) for Pecans and Hickories is another good source for information. The NCGR is dedicated to the collection, maintenance, and characterization of world genetic resources of the *Carya* genus. Their major objective is the development of improved pecan cultivars and rootstocks for all U.S. production areas. For more information, contact Dr. L. J. Grauke, Route 2, Box 133, Sommerville, Texas 77879 (email: ljg@tamu.edu).

SPECIES DESCRIPTIONS

***Carya aquatica* (Water Hickory)**
Tree to 96 feet. In low, wet, swampy areas in east Texas to Florida, north to Illinois. Stratify seed in moist sphagnum moss for 90 days, then sow individually in "bullet tubes." Germination is slow, but usually completed within 2 months. Five months are required to make a finished one-gallon plant. Cold chilling seems to affect seedling vigor. After mild winters, stem growth on young plants is irregular and poor (Bronstad, personal communication, 1999).

***Carya cordiformis* (Bitternut Hickory, Pignut Hickory)**
Tree to 96 feet. Nut has a thin bitter shell and bright reddish brown kernels. Low wet woods near streams in east Texas, east to Florida and New England. Most rapid growing of all hickories and a good shade tree.

***Carya illinoinensis* (Pecan, Nogal, Nueces)**
Tree to 160 feet with sweet edible nut. In bottomlands near streams or rivers and in moist woods from central and northwest Texas east to Alabama, elsewhere under cultivation.

***Carya ovata* (Shagbark Hickory, Nogal Mofudo)**
Tree to 64 feet with light gray bark, which separates in sheets from the tree. Rich woodlands, near streams and swamps in east Texas to Florida. Next to the pecan, this species has the best-tasting nut and is the most common hickory produced commercially. Follow instructions for *C. aquatica*. Shagbark Hickory will make a finished one-gallon container in 5 months after being removed from the bullet tube (Bronstad, personal communication, 1999).

***Carya tomentosa* (Mockernut Hickory)**
Tree seldom reaching 96 feet. Dry or moist woods in east Texas to Florida.

Cassia wislizenii

Wislizeni Senna, Cassia, Palo Prieto, Pinacate

FABACEAE (LEGUME FAMILY)

GENERAL DESCRIPTION

Wislizeni Senna is an attractive western shrub reaching 5–10 feet tall with many short, rigid, leafy branches rising from the base. Dark green compound leaves are spirally arranged on spurs, each with three to seven leaflets.

FLOWERS AND FRUIT

Bright yellow clusters of showy flowers are borne in crowded panicles at the ends of dark stems from late spring intermittently through the summer, depending on rainfall. Fruit is a pod containing numerous seeds each ⅙–¼ inch long.

NATURAL HABITAT, RANGE, AND PREFERRED SITE

Wislizeni Senna is found mainly in igneous soil between 3,000 and 4,000 feet in the Trans-Pecos area of Texas, also in New Mexico, southeast Arizona, and northern Mexico. It must have full sun and a well-drained site. It is adapted as far north as Dallas, if planted in a raised bed. The main limits to the use of this plant are wet winters. Wislizeni Senna cannot stand to have its roots continually wet (Simpson, personal communication, 1986). Wislizeni Senna is geared for blooming during desert monsoons, so it is best to let the plant experience a thoroughly dry rest period between bloom periods. Regular irrigation and high humidity seem to reduce flowering.

COLLECTION AND STORAGE

Collect the pods in late summer or after the intermittent blooming periods when they have turned brown and begun to dry but before they split open and disperse the seeds. Remove the seeds by hand, then air dry 1 or 2 days, and fumigate before storing. Store in sealed containers at room temperature or in the refrigerator. Seeds will remain viable for at least 2 years.

PROPAGATION

Seeds

Wislizeni Senna readily germinates from fresh untreated seeds and is fast growing. Some growers suggest gently nicking the seed to hasten rooting (Manning, personal communication, 1999).

Germination usually occurs within 7 days. Carefully monitor the watering regime: seedlings are very susceptible to damping off. Seedlings may be transplanted when the second set of true leaves appears. Select containers that encourage air pruning of the rapidly growing taproot (see Chapter V). Seeds planted close together in shallow containers often develop roots that quickly become tangled with other seedlings.

Seeds may be planted outdoors after all danger of frost is past or earlier in a cold frame or greenhouse. Place seedlings in strong sunlight to prevent spindly growth. Plants may be pinched back to form more bushy compact growth, or they may be trained as a tall specimen shrub. Plants require 2 full years to reach a five-gallon container size (Gass, personal communication, 1999).

Other species of *Cassia* (see Notes) have harder seed coats, and germination is hastened and more uniform when seeds are nicked or soaked in concentrated sulfuric acid for 5–15 minutes. Plant the seeds ¼–½ inch deep in plant cells or containers with well-drained soil media. Sowing in spring is best for Lindheimer's Senna (*C. lindheimeriana*) so that a showy blooming plant is ready for sale by fall. Smaller plants sown over winter do not have the same appeal (Will, personal communication, 1999).

Cuttings

Although Wislizeni Senna can be grown from cuttings, production of large numbers of plants is easiest from seed. To grow vegetatively, take semihardwood cuttings of the current season's growth in late summer. Select thick, sturdy tip cuttings 4–6 inches long. Treat with IBA (5,000–8,000 ppm) and keep the cuttings under intermittent mist. Newly rooted cuttings should be given cold-frame protection over winter. New vigorous stem growth will resume the following spring (Simpson, personal communication, 1986).

Transplanting

Wislizeni Senna is typically difficult to successfully transplant from its native site.

NOTES

Wislizeni Senna is an outstanding specimen plant for south and west Texas. Masses of brilliant yellow flowers make an attractive contrast to the small dark green leaflets and smooth green branches. Its native desert habitat has programmed Wislizeni Senna to bloom on a "boom or bust" water cycle. It makes more flowers if allowed to become bone dry, then watered deeply. It does not bloom reliably in Austin (McNeal, personal communication, 1999). It is a dependable grower in poor soil and is heat and drought tolerant.

A related species, Gregg Senna (*C. greggii*), is also worthy of cultivation. It is a small thornless shrub to 3 feet with twisted, spreading limbs. Leaflets appear in two to five pairs. Unlike the dense flower clusters of Wislizeni Senna, the flowers of Gregg Senna are borne solitarily on slender axillary pedicels. This is a rare species, known only in Jim Wells County.

Two other species of *Cassia*, Lindheimer's Senna (*C. lindheimeriana*) and Two-leaved Senna (*C. roemeriana*), are also worthy of cultivation. They are bushy perennials with yellow flowers blooming from summer through fall. In fields and pastures, these sennas improve the soil by fixing nitrogen, and their seeds provide an important source of food for birds. In central Texas, *C. lindheimeriana* has fuzzy silvery leaves, while in west Texas the foliage is bright green. This ecotypic variation makes the same species look radically different, depending on its location. Pinch back young seedlings after they are 6–8 inches long to encourage branching. Otherwise the plant will develop a single long cane (Will, personal communication, 1999).

Castanea

Chinquapin

FAGACEAE (BEECH OR OAK FAMILY)

GENERAL DESCRIPTION

Chinquapins are trees or tall shrubs to 49 feet. Leaves are glossy, dark green, deciduous, conspicuously straight-veined, and unlobed.

FLOWERS AND FRUIT

Male and female flowers grow on the same tree in early spring after the new leaves emerge. Fruit is a nut enclosed in a prickly husk that splits open and quickly drops the nut when ripe. Each nut is about ½ inch in diameter.

NATURAL HABITAT, RANGE, AND PREFERRED SITE

Chinquapins are found in sandy thickets and woodlands from Florida to deep east Texas, north to Arkansas and Massachusetts.

COLLECTION AND STORAGE

Collect the ripe burrs or husks as they begin to dry but before they split open and drop the nut. The seeds are mature when firm, filled out, and glossy brown. Spread the unopened husks to dry in the sun or on racks in a warm shed. Collection of chinquapin nuts is often difficult because they are a favorite food of deer, squirrels, and other animals.

Chinquapin nuts lose their viability rapidly and should be planted immediately for best results. Seeds stored longer than a year seldom germinate well. Seeds may be briefly stored in moist sphagnum moss or stratified over winter.

PROPAGATION

Seeds

Germination of chinquapins is delayed by a dormant embryo. Dormancy requirements may be met by fall sowing or cold stratification for 30–60 days at 41° F immediately after collection. Remove the husks before sowing. Natural germination usually occurs in the spring. Outdoor beds should be protected from squirrels and other animals by a wire mesh screen. The best seedbed is continuously moist but not soggy and consists of well-tilled sandy loam and organic compost. Cover the bed with light mulch until germination begins. Seedlings benefit from light shade. Germination rates are reported to be fair (USDA 1974).

Cuttings

Cuttings made from juvenile wood of *Castanea* have been reported to root, while wood from older trees seldom produces roots. A related species, American Chestnut (*C. dentata*), has been rooted from cuttings taken from 3-year-old seedlings in early summer. These cuttings were soaked for 24 hours in IBA (40 mg/l), then placed in a shaded cold frame under intermittent mist. Rooted cuttings subsequently required careful watering and fertilizing the first year in order to survive.

As a group, chestnuts respond well to bench grafting in a greenhouse. Rootstocks must be dug early in the spring, brought into the greenhouse, and grafted immediately. A single splice or whip graft on scions of the same diameter produces the best results.

Transplanting

Large chinquapins are difficult to transplant because of their deep taproots. However, young seedlings lined out in loose soil and periodically root pruned prior to transplanting may be successfully balled and burlapped in winter.

NOTES

Chinquapins produce some of the sweetest of all native nuts. Our Texas chinquapins are attractive small specimen trees for rich loamy soil in the eastern third of the state. They are attractive when in flower and in the fall with the light green burrs among dark green foliage. Unfortunately, like the American Chestnut, they are susceptible to the dreaded chestnut blight.

A related species, *C. pumila var. asheii*, is rare in Texas and is distinguished by becoming mature when less than 6 feet tall. It tends to form clones from shallow rootstocks that can be increased by division in the winter (Lowrey, personal communication, 1986).

SPECIES DESCRIPTIONS

Castanea alnifolia (Downy Chinquapin)

Shrub or small tree usually less than 7 feet. Rolling hills and thickets in east Texas, east to Florida, and north to Arkansas.

Castanea pumila (Chinquapin)

Tree or large thicket-forming shrub to 50 feet. Sandy open woodlands and thickets in east Texas to Florida.

Castela erecta

Chaparro Amargoso, Goatbush, Bisbirinda

SIMAROUBACEAE (QUASSIA FAMILY)

GENERAL DESCRIPTION

Chaparro Amargoso is a spiny, many-branched small- to medium-sized shrub sometimes reaching 10 feet, with grayish white thorn-tipped branches. The small leaves are attached closely to the stem in small bunches, and are very bitter to taste. They are silvery on the undersides.

FLOWERS AND FRUIT

Tiny four-petaled red to pink flowers cover the shrub from March to May and are followed by showy, almost translucent flattened red drupes with a solitary seed.

NATURAL HABITAT, RANGE, AND PREFERRED SITE

Chaparro Amargoso is common in mesquite thickets, gravelly hills, and prairies throughout south Texas. It is cold tolerant as far north as San Antonio.

COLLECTION AND STORAGE

Collect the fruit from May to July, and clean by mashing on a screen with a rolling pin or in a blender fitted with a rubber blade. Spread the pulp and seed on a screen, then wash off the pulp. Air dry the seed before placing in cold storage. Store the seed in the refrigerator until the following February or March.

PROPAGATION

Seeds

Seed planted right after harvest need no pretreatment in order to germinate (McNeal, personal communication, 1999). However, germination is best at moderate temperatures (75–80° F), so storing the seed and sowing in a greenhouse the following spring is most productive. Direct sow the seeds in a container.

After germination, seedlings tend to be slow growing. Observation indicates that applications of chelated iron speed the growth rate (Best 1999).

NOTES

Because of its bitter taste, Chaparro Amargoso is not browsed by wildlife. This tough, thorny plant is very drought resistant. It provides good habitat for small wildlife and provides nesting sites for birds. The bright red berries are attractive against the dark green leaves. Occasionally in the fall the plant is attacked by a bag worm. The juvenile leaf morphology is very different from that of mature leaves (Best, personal communication, 1999).

Chaparro Amargoso has many uses historically as a medicinal plant. Extracts were used for fever, skin disease, yellow jaundice, and amoebic infections (R. B. Taylor, Rutledge, and Herrera 1997).

Chaparro Amargoso is very drought tolerant, and the abundant, glossy small fruit against the dark green leaves and gray stems is very attractive. It can be used as a specimen shrub, low background border plant, or as a barrier plant.

Catalpa speciosa

Catalpa, Cigar-tree

BIGNONIACEAE (TRUMPET-CREEPER FAMILY)

GENERAL DESCRIPTION

Catalpa is a large tree which can reach 98 feet, though usually it is less than 49 feet tall. The branches form a pyramidal crown, and the bark is reddish brown, breaking into thick scales. Leaves are deciduous, broadly oval in shape, 6–12 inches long, bright green and papery smooth.

FLOWERS AND FRUIT

Large and showy flowers bloom from March through June, borne in few-flowered panicles. Each bell-shaped flower is 2 inches long and 2½ inches wide. The corolla is white to lavender on the outside with two conspicuous yellow stripes inside the throat, and pale purplish blotches on the edges. Fruit is a persistent capsule up to 18 inches long containing many compressed and papery thin seeds, each ⅙ inch long.

NATURAL HABITAT, RANGE, AND PREFERRED SITE

Catalpa grows in damp woods, on the edges of swamps and streams from southern Illinois to east Texas. It is also widely adapted and planted much farther west in a variety of different soils and sites. In east Texas, Catalpa sometimes escapes cultivation and is found in old fields and pastures.

COLLECTION AND STORAGE

Collect the fruits after the capsules turn brown and begin to dry. Beat the capsules lightly or crush inside a bag, then separate the seeds by shaking. Good seed crops are borne every 2–3 years. Commercial seed-bearing age averages 20 years. Seeds of a related species, *C. bignoniodes*, remained viable for 2 years when held in cold dry storage.

PROPAGATION

Seeds

Germination of Catalpa is often delayed because of an immature seed embryo that requires a period of after-ripening. Seeds left on the tree and collected in February may germinate better than fall-collected seeds because they may be more mature. However, delayed harvest often results in collecting seeds that have been infested by insects. An after-ripening period may be provided by keeping the seeds in dry cold storage (50° F) until spring planting.

Mature seeds should be sown in the spring outdoors after all danger of frost is past. Cover the seeds with ¼ inch of soil and gently press in before watering. Germination usually occurs within 2 weeks. Seeds may be started earlier indoors. Germination rates with fresh seeds have been reported to be as high as 80% (USDA 1974).

Cuttings

Catalpa will root from semihardwood cuttings taken in late summer (Bailey and Bailey 1947). Most species of Catalpa may also be propagated by root cuttings taken in December. The roots are cut into 1-inch sections and planted in a rich soil mixture of equal parts sandy loam and peat. They are covered first with a thin layer of sand and finally with another thin layer of the loam/peat mixture. The rooting bed should be kept moist but not soggy. Shoot development begins the following spring.

NOTES

Catalpa is rapid growing and relatively short lived. The abundant showy white flowers and large papery leaves make it a very ornamental specimen tree that will adapt to many different soils and sites. It is only moderately drought tolerant. The wood is relatively brittle and often breaks during severe windstorms. It is susceptible to periodic attacks by the Catalpa sphinx moth caterpillar, which may defoliate the tree. Catalpa is occasionally attacked by a leaf blight that causes sudden blackening and dying of the leaves in early summer (Bailey and Bailey 1947).

Ceanothus

Ceanothus, Redroot, Jersey-tea

RHAMNACEAE (BUCKTHORN FAMILY)

GENERAL DESCRIPTION

Ceanothus spp. are shrubs, often multi-trunked, sometimes with weak or spindly stems and thorns. See Species Descriptions.

FLOWERS AND FRUIT

Individual flowers and fruit are small but are showy because they are displayed in such prolific masses (see Species Descriptions). Fruit is a capsule containing three seeds.

NATURAL HABITAT, RANGE, AND PREFERRED SITE

Ceanothus is found in eastern, central, and west Texas as well as elsewhere in the United States. See Species Descriptions for individual range and habitat. Generally, *Ceanothus* cannot tolerate heavy shade or a poorly drained site.

COLLECTION AND STORAGE

Collect seeds from the most vigorous plants in late summer and early fall. Most plants begin bearing seeds after 1 year and produce reliable seed crops each fall. Plants should be carefully observed as the seeds approach maturity because when completely dry the capsules disperse their seeds rather violently by a sudden ejection. Gathering seeds from the ground is difficult. Some recommend tying cloth bags around each cluster of capsules to catch the seeds as they are forcibly ejected. Seeds gathered when they are too green germinate poorly.

PROPAGATION

Seeds

Germination for many species of *Ceanothus* is delayed by an impermeable seed coat or dormant embryo or a combination of both conditions. Best results are achieved when the seeds are cleaned and planted immediately after harvesting (McNeal, personal communication, 1999). Hard-seeded species must be scarified before stratification. Soaking the seeds in hot water (180–200° F) before stratification or planting has been effective in reducing the hard seed coats of several species. Seeds should be allowed to soak in cooling water for 24 hours prior to planting.

Soaking seeds in concentrated sulfuric acid will also effectively scarify them, but exact guidelines for the duration of the acid treatment are lacking.

Seeds, whether scarified or not, should be stratified for 60–90 days at 41° F prior to sowing.

Sow seeds no deeper than twice their diameter. *Ceanothus* prefers soil with a pH of 6.0–7.0. Many species are particularly susceptible to damping-off fungi and require careful watering and periodic drenching with appropriate fungicides. They are also very moisture sensitive: the containers cannot be allowed to become too wet or too dry. It may require a year to 18 months for a seedling to reach a robust one-gallon container size (McNeal, personal communication, 1999). Young plants usually grow best if held in containers during the first summer following germination and then should be set out in late winter or early spring. Set plants shallowly in the soil with the root crown placed just below the soil line.

Cuttings

Although *Ceanothus* will root from cuttings, this method is not nearly as successful as seedling production (McNeal, personal communication, 1999). Select firm, semihardwood shoots of the current season's growth, with or without a heel. Insert the cuttings close together in a cold frame. Cuttings will be rooted and ready to plant outdoors in spring. Often the cuttings will develop a single, long, brittle root that is easily broken during transplanting. To avoid injury, remove the cuttings from the rooting bed just as the root is emerging. Plant the cutting in a well-drained soil mixture. Pinch back the tips of the stems to encourage bushy growth.

Softwood cuttings taken earlier in the growing season will also root under intermittent mist. Application of IBA is recommended.

NOTES

Several Californian and Mexican species of *Ceanothus* have been in cultivation for some time. They are commonly called French Lilacs. In colonial and Civil War days, the leaves were used as a substitute for tea. A red dye is obtained from the roots. Many species of *Ceanothus* provide wildlife food and cover. The western species have potential as drought-tolerant ground covers and soil stabilizers. Desert Ceanothus, *C. greggii*, has potential as a hedge plant for dry landscapes.

SPECIES DESCRIPTIONS

***Ceanothus americanus* (Jersey-tea)**
Low-growing shrub 2–4 feet with a woody base and herbaceous spreading branches. Small white flowers are held in dense clusters at the ends of branches. Jersey-tea is native to sandy soil, forest openings, and prairies from Georgia to central Texas. Prefers partial shade in a well-drained rich soil.

***Ceanothus greggii* (Desert Ceanothus)**
Shrub 3–6½ feet with small, half-evergreen, leathery leaves and crowded fragrant clusters of small white or blue flowers. Desert Ceanothus is native to arid mountains in the Trans-Pecos, south to Mexico. Prefers full sun. It provides browse for deer, elk, and rabbits. Chipmunks and other small animals, as well as quail, eat the small seeds.

***Ceanothus herbaceus* (Redroot)**
Similar to *C. americanus* but less woody, growing to a height of 3 feet, with narrow leaves and shorter flower clusters. Well-drained clays and sandy loams in prairies or crevices of limestone rock in the central Panhandle and Edwards Plateau. Good browse plant, and seeds eaten by a number of birds.

***Ceanothus fendleri* (Desert or Fendler Ceanothus)**
Low shrub seldom over 3 feet with bluish gray, smooth, thorn-tipped branches. Flowers in showy white masses. Native to high elevations of the Trans-Pecos, also Colorado. In cultivation since 1893 and considered the most hardy of the western species. Used in rock gardens and for sand bank planting.

Celastrus scandens

American Bittersweet

CELASTRACEAE (STAFF-TREE FAMILY)

GENERAL DESCRIPTION

American Bittersweet is a high-climbing shrub or woody vine reaching 30 feet, often forming thickets by means of underground stolons. The primary stem may grow as thick as 10 inches.

FLOWERS AND FRUIT

Flowers are small and greenish, borne in short panicles. The fruit is showier than the flowers, consisting of an orange or orange-yellow round capsule that splits open to expose a conspicuous crimson aril. The capsule contains three to six seeds ¼ inch long. Fruit is held in drooping clusters and is persistent throughout the autumn.

NATURAL HABITAT, RANGE, AND PREFERRED SITE

American Bittersweet is found in many different types of soils in thickets, woods, and fencerows from west central Texas to canyons in the mountains of the Trans-Pecos, as well as Georgia, Alabama, and Louisiana. It will grow in sun or shade.

COLLECTION AND STORAGE

American Bittersweet fruit ripens from late August through October. Collect the seeds as soon as the capsules separate and expose the arils. Spread the fruits in shallow layers and air dry for 2–3 weeks. Remove seeds from the capsule by flailing or rubbing on a screen and then dry for another week. The dried arils may be left on the seeds. Dried seeds stored in sealed containers at 34–38° F have reportedly remained viable for up to 8 years (USDA 1974).

PROPAGATION

Seeds

Seeds may be sown in the fall or stratified for 2–6 months at 41° F and sown the following spring. Germination rates are irregular, varying from 9% to 93% (USDA 1974). Germination usually occurs within 20 days. Seedlings are very susceptible to damping-off fungi.

Cuttings

American Bittersweet also may be propagated by root cuttings, layers, and suckers, which are often freely produced by the parent plant. In addition, both hardwood and softwood cuttings of American Bittersweet will produce new plants.

Transplanting

Large plants can often be divided into separate clumps if the soil around the root is easily dug.

NOTES

The brightly colored fruit is showy and persistent throughout most of the winter. American Bittersweet is a good plant for covering trellises, trees, or rocks. It has been in cultivation since 1736. The fruit is eaten by many species of birds as well as the rabbit and fox squirrel.

Celtis

Hackberry, Sugarberry, Palo Blanco

ULMACEAE (ELM FAMILY)

GENERAL DESCRIPTION

Celtis spp. are deciduous trees or semideciduous shrubs with very interesting bark. It is smooth, gray, mottled, or covered with corky or warty protuberances and fissures.

FLOWERS AND FRUIT

Flowers are generally inconspicuous, appearing with the new leaves on young branchlets. Fruit is a round or oval drupe that for some species ripens in early autumn and often persists on the tree through winter. The drupe usually contains a single bony nutlet.

NATURAL HABITAT, RANGE, AND PREFERRED SITE

Celtis grows in a variety of soils. See Species Descriptions for individual range and habitat. Larger species do best in rich, moist, alluvial soil, while smaller species are more drought tolerant. Hackberries generally will not tolerate sites with standing water or a permanently high water table.

COLLECTION AND STORAGE

Pick mature fruits by hand from the tree in late summer until winter. The plant may also be flailed and the fruit dropped onto cloths. Air dry the seeds with the pulp on or soak them until the pulp begins to ferment and soften. Then rub the pulp off on a screen or in a strainer. Viability is best maintained by storage in sealed containers at 41° F.

PROPAGATION

Seeds

Some Hackberry species have a dormant embryo and must be stratified at 41° F for 60–90 days before germination will proceed. Netleaf Hackberry (*C. reticulata*) may require up to 120 days of moist chilling. Seeds that have been cleaned from the pulp apparently respond more uniformly to stratification than uncleaned seeds (USDA 1974).

Cleaned seeds of Desert Hackberry (*C. pallida*) have been sown directly into seedbeds or plant cells in the fall, then kept in a cold frame over winter. Seeds will emerge strongly when temperatures begin to warm the following spring (Gass, personal communication, 1999).

Seeds can also be planted directly outdoors in the fall. Plant seeds ½ inch deep in a loose, fertile, and well-drained seedbed. Keep the soil moist but not soggy until germination begins.

Cuttings

Hackberry is most easily rooted from juvenile wood or from root sprouts or suckers that have coppiced from the root crown (see Chapter V). However, seedling production is the best method for generating large numbers of plants.

NOTES

Though generally considered "trashy trees," Hackberries do have a place in the natural landscape because their dry, sweet fruit is eaten by a number of birds and other animals. Their foliage, especially in desert regions, also provides good cover for wildlife and durable shade for the yard. Hackberries are valuable as fencerow plants because they are extremely drought tolerant and provide shade for livestock. The main enemies of the Hackberry are nipple gall (*Pachypsylla celtidismamma*), witch's broom, borers, mistletoe (*Phoradendron spp.*), and cotton root rot (Arnold 1999).

SPECIES DESCRIPTIONS

Celtis laevigata (Sugarberry, Hackberry)

Tree 60 feet or larger with a broad crown and grayish bark with warty knobs or growths. Sugarberry will be found on almost any soil type as long as there is fair drainage. In the Rio Grande Delta, Sugarberry grows only on sites where there is available moisture. It is the largest and most imposing of the Texas hackberries. Cold hardy to USDA zone 5.

Celtis occidentalis (Hackberry)

Tree or shrub of variable size 51 feet or larger. Sandy or rocky banks of rivers in canyons of the Texas Panhandle and Oklahoma. For an interesting discussion of this peripheral species, see Simpson's (1988) *A Field Guide to Texas Trees.*

***Celtis pallida* (Granjeno, Huasteco, Desert Hackberry)**
Shrub rarely as high as 25 feet with numerous spiny branches. Unlike other hackberries, Granjeno's habitat is not restricted to watercourses or wet sites. It can be found on mesas, foothills, thickets, and brushlands in west and south Texas, west to Arizona. Used in erosion control, it is also a valuable wildlife and honey plant. Cold hardy to USDA zone 7. Germination rates of Granjeno are good if the seed is filled out. Seeds prefer to germinate in spring (70–85° F) (Best 1999).

***Celtis reticulata* (Netleaf Hackberry, Acibuche, Palo Blanco)**
Small tree or tall shrub rarely to 51 feet. Grows along watercourses, near tanks, canyons, and other habitats, though not always dependent on sites with steady moisture. Its range extends throughout the Trans-Pecos, northern Mexico, Oklahoma, Colorado, west to California and Washington. Palo Blanco is characterized by gray bark, a strongly veiny pattern on the underside of the leaves, and orange or bright red fruits. A larger leafed form of this species occurs in east Texas. At least two species of hackberry butterflies rely on the foliage for butterfly food (Bowers 1993). The fruits were eaten by Native Americans and are also enjoyed by many forms of wildlife. Netleaf Hackberry is reportedly tolerant of cotton root rot fungus.

***Celtis tenuifolia* (Dwarf Hackberry)**
Shrub or small tree to 25 or more feet. Hardwood slopes along streams in open woodlands in east Texas from San Augustine south.

Cephalanthus occidentalis

Button-bush, Rosa de Juan, Jazmin

RUBIACEAE (MADDER FAMILY)

GENERAL DESCRIPTION

Button-bush is a fast-growing, cold-hardy shrub or small tree with many stems rising from the base to form a broad, rounded mound. It may grow as high as 18 feet tall and 10 feet wide, but is usually much smaller.

FLOWERS AND FRUIT

Small fragrant flowers are held in tight spherical heads from June through September. Fruit is a cinnamon-brown colored round cluster of spicy-smelling capsules. Each capsule contains two to four small nutlets.

NATURAL HABITAT, RANGE, AND PREFERRED SITE

Button-bush grows in low, wet areas throughout most of Texas, east to Florida, west to California and northern Mexico. It is most common along rivers, swamps, ponds, and wet canyons, in full sun to partial shade. It will adapt to a wide variety of landscape use, including parking lots, if adequately irrigated.

COLLECTION AND STORAGE

Gather seeds in late summer or early fall before the seed balls dry and break apart. Separate the seed by putting the fruits in a bag and lightly beating them. Information on seed storage and longevity is lacking.

PROPAGATION

Seeds

Fresh seeds will germinate without pretreatment in 30–40 days, although germination rates vary greatly and are generally not high. Better results may be achieved by breaking up the seed heads, mixing them with perlite, and setting in the refrigerator for 30 days (McNeal, personal communication, 1999). Sprinkle the seed with the perlite directly into the plant cells and plant immediately.

Cuttings

Button-bush is easily rooted from both softwood and hardwood cuttings. Softwood tip cuttings taken before the flowers appear are easiest to root. These are taken after the first flush of growth (late May/June), just as it is beginning to harden off. Treat with 3,000 ppm IBA and place under mist. Cuttings will produce a one-gallon plant by October. Pinch young rooted cuttings back to encourage branching (Pfeiffer, personal communication, 1999). Semihardwood cuttings taken in late July and treated with IBA (5,000 ppm) rooted in 3 to 4 weeks in high percentages (Dirr and Heuser 1987). Stock plants held in a greenhouse and routinely cut back provide a source of easily rooted cutting material. Otherwise, Button-bushes in the wild are slow to come out in spring and produce a good source of softwood cutting material.

Transplanting

Small plants may be dug in the spring. Large clumps of older plants may be separated in early spring (K. S. Taylor and Hamblin 1963).

NOTES

Button-bush thrives in any good garden soil, especially a moist, sandy loam. It is a good shrub for screening in poorly drained places and will grow in either sun or shade. The flowers are fragrant and a favorite of both butterflies and hummingbirds. The seeds are eaten by at least 25 species of birds, especially water birds (Vines 1970).

Ceratoides lanata

Winterfat, Feather Sage, Lamb's Tail

CHENOPODIACEAE (GOOSEFOOT FAMILY)

GENERAL DESCRIPTION

Winterfat is a cottony-looking low shrub with a woody base and herbaceous stems reaching 1–3 feet tall. The narrow blue-green leaves are woody with white to rust-colored hairs. There is marked ecotypic variation among plants.

FLOWERS AND FRUIT

Inconspicuous spikes of male and female flowers appear on separate plants in spring through mid-summer. As they ripen into fruits in the fall and winter, silvery hairs begin to elongate on the fruiting spike and are very showy, especially when backlit by the sun. Female flowers are showiest. Each small, bladdery one-seeded fruit develops a long silky thread.

NATURAL HABITAT, RANGE, AND PREFERRED SITE

Winterfat is native to high alkaline deserts and slopes in west and northwest Texas, usually at altitudes of 4,000–8,000 feet in the Guadalupe Mountains, the west side of the Davis Mountains, and also in the mountains near Van Horn. Winterfat's range also extends west to New Mexico and California and north to Washington State. Winterfat requires full sun and well-drained soil. It prefers the cool dry temperatures of higher elevations. Although it will grow in Dallas, it never really thrives there or is as attractive as in those areas with cool nights, similar to its native habitat (Simpson, personal communication, 1986).

COLLECTION AND STORAGE

Winterfat plants bear seeds their first year, and good crops are reliably produced each year. Seeds are reported to number from 54,000 to 210,000 per pound, depending on location. Seeds may be gathered by hand or with vacuum strippers from late summer until fall. They must be well dried before storage. Removal of the hairy utricle or fruit before storage is not necessary. Large amounts of seeds may be cleaned using a hammermill with a 5–6 inch screen run at 1,000–1,200 rpm. Seeds lose viability by as much 50% the first year if stored at room temperature. Seeds should be stored in sealed containers at 40° F. Refrigerated seeds may retain viability for as long as 8 years (Vories 1981).

PROPAGATION

Seeds

Germination of Winterfat is delayed by a dormant embryo, and some seed lots also require after-ripening of up to 4 months before stratifying and sowing in the early spring (Manning, personal communication, 1999).

Stratify seed for 2–3 months at 38–41° F before planting. Seeds may also be planted outdoors in the fall or in the spring after stratification. In Colorado, it is not unusual to find Winterfat seedlings germinating beneath late winter snows. In germination tests in the laboratory, average daily temperatures of 50–80° F proved to be the optimum range for germination. Under these conditions, 6–42% of the seeds germinated in 6 days. Under less controlled conditions, germination rates are often poor. Pretreated seeds to be sown outdoors should be planted in early spring before temperatures become too warm.

Cover seeds with ⅛ inch of fine sifted sand. Seeds will not germinate when planted deeper than ½ inch.

Winterfat may be directly field sown, using 3–4 pounds of seeds per acre. Winterfat germinates best in a moist environment. The ability of the seedlings to withstand moisture stress increases as the average temperature decreases, and this is another advantage to early spring planting. Seedlings tend to be slow growing and susceptible to damping off when planted in a greenhouse. Spider mites can also be a problem (Manning, personal communication, 1999).

Cuttings

Winterfat will root from softwood cuttings treated with IBA and kept under intermittent mist. Specific information is lacking. Carefully watch the watering regime and reduce the watering intervals as cuttings begin to callus and initiate roots.

NOTES

Winterfat has been in cultivation since 1895 and has been used as a low-growing ornamental with attractive, fuzzy silver fruit and persistent foliage. It is perhaps most valued as an important winter forage plant for livestock, deer, and elk, and also in revegetation planting for erosion control. The leaves become dry in the fall but remain on the plant for most of the winter, making it a highly prized forage plant, especially for sheep, when other plants are scarce. It is best adapted to dry soil in the mountains of the Trans-Pecos or the High Plains.

In landscape use, Winterfat is best in fall and winter, when the showy fruit really stands out while other plants are dormant. To keep the plant bushy, cut the plant back to the ground in early spring before new growth occurs (Mielke 1993).

The Navaho parboiled its leaves and ate them to relieve blood expectoration. It was thrown on the hot stones of their sweat houses, along with sticky-flowered rabbitbrush for aroma (Elmore 1976).

Cercidium texanum

Texas Palo Verde, Retama China

FABACEAE (LEGUME FAMILY)

GENERAL DESCRIPTION

Texas Palo Verde is a very thorny, drought-resistant, deciduous multi-trunked shrub or small tree, sometimes growing as tall as 24 feet in south Texas. Palo Verde frequently develops a short crooked trunk with low, semiprostrate branches. The bark is smooth and green. Leaves are twice-pinnately compound, with one to three pairs of small, narrowly obovate pinnae. During drought, Palo Verde will drop its tiny leaves, and green bark will provide the photosynthesis.

FLOWERS AND FRUIT

Palo Verde blooms cover the plant from March to November, especially after rains. Each flower has five bright yellow petals, one of which is contracted into a long claw with a red spot at the base. During the times of heaviest bloom, the fallen petals form an iridescent yellow skirt below the plant, reflecting light upward against the bright green trunk to create a spectacular effect. Fruit is a legume, 1–2 inches long, flattened and constricted between the seeds, usually numbering three or four per pod. Each seed is ¼ inch long.

NATURAL HABITAT, RANGE, AND PREFERRED SITE

Texas Palo Verde is very common on alkaline sandy loam or clays on brushy plains in the Rio Grande Plains in southern Texas.

COLLECTION AND STORAGE

Gather the pods from May to August as they begin to turn yellow-brown and dry. Mature seeds will be firm, filled out, and brown. Seeds are often infested by the larva of bruchid beetles while still in the pod, so early collection and fumigation of stored seeds is recommended.

PROPAGATION

Seeds

A hard seed coat inhibits germination. Large numbers of Palo Verde seedlings have been grown by first soaking the seed in sulfuric acid for 35–40 minutes, followed by 1–4 days aeration. Aerated seeds are then encouraged to swell and begin to sprout in pregermination trays. Remove emerging seedlings and place in individual containers at least 4–6 inches deep, with well drained soil media (Best 1999).

Seedling survival and vigor is improved when the roots are air pruned. Texas Palo Verde seedlings are slow growing at first and very susceptible to damping-off fungi and root rot (Lowrey, personal communication, 1986). Careful watering and inoculation with beneficial bacteria may improve survival rate.

Cuttings

Texas Palo Verde has been successfully rooted from semihardwood cuttings taken in the fall, treated with IBA, and placed under mist (Lowrey, personal communication, 1986). Fall-rooted cuttings require cold-frame protection over winter. Softwood cuttings taken in summer will also root. Specific information on rates of rooting and survivability are lacking.

Transplanting

Occasionally you will see large specimen Palo Verde trees balled and burlapped from the field for sale by nurseries. For the individual, however, only small plants (3 feet) are practical for transplanting, and then only if the taproot is unbroken.

NOTES

Texas Palo Verde is an appropriate plant for hot dry sites and poor soil. Its frequent showy blooms and green bark make it a worthy specimen plant. Texas Palo Verde has long been confused with *Cercidium floridum* (Blue Palo Verde), which grows in Arizona. Texas Palo Verde has been merged by taxonomists with *Cercidium macrum* (Border Palo Verde). *C. macrum* is a larger and more treelike form adapted to wetter sites. To make matters even more confusing, other botanists have merged both species into the closely related *Parkinsonia texana*, where they are listed as two varieties: *P. texana var. texanum* (Texas Palo Verde) and *P. texana var. macrum* (Border Palo Verde). Separation of these varieties often depends on legume and flower characteristics (Simpson 1988). However you name them, Palo Verdes are some of the most prolific and drought tolerant of western trees and shrubs. Even without flowers, the sculptural aspect of their twisting branches and bright green bark is a valuable contribution to a desert garden. In habitat reclamation, Texas Palo Verde, along with its close relative *Parkinsonia aculeata* (Retama), is one of the first colonizing species to return to disturbed sites, providing perch sites for birds and light shade that contributes to the development of a brush canopy. At one site in dry loamy soils in the Rio Grande Delta, *Cercidium macrum* was observed to grow 8 feet tall and 15 feet across in only 4 years (Best, personal communication, 1999).

Cercis

Redbud, Árbol de Judío

FABACEAE (LEGUME FAMILY)

GENERAL DESCRIPTION

Redbuds are small to medium-sized deciduous trees with simple, heart-shaped leaves (see Species Descriptions).

FLOWERS AND FRUIT

The whole tree is covered with pink or purplish flowers borne in tight clusters up and down the branches in early spring before the leaves appear. Fruit is a stiff legume with several small seeds ripening in late summer through early fall.

NATURAL HABITAT, RANGE, AND PREFERRED SITE

There are three varieties of *Cercis canadensis* in Texas, each with a distinct range and habitat (see Species Descriptions).

COLLECTION AND STORAGE

Seed quality and availability varies from year to year and population to population. It is unusual for redbuds to produce good seed crops every year. Seed and flower production is affected by late frosts and drought that may cause the seed to abort. The tree may appear to bear plenty of pods, but the seed inside will be inert or hollow. In addition, some redbud seeds from certain populations can be badly infested by weevils. Although the pods remain on the tree throughout the winter, most growers recommend gathering the seed by the end of August or no later than the beginning of September (Janzow, personal communication, 1999).

Others suggest gathering the seed even earlier, before they are fully hardened and barely turning brown to avoid weevil infestation and eliminate the need for scarification (McNeal, personal communication, 1999).

Because of the erratic supply of seeds, it is often necessary to gather large amounts to insure adequate seedling production. Inert or empty seeds can be separated from the lot before sowing by soaking in water. Sound seeds will sink, while poor seeds will float. The flotation test should not be done before storage. Air dry seeds a few days and then store in sealed containers at room temperature for 1 year; store at 41° F if seeds are to be kept for a longer period. Seed stored in the refrigerator will remain viable for at least 3 years (Janzow, personal communication, 1999). Fumigation using pest strips is effective for protecting seed during storage.

PROPAGATION

Seeds

Germination of redbud is delayed by a hard seed coat and a dormant embryo. High germination rates were achieved by one grower by first scarifying the seeds for 30 minutes in concentrated sulfuric acid. Scarified seeds were carefully washed and briefly air dried before being aerated for 2–3 days (see Chapter III). As the water in the aeration jars discolored, it was replaced with fresh water. The seeds were watched carefully to detect swelling during the aeration period. Seeds that had imbibed were removed and stored for 60 days in plastic bags containing moist but not soggy fine-grade perlite. Seeds began to sprout toward the end of the 60-day period while still in cold storage and were then carefully removed individually with tweezers and planted in separate 2½- × 2½- × 3-inch-deep containers. Only the sprouted or swelled seeds were planted (Janzow, personal communication, 1999). Seedlings were later transplanted when they had three true leaves and roots were showing at the bottom of the pots. Another method included scarifying the seed in acid for 30 minutes followed by cold stratification for 30 days at 41° F (McNeal, personal communication, 1999). After the cold treatment, seeds were planted in individual plant cells. Germination of pretreated seeds usually occurs within 3 weeks.

Dan Hosage has yet another twist on germination of *Cercis*. He scarifies the seeds up to 45 minutes, after first testing small lots at 15-minute intervals to determine optimum treatment time. Following scarification, he carefully rinses the seeds and spreads them on newspapers to lightly dry them. Then he puts the seeds in a saucer and covers them with boiling water. He leaves the seeds in the cooling water overnight and plants in individual containers the next day. He believes that the shock of the boiling water activates the internal protein complex of the seed, and that seeds show a strong preference to germinate if exposed to sunlight during imbibition. After germination, seeds were planted ¼ inch deep in well-drained soil.

Robbi Will adds "Superthrive" to the boiling water as it cools after being poured over the seeds. She found that it made germination more uniform and vigorous.

Seedlings benefit from light shade the first season. In some cases, redbuds will grow to a salable one-gallon container size in 5–7 months. A five-gallon plant can be produced in 12–16 months (Pfeiffer, personal communication, 1999). Mexican Redbuds can take as long as 2 years to reach the same size (Hosage, personal communication, 1999).

Redbuds seem to benefit from containers that promote air-root pruning. One grower experienced significant differences in stem height and sturdiness when redbud seedlings were planted in Whitcomb "Rootmaker"™ pots (Will, personal communication, 1999). It is not known whether rhizobium inoculation would further improve growth rates for this genus.

Cuttings

Redbud is difficult to root, but some success has been experienced using juvenile wood or root sprouts taken from seedlings in late spring and summer. Softwood and semihardwood cuttings root less easily. All cuttings should be treated with IBA and placed under intermittent mist. However, rooted cuttings seldom develop into strong, well-shaped plants (McNeal, personal communication, 1999).

Several interesting and unusual redbud forms have been clonally reproduced from tissue cultures. These include the graceful dwarf Texas Redbud, Traveler™ (Hosage, personal communication, 1999), and a cultivar of Mexican Redbud, 'Tipton Flame,' named after Jimmy Tipton.

'Tipton Flame' was chosen for its strong purple-pink flower color and more importantly, the long-lasting dark purple color of its pods. Its leaves are very rounded with wavy edges, and very glossy. A one-gallon container size plant can be produced in one summer's growth from tissue culture. Once established, young plants produced from tissue culture seem to be more vigorous than seedlings and will produce a 10-foot tree in just 3 years in the field (Mackay, personal communication, 1999).

Tissue culture has proven to be a more effective way of clonally reproducing superior forms of redbuds, and we will probably see more and more of these introduced into the nursery trade in the near future.

Transplanting

Redbuds can be transplanted from the field if enough soil is available to guarantee an intact root ball. Winter is the best time for moving established trees.

NOTES

Redbud has long been a familiar and well-loved small ornamental tree. However, each variety is appropriate for very different parts of the state (see Species Descriptions). The consumer should make sure that the nursery knows exactly what kind of redbud it has in stock, and where it came from. In the zones where the species overlap, redbuds have been known to hybridize.

In Mexico, the acid flowers are pickled and used for salads or eaten fried. The seeds and foliage provide forage for wildlife. A fluid extract from redbud bark has an active astringent which has been used for treating dysentery (Powell 1988).

Botryosphaeria canker (a fungus) is the main problem limiting the life expectancy of these trees (Arnold 1999). *Verticillum* wilt and root rot can be problems as well.

SPECIES DESCRIPTIONS

Cercis canadensis var. canadensis (Eastern Redbud)

Eastern Redbud is characterized by large, thin, dull green leaves, sometimes up to 5 inches long and wide. The trunk is usually straight, with a broadly rounded or flattened crown. The flowers are generally purplish red, though individual trees may have flowers that are bright pink to red or occasionally white (Simpson 1988). Eastern Redbud sometimes reaches 40 feet in height. It grows in east Texas with 35 or more inches of rain, in well-drained sands and sandy loams, and in the heavy black clays of the Blackland Prairies. If planted on thin soils in areas with less rainfall, Eastern Redbud's leaves will become burned by late summer, possibly even defoliating during periods of extended drought.

Cercis canadensis var. mexicana (Mexican Redbud)

In Texas, the Mexican Redbud reaches 25 feet tall under favorable conditions. In Mexico, it is found in a very diverse subtropical forest along with oaks and pines near San Luis Potosi. In this location, Mexican Redbud may reach 60–80 feet and bear large leaves. Mexican Redbud may be the more ancestral form of this species as opposed to being a variety or subspecies of the Eastern Redbud (Ogden, personal communication, 1999). Mexican Redbud leaves are heart shaped with a leathery texture and wavy edges. The new leaves are fuzzy, turning a dark glossy green as they mature. Mexican Redbud often flowers four times a year, in response to desert monsoons.

In Texas, Mexican Redbud often grows as a multi-trunked shrub and is sometimes found in the southern edge of the Trans-Pecos on alkaline soils, where it typically receives 12–20 inches of annual rainfall.

***Cercis canadensis var. texensis* (Texas Redbud)**

Texas Redbud is commonly found as a multi-trunked tall shrub or small tree growing on thin limestone soils in central Texas. Its leaves are thicker, smaller, and glossier than those of the Eastern Redbud and the flowers more intense in color.

The cultivar 'Sanderson' is the most desert-adapted selection of Texas Redbud introduced into the nursery trade so far. It has small, half-dollar-sized leaves that are very pubescent when young, maturing to an attractive silver-green color. It is insect free, and a good addition to especially hot, dry sites.

Cercocarpus montanus var. argenteus

Silver-leaf Mountain Mahogany, Palo Duro

ROSACEAE (ROSE FAMILY)

GENERAL DESCRIPTION

Silver-leaf Mountain Mahogany is a shrub or small tree 3–18 feet tall with rigid, upright branches and evergreen leaves. Leaves are small, dark green above and covered with dense wool below.

FLOWERS AND FRUIT

Small, greenish white flowers are borne singly or in twos or threes in the leaf axils from May through June. Fruit is a soft, fuzzy, cylindrical achene with a long, showy, feathery style at the tip. Silver-leaf Mountain Mahogany is showiest when in fruit in late summer and early fall because the dense clusters of white, silky-tailed fruit create a striking contrast to the dark evergreen leaves.

NATURAL HABITAT, RANGE, AND PREFERRED SITE

Silver-leaf Mountain Mahogany is native to the limestone soil of the Edwards Plateau, Rolling Plains, High Plains, and Trans-Pecos regions of Texas, as well as throughout most of the western United States and northern Mexico.

COLLECTION AND STORAGE

The feathery style of the achene has a sharp point like a threaded needle and can be blown many yards from the parent plant. The point of the "needle" is at the heavy end and lands first when the achene hits the ground. Then the "thread" or style hygroscopically twists and turns according to changes in humidity and thus screws the little needle or seed into the ground. The style drops off once the seed is positioned for germination (Simpson, personal communication, 1986). Because of this method of seed dispersal, timing of collection is important. Once the seeds have ripened and begun to dry, a single windstorm can disperse an entire crop. Seeds average 59,000 per pound and mature in August and September.

Collect the seeds by shaking them onto canvas or into a hopper. The largest and best quality seeds may be found on less fertile soil where Silver-leaf Mountain Mahogany plants are not abundant. It is not necessary to remove the styles from small amounts of seeds before storage or planting.

Seeds stored in sealed containers at 41° F will retain viability up to 7 years, depending on seed source and time of collection. Seed quality varies from year to year and across localities.

PROPAGATION

Seeds

Germination of Silver-leaf Mountain Mahogany is delayed by three factors: a chemical inhibitor in the seed coat, a hard seed coat, and a shallow embryo dormancy. Stratification is not always imperative for all seed lots but generally produces more uniform germination rates. In one study, fresh seed with the outer sheath removed and the seed gently nicked but not cold stratified did not germinate (Manning, personal communication, 1999).

One seed lot of Silver-leaf Mountain Mahogany seed gathered near Junction, Texas, germinated readily from untreated seed (McNeal, personal communication, 1999). Generally, scarification for 10–20 minutes in concentrated sulfuric acid followed by 5–10 minutes of rinsing will dissolve the inhibitors and reduce the seed coat.

Follow scarification with 30 days stratification at 41° F. Plant the seeds ¼–½ inch deep in well-drained soil. Scarified seeds may be planted outdoors in the fall or stratified and planted in early spring. In one study, 88% of pretreated seeds germinated in 28 days. However, germination may take 60 days to complete. Large seeds germinate better than small ones.

One method suggests that seed be directly sown into flats in October or November after harvesting. Keep the flats in a cold frame over winter. Seedlings emerge the following spring (Gass, personal communication, 1999).

Young seedlings require partial shade until they are established, but then should be planted in full sun to make a sturdy container plant. *Cercocarpus* seedlings tend to be slow growing, requiring up to 2 years to make a one-gallon plant (Gass, personal communication, 1999). Seedlings are very susceptible to overwatering and to soil pathogens. Water carefully and treat the seedbed with a fungicide.

Cuttings

Silver-leaf Mountain Mahogany will root from softwood cuttings taken in the spring from flexible wood that is firm toward the base. These should be treated with IBA and kept under intermittent mist. In one study, 60% of the cuttings treated as above rooted in 3 weeks (Simpson, personal communication, 1986).

NOTES

The compact habit, evergreen leaves, and attractive fruit make Silver-leaf Mountain Mahogany an outstanding ornamental plant. It is browsed by many animals, so it seldom reaches its full height in nature. The wood is dense but brittle. True Mountain Mahogany, *C. montanus*, is a highly variable species and is represented by three varieties, each with horticultural potential.

Chilopsis linearis

Desert Willow, Flor de Mimbre

BIGNONIACEAE (TRUMPET-CREEPER FAMILY)

GENERAL DESCRIPTION

Desert Willow is a graceful open-branched small tree or spreading multi-trunked tall shrub up to 30 feet tall, though usually smaller. Leaves are deciduous, long and narrow, and light green in color. Stems are smooth, slender, and light colored.

FLOWERS AND FRUIT

Desert Willow produces many fragrant showy flowers in dense clusters at the ends of the branches throughout the summer. Each flower is shaped like a large ruffled trumpet, variously colored from pale pink or white to deep rose, often having pink or purplish stripes on the throat. The fruit is a long woody capsule containing many flattened, oval, and feathery winged seeds.

NATURAL HABITAT, RANGE, AND PREFERRED SITE

Desert Willow is commonly found along watercourses and in dry streambeds in west-central and far west Texas to California. It requires full sun and a well-drained site. Desert Willow will grow in infertile or shallow soil but prefers limestone soil. It is very drought tolerant and grows best in full sun. In shade it may become weak and leggy, and produce few blooms.

COLLECTION AND STORAGE

Gather the seeds by hand from late summer through autumn when the pods have dried and turned brown but before they have split open and the light, feathery seeds are dispersed by the wind. Seeds may be extracted from the pods by spreading them in thin layers to air dry for a few days and then beating them lightly in a sack. After thrashing, the seeds may be separated by screening and fanning. Desert Willow loses viability rapidly, but dry storage in the refrigerator is usually adequate for keeping seeds over winter. For best results sow the seeds indoors immediately following collection.

PROPAGATION

Seeds

Desert Willow germinates readily from freshly gathered seeds. Soaking the seeds in water for a few hours prior to sowing may improve germination (Dewerth 1955). Scatter the seed thinly in the flat or in individual containers, but do not bury. Seeds need light to germinate (Will, personal communication, 1999). Seeds usually germinate within 1–3 weeks, and viability averages 40%.

Seeds should not be planted too thickly in the flat or nursery row. Seedlings 4 inches long may be transplanted to separate one-gallon containers. Seedlings quickly become spindly if kept in the flat too long or not given enough light. The soil mix should be well drained and the plants must have strong sunlight. Seedlings will respond to small yet regularly applied amounts of fertilizer. Heavy applications of fertilizer may cause Desert Willow to become too brittle or leggy or may inhibit blooming.

Seedling growth and survival during later transplanting to larger containers or in the field is improved if seedlings are initially placed in containers that promote root air pruning.

Root girdling in the container is a problem often seen with Desert Willows. Because of their rapid growth rate, a tree may appear tall and healthy in a pot, only later displaying stunted growth or difficulty in thriving after being planted out. This is often because the roots have encircled the bottom of the pot and later have never broken out of the spiral into the larger hole. Even 2–3 years later, these trees will be stunted, and you can easily shake the trunk from side to side. If a long period of time has gone by since the tree was originally planted, we find it better just to replace it with a new, well-rooted plant.

One grower noticed significant improvement in growth rate, root anchoring, and stem development when plants were held in Whitcomb "Rootmaker"™ pots (Will, personal communication, 1999).

Cuttings

Desert Willow is easily rooted from semihardwood cuttings of the current season's growth taken in late May and June. The cuttings should be treated with 5,000 IBA in alcohol solution and kept under intermittent mist (Pfeiffer, personal communication, 1999). As the cuttings begin to callus and form roots, reduce the frequency of misting to encourage the cuttings to harden off and avoid stem rot. Cuttings usually root in 2–3 weeks.

Root development is best in a light soil mix rather than straight perlite alone. Roots tend to be brittle and a soil blend encourages branching (Will, personal communication, 1999).

Cuttings taken at the beginning of the summer will yield a sturdy five-gallon container sized plant within 1 year. Cuttings taken at the end of the summer as the plant becomes dormant sometimes tend to rot during the winter in the greenhouse because temperatures are too cool. Desert Willow requires warm temperatures for active growth.

In Arizona, winter temperatures are not as inhibiting and sometimes help a grower get a jump on spring production (Gass, personal communication, 1999). Bottom heat may prove beneficial to speed rooting.

Transplanting

Desert Willow is easily transplanted from the field if enough soil is available to secure an intact root ball. Cut back the branches by one-third the overall length to reduce transplant shock.

NOTES

Desert Willow is a fast-growing and attractive ornamental tree. Its showy flowers, willowlike leaves, and graceful habit make it a wonderful specimen for a courtyard or against a wall. Heavy watering and fertilizing tends to promote over-rapid growth, weaker branches, and fewer flowers. Desert Willow may also develop root rot on wet sites, especially if the site remains wet for long periods in the winter (Will, personal communication, 1999).

In the field, Desert Willow is resistant to cotton root rot fungus. Occasionally it can be infested with aphids and white wing moth (Arnold 1999). It is a good idea to let the tree dry out completely between waterings to encourage a flush of new flowers, as would occur in its native habitat where Desert Willow responds to infrequent but heavy summer rainstorms. Trimming the spent flowers and seed pods from the tips of the branches will also stimulate more flowering on the new wood.

Desert Willow may sucker many new stems from the base, but can be trained into a stronger form by periodically cutting out the weaker new stems and selecting the dominant or larger stems. Interior twigs can also be removed to give the plant a neater overall appearance. In the winter, Desert Willow can be trimmed back by as much as one-third from the top to encourage secondary branching and more blooms.

Plant Desert Willow as a fast-growing shade tree or as a specimen in naturalistic landscapes, where it provides shelter for nesting and nectar for hummingbirds (Mielke 1993). It has been frequently planted along highways in west Texas and the Panhandle. It is also useful in erosion control and has been in cultivation since 1800 (Lenz 1973). Desert Willow is hardy to at least 10° F, though new growth may be burned back (Mielke 1993).

Desert Willow exists in many different color forms, some of which have been clonally reproduced and are available from nurseries. Two ornamental selections of Desert willow, 'White Storm' and 'Dark Storm,' were developed by Benny Simpson at the Texas A&M Research and Extension Service Center at Dallas. 'White Storm' has pure white flowers and fine-textured foliage. 'Dark Storm' has nearly solid dark pink-magenta flowers. Paul Cox discovered another strong form growing at the San Antonio Botanical Gardens and named it 'Bubba.' It has dark purple flowers and appears to have a more muscular trunk and branches. Another cultivar, 'Burgundy Lace,' is similar to 'Bubba,' except it has two-toned white and pink-magenta flowers, and it may be self-incompatible as it tends to develop fruit only in the presence of other cultivars (Arnold 1999). Leucretia Hamilton™ is a cultivar chosen by Mountain States Wholesale Nursery because it has a smaller overall size and longer bloom period, with virtually no pod production. Its flowers are purple with a white throat. The selection Warren Jones™, also of Mountain States Wholesale Nursery, has lighter lavender flowers that are grouped in very large clusters. It will reach 25 feet, with a more upright rather than spreading form. Like the smaller Leucretia Hamilton™, this form is very floriferous and produces few seed pods.

Chionanthus virginica

Fringe-tree, Old-man's Beard

OLEACEAE (OLIVE FAMILY)

GENERAL DESCRIPTION

Fringe-tree is a deciduous tree or tall shrub to 32 feet with stout branchlets. Dark green oval leaves are shiny on top and fuzzy or pale on the undersurface. The leaves turn golden in the fall.

FLOWERS AND FRUIT

In the early spring, graceful drooping panicles of delicate white flowers cover the plant just before the emergence of new leaves. Male trees are showier than female trees (Wasowski 1994). The fruit is a purple drupe containing one seed, ⅓ inch long.

NATURAL HABITAT, RANGE, AND PREFERRED SITE

Fringe-tree grows in damp woods, thickets, or on sandy bluffs in east Texas, east to Florida, north to Oklahoma and Ohio. It thrives best in rich moist soil and partial shade.

COLLECTION AND STORAGE

Collect fruits from July to September when they have turned purple but before they fall from the tree. Clean the seeds from the pulp and keep in cold moist storage. Seeds held in cold stratification may remain viable for 1–2 years (USDA 1974).

PROPAGATION

Seeds

Natural germination of Fringe-tree usually occurs the second spring following seed fall. Dormancy is deep seated and appears to involve hard bony endocarp, inhibitors in the endosperm, and dormancy in the shoot portion of the embryo. The seeds must first be exposed to a period of warm moist temperatures (68° F) for 2–3 months. During this period of warm stratification, the radicle emerges while the shoot remains dormant. After the warm period, the seeds should be stratified for 2–3 months at 41° F to overcome shoot dormancy. In nature these alternating periods of warm and cold temperatures occur during the first summer and second winter after seed fall.

Scatter the seeds thinly over the seedbed and cover with ¼–½ inch of firmed soil. Care should be taken when planting the seeds to separate the seedlings that may have emerged during stratification. Plant these in separate containers to avoid breaking the new roots.

The best outdoor seedbed consists of rich, moist, loamy soil that has been well worked. Cover with light mulch to conserve moisture until the shoot emerges. Seedlings require light shade until well established.

Cuttings

Fringe-tree is very difficult to root from cuttings. Several tests with different types of cuttings, age of stock plant, and hormone treatments all failed to produce results (Dirr and Heuser 1987).

NOTES

Fringe-tree was introduced into cultivation in 1736 and is planted as an ornamental throughout the southern United States. The twigs and foliage are often preferred browse material by many animals in the Gulf Coast Plain, but the plant is only moderately tolerant of browsing and may die if over one-third of the annual growth is removed (Vines 1970). Birds eat the fruit of the female tree.

Choisya dumosa

Mexican Star-leaf Orange, Zorillo

RUTACEAE (CITRUS FAMILY)

GENERAL DESCRIPTION

Mexican Star-leaf Orange is a mounded evergreen shrub 1–3 feet tall and wide, with dark green palmately compound leaves each with 5–10 narrow needle-like leaflets. The leaves are leathery in texture with aromatic glands on the toothed edges.

FLOWERS AND FRUIT

Mexican Star-leaf Orange produces profuse numbers of fragrant orange or white flowers with golden stamens. They are borne in crowded clusters at the axils of the leaves and bloom from summer to fall. Fruit is a follicle with two to five divergent carpels each containing one or two tiny seeds. When ripe, the fruit is brownish green, and the seeds are black.

NATURAL HABITAT, RANGE, AND PREFERRED SITE

Mexican Star-leaf Orange is found in scattered locations in the mountains of the Trans-Pecos and in New Mexico and northern Mexico. It is most common as an understory plant in Texas in the pinyon belt of the Glass and Guadalupe Mountains at altitudes of 4,500–7,000 feet.

COLLECTION AND STORAGE

Collect the fruits of Mexican Star-leaf Orange in late summer or early fall. Do not allow the seeds to dry out before sowing or storage. Mexican Star-leaf Orange seeds can lose viability unless stratified immediately after collection or kept in sphagnum moss in polyethylene bags at 40° F.

PROPAGATION

Seeds

Production of Mexican Star-leaf Orange is most successful when fresh seeds are planted immediately after collection. Seed can also be stratified for 30 days and then planted after the soil has warmed (60° F) or earlier in a greenhouse (Manning, personal communication, 1999).

Mexican Star-leaf Orange must have well-drained mineral soil. Keep soil slightly moist until the seedlings emerge. Both extremely wet or dry conditions should be avoided during the young seedling stage. After the seedlings are 8–12 inches tall, they are ready to be transplanted from the seed flat to the nursery row or container. Plant the seedlings at the same depth as they grew in the seedbed in rows 9–12 inches apart. Carefully monitor irrigation: Mexican Star-leaf Orange is very sensitive to overwatering while in a container.

Cuttings

Mexican Star-leaf Orange will root from tip cuttings taken in early spring before new growth begins or semihardwood cuttings taken after flowering in late summer. These cuttings should be 4–8 inches long, with the basal cut made at a node. Cuttings root best in well-drained media placed under mist. Application of IBA improves rooting. As the cuttings begin to root, gradually reduce the misting intervals: cuttings are very susceptible to rotting (Phillips 1995b).

NOTES

Mexican Star-leaf Orange is a desirable ornamental plant because of its compact size, showy, long-blooming white flowers, and evergreen aromatic leaves. It is extremely heat tolerant, and it is cold hardy to 0° F. It is deeply rooted and has a moderate growth rate. To encourage compact and bushy growth, regularly tip prune Mexican Star-leaf Orange after blooming (Simpson, personal communication, 1986). This shrub requires extremely well drained mineral soil and prefers full sun.

Chrysactinia mexicana

Damianita, Hierba de San Nicolas

ASTERACEAE (SUNFLOWER FAMILY)

GENERAL DESCRIPTION

Damianita is a low-growing, evergreen, tap-rooted shrub forming a dense mound 1–2 feet high and about 2 feet wide. The dark green needle-like leaves are smooth and aromatic.

FLOWERS AND FRUIT

Numerous golden-yellow daisylike flowers are held on the ends of slender pedicels from April to September. Fruit is a slender achene.

NATURAL HABITAT, RANGE, AND PREFERRED SITE

Damianita grows in dry limestone soils in the Edwards Plateau, Trans-Pecos, and New Mexico. In cultivation, it will tolerate sandy, loamy, or caliche soils, as long as they are well drained. Damianita does not thrive in overly rich or irrigated soil. It is cold tolerant to near 0° F, and does best in full sun. It does not like to have its roots wet, especially during the winter.

COLLECTION AND STORAGE

Collect the dry flower heads from April to June after the intermittent blooming periods and then store in paper bags or sealed containers in a cool dry place. Seed viability diminishes after the first season.

PROPAGATION

Seeds

Damianita is easily grown from seed, and germination rates are high when seeds are planted during warm weather (McNeal, personal communication, 1999). Scatter the seed thinly over the seedbed or in individual plant cells and press in, but don't bury them.

After germination, they are relatively slow growing, requiring 8 months to make a full 4-inch pot, and 1½ years to make a good-sized one-gallon plant. Damianita is very sensitive to overwatering. Plant the seeds directly into plant cells in the fall and keep them in a cold frame until spring (Gass, personal communication, 1999).

Damianita requires a relatively long time to finish rooting out in the small plant cell. Once it is in a 4-inch pot or one-gallon container, growth rate increases rapidly (Pfeiffer, personal communication, 1999). Damianita does not like pine-bark-based soil mix. The best soil blends include decomposed granite and a minimum of organic material (Kirwin, personal communication, 1999). Lightly tip prune young plants to encourage branching, and reduce the watering after cutting or plants will rot. Seedlings benefit from a slow-release fertilizer in the soil mix, but at the same time tend to get woody quickly in a container, making them less appealing to the consumer (Will, personal communication, 1999). Younger, freshly rooted plants are easier to sell.

Cuttings

Individual or container-grown plants are also easily propagated from softwood cuttings taken in summer, treated with IBA (3,000 ppm) and rooted in separate containers under intermittent mist. Reduce the frequency of misting as soon as rooting occurs to avoid stem rot.

Transplanting

Damianita may be easily transplanted in the winter if cut back and given moisture.

NOTES

The narrow, fragrant, evergreen foliage is reminiscent of the more familiar Mediterranean ground cover, Santolina. However, the blooms of Damianita are showier and more prolific, and the plant is slightly more upright. It is an excellent border plant for a flower bed or a ground cover for hillsides or hot exposed areas like median strips and roadsides. Damianita is especially showy in mass plantings.

Citharexylum berlandieri

Negrito, Fiddlewood, Orcajuela, Encorba Gallina

VERBENACEAE (VERBENA FAMILY)

GENERAL DESCRIPTION

Fiddlewood is a shrub or small tree usually no larger than 18 feet with heavy gray branches and small oval leaves.

FLOWERS AND FRUIT

Clusters of fragrant white flowers are held at the ends of branches, or at the axils of the leaves. Fruit is a round drupe turning orange-red and then black when ripe, each containing two-seeded nutlets. The plant is quite showy when bearing the rich clusters of bright, shiny red fruit.

NATURAL HABITAT, RANGE, AND PREFERRED SITE

Fiddlewood is an uncommon plant native to the palm groves, clay dunes, and thickets in coastal shrub lands of the southern Rio Grande Plains.

Collection and Storage

Fruit ripens throughout the summer, following the intermittent blooms that usually follow rains. Collect the fruit as it turns black and air dry a few days on screens. Keep in paper bags or ventillated containers. Information is lacking on longevity of seed viability.

PROPAGATION

Seeds

Fiddlewood is easily grown from seed, but vegetative production is preferred because cuttings root at almost 100% (McNeal, personal communication, 1999). Depulp the fresh seeds and then aerate them for 1–2 days or until imbibition occurs. Sow thinly on well-drained seed flats in a greenhouse in the fall or outdoors in the spring when the temperatures have warmed (Best, personal communication, 1999).

Cuttings
Fiddlewood is easy to root from softwood cuttings. Make cuttings 3–4 inches long and remove the leaves from the lower half. Treat with IBA (1,500 ppm) and keep under mist. Rooting will occur within 2 weeks. Like its close relative, Lantana, Fiddlewood will make a one-gallon plant from a cutting in 5 months (McNeal, personal communication, 1999).

NOTES

Fiddlewood is cold hardy to San Antonio, though in hard winters it will freeze to the ground, sending up new shoots when the weather turns warm again. Fiddlewood is a desirable landscape plant because even in the hottest, driest weather, the leaves remain glossy green and do not wilt. It prefers south-facing, hot locations. The flowers are fragrant and attract butterflies. The abundant glossy fruit makes a showy contrast against the dark green leaves.

Clematis

Clematis, Virgin-bower, Barba de Viejo

RANUNCULACEAE (CROWFOOT FAMILY)

GENERAL DESCRIPTION

Clematis spp. are herbaceous, perennial vines climbing by means of twining petioles. Leaves are opposite, simple, or variously compound.

FLOWERS AND FRUIT

Clematis bears single flowers or clusters at the ends of branches. Instead of petals, they have petal-like sepals, some showy and colored, and are also distinguished by having numerous extended stamens. Fruit is an achene with a long, feathery style, which in some species (*C. drummondii*) is its showiest feature. The achenes are held in tight clusters and ripen in late summer or early fall.

NATURAL HABITAT, RANGE, AND PREFERRED SITE

Clematis grows on rich soil or shady limestone cliffs, climbing on shrubs, fences, or creek banks throughout much of Texas, the Deep South, and the southwest United States. See Species Descriptions for individual range and habitat. Most species will grow in full sun or light shade.

COLLECTION AND STORAGE

Gather the seeds when they are no longer green but before the cluster of achenes completely dries and the seeds fall to the ground. Seeds may remain viable up to 2 years without refrigeration (Gill and Healy 1974).

PROPAGATION

Seeds

In general, *Clematis* seeds should be planted in containers outdoors in the fall or stratified in moist media at 41° F for 60–90 days. Clematis prospers in fertile, light, loamy soil that is well drained. The seeds should be only lightly covered.

One method recommends sowing multiple seeds of *C. texensis* and *C. pitcheri* in five-gallon pots in the fall following collection. Keep in the container for a year, and then remove them to individual one-gallon containers the following February. Carefully place the crown of the plant just slightly below the soil surface (Janzow, personal communication, 1999).

Cuttings

Clematis is slow to root from cuttings, and roots in low numbers. Cuttings will only root from the nodes. Best results are achieved using semihardwood cuttings with two nodes, taken in spring before the wood snaps when broken (McNeal, personal communication, 1999). Treat the cuttings with 5,000 ppm IBA solution.

Transplanting

Clematis can be transplanted from the field in winter if enough soil is dug around the roots to make an intact root ball. Cut the top back by two-thirds before replanting.

NOTES

The unusual, long-blooming flowers and interesting fuzzy clusters of seeds make this plant a worthy ornamental wherever a delicately branched vine is needed for arbors, trellises, fences, or over other foliage.

There is much variability in the attractiveness of the flowers. Texas Clematis (*C. drummondii*) is a small-flowered woody vine and is not much modified by domestication. However, it is hardy and drought tolerant. *C. texensis* and *C. pitcheri* have the showiest flowers.

Native clematis should be cut back to two or three nodes each winter and should not be overfertilized.

SPECIES DESCRIPTIONS

Clematis drummondii **(Virgin-bower, Old-man's Beard, Barba de Viejo)**
Light, fairly long-spreading, aggressively vine-producing, prolific achenes with long fuzzy tails. *C. drummondii* is native to dry soil along roadsides and rocky canyons in central, south, and west Texas. It is one of the easiest native clematises to grow from seed (McNeal, personal communication, 1999).

Clematis pitcheri **(Pitcher or Purple Clematis)**
Slender, high-climbing vine with dull purple to brick-red-throated, urn-shaped flowers. Purple Clematis grows in thickets, open woodlands, and along streams mostly in central Texas and north to Canada. It is fast grow-

ing and has long-blooming and interesting flowers. It is happiest in dappled light on the edges of woods, but is also fairly heat and drought tolerant. Cold stratify seed before planting.

***Clematis texensis* (Scarlet or Texas Clematis)**
Herbaceous or slightly woody vine with brilliant red, bell-shaped flowers held in one to seven clusters. Endemic to limestone bluffs along streams in the Edwards Plateau. This is the most attractive of all the native clematis species. Does best in full sun and alkaline soil. Blooms occur from early summer to frost. Scarlet Clematis sprouts from base in spring and blooms on new growth. Seed of this *Clematis* has a double-dormancy requirement, and may take up to 18 months to germinate (McNeal, personal communication, 1999).

Clethra alnifolia

White Alder, Sweet Pepper-bush, Summer-Sweet

CLETHRACEAE (WHITE ALDER FAMILY)

GENERAL DESCRIPTION

Sweet Pepper-bush is a small shrub or small tree to 10 feet with brown bark and alternate, oval-toothed leaves. It is a somewhat straggly understory bush, with wandlike ascending branches.

FLOWERS AND FRUIT

Sweet Pepper-bush's showiest feature is the fragrant white or pink flowers which bloom from June to September. They are borne in crowded upright clusters 3–8 inches long. Fruit is a capsule rarely more than ⅛ inch in diameter containing several minute seeds.

NATURAL HABITAT, RANGE, AND PREFERRED SITE

Sweet Pepper-bush grows in swamps, around lakes, and in wet woods and thickets in southeast Texas, east to Florida, and north to Maine. It prefers wet, sandy, acidic soil and partial shade.

COLLECTION AND STORAGE

Collect the capsules by hand from the bush in late summer or early fall when they are no longer green but before they have completely dried and shattered, dispersing the seeds. To remove the seeds, allow the capsule to air dry a few days until it becomes brittle, then gently crush in a bag. Cool dry storage is best. Information on seed longevity is lacking.

PROPAGATION

Seeds

Sow seeds in moist sand or a peat/vermiculite mix outdoors in early spring or late winter in a cold frame or greenhouse. Sweet Pepper-bush germinates best in cool temperatures. Keep the seedbed damp.

Cuttings

Several species of *Clethra* are propagated by softwood cuttings and layers. Basal shoots taken in mid- to late summer often provide the best cutting material (Bailey and Bailey 1947).

NOTES

Sweet Pepper-bush is rarely attacked by insects or diseases (Vines 1970). It should be fertilized every 2–3 years in the spring. Sweet Pepper-bush was introduced into cultivation in 1906. The cultivar, *C. alnifolia var. rosea*, has distinctively pink flowers.

In some regions this plant is known as "poor man's soap" because the flowers, when crushed in water, form a lather (Correll and Johnston 1970).

Colubrina texensis

Hog-plum, Snakewood, Guajalote

RHAMNACEAE (BUCKTHORN FAMILY)

GENERAL DESCRIPTION

Hog-plum is a rounded shrub 3–10 feet tall with small deciduous leaves. Its most interesting feature is the sinuate grooves on the twisting branches of the mature plant, which resemble patterns on a snake's skin.

FLOWERS AND FRUIT

Inconspicuous greenish white flowers are borne singly or in small clusters from late spring to early summer. Fruit is a drupe that separates when ripe into two or three nutlets, each containing one seed. Seed is dark brown, smooth, and shiny when mature.

NATURAL HABITAT, RANGE, AND PREFERRED SITE

Hog-plum is locally abundant in the Rio Grande Plains and less common in north-central Texas, the southern part of the Trans-Pecos, and northern Mexico. Prefers full sun and dry soil. It is cold hardy as far north as Dallas.

COLLECTION AND STORAGE

Gather fruit as it turns black-brown but before it splits apart. The hard fruit may remain on the shrub for many months after it becomes mature. If the pulp is still fleshy, it should be removed or allowed to dry on the seed. Fruit collected later in the season is usually dry enough to store intact with the seed. Cold dry storage is adequate to preserve viability for one season.

PROPAGATION

Seeds

Germination of Hog-plum growing in the northern part of its natural range is often delayed by a dormant seed embryo and hard seed coat. Seed collected from plants in the Rio Grande Valley do not require cold stratification. Scarify the seed for 90 minutes in sulfuric acid (Best, personal communication, 1999). For those seeds requiring cold stratification, store seed immediately after scarification in moist bags of perlite in the refrigerator for 30–40 days prior to sowing. Seed may also be sown directly outdoors in the fall following collection, but expect germination to occur at staggered intervals over two seasons. Hog-plum has a moderate growth rate. Five-month-old seedlings have been successfully transplanted as liners to the field in revegetation projects (Best 1999).

Cuttings

Hog-plum will root from semihardwood tip cuttings taken from the current season's growth and placed under mist. Treat with IBA (5,000 ppm) and remove all leaves from the lower half of the cutting. Rooting occurs within 3 weeks. Specific information on rooting percentages and further production is lacking.

NOTES

Hog-plum is useful as a hedge or border plant in dry, poor locations. It is disease tolerant (Friend 1942). If unpruned, Hog-plum will become lanky and sparsely branched. Selective pruning and removal of dead branches encourages a dense branching habit and more compact growth. The fruit is eaten by birds and other wildlife, including deer and javelina, and the plant also provides an important nesting habitat.

Condalia hookeri

Bluewood Condalia, Brasil, Capul Negro

RHAMNACEAE (BUCKTHORN FAMILY)

GENERAL DESCRIPTION

Brasil is a spiny evergreen shrub or small tree 6–30 feet with multiple stems or trunks. Shiny light green leaves are crowded on spine-tipped branches. Brasils often grow close together, forming impenetrable thickets.

FLOWERS AND FRUIT

Small inconspicuous greenish flowers are followed by purple-black fruit that ripens throughout the summer. Each fleshy drupe contains one small seed.

NATURAL HABITAT, RANGE, AND PREFERRED SITE

Brasil is a major component of the mattoral (shrub land) plant community of the Rio Grande Plains in Texas. It also grows in dry soils and full sun south to northern Mexico, north to Travis County.

COLLECTION AND STORAGE

Because Brasil blooms over a long growing season, ripe fruit can usually be found on the plant from April to October. Collection of large amounts of fruit all at once is sometimes difficult. Gather the fruit when it has turned a black or purplish color. The pulp can either be removed by rubbing on a screen or dried completely on the seed before sowing or storage. Do not try to clean the seed in a blender unless the blades are covered with rubber tubing, or the seeds will be damaged. Information is lacking on optimum storage conditions and seed longevity.

PROPAGATION

Seeds

First-year seeds sown immediately after collection but before they have had a chance to dry will germinate promptly (Lowrey, personal communication, 1986). In one study, Brasil seed from the Rio Grande Valley sown 2–3 months after collection still germinated in good percentages (Best 1999). The longer the seed is stored, the lower its viability.

Brasil seeds collected in the northern part of its range should be stratified for 30 days at 41° F to encourage more uniform germination. Germination is best under moderate temperatures. Germination in south Texas is enhanced by rainfall. Seed may also be sown outdoors in the fall immediately after collection or in early spring for stored seed.

Seeds of a related species, *C. warnockii,* germinated 30% from untreated seed (Manning, personal communication, 1999).

Cuttings

Brasil will root from semihardwood cuttings treated with IBA and placed under intermittent mist. Detailed information on exact techniques is lacking.

Transplanting

Small plants under 3 feet may be transplanted in the winter with little loss in growth if the site is not too rocky for digging (Lowrey, personal communication, 1986).

NOTES

Brasil is rarely completely deciduous. The new leaves appear in early spring as soon as the older leaves finally drop. In south Texas, it is evergreen. With its persistent foliage and dense branching, Brasil makes a good screen, hedge, or wildlife habitat plant. Even in the driest conditions, the Brasil leaves still appear fresh and light green.

The sweet fruit is eaten by the gray fox, raccoon, and various birds, including the bobwhite and scaled quail. The leaves contain about 15% crude protein and are frequently browsed by white-tailed deer (Everitt and Drawe 1993). The wood of this plant yields a blue dye, thus giving the plant one of its common names. Brasil has been successfully planted as far east as Houston (Lowrey, personal communication, 1986).

Cordia boisseri

Wild Olive, Anacahuita

BORAGINACEAE (BORAGE FAMILY)

GENERAL DESCRIPTION

Anacahuita is a small tree with a broadly rounded top and thick, crooked branches. It sometimes forms a tree 30 feet high, but is more often seen as a large multi-trunked shrub.

FLOWERS AND FRUIT

Showy, trumpet-shaped white flowers 3 inches long with a yellow throat are held in loose clusters at the ends of branches. Blooms may appear year round, although the main flowering season is from late spring through early summer, and after rains. The large, papery-white flowers are lovely in contrast to the dark foliage and bare dark stems and trunk. Fruit is a sweet, fleshy drupe maturing July through September and is eaten by wildlife and livestock. Each drupe contains one to three hard oval seeds ¼–½ inch long.

NATURAL HABITAT, RANGE, AND PREFERRED SITE

Anacahuita is native to the plains of far south Texas, from Boca Chica on the lomas near Brownsville, La Sal Vieja, and La Sal del Rey, to McAllen, where it is common along roadsides and stream banks, in thickets, and on gravelly caliche slopes, although some populations in Cameron County are found growing in heavy clays. From Laredo toward Sabinas Hidalgo in Mexico, Anacahuita is a characteristic mattoral (shrub land) species. It is adapted as far north as San Antonio, although in especially cold winters the top branches may freeze back. There are also a few specimens in Austin that are 18 feet tall on a wooded lot and seem to have survived the coldest winters without obvious die-back.

Anacahuita is commonly planted along roadsides and in median strips in the Rio Grande Plains. It prefers full sun and well-drained soil. It is very drought tolerant. Sometimes during extended drought it may drop its leaves but will refoliate when rains return.

COLLECTION AND STORAGE

Collect the fruit as soon as it turns yellowish white or light brown and the seed inside feels hard and filled out. Seeds should be carefully cleaned and air dried before being stored in a cool dry place. Leave the fruit in buckets of water 1–2 days to soften the pulp. Then scrape them on screens with wooden boards. Lisa Williams of the Nature Conservancy developed an ingenious and effective technique for cleaning seeds. She sandwiched the seeds between two ¼-inch screens and then left the screens over a Harvester ant mound. The ants did an excellent job of cleaning the seed (Best, personal communication, 1999). Some growers place the drupes on a board with a specially made groove and then whack them with another board to crack open the hull and extract the seed. While this does release the seed, over half are usually destroyed. Generally Anacahuitas are common enough and prolific enough to make gathering large amounts of seed to compensate for damage possible.

PROPAGATION

Seeds

After-ripening and seed dormancy requirements of Anacahuita seed vary from year to year and also from site to site. Therefore, it is impossible to recommend a single foolproof method that will yield uniform results. Everyone who has worked with Anacahuita has germinated the seed at least once, thinking they have perfected the technique, only to find that future collections do not respond in the same way. What may explain the differences between batches is the degree to which the hulls have been degraded by bacteria and weathering. Fresh, well-cleaned seed that has not had the pulp rotted off naturally over a season or two is difficult to germinate (Best 1999).

Acid scarification does not have consistent success because the thickness of the wooden husk varies with each crop. There seems to be a "trap door" mechanism in each drupe, which is sealed with a gluelike material that keeps water out and thus delays imbibition. Bacteria present in the natural weathering process that seed experience as they fall from the tree and lay on the ground may break down this glue. Some batches germinate in 6 weeks, while others take up to 2 years to sprout. Whatever pretreatment the seed are given, after they begin to germinate, they will come up in 5–10 days, and are very fast growing. Eight- to ten-inch seedlings planted in the fall grew 6–10 feet tall and equally broad in 2 years (Best 1999). These seedlings were not given supplemental irrigation and had to compete with aggressive weeds. One key to their success was that the roots of the seedlings were air pruned and thus the seedlings developed dense, robust root systems.

Anacahuita seedlings will flower in 1–2 years.

Cuttings

Anacahuita may be propagated from softwood or semihardwood cuttings taken in the summer and treated with IBA. These should be 4–6 inches long with the leaves removed from the lower half and placed under intermittent mist.

Transplanting

Small trees under 15 feet have been successfully transplanted from the wild.

NOTES

The showy flowers, dense branching, and persistent foliage make Anacahuita an outstanding ornamental plant for hot, dry areas with mild winters. It is well suited as a specimen plant or in a group along highways and other situations requiring low-maintenance plants. Anacahuita is also an important nectar plant for migrating butterflies.

Cornus

Dogwood

CORNACEAE (DOGWOOD FAMILY)

GENERAL DESCRIPTION

Dogwoods are shrubs or small trees with opposite, prominently veined, deciduous leaves. Slender branches spread to form an open crown.

FLOWERS AND FRUIT

Flower size varies according to species (see Species Descriptions). Each flower has four white, pink, or light green petals. Fruit is a small drupe, either red or white when ripe, containing a two-seeded stone.

NATURAL HABITAT, RANGE, AND PREFERRED SITE

Members of this genus are most often found in open woods and stream banks in the eastern half of the state, west to the Edwards Plateau. See Species Descriptions for individual range and habitat. Dogwoods thrive best in loose loamy soil that contains a fair amount of organic material. Rough-leaf Dogwood, *C. drummondii,* grows best in limestone or alkaline soil, but the other species require acid soil and moist conditions, without which the leaves may appear burned or chronically chlorotic and the overall growth may be stunted.

COLLECTION AND STORAGE

Fruits ripen in late summer or early fall. Rough-leaf Dogwood (*C. drummondii*) can be collected as late as November or December (Hosage, personal communication, 1999). Harvest the seed of Flowering Dogwood (*C. florida*) when the fruit is soft enough to squeeze and release the seed inside. Collection may be competitive with birds and other wildlife that favor the fruit. Seeds may be gathered by hand as soon as ripe by stripping and shaking the branches. Fruits of Flowering Dogwood, *C. florida*, should not be collected from isolated trees because many may be self-sterile and contain empty seeds (USDA 1974).

Remove the pulp before sowing or storage. It is not necessary to remove the seeds from the stones as long as they are carefully air dried. In one report, clean, air-dried stones of Flowering Dogwood have been stored in sealed containers at 38–41° F for 2–3 years without significant loss in viability (USDA 1974).

PROPAGATION

Seeds

The seeds may be sown immediately outdoors after collection in the fall or stratified for 30–60 days at 41° F and sown the following spring. Natural germination of untreated seeds usually occurs in the spring, but sometimes seeds will not germinate until the second spring following seed fall.

Germination of Rough-leaf Dogwood is delayed by embryo dormancy and an impermeable pericarp (stone). The stones should first be soaked in sulfuric acid for 1–3 hours, depending on seed lot. Follow scarification with cold stratification for 60–90 days (Hosage, personal communication, 1999). Warm stratification at 68° F for at least 60 days may be substituted for the acid treatment, though usually with less uniform results.

Cover the seeds with ¼–½ inch of fine, loose soil. Seeds sown outdoors should be mulched over winter until germination begins.

Cuttings

Dogwoods will root from softwood or semihardwood cuttings taken in summer, hardwood cuttings in winter, and suckers and divisions and by layering in early spring (Gill and Healy 1974). Cuttings of juvenile wood root best. Semihardwood cuttings 4–5 inches long of *C. drummondii* rooted nearly 100% after being treated with 3,000–5,000 ppm IBA (McNeal, personal communication, 1999). Seedlings tend to be more treelike, with a single leader than plants produced from cuttings. Cuttings require 18 months to make a five-gallon container plant. Periodic light tip pruning after each flush of growth is helpful in developing a tree with stronger branching and better overall shape (Pfeiffer, personal communication, 1999).

Softwood or semihardwood cuttings of Flowering Dogwood should be taken from terminal shoot tips in early summer. These should be 5–6 inches long with a terminal pair of leaflets and the bottom leaves removed. Wound the cuttings and treat with 0.3–2.0% IBA talc. Place in well-drained media under mist and expect rooting to occur in 5–8 weeks at high percentages. Leave rooted cuttings of this species in the cutting bed over winter before transplanting into separate containers early the following spring. Cuttings that were lifted too soon reported 90% mortality (Dirr and Heuser 1987).

Rooting in individual containers from the start might be worthwhile. Once the cuttings have rooted, they should be regularly fertilized with a dilute solution of soluble fertilizer and kept in the rooting bed several months. Selecting tip (terminal) stems for cutting material is important because their rooting percentages are highest and they produce a straight-trunked tree.

Dogwoods can also be successfully grafted during the winter or early spring months. Selection of the scions should be restricted to wood of the previous growing season. Scions may be collected 3–4 weeks in advance and stored in plastic bags with sphagnum moss to prevent drying. The scions should be about the same diameter as a pencil, 8–12 inches long, with three or four buds. These may be grafted using any of the common techniques, such as whip and tongue, side, or bare-root.

Attempts to graft the Flowering Dogwood onto the more drought- and alkaline-soil-tolerant Rough-leaf Dogwood have not yet proven to be successful. Rough-leaf Dogwood is often rhizomatous and may be increased from root cuttings.

Transplanting

Dogwoods transplant better with a root ball than they do bare rooted. Rough-leaf Dogwood is easily transplanted because of its spreading, rhizomatous roots. Field-grown plants, 2–3 years old, are suitable for potting into large containers or for moving to a permanent location. Dogwoods should be planted out in late winter or no later than early spring. Prune only after flowering in late spring.

NOTES

The name "Dogwood" comes from an old use of the plant. A decoction of a related species, *C. sanguinea*, was used in England to wash mangy dogs. This genus contains one of the most attractive native ornamentals, Flowering Dogwood, from which many superior horticultural selections have been bred.

Flowering Dogwood is helpful in limiting movement of nutrients, particularly calcium, through the soil profile and keeping them available in the rooting zone of other species. The leaves of dogwoods decompose rapidly and help to rebuild the soil (Gill and Healy 1974). Dogwoods also provide valuable food for a number of species of wildlife.

SPECIES DESCRIPTIONS

Cornus drummondii **(Rough-leaf Dogwood)**

Shrub or small tree to 16 feet with creamy yellow flowers and clusters of hard white fruit. Damp woodlands, thickets, and creeksides in alkaline soil in the eastern half of Texas, east to Florida. Rough-leaf Dogwood is a good plant to use for erosion control along stream banks or woodland slopes because it tends to sucker from lateral roots and form thickets. For this same reason, it is not a good landscape plant for a shrub border or near a lawn. Fruit is eaten by several birds. The leaves turn maroon in the fall.

Cornus florida **(Flowering Dogwood)**

Large shrub or small tree to 38 feet with a spreading crown and large, showy white or sometimes pink flowers. In woodlands in east Texas, adapted west to central Texas if planted in acid soil and given adequate water. Does best in fertile, well-drained soil with a light texture. Flowering Dogwood was first cultivated in 1731. One-year seedlings can be transplanted to most sites. The leaves are dark green in the spring, turning to scarlet and crimson in the fall. Seeds turn a bright red also in the fall. Seeds eaten by many birds.

Cornus racemosa **(Gray Dogwood)**

Shrub or small tree to 16 feet, often forming thickets, with small greenish white flowers in open cymes. Young twigs are reddish. Moist or wet soil on slopes in thickets and along streams in east Texas north to New England. Will adapt to drier sites and is used in erosion control, wildlife habitats, and as bird food.

Cotinus obovatus

Smoke Tree

ANACARDIACEAE (SUMAC FAMILY)

GENERAL DESCRIPTION

Smoke Tree is a small deciduous tree or tall multi-trunked shrub reaching 32 feet. Bark is grayish and scaly, and the wood is hard. The oval-shaped leaves are smooth and glaucous-green in summer, turning gold, scarlet, and orange in the fall. Spectacular fall color is often more impressive than spring flowering.

FLOWERS AND FRUIT

Smoke Tree flowers from April to May and is covered with fluffy pink "smoke" created by the fuzzy pink petioles of the inconspicuous flowers crowded at the ends of the branches. Flowers are staminate, pistillate, or perfect. The seeds are less than ⅙ inch in diameter.

NATURAL HABITAT, RANGE, AND PREFERRED SITE

Smoke Tree occurs on the hard limestone of Bandera, Kendall, Kerr, and Uvalde counties in the Edwards Plateau. It is a relict tree from the Miocene epoch approximately 25 million years ago (Simpson 1988). At one time, its distribution extended continuously north to Arkansas and Missouri, and northeastern Alabama. Smoke Tree prefers full sun and well-drained alkaline soil. It is adapted as far north as Dallas, but to thrive there, it must be given south-wall protection. If planted in rich soil and fertilized, Smoke Tree may become brittle and easily damaged in windstorms.

COLLECTION AND STORAGE

Seeds ripen shortly after the flowers bloom and are quickly dispersed by wind, usually by the end of May (Janzow, personal communication, 1999). Seed quantity and quality can vary markedly from year to year and also across populations. Collect the seeds in late April by clipping the entire fruiting panicle from the tree. Since the seeds of Smoke Tree are often infertile or empty, large amounts of seeds must be collected in order to produce a reasonable number of seedlings.

Test seed viability immediately after collection by flotation. Discard any seeds that float. Spread the seeds out in thin layers to air dry a few days before storing or planting. When dried, the fuzzy panicles will detach and may be separated by light beating of the seeds in a bag.

Seeds of a related species, European Smoke Tree (*C. coggygria*), have been stored satisfactorily for several years in sealed containers at room temperature (USDA 1974).

PROPAGATION

Seeds

Smoke Tree germinates best from freshly gathered or first-year seeds. Germination is delayed because of a hard seed coat and a dormant embryo. Germination rates of almost 90% were achieved when the seeds were first scarified for 25 minutes in concentrated sulfuric acid followed by cold moist stratification in screened perlite for 60 days in the refrigerator. Seeds were pretreated in November and removed from cold stratification in March. They were kept at room temperature still in the bags of perlite for a few weeks before sowing into individual containers (38-count "Pro-Trays") at the first of February. The seed trays were kept in the greenhouse, and seedlings began to emerge in 2–3 weeks. Seedlings were transplanted into one-gallon containers in April and were ready to sell as one-gallon plants by the end of August. Seedlings prefer light shade (Janzow, personal communication, 1999).

Another method recommended soaking the seeds in concentrated sulfuric acid for only 15 minutes followed by stratification for 60–80 days at 38–41° F (McNeal, personal communication, 1999).

One grower suggests 30 minutes of acid scarification. Testing the seed in batches at 15-minute intervals may provide the optimum time for acid treatment, if seeds are abundant. Seeds sown outdoors following collection without treatment may take two springs to germinate.

With some seed lots, warm moist stratification at 68° F for 150 days has been substituted for acid scarification, although with less successful results.

Smoke Tree seedlings are very slow growing, and young plants are extremely sensitive to both desiccation and damping-off fungi encouraged by excessively wet soil. Regular applications of fungicide are recommended. The soil media should be well drained but not arid. Cover the seeds with ¼ inch of soil and gently press in before watering. Seeds sown outdoors should be covered with a light mulch until germination begins.

Pretreated seeds of Smoke Tree may be planted indoors in late winter or outdoors in early spring. Seeds must be planted well before the onset of hot weather. Early emerging seedlings may need cold-frame protection.

Young trees in nursery production often suffer from root girdling. Air-root pruning and application of beneficial microorganisms such as biological microorganisms may make a big difference in speeding up shoot growth as well as survival of the plant as it is moved up to larger containers or into the landscape. The potting soil must be extremely well drained, and adding a mineral component to the mix such as decomposed granite has proven beneficial in some cases (Kirwin, personal communication, 1999). Once Smoke Tree has reached a five-gallon size, lightly tip prune the branches to encourage sturdier growth and a tighter form.

Cuttings

Smoke Trees are most successfully rooted from succulent softwood cuttings taken in May right after flowering. These should be green but beginning to harden off at the base of last year's growth. One method used 5,000 ppm IBA solution and achieved rooting in 10–14 days.

New roots tend to be brittle, so it is important to use a light soil mix. However, straight coarse perlite was unsuitable because it promoted fewer, less-branched brittle roots than a mix having some peat or sterile soil mix in combination with perlite (Pfeiffer, personal communication, 1999).

Another method recommends making a 45° angle cut on the cutting followed by treatment with 5,000 ppm IBA/NAA "quick-dip" solution. Cuttings broke new roots from the internode usually within in 30 days (Hosage, personal communication, 1999).

Still another grower achieved rooting rates of 70% using alcohol-based rooting hormone solution and individual containers which were better for transplanting the brittle-rooted cuttings (McNeal, personal communication, 1999).

Cuttings made from juvenile wood, adventitious shoots, or suckers have also been rooted, but at lower rates. Woodier cuttings tended to rot in the mist bench (Pfeiffer, personal communication, 1999).

After cuttings have reached 15 inches or so, prune them back by one-third to encourage branching. A cutting made in the spring will become a one-gallon container by late summer. Do not try to move the plant into larger containers while temperatures are still high. Better results are achieved when plants are moved up in late fall or winter into five-gallon containers (Pfeiffer, personal communication, 1999).

Transplanting

The rocky sites where Smoke Trees habitually grow make them difficult to transplant from the wild.

NOTES

Smoke Tree is a unique, small flowering tree. It is ornamental in every season. In spring it is covered in a cloud of red or purplish flower stems. In the fall the leaves turn brilliant shades of burnished gold, orange, or scarlet. In winter and all year round, the dark flaking bark, gnarled and twisted limb structure, and overall interesting habit contribute to its value as an outstanding specimen plant. It is drought and disease tolerant and will grow in many different locations. In nature it looks its best when it grows on the north side of hills in partial shade or on the east sides of steep canyons where it is protected from harsh afternoon sun (Janzow, personal communication, 1999). Deer are fond of browsing this plant, which accounts for its scarcity in the Hill Country.

Cotinus is the ancient Greek name for the olive tree; its inner red wood is similar to that of the Smoke Tree. The wood of Smoke Tree produced a water-soluble orange-brown dye that was in great demand during the Civil War. The wood is very durable, and many Smoke Trees were cut down to make fence posts and tool handles.

Coursetia axillaris

Baby Bonnets, Couaxi, Coursetia

FABACEAE (LEGUME FAMILY)

GENERAL DESCRIPTION

Coursetia is a compact, densely branched shrub or small tree 3–9 feet tall with a cluster of stems, each about an inch thick rising from the base, spreading out in a vase-shaped form. The young branches are ashen in color, covered with flat, bristly hairs, yet without thorns. The leaves are pinnately compound, consisting of three to five pairs of small, oval leaflets. Coursetia freely coppices from the root collar without being cut. Once it reaches a certain height, instead of growing taller, it produces more stems from the base, reaching a maximum of 12 feet across. The leaf morphology of Coursetia changes with the amount of water and sunlight it receives. Under irrigation and in partial shade, the leaves are large and glabrous, and in dry sunny locations (its more typical habitat), the leaves are small and pubescent. During severe drought and hard freezes, the plant will defoliate (Best 1999).

FLOWERS AND FRUIT

The majority of flowers appears in February and may vary from magenta to pink or whitish flowers within the same population. They are borne singly or in short clusters. Each flower is delicate, sweet-pea shaped, and develops into a small (1–2 inch), flat reddish brown legume, containing one to five seeds. Seed ripens in March and April and can appear on the plant at the same time as the flowers. Coursetia will flower by the second year in its native habitat, and with more care under cultivation, blooms may appear the first year.

NATURAL HABITAT, RANGE, AND PREFERRED SITE

C. axillaris is a peripheral and rare plant in Texas, found infrequently in scrubby vegetation on caliche ridges in the Rio Grande Plains in south Texas. It is also found in Mexico in Tamaulipas. Twenty miles south of Reynosa it becomes a common roadside plant. In the Rio Grande Delta, Coursetia is most often found growing in small, isolated populations of a few dozen to a few hundred plants (Best, personal communication, 1999). It is largely restricted to well-drained sites (rather than flat, alluvial flood plains) in full sun. Coursetia tolerates limey soils such as caliche and also shows some tolerance of salinity.

COLLECTION AND STORAGE

As the pod dries, it twists open slightly to drop the seed. To avoid losing the seed, begin collection when the pods turn brown, but before they have completely dried. Spread the small pods between two ⅛-inch screens to complete the drying. Seeds will dehisce naturally if left in the sun.

PROPAGATION

Seeds

The seeds can be tested for viability by soaking in water (see Chapter III). Seed exposed to the sun for several months usually imbibe water immediately. For those batches of seed that resist imbibition, careful quick scarification for 1–5 minutes in 93% technical grade sulfuric acid followed by aeration for a minimum of 1–2 days or until imbibition occurs is effective (Best 1999).

Hot water scarification is not recommended. By the time the seeds have been exposed to 100° F water long enough to imbibe water (4 minutes), most have been damaged.

Simple weathering of the seed a few months in sunlight followed by aeration is usually sufficient pretreatment.

The length of time necessary for aeration will vary from one collection to the next. Some will imbibe in 15 minutes while others may take a day or two. Sow immediately in pregermination trays (see Chapter III). Check the seed while in the pregermination trays and each day remove and plant those seeds which have imbibed.

Gently press seed ¼ inch deep into individual containers. Be careful not to bury the seed. Seed will complete germination in 4–10 days (Best 1999).

NOTES

The delicate pink sweet-pea–like flowers covering the plant, the dense irregular form, and extreme drought tolerance combine to make Coursetia a desirable addition to a naturalistic landscape. It can be planted as a hedge or used as a large airy specimen shrub. It should not be sheared, except to remove dead branches. Coursetia tends to be slow growing and must be planted in full sun in well-drained soil.

Cowania ericaefolia

Heath Cliff-rose

ROSACEAE (ROSE FAMILY)

GENERAL DESCRIPTION

Heath Cliff-rose is an intricately branched evergreen shrub reaching 3 feet. The bark is dark brown and fissured, and the evergreen leaves are small and needle-like, gathered in clusters along the stem.

FLOWERS AND FRUIT

Flowers characteristic of the Rose family are held at the ends of short branches. The petals are creamy white or yellowish, appearing from April to October, usually after rains. The flowers have a fragrance like musk roses and are attractive to honeybees and other insects. Fruit is also showy; 5–12 achenes are held together in a feathery cluster by silver or tawny-colored styles, each ½ to 1½ inch long. These showy plumes aid in spreading the seeds by the wind. A single flower may produce as many as 10 plumed achenes.

NATURAL HABITAT, RANGE, AND PREFERRED SITE

Heath Cliff-rose is found growing in crevices among limestone boulders at elevations of 2,400–4,600 feet in the mountains of the Trans-Pecos, west to California, through Nevada, Utah, and Arizona, and into western New Mexico and southwestern Colorado.

COLLECTION AND STORAGE

Collect seed after the blooming periods that occur intermittently throughout the summer, especially after rains. Air dry before storage. After drying, the plumes can be rubbed off.

PROPAGATION

Seeds

Heath Cliff-rose seeds have an internal dormancy that can be broken by moist chilling the seeds for 2–3 months prior to planting in cool soil in

March or April. Seeds planted without pretreatment germinated at rates of 20% (Manning, personal communication, 1999).

Seedlings are slow growing and require careful lifting from the flat to liners. They must have a well-drained mineral soil. Small seedlings do not thrive in extreme temperatures, so it is important to propagate the seeds as early as possible to get them established. Provide light shade for the first year.

Cuttings

Semihardwood cuttings taken from May/June and treated with 3,000–5,000 ppm IBA root best. The biggest challenge is to find enough new wood on these slow-growing desert plants from which to take cuttings. Rooting can be slow and erratic. Keep rooted cuttings in a one-gallon container for a year before planting out (McNeal, personal communication, 1999).

NOTES

This plant is sometimes confused with Apache Plume (*Fallugia paradoxa*), which also has plumed seeds. Heath Cliff-rose is most often seen as a small tree or larger shrub with deep-branching taproots that anchor the soil between rocks and help it survive dry spells. It will look better in the summer if given a deep watering monthly, but be careful not to overwater it, especially if the soils are heavy.

Heath Cliff-rose looks best at higher elevations with cooler summer nights. Moving it to areas of high rainfall and humidity encourage it to sprawl and suffer from root rot. It is tolerant of temperatures below zero. The leaves of Heath Cliff-rose have resinous compounds that give it a bitter taste and pungent odor, yet despite these chemicals it is still browsed by deer, especially in the winter. Heath Cliff-rose is also the sole diet of the Fotis hairstreak, a small, dark brown butterfly (Bowers 1993).

Crataegus

Hawthorn

ROSACEAE (ROSE FAMILY)

GENERAL DESCRIPTION

The hawthorns represent a taxonomically complex and controversial group of small trees and multi-stemmed shrubs. See Species Descriptions for individual descriptions.

FLOWERS AND FRUIT

Hawthorn flowers are characteristic of the rose family. They appear either in early spring before the leaves emerge or in early summer. Fruit is a berrylike pome turning red, blue, or yellow when ripe. Spring-blooming species ripen in early summer, while later-flowering species ripen after mid-September. Summer-ripening fruits usually have a soft, pulpy flesh that quickly decomposes. Fall-ripening fruits may remain hard until the following spring, even after dropping from the parent plants (see Species Descriptions).

NATURAL HABITAT, RANGE, AND PREFERRED SITE

Most Texas hawthorns grow in the eastern third of the state in open woods, fencerows, stream banks, and on the edges of fields. A few species occur in the mountains of west Texas and northern Mexico. See Species Descriptions for individual range and habitat.

COLLECTION AND STORAGE

Fruits may be hand-picked or shaken from the plant from mid-summer until the first frost, depending on species. Clean the seeds from the pulp to avoid mold and fermentation. Large amounts of seeds may be cleaned in a mechanical macerator. Air dry seeds at room temperature 1 or 2 days before storing. Store seeds in sealed containers at 45° F. The cleaned seed may be stored in sealed containers for 2–3 years in the refrigerator.

PROPAGATION

Seeds

Propagation of *Crataegus* can be problematic because some species have an immature embryo that requires a period of warm stratification to complete after-ripening. This period of after-ripening may or may not be combined with a cold dormancy requirement and a hard seed coat. It is common for hawthorn seeds to require a combination of scarification and various periods of cold and warm stratification before they will germinate.

Germination is often slow and in low percentages. To achieve maximum germination rates for many species of *Crataegus*, a three-step pretreatment process must be followed. First, the seed should be scarified in concentrated sulfuric acid. Next, the seed should be placed in warm moist storage for up to 120 days or planted outdoors in early fall. Finally, the seeds should be exposed to cold temperatures by remaining outdoors or by being held in cold storage for 100–300 days.

Some species, like Mayhaw (*C. opaca*) and Parsley Hawthorn (*C. marshallii*), require no scarification prior to stratification. Consult Species Descriptions for known guidelines for particular plants. Seeds held in dry storage and planted without pretreatment in the spring seldom germinate well. Germination of hawthorns is often staggered and may begin while the seeds are still in cold stratification.

For eastern species, the seedbed should contain a well-drained soil mix with a high proportion of well-cured compost or organic matter. Apply a light mulch to conserve moisture until germination is well advanced. Do not leave young plants in the seedbed for longer than 1 year because they form long roots and then are hard to transplant. Seedlings are relatively slow growing and subject to many soil-borne pathogens while young.

Cuttings

Hawthorns are difficult and slow to root. Some of the rhizomatous species have been propagated from root cuttings. Cuttings of *Crataegus* are rarely successful (Dirr and Heuser 1987).

NOTES

Hawthorns have many attributes that make them outstanding landscape plants. However, research is needed to develop successful propagation methods so that nursery production for more of our native species is feasible. Hawthorns make good screens and hedges. The flowers, fruit, and foliage are both ornamental and important to wildlife. They are tolerant of a number of different sites and have been used to stabilize spoil banks, make shelter beds, and to achieve other forms of erosion control.

Several hawthorns have been in cultivation. Hawthorn fruits are consumed by a number of birds and animals, and their foliage provides cover for wildlife.

Hawthorns benefit from frequent pruning. Side branches should be pruned severely to encourage mature plants to be full at the center; hawthorns should also be trained to a single trunk (Bailey and Bailey 1947).

SPECIES DESCRIPTIONS

***Crataegus brachyacantha* (Blueberry Hawthorn)**

Tree to 48 feet with oblong leaves, numerous white flowers, and bright blue fruit ripening in August and September. Found in rich soil near streams in east Texas, Louisiana, and Arkansas.

***Crataegus crus-galli* (Cockspur Hawthorn)**

Shrub or tree to 26 feet with clusters of showy white flowers and greenish or dull red fruit ripening in October. Limestone bluffs and hilltops, thickets, and fencerows in east and north-central Texas. Hard seeds require acid scarification for 2–3 hours followed by warm stratification at 70° F for 21 days, and finally cold stratification at 36° F for 21–135 days (USDA 1974).

***Crataegus marshallii* (Parsley Hawthorn)**

Shrub or small tree to 25 feet with slender, thorny, or sometimes thornless branches. Leaves sharply lobed. Flowers numerous, held in dense cymes, followed by bright red fruit ripening in September and October. Sandy woods and hillsides in east Texas to Harris County, east to Florida. Collect the fruit in late fall or early winter. Stratify in perlite for 90 days, then sow individually into "bullet tubes." Germination rates are usually excellent. From a rooted bullet tube to a finished one-gallon takes 8 months (Bronstad, personal communication, 1999).

***Crataegus opaca* (Mayhaw)**

Shrub or small tree to 28 feet. Very showy pink or white flowers held in clusters in February. Fruit rosy red, large, ripening in late April through May. Most often near swamps or in low ground filled with water part of the year in east Texas to Alabama. Fruit is eaten by birds and also makes an exceptionally delicious preserve. Mayhaw can be planted as an ornamental shrub or hedge for a poorly drained, shady place.

Collect seeds in April or May, clean, and sow immediately. Fresh seed planted before the seed has air dried will germinate in high percentages.

Drying appears to induce dormancy. If the seeds stay in the fruit or sit in a bag, they will require another year to germinate. Once the seedlings are rooted in a bullet tube, they grow fairly quickly. For orchard production, space the trees at intervals of 20 feet. Mayhaw will adapt to any site with deep soil that would also accommodate an apple, pear, or peach tree.

***Crataegus reverchonii* (Reverchon's Hawthorn)**
Tree 20–26 feet with dark oval leaves and white flowers, 1 inch across, held in showy compact corymbs in spring. Plant is sometimes multi-trunked with reddish peeling bark. Berries are bright red and persistent after the leaves fall. In deep soil in rich woods in northeast Texas. Sun and partial shade.

***Crataegus spathulata* (Little-hip Hawthorn)**
Shrub or tree 16–22 feet high with oval leaves having a conspicuous winged petiole near the base. White flowers and yellow fruit. Sandy or sandy clay woods in east Texas to Florida.

***Crataegus tracyi* (Mountain Hawthorn)**
Bushy tree, 14 feet, with oval leaves, corymbs of 7–10 flowers, and orange-red fruit ripening in September and October. Endemic to rocky banks of streams in the Edwards Plateau and the Trans-Pecos. Seeds of Mountain Hawthorn require 4½ hours of acid scarification followed by up to 60 days of warm stratification and 100–320 days of cold stratification. This species germinates best at relatively low temperatures, and seeds often germinate while still in cold stratification and then must be removed individually.

***Crataegus viburnifolia* (Viburnum Hawthorn)**
Tree to 35 feet with gray scaly bark and unarmed branchlets. Leaves large ovate or oval. Flowers opening in March in corymbs of 5–12 blossoms, followed by large yellow fruit. Endemic to low wet woods in southeast Texas, especially near the bottomlands of the Brazos River near Wharton and Columbia. Named for the large viburnum-like leaves. Seeds stratified over winter germinate promptly in spring without scarification.

Cupressus arizonica var. arizonica

Arizona Cypress, Arizona Rough Cypress, Cedro Blanco, Pinobete, Cedro de la Sierra

CUPRESSACEAE (CYPRESS FAMILY)

GENERAL DESCRIPTION

Arizona Cypress is an evergreen tree that can grow to 90 feet when located in protected canyons, though typically it is less than half that size. The trunk can be as large as 5 feet in diameter with short horizontal branches forming a fairly tight conical shape in the younger tree, gradually opening up as the tree matures. The bark on the young branches breaks into thin irregular scales, and on the older trunk and branches, it peels off in long shreds, revealing a very attractive smooth mahogany or cinnamon-colored underbark.

FLOWERS AND FRUIT

Male and female flowers appear in spring on different branches on the same tree. Fruit is a cone ¾–1 inch long, carrying numerous dark reddish-brown seeds. The cone matures in the second season, and old cones are persistent.

NATURAL HABITAT, RANGE, AND PREFERRED SITE

In Texas, Arizona Cypress is known only from high forested canyons in the Chisos Mountains in the Big Bend National Park in Brewster County. It is not known why Arizona Cypress occurs only in this location in Texas. The group in the park is a healthy reproducing population, with many seedlings evident on the forest floor of the canyon (Simpson 1988). Its range extends into southwest New Mexico, west to southern California and northern New Mexico.

Arizona Cypress will adapt to a variety of sites, but does best at altitudes of 3,000–8,000 feet in dry, well-drained soil on slopes in the sun. Arizona Cypress has been used as a shade tree in some of the world's hottest, driest locations. It is the most widely planted tree in west Texas and the southern High Plains, used both as a dense windbreak and a specimen tree (Simpson 1988). Arizona Cypress can be grown in most regions of the state. It is tolerant of full sun, reflected heat and light, and, once it is established, can survive on as little as 15 inches of rainfall a year. It has some tolerance of salty irrigation and is very adaptable to a variety of soil pH. Overwatering and overfertilization can promote excess and weak growth.

COLLECTION AND STORAGE

Seed production is generally prolific each year, with the cones persisting on the branches through the winter. Seeds also remain attached inside the cone for several years with their viability intact. Cones contain about 48–112 seeds each. Mature cones are brown, the older ones gray. Remove the seeds by drying on wire racks. Seed may be stored for 2–3 years in sealed containers at 40° F (Vines 1970). A pound of cleaned seed contains about 40,000 seeds, with a commercial purity of 82% and a soundness of 55%.

PROPAGATION

Seeds

Fresh seed readily germinates without pretreatment (Manning, personal communication, 1999). Seed may be planted without pretreatment, but stratification in moist sand at 41° F for 60 days may unify and hasten germination.

In field production, stratified seed is planted in springs in drills and covered with about ¼ inch of soil. Germination usually occurs in 2–3 weeks after spring planting. Plants grow best in deep, well-drained sandy loam that has some mineral component such as decomposed granite. Young seedlings are very susceptible to damping-off fungi.

Cuttings

Arizona Cypress can also be rooted from cuttings taken from juvenile wood (trees under 5 years old). Take 3–4 inch softwood cuttings just before growth resumes in early spring. Remove the sideshoots from the base of the cuttings, and treat with IBA (5,000 ppm). Stick in a peat/perlite medium. Rooting percentages are not usually very high (Dirr and Heuser 1987).

Root under mist with bottom heat (68° F). Semihardwood cuttings taken in late summer or early fall have also been used. Often it will take a long time for any rooting activity to appear in cuttings taken in autumn. They will form root initials over the winter and will root only as new growth is made in the following early summer.

Transplanting

Arizona Cypress can be transplanted from the field in winter if the root ball is kept intact. Large specimens (over 15 feet) do not like to be moved.

NOTES

Arizona Cypress was first cultivated in 1822. There have been many horticultural selections made over the years. These include 'Carolina Sapphire,' which is more adaptable to eastern humid areas. 'Silver Smoke' has an Italian Cypress-like columnal form. 'Blue Ice' has distinctive blue-green foliage, as its name suggests. Possibilities of other selections, such as one with dark green foliage, have not been exhausted (Ogden, personal communication, 1999).

Arizona Cypress grows rapidly (2 feet a year once established) in good soils with adequate (but not excessive) moisture, and slower in more xeric conditions with poor soil. The main enemies of Arizona Cypress are bark beetles and spider mites in the summer. Drought-stressed trees are susceptible to borers. The silvery-gray foliage, especially in the younger tree, makes an extraordinary contrast with the deep burnished red underbark of the trunk. Arizona Cypress is an excellent specimen tree or companion to plants with dark green foliage such as Mountain Laurel (*Sophora secundiflora*), Evergreen sumac (*Rhus virens*), Pointleaf Manzanita (*Arctostaphylos pungens*), and Wright's Silk Tassel (*Garrya wrightii*).

Cyrilla racemiflora

Leatherwood

CYRILLACEAE (LEATHERWOOD FAMILY)

GENERAL DESCRIPTION

Leatherwood is a tall shrub or occasionally a small tree 32 feet tall with a short trunk and spreading branches. Glossy evergreen leaves turn scarlet and orange in the fall.

FLOWERS AND FRUIT

Fragrant white flowers hang in slender racemes or clusters at the ends of branches in early summer. Flowers and size of racemes may vary greatly from plant to plant. The fruit is an ovoid yellowish brown capsule, ⅛ inch long, containing a single minute globose seed. Fruit ripens late summer to early fall.

NATURAL HABITAT, RANGE, AND PREFERRED SITE

Leatherwood is native to swamps and such other low, wet places as bottomlands, pine barrens, and along stream banks in southeast Texas, and east along the coast to Florida. Leatherwood requires consistent moisture and very acid soils.

COLLECTION AND STORAGE

In nature the seeds are quickly but not uniformly dispersed. In late summer, capsules nearing maturity should be clipped from the branches before they dry and split open. Store in paper bags until the capsules complete drying, then slightly crush to release the seeds. Remove the seeds from the capsules and store in sealed containers in the refrigerator. Germination is best when seeds are planted immediately after collection.

PROPAGATION

Seeds

Sow freshly gathered seed in a flat filled with light potting soil. On top of the flat, spread a thin layer of moist sphagnum moss. Press the seed into the sphagnum and lightly water in. Germination will occur within 2 months. The fungicidal properties of sphagnum moss prevent damping off. Seedlings tend to grow out irregularly. Sow seeds extremely thickly to encourage crowding and etiolation, otherwise seedlings tend to be spindly and floppy. Sparsely sown seedlings may require staking. Leave them in the flat for a whole year. The September following seed collection, bare-root the seedlings directly into one-gallon containers (Bronstad, personal communication, 1999).

Cuttings

Semihardwood cuttings taken in late summer and treated with 1.0% IBA rooted in high percentages (Dirr and Heuser 1987). Softwood cuttings from a 4-year-old plant also rooted well when treated with 3,000 ppm IBA solution. Stick the cuttings in a peat/perlite mixture and keep under mist. Cuttings reportedly transplant readily and grow quickly. Root cuttings taken in winter will also root. Rooting usually occurs within 8 weeks (Doran 1957).

Transplanting

Suckers or offshoots of older plants can sometimes be separated into clumps and relocated. Exact information on rates of successful transplanting from the field is not available.

NOTES

Leatherwood leaves remain mostly green and persistent throughout the year in the southern part of its range. The hardy foliage and delicate racemes of white flowers make Leatherwood worthy of cultivation, especially in low poorly drained locations. The flowers provide a source of food for bees. Under ideal conditions Leatherwood might form a thicket. Because flowers appear on the previous season's growth, prune flowers only right after blooming.

Dalea

Dalea

FABACEAE (LEGUME FAMILY)

GENERAL DESCRIPTION

Daleas are annual or perennial herbs or low unarmed shrubs. Species listed here have small compound leaves that are sometimes covered with fine hairs, giving the plant a silver or gray appearance. Foliage may also be gland dotted and aromatic.

FLOWERS AND FRUIT

Dalea flowers bloom over a long season and are usually showy (see Species Descriptions). Fruit is a one- or two-seeded small indehiscent pod, ripening intermittently throughout the season.

NATURAL HABITAT, RANGE, AND PREFERRED SITE

All daleas mentioned here prefer full sun and well-drained soil. Most are native to gravelly or rocky slopes (see Species Descriptions).

COLLECTION AND STORAGE

Collect the pods from summer to early fall when they are no longer green and are beginning to dry. Pods will appear at the same time as flowers, and not all will be ripe at the same time. Mature seeds will be firm, filled out, and brown. It is difficult but necessary to separate the tiny seeds from the pods before sowing because the pods delay germination. It is not necessary to separate them before storage. If the pods are sufficiently dry, they may be placed in a bag and lightly crushed to release the seeds. Fumigate the seeds before storage. Storage in sealed containers at room temperature is sufficient for at least 1 year.

PROPAGATION

Seeds

Daleas are easily grown from untreated seeds. Sow in early spring in a greenhouse or outdoors after all danger of frost is past. *Dalea* seeds germinate best in warm soil. Seedlings usually emerge within 1–3 weeks.

The seed flat or bed should contain well-drained soil, and care should be taken not to overwater. Seedlings may be transplanted to one-gallon containers when they are 6 inches tall.

Cuttings

Daleas are easiest to produce from cuttings (McNeal, personal communication, 1999). They will root from semihardwood cuttings taken in summer or early fall from wood of the current season's growth. These should be 3–4 inches long and slightly woody toward the base. Treat with IBA (3,000–5,000 ppm) and place under mist. As the cutting begins to callus and form roots, reduce the frequency of misting to encourage it to harden off and avoid stem rot. Rooting is usually accomplished in 4–5 weeks.

Transplanting

Daleas are difficult to transplant from the field because the rocky soils where they typically grow make it hard to remove all the roots intact.

NOTES

Daleas are useful and attractive ornamentals because of their delicate, often silver-gray foliage, and prolific blue or purple flowers. They are able to grow in poor soil and dry conditions. Several species are low growing and especially suitable as a ground cover for stabilizing slopes or rocky sites. Once established, daleas require little maintenance.

Like many perennial shrubs, daleas will produce more blooms and their shapes will be improved if the plants are cut back severely each spring. Daleas should not be fertilized or overwatered because that causes them to be leggy, weak, and to bear fewer blooms. The aromatic glands on the leaves of some species make them less palatable to deer.

Selection of several outstanding Mexican forms of Dalea have been made by Mountain States Wholesale Nursery in Phoenix, Arizona, indicating that the potential of this genus for ornamental forms adaptable to both dry climates and nursery culture has not been exhausted.

SPECIES DESCRIPTIONS

Dalea bicolor var. argyraea (Silver Dalea, Escobilla Cenizo)

An evergreen mounding shrub growing 3 feet by 3 feet. The foliage is covered in fine silvery hairs. From July to September the plant produces dark purple flowers borne in short spikes. Native to rocky limestone soils between 1,500 and 5,000 feet in elevation from western Texas, southern New Mexico, south to Coahuila and Nuevo Leon, Mexico. Silver Dalea is hardy to 10° F. It prefers full sun and well-drained soil, but is more tolerant of dappled sun than many desert plants. The smaller size and fine-textured foliage make Silver Dalea an effective taller ground cover for rocky slopes. Periodic shearing, especially where the plant is receiving extra irrigation, helps to maintain a more branched and dense form.

Dalea formosa **(Feather Dalea, Limoncillo)**
Low, semi-evergreen rounded shrub 2 feet wide and 2 feet high. Small leaves (¼ inch) are divided into even smaller light green leaflets. Flowers are purple, borne in short clusters about 1 inch long. Each flower is surrounded by feathery plumes. Seeds also have feathery tails. Flowers appear from March to September, with the heaviest bloom appearing in the spring, followed by intermittent displays after rains. Feather Dalea is native to gravelly or rocky slopes in much of the Southwest and northern Mexico, including southern Oklahoma, west Texas, southern Utah, New Mexico, Arizona, Colorado, and northern Mexico.

Dalea frutescens **(Black Dalea)**
Rounded, thornless shrub usually under 3 feet. Violet flowers borne in terminal spikes in late summer. From the Rio Grande Plains to lower elevations of the Plains Country, east to Travis County and Oklahoma. Prefers dry, limestone soil in full sun but is fairly adaptable. Rooting methods the same as for *D. greggii.*

Dalea greggii **(Gregg's Dalea)**
Trailing ground cover, usually not over 6 inches, with silver-gray leaflets on long stems that root at the nodes. Flowers reddish lavender to purple. Limestone soil of Brewster, Terrell, and Pecos counties in the Trans-Pecos and nearby Mexico. Useful ground cover for rocky slopes and exposed areas. To encourage fuller growth, shear this plant periodically. In the winter it will have less foliage than in the summer, when it fills out. Do not overwater. Gregg's Dalea is easily rooted from softwood cuttings taken in June/July, treated with 5,000 ppm IBA and placed under mist. Rooting usually takes place in 7–10 days. Rooted cuttings can be moved up to a 4-inch pot or one-gallon container in less than a month. This plant must have a light, well-drained soil mix. Newly rooted plants benefit from 30% shade at first (Pfeiffer, personal communication, 1999).

Dalea scoparia **(Broom Dalea)**
Thornless shrub up to 2 feet with simple leaves and a broomlike open top. Flowers are blue. Native to the deep sands along the Rio Grande of El Paso and Hudspeth counties, also New Mexico and Arizona. Good for erosion control. Needs pruning periodically to encourage compact growth.

Dasylirion

Sotol, Desert Spoon

AGAVACEAE (AGAVE FAMILY)

GENERAL DESCRIPTION

Sotols are large dramatic desert plants frequently confused with yuccas. They are characterized by mounding clusters of many long, pliant, ribbon-like, saw-toothed bluish-green leaves which are spoonlike at the base. Single plants may spread more than 2 feet wide and 2 feet tall, not counting the flower stalk.

FLOWERS AND FRUIT

The tall, thick, flowering stalks elongate in the late spring and bloom from May to August. Male and female flowers are borne on separate plants and are wind pollinated. Each seed is contained within a papery three-winged shell that is also dispersed by the wind.

NATURAL HABITAT, RANGE, AND PREFERRED SITE

Sotols are native to rocky limestone or igneous soil from the western Edwards Plateau to the Trans-Pecos, Arizona, and New Mexico, also northern Mexico. Sotols must have sandy or rocky well-drained soil and full sun. Many will freeze back during hard winters and suffer during lengthy spells of slushy or wet weather unless placed in well-drained, gravelly soils.

COLLECTION AND STORAGE

Gather the seeds when the capsules have dried and are ready to split open and drop the flattened black seeds. Seeds can be collected from September to January. Spread the seeds to dry in thin layers on screens in a protected location to help remove the papery pericarp before storing in sealed containers in the refrigerator. Cleaned seed germinates better than seed with the papery covering left on (Manning, personal communication, 1999). Seeds will remain viable at high percentages for the first 6 months following collection; after that viability decreases rapidly (McNeal, personal communication, 1999).

PROPAGATION

Seeds

Sotols will readily germinate from untreated seeds planted as soon as they are ripe. Either plant in flats or individual containers outdoors immediately after harvest, or keep in dry storage and plant in cold frames in March. Seeds planted in the fall require protection from cold.

Press the seeds into the soil about ¼ inch or less and barely cover with a light sprinkling of sifted sand or vermiculite. Seeds can be planted thickly in the flat. One flat can have as many as 5,000 seedlings (McNeal, personal communication, 1999). Germination rates are usually high. Keep the soil slightly damp but not soggy. Seeds will germinate within 3–4 weeks. Seedlings often remain in a small, grasslike stage for up to 2 years. Some growers leave the seedlings in the flat until the third year or until the third set of leaves is produced, before transplanting to a one-gallon container (McNeal, personal communication, 1999).

Others use slow-release fertilizers on young seedlings to hasten growth and produce one-gallon size plants at the end of the first year (Kirwin, personal communication, 1999).

Seedlings do best in light shade during the first growing season. After they have reached a strong one-gallon size, place them in strong sunlight and take care not to overwater. Keep them in a one-gallon container for at least 2 years, until the leaves become stiff and hardened off. After the second year, sotols grow quickly (Manning, personal communication, 1999).

Transplanting

Young plants are easily separated from the parent clump in winter.

NOTES

The flower stalks of sotols have been a source of renewable building material traditionally used in Mexico for ramadas, corrals, and other temporary structures as well as for fuel. During dry spells the trunks are split open to allow cattle to eat the spongy interior and the leaf bases. The heads of the plants may be eaten roasted or boiled like an artichoke. A liquor is made from the fermented trunks, and the leaves have been used to make baskets and also for thatching.

Sotol flowers are attractive to hummingbirds. Sotols are attractive when planted in naturalistic gardens in arid regions, especially when used in combination with plants such as Cenizo (*Leucophyllum frutescens*), New Mexico Agave (*Agave neomexicana*), Daleas (*Dalea spp.*), Creosote bush (*Larrea tridentata*), and Junipers (*Juniperus spp.*). Sotols are striking ornamental desert plants commonly grown in cactus or succulent gardens but also beautiful in large containers, as dramatic specimens, or in massed plantings along highways and other hot, exposed areas.

SPECIES DESCRIPTIONS

***Dasylirion leiophyllum* (Sotol)**
Plants with a flowering stalk up to 12 feet tall. Leaves less than 3 feet long, wide at the base, smooth and glossy. Greenish white flowers. Limestone hills in the Trans-Pecos, New Mexico, and adjacent Mexico. This species differs from *D. wheeleri* by having the prickles on the leaf margins directed down instead of up. This is the most common sotol of the Trans-Pecos.

***Dasylirion texanum* (Texas Sotol)**
Short trunked, with part of the base underground, and glossy green leaves 2–3 feet long. Flowering stalks are 9–15 feet long. Mostly on rocky limestone hills in the southeastern Trans-Pecos, common in the Edwards Plateau and adjacent Mexico.

***Dasylirion wheeleri* (Desert Spoon)**
Short trunk not over 3 feet and often absent under cultivation. Flower stalk to 15 feet. Leaves nearly 3 feet long with a spoon-shaped base. Limestone or granite slopes in the Trans-Pecos, New Mexico, and Arizona. Common on limestone or granite hills in El Paso County, west to New Mexico and southern Arizona.

Diospyros

Persimmon, Chapote Prieto

EBENACEAE (PERSIMMON FAMILY)

GENERAL DESCRIPTION

Persimmons are shrubs or small trees with deciduous or sometimes persistent leaves. Bark and leaf shape vary with species (see Species Descriptions).

FLOWERS AND FRUIT

Male and female flowers bloom on separate plants from April to June and are not very showy. Fruit is a persistent berry containing as many as 10 seeds.

NATURAL HABITAT, RANGE, AND PREFERRED SITE

Diospyros is represented in Texas by two species that grow in very different habitats in east or west Texas. See Species Descriptions for individual range and habitat.

COLLECTION AND STORAGE

Mexican Persimmon, *D. texana*, ripens from August to October and turns from green to splotchy green to completely purple-black and soft when mature. There is tremendous variability of seed production and quality from year to year, based on the weather. It is best to collect Mexican Persimmon from a variety of populations (Will, personal communication, 1999).

The large, bright pink fruit of Eastern persimmon, *D. virginiana*, is not edible until after a hard freeze. Fruit of both species is eaten by many different kinds of wildlife, so harvesting large quantities of fruit can become a very competitive enterprise.

Some growers have found it helpful to collect the cleaned (or undigested) seeds of both species from piles of scat. Germination rates of Mexican Persimmon are inconsistent with both "scat-cleaned" and green seed. Each crop has its own variables of seed weight, latency (immature embryo), fertility, and seed coat thickness that all affect germination rates (Best, personal communication, 1999).

Clean the fruit immediately after collection to avoid mold and fermentation. It may be necessary to soak hard or slightly green fruit overnight to make it easier to clean. Scrape the softened seed on screens, and then wash the pulp off.

One efficient method for cleaning large amounts of Mexican Persimmon seeds involves sandwiching the softened fruit between two heavy screens and using a power washer hose spray to depulp them (Best, personal communication, 1999). Dry the cleaned seed several days before storing it inside plastic bags. Then place the bags containing the seeds inside a plastic container with a tight fitting lid in the refrigerator. Storing the cleaned seeds under these conditions will be sufficient for at least one season.

It has been suggested that the fruit pulp of persimmons may contain chemical properties that inhibit the seeds from germinating (Meyers 1974).

PROPAGATION

Seeds

Seeds of Eastern Persimmon (*D. virginiana*) should be stratified in moist sphagnum moss for 30–60 days at 36–41° F prior to sowing outdoors or in a cold frame in early spring. Although Eastern Persimmon has a hard seed coat, scarification in concentrated sulfuric acid does not seem to improve germination (USDA 1974). The best seedbed is one containing a deep, loose, well-drained sandy loam with a fair proportion of organic material. Seeds also may be sown outdoors in the fall instead of stratifying over winter in the refrigerator. Germination rates are usually erratic. Persimmon seedlings grow best at an average temperature of 80° F.

Mexican Persimmon (*D. texana*) germinates better from first-year seeds than from stored seeds. Aerate the cleaned persimmon seeds 2–3 days. Then set the seed in pregerminating trays filled with moist vermiculite (see Chapter III). Since seed germination is often slow and erratic, pregermination will reduce the inconvenience of empty seed flats or containers. Check the seeds every day and remove the ones beginning to germinate into individual containers. Germination usually proceeds within 7–21 days. Plant the seeds just at the soil level (instead of burying) with the root pointing down. If buried, the initial thrust of growth of the emerging seedling is sometimes so strong that the stem breaks away from the seed, which remains stuck to the soil. You will notice in the seed flat many separated seeds with the radicle anchoring itself into the soil, but with its stem broken off and no way to regenerate a new one (Best, personal communication, 1999). Seedlings develop long, brittle, unbranched taproots and are most successfully transplanted into larger pots or to the field if first grown in containers that encourage root pruning (see Chapter IV). Germination vigor varies tremendously with seed lots.

Mexican Persimmon is slow growing and sensitive to both damping-off and root rot fungi. Seedling survival depends on careful watering and regular applications of fungicide and chelated iron (Best 1999). Mexican Persimmon needs at least 6 months to reach a good size for transplanting in the field or moving to a larger container. It can take up to 3 years to make a one-gallon container plant, and 5 years to become a reasonable five-gallon plant (McNeal, personal communication, 1999).

Cuttings

Eastern Persimmon may be grown from root cuttings 6–12 inches long and 3 inches in diameter. Bury the cuttings in moist sand over winter and lift when rooting and growth of new shoots is well advanced. Mexican Persimmon is difficult to root from stem or root cuttings.

Eastern Persimmon trees may be grafted by chip budding, cleft grafting, or whip grafting, using the same techniques as for other fruit trees (Hartmann and Kester 1975).

Difficulties surrounding the production of Mexican Persimmon from cuttings make it hardly worth the effort for the commercial grower (McNeal, personal communication, 1999).

Transplanting

Both species of persimmon develop long taproots that make transplanting difficult unless the trees are frequently root pruned prior to moving and the soil around the roots is easily dug.

Mexican Persimmon is most successfully moved in the winter (Lowrey, personal communication, 1986). In central Texas, specimen plants of Mexican Persimmon as tall as 12 feet are frequently dug from the field. Transplant shock typically causes the trees to defoliate, and new growth may be slow. For best results, transplant during the winter, apply root stimulator (see Chapter V), and foliar feed the tree for the first 2 months following transplanting.

NOTES

Eastern Persimmon (*Diospyros virginiana*) is valued for its fruit and attraction for wildlife. There are many cultivars and selections available. The fruit is not edible until it becomes soft and has been exposed to a hard frost.

Mexican Persimmon (*D. texana*) makes an outstanding specimen small tree or large shrub because of its interesting gnarled branches, beautiful peeling outer bark,, and smooth inner bark with shades of gray, white, and pink. Mexican Persimmon is common throughout south and central Texas. It is extremely drought and disease tolerant, and its leaves are often semi-evergreen.

SPECIES DESCRIPTIONS

***Diospyros texana* (Texas or Mexican Persimmon, Chapote Prieto)**
Multi-branched shrub or small tree to 40 feet, with small leathery leaves and small dark purple fruit. Central and west Texas on rocky hills or pastures, east to Harris County. It is a valuable wildlife plant. Deer browse the leaves and the sweet juicy fruit is eaten by birds and mammals. Birds roost and nest in the tree, and the flowers attract many pollinators. Mexican Persimmon is a food source for butterfly larvae as well as a source of nectar for adult butterflies (R. B. Taylor, Rutledge, and Herrera 1997).

***Diospyros virginiana* (Eastern Persimmon)**
Eastern Persimmon can grow to 60 feet, though it is generally smaller. It has a broad crown with spreading branches, large smooth leaves, and large fruit turning pinkish orange when ripe. Native to woods, old fields, and open thickets in east Texas to Florida. Eastern Persimmon can grow on many soil types, ranging from the acid sands of east Texas to the neutral sands and sandy loams of the prairies and the alkaline clay gumbos of the Blackland Prairie (Simpson 1988). It is cold hardy to USDA zone 4 (Arnold 1999).

Color
Plates

TEXAS MOUNTAIN LAUREL
Sophora secundiflora

TRUMPET-CREEPER
Campsis radicans

DESERT WILLOW
Chilopsis linearis

SWEETGUM

Liquidambar styraciflua

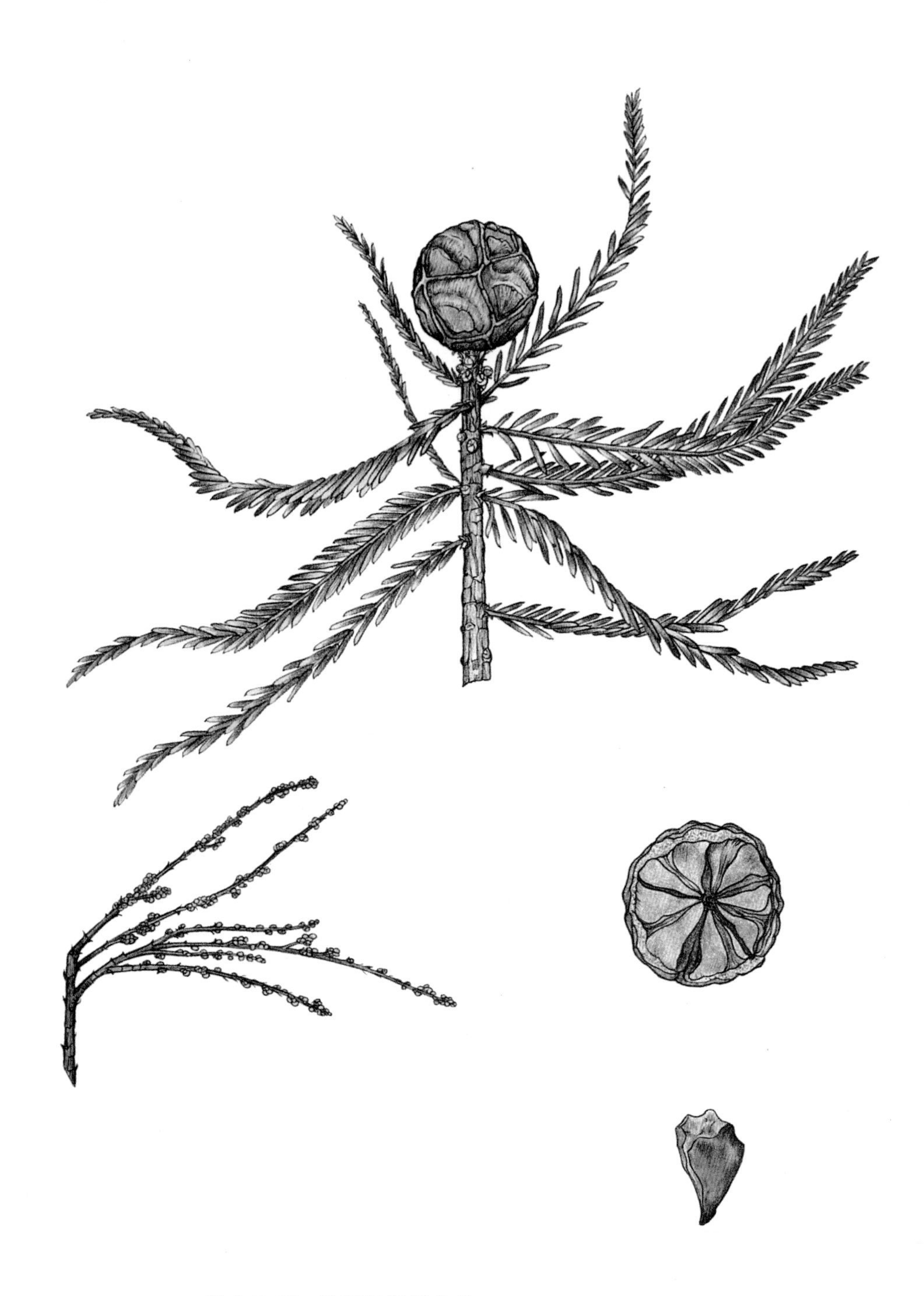

BALD CYPRESS
Taxodium distichum

PRAIRIE FLAME-LEAF SUMAC

Rhus lanceolata

BIG-TOOTHED MAPLE

Acer grandidentatum

SKELTON-LEAF GOLDENEYE DAISY
Viguiera stenoloba

WOOLLY BUTTERFLY-BUSH

Buddleia marrubifolia

AGARITA

Berberis trifoliolata

MADRONE

Arbutus xalapensis

GUAYACAN

Guaiacum angustifolium

FRAGRANT MIMOSA
Mimosa borealis

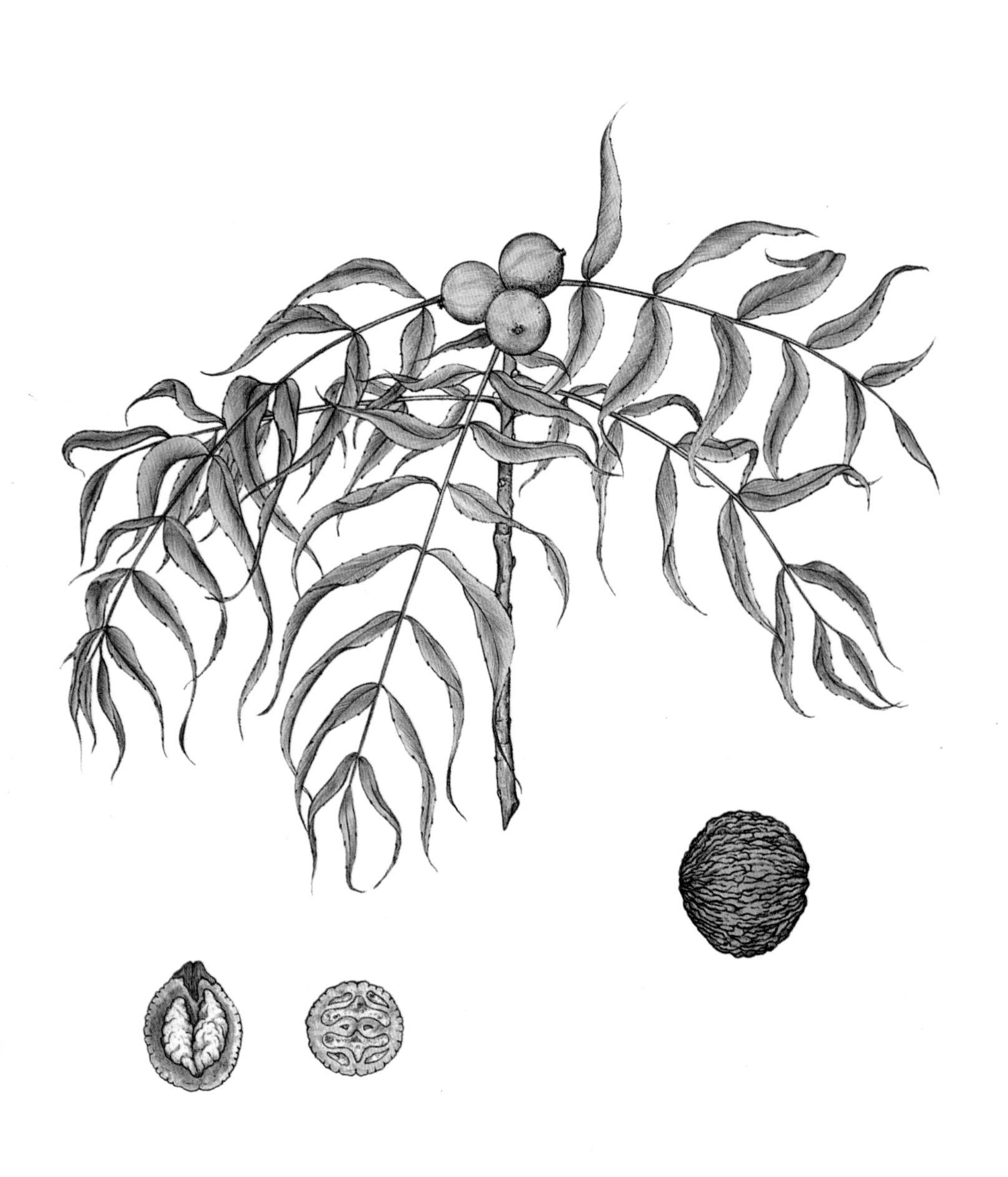

LITTLE WALNUT

Juglans microcarpa

PURPLE SAGE

Leucophyllum frutescens

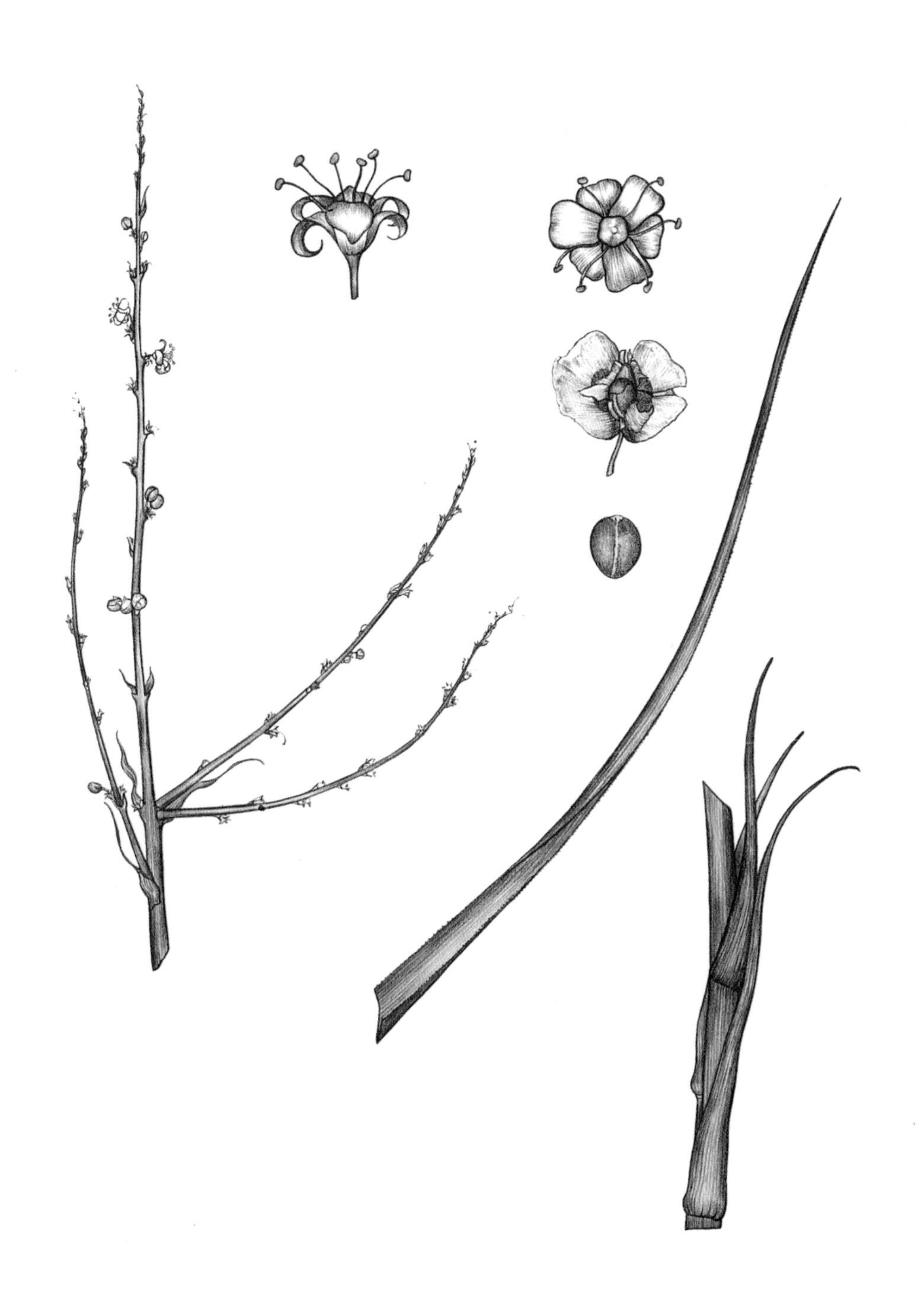

TEXAS SACAHUISTE

Nolina texana

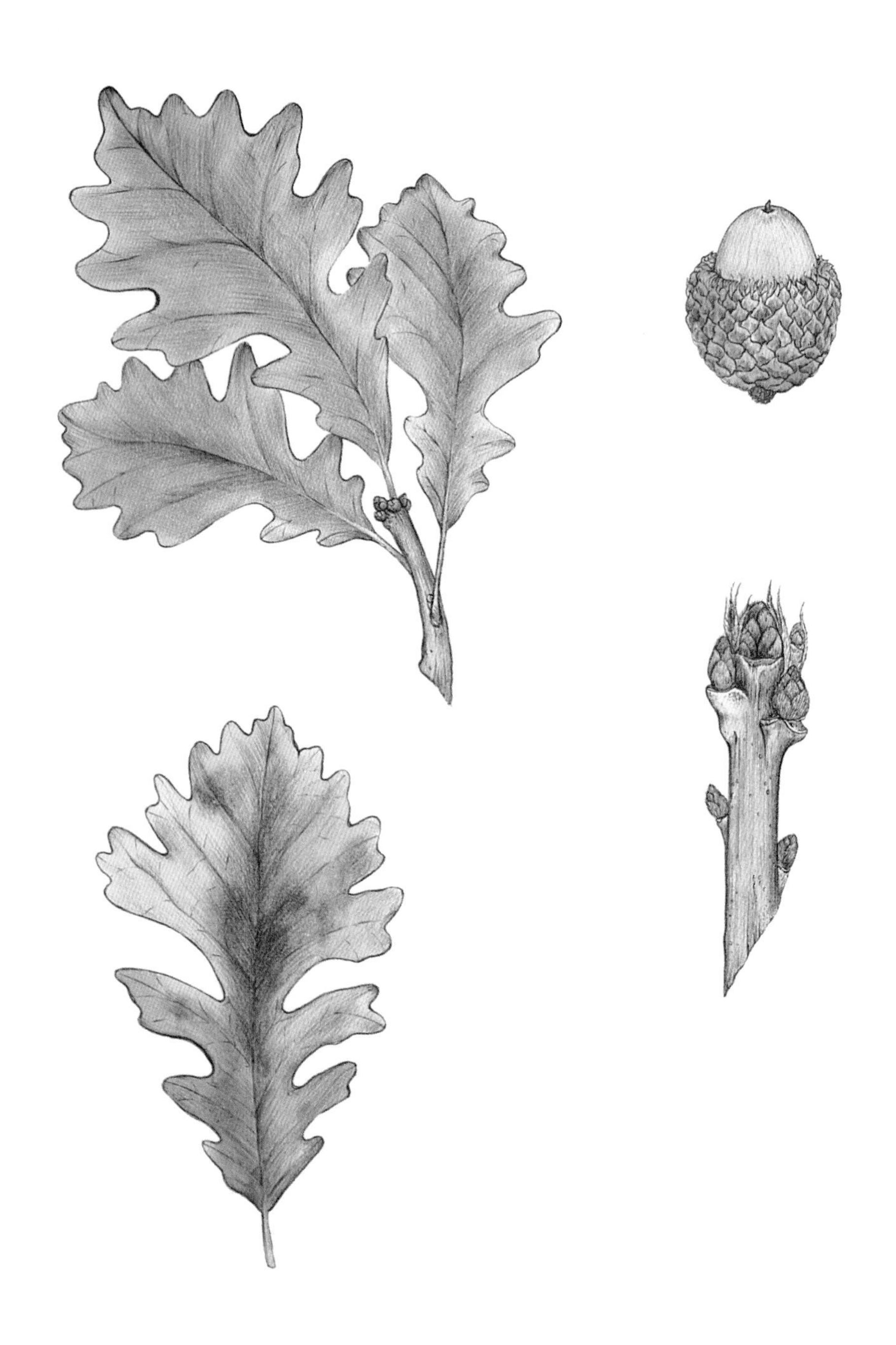

BUR OAK
Quercus macrocarpa

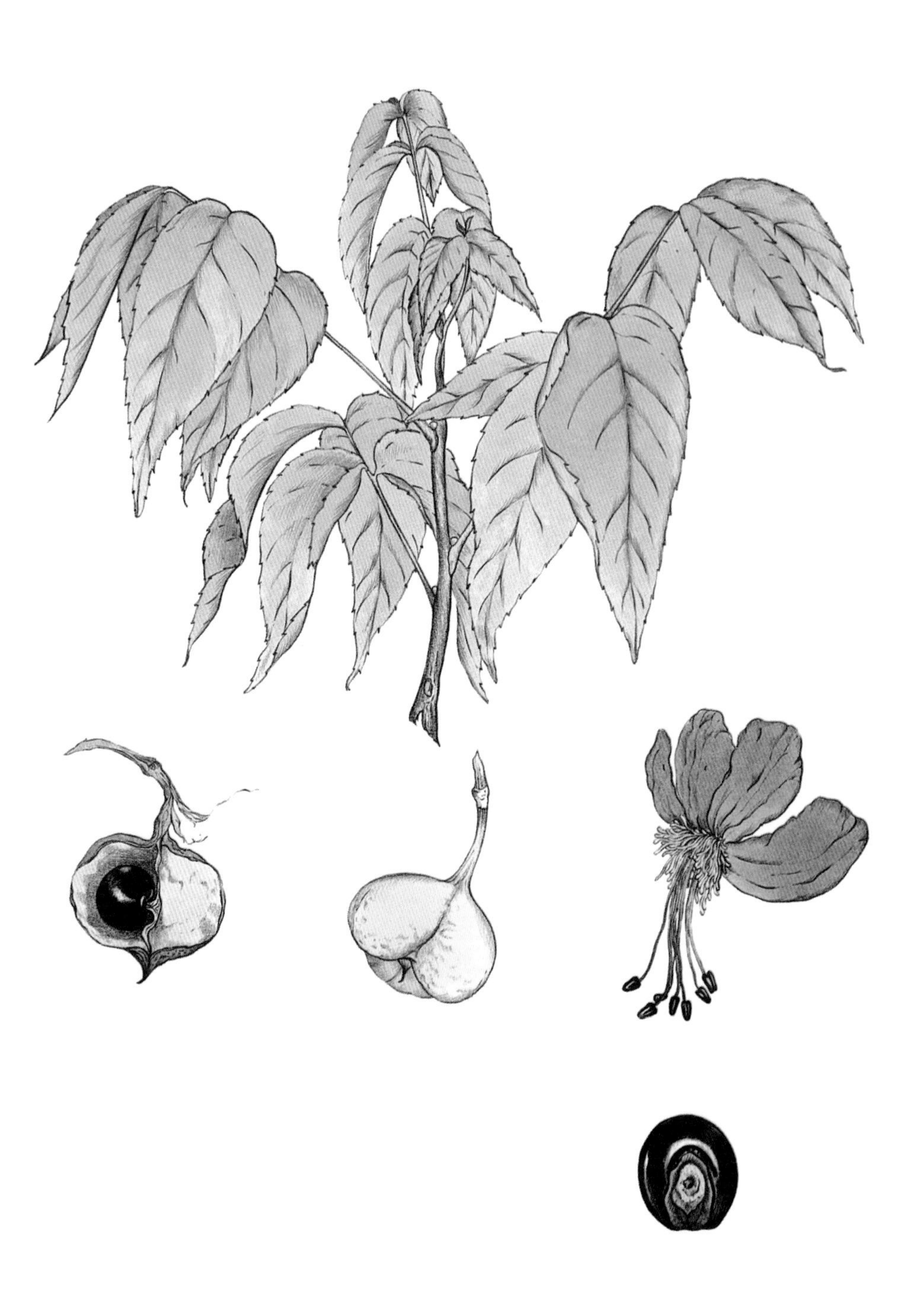

MEXICAN BUCKEYE
Ungnadia speciosa

PITCHER CLEMATIS

Clematis pitcheri

FLAME ACANTHUS

Anisacanthus quadrifidus var. wrightii

AUTUMN SAGE

Salvia greggii

MEXICAN PLUM
Prunus mexicana

SYCAMORE-LEAF SNOWBELL
Styrax platanifolia

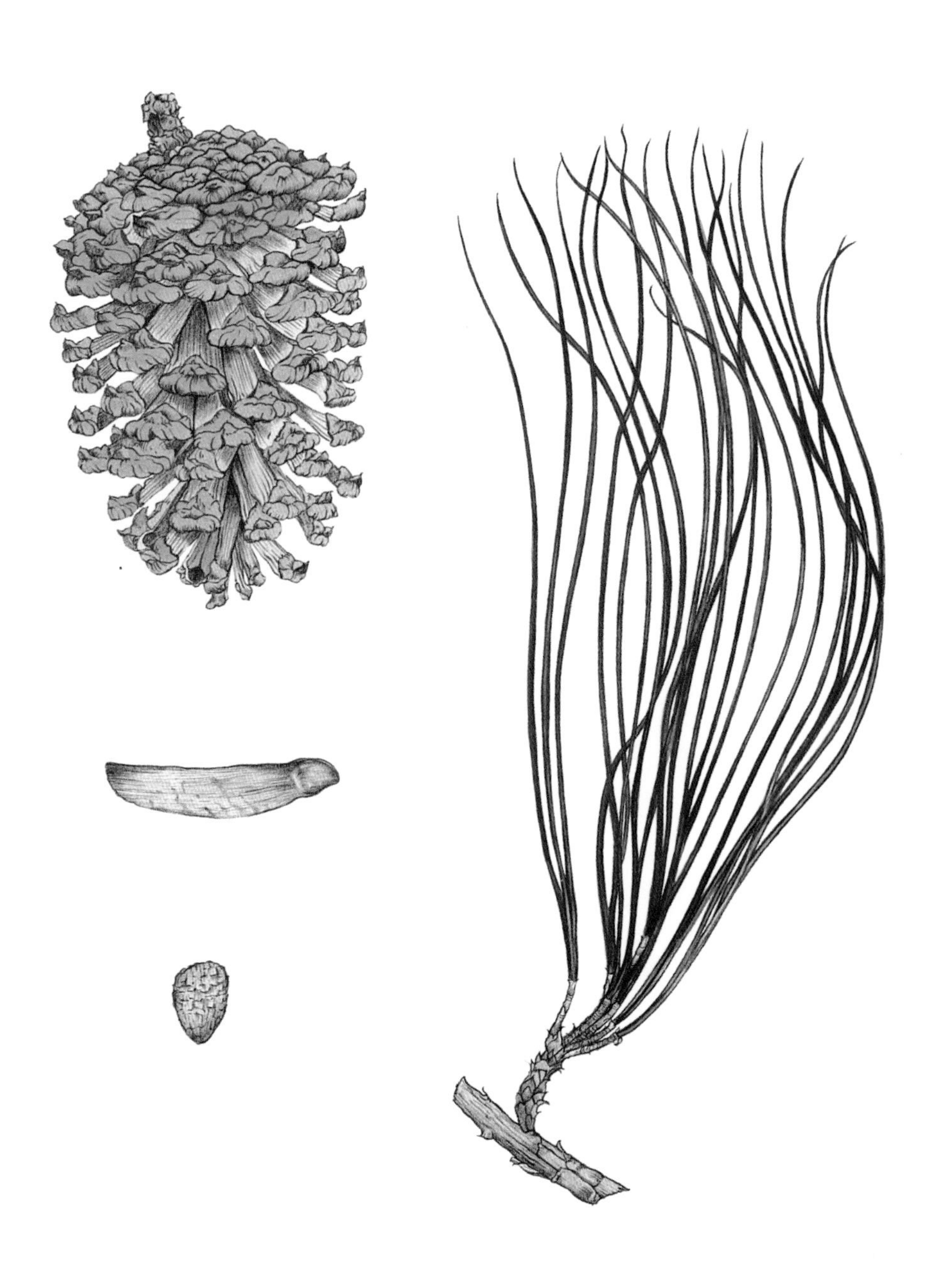

LONGLEAF PINE
Pinus palustris

ROSE-MALLOW PAVONIA

Pavonia lasiopetala

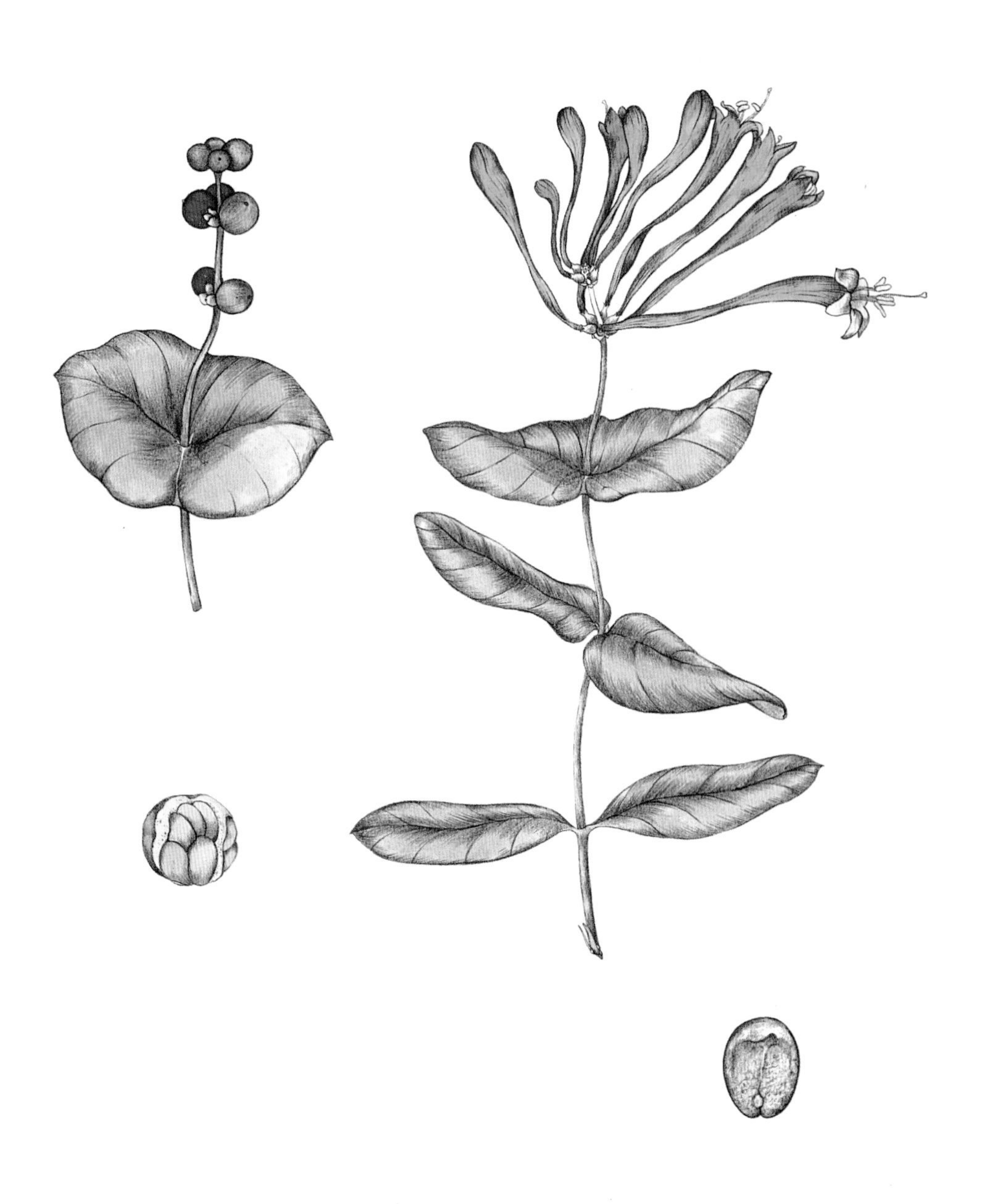

CORAL HONEYSUCKLE
Lonicera sempervirens

RUSTY BLACK-HAW VIBURNUM

Viburnum rufidulum

AMERICAN BEAUTY-BERRY
Callicarpa americana

WILD OLIVE

Cordia boisseri

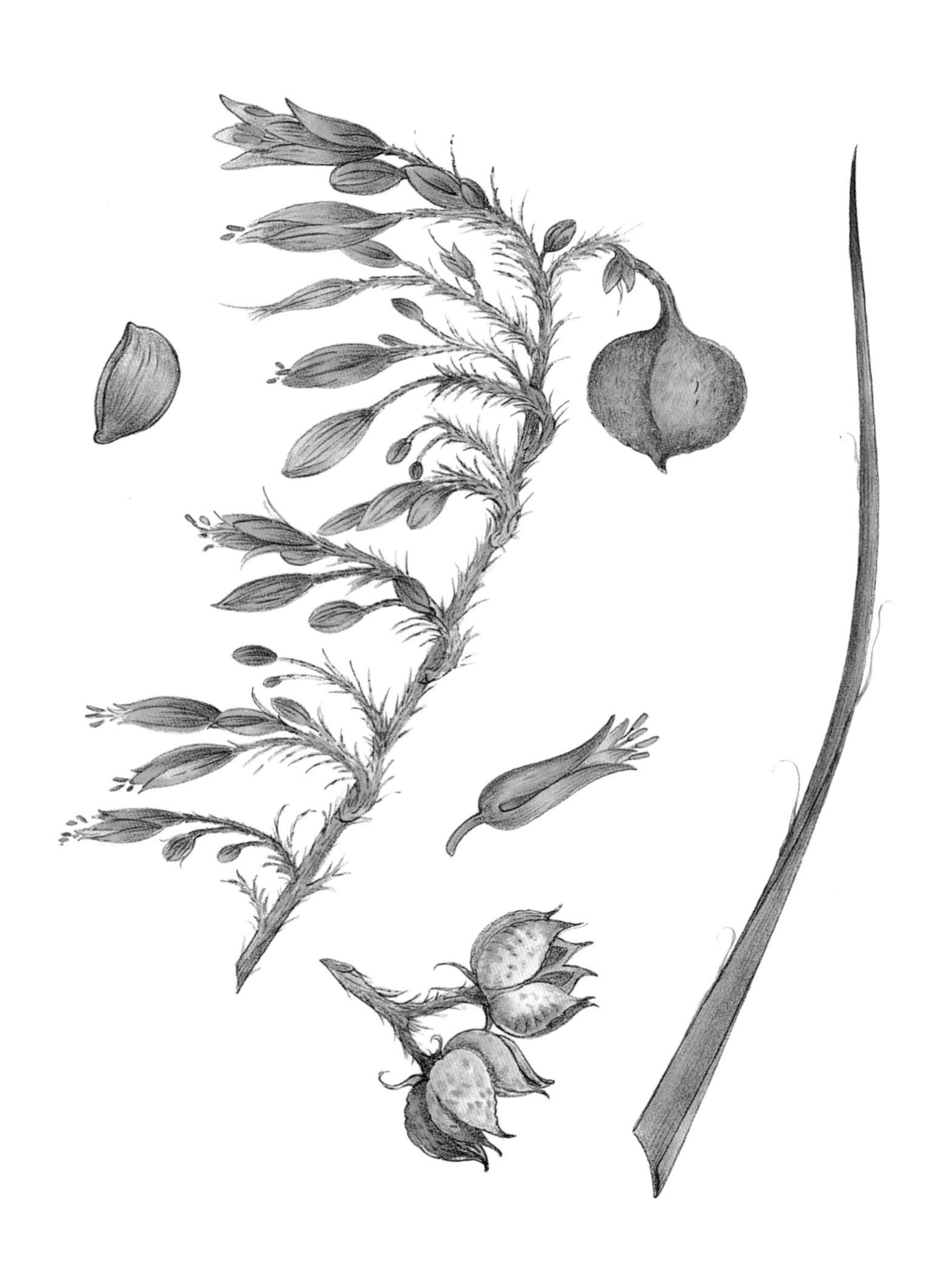

CORAL YUCCA
Hesperaloe parviflora

Ehretia anacua

Sand-Paper Tree, Anacua, Knock-Away Tree

BORAGINACEAE (BORAGE FAMILY)

GENERAL DESCRIPTION

Anacua is a handsome tree to 50 feet or more, often multi-trunked or with suckers clustering around the main stocky trunk. Anacua may form dense stands or thickets, especially along the banks of rivers or streams. Thick-furrowed bark separates into thin gray or reddish scales. Very dark green oval-shaped leaves have a sandpapery feel and provide heavy shade. In the southern part of its range Anacua is evergreen. During hard winters in its northern limits, the tips of branches may be burned back, but in average winters, the old leaves will drop in early spring as new ones emerge.

FLOWERS AND FRUIT

Fragrant small white flowers are held in large showy clusters at the ends of branches in late spring or early summer. In the Rio Grande Delta, Anacua has two main flowering periods: April/May, and again August/September. Ripe fruit appears about 6 weeks later. Individual trees may tend to flower in one period or the other, or occasionally both (Best 1999). Fruit is an orange-red drupe, ¼–⅓ inch wide, containing two seeds.

NATURAL HABITAT, RANGE, AND PREFERRED SITE

Anacua grows in thickets, forests, palm groves, brushlands, and open forests in south Texas north to Travis County, where it is hardy to 10° F. It is well adapted to Houston. Anacua most often grows in calcareous soil but will also thrive in arid, sandy soil (Lowrey, personal communication, 1986).

COLLECTION AND STORAGE

Gather seeds when the fruit has turned an orange or reddish color and is filled out (see above). The pulp may be removed or completely dried on the seeds. Store the dried seeds in sealed containers in the refrigerator. Cleaned seed stored for several years still germinated (Best 1999).

PROPAGATION

Seeds

Anacua germinates readily from first-year seeds. Depulp the seeds in a blender, then aerate them for several days (see Chapter III). Direct sow the seeds into plant cells or containers, with several seeds in a container. Germination will proceed within 10–20 days, after which crowded seedlings may be thinned (Best 1999).

Germination rates in some tests averaged 50% (Lowrey, personal communication, 1986). Seedlings may grow as high as 4 feet the first season if planted in containers filled with a 3:1 mixture of coarse sandy topsoil and composted bark mulch, and periodically fertilized (Lowrey, personal communication, 1986). Generally, however, Anacua trees are quick to germinate but slow growing as seedlings. For the first season, most growth occurs in the root zone (McNeal, personal communication, 1999).

In nature, mature plants often have many new seedlings sprouting from their base. In a container, Anacua has an irregular habit of growing. At first, a leader shoot rises 3 feet, then leans out strongly to one side, then another lateral shoot emerges, rises to the same height, and begins to grow sideways. Eventually one lateral shoot becomes the dominant trunk. Mature trees will have a strong form and main trunk, but in smaller sizes their wacky irregular shape is unconvincing to the consumer and difficult for the grower to modify.

Cuttings

Anacua roots easily from juvenile wood or suckers (Mortensen 1947). It may also be rooted from semihardwood cuttings of the current season's growth, 6–8 inches long, treated with IBA (5,000 ppm), and placed under intermittent mist. However, vegetative production of Anacua often results in weak-rooted, irregularly shaped shrubs that do not form strong trees (McNeal, personal communication, 1999).

Transplanting

Trees up to 23 feet have been successfully transplanted from the wild in winter (Lowrey, personal communication, 1986). Smaller Anacuas are fairly tolerant of transplanting year round, if given extra water. We transplanted an "L"-shaped sucker with a single slender stem 12 inches long and a root 6 inches long 9 years ago to our yard and we now enjoy a robust tree with a dense, rounded crown 17 feet tall.

NOTES

Anacua is valued as an ornamental plant for its many clusters of white flowers and orange-red berries, which are especially showy in contrast to the dark, persistent foliage. They are very drought tolerant and generally not subject to disease (Mortensen 1947). Their extensive root system provides erosion control on stream banks and hillsides.

Mature trees have an interesting, gnarled, and stocky appearance. Old Anacua trees in Victoria, Texas, often are as big as live oaks but with a more upright form and dense crown. Anacua trees in Sabinas Hidalgo, Nuevo Leon, Mexico, reach more than 60 feet tall and 3 feet thick (Best, personal communication, 1999). Anacuas tend to be multi-trunked and often produce many suckering stems from the base that can be pruned into large specimen shade trees. Birds are very fond of the fruit. Occasionally, the leaves are eaten by a beetle. Anacuas cast very dense shade and grass will typically not grow below them.

Erythrina herbaceae

Coral-bean, Colorín

FABACEAE (LEGUME FAMILY)

GENERAL DESCRIPTION

Coral-bean is a shrub sometimes as tall as 6 feet, with slender thorny branches rising up from a woody base. The leaves are deciduous, heart shaped, and glossy green. Each winter, the stems freeze back to the root.

FLOWERS AND FRUIT

Narrow, tubular-shaped, bright red waxy flowers bloom from May to June. They are held on slender stems alone before the leaves appear. Fruit is a persistent legume containing several bright red beans. When ripe, the legume remains attached to the stalk but splits open to reveal the red beans that stay attached inside the pod, even after the rest of the plant has died back.

NATURAL HABITAT, RANGE, AND PREFERRED SITE

Coral-bean is native to sandy woods along the coast of Texas but is adapted as far north as Dallas, also along the coastal southern United States. Prefers a well-drained but not arid site in full or partial sun (Mortensen 1947).

COLLECTION AND STORAGE

Collect the seeds in late summer through early fall when they are firm and bright red. Coral-bean seed has a thick seed coat and will remain viable for several years if fumigated and stored in sealed containers at room temperature.

PROPAGATION

Seeds

Germination of Coral-bean is delayed by a hard seed coat. Scarify the seeds either mechanically or by soaking them in hot water that has been allowed to cool (McNeal, personal communication, 1999). For large amounts of seed, acid scarification for 20–45 minutes is recommended. Aerate seeds following scarification until imbibition occurs (Best 1999).

Pretreated seeds planted indoors or outdoors after the soil has warmed will germinate within 2 weeks. Plant the seeds ½–1 inch deep in a well-drained medium. The flat or container should be 6 inches deep to accommodate the long initial root. If planted in a flat, remove the seedlings to separate containers after the second set of true leaves emerges to avoid crowding and breaking the roots.

Seedlings are sensitive to frost damage. Production of Coral-bean is best achieved if the seeds are started early in a greenhouse and allowed to reach a good size before summer. Coral-bean will grow to a one-gallon size plant within 1 year (McNeal, personal communication, 1999).

Cuttings

Coral-bean may be rooted from softwood cuttings 6–8 inches long taken in summer to early fall. Cuttings will often root at rates of 50% (Bering, personal communication, 1999). Cuttings taken in June and treated with IBA (3,000 ppm) will produce a one-gallon plant by the following spring (McNeal, personal communication, 1999).

Transplanting

Older, spreading plants may be separated in winter by dividing the large underground stem. When transplanting Coral-bean, you need to severely cut back the top.

NOTES

Coral-bean is a good ornamental plant for rock gardens, hot sunny sites, and sandy coastal plantings. Because this plant spreads and grows tall, it is best planted alone as a specimen or background plant. It is also an interesting understory plant, mixed with other shrubs. The tall slender stems with the large waxy cardinal red flowers come as a surprise each year.

Esenbeckia runyonii

Limoncillo, Naranjillo

RUTACEAE (CITRUS FAMILY)

GENERAL DESCRIPTION

Limoncillo is an uncommon to rare (in Texas) small, multi-trunked tree, growing up to 30 feet tall and 2 feet in diameter, though usually smaller. Dark, glossy, green three-foliate leaves are showy, with each oval leaflet 1–3 inches long. Trunk and bark are very unusual, having irregular patches of thin, coppery-colored bark which peel to reveal a greenish inner bark dotted with white lenticels (like the Sycamore).

FLOWERS AND FRUIT

Clusters of small, star-shaped white flowers are held in dense fuzzy panicles and often bloom twice a year. Fruit is a woody capsule about 1 inch long with five carpels. Each carpel has a winged seed coat that twists into two halves when dried, often ejecting the seed a considerable distance. Seeds are black and up to ⅓ inch long.

NATURAL HABITAT, RANGE, AND PREFERRED SITE

Limoncillo is found throughout Mexico and northern Nuevo Leon on talus slopes in deep protected canyons, usually at 2000–3000 feet elevation in the Sierra Madre Mountains. It is also sometimes found in the ecotones between forested canyons and mattoral (shrub land) in Northern Mexico. It is somewhat restricted in its range in Mexico, but common or relatively abundant in the right habitat. Populations observed in the Sierra de Los Picachos at these elevations seem to have survived frequent freezes without major losses (Best, personal communication, 1999).

In Texas Limoncillo is only known in cultivation and from a small stand reported from Cameron County (Richardson 1990, Everitt and Drawe 1993). It is possible that these populations were washed down during floods from the two watersheds in the Sierra Madres that drain into the Rio Grande and were deposited on the edge of resacas (Best, personal communication, 1999).

PROPAGATION

Seeds

Limoncillo is easy to grow from seeds. Most seeds have an air pocket and will float even when viable. Aerate cleaned seeds until imbibition occurs and then seed directly to containers or pregerminate in larger quantities before placing in individual containers (Best 1999).

Seedlings require good drainage and are salt sensitive. Irrigation with tap water in the Rio Grande Valley will cause defoliation because of high saline levels. Limoncillo is slow growing, especially in shady locations. Seedlings planted out in a revegetation program in the Rio Grande Delta without supplemental water only reached 3 feet after 2 years (Best 1999).

NOTES

Like Texas Ebony, Persimmon, and Guayacan, Limoncillo is a slow-growing but long-lived member of the mattoral or shrub land of south Texas and northern Mexico. The potential of selecting trees grown from seed from the Sierra de los Picachos north of Monterrey for their cold hardiness has not been fully explored.

In the Yucatan region of Mexico, the name "Jopoy" was given by the Mayans to a related species, *E. berlandieri*. In northern Mexico, *E. runyonii* is more commonly called "Limoncillo" (Best, personal communication, 1999).

Branches of this plant are used as "estacas" or living fences. Post-sized sections of branch are planted in the ground during the dry season (February), and eventually they root and form a sturdy corral for small animals or fowl, or serve as protection for a garden.

Euonymus americanus

Strawberry Bush

CELASTRACEAE (STAFF-TREE FAMILY)

GENERAL DESCRIPTION

Strawberry Bush is an open-branched shrub to 6 feet with oval, bright green deciduous leaves and slender crooked stems.

FLOWERS AND FRUIT

Flowers bloom from May to June and are greenish purple with distinctively clawed petals. Each flower is held in a cluster of one to three at the end of slender stems. The fruit is much showier than the flowers, consisting of pink fleshy capsules attached to warty-appearing valves or coverings that split to reveal one or two flattened seeds with conspicuous orange-red arils.

NATURAL HABITAT, RANGE, AND PREFERRED SITE

Strawberry Bush grows in moist places along streams, river bottoms, and in rich, poorly drained, moist woods in east Texas, also east to Florida, north to Oklahoma, and northeast to New York.

COLLECTION AND STORAGE

Seeds must be picked by hand just before the fleshy capsules begin to dehisce. Spread the seeds on screens to air dry a few days before storing. The pulpy arils on the seeds can be removed by rubbing them on a screen, but take care not to injure the soft seeds. If the seeds are completely dried, it is not necessary to remove the aril. Seeds will remain viable for several years if stored in sealed containers at 37° F (USDA 1974).

PROPAGATION

Seeds

Germination of Strawberry Bush is best when seeds are cleaned and then stratified immediately for 60–90 days. Drying seems to induce a longer dormancy period. After cold treatment, sow in individual bullet tubes. Germination generally proceeds within several weeks. Strawberry Bush seedlings require a year to make a finished one-gallon container plant (Bronstad, personal communication, 1999). Seeds can also be sown outdoors in the fall after collection. Germination rates are often low.

Cuttings

Three- to four-inch semihardwood cuttings taken from summer through fall, treated with 2,500 ppm IBA "quick-dip," will root at rates of 30–40% (Bronstad, personal communication, 1999).

Another source reported that soaking cuttings taken in September for 24 hours in 20 or 60 ppm IBA resulted in rooting at high percentages within 5 weeks (Dirr and Heuser 1987). Dormant hardwood and root cuttings have also reportedly rooted.

NOTES

The dark green leaves, stiff spreading branches, and showy, pink, warty fruit make Strawberry Bush a desirable ornamental plant, especially for low, shady, and poorly drained areas. It tends to sucker in nature, and these offshoots may be transplanted in winter.

Eupatorium havanense

Fragrant Mist Flower, Eupatorium, Barba de Viejo

ASTERACEAE (SUNFLOWER FAMILY)

GENERAL DESCRIPTION

Fragrant Mist Flower is shrub usually less than 6 feet tall with many slender, light colored stems arising from the base. It has light green deltoid-shaped deciduous leaves with crinkly edges.

FLOWERS AND FRUIT

Fragrant Mist Flower can be a fairly ordinary looking plant until September, when the whole plant is covered with tight bouquets of strong-smelling, fuzzy white flowers. Even more spectacular is the profusion of butterflies, moths, and other insects who abandon other plants in the garden in preference for this plant. Fruit is a five-ribbed blackish achene, 1/16–1/8 inch long.

NATURAL HABITAT, RANGE, AND PREFERRED SITE

Fragrant Mist Flower is commonly found on limestone hills, ravines, the edges of bluffs, and in canyons in the Edwards Plateau and parts of the Trans-Pecos. It is most often seen on the edges of woods, or in canyons near seeps, although it is adapted to poor soil and dry conditions.

In the garden, Fragrant Mist Flower will grow in a wide variety of situations, including full sun and poorly drained areas. It will bloom more if it receives at least a half-day of sun.

COLLECTION AND STORAGE

Collect achenes throughout the fall when they have dried and are no longer green. Air dry the seeds a few days before storing in bags or containers in the refrigerator.

PROPAGATION

Seeds

Fragrant Mist Flower is easily grown from untreated seeds. Sow the seeds thinly in a seed flat containing loose, well-drained soil. Press them lightly into the soil and just barely cover with a sprinkling of fine sand. Seeds will germinate in 1–2 weeks if daily temperatures average 68–86° F (Hartmann and Kester 1975).

Seeds germinate poorly if soil is either too cold or too hot. Best results are achieved if Fragrant Mist Flower is started indoors in early spring, moved outdoors by early April, and given cold-frame protection. Plants started in early spring will usually produce blooms by fall.

Cuttings

Growing Fragrant Mist Flower from cuttings is the quickest and most reliable method for producing new plants. Fragrant Mist Flower readily roots from softwood and semihardwood cuttings taken in summer or fall. The cutting should be woody toward the base with new wood toward the tip that is firm enough to snap if bent sharply. Take cuttings 3–6 inches long with the leaves removed from the lower half, treat with IBA (1,500 ppm), and stick in a rooting bed or container under intermittent mist. Cuttings root within 2 weeks and transplant easily to individual containers. Fall-rooted cuttings require cold-frame protection over winter.

Transplanting

Fragrant Mist Flower is easily transplanted year round if carefully cut back by one-third and given water at its new site.

NOTES

The long-lasting, showy white masses of fragrant flowers appearing during the last hot weather of the season contribute to Fragrant Mist Flower's worth as an ornamental plant. Migrating butterflies and hummingbirds are very fond of these flowers. Fragrant Mist Flower is especially showy if planted in groups or clusters at the edges of beds or as an understory beneath trees in place of grass or ground covers. In the garden, shear Fragrant Mist Flower back by one-half of its overall height to encourage a tighter, more well formed shape and more blooms. Mist flower only blooms on the new wood, so unsheared plants may become twiggy and less interesting over time if not shaped. However, unsheared plants can be effectively used to cascade over rocks or walls.

Several related herbaceous species are also worthy of cultivation: Blue Boneset, *E. azureum,* and Foam Flower, *E. coelestinum*; both have blue flowers and make a nice deciduous ground cover for moist, shady locations. Wright's Mist Flower, *E. wrightii,* is a low-growing, white-flowered species native to rocky sites in the Trans-Pecos. *E. Greggii*, Gregg's Eupatorium, is a small, herbaceous perennial growing to about 2 feet tall and 2–3 feet wide. It has fine-textured leaves similar to some *Verbena* species, and fuzzy lavender-blue flowers. Mountain States Wholesale Nursery in Phoenix, Arizona, has trademarked a selection called Boothill™ which they offer as a hardy ground cover.

Eysenhardtia texana

Texas Kidney-wood, Vara Dulce

FABACEAE (LEGUME FAMILY)

GENERAL DESCRIPTION

Kidney-wood is a multi-trunked shrub 3–10 feet tall. Leaves are deciduous, delicately compound with 15–47 tiny oblong or oblong-lanceolate leaflets. All parts of the plant are gland dotted, smelling like tangerines when crushed.

FLOWERS AND FRUIT

Flowers are fragrant, white to pale yellow, borne in numerous slender racemes extending from the leaf axils or near the ends of branches. Blooming period begins in summer, especially after rains, although the heaviest flowering time is in late August and September. Fruit is a small legume ¼–⅝ inch long, containing one mature seed.

NATURAL HABITAT, RANGE, AND PREFERRED SITE

Kidney-wood is common in brush vegetation in calcareous soil in the Rio Grande Plains, Edwards Plateau, and Trans-Pecos, south to northern Mexico. It is adaptable to many sites, but prefers full sun or light shade and well-drained soils. When planted in dense shade, kidney-wood may become spindly with few blooms. Kidney-wood is a fast grower in moist situations. In its natural habitat, it is very drought tolerant, though during extended dry periods it may temporarily defoliate (Lowrey, personal communication, 1986).

COLLECTION AND STORAGE

Collect the pods when they have turned brown and somewhat dry. Since blooming may be intermittent, collection may be accomplished over a long period of time as different crops of legumes mature. The pod is thin and papery, and so it is not necessary to remove the seed before planting or storage.

Thoroughly air dry the pod for several days before storing in bags or containers at room temperature. Fumigation is recommended to prevent weevil damage.

PROPAGATION

Seeds

Texas Kidney-wood is easily grown from first-year seeds. No pretreatment is necessary. Slightly crush the pods and plant them together with the seeds outdoors in late March or earlier in a greenhouse. Sow seeds ¼–½ inch deep in flats containing well-drained soil. Germination usually occurs within 2–3 weeks. Kidney-wood does not germinate well in cold temperatures, yet seedling survival is also poor if the temperatures are too high. Daily average temperatures of 68–86° F produce the best seedlings.

Seedlings grow best in individual containers 6–8 inches deep that promote air pruning. When crowded in a seed flat, seedlings can be relatively slow growing and susceptible to damping-off fungi. Kidney-wood will respond to fertilizing. Texas Kidney-wood is very fast growing and will make a nice one-gallon sized plant within 18 months of germination. Shear the young plants when they reach 2 feet to encourage them to fill out. This will also produce more flowers (Kirwin, personal communication, 1999).

Cuttings

Texas Kidney-wood is easily rooted from softwood or semihardwood cuttings taken in summer and early fall. These should be 4–6 inches long, with the leaves from the bottom halves removed. Treat cuttings with IBA (3,000–5,000 ppm) and place under intermittent mist. Rooting usually occurs within 3–4 weeks.

Transplanting

Small plants under 3 feet are easily moved if an adequate ball can be maintained around the roots and if subsequently cut back and cared for the first season.

NOTES

Texas Kidney-wood is a good plant for rocky, calcareous soil on slopes or in dry beds in full sun. Like many brush plants of central and south Texas, kidney-wood tends to sucker from the base with new stems once it has reached its maximum potential height. Eventually it forms a broad spreading shrub. Kidney-wood responds to pruning and can be shaped into a stronger branched specimen tree. Its fragrant blooms, delicate foliage, and interesting branching habit all have ornamental value. To encourage more blooms and a more compact habit, kidney-wood should be periodically cut back. It is a useful honey plant, and dyes have been made from its wood. Texas Kidney-wood is highly preferred for browsing by white-tailed deer.

A related species, Spiny Kidney-wood (*E. spinosa*), is also worthy of attention. It is an uncommon shrub 3 feet tall or less that is native to scattered locations in Presidio County. Twiggy and intricately branched with very tiny leaflets, Spiny Kidney-wood also bears bluish purple flowers in spikelike racemes from the axils of the leaves. Spiny Kidney-wood makes an excellent low-growing shrub or ground cover for rocky soil and hot, exposed places. It is heavily browsed by deer and livestock.

Fagus grandiflora

American Beech, Beechnut

FAGACEAE (BEECH FAMILY)

GENERAL DESCRIPTION

American Beech is a large, deciduous tree to 112 feet with a trunk more than 3 feet in diameter and close, smooth, ash gray bark. Branches spread horizontally to form a rounded top and dense growth.

FLOWERS AND FRUIT

Inconspicuous flowers appear in separate staminate and pistillate clusters from March to April. Fruit is a burrlike involucre that is full grown by the end of the summer but may not turn brown or completely open until the end of November. Each fruit contains two sweet brown nuts ¾ inch long. Good seed crops are produced every 3–4 years.

NATURAL HABITAT, RANGE, AND PREFERRED SITE

Beech trees are native to rich soil in hardwood forests, often along streams or riverbanks in east Texas, east to Florida, north to Massachusetts. American Beech is usually an indicator of climax vegetation in mature, undisturbed woodlands. Prefers rich, loamy soil with a slight lime content. Beech trees reproduce best in nature in dense shade.

COLLECTION AND STORAGE

Fruit is persistent on the branch and can be identified as ripe when it splits open into four valves to disperse the nutlets. Seed dispersal usually occurs after frosts. The seeds may be gathered from the ground or, if possible, by hand from lower branches. Remove the involucre or burr and either stratify or sow immediately. Germination capacity is severely reduced if the seeds are exposed to high temperatures or allowed to dry during storage.

PROPAGATION

Seeds

Germination of beechnuts is delayed by embryo dormancy. Stratify seeds for 90 days at 41° F prior to early spring sowing outdoors or in a greenhouse. Often germination will begin during cold storage, and seeds must be gently transferred from the stratification medium into containers or beds deep enough to accommodate the long taproot. Optimum temperature for the completion of germination after stratification is 68° F. Germination is usually completed within 60 days (USDA 1974). Seeds also may be sown immediately after collection in prepared outdoor beds. Sow seeds no deeper than ½ inch in moist loamy soil, rich in humus with a light lime content. Outdoor beds should be lightly mulched until spring. Seedlings benefit from light shade during the first season.

Cuttings

Beeches are generally difficult to propagate from cuttings, although some success has been achieved in rooting softwood cuttings of European Beech, *F. sylvatica* (Doran 1957).

Transplanting

One- to three-year-old plants growing in deep sandy loam are easily transplanted in winter. Field-grown seedlings of *Fagus* should be transplanted every second or third year, otherwise they produce long taproots that make moving them later very difficult (Hartmann and Kester 1975).

NOTES

The dense, leathery leaves of this species provide very good shade. The new leaf buds are an attractive coppery color, and the leaves make a fine autumn display. Beechnuts are eaten by many forms of wildlife. American Beech is a classic old-time shade tree for those areas with deep, rich soil and adequate rainfall. In its natural habitat, beech sprouts easily from the roots and may form thickets, providing valuable erosion control along streams, rivers, and bayous.

Fallugia paradoxa

Apache Plume

ROSACEAE (ROSE FAMILY)

GENERAL DESCRIPTION

Apache Plume is a slender deciduous or semi-evergreen, multi-branched shrub up to 6 feet tall but typically smaller, especially on dry sites. Leaves are triangular shaped with fuzzy undersurfaces.

FLOWERS AND FRUIT

Showy white flowers with numerous stamens bloom from May through August. The fruit is an achene with a long feathery style or tail and is the showiest aspect of the plant. Flowers bloom intermittently after rains, often appearing at the same time as the ripening fruit. During seasons of heavy seed production, these clusters of fuzzy fruits give the plant an attractive, purplish gray, smoky appearance.

NATURAL HABITAT, RANGE, AND PREFERRED SITE

Apache Plume is native to dry, gravelly, or rocky soil in full sun in the western part of the Edwards Plateau and the Trans-Pecos, west to New Mexico and California. Apache Plume is abundant in the foothills of the Chisos Mountains in Brewster County. It prefers to grow in gravelly soils. When planted in heavier soils with a lot of organic content (i.e., typical garden soil blends), Apache Plume becomes weedy and produces fewer flowers. Deer like to browse it. Apache Plume is very cold tolerant.

COLLECTION AND STORAGE

Collect the seeds from August through November when the purplish styles of the fruit turn white and the plump seeds readily fall from the branches. Fruits may be stripped by hand or shaken onto canvas. It is not necessary to remove the styles prior to sowing or storage. Air dry the seeds and store them in cloth or burlap bags in a dry, well-ventilated place. Seeds stored in this manner may retain viability for up to 3 years. In one study, seed count averaged 54,000 per pound (Vories 1981).

PROPAGATION

Seeds

Apache Plume germinates promptly without pretreatment from fresh seeds that have not been allowed to dry out. Dried or stored seeds must be stratified for 30 days at 41° F to break a delayed dormant condition occurring after harvest.

Press seeds into the soil and just barely cover with ⅛–¼ inch of sifted sand. The soil medium should be very well drained. Outdoor sowing is best accomplished from July through October for fresh seeds or February through April for stored and stratified seeds. Germination usually occurs within 60 days; most germinate the first 4–10 days (Vories 1981). Seed quality and germination rates vary greatly among seed lots.

Seedlings are initially slow growing and very susceptible to damping-off fungi and overwatering.

Cuttings

Apache Plume will root from semihardwood cuttings taken from May to June and treated with relatively low concentrations of IBA solution (3,500–5,000 ppm). Cuttings taken at this time should be overwintered and will be a one-gallon sized plant the following spring (McNeal, personal communication, 1999) Apache Plume can also be grown by layering the suckers that freely appear on the horizontal roots. Plants may be established in field plantings from year-old rooted cuttings. These should be placed in an open, sunny, well-drained location, allowing for the eventual spread and shading of nearby plants.

Transplanting

Plants under 3 feet can be transplanted from easily dug sites in the winter.

NOTES

Apache Plume is valued as an ornamental for its fragile, showy white flowers and graceful, persistent, feathery fruit. It is drought tolerant and hardy as far north as Massachusetts. Apache Plume is an important forage plant for wild and domestic animals and is excellent in controlling erosion in arid situations. Apache Plume is an attractive specimen shrub when planted together with other plants that prefer the same dry conditions, such as *Agave*, Creosote Bush (*Larrea tridentata*), Little-leaf Sumac (*Rhus microphylla*), Goldeneye Daisy (*Viguiera stenoloba*), and ocotillo (*Fouquiera splendens*).

It is best suited as a background or specimen plant, and under favorable conditions, it tends to self-layer and form spreading clumps. If given too much water and fertilizer, Apache Plume may become weedy and aggressive. Apache Plume looks best if the entire plant is cut back to the ground every third or fourth year to encourage a new flush of growth (Mackay, personal communication, 1999). In the intervening year, remove the dead inner twigs. Do not prune into a ball. The fresh seeds will germinate in any moist site, which means that volunteer seedlings may have to be controlled in a shrub bed (Tipton, personal communication, 1986). Apache Plume often produces blooms the first spring following germination.

Apache Plume was introduced into the Royal Botanical Gardens in Kew, England, in 1877 by the botanical explorer J. D. Hooker, who collected it in Colorado with Asa Gray.

Fendlera rupicola

Cliff Fendler-bush

SAXIFRAGACEAE (SAXIFRAGE FAMILY)

GENERAL DESCRIPTION

Cliff Fendler-bush is a rather inconspicuous (until it blooms) deciduous to semi-evergreen shrub up to 6½ feet tall with intricate branching and narrow lanceolate leaves.

FLOWERS AND FRUIT

Attractive flowers are composed of four separate white or pink-tinged petals each up to ¾ inch long with stamens nearly as long as the petals. Flowers appear alone or in graceful hanging clusters of two or three. Fruit is a four-valved brown capsule.

NATURAL HABITAT, RANGE, AND PREFERRED SITE

Cliff Fendler-bush grows on ledges, slopes, and among boulders in canyons in both igneous and limestone soil in the Trans-Pecos, also west to Colorado, New Mexico, and Arizona. It will adapt to well-drained sites as far north and east as Dallas (Simpson, personal communication, 1986).

COLLECTION AND STORAGE

Collect the capsules in late summer or early fall after they turn brown but before they split and drop the seeds. Air dry the seeds a few days and store in sealed containers in the refrigerator.

PROPAGATION

Seeds

Plant fresh seeds outdoors in well-drained beds soon after collection or store and stratify for 60–90 days at 41° F before sowing in a greenhouse or cold frame in early spring.

Cuttings

Cliff Fendler-bush will root from semihardwood cuttings of the current season's growth taken after the plant has bloomed. Treat with 3,000–5,000 ppm IBA and root under mist. After rooting begins, gradually reduce the misting intervals to harden off the cutting and minimize rotting.

NOTES

Cliff Fendler-bush is most prized for its outstanding flowers, which blanket the entire plant in white sheets. Under cultivation it may become lanky and is improved by annual pruning after the blooming period. It is drought tolerant and prefers full sun. The big, mock-orange-type flowers are attractive, but the rest of the plant is nondescript. Still, it briefly sets itself apart from the common mosaic of plants when it comes into bloom in May.

Benny Simpson and Sue Tracy discovered a single gangly plant growing out from the midst of a Texas Mountain Laurel on her ranch in Medina County, Texas. Previously, Cliff Fendler-bush was thought to grow only in the Trans-Pecos. The fact that they found only one specimen suggests that Cliff Fendler is one of unknown numbers of plants whose numbers and range are threatened by overpopulation of deer in the Texas Hill Country.

Forestiera

Desert Olive, Wild Privet, Panalero

OLEACEAE (OLIVE FAMILY)

GENERAL DESCRIPTION

Members of this genus are either shrubs or small trees. Leaf size and shape vary among species (see Species Descriptions).

FLOWERS AND FRUIT

Male and female flowers are borne on separate plants. Both types of flowers are greenish yellow, inconspicuous, and held in clusters in the leaf axils. Flowering occurs in early spring before the appearance of the leaves. Fruit is a slow-maturing drupe turning purple-black when ripe and contains a single stone ¼–½ inch long.

NATURAL HABITAT, RANGE, AND PREFERRED SITE

Members of this genus are mostly found in brushy grasslands or open woodlands in southern or western Texas. See Species Descriptions for individual range and habitat. Most species are common in overgrazed or disturbed areas and will thrive in poor soil.

COLLECTION AND STORAGE

Harvest fruit when it turns dark purple or black during the summer or early fall. In south Texas, fruit can be found on the plant almost any time of year. Remove the pulp by washing or dry on the seeds before storage. Do not clean the seeds in the blender: they are soft and easily damaged. Seeds of *F. angustifolia* dried and stored in the refrigerator still germinated after 3 years (Best 1999).

PROPAGATION

Seeds

Forestiera will typically germinate from first-year seeds without treatment, although one seed lot of Panalero (*F. angustifolia*) exhibited latency and required an after-ripening period of 3 weeks to allow the seed embryo time to mature. To propagate Panalero, first aerate the seed for 1–2 days and then direct sow in containers. Germination is completed in 3–4 weeks with rates as high as 70–90% (Best 1999).

Transplant seedlings from the flat or pregermination trays into separate containers when 1–2 inches tall. Seedlings benefit from light shade during the first season and will also respond to regular applications of water-soluble fertilizer.

Cuttings

Texas Elbow-bush (*F. pubescens*) and Narrow-leaf Forestiera (*F. angustifolia*) will root easily from softwood and semihardwood cuttings. Best results are achieved when cuttings are 4–6 inches long with the leaves removed from the lower halves of the stems and placed under mist. Treat the cuttings with 3,500–5,000 ppm IBA. Rooting is usually accomplished within 3 weeks (McNeal, personal communication, 1999).

F. acuminata will root from 3–4 inch semihardwood cuttings taken as a new flush of growth just hardens off. Treat with a 1,500–2,500 ppm IBA "quick-dip." Rooting occurs fairly quickly (Bronstad, personal communication, 1999).

Transplanting

Forestiera is easily transplanted year round if cut back severely and given adequate water. Texas Elbow-bush (*F. pubescens*) often self-layers and forms thickets, so separating a single plant may seem difficult at first. Yet the roots are far ranging, shallow, and easily dug.

NOTES

Members of this genus are among the most sought after browse plants in south and western Texas by both wild and domestic animals. The ripe fruits are eaten by a number of birds. The early blooms in February are an important source of food for bees as they begin to build up their brood for spring production. Despite the horticultural potential of this genus, nurseries typically have had a difficult time selling our hardy native privets to the public. Most species, except for Swamp Privet (*P. acuminata*), are tolerant of poor soils and dry conditions.

SPECIES DESCRIPTIONS

***Forestiera acuminata* (Swamp Privet, Texas Adelia)**

Spreading shrub or small tree to 30 feet with male and female flowers on separate plants or sometimes together. Female flowers appear in March and occur on a short panicle in clusters of up to 32 small flowers. Leaves are oblong with a distinct point. Native to swamps or bottomlands in east and southeast Texas, north as far as Illinois. Lynn Lowrey discovered a superior form with larger yellow flowers, now grown by Doremus Nursery in Warren, Texas.

***Forestiera angustifolia* (Narrow-leaf Forestiera, Panalero)**
Evergreen shrub to 4 feet with many short, rigid branches. Locally abundant in brush in the coastal areas of the Rio Grande Plains. Prefers well-drained soil and full sun. Coyote, raccoon, and scaled quail eat the fruit, and the leaves and stems are also frequently browsed by livestock and white-tailed deer.

***Forestiera pubescens* (Texas Elbow-bush)**
Deciduous shrub with arched or drooping branches and light green leaves. Sometimes forms thickets by self-layering. It is one of the first plants to leaf out in the spring. Locally abundant on open pastures or brushy prairies and thickets in north-central Texas to the Edwards Plateau and Trans-Pecos, also Oklahoma and west to California. Also called "Spring Herald" because it is one of the first shrubs to bloom in early February. The wandlike branches are covered in delicate, star-shaped greenish yellow flowers. Texas Elbow-bush is suited for planting as a spreading and gracefully drooping background plant for both full sun and shady locations where grass or ground covers will not grow. Its naturally irregular form can be carefully cut back to encourage denser growth.

Forestiera neomexicana
(New Mexican Forestiera, Desert Olive, Palo Blanco)
New Mexican Forestiera is an attractive multi-trunked tree or tall shrub 3–10 feet tall that can be used in the landscape as either a specimen plant or massed together as a screen (Sonier, personal communication, 1999). It is very hardy and drought tolerant, and adapted to a variety of habitats, including saline flats to canyons of high mountains in the Trans-Pecos, west to California, north to southern Utah, south to Mexico. It has very hard wood, and like many other desert plants, is sometimes called "Ironwood." The Hopi Indians used fire-hardened stems of this plant as digging sticks (Elmore 1976).

***Forestiera reticulata* (Netleaf Forestiera)**
Small- to medium-sized shrub rarely to 11 feet with many stems rising from the base. Leaves persistent, shiny, and dark green. In limestone canyons in the southern part of the Edwards Plateau, south to Mexico. Makes an attractive compact shrub that will thrive in poor soil in full sun. Prune periodically to encourage dense form.

Fouquiera splendens

Ocotillo, Coachwhip

FOUQUIERIACEAE (OCOTILLO FAMILY)

GENERAL DESCRIPTION

Ocotillo is a spiny shrub to 10 feet with many long slender spreading whip-like green stems growing from the base. Each stem is covered with hooked thorns and is leafless most of the year. Following a rain the stems cover themselves with clusters of bright green spatulate leaves that are eventually shed until another rain occurs, when new leaves appear.

FLOWERS AND FRUIT

Flowers bloom from March to June and are scarlet to scarlet-orange tubular-shaped blooms held in close groups at the ends of the stems. Each flower is ½–1 inch long. Fruit is an ovoid capsule containing numerous flat winged seeds.

NATURAL HABITAT, RANGE, AND PREFERRED SITE

Ocotillo is common on dry hillsides or desert flats in the western Edwards Plateau, Trans-Pecos, and west to California. It requires arid or well-drained sites in full sun and is not tolerant of heavy soils or moist sites. Ocotillo is cold hardy to 10° F. East of the Pecos River it rarely blooms, appearing to require the intense dry rest periods the desert provides in its native habitat.

COLLECTION AND STORAGE

Gather the seeds from early to late summer as the capsules turn brown and begin to dry but before they split open. If they are not already dry, spread out for a few days in a shed or garage and then lightly crush the capsules in a bag to release the seeds. Store in sealed containers in the refrigerator.

PROPAGATION

Seeds

Ocotillo will sprout from untreated seeds planted in the fall or spring (Manning, personal communication, 1999). Scatter the seeds thinly in a flat containing a well-drained soil mix. Be careful not to overwater because seedlings easily rot and are susceptible to damping-off fungi. Do not bury the seeds too deeply.

Young seedlings are very susceptible to spider mites. Young plants are slow growing: after 1 year they will only be 6–8 inches high in a one-gallon container. After the second season, however, Ocotillo will have several growth spurts, especially if planted in the ground, and achieve 8–12 inches of growth (Manning, personal communication, 1999).

Cuttings

Ocotillo readily roots from cuttings. Cuttings may be taken at any time and placed in separate pots in straight perlite or a 1:2 mix of peat/perlite. It is important that the rooting medium be well drained and that misting or moisture is kept to a minimum because Ocotillo stems will easily rot before they can root.

Transplanting

Ocotillo plants are usually sold bare-root. Water newly transplanted specimens once a week until they are established. Ocotillo make take a long time to set out new leaves, but some people have success by misting the stems with water for several minutes daily. Never partially prune Ocotillo stalks. If it is necessary to cut a stem, make the cut all the way to the base (Mielke 1993).

NOTES

Ocotillo is one of the most dramatic desert plants. Its graceful stems topped with brilliant clusters of scarlet flowers and exceptional drought tolerance make it a worthy specimen plant for any arid location, especially against the backdrop of a wall. People have used Ocotillo in its native habitat to make living fences and corrals by planting the stems directly into the ground, where they eventually root and become established. The tall spreading stems armed with thorns form an impenetrable enclosure. However, because Ocotillo is so slow growing, conservationists do not recommend harvesting the stems for ornamental landscape use as fences or trellises because widespread collecting could endanger the native population. For trellises or ramadas, substitute sotol (*Dasylirion spp.*) stalks. They are produced every year.

Fraxinus

Ash, Fresno

OLEACEAE (OLIVE OR ASH FAMILY)

GENERAL DESCRIPTION

Ashes are trees with deciduous compound leaves each with five to nine leaflets. Bark is generally smooth and greenish. See Species Descriptions for individual characteristics.

FLOWERS AND FRUIT

Male and female flowers grow on separate plants. Small greenish yellow flowers are borne in crowded panicles or racemes. Fruit is a dry, winged samara containing a single nutlet or seed.

NATURAL HABITAT, RANGE, AND PREFERRED SITE

Ashes generally grow on sunny, well-drained, but not arid sites along creeks, canyons, or river bottoms from east to far west Texas (see Species Descriptions).

COLLECTION AND STORAGE

Collect the samaras when no longer green but when they have turned a light yellow color with crisp-textured wings. Avoid collecting samaras from the ground because they are likely to be of poor quality and infested with insects. De-winging before sowing or storage is not necessary, unless to reduce bulk for large seed lots. Thoroughly air dry the seeds and store in sealed containers in a cool dry place. A related species, Green Ash (*F. pensylvanica*), remained viable for 7 years when dried to 7–10% of its fresh weight and stored at 41° F (USDA 1974).

PROPAGATION

Seeds

Ash trees are typically very easy to grow from seeds. Stratify seed from the current season's harvest in moist sand or perlite for 30–60 days at 41° F, and then sow in a greenhouse or outdoors after all danger of frost is past. Seeds may be sown outdoors in the fall after collection in well-tilled and mulched beds. Plant the seeds ¼–⅜ inch deep in well-drained soil. Seedlings benefit from light shade the first season.

Germination rates vary with species and among different seed lots. Some species show both embryo dormancy and an impervious seed coat. Seed collected early in the year and sown immediately could provide the necessary after-ripening time before cold temperatures arrive to fulfill dormancy requirements. Carefully monitor young trees as they advance to larger containers to avoid root girdling.

Several species tend to get aphids as soon as they flush new growth. Ashes will grow at a reasonable rate without high levels of fertilizers (Kirwin, personal communication, 1999).

Cuttings

Many ash species are difficult or impossible to root from cuttings. However, Little-leaf ash, *F. greggii,* has been successfully rooted from juvenile wood obtained from a 6-foot sapling that had not yet flowered. The cuttings were 4–6 inches long, treated with IBA (8,000–10,000 ppm), and placed under intermittent mist, where they rooted in high percentages (Simpson, personal communication, 1986).

Transplanting

Most ashes up to 4 inches in diameter can be easily transplanted in winter if the site permits the taking of a good ball of earth with the roots. Transplanted trees should be pruned back and watered until they adapt to the new site.

NOTES

Ashes are relatively fast-growing shade trees with few diseases and pests. There are several species appropriate to a variety of sites. Ash trees often provide fall color. Fragrant ash (*Fraxinus cuspidata*) in particular should be more widely used in the landscape where a small tree or a mass of fragrant showy shrubs is needed. Texas Ash (*Fraxinus texensis*) is a wonderful hardwood tree that is woefully underappreciated. It makes a fast-growing shade tree with a beautiful form, and foliage that often turns golden yellow in the fall.

SPECIES DESCRIPTIONS

Fraxinus americana (White Ash)

Tall tree to 128 feet. Found along streams in forests from New England south to Florida and west to Texas. Widely distributed but limited to ridges and high flats of old river bottoms. Medium growth rate. Seedlings tolerant of most situations except full shade. Very easily damaged by fire and overgrazing.

***Fraxinus berlandieriana* (Mexican Ash, Fresno, Plumero)**
Small round-topped tree seldom over 30 feet. Grows along wooded streams and in canyons in the Edwards Plateau and Rio Grande Plains. Seldom seen east of the Colorado River. Leafs out earlier and holds its leaves longer than many ashes. Provides medium shade and a rapid growth rate. Fairly resistant to root rot and is cold hardy. Collect seeds in August or September when they turn brown but before they fall. Assay the seeds to see if they are filled out. Seeds that appear mature earlier in the year (June) are not filled out. The samara matures long before the seed. Store them dry until planting. Seed retains viability up to 3 years under refrigeration. Aerate the seeds for 1 day and either pregerminate or sow them "acostado" (lying down), with the tip of the seed slightly pointed downward into the soil, and cover with about ⅓ inch. Germination usually proceeds within 10–20 days. They like moderate temperatures: spring and fall are the best times for planting (Best 1999).

***Fraxinus caroliniana* (Water Ash, Carolina Ash)**
Shrubby tree rarely over 32 feet. In swamps and along rivers in southeast Texas to Florida, north to Arkansas.

***Fraxinus cuspidata* (Fragrant Ash, Flowering Ash)**
Shrub or small graceful tree to 20 feet, typically 12 by 12 feet, sometimes thicket forming. Intensely fragrant pure white flowers hang in 3–4 inch panicles that cover the tree and are showier than Flowering Dogwood flowers. Native to moist canyons at higher altitudes in the Trans-Pecos canyons of the Rio Grande, Pecos, and Devil's rivers; also in the basin of the Chisos Mountains, and in New Mexico and Arizona. Fragrant Ash needs supplemental watering in the summer. It is very difficult to root from cuttings. Most nursery production of this wonderful and overlooked small specimen tree is from seed, but erratic seed set and seed dormancy often result in unreliable production. Seed often shows latency and requires a moist/warm period so the seed embryo can mature, followed by a moist/cold stratification before seed will germinate (Hosage, personal communication, 1999). One method recommends placing the seed in cold stratification for 2–3 months and sowing in early spring. Cover seed with ½ inch of soil. Germination rates are reportedly high (Phillips 1995b).

***Fraxinus greggii* (Little-leaf Ash, Escobilla, Barreta de Cochino)**
Shrub or small tree to 19 feet with smooth, thin, gray bark. On bluffs, talus slopes, rocky hills, and in canyons in West Texas (Brewster County), and west to Arizona. Little-leaf Ash is grown from seed, softwood cuttings, or stump sprouts in the nursery. Air dry the seed after collection and then cold stratify for 30 days. Germination occurs in 30–60 days. It is slow growing (after 1 year, it may only reach 12 inches), but eventually makes a nice smaller specimen tree (Manning, personal communication, 1999).

***Fraxinus pensylvanica* (Green Ash)**
Tree to 64 feet. Found in swamps, along rivers, and in low bottomland forests east from the coast to the Panhandle. Most common in flats and shallow sloughs, rarely in drier uplands. Has a medium growth rate. Moderately susceptible to dying back during drought, especially in the lowest sites with the heaviest soil. Sensitive to grazing, and heart rot often severe in mature trees. It is more tolerant of compaction than *F. americana* (Arnold 1999). Collect the seed from September to October. Store in a moist but not soggy peat/perlite mixture for 90 days. Make sure the medium is not too wet because Green Ash will easily rot during stratification. Monitor the storage bag for radical emergence, then transplant to individual plant cells or containers, as you would for *F. berlandieriana*. Once Green Ash is moved up to a one-gallon container, it has a relatively fast growth rate (Will, personal communication, 1999).

***Fraxinus texensis* (Texas Ash)**
Small tree to 48 feet. Endemic to rocky bluffs of canyons and in open woods near lakes and streams in central and north-central Texas. Closely related to White Ash. Good fall color. See directions for *F. pensylvanica*. Make sure the pretreated seed is lying on its side with the seed tip slightly pointing down (see directions for *F. berlandieriana*). Press into the soil and lightly cover with a fine soil mix (Kirwin, personal communication, 1999). It is possible to produce a good sized one-gallon Texas Ash 1 year from germination, and a 15-gallon plant within 2–3 years (McNeal, personal communication, 1999).

***Fraxinus veluntina* (Velvet Ash, Arizona Ash, Fresno)**
Small- to medium-sized, fast-growing, and relatively short-lived tree to 38 feet. In canyons and along streams in the Trans-Pecos, also west to California and adapted to the Rio Grande Plains. It is resistant to root rot and is cold tolerant.

Garrya ovata subsp. *lindheimeri*

Mexican Silk-tassel

GARRYACEAE FAMILY (SILK-TASSEL BUSH FAMILY)

GENERAL DESCRIPTION

Mexican Silk-tassel is a large evergreen shrub ranging from 5 to 11 feet tall. The leathery oval leaves are dark green and glossy on top, and fuzzy gray beneath. Mature plants are dense and wide.

FLOWERS AND FRUIT

Male and female flowers are on separate plants in early spring (March and April). Fine light-green drooping flower stems resembling corn silk make the male flowers showiest. Female flowers are inconspicuous but later mature into heavy clusters of purple-black fruit, each containing one or two seeds.

NATURAL HABITAT, RANGE, AND PREFERRED SITE

Mexican Silk-tassel grows on slopes, ledges, bluffs, or along ravines in limestone soil in the Edwards Plateau and also on igneous soil in the Trans-Pecos. It can grow in full sun or partial shade. It is very drought tolerant.

COLLECTION AND STORAGE

Female plants of Mexican Silk-tassel are often prolific producers of fruit, but seed viability can vary widely from year to year and from plant to plant. Collect the fruit when it has turned a dark purple-black, from late September to November. Remove the fleshy fruit from the seeds by macerating in a blender with a rubber blade (see Chapter III) or by hand by slightly crushing the fruit and then rubbing on a ¼-inch screen to separate the seed before storing or sowing. Fruit collected later in the season may have partially dried on the seeds and can be stored this way and the pulp removed later during the scarification process. Seeds will remain viable for at least a year if stored in sealed containers or bags in a cool dry place. Information on seed longevity in storage is lacking.

PROPAGATION

Seeds

Propagation of Mexican Silk-tassel can be a challenge because availability of good seed often varies from year to year. Germination rates are typically low or staggered over a very long period. Seedlings are slow growing at first and susceptible to damping-off fungi, especially if the soil medium is heavy and rich in organic material.

Chuck Janzow developed a method that produces higher germination rates. He collected the fruit in late October or November and immediately cleaned the seed to remove most of the pulp. The cleaned seeds were then soaked for 2–3 weeks in glass beakers containing a solution of activated yeast and water (two packages of yeast and a tablespoon of sugar to a gallon of water). The seed/brewer's yeast solution was kept aerated for 2 weeks. The bacteria in the yeast broke down the remaining bits of fruit pulp on the seed, as well as reducing the seed coating itself (see Chapter III). In the third week, one-third of the liquid was poured off and replaced with fresh water. After one more week, the seeds were removed from the solution and planted. The aeration process enabled the seed to imbibe water and eliminated the need to scarify the seed. At this point, the seeds usually have imbibed up to 10–20% are ready to be planted directly into seedbeds outdoors.

Sowing in the fall or winter immediately after collection is recommended because seeds do not germinate well in hot weather. The seedbeds used in Chuck's method were 10–12 inches deep, with three-fourths of their depth below ground level. The beds were filled with "manufactured sand"—a crushed and screened fine limestone material that insured good drainage, and they were kept under a 40% shade cloth. Germination began the following April and continued in staggered amounts until the end of summer (September/October), at which time the seedlings were 4–6 inches tall and ready to be moved into one-gallon containers. These contained a well-drained soil mix that included a slow-release (14-14-14) fertilizer.

Seedlings are sensitive at this stage and transplant losses can be as high as 60%. To minimize losses, transplant in cool, cloudy weather and place the seedlings immediately as they are removed from the seedbed in a solution of water, NAA, and B1 vitamins ("Superthrive") as they await transplanting. As each seedling is placed in a one-gallon container, make sure it is thoroughly watered in. Do not allow seedlings to dry out, even for a minute. Newly planted one-gallon plants are overwintered under shade cloth. By the next (second) spring, they had reached 6–10 inches tall and were ready to be moved up to a five-gallon container. From March to June the plants grew 2–3 feet and were ready to sell (Janzow, personal communication, 1999).

Mexican Silk-tassel has a very poorly developed and slow growing root system, and it is likely that plant vigor and survivability could be greatly improved by inoculating the soil mix with beneficial microorganisms (McNeal, personal communication, 1999).

Young Mexican Silk-tassel plants don't like to be pushed into fast growth. Plants are more successfully moved up into larger containers and into the field if allowed to grow slowly into a sturdy plant. Heavy fertilization only seems to encourage weak growth and susceptibility to disease. Seedlings should be given strong morning sunlight but protected from harsh afternoon light and desiccation (Janzow, personal communication, 1999).

Mexican Silk-tassel is inclined to send out a dominant side shoot or cane, even while the rest of the plant is low in the pot. To encourage more uniform growth, lightly tip prune the plant at regular intervals after the fourth set of leaves appears (Kirwin, personal communication, 1999).

Cuttings

Mexican Silk-tassel has been rooted from semihardwood cuttings taken in late fall and held over winter in a cold frame. Place the cutting under intermittent mist and treat with IBA (10,000 ppm). Silk-tassel readily calluses but is so slow to root that the stem often dies before it can be transplanted. Gradually harden off the plant by reducing watering intervals as soon as the roots begin to appear. Cuttings taken in April and May also rooted when treated with 5,000–10,000 ppm IBA/NAA, but percentages averaged less than 10%. The new roots are often very brittle and easily broken when lifted from the flat. Rooting in individual containers is recommended.

Transplanting

Silk-tassel is typically difficult to transplant from the field, especially because it likes to grow on rocky hillsides.

NOTES

Many people insist on evergreen shrubs in their landscape, and there are relatively few native evergreen plants available in the nursery trade. Mexican Silk-tassel has great potential as a native plant alternative to Burford Holly. Mexican Silk-tassel makes an attractive hedge or screen or understory plant on a rocky site or exposed slope. Like many Hill Country plants, Mexican Silk-tassel spends the first 2–3 years establishing a root system in order to survive on rocky sites. Once established, stem and top growth increase fairly quickly.

While it is often found growing on the edge of forests, in dense shade Mexican Silk-tassel may become tall and lanky. In full sun or if regularly pruned, it will remain dense and compact. It is very drought and disease tolerant. The light green flower stems of the early blooming male flowers are interesting, and later in the fall the heavy clusters of dark purple round fruits make an attractive contrast to the evergreen foliage.

Birds are fond of the fruit, and the dense form of the mature plant provides a refuge for many wildlife species. Garryaceae is related to Cornaceae and has been placed with that family by some authors.

The subspecies Eggleaf Garrya (*Garrya ovata* subsp. *goldmannii*) is similar to subsp. *lindheimeri* except that it has smaller, wavy leaves. It grows on igneous soils at high elevations in the Trans-Pecos. It is not tolerant of alkaline soils.

Another species, Wright's Silk Tassel, *G. wrightii*, has potential as an evergreen specimen plant for a rocky slope or for use in erosion control. It is a compact shrub with gray-green coarse-textured foliage, seldom growing over 6½ feet, but with a potential height of 8 feet tall and 6 feet wide. The leaves are elliptic and smaller than those of the Mexican Silk-tassel. It grows in the crevices of cliffs, among boulders, and on open wooded slopes at elevations between 3,000 and 8,000 feet in the Trans-Pecos, especially in the Franklin Mountains, where it is most often found in igneous rock. However, the leaves of Wright's Silk Tassel from these populations may turn yellow and begin to curl if planted in more alkaline soil (Simpson, personal communication, 1986).

Wright's Silk Tassel can be rooted from semihardwood tip cuttings taken from the first flush of growth in the spring (March) just as it begins to harden off. Cut in 5-inch lengths and treat with 8,000 ppm IBA (talc). Rooting rates of 80% were achieved when the cuttings were rooted in peat pellets, but only 40% of rooted cuttings survived transplanting to a one-gallon container. One-gallon plants required a full season to fully root out into the pot (Manning, personal communication, 1999). Wright's Silk Tassel is slow growing and easily succumbs to a number of seedling diseases (Tipton, personal communication, 1986).

Gochnatia hypoleuca

Chomonque, Ocote

ASTERACEAE (SUNFLOWER FAMILY)

GENERAL DESCRIPTION

Chomonque is a tall, slender evergreen shrub with very noticeable two-colored leaves. The leaves are almost blackish green on top, with a dense white felt underneath. The stems are slender, smooth, and thornless.

FLOWERS AND FRUIT

In the fall, Chomonque bears small clusters of white flowers near the tips of the branches. The fruit is a bristly achene.

NATURAL HABITAT, RANGE, AND PREFERRED SITE

Isolated specimens of Chomonque are found in gravelly soils, caliche, and sands in the mattoral (shrub land) of far south Texas (Zapata, Duval, Jim Hogg, and Starr counties). It is extremely heat and drought tolerant. It will grow in rocky barren sites where other plants may be marginal. Even in the hottest, driest weather, Chomonque will keep its dark green lustrous leaves without wilting (Cox, personal communication, 1999).

COLLECTION AND STORAGE

The bristled achenes of Chomonque may remain on the tree for a long time. Gather the fruit and air dry them between 2 fine screens. The fine hairs on the achenes make them easy to lose in the wind if not weighted down by the top screen. Store dry or in containers in the refrigerator.

PROPAGATION

Seeds

Fresh seed is best for germination. Follow recommendations for *Eupatorium*. Exact information on growth rates and nursery production of seedlings is lacking.

Cuttings

Chomonque is most easily propagated from softwood or semihardwood cuttings taken in the summer from the tips of branches after the plant has flushed new growth, or from sucker shoots growing from the base of the plant. Cuttings should be 3 inches long, treated with 1,500–2,500 ppm IBA, and rooted under mist. Rooting percentages are usually high.

NOTES

Some compare Chomonque's appearance to that of a young olive tree. It is an attractive evergreen shrub for harsh, dry locations. Paul Cox of the San Antonio Botanical Gardens has introduced the selection 'Spank' Chomonque. This cultivar was chosen because of the upright way it holds its leaves, revealing both the dark green tops and the poplar-white undersides at once. It has proven cold hardy in San Antonio, and manages to look its best during the worst part of the summer. Butterflies love the flowers.

Guaiacum angustifolium

Guayacan, Soap-bush

ZYGOPHYLLACEAE (CALTROP FAMILY)

GENERAL DESCRIPTION

Guayacan is an evergreen shrub or small tree that can grow up to 20 feet tall in south Texas, though more often seen 8 feet or less. Thick gnarled branches grow upright to form an irregular and dense crown. The tiny dark green leaflets are crowded along the gray stems. The leaflets fold up at night and in the heat of the day to conserve water.

FLOWERS AND FRUIT

Flowers are deep bluish purple and fragrant, closely attached to the branches in small clusters. Blooms are prolific up and down the stems from March through the summer, especially after rains. Fruit is a capsule ½–1 inch in diameter containing two jet black and rugose seeds, each with a showy, bright red aril. The fruit is often more ornamental than the flower.

NATURAL HABITAT, RANGE, AND PREFERRED SITE

Guayacan is a minor component commonly found in mixed-brush mattoral (shrub land) country throughout south Texas in most habitats and soil types. Its range extends north to Comal County, west to Brewster and Pecos counties in the Trans-Pecos, and also in northern Mexico. Guayacan will grow in poor rocky soil in shade or sun, albeit slowly.

COLLECTION AND STORAGE

Collect seeds from late summer through fall when capsules have turned brown and seeds are also black. Remove the seeds from the capsules and spread to air dry before storage. Make sure the aril is also removed from the seed, or it could cause the seed to rot in storage (Best 1999). Because the seed coats are generally hard, storage in sealed containers at room temperature is sufficient for at least 1 year. Seed stored in the refrigerator for up to 3 years still demonstrated germination rates of up to 85% (Best 1999).

PROPAGATION

Seeds

Germination of some seed lots of Guayacan is delayed by its impermeable seed coat. Seed collected from south Texas populations does not need to be scarified. Aerate the seed 2–3 days and pregerminate on tray (see Chapter III). Duration of acid or hot water treatment for those seed lots requiring scarification will vary among collections. Plant the seeds in separate pots containing extremely well drained soil media. Water the seedlings carefully to avoid damping off (Best 1999).

Guayacan is very slow growing. It may remain under 6 inches tall for 4 years (McNeal, personal communication, 1999). However, growth rates have been dramatically improved by providing chelated iron. Be careful to follow package directions. Only small amounts are necessary (Best 1999).

In one site where Guayacan was used in a revegetation project, certain individual plants reached 8 feet tall and 6 feet wide after 4 years without any supplemental irrigation or attention (Best, personal communication, 1999). In landscape situations with supplemental water and no fertilizers, Guayacan can reach its maximum height in 10 years (Wasowski 1988).

Cuttings

Guayacan will root from softwood or semihardwood cuttings when treated with IBA and placed under mist. Exact information is lacking. Cutting wood is best obtained from nursery-grown or cultivated plants, since plants in their native dry habitat are slow to produce new growth suitable for cutting material.

Transplanting

Guayacan has a deep taproot that helps it survive in the dry rocky sites of its native habitat. Thus larger specimens are difficult to transplant.

NOTES

Guayacan has great potential as an ornamental evergreen hedge plant for dry sites in south and west Texas. The branching and foliage are very dense and compact, and the blooms are showy and fragrant. If placement is staggered along a line, the irregular growth of this plant can merge to form a dense evergreen hedge. Do not try to control Guayacan's shape by pruning. Instead, use the interesting twisted branches as a feature in the garden. The fragrant flowers are also delightful near a patio or walkway.

Guayacan is a good honey plant and provides valuable wildlife cover. It is browsed by deer, sheep, and goats and is a limited food source for birds. Guayacan has very dense, hard wood that is valued for use as fence posts and tool handles, as well as for barbeque wood. Soap reportedly can be made from the root, and root extracts are used to treat rheumatism and venereal disease.

Halesia diptera

Two-winged Silverbell

STYRACACEAE (STYRAX FAMILY)

GENERAL DESCRIPTION

Two-winged Silverbell is a small understory tree with large veiny deciduous leaves and an open crown with a sparsely branching habit.

FLOWERS AND FRUIT

The flowers are showy, creamy white, and bell shaped. They hang in small clusters from last year's wood in March and April. Each flower has four petals and 8 to 16 bright yellow, slightly extended stamens. Fruit is a 2-inch long fruit with two corky wings. Each fruit contains a single seed.

NATURAL HABITAT, RANGE, AND PREFERRED SITE

Silverbells are found in rich, moist acid soils, usually in stream banks in southeast Texas east to Florida, north to Oklahoma, Arkansas, and Missouri.

COLLECTION AND STORAGE

Collect the fruits while still green in late summer (August). De-winging is not necessary, except to reduce bulk for large amounts of seeds. Best germination occurs when seeds are planted immediately after collection. Seeds should be carefully air dried before storage to prevent mold or rotting. Storage is best provided by sealed containers held in the refrigerator. Information on seed longevity is lacking.

PROPAGATION

Seeds

Silverbell is often slow to germinate because the seed embryo is immature and requires a long period of after-ripening followed by cold moist storage to break dormancy. Seeds collected in late summer or early fall and sown immediately in prepared beds outdoors will be able to complete their development before the onset of cold temperatures. Drying after collection seems to induce dormancy and seed may not germinate until the second or third year. Best results are achieved when seeds are sown immediately after collection into community flats outside. Some of the seeds will germinate the following spring, but most will wait until the second season. A big challenge with outdoor sowing is keeping the rodents out of the flats or beds. They are really attracted to the smell of fresh seed (Bronstad, personal communication, 1999).

Another method for pretreating Halesia seeds is to expose them first to warm moist stratification at 60–75° F for 90 days followed by another 90 days or more of cold storage at 33–41° F (Simpson, personal communication, 1986). For some seed lots, cold stratification alone is sufficient pretreatment. Seeds should be removed from stratification and planted before the onset of hot weather.

Seedlings are relatively slow growing the first season, and seem to do best when planted directly from the seed flat into one-gallon containers. Silverbells are sensitive to soil fungi and to salts in irrigation water, and often die from root rot in the summer if the soil medium is too wet. Growing the seedlings in full sun is recommended (Bronstad, personal communication, 1999).

Cuttings

A related species, Carolina Silverbell (*H. caroliniana*), has been rooted from semihardwood cuttings taken in late spring and early summer, treated with 2,500 or 10,000 ppm IBA solution. These were stuck in a peat/perlite bed and kept under mist. Cuttings rooted at high percentages and were easily transplanted to containers (Dirr and Heuser 1987). Silverbell roots better in a rooting bed containing some peat moss rather than sand alone. Root cuttings taken from early spring into autumn have also reportedly done well (Bailey and Bailey 1947).

NOTES

Two-winged Silverbell is an attractive delicate specimen tree. The blooms of Silverbell make outstanding showy displays in early spring, especially when clustered in a group. Prune all Silverbells only immediately after they have flowered because they bloom on last year's wood. They are beautiful companions to Parsley Hawthorn (*Crataegus marshallii*), Fringe-tree (*Chionanthus virginica*), and Drummond Red Maple (*Acer rubrum var. drummondii*). Two-winged Silverbells grow best as an understory plant beneath deciduous hardwood species. In the summer, they receive the shade they need, and in the winter, when the taller tree is leafless, they have enough sunlight to produce an abundance of flowers.

Hamamelis virginiana

Witch-hazel

HAMAMELIDACEAE (WITCH-HAZEL FAMILY)

GENERAL DESCRIPTION

Witch-hazel is a delicate multi-trunked tall shrub or small tree 10–15 feet tall. The leaves are deciduous and straight veined, often turning yellow, purple, or orange in the fall.

FLOWERS AND FRUIT

Witch-hazel is unusual because it flowers in the fall. Small yellow flowers cover the stems in the fall after the leaves have dropped. The fruit is a capsule holding two shiny black seeds.

NATURAL HABITAT, RANGE, AND PREFERRED SITE

Witch-hazels grow in moist but well-drained soils in woods along streams or canyons in light shade. The best looking specimens are found on the moister sites. *H. virginiana* occurs in east Texas, and an isolated population can be found along streams in Bandera County in the Edwards Plateau.

COLLECTION AND STORAGE

The capsule of Witch-hazel splits and forcibly ejects the seed when ripe. Pick the fruits from late August to September before they completely dry and the seeds are lost. Ripeness is usually indicated by a dark orange-brown color and dark attached floral bracts. Seeds mature in late summer before the fruit has fully hardened (USDA 1974). Collect the capsules in the yellow stage before they open and dry them in a closed container.

After collection, sandwich the capsules between two fine screens to allow them to complete drying and release the seeds. Fresh seeds can be stored in sealed containers at 41° F for 1 year without serious loss in viability. For overwinter storage prior to spring sowing, seeds may be directly stratified in moist sand and peat at 41° F.

PROPAGATION

Seeds

Witch-hazel is slow to germinate because of a hard seed coat and an immature seed embryo, which may require up to 6 months after harvest to mature. Under natural conditions some seeds will germinate the first spring, but many remain dormant until the following year. Some seed lots may require up to 2 years to complete germination (McNeal, personal communication, 1999). The trick to breaking the delay in the germination process is to somehow find a way to penetrate the leather-hard coating of the seed after the warm stratification period so that during the period of cold stratification the seed can imbibe water.

One grower recommends stratifying the seed for 90–120 days at 41° F, then planting the seeds individually in "bullet tubes." Seedlings grow to a finished one-gallon size in about 6–8 months. Place containers in full sun. After the first year, Witch-hazel seedlings reach a finished five-gallon size in about 4 months (Bronstad, personal communication, 1999).

For outdoor planting, sow the seeds immediately after collection in September to expose the seeds to a sufficient period of warm temperatures to complete after-ripening. Or, seeds may be pretreated by stratification at 86° F for 60 days followed by cold moist storage at 41° F for 90 days. Remove the seeds from cold stratification in early spring. Germination usually occurs within 60 days.

Sow Witch-hazel seeds thinly using a loose, well-drained soil mix. Cover seeds only lightly and keep moist until germination. Seeds planted in the fall should be lightly mulched over winter and given half-shade the first year.

Cuttings

Witch-hazel is difficult to root from cuttings. Some success can be achieved using semihardwood cuttings taken in late spring and again in early fall after each seasonal flush of growth begins to harden off. Treat with IBA (50 mg/l for 20–22 hours) and place under intermittent mist.

In one study, cuttings made from young 4-year-old plants forced to flush new shoots in the greenhouse proved most successful. These were treated with 1% IBA talc or 1% NAA. Wood collected later in the season that is more hardened off or wood from older trees rooted only in low percentages. Stock plants kept in the greenhouse that are repeatedly coppiced may provide the best cutting material.

NOTES

Witch-hazel was first cultivated in 1736 for its fall flowers, heavy summer foliage, and fall color (Bailey and Bailey 1947). Witch-hazel is an appropriate tree for urban planting because it is tolerant of shade, poor soil, and air pollution.

The wood of Witch-hazel was traditionally used for divining rods. The leaves, bark, and twigs have astringent properties and were distilled for use in medicinal extracts and lotions to lessen bleeding and inflammation. Witch-hazel is browsed by deer and beaver, and the seeds are eaten by a number of birds.

The potential of the central Texas strain of Witch-hazel for a more drought-tolerant specimen understory plant for shade has not fully been explored.

Seedlings raised from seeds gathered from Witch-hazel trees in east Texas seldom adapt well to the drier sites in the western part of this species' range. Therefore, it is important to gather and produce seedlings separately for each extreme of the range.

A related species, Ozark Witch-hazel (*H. vernalis*), is similar in habit and appearance to *H. virginiana*, except that it blooms from mid-winter to spring (January to April) and more often freely sprouts from the trunk. It is found along streams in east Texas, east to Florida and north to Oklahoma. It is easiest to raise from seed. Seventy-five percent on one seed lot germinated following 3 months warm and 3 months cold stratification (McNeal, personal communication, 1999).

Hesperaloe parviflora

Hesperaloe, Coral Yucca

LILIACEAE

GENERAL DESCRIPTION

Coral Yucca has dark, semi-succulent, unarmed gray-green leaves growing in a grasslike clump. The leaves are long and narrow, with fibrous threads along the edges. Coral Yucca grows slowly to form a mound 3–4 feet tall and wide.

FLOWERS AND FRUIT

Slender 5-foot-tall stalks emerging from the center of the plant bear pink or yellow tubular-shaped flowers from spring through the summer. Fruit is a dry capsule containing flattened black seeds.

NATURAL HABITAT, RANGE, AND PREFERRED SITE

There appear to be two disjointed populations of *H. parviflora* (see Notes). In cultivation, Coral Yucca prefers well-drained soils and full sun. It will tolerate shade, but will not bloom as prolifically. Coral Yucca is hardy to 12°.

COLLECTION AND STORAGE

Collect seeds as soon as the capsule has dried, but before it starts to split. Store seed in a cool, dry place.

PROPAGATION

Seeds

Coral Yucca sprouts readily from untreated seed. Sow the seed immediately after harvesting in seed flats, or in individual 4- or 6- inch pots. The container should be at least 4 inches deep and contain well-drained soil media. Plant cells tend to cramp the roots, causing them to grow in knots. Premoisten the soil and then gently press the seed into it, without watering. Keep in a cold frame until the following spring. Some seed will sprout immediately, while others will continue to emerge over the course of a season (Hosage, personal communication, 1999).

Some growers leave Hesperaloe in a flat for a year before moving it into a one-gallon container. Others fertilize the young plant to speed production. After the first 6 months, give the plant strong sunlight.

Transplanting

Harvesting Coral Yucca from the field is discouraged because the native population has already been significantly diminished by collectors who gathered large numbers of this plant for landscape use. Coral Yucca typically grows on rocky sites, and large plants are hard to lift and have poor survival rates.

NOTES

Although called a "yucca," Coral Yucca is a separate species that merely resembles its yucca cousins. In Texas, Coral Yucca seems to be divided into two separate populations, each with its own distinct characteristics (Ogden, personal communication, 1999). One group is found in Val Verde County, in southwestern Texas on the Stockton Plateau near the Devil's River. It is recognized as having shorter leaves that are recurved almost 360° back to their base. The edges of the leaves have curly fibers that peel off. The inflorescences are taller and rarely branched. Flower color tends to be a darker pink, and individual flowers are held more upright.

The second population occurs in the north central part of the Edwards Plateau, in Collin, Haskel, Mills, and San Saba counties.

Coral Yuccas from these locations are generally larger plants with longer, less curved leaves and a more branched flower stalk. Flowers themselves are a lighter pink. It is this form that is most often seen in cultivation, although sometimes the two types have been known to hybridize (Ogden, personal communication, 1999). Ron Gass of Mountain States Wholesale Nursery has also produced a saffron-yellow clone of Coral Yucca (*H. parviflora* 'Yellow').

The succulent flower stems, flowers, and new growth are very attractive to deer, which is one reason there is not an abundance of this plant in its native habitat. Often the only time you will see a Coral Yucca in nature is when it is growing in the midst of a spiny shrub like Black-brush Acacia (*A. rigidula*) or Agarita (*Berberis trifoliolata*), which gives it some protection from browsing animals.

In the landscape, Coral Yucca is an excellent specimen plant for hot, dry areas with poor, well-drained soil. The flowers provide color all summer and are very attractive to hummingbirds. Coral Yucca is suitable for median plantings, slopes, or dry gardens. It has no known insect or disease problems. No maintenance is required other than removing the dry spent flower stalks. If the clumps expand and become too big after several years, divide into sections during early spring.

Hibiscus

Hibiscus, Rose Mallow

MALVACEAE (HIBISCUS OR OKRA FAMILY)

GENERAL DESCRIPTION

Native Texas hibiscus are perennial or, very rarely, annual shrubby plants with conspicuous and often showy flowers (see Species Descriptions).

FLOWERS AND FRUIT

Flowers are large and showy, in several colors (see Species Descriptions). Blooming periods begin with the onset of hot weather and continue intermittently until the first frost. Fruit is a five-part capsule with several seeds in each cell.

NATURAL HABITAT, RANGE, AND PREFERRED SITE

Members of this genus are found throughout Texas in a variety of sites and soil types. See Species Descriptions for individual range and habitat.

COLLECTION AND STORAGE

Gather the seeds as soon as the capsule begins to dry out, but before it splits open and drops the seeds. Capsules ripen intermittently throughout the extended blooming period, and thus several harvests may be necessary in order to gather enough seeds to plant. Spread the capsules on a board or fine screen or in a paper bag to thoroughly air dry before storage. Separate the seeds by rubbing the capsules between two boards or by picking out by hand. Seeds may be stored for at least 1 year if first fumigated or dusted with insecticide and then held in ventilated containers in a cool dry place.

PROPAGATION

Seeds

Some species of *Hibiscus* will germinate from untreated seeds gathered in the previous season, while others require slight scarification (see Species Descriptions). All hibiscus should be planted outdoors after all danger of frost is past and the soil has warmed, or earlier in a greenhouse. The soil in the seedbed must be warm before germination will proceed. Bottom heat may be beneficial to promote early germination. Often germination may be staggered due to differences in seed coats. The most vigorous seeds will emerge within 2 weeks, while other seedlings appear intermittently throughout the growing season.

Sow seeds thinly about ¼ inch deep in well-drained soil. Sowing in small individual containers is recommended. Press the seeds into the surface of the soil and gently water.

Seedlings grow relatively fast if given filtered but strong sunlight and lightly fertilized. Spring-sown seedlings will be large enough for a one-gallon container by the fall and will bloom the following spring. Transplant seedlings from the flat after they have grown their third set of true leaves.

Cuttings

Most hibiscus species are very easily grown from softwood cuttings taken from summer through fall, though some growers believe that they make inferior plants (see *H. cardiophyllus*). The best cutting material is 4–6 inches long, firm toward the base, with the leaves removed from the bottom halves. Place under intermittent mist. Treatment with IBA (3,000 ppm) hastens and improves rooting but is not imperative. Cuttings usually root within 2 weeks. The best rooting medium is a mixture of equal parts peat and perlite. Fall-rooted cuttings will need cold-frame protection over winter.

Transplanting

Hibiscus plants are easily transplanted in the winter if cut back almost to the ground and kept well watered.

NOTES

The species listed here are showy, shrubby perennials that are especially attractive when planted in groups in front of larger shrubs or as specimen plants in beds with other annuals and perennials. Like other shrubby perennials, native hibiscus should be cut back nearly to the base each winter to encourage bushy growth and more blooms. Some mature hibiscus clumps can be divided in the winter.

Most of these hibiscus will live 3 or more years before declining, but they readily reseed themselves in beds so often that the younger plants are on hand to replace the older parent. Most hibiscus are heat tolerant (though still requiring regular watering in the summer) and provide attractive flowers during the hottest part of the season when other wildflowers and shrubs are no longer showy.

SPECIES DESCRIPTIONS

Hibiscus aculeatus **(Pineland Hibiscus)**

A multi-stemmed perennial typically 2–4 feet tall, leaves one- to five-parted, each part being rough and narrow in shape. The large flowers are very showy with rich creamy yellow petals offset by a dark red throat. Pineland Hibiscus grows in moist acid sands in pine savannahs and edges of marshes. It prefers full sun and moist but not soggy soil in the summer. It is less tolerant of oxygen-poor clay than Rose Mallow (*H. moscheutos*) and Texas Star Hibiscus (*H. coccineus*) (Wasowski 1994).

Hibiscus cardiophyllus **(Heart-leaf Hibiscus, Tulipan del Monte)**

Upright, perennial plant 3 feet tall or larger in its southern range, with several leafy stems rising from a woody base. Flowers prolific and exceptionally showy. Brilliant red blooms 2 inches across appear in early summer and bloom intermittently until fall. It is tolerant of dry conditions such as limestone or gravelly soils in pastures, ledges, and hillsides in the Rio Grande Plains, Edwards Plateau, and the southeastern part of the Trans-Pecos. It will adapt to many different sites in cultivation as long as they are well drained, but is not hardy below 20° F. To promote more blooms and less twiggy growth, periodically tip prune.

Seed propagation produces a prettier and shrubbier plant than those generated from cuttings (Pfeiffer, personal communication, 1999). Soak the seed in concentrated sulfuric acid for 15 minutes. Carefully wash and briefly air dry before soaking the seed in gibberilin. Another method is to pour boiling water over the seed and let them soak overnight. Add "Superthrive" to the cooling water.

Plant the seed in a shade house or outdoors in April to May. Seeds need warm temperatures to germinate. Use bottom heat if you want to begin production earlier in the season. Seedlings tend to be slow growing at first and seem to stay in the liner a long time before becoming large enough to move into larger containers.

Seed sown in the fall can go outside in April where growth will proceed rapidly. Taking cuttings from a stock plant usually destroys the mother plant (Will, personal communication, 1999).

Hibiscus coulteri **(Desert Rose Mallow)**

Shrubby perennial to 3 feet with ovate leaves at the base and three-parted, lobed leaves toward the top. Flowers are whitish to lemon or sulphur yellow, sometimes tinged with red or purple. Native to desert areas on hills and slopes of the Trans-Pecos. Blooms throughout the year.

***Hibiscus dasycalyx* (Neches River Rose Mallow)**

This hibiscus is very rare in East Texas, known from only three locations in the Pineywoods. It is threatened by interspecific hybridization by *H. laevis* and *H. moscheutos*, as well as loss of preferred wetland habitat along the Neches River and her tributaries. Neches River Rose Mallow has the most narrow leaves of all the Texas *Hibiscus* species and has white flowers with carmine-red centers in the summer. Fortunately this species has been included by Dr. David Creech and his students in the Stephen F. Austin Mast Arboretum's "Three R's Program," which has targeted certain rare or endangered plants for "Rescue, Research, and Reintroduction." A new population of *H. dasycalyx* has been introduced to Mill Creek Gardens, a natural area, and studies are under way to investigate what simple horticultural methods are successful for establishing nursery-grown plants into a suitable habitat. Initial results of a 2-year study revealed that fertilization of seedlings and placement in a microhabitat which provided consistent moisture via a seep or spring produced plants that were bigger and more successful (Native Plant Society of Texas 1999). For more information check out the Stephen F. Austin Mast Arboretum web page: www.sfasu.edu/ag/arboretum/.

***Hibiscus laevis* (Halberd-leaf Hibiscus)**

Herbaceous perennial 3–8 feet tall with distinctive five-part leaves and large pink or whitish flowers with a purple base. In nature, Halberd-leaf Hibiscus is found in marshes and shallow waters in east and north-central Texas, and north to the Rolling Plains. It will bloom best in full sun. One-year seedlings have one stalk and a few late-flowering seedlings. In the second year it will have three to five stalks and produce blooms all summer.

Hypericum

St. John's Wort

HYPERICACEAE (ST. JOHN'S WORT FAMILY)

GENERAL DESCRIPTION

Hypericum spp. are annual or perennial herbs or shrubs with opposite, tardily deciduous, or evergreen leaves (see Species Descriptions).

FLOWERS AND FRUIT

Hypericum flowers are often showy. Each flower has five yellow or sometimes reddish or purplish petals with numerous showy extended stamens. Fruit is a capsule containing many small seeds.

NATURAL HABITAT, RANGE, AND PREFERRED SITE

St. John's Wort is native to sloping ground in the Pineywoods and along streams in the eastern third of Texas east to Florida, north to New York. See Species Descriptions for individual range and habitat. Many species of *Hypericum* prefer partially shaded situations and bloom longer if not exposed to full sunlight (Bailey and Bailey 1947).

COLLECTION AND STORAGE

Gather the seeds in late August through October when the capsules have turned brown, but before they have dried out completely. Some capsules may remain on the plant throughout the winter. Slightly crush the capsules to release the seeds and air dry at room temperature 1–2 days before storing or sowing. Store seeds in paper or cloth bags in a dry place until the spring (Sheats 1953). Information is lacking on the longevity of seeds in storage.

PROPAGATION

Seeds

Hypericum will readily germinate from first-year seeds. Sow seeds thinly in flats using a loose, well-drained soil mix that does not dry out quickly and yet is not soggy. Cover the seeds lightly with ¼–½ inch of fine sand or soil.

Hypericum germinates best if started in a greenhouse in late winter and transferred after germination to a cold frame to harden off for a month. At that time seedlings may be transplanted to individual containers and placed outside (Sheats 1953). Seeds do not germinate well nor do seedlings survive if planted too late in the season. Seedlings benefit from light shade the first year. Seeds will germinate within 2–3 weeks of planting.

Cuttings

Some species of *Hypericum* are easily rooted from softwood or semihardwood cuttings taken from early summer and again in the fall from the tips of the current year's growth. Treat the cuttings with 1,500–2,500 ppm IBA "quick-dip" and place them under mist in peat/perlite (Bronstad, personal communication, 1999). Cuttings usually root in 4 weeks and transplant readily.

Transplanting

Hypericum can be transplanted in the winter. Cut back top foliage by one-third and keep damp but not soggy until adapted to its new site.

NOTES

Hypericum is a large genus containing many ornamental species used in border plantings, shrubberies, and rock gardens. Some species prefer moist shady locations under specimen trees or taller plants where grass and other ground covers will not grow. Most species are very cold hardy and retain their foliage year round. *Hypericum* is typically not browsed by deer.

Our species do best if planted in deeper soils, given strong morning sunlight, and protection or shade in the afternoon. Occasionally the leaves will become chlorotic in the summer, typically a response to heat stress. Cut back any burned stems and refresh the plant by adding compost and providing plenty of water.

SPECIES DESCRIPTIONS

***Hypericum densiflorum* (Dense St. John's Wort)**

Shrub to 6½ feet, much-branched on top, with slender, upright branches. Flowers are numerous, held in crowded clusters. Native to pinewood slopes and edges of swamps along streams from Florida to southwest Texas.

***Hypericum fasciculatum* (Sand-weed)**

Shrub to 3 feet with evergreen foliage. Flowers singly or in small numbers at the ends of upper branches. Wet places near ponds and lakes in pinelands and forests from Florida to southeast Texas.

***Hypericum frondosum* (Golden St. John's Wort)**
Shrub to 3 feet, widely branching with large, showy golden-yellow flowers. Found in dry, sandy, or rocky thickets and also in wetter soils along streams from southeast Texas to Georgia, occasionally in cultivation. Wood needs to be firm (early summer) before cuttings are taken (Dirr and Heuser 1987).

***Hypericum nudiflorum* (Naked St. John's Wort)**
Shrub to 6 feet, usually shorter. Flowers numerous in open clusters at the ends of branches. Grows in moist sandy woods from east Texas to Georgia.

Ilex

Holly

AQUIFOLIACEAE (HOLLY FAMILY)

GENERAL DESCRIPTION

Members of this genus are typically shrubs or trees with both evergreen and deciduous leaves (see Species Descriptions).

FLOWERS AND FRUIT

Male and female flowers occur on separate plants. The fruit is a round drupe turning either red, black, or orange-red when ripe. Each fruit contains four to eight hard seeds. If you desire a fruiting specimen, make sure you obtain a female tree. Some nurseries do not have their hollies well marked. Some species, like *Ilex vomitoria*, 'Pride of Houston,' have been selected and produced clonally for superior and reliable fruit-bearing characteristics. Doremus Wholesale Nursery in Warren, Texas, is introducing the 'Fontenot Series' of superior female Possum-haw hollies (*I. deciduous*) that are notable for their variation in fruiting colors ranging from amber to orange to deep red.

NATURAL HABITAT, RANGE, AND PREFERRED SITE

Hollies grow in a variety of sites in the eastern half of Texas. See Species Descriptions for individual range and habitat. Many species occur in cultivation and are adapted to a wide range of soils and conditions.

COLLECTION AND STORAGE

Collect the fruits in the fall from September to November when they have filled out and turned their ripe color. They may be gathered by hand or by flailing the fruit onto drop cloths. Clean the seeds and air dry several days at room temperature before storing. Air drying is not necessary if the seeds are to be sown immediately or stratified. Seeds may be successfully stored for at least 1 year if kept in sealed containers at 41° F.

PROPAGATION

Seeds

Holly seeds are often slow to germinate because they may have a hard endocarp surrounding the embryo combined with internal dormancy. In addition, some hollies, like American Holly (*I. opaca*), have an immature embryo at the time of harvest and require a period of after-ripening before the germination process can begin.

Some hollies reproduce best if planted outdoors immediately after they have been collected and before the seeds have had a chance to dry after cleaning. The warm temperatures of fall provide the necessary period of after-ripening while the colder temperatures of winter fulfill the cold dormancy requirement. However, some seeds sown in the fall fail to germinate until the second or third spring. Fall beds should be lightly mulched until germination has begun.

Seeds of some species may be pretreated first by stratifying for 30–60 days at 68–86° F followed by 60–90 days of cold moist storage at 41° F. Germination is also improved for some species of hollies by first scarifying the seeds for a short time in concentrated sulfuric acid prior to stratification. Cover seeds with ⅛–½ inch of soil. Seedlings benefit from shade the first season. See individual species for more guidelines.

Cuttings

Many species of *Ilex* are reproduced from cuttings, but with varying success rates. General recommendations for this genus suggest taking semihardwood cuttings selected from well-matured growth from early summer (May to June) through the year to early spring.

Cuttings taken in fall may be the most successful. These should be tip cuttings with firm wood with a portion of wood from the previous season's growth. Fatter or thicker cuttings root better than spindly ones. Treat with 1,000–3,000 IBA talc or solution for easy to root species.

Species more difficult to root should be wounded first and then treated with 1–2% IBA. Cuttings need to be in a well-drained soil medium (peat/perlite) under mist, and bottom heat may be beneficial. Rooting usually occurs in 4–8 weeks and cuttings should be gradually hardened off to adjust to outdoor conditions.

Transplanting

Most holly species are frequently and successfully transplanted from the wild or from field-grown nursery operations in the winter and balled and burlapped.

NOTES

Several of our native hollies, especially the evergreen forms, have been in cultivation for many years. The smaller and deciduous species deserve further study.

SPECIES DESCRIPTIONS

***Ilex ambigua* (Carolina Holly, Sand Holly)**
Shrub or small tree rarely as tall as 20 feet with deciduous ovate-elliptic leaves. Sandy woods, along streams from Florida, west to Arkansas and east Texas.

***Ilex coriaceae* (Bay-gall Bush, Ink-berry Holly)**
Tree-like evergreen shrub to 16 feet with slender branchlets and purple-black fruit. Swamps and low stream banks from southeast Texas to Florida.

***Ilex decidua* (Possum-haw Holly, Deciduous Holly)**
Shrub or small tree to 32 feet with pale twigs. In the fall bright yellow, red, or reddish orange fruit is borne in prolific clusters closely attached to the stems on female plants. Native to woods, roadsides, and thickets from Florida to central Texas, also in cultivation. Thrives in moist but not soggy sites in full or partial sun. It is fairly adaptable, but looks best in deeper soils that receive some moisture in the summer.

Possum-haw Holly contributes a wonderful form to the winter garden. Its arching branches are dotted heavily with fruit that stays on the stem after the leaves have fallen. To be fully successful, Possum-haw requires careful placement. In a shrub border or lawn, it will sucker out to form a multi-trunked clump, but if allowed to express its own nature, a grove of Possum-haws against the edge of the woods or at the back of the property is truly wonderful. Birds (especially mockingbirds) love the fruit, and deer browse the foliage.

This deciduous species is not particularly easy to root from cuttings. Semihardwood cuttings taken in early summer just as the wood begins to harden seem to root best. The proper degree of wood maturity is critical (Dirr and Heuser 1987). In one study, 5–6 inch long cuttings were taken and treated with 7,500 ppm IBA solution and kept under mist. These were overwintered in a greenhouse and kept under shade another year before being planted out (Dirr and Heuser 1987).

Another grower recommends taking semihardwood cuttings in the summer and treating with 3,000 ppm IBA "quick-dip." Cuttings can take up to 2 months to root. Do not shift cuttings into a liner cell until they have developed a good strong root system, or they'll rot. Rooted cuttings are typically slow (12 months or longer) to finish a one-gallon container. After that, growth rate is more rapid (Bronstad, personal communication, 1999).

Ilex opaca **(American Holly)**
Evergreen tree up to 50 feet, though usually less, with stout, stiff branches and evergreen, spine-tipped foliage. Red or rarely yellow fruit. Moist woods, along stream banks, and in swamps in east and south-central Texas. Understory tree with many horticultural varieties. Has a slow growth rate. Methods for vegetative propagation include taking 4-inch long semi-hardwood cuttings late August through February or early March. Strip all but the two upper leaves, and double wound each cutting. Treat with NAA and NA-acetamide or 1–2% IBA "quick dip" for good root development. Root in peat/perlite under mist. Bottom heat is helpful to rooting. Rooting takes place in 15 weeks. Drench mist bed with fungicides before sticking in the cutting.

Ilex verticillata **(Common Winterberry)**
A deciduous, red-berried holly forming a tall shrub or small tree 25 feet tall. Leaves varying in texture from thin to leathery, usually light green, oval-shaped with a pointed end. Native to swamps and wet woods, riverbanks in east Texas. The most cold hardy of all native hollies (Vines 1970). There are several horticultural forms and varieties of this plant. One of the easiest deciduous hollies to root. Take semihardwood tip cuttings in summer, treat with 7,500 ppm IBA talc. Stick in peat/perlite and keep under mist. Rooting usually occurs in 6–8 weeks in high percentages (Dirr and Heuser 1987). In 2 years, well-branched specimens bearing lots of fruit are ready for sale.

Ilex vomitoria **(Yaupon Holly)**
Shrub or tree with evergreen foliage, single- or multi-trunked with bright red berries on female trees. Common in low woods and thickets along streams and roadsides from Texas and Arkansas east to Florida. Most abundant native holly, widely adaptable.

Semihardwood cuttings taken in late fall and treated with 3,000 ppm IBA solution rooted 50% (Dirr and Heuser 1987). Growers apparently experience quite a bit of inconsistency in rooting success of this species from year to year. Choose healthy, vigorous stock plants and experiment with higher rates of hormone treatment.

Itea virginica

Virginia Sweet-spire, Tassel-white

SAXIFRAGACEAE (SAXIFRAGE FAMILY)

GENERAL DESCRIPTION

Virginia Sweet-spire is a slender branched shrub to 8½ feet with wide oval leaves turning red in autumn.

FLOWERS AND FRUIT

Very showy five-petaled white flowers are held in graceful drooping racemes at the ends of the branches in April and May. Fruit is an oblong capsule with several minute seeds ripening in the fall.

NATURAL HABITAT, RANGE, AND PREFERRED SITE

Virginia Sweet-spire is native to moist sites around lakes or along wooded streams from east Texas to Florida. It prefers acid sandy soil and partial shade.

COLLECTION AND STORAGE

Collect seeds in late summer or early fall and remove from the capsule by allowing the fruit to dry a few days and then lightly crush in a bag. Store the seeds in sealed containers in the refrigerator.

PROPAGATION

Seeds

Pretreatment is not necessary for germination. Seeds are very tiny, and the best germination rates are achieved if they are sown thinly in flats in early spring in a greenhouse. Seeds are delicate and are sometimes difficult to move from the flat. Transplant to containers when seedlings are 4 inches tall. Virginia Sweet-spire grows best if kept in a container for 1 year before being placed at the planting site.

Cuttings

Sweet-spire is very easily propagated from semihardwood cuttings taken in late summer or early fall. Collect cuttings when wood is firm. Take cuttings 3–4 inches long from sideshoots and treat with 1,500–2,500 IBA solution. Stick in peat/perlite and keep under mist (Bronstad, personal communication, 1999). Rooting occurs in high percentages in 4 weeks. Rooted cuttings will make a finished one-gallon plant in 6–8 months. Tip prune plants frequently to encourage bushy instead of lanky growth. Untreated softwood cuttings that are firm at the base and taken in the summer will also root.

NOTES

The long tassels of white flowers and red fall foliage make Sweet-spire an attractive ornamental in a woodland garden or as an understory plant. Since solitary plants can be straggly in shape, mass plantings of this species are most effective.

Juglans

Walnut, Nogal

JUGLANDACEAE (WALNUT FAMILY)

GENERAL DESCRIPTION

Walnuts are trees with furrowed scaly bark and durable dark-colored wood. Their leaves are pinnately compound with numerous long pointed leaflets.

FLOWERS AND FRUIT

Male and female flowers bloom separately on the same tree in spring just before or with the appearance of the new leaves. Fruit is a nut with a woody shell or pericarp enclosed in a thick green husk, ripening in fall.

NATURAL HABITAT, RANGE, AND PREFERRED SITE

Walnuts are found in fields and rich woodlands in east Texas, as well as the stream banks, bottomlands, and canyons of central and west Texas. Walnuts are also cultivated throughout the United States. See Species Descriptions for individual range and habitat.

COLLECTION AND STORAGE

Collect the nuts in late fall or early winter when the husks begin to turn black and split open. During dry years the nuts may drop early. Any husks remaining attached should be removed prior to sowing or storage. It is not necessary to remove the shell of the nuts.

Nuts should be sown immediately or kept in moist sand over winter until spring planting. Nuts lose viability if allowed to dry out.

PROPAGATION

Seeds

Germination of walnuts is delayed by a dormant embryo and a hard seed coat. Embryo dormancy can be broken by either fall sowing outdoors in prepared beds or by stratification at 34–41° F for 60–90 days followed by spring sowing. For indoor stratification, use coarse perlite or moist sand.

Often fall-sown nuts will extend a root during the winter, and shoot growth will be delayed until the warmer temperatures of spring.

Protect outdoor seedbeds from predation by squirrels and other rodents with wire mesh or screen. Keep the seedbed slightly moist and mulched over winter. Cover the nuts with 1–2 inches of soil. For field sowing, the seeds should be planted at the rate of 15 seeds per square foot. Field-grown walnut seedlings should be annually root pruned to produce a more compact root system, which makes them easier to ball and burlap for transplanting (USDA 1974). Container-grown walnuts require a deep pot to accommodate a long taproot. They do not appear to respond favorably to pots with copper-treated interior surfaces (Will, personal communication, 1999). Place seedlings in a five-gallon container by the end of the first growing season.

Cuttings

Improved selections and cultivars of walnuts are routinely propagated by grafting and budding onto established rootstocks.

Transplanting

Field-grown walnut trees are frequently balled and burlapped and sold in winter. Information is lacking on techniques for successfully transplanting mature specimens from the wild.

NOTES

The wood of walnuts is prized as a source of high-grade lumber for making fine furniture and cabinets. The nuts are edible and provide food for wildlife. The most widely planted native species is Black Walnut, *J. nigra.*

Retired horticultural scientist Dr. Loy Shreve of Uvalde, Texas, is widely regarded as the Texas authority on walnuts and other nut-bearing trees. For up-to-the minute information on walnuts, consult the resources for nut species listed under *Carya.*

SPECIES DESCRIPTIONS

Juglans major **(Arizona Walnut, Nogal)**

Tree to 48 feet with a rounded crown and deeply furrowed bark. Leaflets number from 9 to 13. The nut is small and edible with a hard thick shell. Grows along streams and canyons in the Edwards Plateau and Trans-Pecos, also southwest New Mexico, central Arizona, and northern Mexico.

Juglans microcarpa **(River Walnut, Little Walnut, Nogalillo)**

Large shrub or small tree to 20 feet with smooth or lightly furrowed branches forming a broad rounded crown. Along streams and arroyos in south and west Texas from Oklahoma to southeast New Mexico.

***Juglans nigra* (Black Walnut)**
Large tree to 160 feet with wide-spreading branches forming an umbrella-like crown. Nut edible and oily. Fields and rich woodlands in east Texas, from the northeast United States to Florida, west to Texas. Slow-growing but magnificent specimen tree. Deep taproot makes transplanting difficult.

Juniperus

Juniper, Cedar, Cedro

CUPRESSACEAE (CYPRESS FAMILY)

GENERAL DESCRIPTION

Junipers are aromatic evergreen shrubs or trees with reddish wood (see Species Descriptions). Leaves are scalelike needles held oppositely on the stem or in whorls of three.

FLOWERS AND FRUIT

Male and female flowers usually bloom on different plants. Fruit is a berrylike cone turning red to dark purple when ripe with one to several seeds. Seeds of some species ripen the first year while others ripen the second or third year. Average fruit-bearing age is 10–20 years. Seeds are often dispersed by birds, but ripe fruits will sometimes persist on the plant. Good seed crops are produced at irregular intervals (USDA 1974).

NATURAL HABITAT, RANGE, AND PREFERRED SITE

Eastern Red Cedar, *J. virginiana*, and Southern Red-Coat Juniper, *J. silicicola*, are native to the eastern third of the state. Other species occur from central to far west Texas. See Species Descriptions for individual range and habitat.

COLLECTION AND STORAGE

Collect seeds from late summer through fall when the fruit has filled out and turned its ripe color. Gather seeds from several different plants because seed quality often varies from tree to tree. Cut the seeds open and examine them during collection to see if they are filled out and mature. Thoroughly dry or clean seeds immediately after harvesting to avoid mold and overheating.

Species with resinous fruits should be soaked for 1–2 days in a mild lye solution (1 teaspoon per gallon of water) to make them easier to clean. Rinse the seeds thoroughly after soaking and either plant immediately or air dry at room temperature for several days before storing. Store juniper seeds in dry sealed containers at 20–40° F. Under these conditions most species will retain viability for long periods.

PROPAGATION

Seeds

Germination of *Juniperus* is inhibited by a dormant embryo. Some species also have a hard seed coat and chemical inhibitors in the resinous fruit that combine with dormancy to delay germination (USDA 1974). For those species that exhibit only a dormant embryo (*J. ashei*, *J. monosperma*, *J. virginiana*), fall planting outdoors or stratification at 41° F for 30–120 days is typically sufficient pretreatment.

Stratification at freezing temperatures should be avoided because it may either lengthen dormancy or damage the seeds. In one study, germination of Eastern Red Cedar (*J. virginiana*) was improved by first soaking the seeds in a 1% solution of citric acid for 4 days preceding a period of cold stratification (USDA 1974).

Weeping juniper (*J. flaccida*) will germinate readily from cleaned seeds (Hosage, personal communication, 1999).

Species with both a dormant embryo and an impermeable seed coat (e.g., Alligator Juniper, *J. deppeana*) must be scarified prior to stratification or fall sowing. Alligator Juniper seeds can require up to a year of cold stratification before germination will proceed. In one study, seeds stratified for 76 days at 41° F yielded 30% germination rates. Viability of alligator seeds is limited and unreliable (Manning, personal communication, 1999).

Seeds of Red-berried Juniper (*J. pinchotii*) soaked in concentrated sulfuric acid for 45 minutes before cold stratification germinated better than untreated seeds exposed to warm and cold periods of stratification alone (USDA 1974).

Information is lacking on appropriate pretreatment methods for Southern Red-coat Juniper (*J. silicicola*).

For nursery production, juniper seeds are usually sown in late summer or early fall. Spring-sown seeds are removed from stratification by late winter or early spring and then planted out before the soil temperature reaches 70° F. Nursery liners can be planted outdoors in well-prepared beds in rows 6–8 inches apart covered with ¼ inch of soil. Mulch the beds to prevent drying but remove as soon as germination begins. Most species benefit from light shade the first season.

Juniper seedlings may be balled and burlapped from the field after the first or second year. Avoid bare-root transplanting.

Cuttings

Some species of junipers are easily rooted; others root with difficulty, if at all. Although members of this genus play a prominent role in the nursery industry, information is lacking on specific techniques for our native junipers. General guidelines may be useless for junipers growing in the arid Southwest. For a thorough discussion on the main parameters of vegetative propagation of this genus, see Dirr and Heuser (1987).

NOTES

The evergreen foliage, durable wood, and drought tolerance of the western species make junipers excellent landscape plants for both ornamental and wildlife plantings. In their native habitats junipers are often aggressive invaders of overgrazed range and pastures. Junipers are resistant to damping-off and root rot fungi, but all except Ashe Juniper are susceptible to cedar blight, which is very difficult to control. Other diseases that affect junipers but are easier to cure are cedar-apple rust and Cercospora blight. Spider mites can also be a problem during hot weather.

Ashe Juniper provides the main nesting site for the rare golden-cheeked warbler.

Because of their pervasiveness, many people adopt a "scorched-earth" policy toward junipers, believing that the only good juniper is a dead one. In new subdivisions, however, protecting existing junipers is often the only way to screen the view of the neighbor's garage or to hold a hillside. Junipers in the landscape should be considered a valuable part of the native mosaic. They can provide stability to a site under construction and offer valuable shade and protection to newly planted landscapes.

SPECIES DESCRIPTIONS

Juniperus ashei (Ashe Juniper, Rock Cedar)

Large shrub or small tree to 20 feet, usually multi-trunked. Mature fruit dark blue. Common on poor, rocky soil along ravines, arroyos, and in pastures. Quickly invades disturbed or overgrazed sites. From west and central Texas to Arkansas. The shredding bark of older Ashe Junipers provides nesting material for the golden-cheeked warbler.

Juniperus deppeana (Alligator Juniper)

Small tree to 48 feet with distinctive bark furrowed into square or checkered plates. Fruit a reddish brown cone maturing the second year. Leaves bluish green. In open rocky soil on slopes with scrub oak in the mountains and foothills of the Trans-Pecos area, west to central Arizona. One of the most ornamental of all the junipers, it is unfortunately also one of the most difficult to grow.

***Juniperus flaccida* (Weeping Juniper)**
Small tree to 20 feet with stocky furrowed bark and spreading branches bearing graceful drooping stems and leaves. Fruit is reddish brown. Native to forested and rocky slopes of the Chisos Mountains in west Texas to southern Mexico.

***Juniperus monosperma* (One-seeded Juniper)**
Large shrub to small multi-trunked tree up to 20 feet. Characterized by large dark purple fruit. Most often found on steep slopes and broken ground around rimrocks and eroded soil of arroyos and brushlands in the Panhandle and Trans-Pecos, also northward to Oklahoma, Arizona, Nevada, and northern Mexico.

***Juniperus pinchotii* (Red-berried Juniper)**
Large shrub or small tree to 20 feet, multi-trunked, often forming a dense trunk. Fruit reddish or coppery brown. Native to gravelly or rocky soil in open flats and dry hills from central Texas north to the Plains country, also southeast New Mexico and western Oklahoma.

***Juniperus silicicola* (Southern Red-coat Juniper)**
Medium-sized tree to 32 feet or more with ascending branches forming a pyramidal crown. Fruits are deep blue. Native to sandy soils in southeast Texas on the coastal plain west to central Florida. Similar to Eastern Red-coat Juniper, but with slender, more elongated, and pendulous branchlets and smaller leaves and cones.

***Juniperus virginiana* (Eastern Red Cedar)**
Medium-sized to large tree up to 96 feet tall with a single trunk and a pyramidal form. Fruit dark blue to purple. A field or pasture tree in dry forests west to Travis County, north to the Panhandle, Oklahoma, and New York. Near Elgin and McDade, Texas, there is a very interesting columnar-formed population of Eastern Red Cedar. Their shape is similar to Italian cypress, suggesting potential of a horticultural selection with many special landscape applications. Presently these are being dug from the field and not propagated as a nursery crop.

Koeberlinia spinosa

Allthorn, Crucifixion Thorn, Corona de Cristo Junco

KOEBERLINACEAE

GENERAL DESCRIPTION

Allthorn is a rounded tangle of smooth green (mostly) leafless stems. At maturity, it can reach 8 feet tall and 6 feet wide. The twisted stems are stiff and spine-tipped. Tiny leaves drop in early spring.

FLOWERS AND FRUIT

Allthorn bears small inconspicuous flowers from March to October. By fall the plant is covered in clusters of shiny ¼-inch black and red berries which make a nice contrast to the lizard-green stems.

NATURAL HABITAT, RANGE, AND PREFERRED SITE

Allthorn grows on rocky open sites, clay mounds, in mattoral (brushlands) of the southern Rio Grande Plains, and in arroyos in the Trans-Pecos. It also grows west to southeastern California and Arizona, and south to Mexico.

COLLECTION AND STORAGE

Allthorns' thorny stems can make seed collection intimidating, but fruit production is often prolific, so that gathering from the outermost branches is sufficient. Collect fruits in August/September. The trick is beating the birds, who love the fruit. Clean the pulp from the seeds on a screen, and then let them air dry slightly before sowing or storage. Information on seed longevity in storage is lacking.

PROPAGATION

Seeds

Freshly gathered seed planted promptly will germinate 60–70% without treatment. Sow in individual plant cells or 4-inch containers in very well drained soil. Seeds are very slow growing at first, taking a year before they are ready for transplanting into a one-gallon container. Once they have rooted out a one-gallon pot, their growth rate accelerates considerably (Manning, personal communication, 1999). Young seedlings are sensitive to overwatering (Cox, personal communication, 1999).

NOTES

Allthorn is a good example of adaptation to desert conditions. When the tiny leaves are shed during the dry season, the smooth green twigs and large thorns carry on the job of photosynthesis.

Allthorn makes an interesting specimen plant, its fruit is eaten by many birds, and its form lends itself to use as a physical barrier or security barrier. Allthorn is very cold hardy, and must be planted in full sun.

Lantana horrida

Texas Lantana, Hierba de Cristo

VERBENACEAE (VERBENA FAMILY)

GENERAL DESCRIPTION

Lantana is a familiar deciduous shrub usually 3–4 feet tall with rough, dark green leaves that have a very pungent smell when crushed. Except in extreme south Texas, the branches and leaves freeze back each year to the base, eventually forming a broad, spreading clump.

FLOWERS AND FRUIT

Flowers are showy and begin blooming with the onset of hot weather. Their main flowering period lasts from August to September. Flowers are borne in many-flowered, bouquet-like heads of orange, red, and yellow mixed together or occasionally of one color. Fruit is a purple-black drupe containing two small nutlets, ripening in late summer through fall.

NATURAL HABITAT, RANGE, AND PREFERRED SITE

Lantana is native to fields, thickets, swamps, rich sandy woods, gravelly hills, flats, chaparral, and roadsides throughout most of Texas, especially in the south and southwest but rarely in the extreme northwest. Lantana is also cultivated in New Mexico, Arizona, California, and northern Mexico, east to Mississippi. It thrives in any hot dry location with poor soil, such as abandoned fields, vacant lots, roadsides, and old home sites.

COLLECTION AND STORAGE

Collect the seeds as soon as the fruit has filled out and turned dark, primarily in late summer and early fall. Seeds may be air dried with the pulp still on or cleaned before storage. Storage in sealed containers in the refrigerator is adequate for 1 year.

PROPAGATION

Seeds

Lantana will germinate without pretreatment from first-year seeds planted outdoors after the soil has warmed and all danger of frost is past, or earlier in the greenhouse. Germination is often irregular and staggered over a month-long period. Seed quality and vigor may vary greatly from plant to plant each year.

Cuttings

Lantana is most easily reproduced from softwood or semihardwood cuttings of the current season's growth. These should be taken in the summer from sideshoots that are firm toward the base, 4–8 inches long, with the leaves removed from the bottom half. Insert the cuttings into a 1:2 peat/perlite mixture and keep under intermittent mist. Application of IBA improves rooting but is not imperative. Rooting is usually accomplished within 3 weeks.

Fall-rooted cuttings need cold-frame protection until spring.

Lantana may also be propagated from root cuttings taken in late winter before new growth has started.

Transplanting

Lantana is easily transplanted from the field in winter if cut back to the ground and kept damp. Large clumps can usually be divided in winter as well.

NOTES

Lantana is an attractive ornamental plant when used as a low to medium flowering ground cover in rock gardens, median strips, right-of-ways, rocky slopes, or any exposed dry place with poor soil. Its abundant and generous display of flowers during the hottest time of the year provides relief and color during an otherwise bleak and weary season.

Because Lantana will only bloom on new wood, cut back the plant after frost and occasionally during the growing season to encourage a compact form and a flush of new growth that will produce more flowers. Texas Lantana has been known to hybridize with West Indian Lantana or Afrombilla (*L. camara*). Like many other perennial shrubs, Lantana should be cut back to the base each year. Mature plants tend to form large mounds that can be separated into smaller plants in the winter.

The leaves of Lantana are poisonous to livestock, but the seeds are eaten by birds, including bobwhite quail and mockingbirds. It is a food plant for butterfly larvae and source of nectar for adult butterflies. In Mexico, the crushed leaves are sometimes times used to treat snakebite.

A western species, Veiny-leaf or Desert Lantana (*L. macropoda*), is also worthy of attention, especially for dry desert gardens. It is a fuzzy aromatic shrub with slender, brittle wandlike branches and white and pink flowers. It is smaller than Texas Lantana, and is native to gravelly hills and rocky arroyos in central, west, and south Texas. A form of this species (*forma albiflora*) occurs in Star and Cameron counties in far south Texas and in northern Mexico. It is very aromatic and is often used as a mint (Powell 1988).

Larrea tridentata

Creosote Bush, Gobernadora, Hediondilla

ZYGOPHYLLACEAE (CALTROP FAMILY)

GENERAL DESCRIPTION

Creosote Bush is an evergreen shrub occasionally reaching 10 feet, but more often averaging 3–5 feet, with many slender, irregularly branching stems rising from the base. Closely attached dull or olive-green leaflets cover the branchlets. Leaves are coated with a sticky pungent or petroleum-scented resin that gives the plant its most widely recognized English common name. The familiar fresh, spicy smell one recognizes in the Chihuahuan Desert after a rainstorm comes from the Creosote Bush.

FLOWERS AND FRUIT

Small but prolific yellow flowers bloom most abundantly in the spring but also appear intermittently throughout the summer, especially after rains. Each flower has five petals, ¼–⅓ inch long, and 10 stamens. Fruit is a small, rounded, densely fuzzy white capsule that divides into five hard carpels, each containing one tiny seed.

NATURAL HABITAT, RANGE, AND PREFERRED SITE

Creosote Bush is one of the indicator species for the Chihuahuan Desert along with *Agave lechuguilla* (Lechuguilla), *Dasylirion leiophyllum* (Sotol), and *Fouquiera splendens* (Ocotillo). Creosote Bush is probably the most common plant on the alluvial plains of the Trans-Pecos and is less frequently found in the mountains of that region eastward to the Edwards Plateau. It grows throughout the warm deserts of North America from California, Nevada, Arizona, and New Mexico west to Texas and south to northern Mexico.

Creosote Bush is generally found on gravelly plains, sandy soil, and rocky slopes. It must have well-drained soil in order to thrive. Its requirement for well-aerated soils makes it difficult to grow successfully in a container. Creosote Bush is extremely drought tolerant and under cultivation will respond to increased watering and fertilizing by either dying from root rot or becoming lankier and producing dark green leaves and fewer blooms.

COLLECTION AND STORAGE

Collect the ripe fruits in late spring through summer by stripping the plants. Air dry and fumigate the fruits before storage. Seeds may be stored with or without the hard fruit covering or carpel. In one report, seed viability was not affected after 4 years of dry storage at room temperature (USDA 1974).

PROPAGATION

Seeds

Creosote Bush is slow to germinate because of the hard covering of the fruit capsule (carpel). Seed coat inhibitors are efficient devices used by many desert species to insure that germination does not occur until there is sufficient moisture in the ground.

Hulling the seeds improves germination dramatically. In one study, 45% of soaked unhulled seeds germinated after 11 days compared to an 85% germination rate of the hulled seeds (Tipton 1984). Large amounts of hulls may be removed in a mechanical huller.

For fewer seeds, the carpel may be broken by filing off one end with sandpaper. Average number of extracted seeds per pound is 170,000 (USDA 1974). Aerating unhulled seeds in water for up to 48 hours also often improves germination (McNeal, personal communication, 1999).

Creosote Bush seedlings are very sensitive to watering in the greenhouse. The seed flat should contain a light, well-drained soil mix, and care should be taken not to overwater. Treat the soil mix with a fungicide and inoculate with beneficial microorganisms (Gass, personal communication, 1999). Salable one-gallon plants can be produced in 1 year from seed. Five-gallon plants take 2 years (Gass, personal communication, 1999).

Cuttings

Creosote Bush is slow and difficult to root from cuttings. Detailed information on successful techniques is lacking. It is likely that the best cutting material could be obtained from juvenile wood of nursery-grown stock plants or plants forced in the greenhouse.

Transplanting

Creosote Bush is extremely difficult to transplant from the field because of a long taproot. Transplanting foliar-pruned small shrubs without prior root pruning in early spring or late winter proved to be most successful (Tipton, personal communication, 1986). Do not let the root system dry out at all during the digging process. Soak the roots of small plants in water immediately after transplanting.

NOTES

Creosote Bush is the dominant evergreen shrub of most desert landscapes. With minimal irrigation, plants grow rapidly into large shrubs providing dappled shade and screening even in a parched setting. Creosote Bush has been used in soil stabilization and as shelter for the desert tortoise; the seeds are eaten by a variety of desert animals (Wasowski 1995).

The resins on the leaves as well as its tendency to defoliate during drought, like most desert plants, make Creosote Bush one of the most drought tolerant of species. Creosote Bush can continue to manufacture the sugars needed for growth long after the dryness of the soil has forced other plants into dormancy. Thus the plant is ready immediately to flush new growth to take advantage of sudden and infrequent rains (Bowers 1993).

Creosote Bush can be very long lived. As the older stems in the center of the bush die, new stems from the edge of the plant emerge from the original rootstock, perpetuating a clone that may be as old as 100 years (Bowers 1993).

The dark green foliage, bright yellow flowers, and showy white fruit make this plant an outstanding ornamental for arid regions of west Texas. Creosote Bush is strongly aromatic after rains. Occasionally Creosote Bush is mistakenly called Greasewood.

Creosote Bush was used in traditional folk medicine as a dressing for cuts and bruises on both humans and livestock. The leaves are reportedly poisonous to sheep, and the plant is not browsed by livestock. However, an edible livestock feed has been developed from Creosote Bush, and a valuable antitoxin has been commercially extracted from the plant (USDA 1974).

Leitneria floridana

Corkwood

LEITNERIACEAE (CORKWOOD FAMILY)

GENERAL DESCRIPTION

Corkwood is a shrub or small tree to 20 feet with slender stems and very lightweight wood. Bark is brown and smooth when young, becoming fissured with age. Leaves are deciduous, narrowly oval, and more or less scattered along the stem.

FLOWERS AND FRUIT

Male and female flowers are greenish white and inconspicuous. Fruit is a leathery drupe, 1 inch long, containing a single seed that ripens from late summer into fall.

NATURAL HABITAT, RANGE, AND PREFERRED SITE

Corkwood is rare in Texas, found only infrequently in brackish or fresh water swamps near Port Arthur, High Island, and Matagorda Island; also east to Florida, north to Georgia and Missouri. Corkwood prefers low, moist, or poorly drained areas with sandy soil in full or partial sun.

COLLECTION AND STORAGE

Seed collection is sometimes difficult because Corkwood does not set seeds in large quantities each year. Seeds may be stored with the pulp dried on or cleaned. Keep in sealed containers in the refrigerator. Information on seed longevity in storage is lacking.

PROPAGATION

Seeds

Sow seeds thinly in 6-inch pots using one part peat and one part fine sand. The seeds should be sown early in the spring in a greenhouse or cold frame. Press the seeds into the soil and cover lightly with ¼ inch, then gently water in. Keep the soil moist during germination. When seedlings are 3 inches tall, move them outdoors to a protected and lightly shaded location. Germination rates vary widely among seed lots. Prune plants at regular intervals to encourage bushy growth. In one report, 3 months of cold stratification improved germination (Dirr and Heuser 1987).

Cuttings

Corkwood is most easily and reliably reproduced from softwood or hardwood cuttings. Softwood cuttings should be 3–4 inches long, and the leaves should be removed from the bottom halves of the cuttings. Treat with 3,000–8,000 ppm IBA talc plus thiram and keep under intermittent mist. Rooting is usually accomplished within 3 weeks.

Cuttings taken in the winter from roots may also be used. These should be 1½ inches long, tied together in small bundles, and placed in a box of moist sand in a cold frame. Rooting takes place within 2 weeks of the appearance of the first shoots (Sheats 1953).

Dormant cuttings rooted in the greenhouse in the winter should be gradually hardened off in a cold frame before planting outside in the spring.

NOTES

The graceful stems, attractive light green leaves, and tolerance of poorly drained sites make Corkwood a valuable landscape plant, especially for wetlands and marshy areas. Because Corkwood is rare in Texas, it should be protected and increased through cultivation as an ornamental.

Corkwood will often form colonies by sending up shoots from far-ranging roots and thus is effective in erosion control near a beach or pond. Corkwood can be allowed to grow tall and lanky or be pruned back periodically to make a shorter, more compact screen or group planting. Corkwood was traditionally valued as a source of fishing corks or floats for nets.

Leucaena retusa

Goldenball Leadtree, Guaje

FABACEAE (LEGUME FAMILY)

GENERAL DESCRIPTION

Goldenball Leadtree is a deciduous small tree or large shrub typically 6–12 feet tall with irregular light-colored branches and brittle stems. In nature Goldenball Leadtree is often multi-trunked but under cultivation may be pruned to form a single-trunked specimen.

FLOWERS AND FRUIT

Showy flowers appear as bright yellow puffballs held in clusters at the ends of the branches. Goldenball Leadtree blooms primarily from May to June and also intermittently throughout the summer and fall, especially after rains. Fruit is a long legume containing several shiny brown seeds, each ¼ inch long. When ripe, the pod twists open to disperse the seeds. Seeds are often infested with weevils.

NATURAL HABITAT, RANGE, AND PREFERRED SITE

Goldenball Leadtree grows in scattered locations in dry canyons and on limestone slopes in the western part of the Edwards Plateau, as far east as Kendall, Uvalde, and Real counties, west to the Davis and Chisos mountains of the Trans-Pecos, south to northern Mexico.

Goldenball Leadtree is nowhere abundant, but when found is usually growing with other trees in scattered groups or populations. One reason for its scarcity is that it is a favored browse plant of deer and goats. Goldenball Leadtree can survive on as little as 12–15 inches of rain a year and is cold hardy as far north as Dallas if given south-wall protection.

COLLECTION AND STORAGE

Gather the pods in late summer when they are brown and beginning to dry but before they have split open and dropped the seeds. Avoid gathering seeds from the ground. Spread seeds to dry 1–2 days and then fumigate before storing in sealed containers at room temperature. Seeds will remain viable for at least 2 years.

PROPAGATION

Seeds

Goldenball Leadtree is easily grown from first-year seed. Seeds generally do not require pretreatment. Slight scarification may speed germination but is not necessary and may result in weakened or deformed seedlings. Some seed lots germinate faster if first soaked in hot water and left until it has cooled and imbibition has started. Untreated seeds will germinate in 2–3 weeks when planted in the greenhouse or in late spring after all danger of frost has passed.

Planting the seed immediately after collection is the best way to avoid damage done to stored seeds by weevils (Gass, personal communication, 1999). Cover seeds with no more than ½ inch of soil. Best results may be achieved if seeds are planted separately in small pots which promote air pruning rather than in a seed flat. Transplant the seedlings to one-gallon containers after they are 6 inches tall.

Goldenball Leadtree germinates quickly but tends to grow slowly and remains spindly for a long time. Growers have typically had a difficult time discovering production methods that encourage reliable vigorous growth. Even fertilization has not seemed to make a dramatic difference. Some growers suspect that rhizobium inoculants applied to the soil mix might produce a stronger container plant because Goldenball Leadtree grows much more vigorously once it is removed from the container and placed in the ground.

Some growers have experienced more vigorous growth and better survival when seedlings were grown in Whitcomb "Rootmaker"™ pots and also in containers with copper-treated interior surfaces (Will, personal communication, 1999).

Keep the seedling in a one-gallon container for a year before moving it up to a five-gallon pot. At this stage, the growth rate of this plant often speeds up. Light tip pruning of the plant will promote better branching and form. It may be necessary to stake young seedlings at the planting site for the first season to insure that they grow upright.

Cuttings

Goldenball Leadtree may be grown from semihardwood cuttings taken in summer, treated with IBA (8,000 ppm), and kept under mist. Exact information on rooting rates and survivability is lacking.

Transplanting

The long taproot of this plant makes transplanting from the hard rocky soil of its native site difficult. Transplanting should be confined to small plants selected from field-grown nursery sites in the winter. In north Texas, Goldenball Leadtree should be planted in a protected area to protect the brittle stems from windstorms and extreme cold.

NOTES

The prolific yellow blooms, the interesting branching habit, and attractive light green foliage make Goldenball Leadtree an outstanding choice as an ornamental for rocky, dry, and sunny locations, especially slopes and other exposed areas. Its potential as a medium-sized specimen flowering tree has not been fully explored. If production methods can be successfully developed, this plant, like Yellowbells (*Tecoma stans var. angustata*), will sell itself. Goldenball Leadtree is cold tolerant as far north as McKinney, Texas, and would probably adapt to the southern High Plains (Simpson, personal communication, 1986). It is one of the top browse plants of choice for deer.

A related species, Tepeguaje (*L. pulverulenta*), is a widely planted native ornamental tree found in the extreme southern Rio Grande Plains (Cameron and Hidalgo counties), south to Mexico. It is not cold hardy very far north of its natural range. It has smooth, gray-brown branches forming a broad rounded crown with large, delicate twice-compound leaves consisting of many fine leaflets. The flowers bloom from March to June and are creamy white balls held in clusters. The tree produces many papery pods that drop continuously. Tepeguaje is one of the fastest growing trees in the world. In a little over a year from seed, this tree can grow more than 10 feet tall with a 10-foot canopy spread (Best, personal communication, 1999). Tepeguaje is useful in revegetation projects because it so quickly provides a canopy for birds to perch and nest on, which in turn begins the process of animal-ingested seed planting, and it also helps to shade out invasive grass and weeds, thus reducing competition for slower growing woody species that have been planted at the same time. Tepeguaje will germinate readily from seeds that have been acid scarified for 10–15 minutes (Best 1999).

Leucophyllum

Cenizo, Purple Sage, Texas Ranger

SCROPHULARIACEAE (SNAPDRAGON FAMILY)

GENERAL DESCRIPTION

Cenizos are densely branched shrubs with evergreen leaves typically covered with heavy white woolly-branched hairs that give them a silver-gray or greenish white appearance.

FLOWERS AND FRUIT

Showy bell-shaped flowers come in many colors and are attached close to the leaf axils. Colors range from white to pinkish purplish to deep violet. Cenizo will have several blooming periods usually after spells of high humidity or rain. Fruit is a small dry capsule containing tiny seeds.

NATURAL HABITAT, RANGE, AND PREFERRED SITE

Cenizo grows on arid sites from the western edge of the Edwards Plateau, the southern part of the Trans-Pecos, and south through the Rio Grande Plains, New Mexico, and northern Mexico. There are also many forms and selections in cultivation throughout the Southwest. See Species Descriptions for individual range and habitat.

COLLECTION AND STORAGE

Seeds are very tiny and can be tricky to collect in large amounts because as soon as the capsule dries and splits open, all the seeds are blown away within a few days. Gathering from a concentrated population of Cenizos is generally the best strategy as inevitably many of the capsules will already be empty. Seed can be collected in south Texas almost every month of the year. Both seed capsules and flowers will occur on the plant at the same time. Seeds stored in a cool dry place will remain viable for at least 1 year.

PROPAGATION

Seeds

Plant the seeds in a greenhouse immediately after collection in late summer or store over winter and plant outdoors in early spring after all danger of frost is past. Seed can also be started earlier in a greenhouse. Bottom heat may speed germination. Be sure the soil medium is well drained. Sprinkle the seeds densely on top of the seed flat (about 1,000 seeds to an 18 × 2 inch sized flat). Press the seeds in the soil without covering them and then tamp them in. Water gently but thoroughly. Seedlings usually emerge within 1–2 weeks. Seedlings don't appear to be particularly susceptible to damping-off fungi, but instead often show a failure to thrive, especially when planted in sterile potting soil mix.

Chris Best discovered that when he mixed native soil gathered from around the drip line of a mature Cenizo shrub in a 1:1 ratio with vermiculite, he had markedly more vigorous seedlings than when seeds were sown in sterile soil media alone. In the native soil mix, Cenizo seedlings grew quickly and were then transplanted into 6-inch plant bands, using the same soil blend supplemented with slow-release fertilizer (13-13-13). After 6 months seedlings had grown 18 inches tall and were then pinched back before being set in the field.

Cuttings

L. frutescens ('Greencloud,' 'White Cloud,' and hybrid 'Raincloud') will readily root from semihardwood cuttings of the current season's growth (new growth that has begun to harden off). *L. candidum* (Violet Silverleaf, 'Silvercloud,' 'Thundercloud'), *L. laevigatum*, *L. zygophyllum*, *L. langmaniae*, *L. pruinosum*, and *L. revolutum* are more difficult to propagate (Gass, personal communication, 1999).

In Arizona, cuttings are taken from June to September. These are 3–4 inches long with the leaves from the bottom half of the stem removed. They are then treated with IBA "quick-dip" solution (3,000–5,000 ppm) and placed in individual pots containing a 1:1 peat/perlite mixture.

Other growers in Texas take cuttings from April to July. They have observed that in late July the wood starts to harden off and is more difficult to root. Production is then paused until the fall, when a new flush of growth is produced by the parent plant. Treatment of the cuttings is the same as above (Pfeiffer, personal communication, 1999). Be careful not to stick the cuttings too deeply in the rooting medium and keep under intermittent mist. Rooting generally occurs within 3–4 weeks. As the cuttings begin to callus and form roots, gradually reduce the intervals of misting to harden the plants off and minimize the risk of stem rot. Turn the mist system off at night. Cuttings seem to root better in a peat/perlite mixture than in straight perlite alone. Cuttings taken during the hottest part of the summer can be very sensitive to watering regimes and require very careful hardening off as they move from the mist bench to the shade house.

A cutting taken in the summer will yield a five-gallon plant in a year. A one-gallon plant can be produced by the fall from a summer cutting (Gass, personal communication, 1999). Once cuttings have grown to 6 inches, pinch them back by half to encourage them to branch. Otherwise, a long whiplike young plant that will not be as sturdy or well formed will develop (Kirwin, personal communication, 1999).

Rooted cuttings of the 'Greencloud' and 'Silvercloud' selections can be planted directly into one-gallon containers after first being carefully acclimated from the mist house environment. Give the newly potted one-gallon plants 30–50% shade for at least 1–2 weeks and continue to provide frequent misting, though at ever-reducing intervals, until the leaves have hardened off (Kirwin, personal communication, 1999).

As Cenizo is moved up to five-gallon containers, periodic pruning of the branch tips (as opposed to radical shearing) will encourage a better form and more compact growth. Pruning should be carefully done to avoid both a contorted "meatball" shape and significant plant die-off. Reduce watering right after shearing. Cutting the plant over one-third of its new growth reduces its capacity to absorb water and makes it susceptible to rot if watering is not adjusted. It is also vital to separate the pots to provide adequate air flow among the rows and to allow the plants a chance to develop a symmetrical form.

NOTES

This genus contains some of the most ornamental of all native Texas plants. Their showy, prolific blooms, interesting silvery to gray-green evergreen foliage, and drought tolerance make them suitable for any full sun and arid situation. They are also generally unpalatable to deer and other browsing animals.

Cenizos must have well-drained alkaline soil and full sun to thrive and look their best. In shady situations, Cenizos become leggy and unattractive. If planted in acid soil, dolomitic limestone should be added to the beds to adjust the pH. In western areas, gypsum is the best soil amendment to add if supplemental calcium is needed.

L. frutescens will adapt to areas outside their natural range that receive higher amounts of rainfall, but it is a good idea to place them in raised beds to prevent root rot. Other *Leucophyllum spp.* are even less tolerant of poor drainage, and will not survive unless they are placed in gravelly arid soils.

In the nursery, the more silvery-leaved forms of *Leucophyllum* do not thrive in a standard pine-bark potting soil mix (Kirwin, personal communication, 1999). Also, Cenizos do not like to be placed in a shrub border near a lawn and receive the same irrigation.

L. frutescens has been in cultivation for many years and easily adapts to prepared sites as far east as Houston, if planted in raised beds (see above). Do not fertilize or amend the soil with heavy amounts of organic material. This will only encourage the plant to become leggy and produce fewer blooms.

Cenizo can be pruned to encourage a smaller, more compact form, but it seems a shame to ruin its natural shape entirely by shearing it into a tight globe, as one so frequently observes in Arizona and west Texas. Any pruning should be done in late winter or early spring and again in early summer if needed. Cenizos will lose some of their leaves during the winter, but will densely refoliate with the return of warm weather. Once established, Cenizos require little maintenance.

L. frutescens is hardy to 5° F. Cenizos are not susceptible to many insects or diseases except the cotton rot (or Texas root rot) fungus. Benny Simpson, plant scientist at the Texas A&M Research and Extension Service Center at Dallas, developed five particularly showy selections of *Leucophyllum* that were released to the nursery trade. Since he pioneered these initial introductions, other growers have also produced outstanding selections of different species.

Several closely related Mexican species deserve mention as well because of their outstanding potential in ornamental landscape use, and for the several selections that have been released by Mountain States Wholesale Nursery in Phoenix, Arizona. *L. laevigatum* (Chihuahuan Rain Sage) grows to 4 feet by 5 feet, with tiny, slightly cupped, grayish green leaves closely attached at the stem. The slender, spare branches are also green and provide a good backdrop for the fragrant, ½ inch long, lavender-blue flowers. Chihuahuan Rain Sage is less dependent on humidity and warm temperatures for blooming than other *Leucophyllum* species, so flowers often appear on the plant all summer long. It is native to the wide shrub deserts of Durango and Chihuahua.

L. pruinosum (Sierra Bouquet™) was selected for the intense "grape bubble gum" fragrance of its flowers. It has bluish gray foliage and a rather sprawling growth habit with open branching, potentially reaching 6 feet tall and wide. It is hardy to 10° F. *L. pruinosum* is native to the gypsum desert in southern Nuevo Leon and Tamaulipas. It is a beautiful silvery plant, but it will only thrive in truly desert areas. It is a marginal performer in gardens north or east of San Antonio (Ogden, personal communication, 1999).

L. zygophyllum (Cimarron™) is bigger than 'Thundercloud.' It is very cold hardy and has survived winters in Wichita Falls and Albuquerque, where it was 3° F. The foliage is gray and very pubescent. The flowers are deep violet blue.

L. langmaniae (Rio Bravo™) is a medium to large shrub growing 5 feet tall and wide. Plants resemble *L. laevigatum*, but have larger, lusher leaves and a rounded, denser growth habit. Leaves are up to 1 inch long and ½ inch wide. Lavender-blue flowers appear from early summer to frost, especially after summer rains. Rio Bravo™ was chosen from several clones for its richer green foliage and deeper lavender flowers. It is hardy to 10° F, if hardened off in the fall. *L. langmaniae* is the common Cenizo of the eastern Sierra Madres around Monterrey and is probably the best species for humid subtropical areas like central Texas. However, it tends to suffer along the Texas Gulf Coast, where *L. frutescens* will thrive (Ogden, personal communication, 1999).

SPECIES DESCRIPTIONS

Leucophyllum candidum **(Violet Silver-leaf)**

Dense shrub usually 4 feet or less with deep violet-purple flowers and small, cupped, fuzzy silver leaves. The foliage of Violet Silver-leaf is more silver-white than *L. frutescens*. This species is intricately branched and very floriferous. Native to gravelly hills in Big Bend National Park and the adjacent Black Gap Wildlife Refuge in Brewster County, also northern Mexico. 'Silvercloud,' a cultivar of *L. candidum*, was developed by Benny Simpson. It was selected for its distinctive deep purple flowers and intense silvery to almost white foliage. This plant forms a dense rounded bush that usually remains under 3 feet without pruning. It is not cold hardy in El Paso and will rot with irrigation. 'Thundercloud' is another cultivar of this species and was selected as a more dwarf form of 'Silvercloud.'

Leucophyllum frutescens **(Cenizo, Purple Sage, Texas Silver-leaf, Texas Ranger)**

The largest of all the Cenizos, *L. frutescens* is a shrub up to 8 feet tall, with fuzzy, grayish green or gray-white leaves. Flower color ranges from white to pink-lavender or purple. Abundant on rocky limestone hills, bluffs, ravines, and brushlands in the Rio Grande Plains and southern part of the Trans-Pecos. Hardy to 5° F. A cultivar of this species, 'Green Cloud,' was developed by Benny Simpson at the Texas A&M Research and Extension Service Center at Dallas. It was selected from the wild in Cameron County for the dark green of the leaves instead of the more common silver color, as well as its showy purple-violet flowers. 'Green Cloud' is adapted to all areas of the state except the High and Rolling Plains.

'Greencloud' has a more extensive and well-developed root system than most selections of *L. frutescens*. It needs to be sheared at regular intervals to control its growth and carefully watched to make sure it doesn't become root bound. Take one-gallon sized plants and, holding them toward their base like a bouquet or ponytail, shear them across the top. This encourages a somewhat pyramidal form and lets in more air and light (Kirwin, personal communication, 1999). Another cultivar, 'White Cloud,' was also selected and tested by Benny Simpson. It was bred for outstanding large white flowers that are particularly showy against the silvery foliage. The clone 'Compacta' is a somewhat smaller form, generally maturing to about 4 feet tall and equally as wide. The clone 'Bert-star' (Silverado™) has recently been marketed and widely promoted as a substitute for 'Compacta.'

Silverado™ seems to be easier to grow in containers using pine bark soil blends (Ogden, personal communication, 1999). *L. frutescens* is the most tolerant of irrigation of all the Cenizos. 'Convent' Cenizo was a selection made at the Uvalde Experiment Station for its large, beautiful dark rosy-purple blooms. Another selection, variously called 'Lynn's Everblooming,' 'San Jose Cenizo,' or, as more recently proposed by Ron Gass of Mountain States Wholesale Nursery in Phoenix, 'Lynn's Legacy,' appears to be a natural hybrid of *L. langmaniae* and *L. frutescens*. It seems to be sterile, and thus puts all its energy into repeatedly producing a profusion of large, cupped lavender-blue blossoms instead of seeds. 'Lynn's Everblooming' was collected by Lynn Lowrey in San Ysidro Canyon in Nuevo Leon, Mexico. 'Lynn's Everblooming' has an average size of 4–5 feet tall with the same width. It must have full sun and dry soil. It will not tolerate being on the edge of an irrigated lawn.

***Leucophyllum minus* (Big-Bend Silver-leaf)**

Small shrub only growing to 3 feet with hairy silvery leaves and violet-blue flowers. It has very tight growth. It is the most cold hardy of all *Leucophyllum*. It is native to the Trans-Pecos west to New Mexico and northern Mexico, where it grows on gravelly plains and foothills at elevations between 2,300 and 6,600 feet. It is hard to root because plants in their native habitat produce little softwood rooting material. Hybrids of *L. minus* and *L. frutescens* show great hybrid vigor and are easier to root. 'Raincloud' is a recent selection of this hybrid and is distinguished by having intense blue-violet flowers.

Leucothoe racemosa

Sweetbells, Fetter-bush, Leucothoe

ERICACEAE (HEATH FAMILY)

GENERAL DESCRIPTION

Sweetbells are deciduous shrubs to 13 feet tall with wide-spreading, upright branches. Leaves are oblong shaped, with finely serrate margins.

FLOWERS AND FRUIT

Delicate white cylindrical tube- or urn-shaped flowers hang in single-rowed racemes from twigs of the previous season's growth beginning in April through the summer. The fruit is a capsule ⅓ inch long and containing several seeds.

NATURAL HABITAT, RANGE, AND PREFERRED SITE

Sweetbells are native to moist thickets, swamps, and sunny lakeshores in southeast Texas, east to Florida, north to Massachusetts. They prefer moist, sandy, acid soil in partial shade but will grow in the open if the soil is not too dry.

COLLECTION AND STORAGE

Collect the capsules in the summer when they are filled out but before they have split and dropped the seeds. Crush the capsules to release the seeds and air dry at room temperature before storing in sealed containers in the refrigerator. Information on seed longevity in storage is lacking.

PROPAGATION

Seeds

Sweetbells will germinate from freshly gathered untreated seeds. Sow the seeds in late winter or early spring in the greenhouse in a mixture of sphagnum moss and fine sand. Press gently into the soil mix and cover with a sprinkling of fine sand.

Cuttings

Propagation of Sweetbells is also accomplished by division, softwood cuttings, and underground runners. Application of IBA may improve rooting but is not imperative. A related species, Drooping Sweetbells (*L. fontanesiana*), was rooted from cuttings taken in November and December, treated with 3,000 ppm IBA talc, stuck in peat/perlite, and kept under mist. Rooting rates were high. Cuttings taken in June, treated with 1,000 ppm IBA, and stuck in peat/sand under mist also rooted very well. IBA treatment only slightly speeded up rooting (Dirr and Heuser 1987). Leaf bud cuttings of Drooping Sweetbells taken in June have also been rooted (Doran 1957). It is likely that these methods could be applied to other species of *Leucothoe*.

Transplanting

Sweetbells often form clumps or colonies in nature that are easily separated and transplanted in early spring.

NOTES

Formerly called *L. elongata*, this species has been in cultivation since 1736 (Vines 1970). It is often planted as a low ornamental hedge or single specimen plant. Sweetbells tend to form colonies resulting in showy mass plantings, especially when the plants are bearing their delicate wands of graceful white flowers. *Leucothoe* sprays have been traditionally used in the florist trade. Sweetbells should be pruned only after the blooms appear in spring because the blooms grow on last year's wood. Because Sweetbells are often thicket forming, they are useful in erosion control for stream banks, swamps, and lakes.

Other common names for this plant are Fetter-bush, Leucothoe, White-osier, and Pepper-bush. Leaves are reportedly poisonous to livestock. Brown blotches on the leaves are evidence of winter drying, which may be followed by gray areas of conspicuous black fruiting bodies of a secondary fungus.

Lindera benzoin

Spicebush

LAURACEAE (LAUREL FAMILY)

GENERAL DESCRIPTION

Spicebush is a deciduous shrub or small tree 16 feet or taller with many slender branches and stems growing from the base. The branches remain light green and smooth throughout the year. Large oval-shaped leaves are dark green and lush appearing, and also very fragrant when crushed.

FLOWERS AND FRUIT

Small yellow flowers appear in tiny clusters close to the stem in early spring before the new leaves appear. Fruit is a fleshy oval drupe ⅓ inch long containing one light-brown seed. The bright red clusters of fruit contrast vividly with the smooth dark leaves in late summer and early fall.

NATURAL HABITAT, RANGE, AND PREFERRED SITE

Spicebush prefers sandy or moist soil in woods, swamps, and along streams. It is mainly found in east Texas and occasionally in the deeper soil of moist canyons, creek banks, and protected shady arroyos near springs in the Edwards Plateau in central Texas. Its range extends east to Florida, north to Arkansas and Missouri. East Texas selections of Spicebush are not successfully introduced to the drier habitats of central Texas. Central Texas plants have shown a remarkable tolerance for dry sites and thin alkaline soils as long as they receive some shade (McNeal, personal communication, 1999).

COLLECTION AND STORAGE

Collect the seeds in late summer through October when the fruit has turned red. Clean the seeds immediately to avoid losses due to fermentation. The pulp can be soaked in warm water with a small amount of detergent to dissolve the resinous pulp and make the seeds easier to clean. Seeds may be rubbed on a screen or cleaned in a blender with rubber blades (see Chapter III). Store seeds in moist sand or sow immediately after cleaning.

Seeds allowed to dry out or kept in dry storage lose viability rapidly. Seeds average between 4,500 and 4,600 per pound (USDA 1974).

PROPAGATION

Seeds

Spicebush has a seed dormancy requirement that can be met by either fall sowing outdoors immediately after harvesting or stratification in moist sand or sphagnum moss for 30–60 days. Sow in the greenhouse in the fall or in a cold frame in early spring.

Cleaned seed sown in flats left in a cold frame in late winter will germinate in 2–3 months. They are easily lifted out of the tray into individual containers (McNeal, personal communication, 1999).

Spicebush has an average germination rate of 70–80% for first-year seed. Germination rates are higher in cooler temperatures. The seedbed should contain well-prepared sandy loam with a considerable amount of organic matter. Cover the seeds with ½ inch of soil and protect the seedbed with a light mulch until germination begins. Seedlings should have light (30%) shade the first season. Seedlings are generally fast growing and may be 2 feet or taller after the first season.

Cuttings

Spicebush may also be propagated from cuttings of mature sideshoots of the current season's growth. Take cuttings 2 or 3 inches long, firm toward the base, made with a heel. Insert them close together in a well-drained rooting bed and keep under intermittent mist. Rooting generally occurs within 25–35 days. Application of root-promoting hormones hastens and improves rooting. Spicebush also may be propagated from sprouts and suckers.

NOTES

The small yellow flowers, persistent glossy leaves, and red fruit make Spicebush an attractive ornamental for shady moist places. Spicebush can be used along with Yaupon Holly (*Ilex vomitoria*), Possum-haw Holly (*Ilex decidua*), and Carolina Buckthorn (*Rhamnus caroliniana*) as a tall understory plant in a woodland garden or as a single broad-spreading specimen. Spicebush is reported to have a growth rate of 1–2 feet a year. It is a useful plant for wetlands, and careful selection of ecotypes offers opportunities for adapted plants for drier sites.

larval host for spicebush swallowtail

Liquidambar styraciflua

Sweetgum, Balsamo, Copalme

HAMAMELIDACEAE (WITCH-HAZEL FAMILY)

GENERAL DESCRIPTION

Sweetgum is a very ornamental shade tree growing 40–60 feet tall with an upright oval crown and showy star-shaped leaves turning yellow, orange, to red-purple in the fall.

FLOWERS AND FRUIT

Sweetgum flowers are inconspicuous, blooming from March to May. Fruit is a woody cluster of dehiscent capsules, maturing in September to October. Each capsule contains one or two winged seeds. Good seed crops are produced every 3 years, with light crops produced in between (USDA 1974).

NATURAL HABITAT, RANGE, AND PREFERRED SITE

Sweetgum is most often found in wet situations and swampy woods in east and south central Texas, west to Lee County. In the eastern part of its range, Sweetgum is frequently one of the first pioneer species to invade an old field or disturbed area. Sweetgum grows best on clay loam ridges of newer alluvium and next best on well-drained silty clay loam flats. It also grows well on lower and middle upland slopes. Sweetgum is not suitable as an understory plant. On poor or excessively dry sites, the top may die back as the tree matures. It is a majestic specimen for roadside plantings in those areas with adequate annual rainfall.

If the soil is deep enough, Sweetgum will adapt to a high pH. It will become chlorotic and fail to thrive in shallow alkaline soils.

COLLECTION AND STORAGE

The fruiting heads turn from green to yellow or brown as they ripen. The capsules then open to disperse the winged seeds. Collect the mature fruiting heads from standing trees before the heads have completely dried. Capsules picked before they are completely mature may be ripened by storing them in a moist medium at 41° F for about 30 days (USDA 1974).

Spread out the fruiting heads to dry until they release the seeds, usually 5–10 days at 68° F. Shake or lightly beat the heads in a sack to release the seeds. Air dry the seeds thoroughly before storage in sealed bags or containers held at 35° F. Properly stored seeds will remain viable for at least 4 years (USDA 1974).

PROPAGATION

Seeds

Sweetgums have a short embryo dormancy that is most likely triggered by drying during collection or storage. Seeds should either be planted in beds outdoors immediately after they are collected or stratified for 1–2 months at 41° F (Hartmann and Kester 1975). Remove seeds from stratification in the early spring and gently press them into the soil media. Barely cover the seeds with ¼–½ inch of fine sand. The seedbed should be kept moist and shaded. Seedlings are often sensitive to alkaline water used in irrigation.

Cuttings

Leafy semihardwood cuttings treated with 8,000 ppm IBA talc can be rooted under mist. Treatments with NAA have also been helpful in promoting rooting (Hartmann and Kester 1975). Cultivars of this tree are vegetatively propagated by budding on seedlings of the species (Dirr and Heuser 1987).

NOTES

Sweetgum is a desirable ornamental shade tree because of its open crown, large colorful leaves, and relatively rapid growth. It is long lived and generally free from insects and diseases. The main problem with Sweetgum is its susceptibility to iron chlorosis on thin or rocky soils with a high pH. It is not well adapted to the western two-thirds of Texas.

Sweetgum was first cultivated in 1681. The gum of this tree is an ingredient in traditional preparations of various ointments and syrups for the treatment of dysentery and diarrhea (Vines 1970). The wood is used in flooring, furniture, and veneers. Numerous birds are known to eat the fruit (Van Dersal 1938).

Liriodendron tulipfera

Tulip-tree, Tulip Poplar

MAGNOLIACEAE (MAGNOLIA FAMILY)

GENERAL DESCRIPTION

Tulip-tree is a large deciduous shade tree with a potential height of 100 feet and a diameter of 7 feet. The large leaves are dark green and shiny, turning yellow in the fall, and are easily recognized by distinctive notched lobes.

FLOWERS AND FRUIT

Tulip-tree flowers are large and showy, almost 3 inches across, forming a yellow-green "tulip." Fruit is an elongated cone composed of 80–100 overlapping, woody, winged carpels or samaras each containing one to two seeds. Cones turn light brown when ripe in late summer until early fall. As the cones mature they dry and break apart, scattering the samaras. There is great variation in the number of filled seeds.

NATURAL HABITAT, RANGE, AND PREFERRED SITE

Tulip-tree can be found in rich moist woods from east Texas to Florida, north to Massachusetts. It is also widely cultivated and occasionally escapes cultivation to become naturalized in fields and woodlands. Tulip-tree prefers moist but not soggy acid soils. Even mature trees will become stressed and defoliate in the summer if the ground is too hard and dry (Wasowski 1994).

COLLECTION AND STORAGE

Collect the cones from the trees before they completely dry. Cones from the upper part of the tree generally have more seeds than those below. The percentage of filled seeds per cone is often low because of incomplete pollination, so collecting large amounts is necessary to insure adequate production. Thoroughly air dry cones to separate the samaras for storage. Drying may take as long as 20 days, depending on temperature and humidity (USDA 1974).

Dried cones can be separated by shucking, flailing, or running through a hammermill or macerator. Store dried samaras in sealed containers at 36–40° F. Properly stored seeds will remain viable for several years.

PROPAGATION

Seeds

Germination of Tulip-tree is delayed by a dormant embryo. Dormancy may be broken by fall sowing outdoors immediately after collection or stratification for 60–90 days at 36° F. Seeds should not be allowed to dry out. After pretreatment, Tulip-tree germinates best in average daily alternating temperatures of 68–86° F.

Space seedlings in nursery rows at an average rate of 30–35 seedlings per square foot (USDA 1974). Cover seeds with ¼–½ inch of fine soil or sand. Seedlings benefit from light shade the first season.

Cuttings

Horticultural varieties of Tulip-tree are produced by budding, grafting, and layering. Leafy stem cuttings taken in the summer will root in fairly good percentages when treated with IBA and kept under intermittent mist (Hartmann and Kester 1975). Cuttings made from mature trees are difficult to root (Dirr and Heuser 1987).

Transplanting

Young Tulip-trees are very difficult to transplant so they should always be propagated in containers or dug, balled, and burlapped for transplanting from the nursery row in late winter or early spring (Hartmann and Kester 1975).

NOTES

Tulip-tree has been in cultivation since 1663 and is a showy ornamental as well as a valuable timber tree. It is relatively insect and disease free and exhibits spectacular fall foliage. Tulip-tree is intolerant of compacted soil and should not be placed in confined beds or planters near pavement.

Hummingbirds and butterflies enjoy the flowers. The leaves provide food for tiger and spicebush swallowtail butterfly larvae (Wasowski 1994).

Lonicera

Honeysuckle

CAPRIFOLIACEAE (HONEYSUCKLE FAMILY)

GENERAL DESCRIPTION

Honeysuckles are erect or climbing shrubs or vines with a woody or herbaceous base and smooth stems.

FLOWERS AND FRUIT

Tubular-shaped flowers are showy and fragrant, with color varying among species (see Species Descriptions). Fruit is a round, several-seeded drupe.

NATURAL HABITAT, RANGE, AND PREFERRED SITE

Honeysuckles are found on a variety of sites, depending on species, including woods, thickets, slopes, cliffs, and sandy soil. See Species Descriptions for individual range and habitat.

COLLECTION AND STORAGE

Collect the seeds in late summer to early fall when the berries turn red or bluish green. Birds and other wildlife are fond of the fruit and may compete for the harvest. Clean the seeds immediately after collection to avoid fermentation and overheating. Some species with less fleshy fruit may be spread out in thin layers for several days and the pulp dried on the seeds. Store seeds in sealed containers held at 34–38° F.

PROPAGATION

Seeds

Germination of honeysuckle is delayed by a dormant embryo, hard seed coat, or the combined effects of both conditions. Pregermination requirements also vary among different lots of the same species.

For the species listed here, prompt germination is encouraged by stratification for 2–3 months at 40° F. Seeds also may be sown soon after harvest in outdoor beds. Cover seeds with ⅛–¼ inch of soil and cover with light mulch until germination begins.

Cuttings

The easiest and most reliable way to propagate honeysuckle is by softwood or semihardwood cuttings taken from summer to fall. These should be 3–4 inches long, slightly woody at the base, with a pencil-sized diameter. The wood should be firm enough to snap if bent sharply. Make the basal cut just below a node, except when rooting cuttings of Coral Honeysuckle (*L. sempervirens*), which should be taken internodally. The best cutting material for Coral Honeysuckle is taken from new growth in winter, when the canes develop shorter internodes (Will, personal communication, 1999). Application of IBA (3,000–5,000 ppm) speeds and improves rooting but is not imperative. Wounding of the stem by pulling the lower leaves off and taking a little of the outer epidermal layer of bark also seems to stimulate rooting (Hosage, personal communication, 1999).

Insert cuttings in a well-drained medium, such as two parts perlite to one part peat moss, and place under intermittent mist. Rooting usually occurs within 2 weeks. Rooted cuttings may be directly planted in a prepared bed or separate containers.

Layering of the viney types of honeysuckle is very easy because roots form naturally wherever the canes touch moist or loose soil.

Transplanting

Honeysuckle is easily transplanted from the field. Cut canes back to the third leaf node and keep well watered. Rooted canes may also be separated from the parent plant and planted individually.

NOTES

Some native honeysuckles provide an attractive covering for arbors, trellises, and fences. Others are planted as tall ground covers, slope stabilizers, and small shrubs. Flowers are generally long blooming, showy, and attractive to butterflies and hummingbirds.

SPECIES DESCRIPTIONS

Lonicera albiflora var. albiflora (White Bush Honeysuckle)

Smooth, somewhat bushy plant to 4 feet with semi-evergreen foliage and white to yellowish white flowers. Grows on rocky slopes, cliffs, roadsides, and cedar brakes in central and north-central Texas, also Oklahoma. White Bush Honeysuckle is a good low-growing shrub for hot rocky places and thin soil. It is a good companion plant to Fragrant Mist Flower (*Eupatorium havanense*), American Beauty-berry (*Callicarpa americana*), and Beargrass (*Nolina spp.*). Overhead watering may contribute to powdery mildew on this species. It also does not thrive in standard nursery pine bark soil mix.

***Lonicera sempervirens* (Coral or Evergreen honeysuckle)**
Twining shrub with smooth glossy leaves and branches. Coral-red flowers are held in whorls of four to six. Fruit is bright red and also showy. Coral Honeysuckle is native to woods and thickets in east Texas to Florida, north to Massachusetts, and also in cultivation. Not as aggressive or wide spreading as Japanese Honeysuckle. It is more suited for climbing on a fence or trellis. Stays green and blooms as early as January.

Lycium

Wolfberry, Desert-thorn, Tomatillo, Cilindrillo

SOLANACEAE (NIGHTSHADE FAMILY)

GENERAL DESCRIPTION

Wolfberries are erect or spreading shrubs, usually with thorns. Young branchlets have thick grayish green leaves attached close to the stem.

FLOWERS AND FRUIT

Flowers are small, bell shaped, and not as showy as the fruit, which is a shiny, bright red berry containing many small seeds.

NATURAL HABITAT, RANGE, AND PREFERRED SITE

There are about 100 species of *Lycium* found in arid and semi-arid regions of the New World (Powell 1988). Texas has six species, and five of them occur in the Trans-Pecos. See Species Descriptions.

COLLECTION AND STORAGE

Gather the fruits from late spring through early summer when they have filled out and turned red or purplish. Clean seeds and air dry completely before storage. Store in sealed containers in the refrigerator.

PROPAGATION

Seeds

First-year *Lycium* seeds germinate promptly in the spring (late February to March) without pretreatment. Sow seeds thinly in well-drained soil, and take care not to overwater. Germination usually occurs within 2 weeks. Periodically pinch back the young plants to encourage bushy growth.

Germination of Berlander Wolfberry (*L. berlandieri var. berlandieri*) is improved if the cleaned seeds are aerated in a solution of potassium nitrate (1 tablespoon per one gallon of water) for 2–3 days. Rinse seed thoroughly and plant immediately. *Lycium* likes to germinate in moderate temperatures (70–80° F). Germination of outdoor seedbeds seems to be stimulated by rainfall (Best 1999).

Cuttings

Some species of *Lycium* may be propagated from semihardwood cuttings taken in the summer with a slight heel. Treat with IBA (3,000 ppm or less), stick in a well-drained soil mix, and keep under intermittent mist. Carolina Wolfberry (*L. carolinianum var. quadrifidium*) can be expected to root in fairly high percentages (Sheats 1953).

NOTES

Lycium is an important source of food and cover for wildlife, and it is also browsed by livestock. Native Americans harvested the fruits and used the plants for a variety of medicinal purposes.

SPECIES DESCRIPTIONS

Lycium berlandieri var. berlandieri
(Berlander Wolfberry, Tomatillo, Cilindrillo)

Shrub to 6 feet, with dark green spatulate leaves and pale yellow flowers. Compared to some other species of *Lycium*, the stems of Cilindrillo are nearly unarmed and the plant less dense. Cilindrillo occurs on limestone and clay dunes, arroyos, and shrub land in the Rio Grande Plains and Coastal Prairie, and on arid gravelly hills throughout the Trans-Pecos. White-tailed deer and occasionally livestock browse on the leaves, and many birds and small mammals such as chachalacas and raccoons eat the fruit (R. B. Taylor, Rutledge, and Herrera 1997).

***Lycium carolinianum var. quadrifidium* (Carolina Wolfberry)**

Shrub about 3 feet tall, spiny, with open branching. Leaves thick and fleshy. Lavender flowers appear January through November followed by a bright red berry. Native to the Rio Grande Plains and Coastal Prairies, around ponds, marshes, and salt flats; also grows on chaparral-covered hills. In moist areas, Wolfberry grows quickly and is very useful in erosion control.

***Lycium pallidum var. pallidum* (Pallid Wolfberry)**

Lycium pallidum var. pallidum is distinctive of all the desert wolfberries because the leaves are larger and tend to be evergreen, and the flowers are bigger. They are bluish white and waxy. The bark is reddish brown, and the stems are armed with ferocious thorns. Pallid Wolfberry produces abundant amounts of juicy fruits in the late spring and summer. Birds and other wildlife including bear feast on the berries, and they were also harvested by Native Americans (Bowers 1993).

In Texas, Pallid Wolfberry grows on rocky slopes and canyons in both igneous and limestone soils in the Franklin Mountains, west to California and Utah.

Lyonia

Huckleberry

ERICACEAE (HEATH FAMILY)

GENERAL DESCRIPTION

Huckleberries are shrubs to 13 feet. Our species of huckleberries are deciduous with slender, erect branches. See Species Descriptions for individual characteristics.

FLOWERS AND FRUIT

Flowers are white to rose colored, held in leafless racemes or panicles in early spring. Fruit is a capsule ⅛–⅓ inch long containing several tiny seeds.

NATURAL HABITAT, RANGE, AND PREFERRED SITE

Most huckleberries are found in bogs or low areas, along wooded streams in east Texas and throughout the southern United States, north to Oklahoma, Arkansas, and Pennsylvania. They prefer moist acid soil and partial shade.

COLLECTION AND STORAGE

Gather the seeds in September when the capsules have turned brown but before they have split to disperse the seeds. Seeds may be stored over winter in sealed containers at room temperature. Refrigeration is recommended for longer periods of storage.

PROPAGATION

Seeds

Huckleberry seeds have a dormancy requirement that can be met by either direct fall planting outdoors or stratification for 40–60 days at 41° F. The seedbed should contain a rich sandy loam with a slightly acid pH. Do not bury the seeds too deeply.

Cuttings

Huckleberries are also grown from semihardwood cuttings and layers taken in summer. For best results, treat the cuttings with IBA and place under intermittent mist.

NOTES

Huckleberries make attractive low understory plants, especially when planted in groups. They will thrive in poorly drained and shady locations. In late spring to early summer, the small delicate racemes of white flowers are showy, and in the fall, the leathery oval leaves take on colored tints.

SPECIES DESCRIPTIONS

Lyonia ligustrina **(He-huckleberry)**
Shrub to 13 feet, sometimes treelike, with thin elliptic leaves and white flowers in terminal panicles. Bogs and low areas in sandy soil along streams in east Texas to Florida, also Oklahoma and Arkansas. In cultivation since 1748.

Lyonia mariana **(Stagger-bush)**
Erect shrub to 6½ feet with elliptic-ovate leaves and white to pinkish flowers held in racemes. Peaty or sandy pinewoods usually in moist acid soil from Florida to south-central Texas, north to New England. Foliage is poisonous to young grazing animals. Has been in cultivation since 1765.

Magnolia

Magnolia

MAGNOLIACEAE (MAGNOLIA FAMILY)

GENERAL DESCRIPTION

Three species of *Magnolia* occur in Texas. They are trees or rarely tall shrubs 32–96 feet tall with bitter aromatic bark. See Species Descriptions for individual characteristics.

FLOWERS AND FRUIT

Magnolias are known for their showy, large, and fragrant flowers. A woody conelike fruit opens when ripe to reveal fleshy red seeds hanging from a fuzzy aril inside the carpel.

NATURAL HABITAT, RANGE, AND PREFERRED SITE

Magnolias grow in low moist woods, especially along streams in the Pineywoods of east Texas, east to Florida, and in cultivation farther west. See Species Descriptions for individual range and habitat. Magnolias thrive in rich, porous, acid, sandy or peaty loam soils. Under cultivation Southern Magnolia (*M. grandiflora*) will adapt to different soil types and conditions provided soils are relatively deep and the trees are watered and fertilized regularly, especially while getting established. Young plants do best when shaded from afternoon sun. In heavy shade, magnolias tend to become open and gangly. In shallow or poor soils, supplemental fertilization is recommended. Southern Magnolias are moderately tolerant of heat and salty irrigation water (Arnold 1999).

COLLECTION AND STORAGE

When ripe the seeds are bright red, fleshy, oily, and soft on the outside but stony in the inner portion. Gather the seeds as soon as they are ripe from early September through October. Clean the seeds before storage. Seeds lose their viability rapidly if held in dry storage at room temperature, so they must be placed in moist sand or sphagnum moss in the refrigerator immediately after cleaning. Cold moist storage will also serve as the stratification necessary to pretreat the seeds before germination.

PROPAGATION

Seeds

Germination of magnolias is delayed by a dormant embryo that requires fall sowing outdoors immediately after collection or cold moist stratification at 41° F for up to 120 days before spring sowing. Seeds frequently split open and begin to germinate while still in cold moist storage.

Seeds of the Cucumber Tree (*M. pyramidata*) are collected in midsummer and stratified for 120 days in the refrigerator. After cold moist treatment, they are planted individually into seed cells. Seedling roots fill out seed cells within 3 months and are ready to be planted into one-gallon containers within 6 months of initial sowing. Make sure the soil medium is well drained; seedlings do not like to be kept too wet. After the seedling is placed in a one-gallon container, the growth rate accelerates. Eight-year-old seedlings have been known to reach 25 feet tall when planted in a well-drained location (Bronstad, personal communication, 1999).

The best seedbed for outdoor sowing is a sheltered, partially shaded area containing loose sandy loam with a good percentage of organic matter. For greenhouse propagation, peat moss and fine sand or perlite make a suitable soil mix. Cover the seeds with ¾–1 inch of soil.

Seedlings grow slowly at first. Planting seeds in individual containers is recommended. Keep the containers moist but not too soggy, and partially shaded.

Cuttings

Magnolias root best from juvenile wood. One method for vegetatively propagating the deciduous forms of magnolia recommends taking semihardwood tip cuttings 3–6 inches long in the summer just after the first spring flush begins to harden. Treat with 5,000 ppm K-IBA after wounding the cutting, and then stick in a rooting bed consisting of 70% perlite and 30% finely composted pine bark. Rooting is slow: often 4–5 months are required to produce a fully rooted cutting. Once the radicle emerges, reduce the watering to avoid rotting (Bronstad, personal communication, 1999).

Cucumber Tree (*M. pyramidata*) is difficult to root, especially with cuttings collected from older trees. One method recommends using rooted plants as stock plants for future cuttings to maintain reintroduced juvenility. Take 4–6 inch long semihardwood cuttings with end bud set in late summer or early fall. Leave two to three top leaves and treat with 10,000 ppm NAA-50% ethanol in a 5-second dip. Stick the cuttings 4 inches deep in coarse or horticultural perlite and place under mist with a polytent covering the mist table. Keep the table under 53% shade. Rooting takes 10–12 weeks (Dirr and Heuser 1987).

The cultivar 'Little Gem' can be rooted from semihardwood cuttings, using the same treatment as for *M. pyramidata* (Bronstad, personal communication, 1999).

Transplanting

Magnolias are difficult to transplant from the field and must be carefully balled, burlapped, and replanted so as to avoid breaking and bruising the roots. Native magnolias should be moved in early spring, just before new growth begins. Prune after blooming during the growing season because dormant magnolias do not easily heal their wounds.

NOTES

Many members of the magnolia family have long been valued as ornamental plants for the beauty of their flowers and foliage and their quick adaptation to cultivation. Several outstanding cultivars of this genus have been selected. Magnolias like to have their roots shaded: they often drop a large amount of their leathery leaves to help keep the roots cool. It is a mistake, therefore, to prune lower limbs up high and to meticulously rake all the leaves below. Magnolias are not particularly tolerant of root zone compaction and should be protected out to their drip line during construction.

Various leaf spot diseases may occur on magnolias, but they are rarely serious enough to warrant spraying. After a wet spring, a parasitic algae entering through surface wounds forms reddish brown or orange cushion-like patches on leaves, twigs, and fruit. The Comstock mealy bug sometimes injures magnolias but can be controlled with a dormant spray (Arnold 1999).

SPECIES DESCRIPTIONS

Magnolia grandiflora **(Southern Magnolia)**

Evergreen pyramidal or cylindrical tree to 110 feet with glossy stiff leaves and large, showy, creamy white flowers. This species grows in moist but well-drained soils of the rich bottomlands and gentle hills of the southeastern Pineywoods. Southern Magnolia has a fleshy root structure, and larger trees are difficult to dig from the wild. It can be planted as far north as Lubbock and Amarillo, although it sometimes suffers from winter desiccation there.

Magnolia pyramidata **(Pyramid Magnolia, Cucumber Tree)**
Tree to 30 feet, with deciduous leaves 9 inches long and 4 inches wide. It flowers when only a few feet high. Pyramid Magnolia is rare in Texas, occurring only on deeply wooded sandy ridges in Jasper and Newton counties. It is not seen in cultivation very often in Texas, although it has been grown in the warmer parts of Europe for many years. It requires a lot of shade, along with acidic, sandy, moist soils (Simpson 1988).

Magnolia virginiana **(Sweetbay Magnolia)**
Slender semi-evergreen tree to 80 feet with elliptic leaves and white flowers having a lemon fragrance. It is native to swamps and low woods, along boggy streams, and on seepage slopes in east Texas to Florida. It can survive on drier sites but is not as adaptable to drier, high limestone clays as is *M. grandiflora* (Simpson 1988).

Cuttings from young trees rooted better than wood collected from mature trees. Take softwood cuttings in early summer and treat with 5,000–8,000 ppm IBA talc, place under mist in a peat/perlite rooting bed (Dirr and Heuser 1987).

Malpighia glabra

Barbados-cherry, Cereza, Huacacote

MALPIGHIACEAE (MALPIGHIA FAMILY)

GENERAL DESCRIPTION

Barbados-cherries are extremely variable in form, appearing both as upright shrubs as tall as 9 feet with many stems from the base and as low-growing mounding shrubs that make a woody ground cover. Small, pointed oval leaves also vary in size. In the southern part of its range, Barbados-cherry may be evergreen.

FLOWERS AND FRUIT

Barbados-cherry flowers are delicate and attractive. They are pink with five petals and bloom intermittently from March to October. The fruit is an edible and showy glossy red drupe containing three stones. Fruit and flowers are often on the plant at the same time.

NATURAL HABITAT, RANGE, AND PREFERRED SITE

Barbados-cherry grows in thickets, brushlands, palm groves, roadsides, and salty clay areas in the Rio Grande Valley and elsewhere in cultivation.

COLLECTION AND STORAGE

Gather the drupes when they turn red and are filled out. Clean the seeds from the fruit and allow them to air dry on screens a day or so before storing in sealed containers in the refrigerator. Seeds to be planted immediately do not have to be dried first.

PROPAGATION

Seeds

Barbados-cherry will often germinate from first-year seeds planted in a greenhouse or outdoors after all danger of frost is past. However, some seed lots exhibited an after-ripening requirement of 3 months before germination (Best 1999). Care must be taken not to overwater the seedlings.

Transplant to a separate container as soon as the plant has its third set of true leaves.

Both cuttings and seedlings benefit from light shade the first growing season. Periodically tip prune plants to encourage more branching. Barbados-cherry tends to grow slowly in a container, requiring a year to make a one-gallon plant, but takes off once planted in the landscape (Will, personal communication, 1999).

Cuttings

Barbados-cherry is easily rooted from softwood cuttings taken in June. These should be 2 inches long, treated with 5,000 ppm IBA and placed under mist (Pfeiffer, personal communication, 1999). Cuttings can be taken at almost any time of year, but the more hardened off the wood is, the more difficult it is to root (McNeal, personal communication, 1999). To avoid rotting, gradually reduce the amount of misting as rooting begins to harden the cutting off. Newly rooted cuttings grow best if initially kept under partial shade.

Transplanting

Barbados-cherry can be easily transplanted in late winter or early spring if cut back to one-half of its overall height and kept well watered.

NOTES

Barbados-cherry is valued as an ornamental plant because of its showy fruit and long blooming period. Its many different forms of leaf size, growth habit, and cold hardiness have not been fully developed in the nursery trade. Barbados-cherry is typically not cold hardy north of Austin, Texas.

In cultivation, Barbados-cherry can serve as an attractive dense evergreen shrub that can be planted in masses in both full sun or dappled shade. It should be sheared periodically to encourage bushy growth. In south Texas, Barbados-cherry forms a dense ground cover when mowed. It can be kept mowed at 2 feet tall (Best, personal communication, 1999). The fruit is edible and is sometimes made into preserves as well as eaten by birds, coyotes, and raccoons.

Malvaviscus arboreus var. drummondii

Turk's Cap, Manzanilla

MALVACEAE (MALLOW OR HIBISCUS FAMILY)

GENERAL DESCRIPTION

Turk's Cap is a spreading herbaceous perennial shrub with a woody or semiwoody base and many tall upright stems. It may grow as tall as 10 feet in the southern part of its range, though it is more commonly seen as a shrub 4 feet wide with an equal spread. Turk's Cap has large dark green leaves with velvet hairs on the underside.

FLOWERS AND FRUIT

Flowers consist of five red petals twisted into a loose whorl or tube with extended stamens. The heaviest blooming occurs during hot weather at the end of the summer and early fall, although some cultivars have been selected that bloom throughout the summer. In fall a mealy, berrylike red fruit is produced that splits when ripe into five carpels, each containing one seed.

NATURAL HABITAT, RANGE, AND PREFERRED SITE

Turk's Cap is often seen in low, sandy, and partially shady sites along streams and on the edges of woods and limestone ledges from the southern part of the Edwards Plateau south and east to Florida and south to Mexico. In south Texas, Turk's Cap flowers throughout the year. Under cultivation Turk's Cap will adapt to and thrive in many different sites, including full sun and heavier soil.

COLLECTION AND STORAGE

Collect the seeds as soon as the fruit turns ripe and is filled out. Spread the fruit in single layers on screens to dry and separate. After a few days of drying, the pulp will begin to shrivel and may be easily rubbed off the seeds. Unless the seeds are to be immediately sown, do not soak the fruit to remove the pulp. This will cause the seeds to swell and rot during storage. After thoroughly drying, fumigate the seeds and store in ventilated containers or paper bags at room temperature. Seeds to be stored for long periods of time should be refrigerated in sealed containers.

PROPAGATION

Seeds

Turk's Cap will germinate promptly from fresh untreated seeds planted outside after all danger of frost is past and the soil has warmed, or indoors in a greenhouse. Like other members of the okra or hibiscus family, germination of Turk's Cap is inhibited by cold temperatures. Cover the seeds no deeper than ¼–½ inch using a well-drained soil mix. Germination usually proceeds in 2 weeks.

Seedlings may be easily transplanted from the flat after they have developed their second set of true leaves. Seedlings benefit from light shade during the first growing season. Care should be taken to keep water off the leaves and to remove the seedlings from the greenhouse as soon as possible to avoid problems caused by powdery and downy mildew. Seedlings respond to applications of soluble fertilizers, and seedlings germinated in spring will make a one-gallon plant before fall.

Cuttings

Turk's Cap is easily propagated from softwood cuttings taken in summer to fall from strong sideshoots. These should be 4–6 inches long with the leaves from the bottom halves removed, treated with IBA (1,500 ppm), and placed under intermittent mist. Rooting is usually completed in 3 weeks. Prune seedlings, rooted cuttings, and full-grown plants severely in winter and periodically during the growing season to encourage bushy growth and more blooms.

Transplanting

Large clumps of Turk's Cap may be easily divided in early spring. If it is moved during warmer weather, be sure to cut the tops back severely and keep it well watered.

NOTES

When periodically cut back, Turk's Cap is an excellent tall ground cover and bedding plant. If allowed to grow tall and lanky, it becomes a background or understory plant beneath specimen trees where grass will not grow. The bright red flowers and applelike fruit are particularly showy during the hot time of the year. Several good companion plants to Turk's

Cap in the woodland garden include Pigeon Berry (*Rivinia humilis*), Tropical Sage (*Salvia coccinea*), Cedar Sage (*Salvia roemeriana*), and Inland Sea Oats (*Chasmanthium latifolium*).

The fruit is edible, either raw or cooked, and the leaves have many uses in traditional medicine. Hummingbirds, butterflies, and other wildlife are also attracted to this plant. The fruit is eaten by a number of birds, and the leaves are occasionally browsed by livestock. A selection called Super Bloomer™ is a more compact and floriferous form that produces blooms nearly all summer long.

Melochia tomentosa

Woolly Pyramid Bush

STERCULIACEAE (CHOCOLATE FAMILY)

GENERAL DESCRIPTION

Woolly Pyramid Bush is a herbaceous shrub with a woody base growing 4–5 feet tall in the Rio Grande Valley. Outside of its natural range it is generally smaller and will freeze back to the base each winter. The stems and leaves are covered with a fine pubescence. Leaves are narrowly oblong with scalloped edges and felty white undersides.

FLOWERS AND FRUIT

Woolly Pyramid Bush stays in flower from May to frost, bearing lovely five-petaled raspberry-colored flowers. The fruit is a capsule separating into five sections, each containing a pyramid-shaped seed.

NATURAL HABITAT, RANGE, AND PREFERRED SITE

Woolly Pyramid Bush is found in isolated populations in open woodlands and mattoral (brushland) in the southern Rio Grande Plains. It thrives in loose, gravelly soils and full sun. It will tolerate partial shade, but may become leggier with fewer blooms.

COLLECTION AND STORAGE

Collect the seeds at repeated intervals throughout the long blooming season. Air dry a few days before sowing or storage. Information is lacking on seed viability in storage.

PROPAGATION

Seeds
Information is lacking on growing this species from seed.

Cuttings
Woolly Pyramid Bush roots easily from semihardwood cuttings taken from spring through fall. Make cuttings 3 inches long and treat with 1,500 ppm

IBA talc before placing under mist. Rooting will occur within 3 weeks, and plants are easily transplanted.

NOTES

This little ever-blooming herbaceous shrub is a current favorite of Paul Cox of the San Antonio Botanical Gardens. In hot dry weather in poor soils, Woolly Pyramid Bush still manages to produce blooms and fresh foliage. The rich violet to fuchsia color of the flower is a nice contribution to the perennial border.

Mimosa

Mimosa, Uña de Gato, Cat's Claw

FABACEAE (LEGUME FAMILY)

GENERAL DESCRIPTION

Members of this genus are low-growing shrubs 3–6 feet tall armed with scattered curved thorns. Tiny delicate pinnately compound leaves are closely attached to the crooked stems (see Species Descriptions).

FLOWERS AND FRUIT

Small white, pink, or reddish puff-ball flowers cover the plant in spring. Fruit is a small flattened pod containing several seeds.

NATURAL HABITAT, RANGE, AND PREFERRED SITE

Species listed here are found in west-central and west Texas, New Mexico, Arizona, and northern Mexico. See Species Descriptions.

COLLECTION AND STORAGE

Collect the pods beginning in early summer (June) through fall depending on season and blooming periods. Seeds are mature when they are filled out and have turned dark brown. When ripe, the pods also turn brown and dry, twisting open to release the seeds. Collect the pods as they begin to dry and avoid collecting from the ground. Spread the seeds in single layers to air dry before storage. Fumigate or dust with insecticide before placing in ventilated containers at room temperature. Under these conditions, seeds will remain viable for at least 2 years because of their hard seed coats.

PROPAGATION

Seeds

Germination of most species of *Mimosa* is slightly delayed by a thick seed coat. Before sowing, seeds should be either mechanically scarified or soaked in concentrated sulfuric acid. Length of time for acid depends on species and seed lot. Test each seed lot at increasing 3-minute intervals to determine optimal treatment time. Aerate the seed following scarification 1–2 days, or until imbibition occurs. Sometimes soaking in hot water is sufficient treatment (McNeal, personal communication, 1999). Sow the seeds in a well-drained soil mix in individual containers that allow adequate room for a slender but long initial taproot. Most species of *Mimosa* will make a finished one-gallon plant in 1 year.

Cuttings

Mimosa is also easily rooted from semihardwood cuttings taken in the summer and early fall, treated with rooting hormones, and kept under intermittent mist (Simpson, personal communication, 1986).

Transplanting

Large plants over 4 feet are usually difficult to transplant because of a long woody taproot and usually rocky native environment. Smaller plants may be transplanted during winter if cut back by one-half their overall height. Make sure the location is well drained.

NOTES

The delicate foliage, profuse flowers, and interesting form all contribute to this species' worthiness as a small specimen for planting in really rough places such as rocky slopes and arroyos. Mimosas can be used as airy background shrubs in desert gardens and roadsides. Mimosas will also tolerate partial shade. Regular pruning encourages the growth of more branches and flowers. Do not place in heavy wet soils or close to sidewalks. Once established, *Mimosa* requires very little supplemental watering.

These true native mimosas should not be confused with the more widespread exotic tropical tree also called mimosa, *Albizia julibrissin*.

SPECIES DESCRIPTIONS

Mimosa biuncifera **(Cat's Claw, Uña de Gato)**

Rounded or straggly shrub with irregularly branching stems armed with numerous slightly curved prickles. Flowers are fuzzy pinkish globes appearing from early April intermittently to September. Common in the Trans-Pecos, less frequent in the Plains Country and the Edwards Plateau; also found in New Mexico and Arizona. Grows in full sun in thin or rocky soil. May be used in erosion control on rocky slopes or as an ornamental shrub. It is browsed by deer and its seeds are eaten by quail. The spiny thicket-like growth habit of this plant provides shelter for wildlife. Flowers provide nectar for bees, and the seeds are eaten by various mammals.

Mimosa borealis **(Fragrant Mimosa)**

Shrub to 3 feet, sometimes slightly more. Flowers pink, fuzzy, and fragrant, blooming from March intermittently through the summer. Most common mimosa in the Edwards Plateau, also in Oklahoma and New Mexico. Prefers full sun and well-drained soils.

Mimosa dysocarpa **(Velvet-pod Mimosa, Gatuño)**

Shrub 3–6½ feet with short and numerous prickly branches. Leaves pubescent on both sides. Pod very fuzzy and slightly constricted between the seeds. Flowers borne in showy, pink cylindrical spikes. Common to brushy hillsides of the Davis and Chisos mountains in west Texas, also New Mexico and Arizona. Velvet-pod Mimosa is easily germinated from first-year seed that has been gently nicked with a knife. It can be planted in the fall in a greenhouse, or in spring. It is a fast grower (Manning, personal communication, 1999).

Mimosa emoryana **(Emory Mimosa)**

Small shrub most easily recognized by the yellowish spines on the fruits and the pubescent foliage. The flowers are pinkish globes. Emory Mimosa is found on rocky limestone or igneous sites in the Trans-Pecos and northern Mexico.

Mimosa pigra **(Zarza, Coatante)**

A shrub up to 6 feet tall with many branches armed with stiff prickles. Small clusters of puffy pink flowers appear at the leaf axils from March to November. It is locally abundant in dry lake beds and resacas and other seasonally inundated areas of clay soils in extreme south Texas.

M. pigra became a destructive invasive species when introduced to Australia (Best, personal communication, 1999).

Morus

Morus, Mora, Mulberry

MORACEAE (MULBERRY FAMILY)

GENERAL DESCRIPTION

Mulberries are deciduous trees or tall shrubs with scaly bark (see Species Descriptions).

FLOWERS AND FRUIT

Flowers are inconspicuous, developing into blackberry-like fruits consisting of many small, compressed drupes each with a small seed. Fruits ripen and drop from the tree from May through August.

NATURAL HABITAT, RANGE, AND PREFERRED SITE

Morus is represented in Texas by two native species: one in east Texas, the other in west Texas, and their range occasionally overlaps in central Texas. See Species Descriptions for individual range and habitat.

COLLECTION AND STORAGE

Collect the fruits in summer when they have turned red or dark purple. Shake onto a drop cloth and rub them on a screen under running water to remove the seeds. Seeds must be cleaned before storage to avoid fermentation. A mechanical macerator may also be employed to clean large amounts of seeds. Thoroughly air dry the seeds and store at 41° F in sealed containers.

PROPAGATION

Seeds

Germination of mulberry seeds is delayed by a dormant embryo. Seeds may be fall sown outdoors after collection or stratified for 90 days at 41° F and planted in the spring or earlier in a greenhouse.

For outdoor sowing, the best seedbed is a moist, rich, loamy soil. Seedbeds should be slightly mulched and kept moist until germination begins. Germination of pretreated seeds planted in the spring usually occurs within

2 weeks. Optimum temperatures for germination are within the daily alternating range of 68–86° F (Gill and Healy 1974).

One-year-old seedlings may be used for field planting. Seedlings should be dug about 10 inches deep with a sharp-bladed shovel because the main roots are very stout and tough.

Cuttings

Mulberry may also be propagated by semihardwood cuttings taken in late summer or early autumn. Treat the cuttings with IBA (100 mg/l IBA for 24 hours or Hormodin 3) and place in a well-drained medium under mist.

Some species of *Morus* have been propagated from suckers sprouting from the base of the tree.

NOTES

Native mulberries are seldom planted in the home landscape because their wide-ranging fibrous roots and messy fruits are considered undesirable. However, mulberries are wonderful plants for wildlife. If permitted a space at the edge of the property, or in an alley or behind the garage, they will attract many birds. Deer are very fond of the foliage. Children like to climb the stout limbs and pretend they are raccoons gobbling the sticky sweet purple fruit.

SPECIES DESCRIPTIONS

Morus microphylla (Mountain Mulberry)

Large spreading bush or small understory tree to 23 feet. As a shrub, it may be multi-trunked. Leaves light green with serrated edges. The edible fruit is purple or blackish when ripe. Native to canyons in limestone or igneous slopes in the western two-thirds of Texas. Mountain Mulberry is the most drought tolerant member of this genus. Deer love to browse this plant.

Morus rubra (Red Mulberry)

Tree to 64 feet with a short trunk and stout spreading branches to form a broad, round-topped crown. Leaves broadly oval and dark green, sometimes turning yellow in autumn. Fruit dark purple. Uplands woods and flood plains from Massachusetts to Florida west to central Texas. Grows best in pH range of 6.0–7.5. Fruit favored by songbirds. Roots shallow and far ranging, sometimes causing problems in sewer lines and pavements.

Myrica cerifera

Wax-myrtle, Southern Bay-berry, Árbol de la Sierra

MYRICACEAE (WAX-MYRTLE FAMILY)

GENERAL DESCRIPTION

Wax-myrtle is a fast-growing evergreen shrub or multi-trunked small tree sometimes growing as tall as 38 feet. It has dull dark green or yellowish green leaves that are heavily coated on both sides with spicy aromatic resinous dots. Wax-myrtle often forms suckering colonies of several plants.

FLOWERS AND FRUIT

Inconspicuous male and female flowers are borne on separate plants in the spring. On female plants small clusters of small, round, hard bluish gray waxy drupes appear from October to November.

NATURAL HABITAT, RANGE, AND PREFERRED SITE

Wax-myrtle is native to streams, lakes, and bogs in wet pine barrens and woodlands of east Texas, east to Florida, north to Arkansas and New Jersey. Wax-myrtle prefers partial shade and a moist and sandy fertile soil but will adapt to drier locations, including relatively infertile soil and soil with a high salt content. When pushed to the western edge of its range, wax-myrtle will require supplemental summer watering.

COLLECTION AND STORAGE

Collect the fruit in September or October when it turns bluish green. The fruit can be beaten from the bush onto a drop cloth or collected by hand with clippers. The waxy covering can be left on the seeds to be stored over winter but removed before sowing or stratification. The wax must be removed if water is to be imbibed. Soaking the seeds in a dilute mixture of lye and warm water (1 teaspoon lye to 1 gallon water) is an effective way to dissolve the coating. Store seeds in sealed containers in the refrigerator. Dewaxing can also be achieved by vigorously rubbing the fruit on a screen.

PROPAGATION

Seeds

Germination of wax-myrtle is delayed by a dormant embryo. Pretreat seeds by sowing outdoors in the fall or stratifying in moist peat for 60–90 days at 34–41° F. Natural germination occurs in the spring following seed fall. Outdoor sowing should be delayed until late fall or early winter to avoid frost damage to early germinating seedlings. Transplant seedlings from the flat when they are 2 inches tall. Mulch outdoor seedbeds over winter. Both seedlings and cuttings benefit from light shade the first growing season.

Cuttings

Wax-myrtle will root in high percentages from 3–4 inch semihardwood cuttings taken from late spring through early summer and again in the fall after a flush of growth has hardened off. These should be treated with a 1–1.5% IBA solution. IBA in solution has proven to be more effective than the talc form.

Some growers find that a heeled cutting roots best. After rooting occurs, reduce the frequency of misting and harden off. Fall-rooted cuttings should remain in a cold frame over winter (Dirr and Heuser 1987).

Transplanting

Wax-myrtle plants up to 5 feet have been successfully transplanted bareroot in the winter. Cut back the tops by two-thirds to a maximum height of 2 feet. Trim the roots and then place the plant in a container. Transplanting is more successful on cool damp days and also when the roots are treated with a root stimulator (Lowrey, personal communication, 1986). Balled and burlapped plants may be transplanted in the summer if placed in a shady location and then pruned slightly and kept moist. Pruning to remove dead limbs or promote bushy growth should be done in spring.

NOTES

Wax-myrtle makes a good evergreen hedge or background plant and will adapt to all but the most arid or rocky sites. The waxy blue fruit of the female plant is showy and produces scented bayberry candles. It is tolerant of poorly drained sites and exhibits reasonable drought tolerance once established.

Wax-myrtle is important for reforestation purposes because of its nitrogen-fixing root nodules, which contain actinomycetes that work to improve the soil.

A related species, Dwarf Wax-myrtle (*M. pusilla*), is also worthy of cultivation. It is a stoloniferous evergreen shrub typically growing less than 6 feet tall. This species may form colonies on sandy sites. Dwarf Wax-myrtle is native to moist or dry sites in the Pineywoods of east Texas, east to Florida, and north to Delaware and Arkansas. It will adapt to heavier soil and is hardy in Dallas.

Dwarf Wax-myrtle cuttings taken April to May and treated with 8,000 ppm IBA root best. Be careful not to take cuttings too early or too late: timing is very important in establishing rooting. Select fresh new growth that is still very pliable at the tip, but just beginning to harden off at the base. Cuttings may take a year to make a finished one-gallon plant. Strongest growth spurts occur during the cooler months. Use a lighter soil mix to promote faster root development (Pfeiffer, personal communication, 1999).

Nolina

Beargrass, Sacahuiste, Basketgrass

LILIACEAE (LILY FAMILY)

GENERAL DESCRIPTION

Nolina is a grasslike plant growing in a clump with long, coarse-bladed leaves.

FLOWERS AND FRUIT

Flowers are whitish to pink, held in clusters either on stems or near the base of the plant (see Species Descriptions). Blooming occurs from early spring to late summer depending on species and seasonal conditions. Fruit is a capsule divided by three papery walls. Seeds are smooth, flattened, and black.

NATURAL HABITAT, RANGE, AND PREFERRED SITE

Nolina is native to slopes and ravines in limestone or igneous soil from the Edwards Plateau west throughout the Trans-Pecos and the northern part of the Rio Grande Plains. Its range extends into New Mexico and Arizona (see Species Descriptions). *Nolina* does not usually grow on flat mesas or sandy flats, as does the yucca, but is generally confined to exposed locations on rocky slopes. Nolina grows in both full sun and shade. It must be planted in a well-drained location.

COLLECTION AND STORAGE

Collect the seeds when the pod or capsule begins to dry but before it splits open. Carefully spread the seeds out in thin layers and dry at room temperature. Seeds will remain viable for at least 1 year if stored in sealed containers in the refrigerator. Seeds of *N. lindheimeriana* kept in dry storage for 9 years still germinated (Manning, personal communication, 1999).

PROPAGATION

Seeds

Nolina is easily germinated from freshly gathered seed. Germination is more uniform if the seed are first stratified for 30 days in moist perlite in the refrigerator. Plan the timing of cold stratification so that the seeds are ready to plant in late January or February in a cold frame. Seeds germinate best when temperatures are cool. Plant the seeds thinly in well-drained soil in a flat or in separate 4-inch containers.

After germination, seedlings are slow growing and will take up to 2 years to make a finished one-gallon plant. *Nolina* seedlings do best if given light shade the first season. Avoid overwatering. Seedlings will respond to light applications of fertilizers.

Cuttings

Instead of cuttings, individual offshoots are separated from large clumps of mature plants in the winter.

NOTES

Nolina is an excellent plant to use in dry shady locations. It can be used as a tall mounding ground cover or an erosion control plant on rocky hill-sides. The larger nolinas make strong evergreen specimen plants for sun or shade. Once established they are very drought tolerant and the stiff grass-like leaves remain on the plant throughout the year.

It is reported that sheep and goats are sometimes poisoned by the leaves of this plant. Grazing animals are particularly fond of the young inflores-cences, which may account for the scarcity of plants in some localities (Correll and Johnston 1970). Native Americans used fibers from the long leaves of many species for weaving baskets and mats.

SPECIES DESCRIPTIONS

Nolina erumpens (Foothills Nolina, Basketgrass)

This is one of the larger *Nolina*, growing 4 feet high and 6 feet wide. Heavy clusters of small greenish white flowers are held on a short thick 2-foot stalk from March to early summer. Leaves are 2–3 feet long and create a large mound. Native to limestone or clayey rocky soil along arroyos or grassy hills at 2,100–7,500 foot elevation in the Trans-Pecos. This large nolina makes a striking specimen plant and works well in the landscape when planted with agaves, yuccas, and desert shrubs with ephemeral blooms.

Nolina lindheimeriana (Devil's Shoestring, Lindheimer's Nolina)

Devil's Shoestring is recognized by its stout flowering stem, which ex-tends 3 feet from the mound of thin flat leaves. Endemic to limestone slopes and ravines in open woods in the eastern half of the Edwards Plateau.

***Nolina micrantha* (Beargrass)**
Distinguished by a slenderly branched and twiggy inflorescence and reddish purple flower parts. Native to rocky slopes and open sandy soils and grasslands in the Trans-Pecos and northern Mexico. This is the common species of the Guadalupe Mountains (Powell 1988).

***Nolina texana* (Texas Sacahuiste, Bunch-grass)**
Texas Sacahuiste has a short flowering stem nestled in among the numerous thin leaves. Often seen draping over the ground or limestone ledges. Blooms March to late July. In rocky soil from central Texas to the upper Rio Grande Plains and west to the Trans-Pecos.

Nyssa

Tupelo, Sour-gum

CORNACEAE (DOGWOOD FAMILY)

GENERAL DESCRIPTION

Members of this genus are trees to 96 feet or more with simple, alternate leaves (see Species Descriptions).

FLOWERS AND FRUIT

Male and female flowers are greenish yellow or white, appearing in early spring. Fruit is an ovoid to ellipsoid, blue-black fleshy drupe, ripening late summer through early fall.

NATURAL HABITAT, RANGE, AND PREFERRED SITE

Nyssa are native to swamps, moist woods, and along streams in east Texas, east to Florida, north to Missouri and Indiana.

COLLECTION AND STORAGE

Collect the fruits in late summer or early fall by either shaking the fruits onto drop cloths or collecting them from around the base of the tree. For *N. aquatica*, the dark reddish purple drupe ripens from September to October and fruit drop occurs from October to November. For *N. sylvatica var. sylvatica*, the bluish black fruits ripen from late September through early October. Although the removal of the pulp does not seem to be essential, the fruit is generally run through a macerator (Dirr and Heuser 1987). Clean the seeds by removing the pulp and then air dry for 1–2 days. Large amounts of seed can be cleaned in a macerator and the pulp floated off. Stratification in moist sand at 41–58° F will preserve viability up to 1 year.

PROPAGATION

Seeds

Germination of *Nyssa* seeds is delayed by a dormant embryo that must be either fall sown immediately after collection or stratified for 30–60 days at 41° F. Dormancy will vary among seed lots. Keep the seeds moist during storage and after sowing. Seeds that are allowed to dry out often exhibit a secondary dormancy that may delay germination another year.

The best seedbed is a moist, muddy soil that will not crust over when dry. Cover the seeds with ⅓–1 inch of firm soil. Seedlings benefit from partial shade. Stratified seeds were reported to have a germination rate of 38–50% (USDA 1974). Spring sowing after stratification is recommended.

Cuttings

For *N. sylvatica var. sylvatica*, softwood cuttings harvested from forced greenhouse stock plants in late winter root best. Cut in 1½ inch lengths, treat with 8,000 ppm IBA talc, and stick in sand under mist. Bottom heat is recommended. Rooted cuttings are generally ready for transplanting in 6 weeks (Dirr and Heuser 1987).

Transplanting

The sparse fibrous root system of tupelos make transplanting large specimens from the wild difficult. For seedlings lined out in nursery rows, periodic root pruning is helpful in stimulating secondary root growth prior to the final transplanting (USDA 1974).

NOTES

Tupelos are tall narrow-crowned trees appropriate for planting in any low, poorly drained area or areas with compacted soil in the eastern third of Texas. The fruit is eaten by several species of birds, and the flowers are a source of bee food.

SPECIES DESCRIPTIONS

Nyssa aquatica (Water Tupelo)

Relatively fast-growing, long-lived large tree to 100 feet tall with a wide-spreading and shallow root system. While still a young tree, its base begins flaring, becoming much wider than Bald Cypress or Swamp Tupelo. The flaring base gives the tree much stability in a watery habitat and permits it to tolerate compacted low-oxygen soils even in urban or construction areas (Simpson 1988). Its leaves are large, smooth, and dark green. Native to swamps and along streams from Florida to east Texas. Water Tupelo is an important honey and timber plant.

Nyssa sylvatica var. sylvatica (Blackgum, Black Tupelo)

Large tree to 140 feet with horizontally spreading branches. It is the first tree to color in the fall, turning brilliant red. In the winter the tree bears clusters of shiny blue to black fruit that are eaten by wildlife. Native to swamps, low woods, and poor sandy soil in east Texas to Florida. Blackgum is more tolerant of drier sites than *N. aquatica*.

Ostrya virginiana

American Hop-hornbeam

BETULACEAE (BIRCH FAMILY)

GENERAL DESCRIPTION

American Hop-hornbeam is a tree typically 20–30 feet tall, rarely 75 feet, with a twisting trunk, arching branches, and cinnamon-colored shedding bark. Leaves are 3–5 inches long and turn yellow in the fall.

FLOWERS AND FRUIT

Male and female flowers appear in separate greenish yellow catkins just before or with the appearance of new leaves. Fruit is an ornamental hanging hoplike cluster.

NATURAL HABITAT, RANGE, AND PREFERRED SITE

Native to dry upland woods in east Texas, east to Florida, north to Massachusetts. Hop-hornbeam can grow in very dense shade and is most often found as an understory plant. If given shade, this plant adapts well to compacted soil around campgrounds, picnic spots, and other high-use areas. It prefers rich acid soil but is somewhat lime tolerant. Hop-hornbeam does not thrive in heavy wet soils (Wasowski 1994).

COLLECTION AND STORAGE

Collect the seeds when the papery hanging fruit begins to dry out and turn a light greenish brown color, usually from late summer through October. Seed should be harvested and sown just as the endosperm is going into the mealy stage and before the seed coat becomes hard (Dirr and Heuser 1987). Use care when breaking the fruiting structures apart: the inflated bracts that enclose the seed have stinging hairs at each base. Spread the fruit in shallow layers to complete drying. Beat the fruit lightly in a sack and separate from the debris by winnowing. Cold stratification is the best means of storing seeds over winter.

PROPAGATION

Seeds

Germination of hop-hornbeam is delayed by an immature seed embryo that requires a period of after-ripening which must be followed immediately by cold stratification to break a late-developing embryo dormancy. The most direct method is to sow the seeds outdoors immediately after collection so that the seeds are exposed to warm temperatures required for after-ripening. Or, pretreat the seeds by stratifying in moist sand or peat at alternating temperatures of 68–86° F followed by up to 140 days at 41° F (USDA 1974). Remove the seeds from stratification in early spring and plant in a cold frame or greenhouse. Germination is poor in hot temperatures. In one report, seeds harvested while immature germinated 100% (Dirr and Heuser 1987).

For outdoor planting sow the seeds ⅓–½ inch deep and cover with light mulch until germination begins. Keep seedlings well watered and under light shade.

NOTES

Hop-hornbeam is grown for its ornamental summer fruit. It is adaptable to a variety of sites, and its fruit is eaten by songbirds and small mammals (Wasowski 1994).

Western Hop-hornbeam (*O. knowltonii*) is also worthy of attention. It is a small rare tree from the canyons in the Guadalupe Mountains of the northern Trans-Pecos in west Texas at altitudes of at 5,000–7,000 feet. It is also found in southeastern Utah, northern Arizona, and southeastern New Mexico. Even more rare is the Chisos Hop-hornbeam (*O. chisosensis*). It is a medium-sized tree found only in the Chisos Mountains of the Big Bend National Park. In one study, fresh seed planted in the fall germinated very well, but seedling survival to a one-gallon container was a failure (Manning, personal communication, 1999).

Parkinsonia aculeata

Retama, Mexican Palo Verde, Lluvia de Oro

FABACEAE (LEGUME FAMILY)

GENERAL DESCRIPTION

Retama is a small, slender specimen tree sometimes growing as tall as 36 feet in the southern part of its range. Its most noticeable feature is the bright green bark that turns brown on older wood. Spiny branches have long graceful drooping bipinnate leaves 8–16 inches long.

FLOWERS AND FRUIT

Bright yellow flowers are held in loose clusters 5–6 inches from late spring through the summer, making a nice contrast to the green bark. Fruit is a long persistent pod with flattened constrictions between the seeds and tapered at the ends. Seeds are ⅓ inch long with a green or speckled brown seed coat.

NATURAL HABITAT, RANGE, AND PREFERRED SITE

Retama is a frequent invader of pastures and disturbed poor soil, particularly in low and poorly drained areas in south Texas to central Texas. It is also widespread throughout the southern United States.

COLLECTION AND STORAGE

Seeds ripen from late April through October after each intermittent blooming period. Seeds are ripe when they are firm, filled out, and have turned a sandy brown color. Pods are green to light brown and dry when mature. Remove seeds when ripe by crushing the dried pods between two boards. Fumigate before storing. Seeds may be infested while still on the tree, so prompt and repeated collection is recommended.

PROPAGATION

Seeds

Retama seeds require no pretreatment in order to germinate. However, germination rates are higher if the seed is soaked in hot water (100° F) for

1 minute (Best 1999). Adding "Superthrive" to the cooling water also proved beneficial to one grower (Will, personal communication, 1999).

Germination will occur within 2–3 weeks if soil temperatures are warm. Plant in individual containers at least 8 inches deep to accommodate a relatively long taproot. Use a well-drained mineral soil mixture. Seedlings may be directly transplanted to a one-gallon container when they are 4 inches tall. Retama is fast growing and will make a five-gallon container plant by the following spring. To promote optimum growth, place in strong sunlight and fertilize periodically. Like most tap-rooted legume species, Retama has greater survival rates if grown in containers that promote root air pruning. Inoculation of the soil medium with rhizobium may also be beneficial.

Cuttings

Retama will root from semihardwood cuttings taken in summer, treated with IBA, and placed under intermittent mist.

Transplanting

Large specimens are difficult to transplant because of a long taproot. Careful selection of the transplanting site combined with such continued maintenance as cutting back and watering is necessary to achieve plant survival.

NOTES

Retama is one of the fastest growing woody plants in south Texas. It can reach 21 feet tall in 4 years or less (Best 1999). It is very drought tolerant, and the brilliant clusters of yellow flowers and green bark are continuously showy. Retama is especially suited for planting in poor soil or in infrequently maintained areas such as parking lots, roadsides, and median strips. It may be trained to a single trunk or periodically cut back to form a large, spreading shrub.

During periods of severe drought, Retama may shed all its leaves. The green stems will then manufacture chlorophyll and take over the feeding of the plant until rains occur and the plant refoliates. Retama is frost tender in far north Texas but will grow in Dallas if given south-wall protection. Some people object to the thorns and fallen pods, but this hardworking tree provides an interesting texture and vivid colors in situations not tolerated by most plants. It is ideal for planting in full sun with other chaparral plants like Cenizo (*Leucophyllum frutescens*), Mesquite (*Prosopis glandulosa*), Black-brush Acacia (*Acacia rigidula*), or Guajillo (*Acacia berlandieri*). It will adapt to any soil as long as it is moderately well drained. It is heat, drought, and salt tolerant, and must be grown in full sun.

A very beautiful specimen tree, Desert Museum Palo Verde, was first noticed at the Sonoran Desert Museum near Tucson, Arizona. It was an accidental cross of *Cercidium floridum* (Blue Palo Verde), *Cercidium microphyllum* (Foothills Palo Verde), and *Parkensonia aculeata*. It has the best characteristics of its parents: very bright green trunks, extended blooming period and prolific flowers, and strong, muscular form. It is now in the nursery trade, grown on rootstocks of *C. floridum*, which gives it sturdier resistance to windstorms and a cold tolerance of temperatures down to the low teens (Gass, personal communication, 1999). (See *Cercidium*.)

Parthenium argentatum

Guayule, Afinador

ASTERACEAE (SUNFLOWER FAMILY)

GENERAL DESCRIPTION

Guayule is a rounded evergreen shrub 3 feet tall and 4 feet wide with intricate, silvery-tipped branches. Leaf shape may vary widely. Leaves are covered with silver hairs and held on long petioles.

FLOWERS AND FRUIT

Yellowish white flowers are borne in conspicuous flat-topped clusters above the leafy stems from spring to fall. Guayule blooms continuously under conditions of long days, high temperatures, and sufficient moisture. Fruit is an achene.

NATURAL HABITAT, RANGE, AND PREFERRED SITE

Guayule is common in portions of the Chihuahuan Desert in the Trans-Pecos area of west Texas and northern Mexico. It prefers full sun and well-drained limestone soil. It is very drought tolerant once established, and cold hardy down to 15° F.

COLLECTION AND STORAGE

Clip flower heads in late summer and September after blooming, as they begin to dry. Spread on screens to thoroughly air dry, then separate the achenes by crushing. Procedures to harvest large amounts of guayule seeds have been developed using a vacuum insect net; the seeds are then cleaned by a series of screening, threshing, and forced air separations (Tipton, Craver, and Blackwell 1981). Achenes may be sown immediately or dried for storage.

PROPAGATION

Seeds

Guayule seeds exhibit a double dormancy. The inner seed coat is impermeable to gas exchange, which may be overcome by a weak oxidizing agent.

Embryo dormancy is 2 months in duration (Tipton, Craver, and Blackwell 1981). To pretreat the seeds, soak the cleaned seeds overnight in water and then in a .5% solution of sodium hypochlorite for 2 hours to thin the seed coats. Household bleach diluted to 1 part bleach in 10 parts water is a source of sodium hypochlorite. After the seeds have been soaked in the bleach solution, they must be carefully rinsed under running water for 2 hours. Thorough rinsing is very important because as the bleach degrades, it leaves a residue of sodium chloride on the seeds that is very toxic to emerging seedlings. Insufficiently rinsed seeds will germinate poorly.

After scarification, stratify for 60 days at 41° F. Then remove seeds and plant in a well-drained soil mix. Gently press the seeds into the soil but do not bury, because they require light to germinate. Pretreated seeds will begin to germinate within 3 days at rates up to 60–70% (Tipton, personal communication, 1986).

Seedlings are initially very small and weak and extremely susceptible to fungus attacks and desiccation. Broadcast sowing of seeds in the field seldom produces good stands of seedlings. Seedlings are also sensitive to high salinity levels often present in irrigated water in the areas where they naturally grow.

The most effective way of producing guayule in large numbers is to sow seeds in individual containers in a greenhouse in early spring using a well-drained medium, such as peat/perlite, and set out in the field later.

Three- to five-month-old seedlings are usually large enough to be set out in irrigated field plots and will bloom within the first year. In one study, seedlings benefited by a 15-16-17 soluble fertilizer applied every time they were irrigated until planted in the field (Tipton, personal communication, 1986).

Cuttings

Guayule is difficult to root from stem cuttings. The best results have been achieved using tender softwood tip cuttings taken in early spring and treated with 10–15 ppm IBA or Hormodin 2 (Tipton, personal communication, 1986). Once the tissue hardens off and the thick rubbery resin begins to flow, rooting is very difficult to achieve.

NOTES

Guayule is a shrub that produces a high-quality substitute for rubber. It is one of the secondary plant chemicals which are vital in deterring insects and perhaps browse species of mammals (Bowers 1993). Commercial interests and the United States government through the Emergency Rubber

Project investigated guayule rubber production from 1922 to 1959. Many acres of guayule were planted in the Southwest and California to lessen the country's dependence on foreign rubber sources during the war. Later, when energy was cheap and abundant, and methods for producing synthetic rubber were developed, the guayule fields were destroyed or abandoned. Guayule also has great potential as a resource-efficient ornamental plant. Its silver foliage makes a nice contrast to dark-leaved plants. It can be massed together as a ground cover and used on slopes for erosion control. After 3 or 4 years, guayule should be cut back to improve its form and encourage more blooms.

A close relative of guayule, Mariola (*Parthenium incanum*), is a smaller shrub useful for erosion control or highway planting. Its natural range extends from Arizona to Texas, typically on limestone or caliche soils. It also contains rubber and has been used to a small extent commercially.

Parthenocissus quinquefolia

Virginia Creeper, Guaco

VITACEAE (GRAPE FAMILY)

GENERAL DESCRIPTION

Virginia Creeper is a woody vine that climbs by means of adhesive discs on its stems. It has palmately compound leaves that turn crimson, scarlet, or orange in autumn.

FLOWERS AND FRUIT

Each individual flower is small and inconspicuous but hangs in heavy clusters of up to 200 flowers from May to July. In late summer and fall these develop into bluish black clusters of berries, each containing 1–3 ¼-inch seeds.

NATURAL HABITAT, RANGE, AND PREFERRED SITE

Virginia Creeper grows in woods and on rocky banks in open woodlands, on fences, and at the edge of forests in the eastern half of Texas, east to Florida, and north to New England. It prefers moist soil but is adaptable to many soil types. Virginia Creeper does best in partial but not dense shade. It can tolerate full sun if given adequate water.

COLLECTION AND STORAGE

Collect the fruits in September or October after they have turned bluish black by hand stripping them from the vines. The seed coat is thin, and care should be used when cleaning so as not to damage the seed. Extract the seeds from the pulp by mixing them with water in a blender fitted with a rubber blade or by gently rubbing them on a fine screen. Then spread them out to dry before storage. Store the seeds in sealed containers at 42° F.

PROPAGATION

Seeds

Germination of Virginia Creeper is delayed by a dormant embryo. Plant the seeds outdoors in the fall or stratify in a sterile soil mix with perlite for

60 days at 41° F before planting in the spring. Cover the seeds with ⅓ inch of soil. The seedbed should be moist but well drained. Most seeds germinate within 15 days after cold treatment.

Cuttings

Virginia Creeper is easily rooted from semihardwood cuttings. Take cuttings in late spring through the summer from wood that is just beginning to harden off. In one report, single-leaf bud cuttings taken in the summer, treated with 3,000 ppm IBA talc, and stuck in a sand/peat mixture rooted in high percentages (Dirr and Heuser 1987).

Semihardwood cuttings will often make a salable 4-inch pot plant ready to plant out within 4–6 weeks from rooting during the growing season (McNeal, personal communication, 1999). Select cuttings without tendrils because no buds form at nodes with tendrils. Virginia Creeper will also root from hardwood cuttings.

NOTES

Virginia Creeper is an excellent ground cover for deeper loamy soil and partial shade. It will grow on rocky sites, but the foliage will not be as lush. It has been cultivated since 1622. This vine will also grow on trellises and walls and makes an especially attractive plant with colorful fall foliage. Virginia Creeper provides food for numerous species of birds and other wildlife.

A related species, Seven-leaf Creeper (*P. heptaphylla*), is also worthy of cultivation. It tends to be bushier than Virginia Creeper and is more suitable as a ground cover, while Virginia Creeper likes to climb on a trellis or wall. Seven-leaf Creeper has seven to nine narrower leaflets which also turn red in the fall. Seven-leaf Creeper is endemic to woods and river bottoms in the Edwards Plateau. Take cuttings during the first part of the year. Cuttings taken in fall tend to sit on the mist bench and rot over winter (Pfeiffer, personal communication, 1999).

Pavonia lasiopetala

Rose-mallow Pavonia, Rock-rose

MALVACEAE (MALLOW FAMILY)

GENERAL DESCRIPTION

Rose-mallow Pavonia is a small perennial shrub with many herbaceous stems rising from a woody base. It may grow as high as 4 feet tall with a spread of 3 feet.

FLOWERS AND FRUIT

Miniature hibiscus-like pink flowers open in the morning as soon as warm weather begins in late spring and continue to bloom intermittently until a hard freeze occurs. Fruit is a capsule containing five seeds.

NATURAL HABITAT, RANGE, AND PREFERRED SITE

Rose-mallow Pavonia grows in shallow limestone and rocky woodlands and at the edges of thickets in the Edwards Plateau and south Texas. It prefers full sun and well-drained soil, but will also tolerate dappled light. If protected from afternoon sun, the blooms will last longer. Blooms occur on new wood, so frequent pruning promotes more compact growth and flowers.

COLLECTION AND STORAGE

Collect the seeds after intermittent blooming periods as soon as the capsules begin to turn brown but before they completely dry and split apart. Seed kept in paper bags in a cool, dry place will remain viable up to 2 years.

PROPAGATION

Seeds

Most fresh pavonia seeds will germinate within 2–3 weeks if the soil is warm. However, germination rates for the remainder of the same seed lot may be delayed or staggered over a period of several months. This indicates a variation in seed coat thickness even among seeds collected at the same location.

More uniform germination may be achieved if seeds are soaked in hot water before planting. Acid scarification for 3–5 minutes followed by overnight soaking in gibberilin may also provide more uniform germination rates for some species (Will, personal communication, 1999). See guidelines for *Hibiscus cardiophyllus*.

Gently press the seeds into the soil and cover with ¼ inch of soil. Seedlings may be transplanted to one-gallon containers after they have produced their third set of true leaves.

Cuttings

Rose-mallow Pavonia is also easily grown from softwood tip cuttings taken May through July. These should be 3–6 inches long and cut just below a node. All but the top leaves should be removed. Application of IBA (3,000–5,000 ppm) speeds up the rooting process.

Semihardwood cuttings will also root, but they require more rooting hormone and are less reliable (Pfeiffer, personal communication, 1999). Place the cuttings under intermittent mist. Rooting occurs within 3 weeks, and the cuttings may be transplanted to one-gallon pots in 4–5 weeks. Cuttings with a thicker diameter root better than spindly new shoots. Fall-rooted cuttings need cold-frame protection until spring. Light tip pruning will improve the overall form of the plant.

Both seedlings and cuttings respond to fertilizing. Established plants in the landscape do not require supplemental feeding, other than compost added to the soil once a year.

NOTES

Pavonia is a lovely perennial, especially when planted as an accent plant with Autumn Sage (*Salvia greggii*), Beargrass (*Nolina micrantha*), Verbena (*Verbena spp.*), and Cenizo (*Leucophyllum spp.*). It has a long blooming period and the leaves have an attractive shape. Pavonia freely self-seeds in a bed, and younger plants eventually replace the parent, which declines after 4 years.

To encourage bushy growth and more blooms, Rose-mallow Pavonia should be cut back nearly to the base each winter and also pruned during the growing season if it is becoming too leggy or woody. Occasionally during a wet spring, Rose-mallow Pavonia will get powdery mildew. The best remedy is to keep irrigation off the leaves and to cut the plant back and wait for a new flush of growth as the summer becomes more hot and dry.

Rose-mallow Pavonia can be grown as an annual all over Texas; north of the Red River, it will freeze back to the roots, but resprout in the spring if given mulch and south-wall protection (Wasowski 1988). Several dark pink forms have been selected and sold in the nursery trade.

Persea borbonia var. borbonia

Sweetbay, Red Bay

LAURACEAE (LAUREL FAMILY)

GENERAL DESCRIPTION

Sweetbays are evergreen trees with an average height of 15–25 feet, sometimes taller. The large smooth leaves are aromatic when crushed. Sweetbay occasionally forms dense thickets.

FLOWERS AND FRUIT

Inconspicuous flowers bloom from May to June. Fruit is a dark blue or blackish drupe about ⅓ inch long.

NATURAL HABITAT, RANGE, AND PREFERRED SITE

Sweetbay is most common in Texas in very acid, moist sandy soils in the southeastern Pineywoods and Gulf Prairies and Marshes. A separate population is found in drier sandy loams in full sun in the western Coastal Bend in Kennedy and Kleberg counties (Simpson 1988). Sweetbay is suitable for planting in dunes, maritime woods, calcareous hammocks, and scrub forests (Wasowski 1988).

COLLECTION AND STORAGE

Gather the fruits in the fall when they are filled out and have turned a dark blue to black color. Clean the seeds from the pulp before storing. Cleaned seeds held in sealed containers in the refrigerator will remain viable for at least 1 year.

PROPAGATION

Seeds

Germination of Sweetbay is delayed by a dormant embryo. Sow the seeds outdoors directly after collection or stratify in moist peat or sand for 1 month at 41° F before planting in the spring.

NOTES

The lush evergreen boughs of this plant make Sweetbay a worthy ornamental for east Texas. The large blue or blue-black fruit is eaten by several species of birds, including songbirds, quail, and turkey. Sweetbay leaves provide larval food for Palamedes and spicebush swallowtail butterfly. The leaves are used in cooking (Wasowski 1988).

Philadelphus

Mock-orange

SAXIFRAGACEAE (SAXIFRAGE FAMILY)

GENERAL DESCRIPTION

Native Texas mock-oranges are small shrubs 1–3 feet tall with slender, much-branched stems and peeling bark. The leaves are generally small and pointed and often fuzzy underneath.

FLOWERS AND FRUIT

Mock-orange has delicate but showy fragrant flowers, blooming in April and May, occasionally later. Fruit is a small persistent capsule containing many tiny black seeds.

NATURAL HABITAT, RANGE, AND PREFERRED SITE

Mock-oranges grow on the sides of sheltered canyon walls, among boulders, seeps, and around springs in calcareous and igneous soil in central and west Texas (see Species Descriptions). Mock-orange prefers well-drained but not arid soil and partial shade.

COLLECTION AND STORAGE

Collect the capsules from June to September when they begin to turn brown but before they completely dry and split open to drop the tiny seeds. Seed quality varies from year to year. Dry the seeds first in a paper bag and then separate the seeds from the capsules by crushing with a rolling pin. Seeds are very small—finer than ground pepper. Store the seeds in sealed envelopes in the refrigerator. Seeds will remain viable for at least 1 year.

PROPAGATION

Seeds

Mock-orange will germinate from fresh untreated seeds. However, stratification for 30 days at 41° F may produce more uniform germination. Sprinkle the tiny powderlike seeds across the seed flat or container, then gently press the seeds into the soil but do not cover them. Planting in separate containers or plant cells may reduce losses during transplanting. Use a well-drained and loose soil mix that will not become soggy or dry out too quickly. Drench the flat with fungicide prior to sowing. Seedlings are very sensitive to both drying out and damping off.

Seedlings benefit from light shade the first season. Mock-orange grows very slowly at first and should be carefully transplanted from the seed flat after the third set of true leaves appears. Seedlings are very tiny and sensitive to transplanting. *P. ernestii* is especially intolerant of standard pine bark nursery soil mix. It does better in a well-drained mix containing sand, a small amount of compost, and decomposed granite (Kirwin, personal communication, 1999).

Cuttings

Mock-orange will root from semihardwood cuttings taken in May, or just after the first flush of growth. The cuttings should be 3–4 inches long and slightly woody at the base. Thicker, more developed stems root best. Remove the leaves from the bottom halves of the cuttings and treat with 5,000–8,000 ppm IBA (McNeal and Pfeiffer, personal communication, 1999). Place the cuttings under intermittent mist in individual containers filled with a 1:2 mix of peat/perlite. It is essential that the soil mix be very light. Rooting usually occurs within 24–28 days, but can take as long as 1½ months (Kirwin, personal communication, 1999). Gradually reduce watering intervals as the cutting develops roots. Rooting should be well advanced before any attempt is made to transplant.

Hardwood cuttings may also be taken, but they are slower and more difficult to root. In the dry regions where Texas mock-oranges grow, it can be difficult to find enough new wood suitable for cuttings. Forcing nursery plants to flush new growth is the most realistic solution to producing mock-orange as a container crop (McNeal, personal communication, 1999). Light tip pruning of both cuttings and seedlings is recommended. Once a plant reaches a one-gallon size, it is fairly fast growing (Will, personal communication, 1999).

Transplanting

Mock-orange should not be transplanted unless it is growing in a site with deep soil. Avoid digging plants from rocky crevices and boulders. These plants are not common in the wild, and their numbers are already endangered by heavy browsing from deer, so digging from the field is discouraged unless the plants are threatened by construction.

NOTES

The persistent, delicate foliage and the gracefully drooping branches bearing many showy, fragrant flowers contribute to mock-orange's desirability as a low-growing ornamental for shady protected locations. Mock-orange will adapt to different sites and has been successfully grown in cultivation. It is cold hardy as far north as Dallas. Since blooms occur on the previous season's wood, do not prune until after the flowering season. Pruning will encourage a more compact habit. *P. texensis* responds well to shearing and can be used as an attractive border plant if not placed too close to sprinklers (Kirwin, personal communication, 1999).

There are at least nine species of *Philadelphus* in west Texas with potential ornamental landscape application (see Powell 1988). Deer like to browse this plant.

SPECIES DESCRIPTIONS

Philadelphus ernestii **(Canyon Mock-orange)**
Small shrub with brittle grayish branches and white cumin-scented flowers. Rare and endemic to the Edwards Plateau, where it grows in boulders and cliff banks near springs or wet areas.

Philadelphus microphyllus **(Little-leaf Mock-orange)**
Larger flowers on this canyon plant smell like orange blossoms. Shrub up to 4 feet high. Native to high slopes and canyons in the Chisos and Glass Mountains in the Trans-Pecos region of Texas, also New Mexico, Arizona, Nevada, Utah, and Colorado.

Philadelphus texensis **(Texas mock-orange)**
Small shrub to 4 feet with fuzzy leaves and white flowers. Endemic to the Edwards Plateau but will adapt to heavier soil as far north as Dallas. Produces flowers more prolifically than *P. ernestii*.

Pinus

Pine, Pino, Pinyon

PINACEAE (PINE FAMILY)

GENERAL DESCRIPTION

Pines are hard or softwood trees with evergreen needle-like leaves. See Species Descriptions for individual characteristics.

FLOWERS AND FRUIT

Male and female flowers are borne separately on the same tree. Fruit is the familiar woody cone maturing the second or sometimes third year. Cones either dry on the tree and open to shed the seeds or fall while still closed. Closed cones require additional drying or heat to release the seeds. Seeds are usually ovoid.

NATURAL HABITAT, RANGE, AND PREFERRED SITE

Texas has seven species of *Pinus* (or eight, if you designate *P. remota* as a separate species), four of which occur west of the Pecos River. See Species Descriptions for individual ranges and habitats.

COLLECTION AND STORAGE

Collect cones from the best-shaped and most vigorous trees in the late summer and fall, just before they completely open to drop the seeds. Avoid collecting seeds from immature or green cones. Mature seeds have a firm white to yellow embryo, which nearly fills the endosperm cavity.

After collection, spread the cones in thin layers on racks to dry completely so they will open and release the seeds. Then the cones may be shaken to release the seeds. Seeds of most species of pines will retain viability for long periods of time if stored at a moisture content of 5–10% of fresh weight (USDA 1974).

PROPAGATION

Seeds

Pines are most often propagated from seeds. Natural germination for most species occurs in the spring. Fresh seeds will germinate without pretreatment, though germination is improved by 15–30 days of stratification at 41° F. Dormancy may increase with prolonged storage (USDA 1974).

The best seedbed contains a fertile, well-drained, and well-aerated soil. Seeds may be sown outdoors in late fall or early spring. Fall-sown seedlings are usually larger and better developed after one season than are spring-sown seedlings (USDA 1974). Avoid sowing seeds too early in the fall because early emerging seedlings are vulnerable to frost damage. Or, sow seeds in a protected cold frame.

Seeds are drilled or pressed into the soil and covered with 1–2 inches of soil. Germination of spring-sown seeds is usually complete after 10–50 days. Seedlings of Mexican Pinyon (*P. cembroides*) are very susceptible to damping-off fungi and should be carefully watered and drenched periodically with an appropriate fungicide.

Ponderosa Pine (*P. ponderosa*) seedlings experience a better survival rate when planted in separate containers instead of a flat or directly in the field. In nursery practice, seeds are pretreated and sown in the spring in prepared beds.

Cuttings

As a group, the pines are very difficult to root from cuttings. A few species have been rooted from cuttings made from dormant juvenile wood treated with IBA and kept under intermittent mist. Rooting success decreases when cuttings are taken from trees over 5 years old (USDA 1974). Clones may also vary in their ability to root. The best wood is taken from lateral shoots of young trees in winter. Cuttings appear to root better in a sand/peat or perlite/peat mixture than in sand or perlite alone. Drenching the rooting bed in fungicide prior to inserting the cuttings is recommended. Rooting pine cuttings is a slow process.

For detailed information on nursery production of *Pinus*, see *Seeds of Woody Plants in the United States* and *Direct Seeding Pines in the South*, both U.S. Department of Agriculture handbooks, or consult Dirr and Heuser (1987).

NOTES

Pines are familiar forest trees, valued for timber as well as ornamental plants. The west Texas pines are less commonly propagated, and their potential as specimen plants for more arid regions is relatively undeveloped.

SPECIES DESCRIPTIONS

***Pinus cembroides* (Mexican Pinyon)**

Attractive tree with a pyramidal shape and a maximum height of 70 feet, though more commonly seen 20 or 30 feet tall. It has flexible blue-green needles. This variety is found only in Texas, at high altitudes of 4,000–6,000 feet in the southern mountains of the Trans-Pecos, in both igneous and limestone soils. Mexican Pinyon also grows east of the Pecos River in hot, sloping limestone hills. Some taxonomists designate this population as a separate variety, *Pinus cembroides var. remota* (Remote Pinyon or Papershell Pinyon), or even a separate species, *P. remota*. *P. remota* is a remnant of a larger, continuous population existing during glacial times. Once thought to be found only in isolated populations in the western Edwards Plateau, it is now considered to be the most widespread pinyon in the Trans-Pecos. Papershell Pinyon occurs at lower elevations (5,000 feet) than Mexican Pinyon and is characterized by having thinner skins on the nuts and more fragile cones with sharp-pointed scales (Powell 1988).

Research is needed to develop commercial production methods for this outstanding evergreen tree. Selection of faster growing forms would be very welcome in landscape use as an alternative to the shabby Mondale or Afghan Pine (*P. elderica*) or the old world cedars.

***Pinus echinata* (Shortleaf pine)**

To 96 feet with a long clear trunk and short spreading branches forming a narrow pyramidal crown. Most common on well-drained hillsides, flat woods, and slopes in acid soils in east Texas west to Burleson and Henderson counties, north to Oklahoma, east to Florida. It is the most cold hardy of all the southern pines (Simpson 1988).

Mature cones require 48 hours kiln drying at 104° F for opening. Seeds can be stored for 35 years. Fresh seed may require 15 days of cold stratification. Stored seed may require up to 2 months cold stratification. In nursery practice, seeds are pretreated and sown in the spring.

***Pinus edulis* (New Mexico Pinyon)**

Much smaller than Mexican Pinyon, New Mexico Pinyon is usually less than 40 feet tall. In Texas, New Mexico Pinyon is common on mountain slopes in the far north Trans-Pecos (Guadalupe Mountains) north to Colorado, and west to Arizona and New Mexico, localized elsewhere. New Mexico Pinyon is valued for its delicious edible seeds, and as a durable, irregularly shaped evergreen landscape tree. New Mexico Pinyon is susceptible to a variety of pests when stressed by over-or underwatering. Will grow from fresh untreated seeds. Germination rates are best at temperatures under 72° F (Phillips 1995b).

***Pinus palustris* (Longleaf Pine)**
Tree to 96 feet with short stout branches forming an open crown and leaves in dense bundles of three. Each needle is 8–18 inches long and bright green. Mostly in deep sand or coarse sandy loam in southeast Texas, along the coastal plain to Florida. Slow growing at first but catching up with other species after the third year. Seedlings look like a bristly green pom-pom.

***Pinus ponderosa* (Ponderosa Pine, Western Yellow Pine)**
Tree to 112 feet with a pyramidal open crown. Leaves dark gray-green to dark yellowish green. In canyons and on upper slopes of mountains in the Trans-Pecos, west to the northwest United States, and south to north-central Mexico. Cones ripen in late summer and early fall and will open to release the seed after 4–12 days of air drying or 3 hours of kiln drying at 120° F. Fresh seed has no pretreatment requirements, but stored seed may need up to 2 months of cold stratification before germination will occur.

***Pinus strobiformis* (Southwestern White Pine, Pino Enano)**
Benny Simpson regarded this species as "one of the most graceful, loveliest, and rarest of Texas pines" (Simpson 1988:227). Southwestern White Pine grows to 90 feet tall on high slopes in the Davis Mountains and Guadalupe Mountains. It has smooth whitish gray bark and five-bundled leaves.

***Pinus taeda* (Loblolly Pine)**
Tree to 112 feet with spreading and ascending branches forming a large open crown. In sand and sandy loam or gravelly soil in woods and hills in east Texas west to Bastrop's Lost Pines area, and Burleson, Leon, and Wood counties, also east to Florida and Maryland.

Pistacia texana

Texas Pistachio, Lintisco

ANACARDIACEAE (SUMAC FAMILY)

GENERAL DESCRIPTION

Texas Pistachio is a tall shrub or small tree typically 15–20 feet tall (the national champion tree measured 39 feet in 1976). It has slender, spreading branches and nearly evergreen small compound leaves. New leaves are reddish, later turning dark green and glossy.

FLOWERS AND FRUIT

Male and female flowers grow on separate trees. Male trees almost always outnumber female trees in native populations. On the female plant, clusters of white flowers occur in late spring or early summer followed by 3–4 inch panicles of red to blackish purple inedible drupes ripening in late summer or early fall.

NATURAL HABITAT, RANGE, AND PREFERRED SITE

Texas Pistachio occurs in the Edwards Plateau on hard limestone in the header canyons of the Rio Grande in Val Verde and Terrell counties (Simpson 1988). It is more common in northern Mexico. It will adapt to nearly any site across the southern half of Texas, as long as it is well drained. It is cold hardy to USDA zone 8, or 7b in west Texas (Arnold 1999). In Dallas it will survive with south-wall protection (Simpson, personal communication, 1986).

COLLECTION AND STORAGE

Collect the seeds in late August through September when the fruit turns bright red. Seed quality varies greatly from season to season, and often the seeds are without embryos. In some years, the male flowers bloom before the female ones, and so infertile seeds are formed. Sometimes even in good seed-producing years, the seed doesn't all ripen at once. Fruit should be dark purple or black when ripe. To check the general viability of a certain seed lot, cut a few seeds open to determine if they are filled. Briefly float seeds after harvesting to separate filled seeds from empty. Germination is best from freshly gathered seed.

For short-term storage, dry the seeds with the pulp on, or clean by macerating in a blender fitted with rubber blades or by running them on a screen. Store in sealed containers in the refrigerator.

PROPAGATION

Seeds

Germination of Texas Pistachio seeds is erratic. Germination may be delayed by an immature embryo, a hard seed coat, a cold dormancy requirement, or sometimes all three conditions. Freshly gathered seeds planted before they have a chance to dry out in storage or during cleaning often will germinate within 3–5 weeks. Drying the fruits seems to induce seed dormancy. For direct planting in the fall, sow 5–7 sound seeds per plant cell or liner. Germination usually proceeds within 10–14 days. Growth is rapid until the seedlings have put on five sets of leaves. After that, growth slows down.

Seedlings prefer a light mineral soil mix and will respond to moderate applications of fertilizer. Inoculation of the soil media with beneficial microorganisms could also promote faster growth, better root development, and fewer losses during transplanting (Pfeiffer, personal communication, 1999).

Another method suggests first acid scarifying the seed for 30–45 minutes, followed by cold moist stratification in perlite or sphagnum moss for 30–60 days at 41° F. Check the seeds each week while they are in cold storage. Germination will begin for some seeds in 3–4 weeks while the rest will germinate in lessening amounts over the following 6 months. Every week or so carefully remove with tweezers those seeds that are beginning to germinate. Place them in individual deep (6–8 inches) containers with well-drained soil media. Seedlings are often very susceptible to damping-off fungi (McNeal, personal communication, 1999).

Some growers suggest that 60–80 days of cold treatment alone is sufficient to induce germination (Hosage, personal communication, 1999).

Cuttings

Texas Pistachio roots best from semihardwood cuttings taken June through September. Remove the leaves from the lower half of a cutting and treat with rooting hormone (3,500–5,000 K-IBA solution). Keep under mist and gradually reduce the frequency of the misting as the cuttings begin to callus and form roots to promote hardening off and prevent stem rot. Bottom heat may be beneficial. Root in separate containers because roots are very brittle and easily broken during transplanting (McNeal, personal communication, 1999). Root in a peat/perlite or light soil mix instead of straight perlite in order to encourage better root formation.

Rooting percentages are often low (5–10%). Dormant hardwood or softwood cuttings root less successfully. Fall-rooted cuttings require cold-frame protection during the winter. Refinement of successful vegetative propagation would promote greater production of female trees with showy fruit.

Texas Pistachio has been successfully budded onto a rootstock of Chinese Pistachio, *P. chinensis*, though in low percentages (Lowrey, personal communication, 1986).

NOTES

The persistent shiny foliage and the attractive fruit and flowers of the female plant make Texas Pistachio an outstanding ornamental plant. Even male trees without fruit are appealing. Texas Pistachio may be trimmed up as a single-trunked tall specimen plant or cut back periodically and encouraged to develop several trunks to form an effective tall screen, hedge, or background plant. Texas Pistachio should replace every diseased Red-tipped Photinia currently in the landscape. Good companion plants to Texas Pistachio to make a tall screen include Cenizo (*Leucophyllum frutescens*), Four-winged Saltbush (*Atriplex canescens*), Arizona Cypress (*Cupressus arizonica*), and Texas Mountain Laurel (*Sophora secundiflora*). Although extremely adaptable, Texas Pistachio prefers full sun and well-drained alkaline soil. Deer like to browse new foliage of young plants.

Texas Pistachio was first recorded as *P. mexicana* in 1859 by Dr. John Torrey, the well-known New York botanist. Texas Pistachio is abundant in Mexico but is now only infrequently found in Texas.

Pithecellobium flexicaule

Texas Ebony, Ébano

FABACEAE (LEGUME FAMILY)

GENERAL DESCRIPTION

Texas Ebony is a large evergreen shrub or tree to 48 feet or larger in the southern part of its range. It has dense, heavy foliage and stout branches that eventually form a rounded canopy.

FLOWERS AND FRUIT

Creamy yellow flowers are held in long cylindrical clusters from May to October. These fragrant flowers are very showy in contrast to the dark foliage. Fruit is a large, thick woody legume containing several hard reddish brown beans. The pods begin to ripen after each blooming period and then "pause" in their development until June, when all become ripe at once (Best 1999).

NATURAL HABITAT, RANGE, AND PREFERRED SITE

Texas Ebony is an old growth species native primarily to coastal part of the Rio Grande Plains. It is less common in the brush country north of Laredo. It is associated with several plant communities such as Mesquite-Blackbrush and Mesquite-Granjeno. Texas Ebony can be planted as a specimen tree or large shrub as far north as San Antonio. Further north, it needs south-wall protection from winter freezes (Simpson 1988). Texas Ebony prefers well-drained full or partial sun. It is hardy to 10° F and extremely drought tolerant.

COLLECTION AND STORAGE

Texas Ebony seems to produce prolific amounts of seed one year, followed by a year of "rest" or scant pod production (Best 1999). Although the pods are persistent on the tree throughout the winter, early collection (mid-June to mid-July) is recommended to gather quality seeds before they are infested by weevils.

The pods are very thick and woody, and difficult to open. Cleaning large amounts of seed can be time-consuming. One method for treating seeds included gathering as many pods as possible to provide for those years when seeds are scarce. Take the pods before they begin to split and spread them on tarps in a parking lot or open ground. Hose down the pods periodically with water, and continue to allow them to dry in the hot summer sun. After a week or two, the pods will twist and open. Seed is then removed by thrashing and screening (Best 1999). Fumigate or dust the seeds before storage. Scarified seeds have been successfully stored for several years in the refrigerator.

PROPAGATION

Seeds

Germination of Texas Ebony is delayed by a hard seed coat. Highest and fastest germination rates are gained by soaking the seed in 93% technical-grade sulfuric acid for 30–35 minutes. Test each seed lot separately to determine the optimum time for treatment. Seed germination is also enhanced by three to five immersions in boiling water for 20 seconds, alternating with immersions in cold water (Best 1999). Seeds may also be nicked or filed to allow imbibition.

Pretreated seeds will germinate within 2 weeks when planted in a greenhouse or outdoors after the soil has warmed. Planting seeds in narrow but deep individual containers that provide for root pruning is recommended. Texas Ebony produces a long taproot that will rapidly find any small exit in a container and root into the ground below. Grow bags are not recommended. Texas Ebony is relatively slow growing in comparison to other trees in the legume family.

Cuttings

Information is lacking on specific methods of vegetative propagation of Texas Ebony.

Transplanting

Small trees may be transplanted from the wild, but the larger ones develop a long taproot that makes removal difficult.

NOTES

The dark, dense canopy of Texas Ebony casts heavy shade when full grown. It is resistant to root rot and is tolerant of extreme drought. The wood is very valuable because of its handsome coloration of dark brown streaks against a black background. It is very hard and used for fences, cabinets, furniture, and carvings. The seeds are made into jewelry. In Mexico, the seeds are eaten when green and roasted when ripe and used as a coffee substitute (R. B. Taylor, Rutledge, and Herrera 1997).

Texas Ebony makes an outstanding shade tree, hedge, or specimen plant for a hot sunny area or rock garden. Deer browse the foliage and the seeds are eaten by deer, javelina, rodents, and other small mammals. The foliage provides excellent cover for birds. Bees are fond of the flowers.

A related species, Tenaza, or Guajillo (*P. pallens*), is also worth cultivating, especially for revegetation projects. It is a shrub with ferocious bullhorn spines that can grow 20 feet or more on wet sites, but is more typically seen 3–9 feet tall on drier sites. It has delicate bipinnate leaves and is densely covered with fuzzy mimosa-like flowers from May through August. Tenaza is a very characteristic plant of Tamaulipan forests, where in certain locations it can compose up to 30–40% of the overall plant population (Best, personal communication, 1999).

Pretreat the seed by soaking it in acid for 15–25 minutes. Hot water treatments are not reliable. After scarification, aerate the seed at least 1 day, removing each day those seeds that have imbibed. Tenaza is fairly fast growing in the field (Best 1999).

Platanus occidentalis

Sycamore Plane Tree

PLATANACEAE (PLANE-TREE FAMILY)

GENERAL DESCRIPTION

Most sycamores in Texas are 65 feet or less, with mottled brown outer bark that peels off in large scales to reveal a smooth whitish underbark. Leaves are large, papery, with three to five sharply pointed lobes.

FLOWERS AND FRUIT

Male and female flowers are borne in separate heads on the same tree in the spring. Female flowers develop into a globose head of achenes borne on a long peduncle when ripe. Each achene contains one seed.

NATURAL HABITAT, RANGE, AND PREFERRED SITE

Sycamores grow in the river and creek bottoms in the eastern two-thirds of Texas. It occurs as far west as the Devil's River watershed in Val Verde County and in most of the rivers of the Edwards Plateau. Sycamores are present in all vegetational zones in Texas except the High Plains, the Rolling Plains, and the Trans-Pecos (Simpson 1988). Sycamores will grow in a wide variety of soils as long as they are deep, rich, and moist.

COLLECTION AND STORAGE

Fruiting heads remain on the tree throughout the winter and are most easily collected after the leaves fall until early spring. Heads should be well dried on screens or trays and then placed in a paper bag and crushed to separate the achenes. For over-winter storage, place the seeds in a cool, well-ventilated place in open mesh bags. For longer storage, air dry the seeds 2–3 days and store in airtight containers at 20–38° F (USDA 1974).
Propagation

Seeds

For more uniform germination, stratify seed for 30 days at 41° F before planting. Seedlings benefit from light shade the first season.

For field planting, broadcast or drill the seeds in rows 6–8 inches apart. Cover with 1/6 inch of soil. Keep the seedbed moist and shaded. On neutral to alkaline soil, damping off may be severe and can be prevented with regular applications of fungicide (USDA 1974).

Cuttings

Sycamore roots best from wood taken from young, vigorous stock plants that are cut back each winter and forced to coppice. Make the cuttings as the shoots start to mature. Treat with 8,000 ppm IBA talc and keep under mist in a peat/perlite rooting bed. Higher rates of IBA resulted in stem necrosis. Cuttings are typically well rooted after 45 days (Dirr and Heuser 1987).

Cuttings taken from older trees root at lower percentages. One grower noticed that sycamores grown from cuttings often lack a strong vertical leader trunk and will remain more shrublike instead of developing into a tree (McNeal, personal communication, 1999).

NOTES

Sycamore was first cultivated in 1640. It is among the tallest deciduous trees in the United States. Sycamore is slow growing but long lived. The brown exterior bark is shed by older trees to reveal a very beautiful and dramatic white underbark that provides a showy element in the winter.

When buying a sycamore, try to find out the provenance or origin of the seed from which the tree was grown. Trees grown in east Texas generally are not as tolerant of heat, drought, and disease as the more western ecotypes. Sycamore from the acid soils of the eastern forest belt will often suffer chlorosis on alkaline soils, and also become susceptible to the anthracnose pathogen (Ogden 1992). For western sites with adequate soil, the variety *P. occidentalis var. glabrata* (Western Sycamore) is the better choice. It is a fast-growing landscape tree, less prone to disease, including anthracnose, and is very heat and drought tolerant. Mexican Sycamore (*P. mexicana*) is also gaining favor among horticulturists as another fast-growing shade tree for alkaline soils. It tends to be smaller than *P. occidentalis* and is noted for the silvery undersides of its leaves as well as its beautiful bark. It will hybridize with American Sycamore.

Populus

Cottonwood, Alamo

SALICACEAE (WILLOW FAMILY)

GENERAL DESCRIPTION

Cottonwoods are large fast-growing trees with shallow root systems and large deltoid-shaped deciduous leaves. There are eight species in the United States, five of which are represented in Texas.

FLOWERS AND FRUIT

Catkins of male and female flowers occur on separate trees, appearing before the leaves in the spring. Fruit is a two- to four-valved capsule containing many small seeds, each with a fuzzy or "cottony" tail. For western species of cottonwoods, these wind-borne seeds typically disperse as receding spring floodwaters expose moist sandy soils on their edges and banks, which make ideal seedbeds. Since cottonwood seeds lose viability quickly, the timing of spring floods is critical. Seedlings quickly develop long roots that tap moist sand well below the surface. As the upper layers of soil dry out, the tree has an opportunity to become established (Bowers 1993).

NATURAL HABITAT, RANGE, AND PREFERRED SITE

Cottonwoods occur on stream banks, dry riverbeds, or near any source of water. In Trans-Pecos Texas, a solitary cottonwood often marks the location of a spring, seep, or an underground source of water (Powell 1988). Cottonwood is present in every vegetational area of Texas. For a thorough discussion of cottonwood's range and forms, see Simpson (1988).

COLLECTION AND STORAGE

Collect the capsules just before they open and disperse the feathery seeds. Spread the fruit in thin layers on a screen in a warm room or shed, allowing the capsules to dry and open. Then rub the fruit over a wire screen to separate the seeds.

Longevity of cottonwood seeds is brief, lasting between 2 weeks and a month. Seeds should be placed in cold storage, 41° F, immediately after they are air dried.

PROPAGATION

Seeds

Cottonwood will germinate from fresh seeds without pretreatment. Use well-drained sandy soil in the seed flat or container. Press the seeds in the soil but do not cover. Keep the soil media moist but not soggy; young seedlings are susceptible to both drying out and damping off. Fresh seeds usually begin to germinate within a few hours, and will need consistent moisture to become established. If planting in the field or in containers outside, protect the seedbed from wind and rain until the seedlings' roots are well established, usually 1–2 months.

Cuttings

Cottonwood roots easily from semihardwood cuttings of the current season's growth, taken in mid- to late summer, when stems have begun to harden off. Green or softwood cuttings root less well. Take cuttings of 6–10 inches from the ends of the branches. Make the top cut just above the first bud to avoid stem die-back. The rooting bed should be well-drained sand or straight perlite. Application of IBA improves rooting but is not imperative. Keep the cuttings under intermittent mist. Rooting percentages are usually high. However, rooted cuttings often fail to form a strong leader trunk and remain shrubby in their form.

In the Mexican state of Sonora, young cottonwoods are used as living fences or *estacas*. Farmers attach green cottonwood branches to wire fences that stretch across or follow streams. The branches eventually take root in the moist, gravelly streambed and help to trap rich alluvial soil during times of high water, which can be used later for crop production (Bowers 1993). My friend Bill Worrell in Mason, Texas, took a broken limb of *P. deltoides var. deltoides* that was about 3 inches in diameter and planted it in the granite/gravelly soils of his yard. After 8 years, that limb is now a 25-foot tree.

NOTES

Cottonwood is usually not everyone's first choice for an urban shade tree because its roots can be invasive in sewer lines and eventually can cause sidewalks to buckle. The wood is also weak and will break easily in windstorms. Yet there are still situations where the cottonwood is magnificent, as anyone who has enjoyed the majestic old granddaddy cottonwoods along Limpia Creek on the grounds of Old Fort Davis will testify. Generally, if you have a lot of room and especially a streambed or seep on your property, you can accommodate a cottonwood. The fluttering movement of the leaves as they twist and dance from their long leaf petioles in a breeze can be hypnotic when viewed against a bright summer sky. Cottonwoods can also provide brilliant fall color.

SPECIES DESCRIPTIONS

***Populus deltoides var. deltoides* (Eastern Cottonwood)**
A fast-growing tree that reaches more than 100 feet. Grows in almost any soil type (except swampy) in the eastern half of Texas (Simpson 1988). *P. deltoides var. occidentalis* (Plains Cottonwood) is a smaller version of Eastern Cottonwood. It grows in the harsher, drier climate of the High Plains, and is shorter lived.

***Populus fremontii var. wislizenii* (Rio Grande Cottonwood)**
Reaches 110 feet and grows along watercourses, springs, and drainage ditches in the northwestern Trans-Pecos, west to California.

Prosopis

Mesquite

FABACEAE (LEGUME FAMILY)

GENERAL DESCRIPTION

Mesquites are shrubs or trees with straight sharp thorns and delicate, light green compound leaves (see Species Descriptions). The leaves emerge late, usually after the last frost, and are shed early in fall. Mesquite wood is very hard with a dense, reddish grain.

FLOWERS AND FRUIT

Flowers are held in either fuzzy balls or longer cylinder-shaped spikes. They are yellowish white to yellow, fragrant, and valued as a source of nectar for honeybees. Fruit is a tough, leathery, several-seeded indehiscent pod that is a valuable forage plant for both wildlife and livestock.

NATURAL HABITAT, RANGE, AND PREFERRED SITE

Mesquites occur in almost every county throughout the state, especially south, central, and west Texas, and also Oklahoma, eastern New Mexico, and northern Mexico. Mesquites often invade disturbed or overgrazed land. They are a very drought tolerant group and will grow in poor soil.

COLLECTION AND STORAGE

Although pods remain on the tree all winter, gather them in the summer or early fall as soon as they begin to drop in order to avoid weevil infestations. Seeds should be firm, filled out, and turned a brown color. Remove the seeds by hand from the pod or with a mechanical shredder and then separate the seeds by winnowing.

One method for cleaning large amounts of seeds recommends putting the pods in a hand-cranked corn grinder (Best 1999). Spread the seeds in shallow layers to air dry a few days, and then fumigate before storing. Seeds will remain viable for several years if stored in sealed containers in a cool dry place.

PROPAGATION

Seeds

Mesquite seeds are covered with a hard seed coat and can remain dormant for many decades until conditions become favorable for germination (Simpson 1988). Some growers have had success planting slightly green seed that are fully formed and filled out, but that have not yet turned brown and hard. Dried seeds will germinate faster if first scarified. Nick with a knife or soak in hot water (100° F) for 60 seconds. Repeat hot water treatment if necessary. Follow the hot water soak by aerating the seeds for 1 day. Pregerminate seeds that have imbibed on germination trays (see Chapter III). Remove germinating seeds and plant directly in deep containers that air prune the roots. The containers should be filled with a well-drained soil mix. Seedlings have a long initial root. Pretreated seeds will germinate within 10 days in warm soil (Best 1999). Using a small amount of native soil or inoculating with rhizobium bacteria may promote stronger and more vigorous growth.

Cuttings

Prosopis can be rooted from juvenile wood or suckers treated with IBA. Cuttings taken in June and treated with 4,000 ppm IBA rooted 80–90%. Grafting thornless cultivars onto native stock should be done during active growth. Use scion and stock material that has the diameter of a pencil. Best results are achieved if scion and rootstock are genetically close (Gass, personal communication, 1999).

Transplanting

Large trees are difficult to transplant because of a long taproot. Small trees may survive transplant shock if cut back and kept shaded. Nursery grown root-pruned trees are more easily moved and transplanted.

NOTES

The tree species of *Prosopis* have deep and wide-spreading root systems that are strong competitors for available soil moisture, particularly in dry, overgrazed land. Mesquite often invades depleted or hard-used land to form dense thickets. However, this aggressive characteristic does not eliminate this genus' potential as worthy landscape trees. They provide fragrant flowers and dappled shade that allows grass and other ground covers to grow beneath them. Mesquites make excellent shade trees in extremely hostile situations that are too harsh for other species.

SPECIES DESCRIPTIONS

***Prosopis glandulosa var. glandulosa* (Honey Mesquite)**

Tree to 50 feet with delicate light green foliage providing a light, airy appearance. In late spring and early summer, Honey Mesquite is covered with 2-inch long fragrant blossoms. Mesquite is often thought of as a trash tree because it is such an aggressive invader of fields and lots. But in the right situation, mesquite can be a showy specimen tree. The delicate foliage, interesting asymmetrical spreading form, and extreme drought tolerance are among the attributes of this common plant. Under its dappled shade, grass can grow to the trunk. Mesquite is also the subject of renewed interest because of its value as a fuel, as a high-quality wood for flooring and furniture, and as a wood for barbeques that burns white-hot. For an interesting discussion on the mesquite, see Simpson (1988). Honey Mesquite variety is scattered and infrequent in the Trans-Pecos (Powell 1988). The seeds are eaten by a wide variety of wildlife, and the branches provide a nesting habitat for many birds, including scissor-tailed flycatchers, mourning doves, white-winged doves, and chachalacas. Mesquite fixes nitrogen in the soil and often provides a cooler microclimate under its canopy for wildlife. Mesquite is also a good food plant for butterfly larvae and a nectar source for adult butterflies (R. B. Taylor, Rutledge, and Herrera 1997).

***Prosopis glandulosa var. torreyana* (Western Mesquite)**

Western Mesquite is common west of the Pecos River, where it also sometimes hybridizes with *P. glandulosa var. glandulosa* (Honey Mesquite) and *P. velutina* (Velvet Mesquite). It generally has smaller leaflets than Honey Mesquite.

***Prosopis pubescens* (Screwbean Mesquite, Tornillo)**

Screwbean is considered by some to be the showiest member of this genus. It is a large shrub or small tree 6–32 feet tall with smaller, more delicately compound leaves than Honey Mesquite. The flowers are borne in yellowish white spikes in spring and summer, and the fruit is a spirally coiled legume. Although it can survive in the desert, Screwbean grows best in running streams, seeps, or dry washes, where it can take advantage of intermittent run-offs. Its range extends from the Trans-Pecos area of Texas west to California.

***Prosopis reptans* (Creeping Mesquite, Dwarf Screwbean)**

A low undershrub usually only 2 feet tall. Like *P. pubescens*, it has small delicate leaves and a tight spirally coiled legume. It is found only on saline sand or clay soils in the Rio Grande Plains in south Texas (Best, personal communication, 1999). White-tailed deer browse the leaves.

Prunus

Plum, Cherry

ROSACEAE (ROSE FAMILY)

GENERAL DESCRIPTION

Prunus spp. are deciduous or evergreen trees or tall shrubs (see Species Descriptions for individual characteristics).

FLOWERS AND FRUIT

Flowers are usually white or pink with five petals, held in clusters or alone. Fruit is a one-seeded drupe, dark red or purple when ripe.

NATURAL HABITAT, RANGE, AND PREFERRED SITE

Prunus spp. are most often found in thickets, woods, and edges of fields in the eastern half of the state. A few are distributed in cool canyons and drainages in the mountains of central and west Texas (see Species Descriptions).

COLLECTION AND STORAGE

Collect the fruit when it is filled out, firm, and has turned a lustrous blue-purple or dark red. Harvesting will vary with species and climatic changes each year. Some species should be gathered in mid-summer, and others are not ripe until early fall. Collectors often compete with birds and other wildlife for the edible fruit.

Clean the seeds from the pulp and allow to air dry before storing. Do not heat or dry in direct sun, because overdrying may increase dormancy in some species. Seeds to be immediately fall sown outdoors need not be dried after cleaning. Seeds to be stratified or planted within a few weeks or months should be only surface dried for a few hours or a day, depending on humidity. Viability during long-term storage is best maintained at temperatures of 31–41° F. Seeds of Mexican Plum (*P. mexicana*) lose viability rapidly during storage, especially if allowed to dry out after cleaning.

PROPAGATION

Seeds

Germination of most *Prunus* species is delayed by a dormant embryo that requires a period of cold stratification. Some species, including Mexican Plum (*P. mexicana*) and Escarpment Choke Cherry (*P. serotina var. eximia*), also require a period of after-ripening prior to cold stratification.

One method for growing Mexican Plum seeds recommends collecting the seed in late June or July, cleaning the seed, and placing them immediately in warm moist stratification indoors or in moist sand pits outdoors until the middle of September or early October. Then transfer the seed to cold stratification at 41° F for 60–90 days. During cold storage, check the seeds weekly to determine if any are beginning to germinate. Using tweezers, carefully remove the germinating seeds and plant directly in plant bands or deep plant cells. Germination of pretreated seeds will usually occur within 20 days.

Mexican Plum has also been successfully germinated when seeds were collected in August, cleaned, and then soaked in a bucket of warm water containing active yeast and sugar (2 packages of yeast and 2 tablespoons of sugar to a gallon of water) for 3–4 weeks. Seeds were then rinsed and planted outdoors. Germination began early the next spring (Janzow, personal communication, 1999).

About 70% of the seeds of Creek Plum, *P. rivularis*, and the Flatwoods Plum, *P. umbellata*, are mature at the time of harvest and require little or no after-ripening (Simpson, personal communication, 1986). However, 2 weeks or more of warm moist stratification prior to cold stratification will provide more uniform germination results for most *Prunus* species.

For field growing, sow the seeds outdoors before the end of September to allow plenty of time for after-ripening before the onset of cold or freezing weather. Keep beds mulched until seedlings emerge. Cold stratification should be timed so that the seeds are ready to plant in a cold frame or greenhouse by mid- to late February. Later planting exposes the seeds to high temperatures and drying, which adversely affect germination. Optimum temperatures for germination average 77° F during the day and 50° F at night.

Cuttings

Prunus species may also be grown from dormant hardwood, softwood, semihardwood, and root cuttings. Semihardwood cuttings taken in summer are the easiest to root. These should be taken from the tips of the branches, from new stems that are flexible at the end and just beginning to turn woody at the base. Extremely soft cuttings often rot in the mist bench.

Remove one-half of the leaves and treat the cuttings with 8,000 ppm IBA talc for 24 hours. Stick in a peat/perlite mixture and keep under intermittent mist. Gradually harden off the cuttings as they begin to callus and root by decreasing the frequency of misting intervals. Rooting usually occurs in 30 days.

NOTES

Wild Black Cherries and plums offer many ornamental landscape possibilities. They have attractive spring flowers and often showy, edible fruit. The leaves of several species turn yellow or crimson in the fall. Some species make good specimen trees and other thicket-forming species are effective in erosion control and wildlife habitat reclamation. In ornamental landscape situations they may be used as delicate deciduous screens, especially in low-lying areas such as swales and bar ditches.

SPECIES DESCRIPTIONS

Prunus angustifolia **(Chickasaw Plum, Sandhill Plum)**
Twiggy, thicket-forming shrub or small tree to 13 feet with slender reddish branches, white flowers, and red or yellow fruit ripening from May through July. Found in old fields, edges of woods, and roadsides throughout most of the eastern two-thirds of Texas, east to Florida, north to Oklahoma and Arkansas. Fruits reportedly delicious and much used by Native Americans.

Prunus caroliniana **(Cherry Laurel)**
Upright evergreen tree or tall shrub 15–20 feet, sometimes taller. Tiny creamy white flowers bloom early to mid-spring. Leaves smell like almond extract when crushed, but contain a high content of poisonous hydrocyanic acid. Cherry Laurel is moderately adaptable but requires good drainage. It quickly develops root rot in heavy clay or chronically wet sites. It is tolerant of alkaline soils as long as they are deep. On thin rocky soils, Cherry Laurel will become chlorotic and show signs of heat stress. It is moderately salt tolerant (Arnold 1999). Cherry Laurel is best suited as an east Texas plant, though it will adapt to some sites in central Texas in established landscapes. Best used as an evergreen screen. Deer do not typically browse the foliage. There are several horticultural selections available, including 'Brite n Tite,' a compact, more densely branched form. The black fruit is rather inconspicuous when ripe and will remain on the tree well into winter.

Seeds require a 1–2 month cold stratification period or fall planting before they will germinate. Cherry Laurel will also root from softwood to semihardwood cuttings taken in later spring through September. Apply

3,000–8,000 ppm IBA talc or solution. Dormant cuttings will also root (Dirr and Heuser 1987).

***Prunus havardii* (Havard Plum)**
Shrub with rigid branches and light gray bark, usually to 5 feet, with white flowers. The fruit ripens in July. Endemic to rocky canyons in the Trans-Pecos. This species has unexplored potential as an attractive shrub for west Texas.

***Prunus mexicana* (Mexican Plum)**
Tree to 38 feet, single-trunked, with showy flowers covering the tree in spring, and beautiful banded bark. Fruit reddish purple when ripe in July through September. Leaves turn yellow in the fall. Does not form thickets and is not particularly easy to transplant. Native to river bottoms, thickets, and prairies in northeast and north-central Texas and the Edwards Plateau. Mexican Plum is an excellent moderate-sized specimen tree. On thin soils in full sun, Mexican Plum will show signs of heat stress during droughty months. Because Mexican Plum is an understory tree accustomed to growing at the edges of woods, it looks its best in deeper, well-drained soils and in locations that are shaded from direct exposure to afternoon sun.

***Prunus minutiflora* (Texas Almond, Peach-brush)**
Low shrub with irregular, often zigzag spiny branchlets and tiny bluish gray leaves. Flowers small, appearing with the leaves in groups of one to four. Fruit pinkish red when ripe in June. Endemic to the Edwards Plateau where it is only infrequently found. Needs a well-drained site. Could be used as an ornamental woody ground cover for dry, rocky sites. Good wildlife plant.

***Prunus rivularis* (Creek Plum)**
Slender, thicket-forming shrub with fragrant white flowers and bright red fruit ripening in June. Along streams, roadsides, and edges of woods in the Edwards Plateau and north-central Texas, also Oklahoma. Suckers freely from roots. One method for seed propagation recommends soaking the seed in water for 3 weeks after harvest. Then plant in shaded beds outdoors or in five-gallon pots (about 20–35 seeds per pot) in September. Germination usually begins in the following March (Janzow, personal communication, 1999).

***Prunus serotina var. serotina* (Choke-cherry, Wild Black Cherry)**
Tree to 110 feet, with white flowers held in graceful drooping racemes. Fruit purple-black when ripe in August through October. Leaves turn yel-

low in fall. Widely distributed across eastern Texas in woodlands, thickets, and roadsides in neutral to acid soils. Highly intolerant of shade.

***Prunus serotina var. eximia* (Escarpment Choke-cherry)**
Escarpment Choke-cherry, found in the Edwards Plateau, grows to 45 or 50 feet. It is most often found in moister sites along streambeds or in canyons. Escarpment Choke-cherry is very site specific in its adaptability. Two- and three-year-old trees are susceptible to borers and often lose their leaves in the middle of a dry summer (Hosage, personal communication, 1999). Escarpment Choke-cherry seedlings grow best in a light mineral soil rather than a heavy pine bark mixture.

***P. serotina var. rufula* (Southwestern Black Cherry)**
Southwestern Black Cherry grows to a height of 30 feet, though it is usually much smaller. Native to deep canyons and protected bottomlands of the mountains of the Trans-Pecos in west Texas. Adaptable to alkaline, neutral, and acidic soils. Benny Simpson describes an isolated colony of this species occurring many miles away from its native habitat on the Bexar–Wilson county line in deep Carrizo sands. This mountain species proved poorly adapted to landscape situations in Dallas and San Antonio (Simpson 1988).

Seeds of *P. serotina* were germinated after a 14-day warm stratification period followed by several months of cold stratification. Softwood cuttings taken from juvenile wood were rooted in a sand/peat medium after being treated with 8,000 ppm IBA talc. There was wide variability in rooting percentages among different trees (Dirr and Heuser 1987).

***Prunus texana* (Sand Plum)**
Dwarf, bushy shrub with irregular branches and oval leaves. White flowers appearing with or before the leaves. Fruit fuzzy, ripening in June. Endemic to the Edwards Plateau and the Rio Grande Plains. Will grow in poor or disturbed soil. Good low hedge plant. Could be used in erosion control.

***Prunus umbellata* (Flatwoods Plum, Slow Cherry)**
Small tree to 19 feet with a compact head and slender branches. Flowers white, fruit red, yellow, or dark purple. Uncommon but not rare in east Texas, found in acid sands to sandy loams on the edge of forests and on slopes along creeks, as well as pastures, in the true Pineywoods (Simpson 1988). It is highly intolerant of shade. Prefers moist but well-drained soils. It is the last plum to flower in east Texas. Heavy crops occur only every 3 or 4 years. The plums sometimes don't mature until late August to early October.

Ptelea trifoliolata

Hop-tree, Wafer-ash, Cola de Zorillo, Pinacatillo

RUTACEAE (CITRUS FAMILY)

GENERAL DESCRIPTION

Wafer-ash is a delicate, irregularly branched aromatic shrub growing to 25 feet, though generally smaller. Light green deciduous trifoliate leaves make an interesting contrast to the slender branches and pale bark.

FLOWERS AND FRUIT

You will notice the intense orange-blossom fragrance of the small, greenish white flowers before you notice the flowers themselves. Fruit is a reddish brown flat samara with a single disc-shaped wing surrounding the seeds. Seeds are about ⅓ inch in diameter.

NATURAL HABITAT, RANGE, AND PREFERRED SITE

Wafer-ash is found throughout the state, except in extreme south Texas. In west Texas it is found only in protected canyons. Elsewhere, it is common along streams, roadsides, and fencerows, as well as the edges of woods. Wafer-ash will grow in full sun or partial shade as an understory plant. It is adaptable to a wide range of soils and is moderately drought tolerant.

COLLECTION AND STORAGE

Ripe samaras persist on the tree throughout the winter, but best results are obtained when the fruit is harvested in late summer and early fall (i.e., end of August, first of September), as it begins to dry and turn light yellow-brown. It is not imperative to remove the wings from the seeds before storing or sowing, but large amounts of seeds can be cleaned by shredding them in a small leaf grinder (McNeal, personal communication, 1999). Air dry seeds a few days before storing. Seeds will retain viability for at least 16 months if stored in sealed containers at 41° F (USDA 1974).

PROPAGATION

Seeds

Germination of Wafer-ash is delayed by a dormant embryo. Sow the seeds outdoors in an unheated cold frame after collection or stratify for 30–60 days at 41° F before planting in early spring. The seed will start coming up in the spring (McNeal, personal communication, 1999).

Average germination rate has been recorded as 28% (USDA 1974). One grower sowed seedlings in the fall in five-gallon pots. These germinated the following spring and were easily divided and planted into individual containers. Seedling survival was improved by soaking the seedlings in a solution of B-1 vitamins and NAA mixed with water as they were separated. Care was taken to prevent the container from drying out during the transplanting stage (Janzow, personal communication, 1999).

Cuttings

Cuttings of the cultivar 'Aurea' taken in mid-summer, treated with 8,000 ppm IBA talc, and stuck in a perlite/sand medium under mist rooted 100% (Dirr and Heuser 1987). Local growers interviewed for this book have had less success.

NOTES

Wafer-ash is an attractive tall shrub or small understory tree for both moist conditions and dry rocky sites. The flowers in late spring are exceptionally aromatic. The light green leaves add a fresh texture to the dry landscape and the persistent "silver dollar" fruit is interesting. If grown in full sun and periodically cut back, Wafer-ash will develop a bushy form. It may also be trained to a single trunk with an open spreading crown. Hop-tree provides food and shelter for wildlife, and reportedly the fruit was once used as a substitute for hops. Lynn Lowrey used to grow an outstanding glossy-leafed form of Wafer-ash that he collected in Leaky, Texas.

Pyrus ioensis

Blanco Crabapple

ROSACEAE (ROSE FAMILY)

GENERAL DESCRIPTION

Blanco Crabapple is a tall shrub or small tree to 32 feet with a dense irregular form, sometimes suckering from the base. The oval-shaped leaves have serrated edges and fuzzy undersides. Occasionally they turn burgundy in the fall.

FLOWERS AND FRUIT

The flowers of Blanco Crabapple are typical of the rose family, having five white or pink petals. They appear as attractive bouquets held against the dark green leaves in spring and early summer. Fruit is a fleshy pome, green and waxy, 1 inch in diameter, with two or occasionally three filled seeds each less than ⅓ inch long.

NATURAL HABITAT, RANGE, AND PREFERRED SITE

Blanco Crabapple is endemic to limestone slopes, along creeks, and at the head of arroyos in the Edwards Plateau in central Texas. It prefers well-drained but not arid sites. It is not usually found on hot rocky upland sites, but rather in the deeper soils with more organic matter found at the base of valleys or stream sides.

COLLECTION AND STORAGE

Collect the fruit from September to late October when the pulp is fleshy, but preferably before the fruit has fallen from the tree. Cleaning the fruit is a big chore: the pulp is usually hard, and the seeds must be laboriously cut out. Some growers have waited until the pulp softens, and then mash the fruit with a heavy brick or a pair of pliers (McNeal and Hosage, personal communications, 1999). After careful crushing, the seed will have to be cut out individually.

Blanco Crabapple fruit is very acidic and caustic to the skin on your hands. The seed must be cleaned before sowing or storage to avoid fermentation. Large amounts of hard fruits may be soaked in warm water to soften them and then cleaned in a macerator. Be careful of letting the fruit soften and ferment too long: high temperatures could damage the seed. Air dry seeds on screens at room temperature before storing.

Seeds to be planted immediately do not need to be dried. Seeds to be sown in the spring should be held in stratification over winter. For longer storage periods, keep in sealed containers in the refrigerator (USDA 1974).

PROPAGATION

Seeds

Seeds have a dormant embryo that can be pretreated by either fall sowing in beds outdoors or stratification for 90–120 days at 41° F and planting in early spring. Place cleaned seed in plastic bags containing moist perlite in the refrigerator. Blanco Crabapple does not germinate well in hot temperatures. The best seedbed is one containing a loose sandy loam with a lot of organic matter. Plant the seeds ½ inch deep and cover the bed with a light mulch to prevent drying over winter. Protect seed flats and beds from rodents and squirrels with wire mesh. Remove the mulch once germination begins. Seedlings benefit from light shade the first season. Natural germination of fall-planted seeds usually occurs in early March.

Cuttings

Members of *Pyrus* will root from suckers and softwood cuttings. Sprouts or suckers dug in February will also produce new plants (Simpson, personal communication, 1986).

NOTES

At one time, Blanco Crabapple was much more plentiful in the Edwards Plateau, but overgrazing by deer and domestic animals has severely depleted the natural population. Blanco Crabapple has many of the same showy attributes of the domestic crabapple and, in addition, is able to thrive in dry conditions on limestone or alkaline soil. The flowers are delicate and showy, and the leaves often turn crimson in the fall. It makes an excellent specimen plant. The fruit of Blanco Crabapple produces a delicious jelly or preserve.

Blanco Crabapple has a chilling requirement and does not bloom well in Houston after mild winters. The Southern Crabapple, *P. angustifolia*, is a more consistent bloomer for Houston (Lowrey, personal communication, 1986). It is native to woods and thickets in southeast Texas, east to Florida.

A related species, Red Chokeberry (*P. arbutifolia*), also has ornamental value. It is native to low woods, swamps, and thickets from east Texas to Florida.

Quercus

Oak, Encino

FAGACEAE (OAK FAMILY)

GENERAL DESCRIPTION

Members of this genus are trees or shrubs with deciduous or evergreen leaves. The oaks can be roughly divided into two main groups: black (also called red) oaks and white oaks. The white oaks are the more ancient and widespread of the two groups (Ogden 1992). White oaks produce acorns annually, and the inside of the acorn cup is smooth. White oak bark is generally white and scaly, and the wood is light colored, close grained, and prized as lumber. The black or red oak group is restricted to the New World (Ogden 1992). It is distinguished by having bristle-tipped leaves that often turn colors in autumn. Black oaks require 2 years to produce acorns. The inside of black oak acorns has dense hairs or fuzz, and the bark is black, hard, and furrowed.

FLOWERS AND FRUIT

Male and female flowers are borne separately on the same tree in March and early April just before or with the appearance of the new leaves. Male flowers hang in rust-colored aments or catkins. Female flowers are borne singly or in small clusters. Fruit is a one-seeded nut (acorn). Frequency of acorn production depends on species.

NATURAL HABITAT, RANGE, AND PREFERRED SITE

Oaks are found throughout the state in various soils and sites (see Species Descriptions).

COLLECTION AND STORAGE

Begin collecting ripe acorns from August to December, depending on species, site, and seasonal rainfall. To determine the maturity of the acorn, hold the cup between your thumb and index finger and eject the acorn from its cup by snapping your fingers. If it is mature, the acorn will pop out. If it is too immature, part of the acorn will be left in the cup. Most acorns are sufficiently mature for harvesting in late September to October. The most practical indicator of acorn maturity is the change in color from green to brown.

Best quality acorns are shaken or picked from the tree. Acorns should be gathered from the ground only if very recently dropped or if they have fallen on dry pavement. Avoid collecting acorns that have been in wet leaves or mud for a considerable period of time. Also avoid those with holes, which indicate insect infestation. Infested or wet seeds mixed with sound seeds will contaminate the lot. It is not necessary to remove the cap or shell prior to storage or sowing unless you want to reduce the bulk of large amounts. Acorns should be fumigated before storage to kill weevil larvae (USDA 1974). Acorns to be sown immediately can be soaked in hot water (120° F) for 15 minutes to prevent infestation. During the soaking, the infertile seeds will float to the top and can then be separated from the sound seeds.

Acorns of most white oaks quickly lose viability during storage and should be planted or stratified immediately to prevent drying. Black oaks will remain viable up to 6 months if kept in cool storage. This rapid loss in viability for all oaks occurs because the life processes of the seeds are critically dependent on a high moisture content within the seeds (USDA 1974).

Overdrying is indicated by a crackling and wrinkling of the seed coat. For germination to occur, the moisture content must not drop below 30–50% for white oaks and 20–30% for black oaks. For short-term storage of all oaks, layer them in moist sawdust or sand in a shaded area or pit.

PROPAGATION

Seeds

Oaks are most often propagated from seeds. Most oaks require no pretreatment in order to germinate promptly. They should be planted outdoors or in deep containers immediately after collection. Many oaks promptly extend their roots when planted but require exposure to cold temperatures to initiate shoot growth in spring.

For field sowing, plant the acorns 8–14 inches apart, covered with 1–2 inches of firm soil. Mulch the bed lightly to conserve moisture until germination begins. Protect outdoor beds with wire mesh to prevent predation by squirrels and rodents.

For indoor sowing, use deep containers that promote air pruning of the initial root (see Chapter IV). As the seedling is moved up to larger containers, it continues to be important to air prune the roots. Plants with air-pruned roots are more successfully moved into larger containers and into the field. In contrast, older trees with girdled roots seldom thrive when planted out, even in ideal conditions.

Since oaks are generally slow growing and may be held in a container 5 years or more before being planted in the ground, it is important to provide them with a fertile soil mix and proper nutrients to encourage optimum development. The soil mix must be loose and well drained, but not arid, with a fair amount of organic material. Slowly incorporate soluble fertilizers in the soil mix and apply regular supplemental feedings during the growing season.

Cuttings

In general, oaks are difficult to root from cuttings. However, some success has been achieved with Coastal Live Oak (*Quercus virginiana*). Semihardwood tip cuttings were taken from young trees. These rooted better than mature (acorn-producing) trees. Cuttings taken in the months from May to October rooted equally well. Cuttings taken during the colder months failed to root, as did softwood cuttings. Hormone treatment is required, and 10,000 ppm K-IBA quick-dip solution proved to be the most effective. Pencil-sized or slightly smaller cuttings were the best size material. Cuttings were stuck in a well-drained peat/perlite mixture and kept under mist. Bottom heat during cool weather was beneficial. Misting intervals were reduced as the cutting began to callus and put on roots, typically after 12 weeks.

Juvenility appears to be a major factor in the rootability of *Quercus*; rooting percentages were higher for second-generation cuttings taken from plants themselves vegetatively reproduced. Cuttings made from trees older than 5 years old rooted poorly (Morgan 1979). Studies have shown considerable variation in rooting ability among trees from different geographical areas. The question remains, however, as to whether clonally produced oaks will develop into trees with strong forms, or if they will remain rather shrubby. Information is lacking on the feasibility of clonally reproducing the majority of our native oaks. Selection of outstanding characteristics such as drought tolerance, fall color, form, and disease resistance through the study of superior populations in nature and development of the best methods for reproducing them have not been widely achieved.

NOTES

Texas has 43 distinct species and two varieties of oaks. These represent about 8% of all species found in the world, 17% of all North American oaks, and 74% of all oaks found in the United States alone. Thirty-eight species are considered trees. Of the Texas species, 23 are in the white oak group and 15 are black or red oaks. Black oaks occur only in the New World and are some of the most colorful and outstanding members of this family. In Texas there are 9 dwarf oak species, growing up to 15 feet, and 12 small oaks, up to 30 feet. Texas has 20 live or tardily deciduous species, most of which are western in origin (Simpson 1988).

From a horticultural standpoint, the big difference between a black oak and a white oak is that a white oak is much more drought resistant. Most black oaks will be found growing in the high rainfall belts of east and central Texas or in secluded canyons at higher altitudes in the west.

The white oaks, such as Bur Oak (*Quercus macrocarpa*) and Post Oak (*Quercus stellata*), are much more resistant to the fungal disease oak wilt. The least resistant are the black or red oaks such as Texas or Spanish Red Oak (*Q. buckleyi*), Blackjack Oak (*Q. marilandica*), and Shumard Red Oak (*Q. shumardii*). Live oaks (*Q. fusiformis* and *Q. virginiana*) are extremely susceptible but are slower to die than Spanish and Shumard Red Oaks because their vascular tissues are naturally more constricted, which slows the progression of the fungus. Oak wilt is a deadly fungus (*Ceratocystis fagacearum*) that kills trees by infecting their vascular system. The fungus clogs the tree's water-conducting vessels, eventually blocking water and mineral flow to the foliage. Oak wilt spreads rapidly from diseased trees to adjacent healthy live oak trees through interconnecting root systems or by sap-feeding nitidulid beetles which serve as vectors by carrying spores from fungal mats located beneath the bark of infested Spanish Red Oaks or Blackjack Oaks to fresh wounds on uninfected trees. Not all infected oaks form fungal mats. Generally this occurs within the red oaks, which are infected in the summer and early fall. Live oaks, even if they are infected with oak wilt, do not produce fungal mats and are not thought to contribute to the external, long-distance spread of the disease.

An infected Spanish Red Oak or Blackjack Oak develops symptoms of the disease rapidly. Starting in June and continuing throughout the growing season, the leaves of an infected tree will begin to darken; the leaves quickly begin to turn colors, as though it were autumn. Once the foliage begins to turn, the leaves die within weeks, turning first a rusty bronze and finally brown. Although the tree is dead by the time the foliage has dried, there is still enough moisture in the wood for some months to support the formation of fungal mats beneath the bark. These mats are fruiting structures covered with spores of the oak wilt fungus—a source of new disease.

The late autumn or spring after the red oak has developed the disease, fresh spores are easily transmitted to healthy trees by the beetle. The beetle carries the spores to a healthy tree by coming in contact with a fresh wound or cut. If the newly infected tree is another red oak, the chain of infection can come full circle: the dying tree forms more fungal mats, thus producing another source of spores.

The disease may also spread to adjacent healthy trees through root connections with the diseased tree. This pattern of infection is particularly devastating to the live oaks, because they often grow in clumps or colonies, and their roots are interconnected by natural grafting. But because live oaks do not form fungal mats, a live oak infection center is eventually self-limiting.

Another way oak wilt is spread is through contamination during pruning, where improperly cleaned saws and tools carry the fungal spores from the cut of a diseased tree to a healthy tree.

Treatment of oak wilt is very expensive and has limited success. One only has to drive through the Kerrville area to witness the bleak devastation of a once expansive oak forest to appreciate how serious this disease is when it is concentrated in one area. Oak wilt disease has cut a cruel swath from the Red River to the Nueces, from Midland to Pasadena.

No complete prevention or cure has been developed for live oak wilt. Yet understanding the cycle of disease does offer some opportunities for minimizing losses. A diseased red oak should be destroyed as soon as it is clearly infected with oak wilt. It should be cut down, burned, or buried before the fungal mats can be formed. Thorough removal of the entire tree is often too expensive or physically impossible, and sometimes merely felling the tree may still leave a trunk on the ground with enough moisture to support the growth of fungus. One group in Medina, Texas, developed the "Medina method" for hastening the death and drying of diseased red oaks. They girdle the trees by removing a section of bark near the bottom and spray an herbicide onto the exposed wood to hasten death and dessication. In one study, a group of trees that were girdled in the previous July and August formed no fungal mats when examined in January, effectively ending the disease cycle (Tracy, personal communication, 1999).

Other preventive measures for dealing with oak wilt include pruning oaks only in the winter, painting all wounds or pruning cuts immediately, disinfecting all saws and pruning tools with chlorine after each tree is cut, and avoiding the transport and sale of diseased firewood. Diseased live oaks can be isolated from healthy trees by trenching. A machine rips through the soil at least 100 feet from the most recently infected tree. This is an expensive and traumatic measure and does not completely insure that some infection had not occurred before the rock saw did its work.

Alamo™, a new fungicide, is recommended for high-value trees too close to an infection center to be protected by trenching. Results of this treatment are not conclusive.

Although oak wilt is a major threat to red and live oaks, oak decline is also a serious problem, especially in the urban forest. Oak decline is a disease complex that is most common in the city, where trees are under constant stress from human activities (i.e., pollution, compaction of soil, salt in water or fertilizer, fill soil) in addition to the expected challenges of weather, insects, and diseases. The symptoms of oak decline are a weakening of the tree, a thinning of the canopy, and eventual sprouting along the main limbs and trunk. Death may take as long as 8–10 years after the onset of symptoms.

For both oak wilt and oak decline, the best remedy is prevention. It is important to understand the needs of the tree. It must be properly protected during any construction and provided for after building is completed. When planting a new tree, choose the correct species for the site (see information on *Q. shumardii*). Try to add more diversity of species so that whole areas are not so vulnerable to fungal epidemics.

Once we become familiar with the variety of oaks native to our area, we begin to realize how few species are actually available in our nurseries.

SPECIES DESCRIPTIONS

The following species are not a complete list of all oaks found in Texas or the Southwest. They describe some of the more attractive oaks with potential as landscape plants. For a thorough discussion of the Texas oak tree species, see Simpson (1988).

Quercus alba (White Oak)

Large tree more than 100 feet tall with a broad crown, large leaves, and annual acorns. Grows on the rich, deep, well-drained acid sands, loams, and loamy clays of east Texas, and to a lesser extent on the eastern portions of the Post Oak Savannah, east to the Atlantic, north to Canada. In cultivation since 1724.

Quercus buckleyi (Spanish or Texas Red Oak)

Medium or small tree, often multi-trunked, maturing at 25–30 feet. Spanish Red Oak has thin deciduous leaves that are deeply lobed and turn scarlet or maroon in autumn. Acorns biennial. Endemic to rocky limestone hillsides in the Edwards Plateau west of Interstate Highway 35.

Quercus emoryi (Emory Oak)

Shrub or tree to 60–70 feet in ideal locations, though typically averaging 15–25 feet. Emory Oak has furrowed black bark and semi-evergreen foliage. Annual acorns ripen June through September. Emory Oak grows in deep, well-watered canyons of the Trans-Pecos at elevations of 5,000 feet in the Chisos, Davis, and Limpia mountains of Texas, also in Arizona and northern Mexico. This handsome live oak of west Texas should be more widely cultivated.

***Quercus falcata* (Southern Red Oak)**
Large tree to more than 125 feet with roughly furrowed black bark and thin, papery, deciduous leaves turning scarlet in autumn. Fruit biennial. Southern Red Oak is the dominant oak in the Pineywoods. It is also found in the Post Oak Savannah and eastern Gulf Prairies and Marshes. Southern Red Oak and its varieties range east to the Atlantic and north to New Jersey (see Simpson 1988). Stratify seeds in moist sand or potting soil for 30–60 days at 32–38° F, or plant immediately in the fall.

***Quercus fusiformis* (Escarpment Live Oak, Encino Chaparro)**
Thicket-forming, rhizomatous shrub or small tree sometimes reaching up to 50 feet, depending on the site. Rough black bark and a spreading crown. Leaves evergreen, thick, and leathery. Fruit annual. This is the smaller live oak of the Edwards Plateau, forming mottes in limestone soil. It will hybridize with *Q. virginiana* where their ranges overlap (see Simpson 1988).

***Quercus gambelii* (Gambel Oak)**
Shrub or small tree, occasionally up to 25 feet, sometimes smaller and thicket forming. Leaves deciduous and deeply lobed, very similar to White Oak (*Q. alba*). Acorns produced annually. Slopes and valleys at high elevations in the Chinati, Chisos, Davis, and Guadalupe mountains in the Trans-Pecos, also west to Colorado, Utah, and south to northern Mexico. At lower elevations than its native habitat, Gambel Oak will show signs of heat stress in July and will become susceptible to leaf spot diseases (Simpson 1988).

***Quercus glaucoides* (Lacey Oak, Encino Roble)**
Shrub to medium-sized tree to 35 feet with deciduous, dark bluish or grayish green leathery leaves often turning gold in the autumn. Annual acorns. On upland sites in limestone soil in the Edwards Plateau, also northeast Mexico. Lacey Oak is one of the most attractive of the Texas oaks, and it is extremely drought tolerant. Lacey Oak has a full, rounded form and is an excellent medium-sized tree appropriate for most home landscapes. Lacey Oak is relatively slow growing. It may take several years to form a strong trunk, and it often grows in clusters (Ogden 1992). It is resistant to oak wilt.

Quercus graciliformis **(Graceful Oak)**
Small oak to 25–30 feet tall with slender, graceful branches and semi-evergreen foliage. Leaves thin but leathery. Acorns biennial. Graceful Oak is found only in the Chisos Mountains in Brewster County in the Trans-Pecos. Usually in igneous soil at 5,000 feet elevation and often associated with a high water table.

Quercus gravesii **(Chisos Red Oak, Graves Oak, Encino Colorado)**
Small or large tree to 42 feet with furrowed, hard black bark and deciduous leaves turning scarlet in autumn in its native mountains. Acorns biennial. In igneous soil in the mountains of the Trans-Pecos, usually at 5,000 feet, rarely along arroyos in limestone soil, also in northern Mexico. Chisos Red Oak is closely related to Texas Red Oak (*Q. buckleyi*) and Shumard Red Oak (*Q. shumardii*), although neither occurs west of the Pecos River (Simpson 1988).

Quercus grisea **(Gray Oak, Encino Prieto)**
Small tree to 20 feet or smaller shrub with tardily deciduous, leathery, oval-shaped leaves. Gray Oak is one of the most common species of the Trans-Pecos. It prefers igneous soils, but will also grow on limestone. It is known to hybridize with a number of other oak species (Powell 1988).

Quercus hinckleyi **(Hinckley Oak)**
Intricately branched shrub forming coarse thickets to 3 feet tall with evergreen hollylike leaves that are reddish as they emerge. Hinckley Oaks produce tiny acorns every year. Rare and endemic to dry slopes at higher elevations of mountains in Presidio County. Adapted to Dallas and San Antonio, where it makes a spectacular specimen shrub. Hardy and drought tolerant.

Quercus hypoleucoides **(Silverleaf Oak)**
Showy small tree or tall shrub less than 30 feet with persistent, blue-green or grayish leathery leaves with densely fuzzy undersides. Acorns annual. Endemic to moist canyons at high elevations in the Trans-Pecos.

Quercus incana **(Sandjack Oak, Bluejack Oak)**
Low tree or shrub to 26 feet with stout, crooked branches. Leaves deciduous, moderately thin. Acorns biennial. Sandy uplands in east and central Texas, also along the southern Coastal Plain, north to Virginia. Usually found in dry sandy soil. Group plantings may provide a screen. Attractive fall color.

***Quercus intricata* (Coahuila Scrub Oak)**
Exceptionally showy dwarf live oak under 15 feet with thick ovate leaves and intricate branches. Acorns annual. Dry rocky hillsides in the mountains of the Trans-Pecos.

***Quercus laurifolia* (Laurel Oak)**
Large tree to 125 feet with leaves both evergreen and deciduous. Acorns biennial. Wet forests, especially along streams in southeast Texas, east to Florida. Closely related to *Q. phellos* and *Q. nigra*.

***Quercus macrocarpa* (Bur Oak)**
Large shade tree to 50–100 feet with heavy limbs, broad crown, and large lobed leaves. Bur Oak is easily identified by its large (2-inch) acorns covered with bristly caps. Its broad crown may span 100 feet, casting dense shade below. Native to moist forests or along streams in east and central Texas, east to Florida, and north to Canada. Bur Oak has been in cultivation since 1811. Bur Oak is not recommended for a small lot or placement too near buildings. It sometimes is plagued by anthracnose leaf spot disease and can be difficult to transplant. To look their best, Bur Oaks need moderately deep soils, such as alkaline prairie clays. On thin rocky soils, they will only grow 35–40 feet. Produces a good acorn crop every 2–3 years.

***Quercus marilandica* (Blackjack Oak)**
Two distinct forms of Blackjack Oak occur in Texas. The eastern form grows more than 50 feet tall and has large, three-lobed, club-shaped leaves. It grows only on very acid sands, clay, and sandy loams. The western form grows to 30 feet and is found on sand or gravelly clay soils that are only slightly acid. Both have very handsome dark furrowed bark.

***Quercus michauxii* (Swamp Chestnut Oak)**
Majestic oak to 120 feet native to moist woodlands and river bottoms in eastern Texas. Does not like standing water, but does best in situations that are periodically flooded, especially in winter.

***Quercus mohriana* (Mohr Oak, Shin Oak)**
Small rhizomatous tree less than 15 feet with smooth, oblong or elliptic evergreen leaves and annual acorns. On limestone hills and mountains in west and west-central Texas, north to the Plains Country, also in northern Mexico. Often shrubby and forms mottes in the Rolling Plains, western Edwards Plateau, and most of the Texas counties west of the Pecos River.

***Quercus muehlenbergii* (Chinquapin Oak)**
Straight-growing tree with a narrow crown, up to 90 feet tall with attrac-

tive, dark green, lustrous saw-edged leaves with silvery undersides. Acorns annual, sweet, and edible. Chinquapin Oaks have a variable form: some trees have a wide-spreading canopy, and others are more upright and narrow. In calcareous upland forests of northeast, central, and west Texas; east to the Atlantic; west to southern New Mexico and northern Mexico. A very handsome tree, with possible use in the Texas Panhandle (Arnold 1999).

***Quercus nigra* (Water Oak)**
Medium or large tree to 80 feet with semi-evergreen leaves, rather thick and leathery. Young water oaks are pyramidal, becoming rounded with age. Acorns biennial. Wet forests of east Texas, occasionally along the coast. Water Oak tolerates flooding. It tends to become chlorotic on alkaline soils and is not drought tolerant. In cultivation since 1723.

***Quercus oblongifolia* (Mexican Blue Oak)**
Evergreen tree less than 30 feet, leaves sometimes turning dark crimson in the fall. Acorns annual. In igneous rocky soil on hills and mountains of the Trans-Pecos, also New Mexico, Arizona, and northern Mexico. This tree was unknown in Texas until the 1970s, when it was found in Presidio County. These trees are easily distinguished by the deep blue-green color of their leaves (Simpson 1988).

***Quercus phellos* (Willow Oak)**
Medium or large tree to 100 feet with narrow deciduous leaves. Acorns biennial. Willow Oak will grow on poorly drained hardpan soils in the Post Oak Savannah as well as the flood plains of east Texas. In east Texas to Florida, north to New York. A shade tree in cultivation since 1723.

***Quercus polymorpha* (Mexican White Oak)**
Medium to large oak with rough bark and a broad rounded canopy. Leaves are rather large (3–5 inches long), oblong, with several different forms including irregularly scalloped and tapered shapes. Within its natural range, Mexican White Oak is typically semi-evergreen. According to Scott Ogden, Lynn Lowrey observed that many Mexican White Oaks in Nuevo Leon, Mexico, exhibit distinctive yellowish petioles on their leaves which make them especially ornamental. Mexican White Oak is native to the rugged limestone Sierras of eastern Mexico, with outlying populations as far south as Guatemala and northward just into Texas to one known isolated colony in Val Verde County (although it is reasonable to speculate that other small populations may exist undiscovered along the Devil's and Pecos rivers). In the southern part of its range, Mexican White Oak is found in mixed

cloud forests at high elevations (5,000–9,000 feet). Further north, it is more restricted to desert watercourses at 1,000 feet or less, along with Escarpment Live Oak (*Q. fusiformis*), Monteczuma Cypress (*T. mucronatum*), and Sycamore (*Platanus spp.*). Young trees have a moderate to fast growth rate, with a pyramidal form when young. Mexican White Oaks appear to be widely adapted to any location where Escarpment Live Oak also thrives (Ogden, personal communication, 1999). In the trade, it is also known as Monterrey White Oak.

In the early 1990s the Texas Nature Conservancy was surveying some land along the Devil's River near Dolan Falls in Val Verde County when they discovered a very small isolated box canyon with deep silty gravel deposits supporting several gnarled, spreading oak trees that looked somewhat like evergreen Post Oaks. They asked Benny Simpson to identify them. He went to take a look with John Mac Carpenter, and they were stumped as well. They pressed some specimens and sent the information off to an oak expert, who then identified these few trees as the northernmost population of *Q. polymorpha*. Later, Benny Simpson published a monograph on his findings (Simpson and Carpenter 1992). This group is approximately 250 miles northwest of the nearest Mexican White Oaks growing in the Sierra de los Picachos. Mexican or Monterrey White Oaks in the trade today are typically grown from acorns collected in Mexico or from cultivated trees whose provenance is Mexico. The Val Verde group offers perhaps the most cold-hardy ecotype of this species, but collection at this site is prohibited because it is a preserve. Mexican White Oak, like many oaks, will freely hybridize with other oak species. Several interesting crosses with *Q. rhizophylla*, *Q. canbyi*, and *Q. stellata* have been observed.

***Quercus pungens var. vaseyana* (Vasey Oak)**
Shrub or small tree, usually less than 40 feet tall with evergreen or persistent leathery and sharply toothed bright green leaves. Acorns annual. Dry limestone hills at low elevations in southwest Texas and northeast Mexico. Very good small tree for xeric landscapes.

***Quercus rugosa* (Netleaf Oak)**
Shrub or medium-sized tree with evergreen or semi-evergreen leaves that are thick, leathery, and lustrous dark green. Acorns annual. Uncommon on wooded slopes at high elevations in the Trans-Pecos, west to Arizona and Baja California, also in northern Mexico. Today it is difficult to find pure strains of this oak in nature.

***Quercus shumardii* (Shumard Red Oak)**
Large tree to 120 feet with broad crown and thin, deciduous, lobed leaves

turning scarlet or burgundy in autumn. Acorns produced every 2–3 years. Shumard Red Oak is native to the rich moist bottomland soils of the eastern Cross Timbers, Blackland Prairies, Post Oak Savannah, Pineywoods, and Gulf Prairies. Where its range approaches the Edwards Plateau, Shumard Red Oak has been known to hybridize with Spanish or Texas Red Oak (*Q. buckleyi*). However, it is important to realize that Shumard Red Oak is very poorly adapted to the thinner soils and drier conditions west of Interstate Highway 35 in Texas. They prefer deeper bottomland soils with nearly neutral pH (Ogden 1992). In thinner dry soils, Shumard Red Oaks tend to become very chlorotic, though this condition may not become apparent until a few years after they've been planted in the landscape. When weakened by a poor site, Shumard Red Oaks are very susceptible to a whole host of secondary diseases and infestations.

It is not uncommon to find trees mislabeled in the nursery. Shumard Red Oaks are sometimes labeled as generic "Red Oaks," or even declared to be "Texas Red Oaks." It is important for consumers to question the provenance of the red oaks they are buying to make sure they are getting the species best adapted to their particular site.

Another thing to remember about the Shumard Red Oak, as with some of the other taller oaks, is that it can reach a colossal size and easily overwhelm any home or building if planted too close. Nothing is more painful to view than a majestic oak tree butchered in its prime by brutal pruning because the owner did not anticipate its eventual proximity to a power line, roof, or sidewalk.

***Quercus sinuata var. breviloba* (Bigelow Oak, Shin Oak)**
Large tree to 64 feet with soft gray bark in broad thin scales. Leaves deciduous, thick, leathery, and irregularly lobed. Acorns annual. Moist forests in east Texas and along the watercourses to central Texas. It will form thickets when it occurs in lighter soils or when its roots have been disturbed.

***Quercus stellata* (Post Oak)**
Medium to large tree to 48 feet with thick deciduous leaves. Acorns annual. Dry upland woods, common on acidic sandy soil and gravels in the Llano Uplift in central Texas. One of the dominant members of the Cross Timbers and Post Oak Savannah.

***Quercus velutina* (Black Oak)**
Medium or large tree to 90 feet with deciduous ovate leaves having broad lobes. Acorns biennial. Native to acid sands or sandy loams in upland for-

ests of east Texas to Georgia. It is fairly uncommon, occurring singly or in pairs, but never in groves (Simpson 1988). It is intolerant of shade and has a long taproot.

***Quercus virginiana* (Coastal Live Oak, Encino)**
Large spreading tree to 50 feet with limbs occasionally stretching out and to the ground. Leaves evergreen or semi-evergreen, thick and dark green. This is the familiar Spanish moss-covered oak on southern plantations. Coastal Live Oak occurs east of the Brazos River in the Gulf Prairies and Marshes. At the western boundary of its range, it will hybridize with Escarpment Live Oak (*Q. fusiformis*). Coastal Live Oak grows best on well-drained clay loams and gravelly clay loams. It does not tolerate poorly drained soils or extremely well drained deep sand. Some of the most handsome specimens are found on neutral to slightly acid soils, although this is not often a limiting factor. Live oaks in Dallas were severely damaged by the harsh winter of 1983, when temperatures were below freezing for over 12 days (Simpson 1988).

Rhamnus caroliniana

Carolina Buckthorn

RHAMNACEAE (BUCKTHORN FAMILY)

GENERAL DESCRIPTION

Carolina Buckthorn is a shrub or small tree to 20 feet. Dark green glossy oval leaves hang from delicate branches. Leaves may turn yellow in the fall.

FLOWERS AND FRUIT

Small and inconspicuous flowers bloom in late spring and early summer. Fruit is a showy drupe changing from bright red to blue-black as it ripens. Each fruit contains two seeds ¼ inch long.

NATURAL HABITAT, RANGE, AND PREFERRED SITE

Carolina Buckthorn grows in bottomlands in east and southeast Texas, near streams and canyons in central and south-central Texas, also east to Florida and north to Virginia. It will grow in either acid or alkaline soil in full or partial sun.

COLLECTION AND STORAGE

Collect the seeds in the fall when they turn dark purple. Clean them before sowing or storing. Seeds to be sown immediately need not be dried because drying induces dormancy. Store seeds over winter in sealed containers in a cool dry place.

PROPAGATION

Seeds

Fresh seeds of Carolina Buckthorn require no pretreatment in order to germinate promptly. Stored seeds should be stratified for 30 days at 41° F. Germination of fresh or pretreated seeds will occur within 5 weeks. Seedlings are rapid growing and transplant easily from flats to one-gallon containers. Carolina Buckthorns grown in tree tubes or liners can be directly planted into five-gallon containers (Kirwin, personal communication, 1999).

Because they naturally occur as understory plants, Carolina Buckthorn plants do best if given partial shade the first season. Add slow-release fertilizer to the soil mix, but take care not to overfertilize, or too-rapid growth may weaken the plant.

Plants grown from seed seem more likely to develop into straight single-trunked trees, while cuttings tend to remain more shrublike (Will, personal communication, 1999).

The problem with production of Carolina Buckthorn, as with sumacs, comes after germination: trees 4–5 feet tall in five-gallon containers will suddenly show signs of stress. The terminal shoot turns brown and the leaves acquire a burned look. Rapid death of the plant soon follows. Carolina Buckthorns often have difficulty surviving transplanting into larger containers. Losses of 20–30% at this stage are not uncommon (Pfeiffer, personal communication, 1999). The root system of Carolina Buckthorn is not well developed, and may be improved by inoculating the soil mix with beneficial microorganisms and by growing in containers with copper-treated interior surfaces (see Chapter IV). Plants with air-pruned roots demonstrated better rooting, stronger root stem and root crown interface, and better anchoring in the pot (Will, personal communication, 1999). Without these additional treatments, Carolina Buckthorn is difficult to produce as a reliable nursery crop.

Carolina Buckthorn prefers a well-drained mineral soil mix. Heavier soils only contribute to this plant's sensitivity to soil-borne pathogens.

Cuttings

Carolina Buckthorn will also root from semihardwood cuttings taken from mid-summer through fall. These should be 4–6 inches long, treated with IBA (3,000–5,000 ppm), and kept under intermittent mist. Remove the leaves from the lower half of the cutting. Rooting usually occurs within 5 weeks.

Hardwood cuttings taken in late fall or winter have also been rooted. These were 10–17 inches long, tied in even bundles with the basal ends together, and then buried in boxes of moist sand placed outdoors or in refrigeration. Cuttings callused in 6–8 weeks. In the spring these bundles can be removed, washed, and planted in rows in the open ground, allowing one bud of the cutting to stand above the surface of the soil. Firm the soil around the cuttings and water in well.

NOTES

The fruit of Carolina Buckthorn is showy and favored by many birds. Carolina Buckthorn is an excellent medium-sized specimen tree or understory plant, and can be planted in groups along with Yaupon Holly (*Ilex vomitoria*), Cherry Laurel (*Prunus caroliniana*), Rough-leaf Dogwood (*Cornus drummondii*), and Mexican Buckeye (*Ungnadia speciosa*) to make a screen or natural hedge for shady locations. The glossy, prominently veined leaves are showy and turn yellow in the fall.

Rhododendron

Azalea, Wild Honeysuckle

ERICACEAE (HEATH FAMILY)

GENERAL DESCRIPTION

Azaleas are shrubs or small trees. Species listed here are deciduous. See Species Descriptions for individual characteristics.

FLOWERS AND FRUIT

Showy flowers are held in hanging clusters in early spring. The petals are variously colored white, purple, or red. Each flower is tubular or funnel shaped with showy, extended stamens often twice as long as the corolla. Fruit is an elliptic capsule containing numerous seeds, ripening late summer or early fall.

NATURAL HABITAT, RANGE, AND PREFERRED SITE

Azaleas grow in fine sandy and mostly acid soil in east Texas and throughout the southern United States. Most prefer moist soil and shade. Azaleas cannot tolerate arid locations.

COLLECTION AND STORAGE

Gather the seed capsules in late summer or early fall when they are no longer green, but before they have dried and released the seeds. Store the seeds in sealed containers at 41° F.

PROPAGATION

Seeds

Azalea seeds must be exposed to light and cool temperatures in order to germinate successfully. Combine the seeds loosely with milled sphagnum moss and lightly sprinkle over a flat containing a 1:2 mixture of peat and perlite. Press the seeds in the flat but do not bury. The best time to sow is from mid-winter to early spring in a greenhouse or cold frame. Optimum temperatures for germination are 45–50° F.

Transplant seedlings as soon as they are large enough to handle without damage to the stem or roots. Use a potting soil with a high content of organic matter and an acid pH. It should have a porous consistency to allow drainage and encourage a strong root system, yet the soil should be spongy enough to hold ample moisture.

Cuttings

The familiar cultivated evergreen species of *Rhododendron* are easier to root than the native deciduous species. Best results are achieved with softwood cuttings taken from the first flush of growth in the spring or from "forced" wood of nursery stock plants. Wounding the cutting and treating it with root-promoting hormones (IBA at 75 mg/l for 15 hours or IBA in talc at .8%) improves rooting. Remove half of the leaves and keep the cutting under intermittent mist. A mixture of peat/perlite provides the best rooting bed.

Hoary Azalea, *R. canescens*, and Texas Honeysuckle, *R. prinophyllum*, may be increased by division in the spring and layering in the spring and summer (Lowrey, personal communication, 1986).

NOTES

Wild Azaleas are also called Wild Honeysuckle Bushes because of their long funnel-shaped flowers and extended stamens. Wild Azaleas exhibit a delicate showy display in early spring. They are suitable understory specimen or background plants in locations with rich moist acid soils. The potential for selection of outstanding flower colors and characteristics as well as overall form of our native azaleas has not been fully explored.

SPECIES DESCRIPTIONS

***Rhododendron canescens* (Hoary Azalea)**

Shrub to 10 feet, sparingly branched with deciduous leaves. Flowers produced before or with the leaves, usually pink. In sandy or light soil in and on the edge of bogs or seepage areas in piney woods in east Texas, east to Florida.

***Rhododendron coryi* (Azalea)**

Shrub to 3 feet with a woody rhizome. Flowers are produced after the leaves have emerged and are usually white. Endemic to bogs and low woodlands in southeast Texas.

***Rhododendron oblongifolium* (Texas Azalea)**

Spreading shrub to 8 feet with deciduous hairy leaves. Flowers bloom from

March through May, after the new leaves. Trumpet-shaped, pink to reddish flowers with extended stamens. Sandy or light soil in boggy or wet areas, along streams in piney woods.

Rhododendron prinophyllum **(Texas Honeysuckle, Early Azalea)**
Shrub to about 9 feet, with narrow oblanceolate, dull bluish green leaves. White to pink flowers appear with the leaves. Sandy or light soil in moist locations in east Texas to Florida, north to Canada.

Rhus

Sumac

ANACARDIACEAE (SUMAC FAMILY)

GENERAL DESCRIPTION

Sumacs are shrubs or small trees with compound deciduous or evergreen leaves. They are typically low growing and multi-trunked with spreading branches. Some species are thicket forming (see Species Descriptions).

FLOWERS AND FRUIT

Unisexual and bisexual flowers appear in clusters on the same plant. Blooming occurs periodically spring through summer, but the main blooming period is in late summer or early fall. Fruit is a one-seeded rounded or compressed drupe that turns red when mature.

NATURAL HABITAT, RANGE, AND PREFERRED SITE

Sumacs are found throughout the state in a variety of soils and sites. See Species Descriptions for individual range and habitat.

COLLECTION AND STORAGE

Collect the fruits beginning in late September through December after they have turned a deep red color and the pulp is fleshy and filled out. Remove the pulp before storing or sowing. Store the seeds in sealed containers at 32–41° F for optimum longevity.

PROPAGATION

Seeds

Seeds of most Sumacs have a hard impervious seed coat that requires relatively long periods of acid scarification before germination will occur (see Chapter III). In addition, some species, like Fragrant Sumac (*R. aromatica*), have both a hard seed coat and a dormant embryo and must be stratified for 30–90 days at 41° F after they are scarified. See Species Descriptions for individual guidelines.

Each seed lot should be tested separately to determine the optimum length of scarification treatment. Sow pretreated seeds in a greenhouse in February or in a cold frame in April. Mice are often attracted to the seed and can be a problem in the greenhouse or cold frame. Optimum average temperatures for germination are 86° F for days and 68° F for nights. Pretreated seeds will germinate within 3–4 weeks. Early-sown seedlings are better able to withstand the stress of summer heat.

Plant the seeds ⅓–¾ inch deep. Press them into the soil and lightly water. Very poor germination rates occur when seeds are planted deeper than 1 inch. The soil should be well drained and inoculated with beneficial microorganisms prior to sowing (see Chapter IV). This inoculation has greatly improved survival rates for several species of sumacs, both as they are moved up into larger containers and also when they are planted in the landscape (Gass, personal communication, 1999).

Some sumacs are slow growing and sensitive to overhead watering and damping-off fungi. Best results are often achieved when seeds are planted separately in pots which air prune the roots and thus encourage secondary branching (see Chapter IV). This avoids losses when transplanting small seedlings.

Seedlings benefit from light shade the first season but once established should be given full sun. Seedlings respond well to periodic applications of water-soluble fertilizers. The soil mix in containers must be mineral based and well drained. Many sumac species do not thrive in the typical pine-bark-based soil mix, which seems to contribute to disease susceptibility and rotting (Kirwin, personal communication, 1999). A well-drained mix with a mineral component such as decomposed granite is preferable. Pretreated seeds of Evergreen Sumac (*R. virens*) and Prairie Flame-leaf Sumac (*R. lanceolata*) sown in early March in a cold frame will make finished one-gallon plants by the following fall if given strong sunlight and fertilized regularly (McNeal, personal communication, 1999).

Watch the production carefully: some thicket-forming kinds of sumac quickly become root girdled in the pot. Tip-prune one-gallon plants after they reach 8 inches or so to encourage secondary branches and a sturdier form. After shearing, reduce watering intervals to avoid rotting (Kirwin, personal communication, 1999). Sumacs often grow at a much faster rate after being placed in the ground. It may be necessary to stake container-grown plants the first season.

Cuttings

In general, the deciduous sumacs root more easily than evergreen species. Basic methods for this genus recommend taking semihardwood cuttings early in summer through fall or before the new wood has hardened off to achieve best results. These should be 4–6 inches long with the leaves removed from the lower halves. Treat with IBA (1,000–4,000 ppm IBA talc, depending on condition of wood) and place in a rooting media of peat and perlite (1:2 ratio) under intermittent mist.

Rooting of the deciduous species usually occurs within a month. Decrease misting as the cutting calluses and forms roots to encourage it to harden off. Evergreen Sumac is slower to root, and rooted cuttings are less likely to survive than other sumac species. Best results are achieved using large semihardwood cuttings, 4–6 inches with a pencil-sized diameter, that are woody at the base or taken with a heel. Remove all leaves from the lower half of the cuttings. Treat Evergreen Sumac cuttings with IBA solution (5,000 ppm) and place under intermittent mist. Watch the cuttings carefully and reduce misting if the media gets too soggy, because Evergreen Sumac cuttings tend to rot and die before rooting.

Do not stick the cuttings too deeply. Rooting takes place in 5–8 weeks. New roots on all sumac cuttings are very brittle and should be handled with care. Rooting in individual containers in a peat/perlite mixture rather than in perlite alone is recommended (McNeal, personal communication, 1999). The suckering or thicket-forming species of sumac are easiest to root. These are often rooted from root pieces taken in winter, treated with 4,000 ppm IBA talc plus thiram (Dirr and Heuser 1987).

Transplanting

The thicket-forming species like Prairie Flame-leaf Sumac (*R. lanceolata*) are easily transplanted year round with a minimum of roots if cut back by half and kept watered. Other species that do not form lateral underground stems or suckers are more difficult to transplant once they are taller than 3 feet.

NOTES

Native sumacs make attractive specimen, hedge, or background plants and also play an important role in restoring wildlife habitats. As a group they are rapid and tenacious growers. They vary considerably in height, density, growth rate, and ornamental qualities. Many sumac species do not exhibit strong internodal branching, so shearing them to encourage a topiaried or rounded form is usually unsuccessful. However, careful tip pruning will encourage denser growth. The sumacs should be accepted for the form they attain in nature. Generally, the third year after being planted a sumac will really begin to show some top growth and start to fill out, eventually forming a graceful, broadly arching form.

Do not plant the thicket-forming species in a shrub border: the roots and underground stems will run more than 20 feet and sprout up where you don't want them. Sumacs are generally free from insect, disease, or drought injury.

SPECIES DESCRIPTIONS

Rhus aromatica (Fragrant Sumac)

Deciduous shrub with arching branches growing to 6½ feet with a spread of 4–6 feet. Leaves compound with three light green leaflets having scalloped edges. Pale yellowish white flowers are held in clusters at the ends of branches in April and May. Found nearly throughout the state of Texas, east to Florida, also north to Oklahoma and Nebraska. Cold hardy to USDA zone 4 (Arnold 1999).

Fragrant Sumacs don't set seed as often as most of the other sumac species. For best results, acid scarify for 30–50 minutes, then stratify immediately for 30–60 days at 41° F. Germinate in a cold frame or outdoors after all danger of frost is past.

Spindly seedlings are often a sign of too much fertilizer either in the potting soil or applied as foliar food. Softwood cuttings taken in early summer and treated with 1,000 ppm IBA root readily (Dirr and Heuser 1987).

Fragrant Sumac from the Panhandle has a very different form from central Texas populations (McNeal, personal communication, 1999).

In Massachusetts, a low-growing (30 inches) compact clone of *R. aromatica*, 'Grow-Low,' has been selected for highway plantings. Suckering types from the eastern United States are more easily rooted than our larger local form.

Rhus coppalina (Shining Sumac)

Large shrub or small stoloniferous tree to 32 feet with slender branches creating a spread of 20–30 feet. Leaves deciduous with 7–11 leaflets. Greenish white flowers in dense terminal clusters. Rocky hills and woods in the eastern half of Texas. Cold hardy to USDA zone 5 (Arnold 1999). One of the most handsome of the native sumacs. Dark lustrous summer foliage is followed by brilliant red autumn colors. It is relatively compact as a young seedling but gradually grows more open and spreading to form thickets.

Seed pretreatment varies with seed source, usually requiring acid scarification for 30–45 minutes followed by cold stratification for 90 days. Multi-seed treated seedlings directly into "bullet tubes." Treat the soil medium with fungicide before sowing and reapply every 7–10 days. After the seedlings develop true leaves, foliar feed them every 2 weeks. Move up into one-gallon containers directly from the bullet tubes. Seedlings are very fast growing once they are in the gallon containers. Bullet tubes to finished one-gallon plant is usually accomplished in 3–4 months, and from seeds to finished five-gallon plant in one season. For example, seeds are pretreated in the fall and by March have germinated in the bullet tubes. By July they should be ready to move into one-gallon pots. By late fall they are salable five-gallon container plants (Bronstad, personal communication, 1999).

The suckering or thicket-forming sumacs should not be kept indefinitely in a five-gallon container because they tend to develop irregular, gangly forms and become subject to leaf spot and die-back (Bronstad, personal communication, 1999).

***Rhus glabra* (Smooth Sumac, Scarlet Sumac)**

Shrub or small tree to 10 feet, rhizomatous and forming thickets. Leaves deciduous with 11–31 glossy leaflets. Greenish flowers are held in large, dense, terminal panicles May to July. Smooth Sumac is the dominant sumac in the Blackland Prairies. Also found on dry sandy hillsides in east Texas west to Brazos County. Smooth Sumac can also be found in Arizona and northern Mexico. Cold hardy to USDA zone 4 (3 with proper siting) (Arnold 1999). For propagation guidelines, see *R. coppalina*.

Other methods for growing Smooth Sumac suggest acid scarification for 1–3 hours, followed by immediate cold stratification for 30 days at 41° F. Or pour boiling water over the seed and let the seed soak for 2½ days. Follow the hot water treatment with 3 months cold stratification. Root cuttings are also a valuable method of propagation. Spring or fall harvest of roots may yield different results. For spring harvesting, one method recommends taking ½–1 inch diameter roots cut into lengths of 2–3 inches in early spring (February to early March). Pack the root pieces in boxes of barely damp sand. After callusing (about 3 weeks) the cuttings are removed and set in rows in the field. After sprouting, the cuttings are moderately hilled up (Dirr and Heuser 1987).

***Rhus lanceolata* (Prairie Flame-leaf Sumac)**

Small tree or small thicket-forming shrub to 32 feet with compound deciduous leaves having 13–19 leaflets. Whitish flowers held in heavy terminal heads turn into crimson or red fruit clusters. In limestone soil from north-central Texas to the eastern edge of the Edwards Plateau, west to the Trans-Pecos and New Mexico. Prairie Flame-leaf Sumac is one of the most reliable plants for fall color in central Texas.

Scarify fresh or stored seeds for 30–55 minutes and then keep in a plastic bag containing moist perlite in the refrigerator for 50 days. Plant in early spring. This is one of the easiest sumacs to grow, though Fusarium wilt can be a problem with young seedlings. Young plants do not like soil that is too rich (Hosage, personal communication, 1999). It tends to send out suckers as far away as 20 feet from the parent plant, so avoid planting this species in a shrub border. See *R. coppalina* for guidelines on handling the plant after germination.

***Rhus microphylla* (Little-leaf or Desert Sumac, Agrito, Correosa)**
Much-branched shrub or occasionally a small tree to 16 feet though usually much smaller. Leaves deciduous with five to nine leathery and shiny leaflets. The flowers appear before the new leaves. In dry scrub flats and open uplands in the mesas and foothills in western Texas, also Arizona and northern Mexico. Very drought tolerant. Follow the same seed pretreatment guidelines as for *R. aromatica*.

***Rhus trilobata var. pilosissima* (Squaw Bush, Polecat Bush)**
Leaves are similar to *R. aromatica*, except they are densely covered with a soft pelt of rusty-colored hairs. Squaw Bush is conspicuous in the spring with its clusters of small yellowish flowers that usually open before the new leaves appear. In the fall the leaves turn orange and scarlet. Native to loose sandy soils on hills in the Trans-Pecos and in the Panhandle.

***Rhus virens* (Evergreen Sumac, Lentisco)**
Evergreen shrub or small tree to 10 feet with shiny evergreen leaves. New leaves reddish. Mature leaves sometimes tinged with maroon after first frost. Flowers appear in white or greenish clusters in late summer. Gullies and rocky hillsides or plains in the Edwards Plateau, Trans-Pecos, and northern Mexico. Gather seed from late fall until December. Clean in blender fitted with a rubber blade. Test different seed lots at 15-minute intervals for optimum scarification time. Scarification for 30–45 minutes in concentrated sulfuric acid is typical (Hosage and Janzow, personal communications, 1999). Plant treated seed immediately. Germination may take as long as 30 days. Thirty days of cold stratification following scarification may make germination more uniform. Pretreated seed may also be planted directly outdoors in the winter, and germination will begin in early spring. Evergreen Sumac must have well-drained soil. It does not tolerate the

standard nursery pine bark potting soil mixture. Many growers combine 2–3 one-gallon plants in a five-gallon container to make a single extra-bushy plant. It is slow growing for the first 3 years, but has a more rapid rate of growth once it is placed in a landscape situation. Many growers experience losses of 10% or more when small plants are moved up to larger containers. Inoculation with beneficial microorganisms has significantly improved transplant survival and vigor in the landscape (Gass, personal communication, 1999). Deer will browse young plants, but once plants are established, they will ease off. This is a good wildlife plant.

Sabal

Sabal, Soyate, Palma Real, Palmetto

PALMACEAE (PALM FAMILY)

GENERAL DESCRIPTION

Sabals are slow-growing trunkless shrubs or trees with large fan-shaped leaves (see Species Descriptions).

FLOWERS AND FRUIT

Flower clusters are borne in ascending clusters among the leaves. The berrylike fruits turn bluish black when ripe and contain one to three flattened seeds. The fruits are edible and taste like dates (Best, personal communication, 1999).

NATURAL HABITAT, RANGE, AND PREFERRED SITE

Sabals are native to lowlands, swamps, and river terraces in east, central, and south Texas. See Species Descriptions for individual range and habitat.

COLLECTION AND STORAGE

Collect the seeds in late summer or early fall after they have turned a blue-black color. Often *Caryobruchus* weevils infest the fruit and destroy the seeds. Remove the seeds from the pulp and then air dry at least 1 day before storing in sealed containers in the refrigerator. Seeds up to 3 years old held in cold storage have still germinated (Best 1999).

PROPAGATION

Seeds

In general, freshly gathered sabal seeds will germinate without pretreatment, but several techniques are recommended to improve germination rates.

One method recommends stratifying the seed for 30 days at 38° F before planting. At the Lower Rio Grande Wildlife Refuge, seeds were collected, depulped, and dried before being stored. Prior to sowing, the seeds were aerated 3 days (see Chapter IV) and then placed in pregermination trays. The trays were checked frequently and as soon as the radicle emerged, individual seeds were removed and planted in containers. The root may continue to grow 4–6 weeks before leaves appear (Best 1999).

Seeds require a moist seedbed and are very slow growing. A very small salable one-gallon sized plant may take 2 years to produce (McNeal, personal communication, 1999). Sabals need plenty of water to become established. Some collections of apparently viable seed failed to germinate even after 3 years. One explanation for this was that certain members of the palm family sometimes make sterile seed (that appears normal) because the parents have a basic incompatibility. More study of this phenomenon in native sabals is needed (Best, personal communication, 1999).

Transplanting

Small plants, 1 foot or less, are easily transplanted in both cold and warm weather (Lowrey, personal communication, 1986). Older plants are difficult to transplant because of a deep root system.

NOTES

Sabals are outstanding specimen plants for certain landscape situations (see Species Descriptions). Sabal fruits are edible, varying from sweet and tasty to black-cherry bitter. Sabal palms produce edible "hearts" (the apical bud or growing tip).

Petrified palm wood from the cenozoic deposits in south and east Texas is our official state stone. Native Americans made stone tools from it. For a thorough and fascinating discussion of the Texas sabals, see Newsom (1996).

SPECIES DESCRIPTIONS

Sabal minor **(Dwarf Palmetto)**

Ground-hugging shrub, usually acaulescent, occasionally developing a short trunk to 20 feet. Fan-shaped leaves on spineless stems rise from a central point at ground level. Clusters of white blooms are followed by purple-black fruits. Dwarf Palmetto grows in lowlands, river terraces, and flood plains from east Texas along the coast to Corpus Christi and west to the southeastern Edwards Plateau, where it appears on a few rocky ridges away from habitats more suited to water-loving plants. Its range also extends into Arkansas and North Carolina. Dwarf Palmetto is a rugged plant that tolerates both heat and cold. It has no insect or disease problems.

Sabal mexicana **(Texas Palmetto, Palma Micharros, Palma Real, Soyate)**

This is the common large sabal native to the Lower Rio Grande Valley, south along the Caribbean lowlands to Guatemala. It is a slow-growing trunk-forming species, gradually reaching 35–50 feet tall. It has beautiful blue-green filiferous down-curved leaves held on unarmed leaf stalks attached to a short trunk. As the tree grows and older fronds are shed, they leave behind the old leaf bases that persist on young trunks, giving the tree a distinctive cross-hatched appearance. Fragrant white blooms appear on 7–8 foot stalks in March and April. The fruit, called *micharros*, are dark purple to almost black, about the size of an olive, and hang in heavy clusters.

Texas Palmetto's range extends south to Veracruz, and isolated colonies appear in the Yucatan, where a particularly large-leafed strain (syn. *S. guatemalensis*) can be found around old Mayan sites (Ogden, personal communication, 1999). The northernmost colony occurs along Garcitas Creek near Victoria, Texas. This population was discovered by Robert Read and Landon Lockett in 1989, and is the only naturally occurring *S. mexicana* population remaining north of the Rio Grande Valley. They examined historical evidence that indicated that the population was natural and had not escaped cultivation (Lockett 1999). The Garcitas Creek palmettos appear to be a second growth group descended from a much larger population that was clear cut for timber used in wharves and pilings in the nineteenth century (Newsom 1996).

Texas Palmetto is adapted as far north as Austin, Texas. It is typically a tall stout tree to 51 feet, with a trunk 3 feet in diameter. Native to flatlands along the Rio Grande in Cameron County and along the Rio Bravo to Mier, Tamaulipas, in Mexico. Cold hardy in cultivation from Livingston to Austin and Del Rio. Texas Palmetto will grow in sand or heavy gumbo, and is more tolerant of dry conditions than one would normally assume. Some botanists consider *S. texana* and *S. mexicana* to be two separate species; some combine them under one name—*S. mexicana*.

***Sabal x mexicana Read* (Brazoria Palmetto)**

This third native form of *Sabal* is restricted to a few isolated colonies in Brazoria County west of Houston. It was formerly identified by Robert Vines as *S. louisiana*. When the *S. mexicana* population at Garcitas Creek was compared to the plants in Brazoria, it was discovered that *S. mexicana x S. minor* was a naturally occurring hybrid. This is the only known palm hybrid of its kind in the United States. These hybrid palms are reproducing, but it isn't known if they are confining reproduction among themselves, or if they are backcrossing with *S. minor* (Newsom 1996). Some botanists believe that Brazoria Palmetto probably once occurred extensively on Galveston Island, as larger palms were once recorded there. There may have been more extensive palm lowlands along the Gulf Coast uniting these species 12,000 years ago, before the Gulf of Mexico gradually inundated the present-day coastline (Ogden, personal communication, 1999).

The Brazoria Palmetto has great potential as a landscape plant. It is a moderate size, reaching 16–25 feet, which is a good intermediate size between the trunkless *S. minor* and the tall *S. mexicana*. Twenty-three acres of the Brazoria Palm habitat have been purchased for conservation purposes as part of the San Bernard National Wildlife Refuge, where it is hoped that their numbers will be protected for further research.

Salix nigra

Black Willow, Sauz, Sauz Serrano

SALICACEAE (WILLOW FAMILY)

GENERAL DESCRIPTION

Black Willow is a fast-growing tree to 65 feet or more with narrow leaves that are light green with a pointed tip. Bark is dark brown-black with deep fissures.

FLOWERS AND FRUIT

Three-inch long catkins appear from late winter to early spring. Fruit is a light-brown capsule that splits when ripe to disperse many minute seeds with fuzzy hairs or tails.

NATURAL HABITAT, RANGE, AND PREFERRED SITE

Black Willow is common to wet, poorly drained soils in full sun in the eastern two-thirds of Texas, also east to Florida, north to Oklahoma and Arkansas, and east across the United States.

COLLECTION AND STORAGE

Collect the seeds as soon as the capsules begin to dry and turn from green to yellow-brown. Black Willow seeds begin to lose their viability immediately and should be planted as soon as they are collected and separated from the capsule. Under refrigeration, the maximum length of storage for this species is 4–6 weeks (Hartmann and Kester 1975).

PROPAGATION

Seeds

Black Willow will germinate only from fresh seeds. Seeds require no pretreatment, and germination usually occurs within 12–24 hours after sowing if the seedbed is kept continually moist. Shade the seedlings at first and hold in a cold frame over winter. One-year-old plants may be field planted. Willows are often difficult to propagate in large numbers from seeds (Hartmann and Kester 1975).

Cuttings

Willows are among the easiest of all plants to root from cuttings because they have preformed root initials. They will root from softwood or hardwood cuttings. Black Willow will root from either root or stem cuttings. Hardwood cuttings lined out in early spring before the buds leaf out will root promptly. Application of IBA may increase rooting quality but is not absolutely necessary (Doran 1957).

Transplanting

Black Willow is easily transplanted if kept moist in the new location.

NOTES

Black Willow is a rapid-growing tree. The many disease and insect pests that plague this species make it difficult to recommend it as a landscape plant. However, it is an appropriate tree for planting along dams, levees, and riverbanks for erosion control or revegetation.

Two other western willows, Peach-leaf Willow (*S. amygdaloides*) and Yew-leaf Willow (*S. taxifolia*), also are worth considering for planting in wet areas. Peach-leaf Willow is a showy small tree or large shrub growing in water or along streams in the Plains Country in the Panhandle and in the Trans-Pecos, west to New Mexico and northeast Arizona. It is very striking with yellowish twigs and yellowish green leaves. Yew-leaf Willow is a tall shrub or tree to 38 feet with narrow leaves closely resembling the ornamental yew. It is native to stream banks and wet areas from west Texas to Arizona and northern Mexico. Propagation guidelines for these species are similar to those recommended for Black Willow.

Salvia

Sage, Salvia

LABIATAE (SAGE FAMILY)

GENERAL DESCRIPTION

Salvias are perennial or annual herbs or shrubs usually with aromatic leaves. Species listed here are woody perennial herbs or shrubs.

FLOWERS AND FRUIT

Salvias have showy two-lipped flowers in various colors. See Species Descriptions. Each flower forms a dry papery capsule or sheath surrounding a single, tiny dark seed.

NATURAL HABITAT, RANGE, AND PREFERRED SITE

Salvia grows in a variety of sites. See Species Descriptions for individual range and habitat. Salvias are typically best suited to sunny, well-drained sites.

COLLECTION AND STORAGE

Collect the seeds as the capsules around them begin to dry, but before they have dropped the seeds. Spread the seeds in thin layers to dry a few days before storing in sealed containers in the refrigerator.

PROPAGATION

Seeds
Salvia will germinate from freshly gathered untreated seeds planted outdoors after all danger of frost is past or earlier in a greenhouse. Gently press the seeds into a well-drained soil mix and then barely cover with a sprinkling of fine sand. Do not bury the seeds deeply. Keep the seed flat moist but do not overwater. Seedlings grow rapidly.

Cuttings
Salvia is most easily grown from either softwood or semihardwood tip cuttings. These should be of new growth just beginning to harden off

at the base, 4–6 inches long, taken just below a node with the leaves removed from the lower half. Application of IBA (3,000–5,000 ppm) improves rooting.

With hormone treatment, rooting occurs within 3 weeks, and the cutting may be transplanted into a 6-inch pot or one-gallon container. Application of bottom heat in the spring will hasten rooting (Hosage, personal communication, 1999).

The main enemy of many species of salvias in greenhouse production is downy mildew. It can reduce the success of cuttings by 90% and is very difficult to eradicate in a greenhouse system. To maintain disease-free stock, careful nursery sanitation practices, especially in monitoring the watering regime (downy mildew requires water to germinate), are mandatory. Air circulation among pots is critical, and eliminating standing water among the block of pots also reduces environmental conditions that perpetuate downy mildew. When overhead watering is used, the water bounces up from the contaminated pools onto the leaves, and the cycle is repeated. The red-flowered form of *Salvia greggii* seem the most susceptible of that species, followed by coral, white, and pink, with pink-flowered selections apparently the most tolerant of downy mildew. One possible explanation for this is that the leaves of the pink form tend to be more lanceolate in shape, while the others have broader leaves with more leaf surface to catch the spores (Kirwin, personal communication, 1999).

Another factor contributing to weakened plants may be the use of stock plants that are continually fertilized and kept in the greenhouse to produce cutting material for year-round production. Salvias that are allowed a period of rest or even kept outside and subjected to freeze-back may naturally produce stronger, less disease prone wood (Kirwin, personal communication, 1999). If the disease cycle stubbornly refuses to be controlled, the best remedy is to start over with healthy new parent stock.

Transplanting

Most species are easily transplanted if cut back halfway and kept well watered until they have adjusted to the new location. Older plants in the garden can also be divided in the winter and planted in separate clumps.

NOTES

Native and adapted salvias have quickly become familiar plants in the garden. They are used as tall specimens, background plants, or staple fillers in a perennial border garden. They are typically heat and drought tolerant, and the only maintenance they require is frequent shearing to encourage denser growth and more flowers. Salvias may be pruned year round, but at the very least, they should be sheared back in January and in late July.

Heavy fertilization will encourage more leafy growth but fewer blooms. Salvias are often infested with spider mites during the hottest weather. The best treatment is to cut the plant back, mulch well, and wait for fall rains and cooler nights to reinvigorate the plant.

SPECIES DESCRIPTIONS

***Salvia ballotaeflora* (Mejorana, Blue Shrub Sage, Crespa)**
Much-branched shrub with small aromatic leaves covered with dense white fuzz on the underside. Showy blue or violet flowers are held in small dense racemes in the axils of the upper leaves. Blooms intermittently all summer, especially after rain. Native to rocky, sandy, or gravelly soil in full sun from the Edwards Plateau south to the coast, also in northern Mexico. Very drought tolerant and thrives in poor soil. May grow too leggy if given too much water or fertilizer. Mejorana is a good companion plant to Cenizo (*Leucophyllum frutescens*), Black Dalea (*Dalea frutescens*), Yucca (*Yucca spp.*), and Skelton-leaf Goldeneye Daisy (*Viguiera stenoloba*). The dried leaves are used for flavoring meats and other foods.

***Salvia greggii* (Autumn Sage, Cherry Sage)**
Shrubby, much-branched, woody evergreen shrub to 3 feet. Stems covered with small leaves. Showy flowers, borne in ascending spikes from March to December. Colors vary from orange to pink, red, and white. Native to rocky soil and full sun in central, southern, and western Texas. Very adaptable to other sites in cultivation. Good companion plants include a few strong evergreen plants such as Beargrass (*Nolina spp.*) and Evergreen Sumac (*Rhus virens*), and flowering perennials like Rose-mallow Pavonia (*Pavonia lasiopetala*), old roses, and verbena (*Verbena bipinatifida*).

In the 1930s, nurseries in Texas grew and distributed three different forms of the native Edwards Plateau *S. greggii:* a dark wine, a pink ('Rosea'), and a white ('Alba'). 'Rosea' was recognized by its upright growing form and large leaves. A current selection, 'Big Pink,' resembles and may be identical to this old form, which is still found in old gardens from Dallas to Odessa southward. The wine-colored form is the most common of the heirloom variants and is hardy enough to show up in vintage Oklahoma gardens. The true carmine red forms are more recent selections derived from plants native to the area immediately south and west of Kerrville. These include 'Furman's Red,' 'Keeter's Red,' and 'Scott's Red.' 'Scott's Red' was a seedling variant collected, grown, and distributed by Scott

Ogden. It seems to have more vigor than the other reds and appears less susceptible to downy mildew. 'Red Velvet' is a hybrid of *S. greggii* and a larger-leafed Mexican species, *S. microphylla*. 'Red Velvet' is recognized by its prolific display of larger, deep red flowers and rounded leaves with crinkly edges. 'San Carlos Festival' is another outstanding selection of *S. microphylla* introduced by Yuccado Nursery. 'Dwarf Pink' is a selection of *S. greggii* made by Pat McNeal of Austin, Texas, from a collection taken in Junction, Texas, by Scott Ogden. It is interesting because of its spreading, ground-hugging growth habit. Lynn Lowrey first introduced the orange and salmon shades of *S. greggii*, mostly from specimens taken at higher elevations in northern Mexico (Ogden, personal communication, 1999). Other color forms include the fuchsia 'Raspberry,' a deep purple 'Diane,' and 'Pink Perfection,' which is hardy in Denver, Colorado (McNeal, personal communication, 1999). These are just a few of forms of *S. greggii* that are frequently found in nurseries. This variety points to the still untapped potential for selecting superior forms of salvias and other native plants.

***Salvia regla* (Mountain Sage)**

Tall deciduous shrub to 8 feet. Very showy vermilion red flowers occur in loose terminal racemes from mid-August to October. Attractive to migrating hummingbirds. Rocky slopes at high elevations in Brewster County in the Trans-Pecos. An outstanding cultivar of this species, 'Mount Emory Mountain Sage,' was developed by Benny Simpson at the Texas A&M Research and Extension Service Center at Dallas. *S. regla* is adapted as far north as the Rolling and High Plains. It will grow in dappled light, and is most robust when given strong morning sun but protection from harsh afternoon heat. Cut back each winter to encourage bushy growth. Individual plants live about 4–5 years, or less on heavy soils rich in organic matter. Good companion plants for Mountain Sage include Turk's Cap (*Malvaviscus arboreus var. drummondii*), Tropical Sage (*Salvia coccinea*), native sedges (*Carex spp.*), Fragrant Mist Flower (*Eupatorium havanense*), and Pidgeon Berry (*Rivinia humilis*).

Sambucus canadensis

Elderberry, American Elder

CAPRIFOLIACEAE (HONEYSUCKLE FAMILY)

GENERAL DESCRIPTION

Tall lanky shrub with both woody and herbaceous branches up to 13 feet, often with several stems rising from the base. Leaves are compound with 5–11 large, glossy, narrowly ovate leaves.

FLOWERS AND FRUIT

Showy flowers bloom in early summer in heavy clusters at the ends of the branches. Individual flowers are white with five stamens and five petals. Fruit is an edible berrylike pome containing three small hard seeds, ripening from late July until September.

NATURAL HABITAT, RANGE, AND PREFERRED SITE

Elderberry grows in wet soil in low places along streams or the edges of swamps and on flood plains from east to central Texas, also east to Florida, north to Oklahoma and South Dakota. Elderberry tolerates saturated soil but prefers rich, moist, and well-drained acidic soil, though it will adapt to deeper alkaline soils, especially if there is additional moisture.

Elderberry is a common forest plant but grows best in full sun, where it is one of the first species to invade old fields and logged country. Once established, it is a fast grower and aggressive competitor with weeds and herbaceous species.

COLLECTION AND STORAGE

Collect the seeds in the summer as soon as the fruits ripen and turn a dark blue-black color. Clean the seeds immediately to prevent fermentation. Air dry the seeds a day or two before storing in sealed containers at 41° F. Properly cleaned and stored seeds show little or no loss in viability after 2 years (USDA 1974).

PROPAGATION

Seeds

Germination of elderberry can be delayed by both a hard seed coat and a dormant embryo. However, elderberry from southern states does not normally require acid scarification (Dirr and Heuser 1987).

To achieve good germination, expose the seed to 2 months warm stratification (68° F) followed by 3–5 months cold stratification (41° F). Untreated fall-sown seed may take 2 years to germinate. Seeds can also be scarified in sulfuric acid for 10–20 minutes followed immediately by stratification in moist peat or sphagnum moss at 36–40° F for 2 months (Heit 1971). Freshly collected seeds show less dormancy than stored seeds.

Sow elderberry seeds in shallow rows and cover with ¼ inch of soil. Pretreated seeds usually germinate within 60 days. Seedling growth is often slow during the first year but rapid once the plant is established.

Cuttings

The quickest way to propagate elderberry is from cuttings. Elderberry will easily root from softwood cuttings taken from 1-year-old (juvenile) seedlings. Cuttings may vary in length from 10 to 18 inches and should include three sets of opposite buds. These can be directly field planted in early spring or placed in separate containers.

Semihardwood cuttings taken in late summer from mature plants treated with 3,000 ppm IBA talc and kept under intermittent mist rooted 47% in 7 weeks (Dirr and Heuser 1987). Hardwood cuttings taken in late fall and cut into 6-inch lengths with the basal cutting just below a node will also produce roots. The stems should be from one year old wood and no more slender than a pencil. Treat with 1,000 ppm IBA talc. The taking of a heel is often useful in preventing basal rot. Treat the cutting bed with a fungicide to reduce rotting. Keep cuttings in cold frame and wait until spring until they are rooted.

Transplanting

Small elderberry plants are easily transplanted in winter. Underground runners or suckers may be separated into individual plants at any time of the year if kept well watered.

NOTES

Elderberries will grow in full sun if the soil is well tilled and water is provided. They may be planted in a group as a background hedge, or, if planted alone, they can be pruned to make a treelike specimen plant. Both the flowers and fruit are showy. Elderberry is effective in erosion control on moist sites because it so freely spreads and forms colonies by root suckers. However, this characteristic can make it an annoying plant to have in a shrub border or near a lawn. In the suburban landscape, it is best left in the alley or other marginal areas with hackberries, sumacs, and mulberries. There it can provide abundant food for birds and the inevitable neglect it will receive keeps its invasive tendencies in check. Elderberry is one of the first natural pioneers on some strip-mined sites.

Elderberry has great value in wildlife plantings because the fruit is relished by many species of songbirds, red squirrels, raccoons, mice, rabbits, and other wildlife. Its foliage is browsed by deer. It provides fair escape cover for small birds and other wildlife and is found along roadsides.

There are two west Texas elderberry species that may also have ornamental and wildlife value. Blue Elderberry, *S. caerulea*, is an extremely rare plant in Texas, found only at about 7,000 feet and higher in the Davis and Chisos mountains (Simpson 1988). It is a large spreading shrub or small tree averaging 12 feet.

Another species, Mexican Elderberry or Azumiatl (*S. mexicana*), is a small tree with twisted, gnarled branches bearing flat-topped flower clusters at the ends. It may reach 30 feet and is found along streams and on wooded slopes at much lower elevations than Blue Elderberry in the Trans-Pecos. It is easily cultivated from seeds, cuttings, or root suckers, and is widely grown as a landscape plant in El Paso, where it sometimes escapes cultivation and is seen growing in vacant lots. It is typically not widespread in the desert because it requires more water than is generally provided by rainfall. Mexican Elderberry is used in Mexico for a variety of medicinal purposes (Powell 1988). It is not as drought tolerant as many other southwestern plants, although its drought tolerance increases with age. In the fall, it is sometimes slow to harden off and can be damaged by early frost. It is also plagued by many minor insect and disease pests (Arnold 1999). Because of its interesting form and moderate size, Mexican Elderberry, though overused in some places in west Texas, still has value as a small specimen tree or patio shrub. It roots easily from large branches.

Sapindus saponaria var. drummondii

Soapberry, Jaboncillo, Amole de Bolito

SAPINDACEAE (SOAPBERRY FAMILY)

GENERAL DESCRIPTION

Soapberry is a tree growing to 48 feet tall, though more commonly less than 32 feet, with rough grayish or tan bark and yellow wood. The deciduous leaves are divided into a dozen or more lance-shaped leaflets that look much like walnut leaves.

FLOWERS AND FRUIT

Creamy white cone-shaped flowers are borne in dense showy clusters from March to June. Male and female flowers occur on separate trees. Fruit is a translucent amber globe containing a hard seed. Fruit sometimes remains on the tree over winter.

NATURAL HABITAT, RANGE, AND PREFERRED SITE

Soapberry grows in fields, on the edges of woods, and along streams and fencerows throughout most of Texas and also from Louisiana, north to Kansas, and west to New Mexico. Soapberry tends to grow in moister sites in western Texas and does not grow in the swamps of eastern Texas (Simpson 1988). In east Texas, Soapberry often suckers from the roots, forming groves of trees, especially along sites where there is more moisture.

Western forms of Soapberry are less likely to sucker, except right along watercourses or dry, sandy streambeds. There you will often see Soapberries as copses of saplings. The plants spread by underground rhizomes, and each copse is essentially a clone (McNeal, personal communication, 1999). Soapberry thrives in well-drained soil and in full to partial sun. Soapberry is drought tolerant and relatively free from disease and insects.

COLLECTION AND STORAGE

Collect the seeds in late fall or early winter. Clean seeds before sowing or storage. The saponin-rich fruit produces a large volume of gummy suds that makes cleaning the seed a messy and tedious process.

One method suggests soaking the pulp in hot water mixed with a 1% lye solution. The seed and pulp may require several rinsings and soakings before the seed can be completely separated. For environmental and economic reasons, the lye solution method is recommended over sulfuric acid for cleaning and seed scarification.

Another method takes small amounts of seed and cleans them in a blender. Cover the seed with water and pulse the blender on and off. Wash the seed through a screen to separate.

Another method of cleaning is to sandwich the fruit between two screens set slightly off the ground. Leave the seeds exposed to sunlight, heat, and rain in order to weather and erode the pulp. After about 4 months, the fruit becomes a dry husk that is then easily rubbed off (Best 1999).

Cleaned seed kept in sealed containers in a cool dry place will generally maintain reasonable viability for at least 1 year.

PROPAGATION

Seeds

Germination of Soapberry is delayed by a very hard seed coat and a dormant embryo. Scarify the seeds in sulfuric acid for 45–60 minutes depending on seed lot, then aerate them for 2 days (see Chapter III).

Soapberry from south Texas does not exhibit seed dormancy and may be directly sown or placed in pregermination trays after the scarification treatment (Best 1999).

Seeds collected from trees in the northern part of this species' range will germinate more uniformly if first stratified at 35–45° F for 40–60 days. Germination of pretreated seeds takes place in 30–60 days. Plant seeds ¾–1 inch deep in individual containers. Sow pretreated seeds in late February or early March in a cold frame or outdoors after all danger of frost is past. Seedlings benefit from light shade and periodic fertilizing. Seedlings are slow growing at first. They will make a small but salable one-gallon plant in 1 year (McNeal, personal communication, 1999).

Cuttings

Soapberry can be rooted from semihardwood cuttings taken in April/June. Treat with 1.6% IBA and stick in a 2:1 peat/perlite mixture under mist. NAA, especially at high concentrations, was detrimental (Dirr and Heuser 1987). Division or rooting of suckers or coppices is another method of vegetatively reproducing this species, although the individual plant may remain more shrublike rather than have a strong tree form (McNeal, personal communication, 1999).

NOTES

Soapberry is an attractive and hardy medium-sized specimen tree. It can be planted in staggered groups on berms or roadsides to form graceful groves or thickets. The heavy clusters of white flowers are followed by persistent translucent fruits that make an interesting contrast to the bare branches of winter.

Soapberry is not the best tree to plant in a lawn because it tends to send up suckers even outside the shade of its own canopy, and these are just further stimulated by repeated mowing. Instead, plant Soapberry where a grove or screen is needed, on the perimeter of property, or along roads.

The fruit wall of this plant contains saponins, which were used by Native Americans as soap. This use was adopted by the first settlers as a substitute for lye-based soap (Simpson 1988). In Mexico and in the Southwest, Native Americans have tossed crushed soapberries into streams to stupefy fish and make them easier to catch.

The Soapberry hairstreak butterfly frequents Soapberry groves throughout the Southwest. The caterpillars eat only Soapberry foliage, and time their emergence to coincide with the blossoming of the flowers, their main source of nectar (Bowers 1993).

Sassafras albidum

Sassafras

LAURACEAE (LAUREL FAMILY)

GENERAL DESCRIPTION

Sassafras is a small to medium tree typically 20 feet tall, although in certain rare instances individual trees have been seen reaching 60 feet. It has spicy aromatic bark and roots. Leaves appear in three shapes on the same tree: oval or elliptic, mitten shaped with two lobes, or three-lobed. Fall color is generally good, and the same plant may show three different colors. Sassafras is often multi-trunked. The tree reproduces vegetatively by rhizomes, creating large groves or mottes.

FLOWERS AND FRUIT

Flowers are inconspicuous, held in clusters in March and April. Fruit is a dark blue drupe on a red stalk, containing a single seed ¼–⅓ inch long. Birds are fond of the fruit.

NATURAL HABITAT, RANGE, AND PREFERRED SITE

Sassafras is native to sandy woods, old fields, road cuts, and along fencerows in east Texas, also east to Florida, north to Oklahoma, Arkansas, and Michigan. Sassafras is a pioneer species on disturbed sites and will grow in full sun or partial shade. It is not tolerant of salty irrigation water and will become chlorotic on alkaline soils (Arnold 1999).

COLLECTION AND STORAGE

Collect the fruits beginning in July just as they start to turn from green to reddish brown, and when they are filled out. Fruits are rapidly eaten by birds, so harvest promptly. Only a small percentage of Sassafras trees bear fruit. Clean the seeds from the pulp before planting or storage. Seeds should be briefly air dried but not allowed to overdry if they are to be planted immediately. Seeds lose viability rapidly. Storage in sealed containers at 35–41° F is recommended (USDA 1974).

PROPAGATION

Seeds

Sassafras seeds show strong embryo dormancy and must be stratified at 41° F for 90 days or sown outdoors in the fall before germination can occur. Good results were achieved when seed was collected early (July 4) and stratified immediately for 90 days at 41° F. After removal from cold moist storage, seeds may take as long as 2 months to germinate. Overwinter in a cold frame and then pot up the plants into one-gallon containers the following spring. Growth rates accelerate the second season (Bronstad, personal communication, 1999).

For outdoor sowing, the best seedbed contains rich loamy soil covered with a light mulch. Natural germination occurs in the spring. Sow seeds in rows 8–12 inches apart and cover with mulch. Shading is not necessary. Germination rates are often uneven. Fall-sown seeds germinate late in spring (Dirr and Heuser 1987).

Cuttings

Sassafras may be propagated from root but not stem cuttings. Select large root cuttings in early spring before the plant leafs out. The cuttings should be 2–3 inches long and 1–1½ inches thick with a live stem sprout. Plant the cuttings vertically in fine soil and keep moist. Rooting and new stem growth are accomplished in 5 months. Smaller root cuttings may also be selected.

Dormant root cuttings without sprouts will also root if kept in a greenhouse until spring. These should be ½ inch long and placed horizontally in small containers holding a 2:1 mixture of peat moss and sand. Cover the cuttings with ½–¾ inch of soil. Fill the pots to 1 inch below the rim and cover with paper until new shoots appear. Keep the soil moist and harden off new plants in a cold frame before moving outdoors.

Transplanting

Sassafras freely produces root suckers that can be dug and moved immediately. Best results are achieved if the suckers are root pruned by first digging around them with a spade and leaving them in the ground by the parent tree for one season. Most suckers do not have a good root system and are difficult to transplant unless handled carefully. Larger trees do not move well because of their sparse, far-ranging root system (Simpson 1988). Small plants, less than 5 feet, have been successfully transplanted from thickets in warm weather (Lowrey, personal communication, 1986).

NOTES

Sassafras has been in cultivation since 1630 and has many uses in traditional medicine and folk crafts, such as candles, soaps, and dyes. Sassafras is an appropriate medium-sized tree to introduce to disturbed sites with infertile soil, as in logged or strip-mined areas. Sassafras berries are reportedly eaten by at least 28 species of birds, and the tree provides important cover and browse food for other wildlife.

The interesting foliage, fall color, and delicate winter form make Sassafras a worthy landscape plant for acid sandy soils in more temperate climates.

Schaefferia cuneifolia

Desert Yaupon, Capul, Panalero

CELASTRACEAE (STAFF-TREE FAMILY)

GENERAL DESCRIPTION

Desert Yaupon is a low-growing evergreen shrub 3–6½ feet tall with many small spiny branches covered with numerous small, teardrop-shaped, light green leaves.

FLOWERS AND FRUIT

Inconspicuous male and female flowers occur on separate plants. Fruit is a capsule containing two small seeds. Ripeness is indicated by a translucent orange-red color.

NATURAL HABITAT, RANGE, AND PREFERRED SITE

Desert Yaupon is common throughout the western portion of south Texas in various soil types but prefers heavier soils and rocky hillsides in mixed-brush associations. It is also found in infrequent locations on rocky hill-sides and canyons along the Rio Grande in the southern part of the Trans-Pecos and northern Mexico. Desert Yaupon is very drought tolerant.

COLLECTION AND STORAGE

Collect the seeds when the fruit has turned a bright orange or red color in September through November. Clean seeds by rubbing on a screen or in a modified blender before sowing or storing.

PROPAGATION

Seeds

Desert Yaupon can be grown from freshly gathered untreated seeds sown immediately after collection or from seeds stored over winter and planted in the spring. Collect seed when fruits are deep orange and fleshy. Sow seeds in individual containers. Seedlings are very slow growing. A small salable one-gallon plant can be produced in 1 year (McNeal, personal communication, 1999).

Cuttings

Desert Yaupon is propagated from root sprouts separated from the parent plant (Mortensen 1947). Desert Yaupon plants in the field are slow to produce sufficient new growth for cutting stock. Growing this plant from seed is the preferred method because of the prolific production of fruits.

NOTES

This low-growing evergreen shrub makes an attractive hedge or specimen plant in sunny locations in dry soils. Periodic pruning will encourage more compact growth. The bright, translucent, orange-red berries are very showy in the fall in contrast to the dark evergreen foliage. It is occasionally browsed by white-tailed deer. Birds, including bobwhite quail, scaled quail, and cactus wrens, as well as small mammals, including coyotes and wood rats, eat the fruit. Birds occasionally nest in this shrub. It provides some browse for sheep, goats, and cattle. In Mexico the roots of Desert Yaupon have been used to treat venereal disease (R. B. Taylor, Rutledge, and Herrera 1997).

Smilax

Green-briar, Cat-briar

LILIACEAE (LILY FAMILY)

GENERAL DESCRIPTION

Cat-briars are vines that climb by means of tendrils. They have glossy thick leaves that are often spotted on the upper surface. Stems of some species are woody at the base and armed with sharp thorns.

FLOWERS AND FRUIT

Male and female flowers are greenish yellow or white and held in inconspicuous clusters in spring to early summer. Fruit is a small berry turning bluish black or purple when ripe and containing one or two seeds.

NATURAL HABITAT, RANGE, AND PREFERRED SITE

Cat-briar is common in thickets, flood plains, and hillsides in a variety of soils throughout Texas. See Species Descriptions for individual ranges and habitats. *Smilax* is often an invader of disturbed, overgrazed, or abandoned fields. It will grow in poor soil in the shade but prospers in full sun (Gill and Healy 1974).

COLLECTION AND STORAGE

Collect the fruit in fall or early winter when it is filled out and has turned a blue-black color. Clean the seeds from the pulp and allow them to air dry on screens a few days before storing in sealed containers in the refrigerator.

PROPAGATION

Seeds

Natural germination occurs in the spring. Seeds to be sown in the spring must first be stratified for 30–60 days at 41° F. Cover the seeds lightly with soil. Seedlings should be grown in a container for 1 year and then may be transplanted outdoors.

Cuttings

Smilax may be propagated by root division in the spring (Gill and Healy 1974). Firm the soil around the roots and keep thoroughly moist. Stems may not appear from the rootstock until the second year.

Some species may also be propagated from stem cuttings. Best results are achieved from 6-inch cuttings taken in late spring or early summer during the active growing stage with the leaves fully expanded. Cuttings may also be taken in September from mature wood of the current season's growth. Remove all leaves but the top two. Treat with IBA and place in a 3:1 mixture of peat moss and sand under intermittent mist. Periodic pruning, browsing, and burning stimulate new shoot growth.

NOTES

Smilax's greatest contribution is as a revegetation plant. It is an early succession plant on disturbed sites and remains as an understory vine when the tree canopy is developed. It is useful in covering tree stumps, trellises, and fences along property lines. It is one of the best vines for providing wildlife cover and food. Green-briar is an important browse plant for deer, and the fruit is eaten by many birds (Gill and Healy 1974).

Several species of *Smilax* are vicious thorny shrubs that can form impenetrable thickets. Because of a deep root, they are very hard to eradicate. However, they provide protection for small mammals and nesting birds.

SPECIES DESCRIPTIONS

Smilax glauca **(Saw-briar, Cat-briar)**
Slender climbing vine with blue berries and ovate leaves with fuzzy undersides. Dry to moist sandy woods from Florida to east Texas.

Smilax laurifolia **(Bamboo-vine)**
Evergreen, high-climbing vine with oblong or lanceolate leaves and black berries. Swamps and moist areas in low ground in east Texas, east to Florida.

Smilax pumila **(Sarsaparilla-vine)**
Trailing or low-climbing vine with fuzzy stems, ovate-elliptic leaves, and persistent red berries. Sandy soil in piney woods or hardwood forests from east Texas to Florida.

Smilax rotundifolia **(Green-briar, Stretch-berry)**
Tough, woody, high-climbing vine with persistent, ovate to heart-shaped bright green leaves and blue-black berries. Moist to dry thickets from Florida to the eastern third of Texas. This is perhaps the showiest member of the genus. It is a hardy, attractive vine with large glossy leaves.

Sophora secundiflora

Texas Mountain Laurel, Mescal Bean, Frijolito, Frijolillo

FABACEAE (LEGUME FAMILY)

GENERAL DESCRIPTION

Texas Mountain Laurel is a multi-trunked evergreen shrub or small tree sometimes growing as tall as 18 feet. Leaves are dark glossy green and somewhat leathery.

FLOWERS AND FRUIT

Flowers are very showy, held in dense Wisteria-like clusters of purple blooms. Occasionally in the wild a white or pink form may be observed. Blooms begin to appear in March or early April and smell intensely like grape bubble gum. Fruit is a thick pod containing one or more dark red hard seeds.

NATURAL HABITAT, RANGE, AND PREFERRED SITE

Texas Mountain Laurel is common throughout south and most of west Texas on shallow, gravelly, limestone soils. It is cold hardy to USDA zone 8 (Arnold 1999), and in colder zones it will not flower reliably because late freezes will damage flower buds.

COLLECTION AND STORAGE

Gather the seeds in late summer through the fall when the pod begins to dry and the seeds turn red. Separate the seeds from the pod to reduce bulk and store in bags or containers in a cool dry place. Seeds have a hard seed coat and require no refrigeration to maintain viability for at least 3 years. Sometimes soaking the fresh hard pods in warm water will soften them and make seed removal easier.

PROPAGATION

Seeds

Germination of *Sophora* is delayed by a hard seed coat. Seeds may be filed or mechanically scarified with a knife. Or soak them in concentrated sulfuric acid for 30–90 minutes immediately before sowing.

Pretreated seeds will germinate within 2 weeks in a greenhouse or outdoors after the soil has warmed. Plant the seeds in individual containers that are deep enough to accommodate a relatively long initial root. The soil medium should be extremely well drained and drenched with a fungicide before the seeds are sown. Seedlings do not transplant well from the flat and are also sensitive to overhead watering.

Texas Mountain Laurel seedlings tend to grow slowly the first 2 years. This is part of a natural survival mechanism by which the plant expends most of its resources initially establishing a root system that will enable it to survive the often harsh and rocky conditions of its native site.

In the nursery, Texas Mountain Laurel will respond to fertilizers and grow at a much faster rate. Seedlings should be given light (30%) shade the first spring and summer to encourage more elongated shoot growth. Seedlings grown in full sun tend to crouch down in the pot, expending more of their energy on root growth and protecting tender new growth from burning (Kirwin, personal communication, 1999). In their natural habitat, seedlings are found growing in protected areas below parent trees, or in the cedar duff collected below nearby Ashe Juniper trees.

Cuttings

Preliminary studies of vegetative propagation of Texas Mountain Laurel indicate that while asexual propagation of this species is difficult, success can be achieved by applications of high concentrations of hormone treatments.

In one study, cuttings were made from juvenile wood taken from plants less than 3 feet tall. These were treated with 10,000 ppm NAA "quick-dip," and they rooted at a rate of 16%. The same wood treated with IBA (25,000 ppm) rooted at a rate of 50%. Rooting of cuttings of both species occurred after 8 weeks in a rooting medium composed of one part peat moss, one part perlite, and two parts sand. Cuttings were kept under intermittent mist (Simpson, personal communication, 1986). Information for vegetative propagation of other *Sophora* species is lacking.

Transplanting

Sophora is often difficult to transplant because of the long, sparsely branched root system and rocky sites where it naturally grows. However, most large specimens seen in landscape situations have been field dug. Transplant shock and low survival rates are a definite risk when moving large plants. Transplanted Mountain Laurels must not be planted too low in the ground or placed in a wet spot. Also, they must not be allowed to dry out entirely until they have adjusted to their new site. Application of root stimulators has proven helpful.

Eve's Necklace, *S. affinis*, is easiest to transplant in the winter because it often grows in deeper soil and is deciduous. When transplanting, obtain as large a root ball as possible. The plant should be cut back severely and kept well watered in a shady location. Many transplanted specimens of Texas Mountain Laurel will take a year or longer to resume active growth.

NOTES

Members of *Sophora* are among the most ornamental native species. Texas Mountain Laurel is a popular landscape plant because of its evergreen foliage, showy blooms, and hardy drought tolerance. In some years Texas Mountain Laurel is relentlessly defoliated by Genista moth larva. The best treatment for this is to repeatedly apply biological controls such as Baccilis thuringiensis ("Bt") (Will, personal communication, 1999). Collection of Texas Mountain Laurel seed from northern populations offers potential for selection of more cold hardy genotypes that would extend the range of this plant for use as an ornamental plant in Dallas and the Panhandle.

Other species of *Sophora* worthy of cultivation include *Sophora affinis* (Eve's Necklace). This is a tall shrub, 6–18 feet, with deciduous light green graceful leaflets and hanging Wisteria-like clusters of fragrant pale pink flowers. The fruit is a black constricted "pop-bead" legume. It is native to roadsides and edges of thickets in central and east-central Texas. It will grow in dappled light, although shade reduces its flowering display. Unlike Texas Mountain Laurel, Eve's Necklace is browsed by deer. It grows more rapidly than *S. secundiflora*.

Another species, *Sophora gypsophila var. guadalupensis* (Guadalupe Mountain Laurel), is a small evergreen shrub to 4 feet with small rounded leaflets covered with dense silvery fuzz and small purple flowers. Guadalupe Mountain Laurel is found only in scattered locations on gypsum flats in the Guadalupe Mountains in Culberson County. Though slow growing and very susceptible to damping off, this species would make a handsome ornamental hedge or border plant because of its tight branching, compact growth, silver leathery branches, and purple flowers. Guadalupe Mountain Laurel will not thrive in areas with higher humidity and high night-time summer temperatures. It is also intolerant of poor drainage.

Sophora tomentosa var. occidentalis (Yellow Sophora) is a sprawling, rounded shrub up to 6 feet tall with fuzzy whitish leaves and yellow clusters of flowers that bloom from March to October. It is native though infrequently found in sandy soils along the Coastal Prairie in south Texas. Although frost tender when used much north of its range, this plant makes a very attractive patio plant or shrub with showy flowers and interesting foliage.

Stewartia malacodendron

Silky Camellia

THEACEAE (CAMELLIA FAMILY)

GENERAL DESCRIPTION

Silky Camellia is a delicate deciduous shrub or small tree to 20 feet with many branches growing from the base. Leaves are 2–4 inches long, smooth and lustrous green above with a finely serrated margin and pointed tip. Bark is dark brown to gray and smooth.

FLOWERS AND FRUIT

Very showy flowers bloom in April and May and are white with dark purple stamen filaments and bluish anthers. Fruit is a globose capsule containing five or more smooth seeds.

NATURAL HABITAT, RANGE, AND PREFERRED SITE

Silky Camellia is found in Texas only in isolated sites in far east Texas. It is more frequent but nowhere abundant in wooded banks, hillsides, and along streams in southwest Louisiana, east to Florida. Silky Camellia prefers well-drained but moist soil.

COLLECTION AND STORAGE

Collect the seeds from mid- to late summer as the capsule begins to dry; air dry the capsules and shake out the seeds. Seeds are angular and can sometimes be difficult to shake loose. Store in a cool dry place. Seed loses its viability rapidly and should be sown or placed in pretreatment immediately.

PROPAGATION

Seeds

Propagation of Silky Camellia is difficult because seeds are scarce and hard to come by, and also because germination is delayed by a double dormancy that is not clearly understood. Seedlings are also slow growing and very susceptible to damping-off fungi. Limited observations suggest that the best success might be achieved if seeds are allowed a 3–5 month period of after-ripening or warm stratification followed by cold stratification for 3 months. Seed planted outdoors immediately after collection will germinate in 2 years. Time pretreatment so that the seed are ready for planting in a cold frame in late February or March before temperatures are too high. Sow in a well-drained peat/perlite mix. Press the seeds in the soil and lightly sprinkle with sand or sifted peat moss. Do not bury the seeds deeply. Seedlings should be lightly shaded the first year. Germination rates are characteristically erratic and in low percentages.

Cuttings

Members of this genus can be propagated from semihardwood cuttings and layers. The best results for related species occurred when the cuttings were made in early summer, treated with 8,000 ppm IBA plus 15% thiram or IBA plus 2,500 ppm NAA "quick dip." These were stuck in peat/perlite and kept under mist. Rooted cuttings had difficulty surviving over the winter. Do not transplant the cuttings. Harden them off and keep in a cold frame or cold storage at 34° F in well-drained media. Return the cuttings to a greenhouse in spring and initiate new growth. After putting on new growth, they can be transferred to containers.

NOTES

The large white flowers, glossy leaves, and compact growth habit make Silky Camellia one of the most ornamental native plants for east Texas. This rare and beautiful plant should be protected by increasing its numbers in cultivation.

Styrax

Silverbell, Snowbell

STYRACACEAE (STYRAX FAMILY)

GENERAL DESCRIPTION

Styrax spp. are shrubs or small trees with smooth to densely pubescent deciduous leaves (see Species Descriptions).

FLOWERS AND FRUIT

Small bell-shaped flowers hang in delicate clusters from the leaf axils from spring to early summer. Fruit is a dry three-valved capsule containing one to three hard seeds.

NATURAL HABITAT, RANGE, AND PREFERRED SITE

Styrax spp. grow in both east and west Texas. See Species Descriptions for individual range and habitat.

COLLECTION AND STORAGE

Collect the seeds in early or late summer when they have turned a glossy brown color and the capsule has begun to dry. Once mature, the capsules quickly split and drop the seeds. Avoid collecting seeds from the ground. Store the seeds in sealed containers in the refrigerator.

PROPAGATION

Seeds

Styrax spp. germinate well when planted immediately after collection. *Styrax* seed, like that of *Aesculus*, quickly dries out in storage and loses viability. The internal mechanisms of the embryo that delay germination are increased the longer the seed is stored and dried out before sowing.

New seed planted immediately after sowing germinates promptly (McNeal, personal communication, 1999). Newly emerging seedlings in the fall will need to be protected in a greenhouse overwinter. Another method is to stratify stored seeds for 60–90 days at 41° F and sow in late

January or early February in a greenhouse or cold frame. Occasionally the seeds will germinate during cold moist storage. Check the seeds every week, and, using tweezers, carefully remove seeds showing an emerging radicle and transplant into individual containers. *Styrax* seeds do not germinate well in warm temperatures.

Seeds may also be sown outdoors in the fall. Seedlings are very susceptible to damping-off fungi. Carefully inoculate the seedbed or container before sowing with beneficial fungi (see Chapter III). Avoid overhead watering. Seedlings are very sensitive to burning with highly alkaline irrigation water. Seedlings respond to light organic fertilizer, but overfertilization only encourages weak growth and susceptibility to disease. Sow the seeds in individual 4-inch pots, two to three seeds per pot, or in a deep seed flat containing a well-drained loose soil mix. Young plants require partial shade. Seedlings are very sensitive to both overwatering and drying and are sometimes difficult to transplant from the flat.

Snowbells are slow growing, and may require up to 2 years to make a salable one-gallon plant (McNeal, personal communication, 1999). Snowbells are more successful in the landscape if they are not forced, but instead allowed to grow slowly into a sturdy small plant.

Cuttings

In one report, semihardwood cuttings of American Snowbell (*S. americana*) rooted well when taken in early to mid-summer. Cuttings were soaked in 1,000 ppm IBA solution for 18 hours and rooted in sandy soil. Another method recommends taking tip cuttings of American Snowbell from sideshoots 4–6 inches long with the lower leaves removed. These should be woody toward the base and kept under intermittent mist. Treating cuttings with 4,000 ppm IBA quick dip resulted in 100% rooting (Dirr and Heuser 1987). Information is lacking on vegetative propagation of western *Styrax* species.

NOTES

Styrax spp. are attractive ornamental understory or specimen plants because of their glossy foliage, showy flowers, and delicate form. They are most effective if used in a group at the edge of woods or other protected well-drained locations where they receive shade in the afternoons. Snowbells are a favorite browse plant of deer and goats, and native populations have been seriously reduced by overgrazing. The rare and uncommon forms of Snowbells should be protected by increasing their numbers in cultivation.

SPECIES DESCRIPTIONS

Styrax americana **(American Snowbell)**
Shrub or small tree to 20 feet, widely branched with white flowers. Moist woods and along streams from Florida to east Texas, where it is uncommon.

Styrax platanifolia **(Sycamore-leaf Snowbell)**
Multi-trunked tree to 12 feet with slender branches and small glossy ovate leaves. White flowers in small hanging clusters. Along streams, springs, and canyons in the Edwards Plateau. Some populations of *S. platanifolia*, such as those found in Bandera County, have leaves covered with dense white felt on their undersides (Enquist 1987). Endemic to the Hill Country.

Styrax texana **(Texas Snowbell)**
A slender spreading shrub or small tree to 9 feet with smooth rounded leaves having silvery or pale green undersides. White flowers hang in clusters of three to five. Texas Snowbell is endemic to canyons and creeksides in the Edwards Plateau, where it is only rarely found in localized populations. Because Texas Snowbell is listed as a rare and endangered plant, it is illegal to sell it.

Symphoricarpos orbiculatus

Indian Currant, Snowberry

CAPRIFOLIACEAE (HONEYSUCKLE FAMILY)

GENERAL DESCRIPTION

Indian Currant is a low-growing deciduous shrub that spreads by means of underground stems. Small oval leaves are scattered along slender upright stems. Older branches have shredding bark.

FLOWERS AND FRUIT

Greenish white inconspicuous flowers are followed by deep pink or wine-colored berrylike drupes that may remain on the plant throughout most of the winter. Each drupe has two small seeds.

NATURAL HABITAT, RANGE, AND PREFERRED SITE

Indian Currant grows in woods and thickets along streams and fencerows in various soils throughout the eastern third of Texas. It is also widespread throughout the United States. Under cultivation, it will adapt to a wide variety of sites and locations.

COLLECTION AND STORAGE

Collect the fruits anytime during the fall and winter. If the pulp is still fleshy, clean the seeds before storage. If fruit is collected later in the winter, the seeds may be dried with the pulp on. Air dry the seeds before storage. Dried seeds stored at 41° F will remain viable up to 5 years.

PROPAGATION

Seeds

Indian Currant is slow to grow from seeds because of an impermeable seed coat and also an immature seed embryo. Seeds require both after-ripening and scarification. Soak the seeds in concentrated sulfuric acid for 20–30 minutes and then stratify at 86° F for 120 days. Finally put the seeds in cold moist storage at 41° F for 180 days.

For some seed lots, stratification at 50° F for 180 days following the acid treatment is sufficient (Vories 1981). Sow the seeds ¼ inch deep in well-drained soil. Seedlings do best in light shade. Seeds do not germinate well in hot weather.

Cuttings

Indian Currant roots easily from firm softwood and semihardwood cuttings of the current season's growth taken from mid-summer through fall. Take cuttings 4–6 inches long and woody toward the base or with a heel of older wood. Treat with IBA (1,000–3,000 ppm) and keep under intermittent mist. Rooting is slow but occurs in high percentages (McNeal, personal communication, 1999). Hardwood cuttings taken in winter and treated with 3,000 ppm IBA talc also root easily.

Transplanting

Indian Currant is often increased by separating large clumps or suckers in the winter. These should be cut way back and kept well watered. Roots are not deep.

NOTES

Indian Currant is an old-fashioned garden plant that is regaining popularity as a tall ground cover, border, or woodland understory plant. It is useful in erosion control and provides valuable wildlife food and cover. Indian Currant is attractive in fall because of the abundance of reddish purple fruit and persistent foliage that becomes tinged with crimson after the first frost. There is also a domestic variegated leaf form available.

To promote more berries and bushy growth, cut Indian Currant back to the ground each winter. Indian Currant can get powdery mildew during wet springs. Cut back the plant to encourage a flush of new growth and avoid overhead watering. It may also defoliate during hot weather. Good companion plants for Indian Currant are American Beauty-berry (*Callicarpa americana*), Texas Betony (*Stachys coccinea*), native sedges (*Carex spp.*), and Rusty Black-haw Viburnum (*Viburnum rufidulum*).

Some western species—Guadalupe Snowberry, *S. guadalupensis*, and Fragrant Snowberry, *S. longiflorus*—also have potential as ornamental ground covers or low-growing shrubs. Guadalupe Snowberry is a smooth shrub with bell-shaped flowers. It is endemic to the limestone soil of the Guadalupe Mountains of west Texas. Fragrant Snowberry is a low spreading shrub with large fragrant pink or reddish flowers native to canyon ridges and stream banks of the mountains of the Trans-Pecos, west to Colorado and Oregon.

Taxodium distichum var. distichum

Bald Cypress, Sabino, Ahuehuete

CUPRESSACEAE (CYPRESS FAMILY)

GENERAL DESCRIPTION

Bald Cypresses are large trees reaching 100 feet tall with delicate light green deciduous leaves and slender leafy branches. The trunk often develops erect columnar "knees" from the roots when it grows in swamps or stream banks.

FLOWERS AND FRUIT

Bald Cypress flowers are unisexual; male and female flowers occur on the same branches. Fruit is a sticky, resinous globular cone composed of thick scales that bear two three-angled seeds at their bases. The seeds measure about ½ inch long.

NATURAL HABITAT, RANGE, AND PREFERRED SITE

The populations of Bald Cypress in Texas are disconnected and found on very different sites, where they also take on different characteristics. In east Texas or along the coast it grows in swamps and river bottoms. A narrow band on the map in south-central Texas shows a gap in its distribution until Bald Cypress again appears in the Edwards Plateau, where it is almost always associated with running streams and rivers (Simpson 1988). The central Texas form has intensely blue-green foliage and a rounded crown. Although Bald Cypress will grow in more upland situations under cultivation, it does better in wetter areas. During long dry spells, Bald Cypress may defoliate early.

As with the red oaks, it is very important to know the provenance of the Bald Cypress you are buying. Those grown in east Texas or the southeastern United States are very poorly adapted to the thinner soils and dryer climate of central Texas.

COLLECTION AND STORAGE

Collect the seeds beginning in late September when the cones have turned brown and begun to dry but before they have shattered. Spread the cones on screens or trays to dry until the seeds can be easily separated. Each cone contains approximately 18–33 seeds. Flotation is not a reliable method for testing seed viability because the resin coating on the seeds causes them all to float. Bald Cypress seeds do not retain viability if kept more than a year, even if held at low temperatures. For overwinter storage, keep the seeds in sealed containers at 41° F.

Seeds of a related species, Monteczuma Bald Cypress (*T. mucronatum*) (see Notes), will remain viable for at least 3 years if kept in the refrigerator (Best 1999).

PROPAGATION

Seeds

Propagation of Bald Cypress is achieved primarily by seeds rather than cuttings. Germination is typically delayed by a dormant embryo. Sow outdoors in the fall or stratify for 60 days at 41° F. Germination is sometimes inhibited by the resinous coating of the seeds, which in some years is thick enough to prevent imbibition of water. Before sowing or stratification, remove the resin by soaking the seeds or unshattered cones in a 1% lye solution with water or in hot water just under the boiling point (see Chapter III). Do not clean the seeds this way if you are going to store them because the seeds may have begun to swell and will rot in storage.

Sow the seeds in deep individual containers or outdoors in the fall in well-worked seedbeds containing loose sandy soil with a high percentage of organic matter. For container growing use a light premixed soil blend. Drench the soil with a fungicide to prevent damping off and plant the seeds ¼ inch deep. Keep the seedbed continuously moist but not too soggy. Germination usually takes place in 40–90 days but may be as short as 15 days (USDA 1974). Seeds germinate better in cooler springtime temperatures. Partial shading of the seedlings is recommended. Oddly enough for trees that grow in or around water and wet conditions, Bald Cypress seedlings are very susceptible to damping-off fungi.

Cuttings

Bald Cypress is difficult to root. In one report, softwood cuttings treated with 1,000 ppm IBA and placed under mist rooted in low percentages (Dirr and Heuser 1987). Rooting success appears to be restricted to juvenile wood.

Transplanting

Large specimen trees are difficult to transplant from the wild, but container-grown trees are easily handled.

NOTES

The delicate foliage and stout trunk are just two of the attractive characteristics of this outstanding, long-lived specimen tree. Bald Cypress has been in cultivation since 1640. There is much potential for selecting superior forms of Bald Cypress for foliage, shape, rapid growth, and even fall color. It should be kept in mind, however, that although Bald Cypress has a delicate, pyramidal form when young, it will eventually become a huge, magnificent tree and therefore is not appropriate for a small lot or sidewalk planting. It is a wonderful tree for parks, schools with big grounds, corporate headquarters, river walks, and other locations where its size can be celebrated and enjoyed from a distance.

A closely related species, Monteczuma Bald Cypress (*T. mucronatum*), is also worthy of cultivation. It is an evergreen tree very similar in appearance to Bald Cypress that reaches its northern limits on the banks of the Rio Grande Valley and along resacas in Cameron and Hidalgo counties (Simpson 1988). It will grow on high ground as well as swampy soil. Monteczuma Cypress holds its foliage longer than Bald Cypress and is somewhat tolerant of saline conditions. In Texas, Monteczuma Cypress is generally less than 50 feet tall. North of San Antonio it is not as cold hardy as Bald Cypress and even in Houston's mild winters it will lose its leaves.

In the nursery Monteczuma Cypress has proven to be faster growing than Bald Cypress. The seeds require no pretreatment. Seed can be collected in November (Will, personal communication, 1999). One method recommends aerating the seed for several days (see Chapter IV), and then planting in trays as noted above for *T. distichum* (Best 1999). Monteczuma Cypress will grow from a seedling in a tree tube to a five-gallon container in 6 months, and within a year it can be placed in a 15-gallon container (Kirwin, personal communication, 1999).

Monteczuma Cypress first fills out its root zone and then puts on caliper. Production of this plant has to be carefully monitored because of the plant's rapid growth. It can easily become root bound if not moved up to larger containers at the proper time. Carefully tip prune up to one-third of the foliage when the tree is moved up from a 15- to 30-gallon plant. As with other conifers, tip pruning will encourage the branching to fill out and become dense (Kirwin, personal communication, 1999).

Tecoma stans var. angustata

Esperanza, Yellow-bells

BIGNONIACEAE (TRUMPET-CREEPER FAMILY)

GENERAL DESCRIPTION

Esperanza is an irregularly shaped shrub 3–6 feet tall, with several slender stems rising from a single woody base. Leaves are compound, narrow, and willowlike, with deep notches.

FLOWERS AND FRUIT

Esperanza produces a profusion of showy, large bright yellow tubular-shaped flowers intermittently from April to November. Fruit is a large capsule containing many seeds, each with two large thin wings.

NATURAL HABITAT, RANGE, AND PREFERRED SITE

Esperanza can be found on rocky bluffs, slopes, and canyons throughout much of the southern Trans-Pecos, north to New Mexico, Arizona, California, and south through Mexico. It requires full sun and well-drained soils. Plants from the Trans-Pecos are cold hardy. In winter, the plant may freeze to the ground but return during late spring to produce even more flowers on the new wood.

COLLECTION AND STORAGE

Collect the capsules from late summer to fall when they are no longer green. Separate the seeds from the pods by hand. Air dry the seeds on screens at room temperature 1 or 2 days before storage. Storage in sealed containers in the refrigerator is adequate for over winter.

PROPAGATION

Seeds

Esperanza will germinate from fresh untreated seeds sown within a few weeks of harvest. Stored seeds do not germinate as well. The seedbed or container should have light loose soil and be kept slightly moist but not soggy. Press the seeds in and just barely cover them with sifted sand or fine potting soil. Germination will occur in 7–10 days. Overwatered seedlings are very susceptible to damping off and root rot. Seedlings are fast growing.

Cuttings

Esperanza will root from softwood cuttings taken in late spring and early summer and again in the fall, after each flush of growth. Take cuttings 3–4 inches long that are woody toward the base. Those cuttings with a diameter as big as a pencil seem to root best. Application of IBA (3,000–5,000 ppm) improves rooting. Remove half of the leaf surface and keep under intermittent mist. Fall-rooted cuttings require cold-frame protection over winter.

NOTES

The light green leaves and large brilliant yellow flowers make Esperanza an especially showy ornamental shrub. During hard winters it will freeze back to the base and sprout anew in the spring. Periodic pruning and removal of the spent flowers and pods of this plant encourage bushy growth and more blooms. Like its cousin the Desert Willow (*Chilopsis linearis*), Esperanza may bloom more prolifically if established plants are allowed a dry spell between each deep watering. Both these species are genetically triggered to bloom during monsoon rains in the desert and may be less responsive to steady moisture regimes provided by an irrigation system. Esperanza makes a flashy specimen plant for a sunny, well-drained border garden, around pools or patios, or even in neglected areas such as roadside plantings.

A related species from the Caribbean, *T. stans var. stans*, is sometimes erroneously sold as *var. angustifolia* (sometimes with one of the same common English names—"Yellow-bells"). This is a subtropical form and is not cold hardy north of San Antonio. This variety and the cultivar 'Gold Star' should be treated like summer annuals or patio plants that will have to be replanted every year. We can expect to see many more hybrid crosses and cultivar selections of this genus appearing in the nursery trade in the future.

Tilia caroliniana

Carolina Basswood

TILIACEAE (BASSWOOD FAMILY)

GENERAL DESCRIPTION

Carolina Basswood is a large tree growing more than 90 feet. It has large deciduous oval leaves.

FLOWERS AND FRUIT

Fragrant flowers hang in white clusters from a stalk attached to a leafy bract. Blooms occur in clusters of five or axillary racemes from spring to summer. Fruit is a winged, indehiscent, hard nutlike drupe with one or two seeds.

NATURAL HABITAT, RANGE, AND PREFERRED SITE

Carolina Basswood was once quite extensive in its range, but now only occurs in seven or eight counties on rich, deep moist soils of river bottoms and creeks of the Edwards Plateau and more commonly in the Pineywoods (Simpson 1988). Basswood prefers partial shade and light, moist, and fertile soil.

COLLECTION AND STORAGE

Fruits ripen from September through October. Seeds germinate most easily if fruits are collected as they first turn slightly brown and if the seeds are planted immediately. The fruits can be shaken onto canvas and then spread out to dry. Seeds are hard to collect because they are held so high up in the tree. The persistent bracts attached to the fruit may be removed by hand or by running the fruits through a machine. *Tilia* seeds have a hard pericarp that can be removed by running through a grinder or by sulfuric acid treatment (Dirr and Heuser 1987). Basswood seeds stored at room temperature will remain viable up to 2 years. Seeds to be stored longer should be refrigerated. Seed can show great variability in germination from year to year.

PROPAGATION

Seeds

Tilia seeds are difficult to germinate because of a tough pericarp, impermeable seed coat, and dormancy. Seeds may remain in the ground several years and never produce a good stand of seedlings. Seed treatments that result in consistently good germination have not been developed. Fair germination rates of American Basswood (*T. americana*) were achieved when the pericarp was removed immediately following collection and the seed was then sown in the fall or stratified for 3 months at 41° F. Some growers suggest collecting the fruit early in the season just as the pericarp is beginning to turn grayish brown and treating promptly. Drying appears to harden the seed coat and increase dormancy.

Sow the seeds ¼–⅓ inch deep in a loose, well-drained, but moist seedbed. Untreated basswood seeds sown in the fall or spring usually germinate in 2 or 3 years. Young seedlings need shade the first season.

Cuttings

In Holland, *T. americana* is rooted by mound layering the suckering wood from coppiced stock plants in the summer. American Basswood was also reported to root from softwood and semihardwood cuttings taken in early summer. These cuttings were wounded and treated with a 2–3% IBA quick dip. Stem cuttings are susceptible to leaf abscission, after which they will not root (Dirr and Heuser 1987). Exact information on rooting our species in this climate is lacking.

NOTES

The large oval leaves and fragrant flowers hanging from large leafy bracts combine to make basswood a very attractive specimen tree. Certain members of this genus are also valued as timber trees, and most basswoods are important honey plants. American Basswood (*Tilia americana*) is relatively tolerant of city pollution. Carolina Basswoods grown from seed collected in the scattered and diminishing native populations of central Texas have unexplored potential as a relatively fast-growing shade tree that could add much needed variety to the urban forest, in home landscapes, parks, schools, and street plantings.

Tiquilia greggii

Plume Tiquilia, Hierba del Cenizo, Oreja del Perro

BORAGINACEAE (BORAGE FAMILY)

GENERAL DESCRIPTION

Plume Tiquilia is a leafy mounding shrub with dense branching and silver-gray leaves covered with soft hairs. It grows to 2 feet high with a similar spread.

FLOWERS AND FRUIT

After summer rains Plume Tiquilia is covered with ¾-inch balls of tiny pink or magenta bell-shaped flowers and purplish gray plumed seeds. The flowers open in the morning and again in the evening, and are visited by bees and butterflies.

NATURAL HABITAT, RANGE, AND PREFERRED SITE

Plume Tiquilia is common on limestone slopes and desert flats in the Trans-Pecos, west to New Mexico and south to Mexico. It grows best in full sun and is hardy to 5° F.

COLLECTION AND STORAGE

Plume Tiquilia takes advantage of infrequent sudden summer rain showers to produce blooms repeatedly throughout the season. Flowers and fruit are often on the plant at the same time. The challenge is getting enough seed at one time to make collection worthwhile. A hand lens is necessary to tell if the seed is ready for collection. Ripe seed is plump and filled out, black on one side and lighter colored on the other. Sometimes the plant will be covered in dried flower heads, but all the seed will have dropped out. For best results, collect as many seeds as possible from a large population. Extract the seeds using a series of graduated sieves to separate the tiny seed from the dried flower heads (Manning, personal communication, 1999).

PROPAGATION

Seeds

Freshly gathered untreated seed will germinate in early spring in the greenhouse without pretreatment (Manning, personal communication, 1999). Seedlings tend to be slow growing at first and sensitive to overwatering. They can be delicate and often do not survive transplanting into larger containers. Once they have filled out the one-gallon container, they become hardier. Use a light mineral soil mix and do not overfertilize. A finished one-gallon plant can be produced in a year (Manning, personal communication, 1999).

Cuttings

Information is lacking on rooting Plume Tiquilia from cuttings.

Transplanting

Plume Tiquilia is very difficult to transplant from the wild. Container-grown plants placed in loose gravel or well-drained soil have a better chance of survival.

NOTES

Plume Tiquilia can be massed as a ground cover or planted with other desert shrubs such as Black Dalea (*Dalea frutescens*), Little-leaf Sumac (*Rhus microphylla*), Lechuguilla (*Agave lechuguilla*), Prickly Pear (*Opuntia spp.*), and Skelton-leaf Goldeneye Daisy (*Viguiera stenoloba*). Its soft silvery foliage and purple flowers in summer are a wonderful addition to a dry garden.

Ulmus

Elm, Olmo

ULMACEAE (ELM FAMILY)

GENERAL DESCRIPTION

Elms are deciduous trees with short-petioled straight-veined leaves (see Species Descriptions).

FLOWERS AND FRUIT

For some species, inconspicuous greenish yellow flowers appear in early spring just before the new leaves emerge. Others bloom in autumn (see Species Descriptions). Fruit is a one-seeded, compressed winged nutlet that ripens a few weeks after flowering.

NATURAL HABITAT, RANGE, AND PREFERRED SITE

Elms are most often found along streams and woodlands in various soil types. See Species Descriptions for individual range and habitat.

COLLECTION AND STORAGE

Collect the seeds by sweeping or raking them from the ground soon after they fall or by beating or stripping them from the branches. Air dry the seeds a few days at room temperature before storing. Elm seeds store best when the moisture content is slightly reduced and they are held in sealed containers at 36–40° F (USDA 1974).

PROPAGATION

Seeds

Elms will germinate promptly from untreated seeds planted right after collection. Fall-ripening species germinate uniformly if directly planted in seedbeds in the fall, or stratified at 41° F for 60 days and then planted in a cold frame or greenhouse by late February. The seedbed should be kept moist until germination is well advanced. One-year-old seedlings are usually large enough for field planting.

Cuttings

Softwood cuttings of American Elm, *U. americana*, root well when soaked in IBA (50 mg/l for 24 hours) and then placed in sand under intermittent mist. Without IBA, the cuttings root poorly.

NOTES

Most people are familiar with elms as excellent shade trees, although some of our hardy native species have been overlooked in favor of the introduced Chinese Elm. Cedar Elm, *U. crassifolia*, has a tall narrow crown that is less competitive for space when planted near other, more widely spreading, shade trees. Our elms are susceptible to Dutch Elm disease (*Cerastocystis ulmi*), though the disease is currently restricted to small areas in east Texas (Simpson 1988).

SPECIES DESCRIPTIONS

Ulmus alata (Winged Elm)

Small tree usually less than 70 feet with spreading branches forming a round-topped oblong crown. Found in neutral to acid sands and sandy loams along rivers and creeks in eastern Texas and east to Florida. Common on all but the wettest sites. Winged Elm flowers in early spring, before the leaves appear, and in alternate years is a prolific seeder. It sprouts readily from seed and is a rapid grower (Simpson 1988). It is easily transplanted and relatively free from disease and insects.

Ulmus americana (American Elm)

Tall shade tree to 90 feet in east Texas with spreading limbs forming a wide crown. In western areas, American Elm will reach its potential only if planted in deep soils with a steady source of water. In heavy clays, American Elm tends to develop aggressive surface roots (Ogden 1992). In Texas, American Elm can be found in all vegetational areas except the High Plains and Trans-Pecos (see Simpson 1988). It is susceptible to Dutch Elm disease, which has destroyed most of the trees in this species' northern range. Selections for Dutch Elm disease resistance include 'New Harmony,' 'Princeton,' 'Liberty,' 'Delaware #2,' and 'Washington.' However, information is lacking as to how these selections are adapted to Texas climate. Though native stock is seldom available from nurseries, it is important to select local stock that is adaptable to alkaline soil and heat. The southwestern populations in calcareous soils have not been seriously affected by Dutch Elm disease, but growers are understandably wary of including this species in their inventory (Ogden 1992). American Elm is famous for its magnificent vase-shaped crown, but it must be carefully placed in the landscape. Its size restricts its use to parks or other large-scale sites, and Dutch Elm disease is just one of a whole host of disease and insect pests that plague this species, including Texas cotton root rot.

***Ulmus crassifolia* (Cedar Elm, Olmo)**

Slow-growing tree to 50 feet with a narrow crown and small rough leaves. Cedar Elm sets seed in the fall. It is found in woodlands, ravines, and open slopes in all areas of Texas except the Trans-Pecos and the Rio Grande Plains. Cedar Elm is the most adaptable of our elms. It is tolerant of dry conditions and will grow in rocky limestone soil. It may defoliate or turn yellow in times of extreme drought, but it is very tough and adaptable to poor conditions. It has interesting crooked branches and the leaves turn a golden-bronze in the fall.

Cedar Elm is one of the easiest elms to transplant and has a moderate growth rate (Ogden 1992). Nursery-grown elms in five-gallon containers tend to be a little loose in the pot. Let the trees dry out somewhat between waterings to promote better anchoring in the container (Will, personal communication, 1999).

***Ulmus rubra* (Slippery Elm)**

Tree to 64 feet with spreading branches forming a broad open crown. Leaves dark green, rough, with fuzzy undersides. Mostly found in woodlands and thickets along rivers and streams in the eastern third of Texas, also east to Florida, north to Quebec. Slippery Elm is easily confused with American Elm.

Ungnadia speciosa

Mexican Buckeye, Mona, Monilla

SAPINDACEAE (SOAPBERRY FAMILY)

GENERAL DESCRIPTION

Mexican Buckeye is a tall shrub or small tree, often multi-trunked, rarely as tall as 32 feet. Leaves are compound, long, and narrow, often turning yellow in the fall.

FLOWERS AND FRUIT

Small, fragrant pink flowers appear in closely attached clusters just before the new leaves emerge in spring, much in the same way that redbuds bloom. Fruits are woody pods containing as many as three round, shiny black seeds.

NATURAL HABITAT, RANGE, AND PREFERRED SITE

Mexican Buckeye is commonly found in rocky areas in canyons and on slopes in south-central and southwest Texas, east to Dallas County and west to the Trans-Pecos. It prefers well-drained soil and will grow in either full sun or partial shade. It is drought tolerant and will thrive in areas with limited rainfall.

COLLECTION AND STORAGE

Gather the seeds beginning in August through October when the capsules turn dark reddish brown and begin to open. The mature seeds should be shiny black and hard. Seeds may be gathered from the ground if they have only recently fallen. Avoid gathering seeds that have been in damp leaf litter or have become soft. Remove the seeds from the pods and air dry on screens 1–2 days before storing in bags or ventilated containers. Dusting with an insecticide is recommended. Seeds will remain viable for up to three years without refrigeration.

PROPAGATION

Seeds

Mexican Buckeye will germinate within 3 weeks from untreated seeds.

Since seeds germinate best in warm soil, plant in late winter in a greenhouse or outdoors after all danger of frost is past. Seeds planted in the fall will also germinate promptly but will require cold-frame protection over winter. Scarification of the seed coat is not necessary and often produces weak seedlings.

Mexican Buckeye seeds should be planted in deep containers that allow air pruning in order to accommodate the long initial root and encourage the development of secondary roots (see Chapter IV). Girdled roots are a familiar problem with container-grown plants that have been cramped in seed flats or shallow pots. Cover the seeds with ½ inch of soil and keep moist but not soggy. Seedlings germinated in spring will make a one-gallon plant by fall, especially if regularly fertilized.

Cuttings

Because Mexican Buckeye is so easily grown from seeds and seeds are easily obtained, little research has been invested in developing vegetative propagation methods.

NOTES

The light green foliage, delicate pink flowers, and dense branching make Mexican Buckeye an outstanding small specimen tree for a woodland border, a deciduous screen, or tall background shrub. It is rapid growing, drought tolerant, and resistant to cotton root rot. Trees damaged by mowing will often resprout from the stump. Mexican Buckeye flowers in its third year. Selective pruning will encourage a single trunk if so desired. Mexican Buckeye is best when planted as a spreading tall shrub. Therefore, it is not as successful as a curbside or street planting. The growth characteristics of Mexican Buckeyes in Texas vary according to their location. Mexican Buckeyes from the western part of the Edwards Plateau and southern part of the Trans-Pecos are often much smaller, more compact in growth and leaf size, and have darker pink flowers than trees growing along the Brazos River south of Sealy (Lowrey, personal communication, 1986). A population close to the Devil's River near Comstock, Texas, has smaller leaves and distinctive pinkish red pods that remain on the plant and are showy in winter. Other populations have very dark pink or maroon coloration on the emerging leaves (McNeal, personal communication, 1999). These interesting variations should be more fully explored as horticultural selections.

Vaccinium

Blueberry, Farkleberry

ERICACEAE (HEATH FAMILY)

GENERAL DESCRIPTION

Members of this genus are shrubs or small trees with alternate deciduous or persistent leaves. Most often seen in Texas as a coarse multi-trunked shrub. Some species are thicket forming.

FLOWERS AND FRUIT

Flowers are white, urn- or cup-shaped with pink tinges. The flowers are borne singly or in clusters in early spring or summer. Fruit is a dark blue or black drupe with many seeds ripening in late summer or early winter.

NATURAL HABITAT, RANGE, AND PREFERRED SITE

Most members of this genus are native to sandy soil in the eastern third of Texas. See Species Descriptions for individual range and habitat. Western species are most often associated with a marshy or poorly drained habitat.

COLLECTION AND STORAGE

Collect the fruits in late summer or fall when they turn a dark blue-black color. Clean the seeds and air dry them for 48 hours at room temperature before storing in sealed containers at 41° F. Properly stored seeds will retain viability for up to 12 years (USDA 1974).

PROPAGATION

Seeds

Seeds of some species of *Vaccinium* require no pretreatment, while others have a dormant embryo and must be stratified before sowing in the spring. Stratification for 60–90 days at 41° F as a standard pretreatment is most likely to provide the best germination.

Spread the seeds over a well-drained, slightly acid soil mix such as a 2:1 ratio of peat/perlite. Cover with a thin layer of finely ground sphagnum moss and keep moist until germination is well advanced, usually in 3 or 4 weeks. When seedlings reach ¾ inch, transfer them to individual peat pots or 4-inch pots. Keep the seedlings shaded during the first growing season.

Cuttings

Members of this genus are most commonly propagated by cuttings. Softwood cuttings taken in spring, after the first flush of growth has fully expanded the leaves, root best. Treat these with 8,000 ppm IBA talc and insert in a peat/perlite rooting bed under intermittent mist. Cuttings survive best if allowed to remain in the rooting bed under reduced misting until the following spring. Periodic fertilizing will be necessary to maintain growth and survival.

Vaccinium will also root from hardwood cuttings of firm, vigorous, unbranched shoots of the previous season's growth taken during winter or early spring, before the plant has leafed out. These should have about the same diameter as a pencil with three to four buds and an average length of about 5 inches. Place the cuttings in a 1:1 mixture of sand and milled sphagnum about 2 inches apart with the top bud just showing.

Intermittent mist in a greenhouse or a plastic-covered cold frame is a suitable rooting environment. Bottom heat is beneficial, but application of IBA for some species has not been shown to significantly improve rooting of hardwood cuttings. Roots start to form in about 2 months (Hartmann and Kester 1975).

NOTES

Several native *Vaccinium* have potential as low-growing semi-evergreen ornamental shrubs for sun or shade in moist, acid soils. Members of this genus also provide valuable wildlife food and cover.

SPECIES DESCRIPTIONS

***Vaccinium arboreum* (Farkleberry, Sparkleberry)**

Coarse shrub or small tree to 26 feet with tardily deciduous, oblong-elliptic, leathery leaves and white, spicy-smelling flowers in loose racemes, blooming March through May. Sandy soil in piney woods, open mixed forests, and fields from east to central Texas and the coastal scrub forests, also east to Florida and north to Oklahoma. Fruit is eaten by a number of birds. Some ornamental selections have been developed.

***Vaccinium arkansanum* (Highbush Blueberry)**

Large multi-trunked shrub 6½–13 feet tall with deep green leaves, greenish white flowers, and dull black, edible fruit. Infrequently found in bogs or open flat woods in east Texas, also east to Florida and north to Arkansas. Easily transplants and will readily sucker from a stump. Fruit eaten by many bird species and other wildlife. Also has potential for selection as a commercially grown fruit plant.

Vaccinium virgatum **(Rabbit-eye Blueberry)**
Small shrub, forming thick colonies. Deciduous leaves and pink-tinged flowers. The shiny black fruit is not edible. Along streams and open forests or in boggy areas from east Texas to Florida, north to Arkansas. Good for erosion control along stream banks or marshy areas.

Vauquelinia angustifolia

Chisos Rosewood, Palo Prieto

ROSEACEAE (ROSE FAMILY)

GENERAL DESCRIPTION

Chisos Rosewood is a small evergreen tree to 20 feet with twisted branches and long, narrow, sharply toothed leaves. The shiny dark green leaves make a nice contrast to the deep, chestnut brown, fissured bark of older branches.

FLOWERS AND FRUIT

Showy white fragrant flowers appear in dense clusters from late spring to early summer. Fruit is a five-celled, densely fuzzy, woody capsule.

NATURAL HABITAT, RANGE, AND PREFERRED SITE

Chisos Rosewood is native to rocky slopes and canyons at 3,800–6,500 feet in the Chisos Mountains of the Trans-Pecos, and in mountains in northern Mexico. It must be planted on a well-drained site in full sun, and is not tolerant of alkaline soils. Chisos Rosewood does best at high elevations in the desert, where summer nights are not hot and humid.

COLLECTION AND STORAGE

Gather capsules from September through November as they begin to dry and turn brownish yellow. Seeds can be stored in the capsule, or the capsule can be dried and crushed and the seeds separated. Store seeds in sealed containers in the refrigerator. Seed stored for several years still germinated at reasonable rates (Manning, personal communication, 1999).

PROPAGATION

Seeds

Chisos Rosewood will germinate from fresh seeds planted in the fall as soon as they are gathered. Seeds planted immediately after collection require no pretreatment. Sow the seeds in a greenhouse or cold frame and keep the seedlings protected over winter. Remove seedlings the next spring and transplant into separate containers using a well-drained mineral soil mix.

Give young plants filtered but direct sunlight the first season. Seedlings are very slow growing at first, taking up to 2 years to make a salable one-gallon plant. They do not like to stay wet in the pot, and can be very susceptible to spider mites. Once they are planted in the landscape, supplemental irrigation for the first two seasons will speed growth.

One grower observed that plants growing in a landscape situation for 2½ years grew nearly 10 times their original size (Manning, personal communication, 1999). After the plant is established, watering can be limited to one or two deep soakings a month during the summer (Mielke 1993).

Cuttings

Chisos Rosewood will root from softwood or semihardwood cuttings taken in mid- to late summer, treated with IBA, and kept under intermittent mist (Simpson, personal communication, 1986). Fall-rooted cuttings require cold-frame protection over winter.

NOTES

Chisos Rosewood is among the showiest plants of the Trans-Pecos. The dense evergreen leaves, rich brown bark, clusters of showy, fragrant, rose-like flowers, and attractive fuzzy white fruit are some of this plant's many attributes. Chisos Rosewood is very drought tolerant and would make an attractive ornamental screen. Do not shear this plant. Prune only to remove dead wood. When grown outside its own natural range, at lower elevations with higher temperatures and relative humidity, Chisos Rosewood often becomes disease prone, suffering especially from rose leaf spot (Simpson, personal communication, 1986). In Mexico, the wood and bark have been used to dye skins.

Viburnum

Viburnum, Arrow-wood

CAPRIFOLIACEAE (HONEYSUCKLE FAMILY)

GENERAL DESCRIPTION

Viburnums are shrubs or small trees with deciduous and often glossy leaves (see Species Descriptions).

FLOWERS AND FRUIT

Flowers are usually showy, white or rarely pink, borne in dense clusters in early spring to summer. Fruit is a blue-black drupe containing a single hard stone.

NATURAL HABITAT, RANGE, AND PREFERRED SITE

Most viburnums are found in moist, well-drained soil on the edge of woods in the eastern third of the state. See Species Descriptions for individual range and habitat. Viburnums are shade tolerant and are somewhat adaptable to different soil types as long as there is moisture.

COLLECTION AND STORAGE

Collect the fruit in late summer as soon as it is filled out and has turned a dark bluish black color. The fruit may be air dried with the pulp still on the seed or cleaned and then stored. Cleaning and drying the seed apparently induces dormancy in some species. Viburnum seeds can be stored for at least 10 years if properly dried and sealed in a moisture-proof container at 30–34° F (Dirr and Heuser 1987).

PROPAGATION

Seeds

Many *Viburnum* species are difficult to germinate because seeds have both a cold dormancy requirement and an undeveloped embryo (see Species Descriptions for individual guidelines). In some species these two conditions are combined with an impermeable seed coat. Often natural germination does not occur until the second or sometimes third spring following fruit production. This delay in germination causes long lapses in production of many viburnums in the nursery. The dormancy of the southern ecotypes is more easily broken than that of the northern forms.

Sow viburnum seed outdoors in well-worked beds or containers as soon as they are collected. The warm temperatures of fall will provide the conditions necessary to complete after-ripening and initiate root emergence. The cold temperatures of the following winter will break epicotyl or shoot dormancy. Tests on separate species and seed lots are necessary to determine whether scarification in addition to these other treatments will further improve germination.

Seed planted right after being cleaned from freshly harvested fruit will often germinate at rates greater than 25%. If allowed to dry or if put in storage, germination rates for Rusty Black-haw Viburnum (*V. dentatum*) drop sharply as internal inhibitors kick in (Kirwin, personal communication, 1999).

For container production, viburnums have a higher survival rate if the soil mix is inoculated with beneficial microorganisms (see Chapter IV). The inoculation promotes greater root development and reduces losses as plants are moved up to larger containers (Kirwin, personal communication, 1999).

For field plantings, sow seeds in rows 8–12 inches apart and cover with ½ inch of soil. Lightly mulch seedbeds until seedlings emerge. Screening may be necessary to protect the beds from birds and rodents. Provide shade the first growing season.

Cuttings

Rusty Black-haw Viburnum (*V. rufidulum*) can be propagated from semi-hardwood cuttings taken in late spring to early summer right after flowering when the first flush of growth is just beginning to harden off.

For one grower, rooting occurred at high levels using the "double-dip" method. Cuttings were first dipped in 1,250 ppm IBA followed immediately by 3,000 ppm IBA talc. The liquid IBA promoted the formation of root initials that were then encouraged to develop by the slower reacting talc. Using higher rates of liquid IBA on slow-rooting cuttings can sometimes inhibit rooting as the radicle has a harder time breaking through the callus formed on the end of the stem. Root formation was improved if the rooting bed contained fine light soil mix instead of coarse perlite (Pfeiffer, personal communication, 1999).

Another technique suggests taking the cuttings with three to five nodes from the end with the leaves stripped from the lower half. Dip these in

3,000 ppm IBA plus 500 ppm NAA solution. Stick each cutting into individual plant cells or "Pro-trays" (Hosage, personal communication, 1999).

Some success has also been achieved by taking a heel with the cutting. Remove the buds from the lower halves of the cuttings. Treat with 3,000–8,000 ppm IBA solution and place in a very well drained rooting bed (e.g., peat/vermiculite mixed 1:2). The cuttings are relatively slow to root and the roots are brittle. The less the cutting is handled, the better.

At another nursery, Rusty Black-haw Viburnum cuttings taken in May and treated as above rooted at an average rate of 70–80%. Bottom heat and regular fertilizing help insure survival of cuttings (McNeal, personal communication, 1999). Rooted cuttings make take as long as 1 year to become a finished one-gallon plant. Rusty Black-haw Viburnums grown from cuttings tend to remain shrubby instead of developing a treelike form at maturity. Eventually these new plants will reach a maximum size of 12 feet (McNeal, personal communication, 1999).

Arrow-wood Viburnum was successfully rooted from semihardwood cuttings taken in summer and treated with 1,500–2,500 ppm IBA "quick dip." Rooted cuttings finished a one-gallon container within 8 months (Bronstad, personal communication, 1999). Another method recommends treating semihardwood cuttings taken in early summer, with 8,000 IBA talc plus thiram. These rooted 100% (Dirr and Heuser 1987).

Rooting for many *Viburnum spp.* is slow, averaging 20–38 days for some species (Doran 1957). Because native viburnums produce roots so slowly, the real difficulties in vegetative propagation of this species are getting the rooted cuttings to survive and initiate new growth. These difficulties can be overcome through a program of careful watering, shading, overwintering in a cold frame, and fertilizing.

NOTES

Members of this genus have been widely cultivated for their attractive foliage and showy flowers and fruit. Viburnums provide excellent habitat for wildlife, and the persistent fruits are an important source of food. Many of our native viburnums have been overlooked as outstanding specimen plants. Typically the larger specimens of Rusty Black-haw Viburnum (*V. rufidulum*) one sees in the landscape trade have been field dug from an ever-dwindling native population.

SPECIES DESCRIPTIONS

Viburnum acerifolium (Maple-leaf Viburnum)

Shrub to 8 feet with thin, deciduous, dark green leaves and white flowers in 1–2 inch cymes. Forests of east Texas to Florida, north to Canada. In cultivation since 1736. Seed requires a warm stratification period of 6–17 months followed by 2–4 months cold stratification at 34–41° F. Some growers collect the seed early in the fall and plant immediately. Leave cuttings in rooting bed and transplant after new growth begins in the following spring.

Viburnum dentatum **(Southern Arrow-wood)**
Shrub or occasionally a small tree to 24 feet with ovate deciduous leaves and small white flowers. Woods and thickets from east Texas to Florida and north to New England. Will adapt to different soil types. See *V. acerifolium* for guidelines on germination requirements. Arrow-wood can be propagated from softwood cuttings. Softwood cuttings root in high rates and are easily transplanted. Treat with 1,000 ppm IBA plus 500 ppm NAA solution or 8,000 ppm IBA talc, stick in peat/perlite, and keep under mist. Hardwood cuttings from flowering plants are not recommended. Dormant hardwood cuttings have been used by some nurseries (Dirr and Heuser 1987).

Viburnum nudum **(Possum-haw Viburnum)**
Spreading or erect shrub to 16 feet with long, lustrous leaves. Along streams in moist forests or bogs in piney woods of east Texas, Florida, north to New England. Prefers wet, mucky soil. Fruit is eaten by a number of birds.

Viburnum rufidulum **(Rusty Black-haw Viburnum)**
Showy tall shrub or small tree with glossy dark green, oval leaves. White flowers in showy clusters followed by hanging clusters of blue-black fruit. Edges of woods or streams from east to central Texas, also east to Florida and north to Illinois. Seldom on dry upland sites. Rusty Black-haw Viburnum will grow on heavy clay, but is susceptible to the Texas cotton root rot. Warm stratify the seed for 4 months followed by cold stratification for 3 months. Some seeds will come up right away, while others will take a year and a half to germinate. Every year yields different germination percentages.

Seedlings do not like to be kept too wet. For best results, keep in 4-inch containers for the first season, then move into one-gallons. After 8 months, pot up into four-gallon containers. Seedlings respond to applications of calcium nitrate. This fertilizer helps produce a flush of growth in late summer. Success is also achieved by raising the second-year seedlings in root control bags planted in the field (Bronstad, personal communication, 1999).

Viguiera stenoloba

Skelton-leaf Goldeneye Daisy, Resin-bush

ASTERACEAE (SUNFLOWER FAMILY)

GENERAL DESCRIPTION

Skelton-leaf Goldeneye Daisy is a dense, rounded, shrubby evergreen plant growing 4 feet by 4 feet. The narrow, dark green leaves are closely attached to the slender stem.

FLOWERS AND FRUIT

Brilliant yellow-orange flowers held singly on the ends of slender leafless stalks give the entire shrub a bouquet appearance. Flowers bloom intermittently throughout the summer, but most heavily in the fall. Fruit is an achene.

NATURAL HABITAT, RANGE, AND PREFERRED SITE

Skelton-leaf Goldeneye Daisy is native to rocky dry ground from the western part of the Edwards Plateau to the Trans-Pecos and New Mexico. It will adapt to most well-drained sites in full sun.

COLLECTION AND STORAGE

Gather the achenes as they turn brown and begin to shatter. Spread in thin layers to air dry a few days before storing in sealed containers in the refrigerator.

PROPAGATION

Seeds

Seed propagation of Skelton-leaf Goldeneye Daisy is most often used in wildflower gardens or roadside plantings. Gather large amounts of seeds and spread them on screens or tables to air dry. Dried seeds may be broken apart by gently beating them in a bag. Broadcast sow, or scatter the seeds in an open area that has been lightly raked, then water in well. Sowing in late fall or winter is recommended.

Cuttings

Skelton-leaf Goldeneye Daisy will root from softwood tip cuttings taken after the first flush of growth from April to June, and again in late August to October when the second growth begins. The timing of taking cuttings is critical because the wood of Skelton-leaf Goldeneye Daisy hardens quickly and older, woodier cuttings are more difficult to root. Cuttings should be 2–3 inches long, treated with 5,000 ppm IBA/NAA solution, and kept under intermittent mist. Cuttings are typically slow to root, and rooting rates are often less than 50% (McNeal, personal communication, 1999).

As the cutting begins to callus and form roots, gradually reduce the frequency of misting to minimize stem rot. Once a cutting develops roots, the plant will speed up growth. The best cutting material is usually obtained from nursery-grown or cultivated plants that have been forced to flush more new growth. In its native dry habitat, Skelton-leaf Goldeneye Daisy has moderate growth and does not produce the new succulent shoots that are best for rooting.

Rooting in separate small pots is recommended. Give cuttings partial shade for 2–3 weeks after removing from the mist house to help them harden off (Kirwin, personal communication, 1999).

A small one-gallon plant can be produced in 6 months (Bering, personal communication, 1999). New plants tend to look straggly, but within a year to a year and a half, it is possible to produce a robust and well-formed five-gallon plant. Put the plants in full sun with well-drained soil. Spider mites can sometimes be a problem on nursery stock. This could be a response to too-rich soil medium and overwatering (Kirwin, personal communication, 1999).

Do not crowd the containers as the plants are gaining size; the best looking plants are those that have plenty of air circulation and that have received periodic careful shearing. Skelton-leaf Goldeneye Daisy will respond to tip pruning by filling out to make a bushier plant, but be sure to cut back on frequency of irrigation right after shearing to avoid rotting.

Transplanting

Skelton-leaf Goldeneye Daisy is easily transplanted from its natural habitat in winter if cut back severely and kept watered.

NOTES

Skelton-leaf Goldeneye Daisy is an excellent mounding, flowering evergreen shrub for a perennial garden or border plant. Its prolific brilliant orange-yellow flowers and persistent dark leaves make it attractive year round. Some good companion plants include Agarita (*Berberis trifoliolata*), Goldenball Lead-tree (*Leucaena retusa*), Prickly Pear Cactus (*Opuntia spp.*), and Black Dalea (*Dalea frutescens*). To encourage a bushy compact habit, cut back the plant periodically. It is extremely drought tolerant and will thrive on the rockiest hillsides. The aromatic oils in the leaves discourage browsing by deer. Skelton-leaf Goldeneye Daisy is also an important larval plant for some butterflies.

Vitis

Grape, Uva

VITACEAE (GRAPE FAMILY)

GENERAL DESCRIPTION

Grapes are the familiar deciduous vines with woody trunks that climb by means of tendrils. Leaves are usually rounded or heart shaped, entire or with lobes. Some have fuzzy silver undersides.

FLOWERS AND FRUIT

Fragrant flowers are held in a cluster opposite a leaf, blooming in the spring to early summer. Fruit a two- to four-seeded berry.

NATURAL HABITAT, RANGE, AND PREFERRED SITE

Grapes are found throughout the state, most commonly along stream bottoms, thickets, fencerows, edges of woods, and sandy slopes, especially in disturbed ground.

COLLECTION AND STORAGE

Strip the fruits from the vines in summer through early fall, depending on species. Ripeness is indicated by a deep lustrous blue-black color and pulpy filled-out texture. Clean the seeds before storing at 41° F in sealed containers. Properly stored seeds may remain viable for up to 26 months (USDA 1974).

PROPAGATION

Seeds

Grape seeds have an embryo dormancy that can be broken by either fall sowing outdoors or by stratification at 33–40° F for about 12 weeks. Seeds planted outdoors in the fall will emerge in March. The seedbed should contain rich, loamy, but well-drained soil.

Cuttings

Grapes are most often propagated from cuttings in order to select outstanding clones for fruit preference, vigor, and disease tolerance. Most commercial propagation is achieved from dormant hardwood cuttings. Some types of grapes, such as the Muscadine (*V. rotundifolia*), are difficult to propagate and will root only from leafy softwood cuttings under mist.

To propagate grapes from hardwood cuttings, select wood from the middle and basal parts of the current season's shoots on vigorous mature vines. In Texas, dormant cuttings may be taken from December until the buds begin to swell in February. The cuttings should have about the same diameter as a pencil and a length of 12–16 inches. Application of IBA does not appear to significantly improve rooting on dormant cuttings. Rooted cuttings held in containers for 1 year are usually large enough to transplant to the field.

Softwood or leafy cuttings from vigorous stock plants 4–6 inches long taken in June readily root under mist in about 10 days if given high bottom heat (80–85° F) and treated with IBA (Hartmann and Kester 1975). Grape cultivars are often bench grafted onto hardy, disease resistant, native rootstocks. Scions are grafted on either rooted or unrooted disbudded rootstock cuttings by whip grafting or machine grafting on dormant wood in the winter.

NOTES

The Texas pioneer horticulturist Thomas Volney Munson once saved the French wine industry with native Texas grapes. In addition to many other selecting and breeding programs, Munson was interested in classifying and improving the American grape. He produced some 300 new varieties of grapes. Munson was the second American to receive the French Legion of Honor, which was awarded to him for saving the French vineyards from total destruction by the grape phylloxera disease. From extensive study and breeding of native American grapes, he was able to supply the French vineyards with a resistant rootstock. For more information, contact the Munson Vine Museum, Grayson County College, 5101 Grayson Drive, Denison, Texas 75020.

More recently, Texas Tech and Texas A&M universities, as well as private commercial owners, have developed vineyards in the High Plains, the Davis and Chisos mountains, and the Llano Uplift. It may be that our native grapes have unexplored potential as hardy, drought-tolerant rootstocks suitable for varietal grafting. Grapes not suitable for fruit production have value as hardy vines for arbors, trellises, and as ground covers.

For more information, visit the Texas A&M web site: http://aggie-horticulture.tamu.edu.

SPECIES DESCRIPTIONS

Vitis acerifolia **(Panhandle Grape)**
Low bush vine of the Panhandle and Rolling Plains and the Sierra Tierra Vieja.

Vitis aestivalis **(Pigeon Grape)**
High-climbing vine found in the eastern third of the state. This species has two varieties, *aestivalis* and *lincecumii*.

Vitis arizonica **(Canyon Grape)**
Shrubby, low-climbing vine native to the canyons of the Trans-Pecos and Arizona. Fruits August to October.

Vitis berlandiera **(Spanish Grape)**
Stocky, high-climbing vine of the Edwards Plateau. Fruits August to October.

Vitis cinerea **(Sweet Grape)**
Vigorous, high-climbing vine native to river bottoms in north, central, and east Texas, also east to Florida and north to Illinois.

Vitis cordifolia **(Frost Grape)**
High-climbing vine of north-central Texas, also Oklahoma and east to Florida. Grapes generally need frost to be edible. Susceptible to mildew and root rot.

Vitis monticola **(Sweet Mountain Grape)**
High-climbing vine found only on the Edwards Plateau.

Vitis mustangensis **(Mustang Grape)**
Common, high-climbing, vigorous vine with broad leaves having densely fuzzy undersides. Along streams and forests in the eastern half of Texas; also Oklahoma, Louisiana, and Arkansas.

Vitis palmata **(Missouri Grape, Catbird Grape)**
Slender, high-climbing vine with tender branchlets and flowering shoots. Near ponds, sloughs, or low woods from Louisiana to east Texas, north to Illinois. Prefers a wet site.

Vitis riparia **(Riverbank Grape)**
High-climbing vine of north-central Texas and the Trans-Pecos, also New Mexico, north to Canada.

Vitis rotundifolia **(Muscadine Grape, Scuppernog)**
Vigorous very high climber with relatively small, unlobed leaf blades. Mainly in east and southeast Texas, occasionally as far west as Hopkins and Lamar counties in north-central Texas.

Vitis vulpina **(Fox Grape)**
Vigorous, high-climbing vine with a stout trunk, fruiting October and November. Edge of woods and fields and along roadsides in the eastern third of Texas to Florida, north to New Jersey. Fruit edible after frost.

Yucca

Yucca, Spanish-Bayonet

LILIACEAE (LILY FAMILY)

GENERAL DESCRIPTION

Yuccas are an easily recognized group of plants with simple or branching trunks covered in stiff or corky bark, or sometimes by a persistent thatch of older dried leaves. Dark green narrow leaves are usually spine-tipped, and vary among species from being stiff and large to thin and flexible. Texas has about 20 species of yuccas, some being very large and treelike, others small and without large stems or trunks. Parent plants often develop offshoots that create dramatic groupings of this plant.

FLOWERS AND FRUIT

Large, waxy, bell-shaped flowers hang in usually numerous clusters and vary in color from creamy white to greenish white. Yuccas flower mostly in spring (April/May) or early summer (June/July). Fruit is a dry or fleshy capsule containing many flat, dark seeds.

NATURAL HABITAT, RANGE, AND PREFERRED SITE

Yuccas are native to both arid and humid regions in east and west Texas, and throughout the Southwest. Although many yuccas require a sunny and dry location with light sandy or gritty well-drained soils, some species grow as understory plants or in heavier soils.

COLLECTION AND STORAGE

Yuccas are prolific seed producers and the seeds can be collected during the summer and into the fall when the woody capsule dries and begins to split open to reveal the compartments full of flat, black, disklike seeds. For overwinter storage, keep the seeds in moist sand in the refrigerator. For longer periods of time, put the seeds in sealed containers held at low temperatures.

PROPAGATION

Seeds

Yuccas are easy to grow from fresh seeds. Plant seed shallowly in flats or 4-inch pots containing well-drained soil in the fall following collection in a greenhouse, or in early spring the following year. Seeds will germinate within 2 weeks, with some of the plants continuing to emerge even a few months later. Young plants will remain in a grasslike state for a full season; salable one-gallon plant can be produced in 1½ years (McNeal, personal communication, 1999).

Cuttings

Yuccas may also be grown from rhizomes, stem cuttings, or by digging offsets from the side of an established plant.

Transplanting

Most Yuccas are easy to transplant because new fibrous roots will regenerate quickly from the smooth, rounded knob at the base of the stem (Simpson 1988). Exceptions to this are noted in the Species Descriptions. Yuccas are generally very hardy and free of pests, but if overwatered or handled too roughly during transplanting, become susceptible to snout weevils, which bore into the trunks. Plants will also develop root rot if overwatered.

Another symptom of overwatering of yuccas in the nursery is brown leaf spotting. Let the plant dry out completely between waterings to avoid mottled leaves.

NOTES

The yuccas were an important source of food for Native Americans in the Southwest (Powell 1988). Roots and stems were used as a soap and as a laxative. The leaves of some species have loose, peeling margins that produce a fiber that was used to make cloth, ropes, baskets, and sandals. Flower buds and young flower stalks were eaten both cooked and raw, as were seeds. Seeds and flowers were also ground into a meal. Each yucca species depends on its own special night-flying moth (Tegeticula = Pronuba) for pollination (Powell 1988).

The potential of yuccas for use as specimen trees or distinctive spiky shrubs in the landscape has often been limited to desert or cactus gardens. These dramatic and hardy plants should be used more often to provide both vertical elements as well as unique textures in a shrub planting. Some of the eastern species, such as Twisted-leaf Yucca (*Y. rupicola*), Pale-leaf Yucca (*Y. pallida*), and Arkansas Yucca (*Y. arkansana*), add wonderful texture to the shade garden, though they may bloom less than their counterparts growing in full sun. The larger, treelike yuccas with the potential to form multi-trunks should be carefully situated in the landscape where their powerful form can frame the garden and be truly appreciated. Often people dislike yuccas and regard them as hostile thorny "cactus" because they have outgrown a confined space and their pointed leaves have become a hazard to pedestrians.

The dead, shaggy leaves that cover the trunks on some species can give the plant a shabby appearance, but they do have a purpose. They insulate and protect the trunk and absorb moisture during hard desert rainstorms. When pruned or "tidied up," the trunks of yucca can look like scrawny, corky chicken necks to some, or like palms if you like this look. Clustering large desert shrubs with compatible water needs, such as Creosote Bush (*Larrea tridentata*), Little-leaf Sumac (*Rhus microphylla*), Apache Plume (*Fallugia paradoxa*), and Cenizo (*Leucophyllum frutescens*) can screen the dead foliage. Insecticidal soaps will control aphids, which sometimes infest the flower stalks. A light application of horticultural oil is effective on scale insects (Phillips 1995b). Deer are fond of browsing the flowers of the lower growing yuccas.

SPECIES DESCRIPTIONS

Yucca angustifolia (Narrow-leaf Yucca)

Usually a stemless plant with leaves 2–3 feet long and flower stalks 2–6 feet high. Frequently seen in the Panhandle south to the Edwards Plateau, they also extend to New Mexico, Arizona, and Utah. Narrow-leaf Yuccas will grow in a variety of soils as long as they are well-drained. This yucca is adapted to sunny, well-drained sites as far east as Dallas (Wasowski 1988).

Yucca arkansana (Arkansas Yucca)

One of the smaller yuccas (1–2 feet) with an unbranched flower stalk 3–4 feet high. Leaves are pale green, curved lengthwise, and sometimes twisted. Although spine-tipped like most yuccas, the leaves of Arkansas Yucca are soft and pliable, with shredding white hairs on the edges. It is native to the eastern half of Texas, north to Oklahoma and Arkansas. Arkansas Yucca will grow fast in sandy soils, quickly forming a clump 18 inches high and 2 feet across. On limestone soils it grows more slowly. It will grow in shade as an evergreen understory plant (Wasowski 1988).

Yucca baccata (Datil Yucca, Banana Yucca)

Banana Yucca is typically a stemless plant, occasionally reaching 4 feet high and about 6 feet wide, with the sword-shaped leaves clumped at ground level. The leaves can vary in appearance from curved to straight, bluish to yellowish-green. This yucca's name is derived from the solid green fruits with succulent fruit, which look like short green bananas about 5 inches long and 2 inches in diameter. The capsules of most yuccas are dry and split when ripe. Banana Yucca fruits never split; instead, the seeds are dispersed by small mammals as they eat the fruits. The flowers are borne in large heavy clusters up to 2 feet tall, held in the rosette of leaves between April and June. Flowering is very demanding of the sugar reserves of this plant. Many plants must recuperate a few years before blooming again (Bowers 1993). Banana Yucca is the common yucca found along the Rocky Mountain foothills entering into Texas in the Trans-Pecos and perhaps into the western Edwards Plateau, also west to California and north to southern Utah.

***Yucca constricta* (Buckley Yucca)**
Usually without a trunk, occurring singly or in clumps. Flowers held high above the symmetrical cluster of long, narrow leaves in graceful uncrowded panicles. Buckley Yucca is found in Texas from the eastern edge of the Edwards Plateau southwest to the Gulf of Mexico, west and south in the Rio Grande Plains (Vines 1970). It has a taproot, and even small plants are hard to transplant.

***Yucca elata* (Soaptree Yucca, Palmilla)**
A prominently trunked yucca with a slender leaf crown. Soaptree Yucca grows slowly up to 20 or 30 feet, but is usually smaller. Some authors believe Soaptree Yucca can live as long as 250–300 years. Leaf margins are edged with white filaments. As a young plant, Soaptree Yucca looks like a clump of coarse blue-green grass. As it matures, the bottom leaves die and bend down, covering the trunk while new leaves are borne in symmetrical heads from a central crown. Flower stalks are 3–7 feet long. Soaptree Yucca grows in both limestone and igneous soils throughout most of the Trans-Pecos. It is found most often on mesas and grasslands at altitudes of 4,000–4,500 feet. A taproot makes this species difficult to transplant. It is hardy to −20° F, as well as tolerating hot summer temperatures. The inner bark of the roots and trunk was used as a substitute for soap, giving the plant its common name.

***Yucca faxoniana* (or *Yucca carnerosana* [Carneros Yucca], Giant Dagger, Palma, Spanish Dagger, Palmilla, Palma Barreta, Palma Samandoca)**
Spanish Daggers are the largest yuccas of the Trans-Pecos, in some areas reaching more than 25 feet tall with a trunk 1½ feet in diameter. This plant

flowers only once every 3–4 years and produces flower clusters weighing up to 70 pounds. Spanish Dagger is found in scattered locations in high desert plateaus, rimrock areas, and mountain slopes in both limestone and igneous soils, at altitudes of 2,700–6,700 feet in Texas and northern Mexico. Spanish Daggers have been widely transplanted as ornamental specimen trees. They are slow growing.

Yucca pallida **(Pale-leaf Yucca)**
Pale-leaf Yucca is a clump-forming yucca without a trunk. Its distinctive characteristics are the erect, short, flat, sage-green leaves. It is mostly found growing in the limestone cedar brakes of North Texas (Ogden 1998). Pale-leaf Yucca is used in mass plantings as a shrub border, or to add texture to the landscape.

Yucca rostrata **(or** ***Y. thompsoniana*** **[Thompson Yucca],Beaked Yucca, Big Bend Yucca, Palmita, Soyate)**
Botanists have recently grouped Beaked Yucca with *Y. thompsoniana*. However, gardeners may still find it useful to segregate the two forms for horticultural purposes (Ogden, personal communication, 1999). *Y. rostrata* is recognized as typically having a single trunk about 6–12 feet high with a diameter of 5–8 inches or sometimes developing a few short branches toward the top. Beaked Yucca's leaves are unarmed or without sharp edges. *Y. rostrata* is also recognized by its conspicuously beaked fruits. Beaked Yucca is common in canyons and mountain slopes, mostly in the Black Gap Refuge in Brewster County in the Trans-Pecos. *Yucca thompsoniana* is more heavily branched and generally shorter than *Y. rostrata*, with leaves armed on the edges with sharp, small teeth. Thompson Yucca has been one of the most frequently dug yuccas in the west, where it grows abundantly in the mesa country from Fort Stockton to Big Bend National Park (Warnock 1970).

Yucca rupicola **(Twisted-leaf Yucca)**
A low-growing yucca without a visible stem, appearing as single or clustered heads of twisted, arching blue-green leaves 8–24 inches long. Flowers held on stalks as long as 9 feet, blooming in May. Twisted-leaf Yucca is native to rocky limestone hills or woodlands in the Edwards Plateau. It will grow in full sun (where it blooms best), or as an understory plant. It is very difficult to transplant from the wild, but is sold as a container plant by several nurseries. Twisted-leaf Yucca is very effective on difficult-to-landscape sites such as rocky slopes or escarpments, in shallow soils in groupings with Bear Grass (*Nolina spp.*), Cedar Sage (*Salvia roemeriana*),

Turk's Cap (*Malvaviscus arboreus var. Drummondii*), and Fragrant Mist Flower (*Eupatorium havanense*).

Yucca treculeana (or _Yucca torreyi_ [Torrey Yucca], Old Shag, Spanish Bayonet, Spanish Dagger, Palma)

Torrey Yucca can grow to 25 feet, but is usually much shorter. The western subspecies (formerly *Y. torreyi*) or form of Torrey Yucca grows on caliche ridges in the Trans-Pecos west of Junction and Bracketville. The southern subspecies (formerly *Y. treculeana*) is more common in the Edwards Plateau, north to Lampasas, west almost to Junction, south to Eagle Pass and the Rio Grande Valley, and along the Gulf Coast in a solid population as far as Rockport, and then scattered in smaller, more isolated locations southeast to Victoria. This form is more common in cultivation because it has perfectly symmetrical radiating leaves arranged around the trunk and is more striking in its overall appearance (Ogden, personal communication, 1999).

Zanthoxylum fagara

Lime Prickly-ash, Colima

RUTACEAE (CITRUS FAMILY)

GENERAL DESCRIPTION

Colima is an intricately branched evergreen shrub 5–20 feet tall. The trunk and stems are armed with small recurved thorns. The bright green oblong leaves are compound and dotted with aromatic glands that are bitter to taste.

FLOWERS AND FRUIT

Small yellowish green flowers are produced from March to June and are followed by a bright red smooth and shiny fruit containing one seed. Fruit ripens from mid- to late summer and is very showy in contrast with the fresh green leaflets.

NATURAL HABITAT, RANGE, AND PREFERRED SITE

Colima is common throughout south Texas and is often associated with Honey Mesquite (*Prosopis glandulosa*), Prickly Pear Cactus (*Opuntia*), and Berlander Wolfberry (*Lycium berlandieri*).

COLLECTION AND STORAGE

Gather the fruit throughout the summer after it has turned brown and the seed is black and filled out. Spread out to dry a few days and then separate the seeds by gentle flailing. Seeds will remain viable for 6 months to 1 year if stored in sealed containers at 41° F (Best 1999).

PROPAGATION

Seeds

Germination of Colima seeds is delayed by an immature seed embryo that requires a period of after-ripening before it is ready to germinate. Exact length of warm stratification is not known. However, it does not require scarification. Aerate cleaned seed until imbibition occurs and then sow the seeds in flats or containers in a well-drained soil mix. Sow sparingly and cover lightly with soil (Best 1999). Transplant from the flat when seedlings are 2 inches. Colima has a moderate growth rate.

NOTES

Colima has great unrecognized potential as an ornamental landscape shrub for hot dry locations in south Texas. It could be used as a specimen plant or grouped together to form a dense hedge. It is cold hardy as far north as San Antonio. The small, shiny, oval leaflets appear fresh even in dry conditions. The plant is frequently loaded with bright red fruit.

Even more importantly, Colima is a valuable wildlife plant. White-tailed deer browse on the foliage and young stems. Most birds, including white-winged doves, relish the seeds and many songbirds nest in the larger shrubs. Small animals and reptiles use Colima in association with other species for protective cover. It is a food plant for butterfly larvae and a source of nectar for adult butterflies (R. B. Taylor, Rutledge, and Herrera 1997). The bark and leaves are powdered and used as a condiment. The wood produces a yellow dye.

Zexmenia hispidia

Zexmenia Daisy

ASTERACEAE (SUNFLOWER FAMILY)

GENERAL DESCRIPTION

Zexmenia Daisy is a small, rounded, bouquet-like shrub up to 3 feet tall with an equal spread. It has a woody base and herbaceous upper stems. In mild winters the leaves are persistent, but typically the plant freezes back to the woody base and produces new stems and flowers in late spring.

FLOWERS AND FRUIT

Zexmenia Daisy produces many attractive marigold-colored flowers throughout the summer and fall. These are held on the tips of slender, leafless branches. Fruit is an achene.

NATURAL HABITAT, RANGE, AND PREFERRED SITE

Zexmenia Daisy is common on hillsides and flats in the Edwards Plateau, Rio Grande Plains, and also in the Trans-Pecos and the southern part of southeast and north-central Texas. It prefers full sun but will also grow in dappled light, at the edge of woods.

COLLECTION AND STORAGE

Gather the dry flower heads in late summer before they shatter. Spread to dry and break apart by lightly beating in a bag. Store over winter in sealed containers or paper bags in a cool dry place.

PROPAGATION

Seeds

Seed propagation of Zexmenia Daisy is usually done for wildflower gardens and roadside plantings. Broadcast large amounts of freshly gathered or recently stored seeds over an open area in the fall or early spring.

Cuttings

Zexmenia Daisy will easily root from semihardwood tip cuttings of the current season's growth taken in mid-summer through fall. Treat with 1,000 ppm IBA. Take cuttings 3–4 inches long, firm toward the base, but not brittle. Remove the leaves from the lower half of the cutting and place in a small container or flat filled with a peat/perlite mixture. Make sure the rooting bed is well drained by adding more perlite if necessary. Keep moist or under intermittent mist until rooting begins and then remove immediately to avoid stem rot.

Fall-rooted cuttings will need to be protected in a cold frame or greenhouse. A finished one-gallon plant can be produced in one season, and a cutting rooted in August will make a full five-gallon plant the following summer (McNeal, personal communication, 1999).

Transplanting

Zexmenia Daisy may be transplanted in the winter if cut back to the ground and given occasional moisture.

NOTES

Zexmenia Daisy makes a good addition to a perennial flower garden. It will also serve as a mounding ground cover for poor, rocky sites. Shear the plant regularly and remove spent flowers to control its sometimes sprawling growth habit and to encourage more blooms. If planted in shade, it may become weak and leggy. Do not fertilize this plant once it is transplanted outdoors. Zexmenia Daisy freely reseeds in the garden, and new seedlings can be transplanted or shared with neighbors.

Glossary

Acaulescent: Without a stem or nearly so.

Achene: A small, dry, indehiscent, one-seeded pericarp or fruit.

Acid soil: Soil having a pH below 7.0. Peat and soil with high organic content are usually within the acidic range.

Actinomycete: An organism classified as bacteria or fungi. Some are pathogenic, others are symbiotically associated with plants.

Acuminate: Leaves having a relatively broad body and narrowed to a gently tapering end.

Acute: Sharp pointed.

Adventitious root: A root that is neither primary nor secondary nor arising therefrom. A new growing point on a vegetative structure such as a root, stem, or leaf.

After-ripening: An enzymatic process involved in the maturation of seeds, bulbs, and tubers, which is often necessary for germination or resumption of growth.

Air pruning: The exposure of roots to air through holes in a container, which "burns off" the main root and encourages the formation of secondary feeder roots within the container.

Alkaline soil: Soil having a pH above 7.0. Of, pertaining to, or having the properties of alkali (a soluble mineral salt present in some soils of arid regions).

Alluvial soil: The sedimentary sand, mud, or other soil deposited in the valleys of rivers and streams.

Alternate: Any arrangement of leaves or flowers along the axis singly at different heights (not opposite or whorled).

Ament: A bracted pendulous spike (see catkin). As in birches, alders, cottonwoods, and oaks.

Apetalous: Without petals.

Apex: The growing tip or top growing shoot of a plant.

Aril: The exterior covering or appendage of certain seeds that develops after fertilization as an outgrowth from the point of attachment of the ovule, as in Strawberry Bush (*Euonymus americanus*).

Auxin: A hormonal growth regulator that influences root initiation in cuttings. Auxins are also involved in stem growth, lateral bud inhibition, abscission of leaves and fruits, and activation of cambial cells. Indole-3-acetic acid (IAA), indolebutyric acid (IBA), and naphthaleneacetic acid (NAA) are all auxins. Auxins occur naturally in the plant and are also manufactured commercially as chemical concentrates for vegetative propagation.

Axil: The angle formed by a leaf or branch with the stem.

Axillary: Growing out of an axil, usually refers to a leaf or flower.

Ball and burlap: A transplanting procedure whereby the plant is carefully removed with a ball of soil adhering to the roots. Burlap is wrapped around the ball and secured with heavy twine, which preserves the ball while the plant is being transported to a new planting site.

Biennial: Two years duration from seed to maturity to death.

Bipinnate: Twice pinnate, as the fronds of many ferns and some legumes.

Bract: A more or less reduced leaf subtending a flower, inflorescence, or branch.

Calcareous: Containing an excess of available calcium, usually in the form of the compound calcium carbonate. A limy soil.

Caliche: A crust of calcium carbonate formed on stony soil in arid regions.

Callus: New cells proliferating from cut tissues in response to wounding or cutting of stems or roots. Precursors to the formation of new or adventitious roots.

Campanulate: Bell shaped.

Capsule: A dry, usually many-seeded, dehiscent fruit composed of more than one carpel, which splits at maturity to release the seed.

Caudex: The woody base of an otherwise herbaceous perennial, as in Rose-mallow Pavonia (*Pavonia lasiopetala*).

Caulescent: Having a leafy stem.

Carpel: A simple pistil or one member of a compound pistil.

Catkin: An ament or a scaly or bracted spike.

Chaff: Thin dry scales.

Chilling requirement: A term sometimes substituted for stratification. See Stratification and Embryo dormancy.

Chlorotic: Yellow appearance of the leaves and stem.

Chlorosis: An abnormally yellow color of plant tissues resulting from partial failure to develop chlorophyll caused by a nutrient deficiency or the activities of a pathogen.

Clone: One of a group of genetically identical plants produced by vegetatively propagating a single plant over one or more vegetative generations. Accomplished in woody plants by rooting stem cuttings, budding, grafting, or air layering.

Cold frame: A simple structure like the traditional hotbed made from glass or plastic, a cold frame is designed to condition or harden rooted cuttings for the early germination of spring-sown seeds or to protect seedlings over winter using solar heating and natural ventilation instead of heaters and other equipment.

Cold hardy: Describes a plant that is cold tolerant and will not be killed by normal winter temperatures in a given area.

Cordate: Heart shaped, the lobes pointing outward.

Corolla: The inner perianth of the flower, composed of colored petals, which may be almost wholly united.

Corymb: A flat flower cluster in which the outer flowers open first.

Cotyledon: Seed leaf. The primary leaf or leaves of the embryo, first to emerge during germination.

Cultivar: A variety or race that has originated and persisted under cultivation. Not necessarily a botanical species.

Cuneate: Wedge shaped or triangular, with the narrow part at the point of attachment.

Cyme: A flat cluster of flowers. The central cluster opens first, as in elderberry (*Sambucus*) and viburnum (*Viburnum*).

Cymose: Arranged in cymes.

Damping off: A seedling disease which causes rotting at the stem or below and death of the roots. It is most often caused by Pythium and Rhizoctonia fungi.

Deciduous: Falling off, as petals after flowering or leaves of nonevergreen trees in autumn.

Deltoid: Triangular shaped.

Dehiscent: Splitting open at maturity by valves or slits to discharge contents, such as a capsule discharging seeds or an anther discharging pollen.

Dentate: Toothed, with the nearly equal-sided teeth projecting forward or at right angles rather than upward.

Dichotomous: Repeatedly forking in pairs.

Dioecious: Having staminate (male) and pistillate (female) flowers on different plants.

Distal: Opposite the point of attachment, apical, away from the axis. The topmost part of a plant.

Division: Separation of a plant into several root-bearing pieces or one of such pieces.

Dormancy: In seeds, an inner condition that prevents germination under environmental conditions favorable for growth. A general term for instances when a living tissue that is predisposed to grow does not do so. For example, trees are dormant in winter.

Double dormancy: The condition of a seed that inhibits germination in which dormancy occurs in both the seed coat, which is external, and the embryo, which is internal. This condition requires that the seed first be scarified and then stratified before germination is possible.

Dormant cuttings: Cuttings taken from plants in the winter when active growth has stopped. Hardwood cuttings.

Drupe: A fleshy, usually one-seeded, indehiscent fruit with the seed enclosed in a hard bony endocarp as in dogwood (*Cornus*), Fringe-tree (*Chionanthus virginica*), or plum (*Prunus*).

Ecotype: An individual plant that is suited to only one kind of environment occupied by the species.

Ecotypic variation: Differences within a species determined by evolution in a particular habitat or local environment.

Elliptic: Nearly twice or three times as long as wide, with continuously rounded sides.

Embryo: The incipient plantlet within the seed.

Embryo dormancy: A condition within the seed that delays germination under favorable environmental conditions. It may be caused by one or all of the following factors: immature embryo, chilling requirement, after-ripening.

Endemic: Indigenous or native to a restricted locality. Naturally confined to a certain limited area or region.

Endocarp: The inner layer of a pericarp or covering of a fruit. The bony part of the stone of a cherry or plum is an endocarp.

Endosperm: Storage or nutritive tissue surrounding the embryo in a seed.

Epicotyl: The young stems above the cotyledons or primary leaves.

Excrescence: A small, warty outgrowth.

Fasciculate: Arranged in dense or close bundles or clusters, especially of like organs having a common source. Leaves of Southwestern White Pine are fasciculate.

Fissures: Cracks or fractures, as on the bark of a tree.

Follicle: A dry, one-celled fruit splitting open on one side only.

Fungicide: A chemical compound formulated to kill or inhibit certain fungi.

Funnelform: Of tubular form, gradually widening upward like a funnel.

Genus: The natural group containing distinct species. A group of more than one related species.

Germination capacity: The percentage of seeds that germinate during a period of time when germination is practically complete.

Glabrous: Smooth, without hairs or down.

Glaucous: Having a powdery or waxy coating that appears frosted and tends to rub off.

Graft: The art of joining pairs of plants together in such a way that they will unite and continue growth as one plant. There are several methods of grafting. A budded graft is accomplished by inserting a bud under the bark of the graft host. In a cleft or side graft, the stock is cut off, then split from the top for a short distance before inserting a wedge-shaped scion in one or both sides of the split. In a whip-and-tongue graft, both the stock and scion are cut diagonally, and a split is made in each so that one fits into the other. The graft is then tied securely with a band. In bench grafting, the stored scion wood is grafted onto rootstock plants dug in late fall and stored under moist conditions until the graft is complete. This process is called "bench grafting" because it is often accomplished at benches in the large-scale production of pears, grapes, rhododendron, and other ornamentals.

Habitat: The site or environment that plants or animals natively occupy.

Hardwood cuttings: Dormant cuttings made in winter from firm mature wood after the previous growing season.

Heel: A cutting that is made by including a tapering piece of bark and cambium, or inner, wood from the main stem.

Herbaceous: Pertaining to an herb and opposed to woody. Having the texture or color of a foliage leaf and dying to the ground each year.

Humus: Decomposing organic matter in the soil.

Husk: The outer covering of certain fruits or seeds, such as walnuts.

Hypocotyl: The axis of the seed embryo between the cotyledonary node and primary root.

Imbibe: Absorb or take up moisture or liquid.

Indehiscent: Not splitting open. This term may describe an achene.

Indolebutyric acid (IBA): An auxin that encourages the initiation of adventitious roots on stems.

Inflorescence: The flower cluster of a plant or the disposition of the flowers on the axis.

Involucre: A whorl of bracts subtending a flower cluster, as in the flower heads of sunflowers.

Juvenility: A condition that exists in an immature plant that has not flowered or borne fruit and may possess enhanced vegetative regeneration abilities.

Lanceolate: Lance shaped, much longer than broad, tapering from below the middle to the apex and more abruptly to the base.

Layering: A process of vegetatively propagating a plant by which adventitious roots are caused to form on a stem that it is still attached to the parent plant. The rooted or layered stem is then detached to become a new plant growing on its new roots.

Legume: A dry indehiscent one-celled fruit of the legume family. A pod.

Linear: Resembling a line, long and narrow or of uniform width, as in the leaf blade of grass.

Maceration: A process for removing the soft, pulpy tissue from fleshy fruits.

Mericarp: One of two seedlike carpels of an umbelliferous fruit.

Meristematic cell: An undifferentiated embryonic tissue, which is actively growing and dividing cells.

Monoecious: Having imperfect male and female flowers on the same plant.

Naphthaleneacetic (NAA): A synthetic root-promoting growth regulator or auxin. It is usually applied to cuttings to promote production of adventitious roots.

Node: A joint of a stem. The point of insertion of a leaf or leaves.

Nut: A hard-shelled and one-seeded indehiscent fruit derived from a simple or compound ovary.

Nutlet: This term is applied to any small and dry nutlike fruit or seed which is thicker walled than an achene.

Oblanceolate: Inversely lanceolate.

Obovate: Inversely ovate.

Ovary: The part of the pistil that contains the ovules.

Ovate: Egg shaped.

Ovule: The body in the ovary that becomes a seed.

Palmate: Hand shaped, the lobes or divisions radiating from a common point.

Panicle: A compound floral raceme. A loose, irregularly compound inflorescence as in ash (*Fraxinus*) and buckeye (*Aesculus*).

Papilionaceous: The butterfly configuration of the pea flower with banner, wings, and keel.

Pedicel: The stalk of a single flower in a flower cluster.

Pendulous: Suspended or hanging.

Perennial: Lasting more than 2 years.

Perfect: A flower having both male and female parts.

Perianth: The collective floral envelopes of the calyx and corolla.

Pericarp: The wall of the mature ovary.

Perlite: Gray-white siliceous material of organic origin, mined from lava flows. The crude ore is crushed and screened, then heated in furnaces to about 1,400° F. At this temperature, the small amount of moisture in the particle changes to steam, expanding the particles into small, spongelike kernels. Perlite is used in soil mixtures to improve drainage and to prevent packing.

Persistent: Remaining attached, as in the calyx on a fruit or leaf that remains on the tree past autumn, falling much later than typical deciduous leaves. Semi-evergreen.

Petiole: A leaf stalk.

pH: The soil reaction measured by the concentration of hydrogen ions in the soil. Although not directly influencing plant growth, it has a number of indirect effects such as the availability of various plant nutrients and the activity of beneficial microbial activity. A pH range of 5.5–7.0 is best for most plants.

Pinna(ae): A main or primary division of a pinnate leaf. A single leaflet of the leaf is simply or once pinnate.

Pinnate: Compound, with the leaflets arranged on two opposite sides of a common petiole.

Pistil: The female or seed-bearing organ of the flower, typically consisting of the style, stigma, and ovary.

Pistillate: Provided with pistils and without stamens. Female.

Plant hormone: An organic compound other than a nutrient produced by a plant that, in low concentrations, regulates the plant's physiological processes. It usually moves within the plant from a site of production to a site of action.

Pome: An applelike fruit.

Powdery mildew: A fungal leaf disease that proliferates under conditions of high relative humidity and covers the leaf surfaces with a white powdery mass. Powdery mildews are controlled by preventative cultural practices, sulfur sprays or dusts, and organic fungicides.

Primordia: A member or organ in its earliest condition. Root primordia are undeveloped root initials within the stem or root.

Propagule: Any part of a plant that may be used to propagate it, either sexually, as with seeds, or vegetatively, as with cuttings.

Proximal: Nearest the axis or base. Opposite of distal.

Provenance: Seed source. The origin or site where the seed was collected.

Pubescent: Covered with short, soft hairs. Downy.

Raceme: A simple elongated flower cluster on an elongated axis. Each flower in the cluster has a pedicel.

Rachis: The axis of a spike, raceme, or compound leaf.

Radicle: The portion of the axis of an embryo from which the root develops.

Rhizomatous: Having an underground stem or rootstock, with scales at the nodes and producing leafy shoots on the upper side and roots on the lower side.

River bottom: Flood plain of a river. See Alluvial soil.

Rooting hormone: A substance that encourages the initiation of new adventitious roots on stems and stems on roots, such as indolebutyric acid, napthalenic acid, and auxins.

Root sprout: A stem suckering or sprouting from a root, particularly around the trunk or base of a plant that has been damaged or cut down.

Rootstock: Very elongated rhizomes or underground offshoots. See Stolon.

Rosette: A crowded cluster of radiating leaves appearing to rise from the ground.

Samara: A dry, indehiscent winged fruit. A samara can be one seeded, as in ash (*Fraxinus*), or two seeded, as in maple (*Acer*).

Scarification: A pregerminative treatment to make seed coats permeable to water and gases. Usually accomplished by mechanical abrasion or by soaking the seeds briefly in strong acid or other chemical solutions.

Schizocarp: A pericarp that splits into one-seeded portions or mericarps.

Scion: The part of the graft combination that is to become the upper portion (sometimes the stem).

Seed coat dormancy: Dormancy imposed on seeds by their seed coats through their impermeability to water or gas exchange or mechanical restrictions on growth of the embryo.

Seed lot: An indefinite quantity of seeds having uniform quality, produced at a specific location or within a single seed collection zone and collected from a single annual crop.

Seed set: The amount of seeds or fruit produced by a single plant during a particular harvest.

Semi-evergreen: A characteristic wherein leaves remain on the plant throughout most of the year but are eventually shed, usually in late winter or early spring, as in Live Oak (*Quercus virginiana*). See Persistent.

Semi-hardwood cutting: A stem cutting of the mature wood of the current season's growth taken during the summer and fall. These cuttings are firm and woody at the base.

Sepal: A leaf or segment of the calyx or outer part of the flower.

Serrate: Saw toothed. The teeth of the leaves point forward.

Simple: Unbranched, as a stem or hair; uncompounded, as a leaf; or single, as a pistil of one carpel.

Softwood cutting: A cutting of juvenile or green herbaceous wood during the growing season.

Spatulate: Shaped like a spatula, a knife rounded above and gradually more narrow toward the base.

Spike: A slender sessile flower cluster on an elongated axis.

Stamen: The pollen-bearing male organ of the flower.

Staminate: Having stamens but no pistil. Male.

Stolon: A runner or modified stem, often below ground, rooting at the tip or creeping and rooting at the nodes. A horizontal stem that produces a new plant at its tip. A spreading rootstock.

Stratification: A pregerminative treatment to break dormancy in seeds and to promote rapid and uniform germination.

Strobile: A spiky pistillate inflorescence or the resulting fruit, as in River Birch (*Betula nigra*).

Style: The usually attenuated portion of the pistil connecting the stigma and ovary.

Succulent: Juicy, fleshy, and soft, as some stems and foliage.

Sucker: An underground stem or shoot, eventually rising to a leafy stem; a chance sprout upon a stem.

Taproot: The main descending root of a plant.

Tardily deciduous: See Semi-evergreen and Persistent.

Tendril: A slender, coiling, or twining organ by which a climbing plant grasps its support.

Terminal: Proceeding from or belonging to the end or top (apex).

Trailing: Growing flat on the ground but not rooting in the soil.

Trifoliate: Having three leaflets.

Tomentose: Covered with short, densely matted, woolly hair.

Tuber: A thickened, solid, and short underground stem with many buds.

Umbel: A flat or convex flower cluster in which the pedicels arise from a common point, like rays of an umbrella.

Umbellate: Borne in an umbel.

Understory: The lower layer or stratum of vegetation generally growing in the shade of other species.

Utricle: A small, bladderlike, one-seeded fruit.

Variety: Plants having minor characteristics or variations that separate them from one or more similarly characterized varieties within a species.

Vermiculite: A micaceous mineral that expands when heated. It is able to absorb large quantities of water. A component in potting soil that improves drainage.

Viability: The capacity of a seed to germinate. The potential germinative capacity of a seed lot.

Villous: Bearing long, soft, and unmatted hairs. Shaggy.

Whorl: A ring of similar organs radiating from a node.

Wounding: A process of injuring the base of a cutting to promote callus formation and root production. Sufficient wounding may also be accomplished in some species by hitting the base with a mallet or tool, stripping off the lower leaves, or removing a thin slice of bark from about an inch of the base on two sides of the cutting, exposing the cambium layer but not cutting deeply into the wood.

Bibliography

Ajilvsgi, Geyata. *Wildflowers of Texas.* Bryan, Tex.: Shearer, 1984.

———. *Butterfly Gardening for the South.* Dallas: Taylor, 1990.

Arnold, Michael A. *Landscape Plants for Texas and Environs.* Champaign, Ill.: Stipes, 1999.

Arnold, Michael A., Larry J. Shoemake, and Mitchell W. Goyne. "Seed Selection and Nursery Production Practices Impact Root Regeneration and Tree Establishment." *The Landscape Below Ground II: Proceedings of the Second International Conference on Tree Root Development in Urban Soils.* Ed. Dan Neely and Gary W. Watson. Savoy, Ill.: International Society of Arboriculture, 1998.

Bailey, L. H., and Ethel Z. Bailey. *The Standard Cyclopedia of Horticulture.* 3 vols. New York: Macmillan, 1947.

Baldwin, H. I. *Forest Tree Seed of the North Temperate Regions.* Waltham, Mass.: Chronica Botanica, 1942.

Barker, Phillip A. "The Spectacular Canyon Maple." *Utah Science* 35 (1975):7–10.

Benson, L., and R. A. Darrow. A *Manual of Southwestern Desert Trees and Shrubs.* Tucson: University of Arizona Press, 1945.

Best, Chris. *Revegetation Manual for the Rio Grande Delta.* Unpublished manuscript, 1999.

Bowers, Janice Emily, and Brian Wignall. *Shrubs and Trees of the Southwest Deserts.* Tucson, Ariz.: Southwest Parks and Monuments Association, 1993.

Cheatham, Scooter, and Marshall C. Johnston, with Lynn Marshall. *The Useful Wild Plants of Texas, the Southeastern and Southwestern United States, the Southern Plains, and Northern Mexico.* Vol 1. Austin, Tex.: Useful Wild Plants of Texas, Inc., 1995.

Church, Thomas D., Grace Hall, and Michael Laurie. *Gardens Are for People.* 3d ed. Berkeley: University of California Press, 1995.

Correll, Donovan S., and Marshall C. Johnston. *Manual of the Vascular Plants of Texas.* Vol. 6. Ed. Cyrus Longworth Lundell. Renner, Tex.: Texas Research Foundation, 1970.

Cox, P., and Patty Leslie. *Texas Trees: A Friendly Guide.* San Antonio, Tex.: Corona Press, 1988.

Creech, David, Dawn Parish, and Bea Clack. "Saving the Neches River Rose Mallow, *Hibiscus dasycalyx.*" *Native Plant Society of Texas Newsletter* 17, no. 3 (May/June 1999).

Davidson, H., and Roy Mecklenburg. *Nursery Management: Administration and Culture*. Englewood Cliffs, N.J.: Prentice-Hall, 1981.

Deer, H. J., and W. F. Mann Jr. *Direct Seeding Pines in the South*. U.S. Department of Agricultural Handbook no. 391. Washington, D.C.: U.S. Government Printing Office, 1971.

Dewars, R. F. *Native and Naturalized Woody Plants of Bexar County and Vicinity*. Texas Agricultural Experiment Station Ornamental Horticulture Bulletin no. 11. College Station, Tex., 1973.

Dewerth, A. F. *Woody Plants for Texas*. Texas Agricultural Experiment Station Bulletin no. MO-139. College Station, Tex., 1955.

———. *Groundcovers for Texas Gardens*. Texas Agricultural Progress Report no. 14. College Station, Tex., 1969.

Diggs, George M., Barney Lipscomb, and Robert J. O'Kennon. *Shinners and Mahler's Illustrated Flora of North Central Texas*. Fort Worth: Botanical Research Institute of Texas and Austin College, 1999.

Dirr, Michael A. *Manual of Woody Landscape Plants: Their Identification, Ornamental Characteristics, Culture, Propagation and Uses*. 4th ed. Champaign, Ill.: Stipes, 1990.

Dirr, Michael A., and Charles W. Heuser. *The Reference Manual of Woody Plant Propagation from Seed to Tissue Culture*. Athens, Ga.: Varsity Press, 1987.

Doran, W. L. *Propagation of Woody Plants by Cuttings*. University of Massachusetts Experiment Station Bulletin no. 491. Amherst, Mass., 1957.

Dunn, Stuart, and Ralph J. Townsend. "Propagation of Sugar Maple by Vegetative Cuttings." *Journal of Forestry* 52 (1954):678–679.

Elmore, Francis H. *Shrubs and Trees of the Southwest Uplands*. Tucson, Ariz.: Southwest Parks and Monuments Association, 1976.

Emery, D. "Seed Propagation of Native California Plants." *Santa Barbara Botanical Gardens* 1 (1964):10.

Engstrom, H. E., and J. H. Stoeckeler. *Nursery Practice for Trees and Shrubs for Planting in the Prairie-Plains*. U.S. Department of Agriculture Forestry Service Miscellaneous Publication no. 434. Washington, D.C.: U.S. Government Printing Office, 1941.

Enquist, Marshall. *Wildflowers of the Texas Hill Country*. Austin, Tex.: Lone Star Botanical, 1987.

Everitt, James H., and D. Lynn Drawe. *Trees, Shrubs and Cacti of South Texas*. Lubbock, Tex.: Texas Tech University Press, 1993.

Folkner, Joseph S., and Robert Charles. "Native Trees and Shrubs for Landscape Use in Southern Arizona." *American Horticultural Magazine* 43 (1964):43–49.

Friend, W. H. *Plants of Ornamental Value for the Rio Grande Valley of Texas*. Texas Agricultural Experiment Station Bulletin no. 609. College Station, Tex., 1942.

Geiser, Samuel Wood. *Horticulture and Horticulturists in Early Texas*. Dallas: Southern Methodist University Press, 1945.

Gentry, Howard Scott. *Agaves of Continental North America*. Tucson: University of Arizona Press, 1982.

Gill, J. D., and W. M. Healy. *Shrubs and Vines for Northeastern Wildlife*. U.S. Department of Agriculture Forest Service General Technical Report NE-9. Washington, D.C.: U.S. Government Printing Office, 1974.

Gould, F. W. *Texas Plants: A Checklist and Ecological Summary*. Texas Agricultural Experiment Station Bulletin no. MP-585. College Station, Tex., 1969.

Hartmann, Hudson T., and Dale E. Kester. *Plant Propagation: Principles and Practices*. 4th ed. Englewood Cliffs, N.J.: Prentice-Hall, 1975.

Heit, C. E. "Testing and Growing Western Desert and Mountain Shrub Species." *American Nursery* 133 (1971).

Hipp, B. W., and B. J. Simpson. "Nitrogen Requirements of Container Grown Texas Madrone (*Arbutus xalapensis*)." *Proceedings of the Texas State Horticultural Society*. College Station, Tex., 1985.

Jaynes, R. A., ed. *Handbook of North American Nut Trees*. Knoxville: Northern Nut Growers' Association, 1969.

Johnson, Eric A. *Pruning, Planting and Care: Johnson's Guide to Gardening Plants for the Arid West*. Tucson, Ariz.: Ironwood Press, 1997.

Kenfield, Warren G. *The Wild Gardener in the Wild Landscape*. New York: Hofner, 1966.

Lenz, Lee W. *Native Plants for California Gardens*. Claremont, Calif.: Rancho Santa Anna Botanical Garden, 1973.

Lockett, Landon. "Historical Evidence of the Native Presence of *Sabal mexicana* (*Palmae*) North of the Lower Rio Grande Valley." *Sida* 16 (1995):711–719.

———. "Searching for Sabal." *Native Plant Society of Texas Newsletter* 17, no. 2 (March/April 1999).

Lockett, Landon, and R. W. Read. "Extension of the Native Range of *Sabal mexicana* (*Palmae*) in Texas to Include Central Coast." *Sida* 14 (1990):79–85.

Lynch, Daniel. *Native and Naturalized Woody Plants of Austin and the Hill Country*. Austin, Tex.: Acorn Press, 1981.

Mackay, Wayne A. "Micropropagation of Texas Madrone, *Arbutus xalapensis H. B. K.*" *HortScience* 31, no. 6 (1996):1028–1029.

Mackay, Wayne A., Jimmy Tipton, and Gary A. Thompson. "Micropropagation of Mexican Redbud *Cercis canadensis var. mexicana*." *Plant Cell, Tissue, and Organ Culture* 43 (1995):295–299.

McEachern, George R. "Texas Pecan Orchard Management Handbook." *Proceedings of the Texas Pecan Short Course*. College Station, Tex.: Texas Agricultural Experiment Station and the U.S. Department of Agriculture, 1985.

McHarg, Ian L. *Design with Nature*. Garden City, N.Y.: Natural History Press, 1969.

McKell, C. M., J. R Blaisdell, and J. R. Goddin, eds. *Wildland Shrubs: Their Biology and Utilization*. U.S. Department of Agriculture Forestry Service General Technical Report INT-1. Washington, D.C.: U.S. Government Printing Office, 1971.

Meyers, R. E. *Morphology and Anatomy of Texas Persimmon*. Texas Agricultural Experiment Station Bulletin no. 1147. College Station, Tex., 1974.

Mielke, Judy. *Native Plants for Southwestern Landscapes*. Austin: University of Texas Press, 1993.

Miles, BeBe. *Bluebells and Bittersweet: Gardening with Native American Plants.* New York: Van Nostrand Reinhold Press, 1968.

Mirov, N. T., and Charles J. Kraebel. *Collecting and Handling Seeds of Wild Plants.* Civilian Conservation Corps Forestry Publication no. 5. Washington, D.C.: U.S. Government Printing Office, 1939.

Molinar, Francisco Jr., Wayne A. Mackay, Marisa M. Wall, and Manuel Cardenas. "Micropropagation of Agarita (*Berberis trifoliolata Moric.*). "*HortScience* 31, no. 6 (1996):1030–1032.

Morgan, David L. "Vegetative Propagation of Live Oaks." *International Plant Propagators' Society Combined Proceedings for 1979* 29:113–115.

Morgan, David L., E. L. McWilliams, and W. C. Parr. "Maintaining Juvenility in Live Oak." *HortScience* 15 (1980):493–494.

Mortensen, E. *Ornamentals for Southwest Texas.* Texas Agricultural Experiment Station Bulletin MP-139. College Station, Tex., 1947.

Native Plant Society of Texas. *Native Plant Society of Texas News* 17, no. 3 (May/June 1999).

Natural Vegetation Committee, Arizona Chapter Soil Conservation Society of America. *Landscaping with Native Arizona Plants.* Tucson: University of Arizona Press, 1973.

Nehrling, Arno, and Irene Nehrling. *Easy Gardening with Drought-Resistant Plants.* New York: Dover, 1968.

Newsom, Bill. "Palm Reading: Tall, Dark and Handsome . . . Is There a Native Sabal in Your Future?" *The Useful Wild Plants Newsletter* no. 12 (Fall 1996).

Norland, Elizabeth. "Apache Plume (*Fallugia paradoxa*)." *Leaflets of the Santa Barbara Botanical Garden* 1, no. 2 (1946):1–24.

Oefinger, Simeon W., and Lowell K. Halls. *Identifying Woody Plants Valuable to Wildlife in Southern Forests.* U.S. Department of Agriculture Forestry Service Research Paper no. SO-92. Washington, D.C.: U.S. Government Printing Office, 1974.

Ogden, Scott. *Gardening Success with Difficult Soils: Limestone, Alkaline Clay, and Caliche.* Dallas: Taylor, 1992.

Padilla, A., J. Gleason, W. Anderson, N. Lawnds, W. A. Mackay, O. Mestas, and J. M. White. *Desert Blooms: A Sunscape Guide to Plants for a Water-Scarce Region.* Interactive CD-rom. Las Cruces: New Mexico State University, 1998.

Parks, H. B. *Valuable Plants Native to Texas.* Texas Agricultural Experiment Station Bulletin no. 551. College Station, Tex., 1937.

Perry, Francis. *Complete Guide to Plants and Flowers.* New York: Simon and Schuster, 1974.

Phillips, Judith. *Southwestern Landscaping with Native Plants.* Santa Fe: Museum of New Mexico Press, 1987.

———. *Natural by Design: Beauty and Balance in Southwest Gardens.* Santa Fe: Museum of New Mexico Press, 1995a.

———. *Plants for Natural Gardens: Southwestern Native and Adaptive Trees, Shrubs, Wildflowers, and Grasses.* Santa Fe: Museum of New Mexico Press, 1995b.

Plummer, A. D., D. R. Christensen, and Stephen B. Monsen. *Restoring Big-Game Range in Utah*. U.S. Department of Agriculture Forestry Service Publication no. 68-3. Washington, D.C.: U.S. Government Printing Office, 1968.

Powell, A. Michael. *Trees and Shrubs of Trans-Pecos, Texas, Including Big Bend and Guadalupe Mountains National Parks*. Big Bend National Park, Tex.: Big Bend Natural History Association, 1988.

Renton, P. A. Jr., H. R. Newcomer, and Roy C. Bates. *Gardening in South Texas*. San Antonio: Naylor, 1973.

Richardson, Alfred. *Plants of the Rio Grande Delta*. Austin: University of Texas Press, 1990.

Schama, Simon. *Landscape and Memory*. New York: Knopf, 1995.

Scifres, C. F. "Salient Aspects of Huisache Seed Germination." *The Southwestern Naturalist* 18 (1974):383–391.

Sheats, W. G. *Propagation of Trees, Shrubs, and Conifers*. New York: Macmillan, 1953.

Shoemaker, J. S., ed. *Small Fruit Culture*. Westport, Conn.: A.V.I. Publishing, 1975.

Simpson, Benny J. *A Field Guide to Texas Trees*. Austin, Tex.: Texas Monthly Press, 1988.

Simpson, Benny J., and John M. Carpenter. "*Quercus polymorpha* (*Fagaceae*) New to Texas and the U.S." *Sida* 15 (1992):153.

Simpson, Benny J., and B. W. Hipp. "Influence of Media Composition on Growth Parameters of Texas Madrone (*Arbutus xalapensis*)." *Proceedings of the Texas State Horticultural Society*. College Station, Tex., 1985a.

———. "The Propagation and Transplanting of the Texas Madrone (*Arbutus xalapensis*)." *Proceedings of the Texas State Horticultural Society*. College Station, Tex., 1985b.

Sperry, Neil. *Neil Sperry's Complete Guide to Texas Gardening*. Dallas: Taylor, 1982.

Stark, N., ed. *Review of Highway Planting Information Appropriate to Nevada*. University of Nevada Agricultural Bulletin no. B-7. Carson City, Nev., 1966.

———., ed. *Wildland Shrubs: Their Biology and Utilization*. U.S. Department of Agriculture Forestry Service General Technical Report no. INT-1. Ogden, Utah: Intermountain Forest and Range Experiment Station, 1972.

Struve, Daniel K., Michael Arnold, Richard Beeson Jr., John M. Ruter, Sven Svenson, and Willard T. Witte. "The Copper Connection: The Benefits of Growing Woody Ornamentals in Copper-treated Containers." *American Nurseryman* (February 1994).

Swingle, Charles F. *Seed Propagation of Trees, Shrubs, and Forbs for Conservation Planting*. U.S. Department of Agriculture Soil Conservation Service Report no. TP-27. Washington, D.C.: U.S. Government Printing Office, 1939.

Taylor, Kathryn S., and Stephen F. Hamblin. *Handbook of Wildflower Cultivation*. New York: Macmillan, 1963.

Taylor, Richard B., Jimmy Rutledge, and Joe C. Herrera. *A Field Guide to Common South Texas Shrubs*. Austin, Tex.: Texas Parks and Wildlife Press, 1997.

Texas Grape Growers Association. *Proceedings*. College Station, Tex.: Texas Agricultural Experiment Station, 1984.

Tipton, J. L. "Asexual Propagation of Juvenile *Arbutus xalapensis* in a High Humidity Chamber." *The Plant Propagator* 27 (1981):11–12.

———. "Evaluation of Three Growth Curve Models for Germination Data Analysis." *Journal of the American Society of Horticultural Science* 109 (1984):451–454.

Tipton, J., L. Craver, and J. Blackwell. "A Method for Harvesting, Cleaning, and Treating Achenes of Guayule (*Parthenium argentatum*)." *HortScience* 16 (1981).

U.S. Department of Agriculture Forest Service. *Seeds of Woody Plants in the United States.* Agricultural Handbook no. 450. Washington, D.C.: U.S. Government Printing Office, 1974.

Van Dersal, William R. *Native Woody Plants of the United States: Their Erosion-Control and Wild Life Values.* Washington, D.C.: U.S. Government Printing Office, 1938.

Vines, Robert A. *Trees, Shrubs, and Woody Vines of the Southwest.* Austin: University of Texas Press, 1970.

Vories, Kimery C. *Growing Colorado Plants from Seed: A State of the Art. Vol. 1: Shrubs.* U.S. Department of Agriculture Forest Service General Technical Report INT-103. Springfield, Va.: National Technical Information Service, 1981.

Warnock, Barton H. *Wildflowers of the Big Bend Country.* Alpine, Tex.: Sul Ross State University Press, 1970.

———. *Wildflowers of the Guadalupe Mountains and the Sand Dune Country of Texas.* Alpine, Tex.: Sul Ross State University Press, 1974.

Wasowski, Sally, with Andy Wasowski. *Native Texas Plants: Landscaping Region by Region.* Austin: Texas Monthly Press, 1988.

———. *Native Plants for Dry Climates.* New York: C. Potter Publishers, 1995.

———. *Native Texas Plants: Landscaping Region by Region.* 2d ed. Houston: Gulf Publishing, 1997.

———. *Gardening with Native Plants of the South.* Dallas: Taylor, 1994.

Water for Texas: A Consensus-Based Update to the State Water Plan. Vol. 2: Technical Planning Appendix. Texas Water Development Board Document no. GP-6-2. Austin, Tex., 1997.

Webster, Bob. *The South Texas Garden Book.* San Antonio: Corona, 1980.

Whitcomb, Carl. *Growing Tree Seedlings in Containers.* Oklahoma State University Agricultural Experiment Station Bulletin no. 755. Stillwater, Okla., 1981.

Woodroof, J. G. *Tree Nuts.* 2d ed. Westport, Conn.: A.V.I. Publishing, 1979.

Wyman, Donald. *Shrubs and Vines for American Gardens.* New York: Macmillan, 1969.

———. "When to Collect Woody Plant Seeds." *American Nursery* 28 (1972).

Zak, B. "Ectendomycorrhiza of Pacific Madrone (*Arbutus menziesii*)." *Transactions of the British Mycological Society* 62 (1974):202–205.

Index

Page numbers in italics indicate illustrations

Acacia (Acacia), 73–78
Acacia berlandieri (Guajillo), 76, 383
Acacia constricta (Whitethorn Acacia, Largancillo, Mescat Acacia), 74, 76
Acacia farnesiana (Huisache), 10, 74, 76–77
Acacia greggii (Catclaw Acacia, Uña de Gato), 73, 77, 78
Acacia hirta (Fern Acacia), 77
Acacia neovernicosa (Viscid Acacia), 74, 76
Acacia rigidula (Black-brush Acacia, Chaparro Prieto), 74, 77, 301, 383
Acacia roemeriana (Romer Acacia, Catclaw Acacia, Gatuño), 73, 77
Acacia schaffneri var. bravoensis (Twisted Acacia, Huisachillo), 74, 77–78
Acacia wrightii (Wright's Acacia, Catclaw, Uña de Gato), 32, 73, 77, 78
Acanthaceae (Acanthus family), 115–117
Acer (maple), 9, 12, 14, 26, 79–87
Aceraceae (maple family), 79–87
Acer barbatum (Southern Sugar Maple), 81, 85
Acer grandidentatum (Big-toothed Maple), 79, 80, 81–83, 84, 85–86. *See also color plates*
Acer leucoderme (Chalk Maple), 82, 86
Acer rubrum var. drummondii (Drummond Red Maple), 80, 84, 86, 296
Acer rubrum var. rubrum (Red Maple), 79, 84
Acer rubrum var. trilobum (Trident Red Maple), 86
Acer saccharum (Sugar Maple), 81, 82, 84, 85, 86–87
Acibuche (*Celtis reticulata*), 181–182, 183
Acid scarification, 18–20, 21, 22
Acorns. *See* Oak (*Quercus*)
Active yeast scarification, 21
Adelia vaseyi (Vasey's Adelia), 88–89
Adventitious roots, 39, 42, 46
Aeration procedure, 29–30
Aesculus (Buckeye), 10, 14, 90–93, 478
Aesculus glabra var. arguta (Texas Buckeye), 22, 36, 93
Aesculus parviflora, 91–92
Aesculus pavia var. flavescens (Scarlet Buckeye), 93
Aesculus pavia var. pavia (Red Buckeye), 93
Afghan Pine (*Pinus elderica*), 399
Afinador (*Parthenium argentatum*), 17, 20, 385–387
Afrombilla (*Lantana camara*), 325
After-ripening, 23, 26–27
Agarita (*Berberis*), 10, 136–139
Agarita (*Berberis trifoliolata*), 117, 137, 138, 139, 301, 508. *See also color plates*
Agavaceae (Agave family), 248–250
Agave (Agave, Century Plant, Maguey), 94–98, 135, 154, 273
Agave americana (Century Plant, Maguey), 96–97
Agave americana spp. protoamericana, 96
Agave americana var. marginata, 96
Agave americana var. medio-picta, 96
Agave americana var. striata, 96
Agave americana var. variegata, 96
Agave family (*Agavaceae*), 248–250
Agave havardiana (Havard Maguey), 97
Agave lechuguilla (Lechuguilla), 97–98, 327, 491

Agave lophantha (Big Lechuguilla, Thorn-crested Agave), 98
Agave neomexicana (Apache Mescal, New Mexico Agave), 97, 249
Agave scabra (Rough Maguey, Maguey Cenizo), 98
Agrito (*Rhus microphylla*), 273, 448, 491, 515
Ahuehuete (*Taxodium distichum var. distichum*), 4, *8*, *9*, 12, 32, 379, 483–485. *See also color plates*
Alamo (*Populus*), 39, 409–411
Alamo ™ (fungicide), 428–429
Alba (Autumn Sage), 458
Albizia julibrissin (Mimosa), 368
Alligator Juniper (*Juniperus deppeana*), 13, 319, 320–321
Allthorn (*Koeberlinia spinosa*), 322–323
Alnus serrulata (Smooth Alder, Hazel Alder), 99–100
Aloysia (Bee-brush, White Brush, Jazminillo), 101–103
Aloysia gratissima (Bee-brush, White Brush, Hierba de la Princesa, Jazminillo), 102–103
Aloysia macrostachya (Vara Dulce, Cabradora, Sweetbrush), 103
Aloysia wrightii (Oreganillo), 103
Amaryllidaceae (Amaryllis family), 94–98
Amelanchier (Service-berry, Shadbush, Juneberry), 104–106
Amelanchier arborea (Service-berry), 105
Amelanchier denticulata (Big Bend Service-berry), 106
Amelanchier utahensis (Utah Service-berry), 106
American Basswood (*Tilia americana*), 489
American Beauty-berry (*Callicarpa americana*), 10, 155–157, 350, 482. *See also color plates*
American Beech (*Fagus grandiflora*), 270–271
American Bittersweet (*Celastrus scandens*), 179–180
American Chestnut (*Castanea dentata*), 171
American Elder (*Sambucus canadensis*), 460–462
American Elm (*Ulmus americana*), 493–494
American Holly (*Ilex opaca*), 26, 310, 312
American Hop-hornbeam (*Ostrya virginiana*), 380–381
American Snowbell (*Styrax americana*), 479, 480
Amole de Bolito (*Sapindus saponaria var. drummondii*), 463–465
Amorpha (False Indigo, Indigo Bush), 107–109
Amorpha canescens, 108
Amorpha fruticosa (False Indigo, Indigo-bush Amorpha), 107–109
Amorpha paniculata (Panicled Amorpha), 109
Amorpha roemeriana (Texas Indigo Bush), 109
Ampelopsis (Pepper-vine), 110–111
Ampelopsis arborea (Pepper-vine), 111
Ampelopsis cordata (Heart-leaf Pepper-vine), 111
Amyris (Torchwood, Chapotillo, Lantrisco, Limonaria), 112–114
Amyris madrensis (Sierra Madre Torch-wood, Limonaria), 30, 112, 113, 114
Amyris texana (Texas Torchwood, Lantrisco, Chapotillo), 112, 113, 114
Anacahuita (*Cordia boisseri*), 30, 221–223. *See also color plates*
Anacardiaceae (Sumac family), 228–231, 401–403, 443–449
Anacua (*Ehretia anacua*), 255–257
Anisacanthus (Anisacanthus), 115–117
Anisacanthus linearis (Dwarf Anisacanthus), 116, 117
Anisacanthus puberulus (Pinky Anisacanthus), 116, 117
Anisacanthus quadrifidus var. wrightii (Flame Acanthus, Orange Humming-bird-bush), 7, 11, 116, 117. *See also color plates*
Annonanaceae (Custard Apple family), 124–126
Anthracnose (*Glomerella*), 92
Apache Mescal (*Agave neomexicana*), 97, 249

Apache Plume (*Fallugia paradoxa*), 235, 272–274, 515
Aquifoliaceae (Holly family), 309–312
Araliaceae (Ginseng family), 118–119
Aralia spinosa (Devil's Walking-stick), 118–119
Árbol de Judío (*Cercis*), 6, 10, 32, 192–196
Árbol de la Sierra (*Myrica cerifera*), 372–374
Arbutus menziesii (Pacific Madrone), 122
Arbutus xalapensis (Madrone, Madrona, Naked Indian's Leg), 38, 120–123. *See also color plates*
Arctostaphylos pungens (Pointleaf Manzanita), 242
Arid soils, 2
Arizona Ash (*Fraxinus veluntina*), 285
Arizona Cypress (*Cupressus arizonica*), 129
Arizona Cypress (*Cupressus arizonica var. arizonica*), 240–242, 403
Arizona Rough Cypress (*Cupressus arizonica var. arizonica*), 240–242, 403
Arizona Walnut (*Juglans major*), 316
Arkansas Yucca (*Yucca arkansana*), 514, 515
Arrow-wood (*Viburnum*), 26, 502–505
Ash (*Fraxinus*), 12, 38, 282–285
Ash family (*Oleaceae*), 204–205, 277–279, 282–285
Ashe Juniper (*Juniperus ashei*), 122, 319, 320
Asimina parviflora (Dwarf Paw-paw), 126
Asimina tribola (Paw-paw, Custard Apple), 124–126
Asteraceae (Sunflower family), 131–132, 208–209, 264–266, 290–291, 506–508, 521–522
Atriplex (Saltbush, Chamiso, Costilla de Vaca), 127–130
Atriplex acanthocarpa (Tubercled Saltbush), 129
Atriplex canescens (Four-winged Saltbush), 128, 129, 403
Atriplex confertifolia (Spiny Saltbush, Shadscale), 129–130
Atriplex ovata (Oval-leaf Saltbush), 130
Autumn Sage (*Salvia greggii*), 391, 457, 458–459. *See also color plates*
Azafran (*Buddleia*), 146–148
Azafran (*Buddleia marrubifolia*), 147, 148. *See also color plates*
Azalea (*Rhododendron*), 440–442
Azalea (*Rhododendron coryi*), 441
Azalea family (*Ericaceae*), 120–123, 341–342, 354–355, 440–442, 497–499

Baby Bonnets (*Coursetia axillaris*), 30, 232–233
Baccharis neglecta (False-willow, Seep-willow, Roosevelt Weed, New Deal Weed), 131–132
Bald Cypress (*Taxodium distichum var. distichum*), 4, 8, 9, 12, 32, 379, 483–485. *See also color plates*
Balsamo (*Liquidambar styraciflua*), 345–346. *See also color plates*
Bamboo-vine (*Smilax laurifolia*), 472
Banana Yucca (*Yucca baccata*), 515–516
Barba de Viejo (*Clematis*), 7, 212–214
Barba de Viejo (*Clematis drummondii*), 212, 213
Barba de Viejo (*Eupatorium havanense*), 264–266, 290, 350, 459, 518
Barbados-cherry (*Malpighia glabra*), 360–361
Barberry (*Berberis*), 10, 136–139
Barberry family (*Berberidaceae*), 136–139
Barreta de Cochino (*Fraxinus greggii*), 1, 283, 285
Basketgrass (*Nolina*), 92, 350, 375–377, 458, 517
Basketgrass (*Nolina erumpens*), 376
Basswood family (*Tiliaceae*), 488–489
Bauhinia luinaroides (Orchid-tree, Pata de Vaca, Pata de Cabra), 133–135
Bay-gall Bush (*Ilex coriaceae*), 311
Beaked Yucca (*Yucca rostrata*), 517
Beargrass (*Nolina*), 92, 350, 375–377, 458, 517
Beargrass (*Nolina micrantha*), 377, 391
Bee-brush (*Aloysia*), 101–103
Bee-brush (*Aloysia gratissima*), 102–103
Beech family (*Fagaceae*), 170–171, 270–271, 424–436
Beechnut (*Fagus grandiflora*), 270–271

Berberidaceae (Barberry family), 136–139
Berberis (Agarita, Mahonia, Barberry), 10, 136–139
Berberis haematocarpa (Red Barberry), 138, 139
Berberis repens (Creeping Barberry), 138–139
Berberis swayseii (Texas Mahonia, Texas Barberry), 137, 138, 139
Berberis trifoliolata (Agarita, Paisano Bush), 117, 137, 138, 139, 301, 508. *See also color plates*
Berlander Wolfberry (*Lycium berlandieri var. berlandieri*), 352, 353, 519
Bert-star (Silverado ™), 340
Best, Chris, 19, 336
Betulaceae (Birch family), 99–100, 140–141, 162–163, 380–381
Betula nigra (River Birch), 140–141
Betula populifolia (Gray Birch), 141
Big Bend Service-berry (*Amelanchier denticulata*), 106
Big-Bend Silver-leaf (*Leucophyllum minus*), 340
Big Bend Yucca (*Yucca rostrata*), 517
Bigelow Oak (*Quercus sinuata var. breviloba*), 435
Big Lechuguilla (*Agave lophantha*), 98
Bignonia capreolata (Cross-vine, Cola de Iguana), 142–143
Bignoniaceae (Trumpet-creeper family), 142–143, 158–159, 174–175, 200–203, 486–487
Big Pink (Autumn Sage), 458
Big-toothed maple (*Acer grandidentatum*), 79, 80, 81–83, 84, 85–86. *See also color plates*
Birch family (*Betulaceae*), 99–100, 140–141, 162–163, 380–381
Bisbirinda (*Castela erecta*), 172–173
Bitternut Hickory (*Carya cordiformis*), 166
Black-brush Acacia (*Acacia rigidula*), 74, 77, 301, 383
Black Dalea (*Dalea frutescens*), 247, 458, 491, 508
Blackgum (*Nyssa sylvatica var. sylvatica*), 378, 379
Blackjack Oak (*Quercus marilandica*), 427, 432
Black mold (*Dimerosporum pulchrum*), 163
Black Oak (*Quercus velutina*), 6, 435–436
Black Tupelo (*Nyssa sylvatica var. sylvatica*), 378, 379
Black Walnut (*Juglans nigra*), 316, 317
Black Willow (*Salix nigra*), 454–455
Blanco Crabapple (*Pyrus ioensis*), 422–423
Blue-beech (*Carpinus caroliniana*), 162–163
Blueberry (*Vaccinium*), 497–499
Blueberry Hawthorn (*Crataegus brachyacantha*), 238
Blue Boneset (*Eupatorium azureum*), 266
Blue Elderberry (*Sambucus caerulea*), 462
Blue Ice (Arizona Cypress), 242
Bluejack Oak (*Quercus incana*), 431
Blue Palo Verde (*Cercidium floridum*), 190, 384
Blue Shrub Sage (*Salvia ballotaeflora*), 117, 458
Bluewood Condalia (*Condalia hookeri*), 219–220
Boothill ™ (Gregg's Eupatorium), 266
Boraginaceae (Borage family), 221–223, 255–257, 490–491
Border Palo Verde (*Cercidium macrum*), 190, 191
Border Palo Verde (*Parkinsonia texana var. macrum*), 190
Borers, 182
Botryosphaeria canker, 195
Bottom heat: and germination, 2, 25; and planting, 31; and rooting, 45; and semihardwood cuttings, 47
Bouchea (Bouchea), 144–145
Bouchea linifolia (Groovestem Bouchea), 144, 145
Bouchea spathulata (Spoon-leaf Bouchea), 144, 145
Brasil (*Condalia hookeri*), 219–220
Brazoria Palmetto (*Sabal x mexicana Read*), 452–453
Brite n Tite (Cherry Laurel), 417
Bronstad, Mark, 82
Broom Dalea (*Dalea scoparia*), 247
Bubba (Desert Willow), 23

Buckeye (*Aesculus*), 10, 14, 90–93, 478
Buckeye family (*Hippocastanaceae*), 90–93
Buckley Yucca (*Yucca constricta*), 516
Buckthorn family (*Rhamnaceae*), 176–178, 217–220, 437–439
Buddleia (Woolly Butterfly-bush, Escobilla Butterfly-bush, Azafran), 146–148
Buddleia davidii, 109
Buddleia marrubifolia (Woolly Butterfly-bush, Azafran), 147, 148. *See also color plates*
Buddleia racemosa (Wand Butterfly-bush), 148
Buddleia scordioides (Escobilla Butterfly-bush), 148
Buddleia sessilflora (Tepozán), 148
Bumelia celastrina (La Coma), 150
Bumelia lanuginosa (Gum-elastic Tree, La Coma, Chittamwood), 149–150
Bunch-grass (*Nolina texana*), 377. *See also color plates*
Burford Holly, 288
Burgundy Lace (Desert Willow), 203
Bur Oak (*Quercus macrocarpa*), 5, 7, 427, 432. *See also color plates*
Bush-pepper (*Capsicum annum*), 92, 160–161
Butterfly Bush, 109
Butterfly Weed, 9
Button-bush (*Cephalanthus occidentalis*), 184–185

Cabradora (*Aloysia macrostachya*), 103
Caesalpinia mexicana (Mexican Caesalpinia, Tabachín del Monte), 151–152
Calliandra eriophylla (Fairy Duster, False Mesquite, Charrasquillo), 153–154
Callicarpa americana (American Beauty-berry, Filigrana), 10, 155–157, 350, 482. *See also color plates*
Callicarpa americana var. lactea (White American Beauty-berry), 157
Caltrop family (*Zygophyllaceae*), 292–294, 327–329
Camellia family (*Theaceae*), 476–477
Campsis radicans (Trumpet-creeper, Monapesto), 158–159. *See also color plates*
Canyon Grape (*Vitis arizonica*), 511
Canyon Mock-orange (*Philadelphus ernestii*), 395, 396
Caprifoliaceae (Honeysuckle family), 349–351, 460–462, 481–482, 502–505
Capsicum annum (Chile Pequín, Bush-pepper), 92, 160–161
Capul (*Schaefferia cuneifolia*), 469–470
Capul Negro (*Condalia hookeri*), 219–220
Carex (Sedge), 459, 482
Carex texensis (Cedar Sedge), 161
Carneros Yucca (*Yucca carnerosana*), 516–517
Carolina Ash (*Fraxinus caroliniana*), 284
Carolina Basswood (*Tilia caroliniana*), 488–489
Carolina Buckthorn (*Rhamnus caroliniana*), 6, 10, 344, 437–439
Carolina Holly (*Ilex ambigua*), 311
Carolina Sapphire (Arizona Cypress), 242
Carolina Silverbell (*Halesia caroliniana*), 296
Carolina Wolfberry (*Lycium carolinianum var. quadrifidium*), 353
Carpenter, John Mac, 434
Carpinus betulus (European Hornbeam), 163
Carpinus caroliniana (Hornbeam, Blue-beech, Lechillo, Mora de la Sierra), 162–163
Carya (Hickory, Pecan, Nogal, Nueces), 6, 10, 14, 164–166, 316
Carya aquatica (Water Hickory), 166
Carya cordiformis (Bitternut Hickory, Pignut Hickory), 166
Carya illinoinensis (Pecan, Nogal, Nueces), 166
Carya ovata (Shagbark Hickory, Nogal Mofudo), 166
Carya tomentosa (Mockernut Hickory), 166
Caryobruchus, 450
Cassia (*Cassia wislizenii*), 167–169
Cassia greggii (Gregg Senna), 169

Cassia lindheimeriana (Lindheimer's Senna), 117, 168, 169
Cassia roemeriana (Two-leaved Senna), 169
Cassia wislizenii (Wislizeni Senna, Cassia, Palo Prieto, Pinacate), 167–169
Castanea (Chinquapin), 170–171
Castanea alnifolia (Downy Chinquapin), 171
Castanea dentata (American Chestnut), 171
Castanea pumila (Chinquapin), 171
Castanea pumila var. asheii, 171
Castela erecta (Chaparro Amargosa, Goatbush, Bisbirinda), 172–173
Catalpa (*Catalpa speciosa*), 174–175
Catalpa bignoniodes, 174
Catalpa speciosa (Catalpa, Cigar-tree), 174–175
Catbird Grape (*Vitis palmata*), 511
Cat-briar (*Smilax*), 471–472
Cat-briar (*Smilax glauca*), 472
Catclaw (*Acacia wrightii*), 32, 73, 77, 78
Catclaw Acacia (*Acacia greggii*), 73, 77, 78
Catclaw Acacia (*Acacia roemeriana*), 73, 77
Cat's Claw (*Mimosa*), 367–369
Cat's Claw (*Mimosa biuncifera*), 368
Ceanothus (Ceanothus, Redroot, Jersey-tea), 176–178
Ceanothus americanus (Jersey-tea), 178
Ceanothus fendleri (Desert Ceanothus, Fendler Ceanothus), 178
Ceanothus greggii (Desert Ceanothus), 178
Ceanothus herbaceus (Redroot), 178
Cedar (*Juniperus*), 22, 45, 49, 249, 318–321
Cedar Elm (*Ulmus crassifolia*), 493, 494
Cedar Sage (*Salvia roemeriana*), 161, 364, 517
Cedar Sedge (*Carex texensis*), 161
Cedro (*Juniperus*), 22, 45, 49, 249, 318–321
Cedro Blanco (*Cupressus arizonica var. arizonica*), 240–242, 403
Cedro de la Sierra (*Cupressus arizonica var. arizonica*), 240–242, 403
Celastrus scandens (American Bittersweet), 179–180
Celestraceae (Staff-tree family), 179–180, 262–263, 469–470
Celtis (Hackberry, Sugarberry, Palo Blanco), 181–183, 462
Celtis laevigata (Sugarberry, Hackberry), 182
Celtis occidentalis (Hackberry), 182
Celtis pallida (Granjeno, Huasteco, Desert Hackberry), 182, 183
Celtis reticulata (Netleaf Hackberry, Acibuche, Palo Blanco), 181–182, 183
Celtis tenuifolia (Dwarf Hackberry), 183
Cenizo (*Leucophyllum*), 6, 37, 154, 335–340, 391
Cenizo (*Leucophyllum frutescens*), 37, 76, 129, 135, 147, 249, 336, 337, 338, 339–340, 383, 403, 458, 515. *See also color plates*
Century Plant (*Agave*), 94–98, 135, 154, 273
Century Plant (*Agave americana*), 96–97
Cephalanthus occidentalis (Button-bush, Rosa de Juan, Jazmin), 184–185
Cerastocystis ulmi (Dutch Elm disease), 493
Ceratocystis fagacearum (Oak wilt), 427–429
Ceratoides lanata (Winterfat, Feather Sage, Lamb's Tail), 186–188
Cercidium floridum (Blue Palo Verde), 190, 384
Cercidium macrum (Border Palo Verde), 190, 191
Cercidium microphyllum (Foothills Palo Verde), 384
Cercidium texanum (Texas Palo Verde, Retama China), 189–191
Cercis (Redbud, Árbol de Judío), 6, 10, 32, 192–196
Cercis canadensis, 6, 10, 192
Cercis canadensis var. canadensis (Eastern Redbud), 192
Cercis canadensis var. mexicana (Mexican Redbud), 192, 194
Cercis canadensis var. texensis (Texas Redbud), 194, 196
Cercocarpus montanus (True Mountain Mahogany), 199
Cercocarpus montanus var. argenteus (Silver-leaf Mountain Mahogany, Palo Duro), 12, 197–199

Cereza (*Malpighia glabra*), 360–361
Chalk Maple (*Acer leucoderme*), 82, 86
Chamiso (*Atriplex*), 127–130
Chaparro Amargosa (*Castela erecta*), 172–173
Chaparro Prieto (*Acacia rigidula*), 74, 77, 301, 383
Chapote Prieto (*Diospyros*), 13, 251–254, 261
Chapote Prieto (*Diospyros texana*), 10, 30, 103, 251, 252–254
Chapotillo (*Amyris*), 112–114
Chapotillo (*Amyris texana*), 112, 113, 114
Charrasquillo (*Calliandra eriophylla*), 153–154
Chasmanthium latifolium (Inland Sea Oats), 364
Chenopodiaceae (Goosefoot family), 127–130, 186–188
Cherry (*Prunus*), 10, 12–13, 21, 415–419
Cherry Laurel (*Prunus caroliniana*), 417–418, 439
Cherry Sage (*Salvia greggii*), 391, 457, 458–459. *See also color plates*
Chickasaw Plum (*Prunus angustifolia*), 417
Chihuahuan Rain Sage (*Leucophyllum laevigatum*), 336, 338, 339
Chile Pequín (*Capsicum annum*), 92, 160–161
Chilopsis linearis (Desert Willow, Flor de Mimbre), *8*, 32, 200–203, 487. *See also color plates*
Chinese Pistachio (*Pistacia chinensis*), 403
Chinese Tallow Tree, 76
Chinquapin (*Castanea*), 170–171
Chinquapin (*Castanea pumila*), 171
Chinquapin Oak (*Quercus meuhlenbergii*), 432–433
Chionanthus virginica (Fringe-tree, Old-man's Beard), 52, 204–205, 296
Chisos Hop-hornbeam (*Ostrya chisosensis*), 381
Chisos Red Oak (*Quercus gravesii*), 431
Chisos Rosewood (*Vauquelinia angustifolia*), 500–501
Chittamwood (*Bumelia lanuginosa*), 149–150
Chocolate family (*Sterculiaceae*), 365–366
Choisya dumosa (Mexican Star-leaf Orange, Zorillo), 206–207
Choke-Cherry (*Prunus serotina var. serotina*), 417, 418–419
Chomonque (*Gochnatia hypoleuca*), 290–291
Chrysactinia mexicana (Damianita, Hierba de San Nicolas), 208–209
Church, Thomas, xxiv
Cigar-tree (*Catalpa speciosa*), 174–175
Cilindrillo (*Lycium*), 352–353
Cilindrillo (*Lycium berlandieri var. berlandieri*), 352, 353, 519
Cimarron ™ (*Leucophyllum zygophyllum*), 336, 339
Citharexylum berlandieri (Negrito, Fiddlewood, Orcajuela, Encorba Gallina), 210–211
Citrus family (*Rutaceae*), 112–114, 206–207, 260–261, 420–421, 519–520
Clematis (Clematis, Virgin-bower, Barba de Viejo), *7*, 212–214
Clematis drummondii (Virgin-bower, Old-man's Beard, Barba de Viego), 212, 213
Clematis pitcheri (Pitcher or Purple Clematis), 213–214. *See also color plates*
Clematis texensis (Scarlet or Texas Clematis), 213, 214
Clethra alnifolia (White Alder, Sweet Pepper-bush, Summer-sweet), 215–216
Clethra alnifolia var. rosea, 216
Clethraceae (White Alder family), 215–216
Cliff Fendler-bush (*Fendlera rupicola*), 275–276
Clones, 37
Coachwhip (*Fouquiera splendens*), 273, 280–281, 327
Coahuila Scrub Oak (*Quercus intricata*), 432
Coastal Live Oak (*Quercus virginiana*), 32, 426, 427, 436
Coatante (*Mimosa pigra*), 369
Cockspur Hawthorn (*Crataegus crus-galli*), 238
Cola de Iguana (*Bignonia capreolata*), 142–143

Cola de Zorillo (*Ptelea trifoliolata*), 420–421
Cold dormancy, 23–25, 26
Cold frames, 31, 47, 56, 58
Cold stratification, 23–25, 26
Colima (*Zanthoxylum fagara*), 519–520
Colorín (*Erythrina herbaceae*), 21, 258–259
Colubrina texensis (Hog-plum, Snakewood, Guajalote), 217–218
Common Winterberry (*Ilex verticillata*), 312
Compacta (Cenizo), 340
Condalia hookeri (Bluewood Condalia, Brasil, Capul Negro), 219–220
Condalia warnockii, 220
Consumers, 2–3
Containers: copper-treated, 2, 32; for planting, 31–32; for rooting, 53–54; for seed collection, 11; for seed storage, 14; and transplantation, 62
Convent (Cenizo), 340
Copalme (*Liquidambar styraciflua*), 345–346. *See also color plates*
Coral-bean (*Erythrina herbaceae*), 21, 258–259
Coral-berry (*Symphoricarpos orbiculatus*), 157, 481–482
Coral Honeysuckle (*Lonicera sempervirens*), 350, 351. *See also color plates*
Coral Yucca (*Hesperaloe parviflora*), 300–301. *See also color plates*
Coral Yucca (*Hesperaloe parviflora 'Yellow'*), 301
Cordia boisseri (Wild Olive, Anacahuita), 30, 221–223. *See also color plates*
Corkwood (*Leitneria floridana*), 330–331
Corkwood family (*Leitneriaceae*), 330–331
Cornaceae (Dogwood family), 224–227, 289, 378–379
Cornus (Dogwood), 13, 224–227
Cornus drummondii (Rough-leaf Dogwood), 27, 224, 225, 226, 227, 439
Cornus florida (Flowering Dogwood), 224–225, 226, 227
Cornus racemosa (Gray Dogwood), 227
Cornus sanguinea, 226
Corona de Cristo Junco (*Koeberlinia spinosa*), 322–323
Correosa (*Rhus microphylla*), 273, 448, 491, 515
Costilla de Vaca (*Atriplex*), 127–130
Cotinus coggygria (European Smoke Tree), 229
Cotinus obovatus (Smoke Tree), 6, 228–231
Cotton root rot, 182
Cottonwood (*Populus*), 39, 409–411
Couaxi (*Coursetia axillaris*), 30, 232–233
Coursetia (*Coursetia axillaris*), 30, 232–233
Coursetia axillaris (Baby Bonnets, Couaxi, Coursetia), 30, 232–233
Cowania ericaefolia (Heath Cliff-rose), 234–235
Cox, Paul, 203, 291, 366
Crabapple (*Pyrus*), 7, 10, 12–13
Crataegus (Hawthorn), 236–239
Crataegus brachyacantha (Blueberry Hawthorn), 238
Crataegus crus-galli (Cockspur Hawthorn), 238
Crataegus marshallii (Parsley Hawthorn), 237, 238, 296
Crataegus opaca (Mayhaw), 237, 238–239
Crataegus reverchonii (Reverchon's Hawthorn), 239
Crataegus spathulata (Little-hip Hawthorn), 239
Crataegus tracyi (Mountain Hawthorn), 239
Crataegus viburnifolia (Viburnum Hawthorn), 239
Creech, David, 305
Creek Plum (*Prunus rivularis*), 416, 418
Creeping Barberry (*Berberis repens*), 138–139
Creeping Mesquite (*Prosopis reptans*), 414
Creosote bush (*Larrea tridentata*), 249, 273, 327–329, 515
Crespa (*Salvia ballotaeflora*), 117, 458
Cross-vine (*Bignonia capreolata*), 142–143
Crowfoot family (*Ranunculaeceae*), 212–214
Crucifixion Thorn (*Koeberlinia spinosa*), 322–323
Cucumber Tree (*Magnolia pyramidata*), 357–358, 359

Cupressaceae (Cypress family), 240–242, 318–321, 483–485
Cupressus arizonica (Arizona Ash), 129
Cupressus arizonica var. arizonica (Arizona Cypress, Arizona Rough Cypress, Cedro Blanco, Pinobete, Cedro de la Sierra), 240–242, 403
Custard Apple (*Asimina tribola*), 124–126
Custard Apple family (*Annonanaceae*), 124–126
Cuttings: age of, 42; deciduous hardwood cuttings, 44–45; hardwood cuttings, 43–44, 49, 52; and misting systems, 47, 49, 53, *54*; and plant selection, 49–50; and propagation, 37–43; root cuttings, 46; semihardwood (greenwood) cuttings, 43, 46–47, 49, 52, 53, 55; shade for, *57*, 58; softwood cuttings, 43, 47–49, *48*, 53, 55; transplantation of, 58; types of, *41*, 43; and weather trends, 43. *See also specific plants*
Cypress family (*Cupressaceae*), 240–242, 318–321, 483–485
Cyrillaceae (Leatherwood family), 243–244
Cyrilla racemiflora (Leatherwood), 243–244

Dalea (Dalea), 145, 245–247, 249
Dalea bicolor var. argyraea (Silver Dalea, Escobilla Cenizo), 246–247
Dalea formosa (Feather Dalea, Limoncillo), 247
Dalea frutescens (Black Dalea), 247, 458, 491, 508
Dalea greggii (Gregg's Dalea), *48*, 247
Dalea scoparia (Broom Dalea), 247
Damianita (*Chrysactinia mexicana*), 208–209
Damping-off fungi, 35
Dark Storm (Desert Willow), 203
Dasylirion (Sotol, Desert Spoon), 248–250, 281
Dasylirion leiophyllum (Sotol), 250, 327
Dasylirion texanum (Texas Sotol), 250
Dasylirion wheeleri (Desert Spoon), 250
Datil Yucca (*Yucca baccata*), 515–516
Deciduous hardwood cuttings, 44–45
Deciduous Holly (*Ilex decidua*), 309, 311–312, 344
Delaware #2 (American Elm), 493
Dense St. John's Wort (*Hypericum densiflorum*), 307
Desert Ceanothus (*Ceanothus fendleri*), 178
Desert Ceanothus (*Ceanothus greggii*), 178
Desert Hackberry (*Celtis pallida*), 182, 183
Desert Lantana (*Lantana macropoda*), 326
Desert Olive (*Forestiera*), 30, 42, 277–279
Desert Olive (*Forestiera neomexicana*), 279
Desert Rose Mallow (*Hibiscus coulteri*), 304–305
Desert Spoon (*Dasylirion*), 248–250, 281
Desert Spoon (*Dasylirion wheeleri*), 250
Desert Sumac (*Rhus microphylla*), 273, 448, 491, 515
Desert-thorn (*Lycium*), 352–353
Desert Willow (*Chilopsis linearis*), *8*, 32, 200–203, 487. *See also color plates*
Desert Yaupon (*Schaefferia cuneifolia*), 469–470
Development, and urban landscapes, xxii–xxiii
Devil's Shoestring (*Nolina lindheimeriana*), 375, 376
Devil's Walking-stick (*Aralia spinosa*), 118–119
Dewberry, *7*
Diane (Autumn Sage), 459
Dimerosporum pulchrum (black mold), 163
Diospyros (Persimmon, Chapote Prieto), 13, 251–254, 261
Diospyros texana (Texas or Mexican Persimmon, Chapote Prieto), 10, 30, 103, 251, 252–254
Diospyros virginiana (Eastern persimmon), 251, 252, 253, 254
Dirr, Michael, 3
Dogwood (*Cornus*), 13, 224–227
Dogwood family (*Cornaceae*), 224–227, 289, 378–379
Dormancy: double dormancy, 23, 26–27; and germination, 2, 15, 17, 22–23; and seed storage, 14; and stratification, 23–26; and transplantation, 59; types of, 17
Double dormancy, 23, 26–27

Downy Chinquapin (*Castanea alnifolia*), 171
Drooping Sweetbells (*Leucothoe fontanesiana*), 342
Droughts, xxii
Drummond Red Maple (*Acer rubrum var. drummondii*), 80, 84, 86, 296
Dryopteris (River Fern), 157
Dutch Elm disease (*Cerastocystis ulmi*), 493
Dwarf Anisacanthus (*Anisacanthus linearis*), 116, 117
Dwarf Hackberry (*Celtis tenuifolia*), 183
Dwarf Palmetto (*Sabal minor*), 451, 452, 453
Dwarf Paw-paw (*Asimina parviflora*), 126
Dwarf Pink (Autumn Sage), 459
Dwarf Screwbean (*Prosopis reptans*), 414
Dwarf Wax-myrtle (*Myrica pusila*), 374
Dychoriste linearis (Snake Herb), 145

Early Azalea (*Rhododendron prinophyllum*), 441, 442
Eastern Cottonwood (*Populus deltoides var. deltoides*), 410, 411
Eastern Persimmon (*Diospyros virginiana*), 251, 252, 253, 254
Eastern Redbud (*Cercis canadensis var. canadensis*), 192
Eastern Red Cedar (*Juniperus virginiana*), 318, 319, 321
Ébano (*Pithecellobium flexicaule*), 30, 261, 404–406
Ebenaceae (Persimmon family), 251–254
Eggleaf Garrya (*Garrya ovata* subsp. *goldmannii*), 289
Ehretia anacua (Sand-paper Tree, Anacua, Knock-away Tree), 255–257
Elderberry (*Sambucus canadensis*), 460–462
Elm (*Ulmus*), 14, 492–494
Elm family (*Ulmaceae*), 181–183, 492–494
Emory Mimosa (*Mimosa emoryana*), 369
Emory Oak (*Quercus emoryi*), 429–430
Encino (*Quercus*), 6, 10–11, 14, 30, 42, 424–436
Encino (*Quercus virginiana*), 32, 426, 427, 436
Encino Chaparro (*Quercus fusiformis*), 427, 430, 434, 436
Encino Colorado (*Quercus gravesii*), 431
Encino Prieto (*Quercus grisea*), 431
Encino Roble (*Quercus glaucoides*), 430
Encorba Gallina (*Citharexylum berlandieri*), 210–211
Endangered plants, 5–6, 59
Ericaceae (Heath or Azalea family), 120–123, 341–342, 354–355, 440–442, 497–499
Erythrina herbaceae (Coral-bean, Colorín), 21, 258–259
Escarpment Choke-cherry (*Prunus serotina var. eximia*), 416, 419
Escarpment Live Oak (*Quercus fusiformis*), 427, 430, 434, 436
Escobilla (*Fraxinus greggii*), 1, 283, 285
Escobilla Butterfly-bush (*Buddleia*), 146–148
Escobilla Butterfly-bush (*Buddleia scordioides*), 148
Escobilla Cenizo (*Dalea bicolor var. argyraea*), 246–247
Esenbeckia berlandieri (Jopoy), 261
Esenbeckia runyonii (Limoncillo, Naranjillo), 260–261
Esperanza (*Tecoma stans var. angustata*), 334, 486–487
Euonymus americanus (Strawberry Bush), 262–263
Eupatorium (*Eupatorium havanense*), 264–266, 290, 350, 459, 518
Eupatorium azureum (Blue Boneset), 266
Eupatorium coelestinum (Foam Flower), 266
Eupatorium greggii (Gregg's Eupatorium), 266
Eupatorium havanense (Fragrant Mist Flower, Eupatorium, Barba de Viejo), 264–266, 290, 350, 459, 518
Eupatorium wrightii (Wright's Mist Flower), 266
Euphorbiaceae (Spurge family), 88–89
European Beech (*Fagus sylvatica*), 271
European Hornbeam (*Carpinus betulus*), 163
European Smoke Tree (*Cotinus coggygria*), 229

Evergreen Honeysuckle (*Lonicera sempervirens*), 350, 351. *See also color plates*
Evergreen Sumac (*Rhus virens*), 34, 242, 444, 445, 448–449, 458
Eve's Necklace (*Sophora affinis*), 32, 475
Exotic landscape plants, xxiii, xxv
Eysenhardtia spinosa (Spiny Kidney-wood), 269
Eysenhardtia texana (Texas Kidney-wood, Vara Dulce), 267–269

Fabaceae (Legume family), 12, 14, 34, 73–78, 107–109, 133–135, 151–154, 167–169, 186–188, 232–233, 245–247, 258–259, 267–269, 332–334, 367–369, 382–384, 404–406, 412–414, 473–475
Fagaceae (Beech or Oak family), 170–171, 270–271, 424–436
Fagus grandiflora (American Beech, Beechnut), 270–271
Fagus sylvatica (European Beech), 271
Fairy Duster (*Calliandra eriophylla*), 153–154
Fallugia paradoxa (Apache Plume), 235, 272–274, 515
False Indigo (*Amorpha*), 107–109
False Indigo (*Amorpha fruticosa*), 107–109
False Mesquite (*Calliandra eriophylla*), 153–154
False-willow (*Baccharis neglecta*), 131–132
Farkleberry (*Vaccinium*), 497–499
Farkleberry (*Vaccinium arboreum*), 498
Feather Dalea (*Dalea formosa*), 247
Feather Sage (*Ceratoides lanata*), 186–188
Fendler Ceanothus (*Ceanothus fendleri*), 178
Fendlera rupicola (Cliff Fendler-bush), 275–276
Fern Acacia (*Acacia hirta*), 77
Fetter-bush (*Leucothoe racemosa*), 341–342
Fiddlewood (*Citharexylum berlandieri*), 210–211
Filigrana (*Callicarpa americana*), 10, 155–157, 350, 482. *See also color plates*
Flame Acanthus (*Anisacanthus quadrifidus var. wrightii*), 7, 11, 116, 117. *See also color plates*
Flatwoods Plum (*Prunus umbellata*), 416, 419
Floral arrangements, *68–69*
Flor de Mimbre (*Chilopsis linearis*), *8*, 32, 200–203, 487. *See also color plates*
Flowering Ash (*Fraxinus cuspidata*), 283, 284
Flowering dates, and seed collection, 5
Flowering Dogwood (*Cornus florida*), 224–225, 226, 227
Foam Flower (*Eupatorium coelestinum*), 266
Foothills Nolina (*Nolina erumpens*), 376
Foothills Palo Verde (*Cercidium microphyllum*), 384
Forestiera (Desert Olive, Wild Privet, Panalero), 30, 42, 277–279
Forestiera acuminata (Swamp Privet, Texas Adelia), 278–279
Forestiera angustifolia (Narrow-leaf Forestiera, Panalero), 277–278, 279
Forestiera neomexicana (New Mexican Forestiera, Desert Olive, Palo Blanco), 279
Forestiera pubescens (Texas Elbow-bush), 278, 279
Forestiera reticulata (Netleaf Forestiera), 279
Fouquiera splendens (Ocotillo, Coachwhip), 273, 280–281, 327
Fouquieriaceae (Ocotillo family), 280–281
Four-winged Saltbush (*Atriplex canescens*), 128, 129, 403
Fox Grape (*Vitis vulpina*), 512
Fragrant Ash (*Fraxinus cuspidata*), 283, 284
Fragrant Mimosa (*Mimosa borealis*), 369. *See also color plates*
Fragrant Mist Flower (*Eupatorium havanense*), 264–266, 290, 350, 459, 518
Fragrant Snowberry (*Symphoricarpos longiflorus*), 482
Fragrant Sumac (*Rhus aromatica*), 27, 443, 446, 448
Fraxinus (Ash, Fresno), 12, 38, 282–285
Fraxinus americana (White Ash), 283–284, 285
Fraxinus berlandieriana (Mexican Ash, Fresno, Plumero), 284, 285

Fraxinus caroliniana (Water Ash, Carolina Ash), 284
Fraxinus cuspidata (Fragrant Ash, Flowering Ash), 283, 284
Fraxinus greggii (Little-leaf Ash, Escobilla, Barreta de Cochino), 1, 283, 285
Fraxinus pensylvanica (Green Ash), 282, 285
Fraxinus texensis (Texas Ash), 283, 285
Fraxinus veluntina (Velvet Ash, Arizona Ash, Fresno), 285
Freezes, and native plants, xxii
Fresno (*Fraxinus*), 12, 38, 282–285
Fresno (*Fraxinus berlandieriana*), 284, 285
Fresno (*Fraxinus veluntina*), 285
Frijolillo (*Sophora secundiflora*), *9*, 21–22, 76, 129, 147, 242, 403, 473–475. *See also color plates*
Frijolito (*Sophora secundiflora*), *9*, 21–22, 76, 129, 147, 242, 403, 473–475. *See also color plates*
Fringe-tree (*Chionanthus virginica*), 52, 204–205, 296
Frost Grape (*Vitis cordifolia*), 511
Fruiting dates, and seed collection, 5
Fruit shapes, *7*
Fungicides, 35, 55, 428–429
Furman's Red (Autumn Sage), 458

Gambel Oak (*Quercus gambelii*), 430
Garryaceae (Silk-tassel bush family), 286–289
Garrya ovata subsp. *goldmannii* (Eggleaf Garrya), 289
Garrya ovata subsp. *lindheimeri* (Mexican Silk-tassel), 13, 21, 23, 34, 58, 286–289
Garrya wrightii (Wright's Silk Tassel), 242, 289
Gass, Ron, 301, 340
Gatuño (*Acacia roemeriana*), 73, 77
Gatuño (*Mimosa dysocarpa*), 369
Genetic engineering, 1
Germination: aeration procedure for, 29–30; and chemical inhibitors, 22; and dormancy, 2, 15, 17, 22–23; and indoor sowing, 35; and planting, 28, 29–30; pregermination on moist paper, 30; process of, 15; and pulsing, 26; and scarification, 17–22; and seed collection, 11; and seed ripening, 23; and soil mixes, 23–24, 33; stages of, 15, *16*; and stratification, 23–27; unexplainable nature of, 1. *See also specific plants*
Giant Dagger (*Yucca faxoniana*), 516–517
Ginseng family (*Araliaceae*), 118–119
Glomerella (anthracnose), 92
Goatbush (*Castela erecta*), 172–173
Gobernadora (*Larrea tridentata*), 249, 273, 327–329, 515
Gochnatia hypoleuca (Chomonque, Ocote), 290–291
Goldenball Leadtree (*Leucaena retusa*), 1, 22, 332–334, 508
Golden St. John's Wort (*Hypericum frondosum*), 308
Gold Star (Yellow-bells), 487
Goosefoot family (*Chenopodiaceae*), 127–130, 186–188
Graceful Oak (*Quercus graciliformis*), 431
Grafting, and cuttings, 44
Granjeno (*Celtis pallida*), 182, 183
Grape (*Vitis*), 7, 12–13, 509–512
Grape family (*Vitaceae*), 110–111, 388–389, 509–512
Graves Oak (*Quercus gravesii*), 431
Gray, Asa, 274
Gray Birch (*Betula populifolia*), 141
Gray Dogwood (*Cornus racemosa*), 227
Gray Oak (*Quercus grisea*), 431
Greasewood, 329
Green Ash (*Fraxinus pensylvanica*), 282, 285
Green-briar (*Smilax*), 471–472
Green-briar (*Smilax rotundifolia*), 472
Greencloud (Cenizo), 37, 336, 337, 339–340
Greenhouses: and germination, 25; misting systems in, 56; planting in, 28, 30–31; "wet-wall" greenhouses, 2
Gregg's Dalea (*Dalea greggii*), *48*, 247
Gregg Senna (*Cassia greggii*), 169
Gregg's Eupatorium (*Eupatorium greggii*), 266
Groovestem Bouchea (*Bouchea linifolia*), 144, 145

Grow-Low (Fragrant Sumac), 446
Guaco (*Parthenocissus quinquefolia*), 38, 388–389
Guadalupe Mountain Laurel (*Sophora gypsophila var. guadalupensis*), 475
Guadalupe Snowberry (*Symphoricarpos guadalupensis*), 482
Guaiacum angustifolium (Guayacan, Soap-bush), 261, 292–294. *See also color plates*
Guajalote (*Colubrina texensis*), 217–218
Guaje (*Leucaena retusa*), 1, 22, 332–334, 508
Guajillo (*Acacia berlandieri*), 76, 383
Guajillo (*Pithecellobium pallens*), 406
Guayacan (*Guaiacum angustifolium*), 261, 292–294. *See also color plates*
Guayule (*Parthenium argentatum*), 17, 20, 385–387
Guignardia aesculi (leaf blotch), 92
Gum-elastic Tree (*Bumelia lanuginosa*), 149–150

Hackberry (*Celtis*), 181–183, 462
Hackberry (*Celtis laevigata*), 182
Hackberry (*Celtis occidentalis*), 182
Halberd-leaf Hibiscus (*Hibiscus laevis*), 305
Halesia caroliniana (Carolina Silverbell), 296
Halesia diptera (Two-winged Silverbell), 295–296
Hall, Oza, xxi
Hamamelidaceae (Witch-hazel family), 297–299, 345–346
Hamamelis vernalis (Ozark Witch-hazel), 299
Hamamelis virginiana (Witch-hazel), 11, 297–299
Hard seed coats, 17–22
Hardwood cuttings, 43–44, 49, 52
Hardwood deciduous cuttings, 44–45
Havard Maguey (*Agave havardiana*), 97
Havard Plum (*Prunus havardii*), 418
Hawthorn (*Crataegus*), 236–239
Hazel Alder (*Alnus serrulata*), 99–100
Heart-leaf Hibiscus (*Hibiscus cardiophyllus*), 303, 304, 391
Heart-leaf Pepper-vine (*Ampelopsis cordata*), 111
Heath Cliff-rose (*Cowania ericaefolia*), 234–235
Heath family (*Ericaceae*), 120–123, 341–342, 354–355, 440–442, 497–499
Hediondilla (*Larrea tridentata*), 249, 273, 327–329, 515
He-huckleberry (*Lyonia ligustrina*), 355
Hesperaloe (*Hesperaloe parviflora*), 300–301. *See also color plates*
Hesperaloe parviflora (Hesperaloe, Coral Yucca), 300–301. *See also color plates*
Hesperaloe parviflora 'Yellow' (Coral Yucca), 301
Hibiscus (Hibiscus, Rose Mallow), 302–305
Hibiscus aculeatus (Pineland Hibiscus), 304
Hibiscus cardiophyllus (Heart-leaf Hibiscus, Tulipan del Monte), 303, 304, 391
Hibiscus coccineus (Texas Star Hibiscus), 304
Hibiscus coulteri (Desert Rose Mallow), 304–305
Hibiscus dasycalyx (Neches River Rose Mallow), 305
Hibiscus family (*Malvaceae*), 302–305, 362–364, 390–391
Hibiscus laevis (Halberd-leaf Hibiscus), 305
Hibiscus moscheutos (Rose Mallow), 304, 305
Hickory (*Carya*), 6, 10, 14, 164–166, 316
Hierba de Cristo (*Lantana horrida*), 117, 324–326
Hierba de la Princesa (*Aloysia gratissima*), 102–103
Hierba del Cenizo (*Tiquilia greggii*), 6, 490–491
Hierba de San Nicolas (*Chrysactinia mexicana*), 208–209
Highbush Blueberry (*Vaccinium arkansanum*), 498–499
Hinckley Oak (*Quercus hinckleyi*), 431
Hippocastanaceae (Buckeye family), 90–93
Hoary Azalea (*Rhododendron canescens*), 441
Hog-plum (*Colubrina texensis*), 217–218

Holly (*Ilex*), 49, 309–312
Holly family (*Aquifoliaceae*), 309–312
Honey Mesquite (*Prosopis glandulosa var. glandulosa*), 414, 519
Honeysuckle (*Lonicera*), 38, 42, 349–351
Honeysuckle family (*Caprifoliaceae*), 349–351, 460–462, 481–482, 502–505
Hooker, J. D., 274
Hop-hornbeam, *9*
Hop-tree (*Ptelea trifoliolata*), 420–421
Hornbeam (*Carpinus caroliniana*), 162–163
Hosage, Dan, 193
Hot water scarification, 18, 20–21
Huacacote (*Malpighia glabra*), 360–361
Huasteco (*Celtis pallida*), 182, 183
Huckleberry (*Lyonia*), 354–355
Huisache (*Acacia farnesiana*), 10, 74, 76–77
Huisachillo (*Acacia schaffneri var. bravoensis*), 74, 77–78
Hypercaceae (St. John's Wort family), 306–308
Hypericum (St. John's Wort), 306–308
Hypericum densiflorum (Dense St. John's Wort), 307
Hypericum fasciculatum (Sand-weed), 307
Hypericum frondosum (Golden St. John's Wort), 308
Hypericum nudiflorum (Naked St. John's Wort), 308

Ilex (Holly), 49, 309–312
Ilex ambigua (Carolina Holly, Sand Holly), 311
Ilex coriaceae (Bay-gall Bush, Ink-berry Holly), 311
Ilex decidua (Possum-haw Holly, Deciduous Holly), 309, 311–312, 344
Ilex opaca (American Holly), 26, 310, 312
Ilex verticillata (Common Winterberry), 312
Ilex vomitoria (Yaupon Holly), 309, 312, 344, 439
Indian Currant (*Symphoricarpos orbiculatus*), 157, 481–482
Indigo bush (*Amorpha*), 107–109
Indigo-bush Amorpha (*Amorpha fruticosa*), 107–109
Indoor sowing, 35
Ink-berry Holly (*Ilex coriaceae*), 311
Inland Sea Oats (*Chasmanthium latifolium*), 364
Insect infestation, 10, 12, 14
Itea virginica (Virginia Sweet-spire, Tassel-white), 313–314

Jaboncillo (*Sapindus saponaria var. drummondii*), 463–465
Janzow, Chuck, 21, 287
Jazmin (*Cephalanthus occidentalis*), 184–185
Jazminillo (*Aloysia*), 101–103
Jazminillo (*Aloysia gratissima*), 102–103
Jersey-tea (*Ceanothus*), 176–178
Jersey-tea (*Ceanothus americanus*), 178
Jopoy (*Esenbeckia berlandieri*), 261
Juglandaceae (Walnut family), 164–166, 315–317
Juglans (Walnut, Nogal), 6, 10–11, 14, 22, 315–317
Juglans major (Arizona Walnut, Nogal), 316
Juglans microcarpa (River Walnut, Little Walnut, Nogalillo), 316–317. *See also color plates*
Juglans nigra (Black Walnut), 316, 317
Juneberry (*Amelanchier*), 104–106
Juniper (*Juniperus*), 22, 45, 49, 249, 318–321
Juniperus (Juniper, Cedar, Cedro), 22, 45, 49, 249, 318–321
Juniperus ashei (Ashe Juniper, Rock Cedar), 122, 319, 320
Juniperus deppeana (Alligator Juniper), 13, 319, 320–321
Juniperus flaccida (Weeping Juniper), 319, 321
Juniperus monosperma (One-seeded Juniper), 319, 321
Juniperus pinchotii (Red-berried Juniper), 13, 319, 321
Juniperus silicicola (Southern Red-Coat Juniper), 318, 319, 321
Juniperus virginiana (Eastern Red Cedar), 318, 319, 321

Keeter's Red (Autumn Sage), 458
Knock-Away Tree (*Ehretia anacua*), 255–257

Koeberlinaceae, 322–323
Koeberlinia spinosa (Allthorn, Crucifixion Thorn, Corona de Cristo Junco), 322–323

Labiatae (Sage family), 456–459
Lacey Oak (*Quercus glaucoides*), 430
La Coma (*Bumelia celastrina*), 150
La Coma (*Bumelia lanuginosa*), 149–150
Lamb's Tail (*Ceratoides lanata*), 186–188
Landscaping, xxi–xxv, 3
Land stewardship, xxiv
Lantana (Lantana), 52, 147
Lantana camara (West Indian Lantana, Afrombilla), 325
Lantana horrida (Texas Lantana, Hierba de Cristo), 117, 324–326
Lantana macropoda (Veiny-leaf or Desert Lantana), 326
Lantana macropoda forma albiflora, 326
Lantrisco (*Amyris*), 112–114
Lantrisco (*Amyris texana*), 112, 113, 114
Largancillo (*Acacia constricta*), 74, 76
Larrea tridentata (Creosote Bush, Gobernadora, Hediondilla), 249, 273, 327–329, 515
Lauraceae (Laurel family), 343–344, 392–393, 466–468
Laurel family (*Lauraceae*), 343–344, 392–393, 466–468
Laurel Oak (*Quercus laurifolia*), 432
Leaf blotch (*Guignardia aesculi*), 92
Leaf shapes, *66–67*
Leaf-spot disease (*Septoria hippocastani*), 92
Leatherwood (*Cyrilla racemiflora*), 243–244
Leatherwood family (*Cyrillaceae*), 243–244
Lechillo (*Carpinus caroliniana*), 162–163
Lechuguilla (*Agave lechuguilla*), 97–98, 327, 491
Legume family (*Fabaceae*), 12, 14, 34, 73–78, 107–109, 133–135, 151–154, 167–169, 186–188, 232–233, 245–247, 258–259, 267–269, 332–334, 367–369, 382–384, 404–406, 412–414, 473–475
Leitneriaceae (Corkwood family), 330–331
Leitneria floridana (Corkwood), 330–331
Lentisco (*Rhus virens*), 34, 242, 444, 445, 448–449, 458
Leucaena pulverulenta (Tepeguaje), 334
Leucaena retusa (Goldenball Leadtree, Guaje), 1, 22, 332–334, 508
Leucophyllum (Cenizo, Purple Sage, Texas Ranger), 6, 37, 154, 335–340, 391
Leucophyllum candidum (Violet Silverleaf), 336, 339
Leucophyllum frutescens (Cenizo, Purple Sage, Texas Silver-leaf, Texas Ranger), 37, 76, 129, 135, 147, 249, 336, 337, 338, 339–340, 383, 403, 458, 515. *See also color plates*
Leucophyllum laevigatum (Chihuahuan Rain Sage), 336, 338, 339
Leucophyllum langmaniae (Rio Bravo ™), 336, 339
Leucophyllum minus (Big-Bend Silver-leaf), 340
Leucophyllum pruinosum (Sierra Bouquet™), 336, 338
Leucophyllum revolutum, 336
Leucophyllum zygophyllum (Cimarron ™), 336, 339
Leucothoe (*Leucothoe racemosa*), 341–342
Leucothoe fontanesiana (Drooping Sweetbells), 342
Leucothoe racemosa (Sweetbells, Fetter-bush, Leucothoe), 341–342
Leucretia Hamilton ™ (Desert Willow), 203
Liberty (American Elm), 493
Liliaceae (Lily family), 300–301, 375–377, 471–472, 513–518
Lime Prickly-ash (*Zanthoxylum fagara*), 519–520
Limonaria (*Amyris madrensis*), 30, 112, 113, 114
Limoncillo (*Dalea formosa*), 247
Limoncillo (*Esenbeckia runyonii*), 260–261
Lindera benzoin (Spicebush), 343–344
Lindheimer's Nolina (*Nolina lindheimeriana*), 375, 376
Lindheimer's Senna (*Cassia lindheimeriana*), 117, 168, 169

Lintisco (*Pistacia texana*), 6, 58, 129, 401–403
Liquidambar styraciflua (Sweetgum, Balsamo, Copalme), 345–346. *See also color plates*
Liriodendron tulipfera (Tulip-tree, Tulip Poplar), 347–348
Little Gem (Cucumber Tree), 358
Little-hip Hawthorn (*Crataegus spathulata*), 239
Little-leaf Ash (*Fraxinus greggii*), 1, 283, 285
Little-leaf Mock-orange (*Philadelphus microphyllus*), 396
Little-leaf Sumac (*Rhus microphylla*), 273, 448, 491, 515
Little Walnut (*Juglans microcarpa*), 316–317. *See also color plates*
Lluvia de Oro (*Parkinsonia aculeata*), 191, 382–384
Loblolly Pine (*Pinus taeda*), 400
Lockett, Landon, 452
Loganiaceae (Logania family), 146–148
Longleaf Pine (*Pinus palustris*), *8*, 400. *See also color plates*
Lonicera (Honeysuckle), 38, 42, 349–351
Lonicera albiflora var. albiflora (White Bush Honeysuckle), 350
Lonicera sempervirens (Coral or Evergreen Honeysuckle), 350, 351. *See also color plates*
Lowrey, Lynn, xxi, 85, 109, 340, 421, 433, 459
Lycium (Wolfberry, Desert-thorn, Tomatillo, Cilindrillo), 352–353
Lycium berlandieri var. berlandieri (Berlander Wolfberry, Tomatillo, Cilindrillo), 352, 353, 519
Lycium carolinianum var. quadrifidium (Carolina Wolfberry), 353
Lycium pallidum var. pallidum (Pallid Wolfberry), 353
Lynn's Everblooming (Cenizo), 340
Lynn's Legacy (Cenizo), 340
Lyonia (Huckleberry), 354–355
Lyonia ligustrina (He-huckleberry), 355
Lyonia mariana (Stagger-bush), 355
Maclura pomifera (Osage-orange), *8*
Madder family (*Rubiaceae*), 184–185
Madrona (*Arbutus xalapensis*), 38, 120–123. *See also color plates*
Madrone (*Arbutus xalapensis*), 38, 120–123. *See also color plates*
Magnolia (Magnolia), 13, 49, 356–359
Magnoliaceae (Magnolia family), 347–348, 356–359
Magnolia family (*Magnoliaceae*), 347–348, 356–359
Magnolia grandiflora (Southern Magnolia), 356, 358–359
Magnolia pyramidata (Pyramid Magnolia, Cucumber Tree), 357–358, 359
Magnolia virginiana (Sweetbay Magnolia), 359
Maguey (*Agave*), 94–98, 135, 154, 273
Maguey (*Agave americana*), 96–97
Maguey Cenizo (*Agave scabra*), 98
Mahonia (*Berberis*), 10, 136–139
Mallow family (*Malvaceae*), 302–305, 362–364, 390–391
Malpighiaceae (Malphighia family), 360–361
Malpighia glabra (Barbados-cherry, Cereza, Huacacote), 360–361
Malvaceae (Hibiscus, Okra or Mallow family), 302–305, 362–364, 390–391
Malvaviscus arboreus var. drummondii (Turk's Cap, Manzanilla), 38, 92, 161, 362–364, 459, 517–518
Manfreda (*Manfreda variegata*), 161
Manzanilla (*Malvaviscus arboreus var. drummondii*), 38, 92, 161, 362–364, 459, 517–518
Maple (*Acer*), *9*, 12, 14, 26, 79–87
Maple family (*Aceraceae*), 79–87
Maple-leaf Viburnum (*Viburnum acerifolium*), 504–505
Mariola (*Parthenium incanum*), 387
Master Gardener Program, xxv
Maturity: and cuttings, 42; and seed collection, 5, 6, 21; and seed ripeness, 6, 10; and seed storage, 13
Mayhaw (*Crataegus opaca*), 237, 238–239
McNeal, Pat, 109, 459

Mejorana (*Salvia ballotaeflora*), 117, 458
Melochia tomentosa (Woolly Pyramid Bush), 365–366
Meristematic cells, 39
Mescal Bean (*Sophora secundiflora*), *9*, 21–22, 76, 129, 147, 242, 403, 473–475. *See also color plates*
Mescat Acacia (*Acacia constricta*), 74, 76
Mesquite (*Prosopis*), 412–414
Mesquite (*Prosopis glandulosa*), 12, 383
Mexican Ash (*Fraxinus berlandieriana*), 284, 285
Mexican Blue Oak (*Quercus oblongifolia*), 433
Mexican Buckeye (*Ungnadia speciosa*), 12, 22, 439, 495–496. *See also color plates*
Mexican Caesalpinia (*Caesalpinia mexicana*), 151–152
Mexican Elderberry (*Sambucus mexicana*), 462
Mexican Palo Verde (*Parkinsonia aculeata*), 191, 382–384
Mexican Persimmon (*Diospyros texana*), 10, 30, 103, 251, 252–254
Mexican Pinyon (*Pinus cembroides*), 398, 399
Mexican Plum (*Prunus mexicana*), *8*, 415, 416, 418. *See also color plates*
Mexican Redbud (*Cercis canadensis var. mexicana*), 194, 192
Mexican Silk-tassel (*Garrya ovata* subsp. *lindheimeri*), 13, 21, 23, 34, 58, 286–289
Mexican Star-leaf Orange (*Choisya dumosa*), 206–207
Mexican Sycamore (*Platanus mexicana*), 408
Mexican White Oak (*Quercus polymorpha*), 433–434
Mimosa (*Albizia julibrissin*), 368
Mimosa (*Mimosa*), 367–369
Mimosa (Mimosa, Uña de Gato, Cat's Claw), 367–369
Mimosa biuncifera (Cat's Claw, Uña de Gato), 368
Mimosa borealis (Fragrant Mimosa), 369. *See also color plates*
Mimosa dysocarpa (Velvet-pod Mimosa, Gatuño), 369
Mimosa emoryana (Emory Mimosa), 369
Mimosa pigra (Zarza, Coatante), 369
Missouri Grape (*Vitis palmata*), 511
Misting systems, 47, 49, 53, *54*, 56
Mistletoe, 182
Mockernut Hickory (*Carya tomentosa*), 166
Mock-orange (*Philadelphus*), 394–396
Mohr Oak (*Quercus mohriana*), 432
Mona (*Ungnadia speciosa*), 12, 22, 439, 495–496. *See also color plates*
Monapesto (*Campsis radicans*), 158–159. *See also color plates*
Mondale Pine (*Pinus elderica*), 399
Monilla (*Ungnadia speciosa*), 12, 22, 439, 495–496. *See also color plates*
Monteczuma Bald Cypress (*Taxodium mucronatum*), 434, 484, 485
Mora de la Sierra (*Carpinus caroliniana*), 162–163
Mora (*Morus*), 370–371, 462
Moraceae (Mulberry family), 370–371
Morus (Morus, Mora, Mulberry), 370–371, 462
Morus microphylla (Mountain Mulberry), 371
Morus rubra (Red Mulberry), 371
Mount Emory Mountain Sage, 459
Mountain Hawthorn (*Crataegus tracyi*), 239
Mountain Mulberry (*Morus microphylla*), 371
Mountain Sage (*Salvia regla*), 459
Mulberry (*Morus*), 370–371, 462
Mulberry family (*Moraceae*), 370–371
Munson, Thomas Volney, 510
Muscadine (*Vitis rotundifolia*), 510, 512
Mustang Grape (*Vitis mustangensis*), 511
Mycorrhizal fungi, 34, 122
Myricaceae (Wax-myrtle family), 372–374
Myrica cerifera (Wax-myrtle, Southern Bay-berry, Árbol de la Sierra), 372–374
Myrica pusila (Dwarf Wax-myrtle), 374

Naked Indian's Leg (*Arbutus xalapensis*), 38, 120–123. *See also color plates*
Naked St. John's Wort (*Hypericum nudiflorum*), 308

Naranjillo (*Esenbeckia runyonii*), 260–261
Narrow-leaf Forestiera (*Forestiera angustifolia*), 277–278, 279
Narrow-leaf Yucca (*Yucca angustifolia*), 515
Narrow-leaved evergreen cuttings, 45
Native plant movement, xxi–xxii, xxv
Native plants: cultivars of, 3, 37–38; and landscaping, xxi–xxv, 3; and nursery industry, xxiii, 1–2; and water supply, xxii, xxv, 2
Native Plant Society, xxv
Naturalistic gardening style, xxiv, xxv
Natural world, connection/disconnection to, xxii, xxiv
Neches River Rose Mallow (*Hibiscus dasycalyx*), 305
Negrito (*Citharexylum berlandieri*), 210–211
Netleaf Forestiera (*Forestiera reticulata*), 279
Netleaf Hackberry (*Celtis reticulata*), 181–182, 183
Netleaf Oak (*Quercus rugosa*), 434
New Deal Weed (*Baccharis neglecta*), 131–132
New Harmony (American Elm), 493
New Mexico Agave (*Agave neomexicana*), 97, 249
New Mexico Foresteria (*Forestiera neomexicana*), 279
New Mexico Pinyon (*Pinus edulis*), 399–400
Nightshade family (*Solanaceae*), 160–161, 352–353
Nipple gall (*Pachypsylla celtidismamma*), 182
Nitidulid beetles, 427–428
Nogal (*Carya*), 6, 10, 14, 164–166, 316
Nogal (*Carya illinoinensis*), 166
Nogal (*Juglans*), 6, 10–11, 14, 22, 315–317
Nogal (*Juglans major*), 316
Nogalillo (*Juglans microcarpa*), 316–317. *See also color plates*
Nogal Mofudo (*Carya ovata*), 166
Nolina (Beargrass, Sacahuiste, Basketgrass), 92, 350, 375–377, 458, 517
Nolina erumpens (Foothills Nolina, Basketgrass), 376
Nolina lindheimeri (Prickly Pear Cactus), 103
Nolina lindheimeriana (Devil's Shoestring, Lindheimer's Nolina), 375, 376
Nolina micrantha (Beargrass), 377, 391
Nolina texana (Texas Sacahuiste, Bunchgrass), 377. *See also color plates*
Nopal (*Opuntia*), 135, 491, 508, 519
Nueces (*Carya*), 6, 10, 14, 164–166, 316
Nueces (*Carya illinoinensis*), 166
Nursery industry: and cutting propagation, 37, 38; hazards in, 3; and native plants, xxiii, 1–2; and stock plants, 11; and water supply, xxv
Nyssa (Tupelo, Sour-gum), 378–379
Nyssa aquatica (Water Tupelo), 378, 379
Nyssa sylvatica var. sylvatica (Blackgum, Black Tupelo), 378, 379

Oak (*Quercus*), 6, 10–11, 14, 30, 42, 424–436
Oak family (*Fagaceae*), 170–171, 270–271, 424–436
Oak wilt (*Ceratocystis fagacearum*), 427–429
Ocote (*Gochnatia hypoleuca*), 290–291
Ocotillo (*Fouquiera splendens*), 273, 280–281, 327
Ocotillo family (*Fouquieriaceae*), 280–281
Ogden, Scott, 433, 458–459
Okra family (*Malvaceae*), 302–305, 362–364, 390–391
Old-man's Beard (*Chionanthus virginica*), 52, 204–205, 296
Old-man's Beard (*Clematis drummondii*), 212, 213
Old Shag (*Yucca treculeana*), 518
Oleaceae (Olive or Ash family), 204–205, 277–279, 282–285
Olive family (*Oleaceae*), 204–205, 277–279, 282–285
Olmo (*Ulmus*), 14, 492–494
Olmo (*Ulmus crassifolia*), 493, 494
One-seeded Juniper (*Juniperus monosperma*), 319, 321
Opuntia (Nopal, Prickly Pear Cactus), 135, 491, 508, 519
Opuntia leptocaulis (Tasajillo), 103

Orange Hummingbird-bush (*Anisacanthus quadrifidus var. wrightii*), 7, 11, 116, 117. *See also color plates*
Orcajuela (*Citharexylum berlandieri*), 210–211
Orchid-tree (*Bauhinia luinaroides*), 133–135
Oreganillo (*Aloysia wrightii*), 103
Oreja del Perro (*Tiquilia greggii*), 6, 490–491
Osage-orange (*Maclura pomifera*), *8*
Ostrya chisosensis (Chisos Hop-hornbeam), 381
Ostrya knowltonii (Western Hop-hornbeam), 381
Ostrya virginiana (American Hop-hornbeam), 380–381
Outdoor fall planting, 28
Oval-leaf Saltbush (*Atriplex ovata*), 130
Ozark Witch-hazel (*Hamamelis vernalis*), 299

Pachypsylla celtidismamma (nipple gall), 182
Pacific Madrone (*Arbutus menziesii*), 122
Paisano Bush (*Berberis trifoliolata*), 117, 137, 138, 139, 301, 508. *See also color plates*
Pale-leaf Yucca (*Yucca pallida*), 514, 517
Pallid Wolfberry (*Lycium pallidum var. pallidum*), 353
Palma (*Yucca faxoniana*), 516–517
Palma (*Yucca treculeana*), 518
Palma Barreta (*Yucca faxoniana*), 516–517
Palmaceae (Palm family), 450–453
Palma Micharros (*Sabal mexicana*), 30, 451–452, 453
Palma Real (*Sabal*), 30, 450–453
Palma Real (*Sabal mexicana*), 30, 451–452, 453
Palma Samandoca (*Yucca faxoniana*), 516–517
Palmetto (*Sabal*), 30, 450–453
Palm family (*Palmaceae*), 450–453
Palmilla (*Yucca elata*), 516
Palmilla (*Yucca faxoniana*), 516–517
Palmita (*Yucca rostrata*), 517
Palo Blanco (*Celtis*), 181–183, 462
Palo Blanco (*Celtis reticulata*), 181–182, 183
Palo Blanco (*Forestiera neomexicana*), 279
Palo Duro (*Cercocarpus montanus var. argenteus*), 12, 197–199
Palo Prieto (*Cassia wislizenii*), 167–169
Palo Prieto (*Vauquelinia angustifolia*), 500–501
Panalero (*Forestiera*), 30, 42, 277–279
Panalero (*Forestiera angustifolia*), 277–278, 279
Panalero (*Schaefferia cuneifolia*), 469–470
Panhandle Grape (*Vitis acerifolia*), 511
Panicled Amorpha (*Amorpha paniculata*), 109
Papershell Pinyon (*Pinus cembroides var. remota*), 399
Parkinsonia aculeata (Retama, Mexican Palo Verde, Lluvia de Oro), 191, 382–384
Parkinsonia texana var. macrum (Border Palo Verde), 190
Parkinsonia texana var. texanum (Texas Palo Verde), 190
Parsley Hawthorn (*Crataegus marshallii*), 237, 238, 296
Parthenium argentatum (Guayule, Afinador), 17, 20, 385–387
Parthenium incanum (Mariola), 387
Parthenocissus heptaphylla (Seven-leaf Creeper), 389
Parthenocissus quinquefolia (Virginia Creeper, Guaco), 38, 388–389
Pata de Cabra (*Bauhinia luinaroides*), 133–135
Pata de Vaca (*Bauhinia luinaroides*), 133–135
Pavonia lasiopetala (Rose-mallow Pavonia, Rock-Rose), 29, 38, 390–391, 458. *See also color plates*
Paw-paw (*Asimina tribola*), 124–126
Peach-brush (*Prunus minutiflora*), 418
Peach-leaf Willow (*Salix amygdaloides*), 455
Pea family. *See* Legume family (*Fabaceae*)
Pecan (*Carya*), 6, 10, 14, 164–166, 316
Pecan (*Carya illinoinensis*), 166
Pepper-vine (*Ampelopsis*), 110–111
Pepper-vine (*Ampelopsis arborea*), 111

Persea borbonia var. borbonia (Sweetbay, Red bay), 392–393
Persimmon (*Diospyros*), 13, 251–254, 261
Persimmon family (*Ebenaceae*), 251–254
Philadelphus (Mock-orange), 394–396
Philadelphus ernestii (Canyon Mock-orange), 395, 396
Philadelphus microphyllus (Little-leaf Mock-orange), 396
Philadelphus texensis (Texas mock-orange), 396
Phorandendron, 182
Pigeon Berry (*Rivinia humilis*), 92, 157, 364, 459
Pigeon Grape (*Vitis aestivalis*), 511
Pignut Hickory (*Carya cordiformis*), 166
Pinacate (*Cassia wislizenii*), 167–169
Pinacatillo (*Ptelea trifoliolata*), 420–421
Pinaceae (Pine family), 397–400
Pine (*Pinus*), 45, 397–400
Pine family (*Pinaceae*), 397–400
Pineland Hibiscus (*Hibiscus aculeatus*), 304
Pink Perfection (Autumn Sage), 459
Pinky Anisacanthus (*Anisacanthus puberulus*), 116, 117
Pino (*Pinus*), 45, 397–400
Pinobete (*Cupressus arizonica var. arizonica*), 240–242, 403
Pino Enano (*Pinus strobiformis*), 400
Pinus (Pine, Pino, Pinyon), 45, 397–400
Pinus cembroides (Mexican Pinyon), 398, 399
Pinus cembroides var. remota (Remote Pinyon, Papershell Pinyon), 399
Pinus echinata (Shortleaf pine), 399
Pinus edulis (New Mexico Pinyon), 399–400
Pinus elderica (Afghan Pine, Mondale Pine), 399
Pinus palustris (Longleaf Pine), *8*, 400. *See also color plates*
Pinus ponderosa (Ponderosa Pine, Western Yellow Pine), 398, 400
Pinus strobiformis (Southwestern White Pine, Pino Enano), 400
Pinus taeda (Loblolly Pine), 400
Pinyon (*Pinus*), 45, 397–400
Pistacia chinensis (Chinese Pistachio), 403
Pistacia texana (Texas Pistachio, Lintisco), 6, 58, 129, 401–403
Pitcher Clematis (*Clematis pitcheri*), 213–214. *See also color plates*
Pithecellobium flexicaule (Texas Ebony, Ébano), 30, 261, 404–406
Pithecellobium pallens (Tenaza, Guajillo), 406
Plains Cottonwood (*Populus deltoides var. occidentalis*), 411
Plane-tree family (*Platanaceae*), 407–408
Planting: aeration procedure, 29–30; containers for, 31–32; fall planting, 28, 30–31; and field sowing, 35–36; in greenhouse, 28, 30–31; and indoor sowing, 35; and maturity, 21; and seedling transplantation, 36; and soil mixes, 33–34; spring planting, 29
Platanaceae (Plane-tree family), 407–408
Platanus (Sycamore), 434
Platanus mexicana (Mexican Sycamore), 408
Platanus occidentalis (Sycamore Plane Tree), 407–408
Platanus occidentalis var. glabrata (Western Sycamore), 408
Plum (*Prunus*), 10, 12–13, 21, 415–419
Plumero (*Fraxinus berlandieriana*), 284, 285
Plume Tiquilia (*Tiquilia greggii*), 6, 490–491
Pointleaf Manzanita (*Arctostaphylos pungens*), 242
Polecat Bush (*Rhus trilobata var. pilosissima*), 448
Ponderosa Pine (*Pinus ponderosa*), 398, 400
Populus (Cottonwood, Alamo), 39, 409–411
Populus deltoides var. deltoides (Eastern Cottonwood), 410, 411
Populus deltoides var. occidentalis (Plains Cottonwood), 411
Populus fremontii var. wislizenii (Rio Grande Cottonwood), 411
Possum-haw Holly (*Ilex decidua*), 309, 311–312, 344

Possum-haw Viburnum (*Viburnum nudum*), 505
Post Oak (*Quercus stellata*), 427, 434, 435
Prairie Association, xxv
Prairie Flame-leaf Sumac (*Rhus lanceolata*), 10, 32, 444, 445, 447–448. *See also color plates*
Pregermination, 22
Prickly Pear Cactus (*Nolina lindheimeri*), 103
Prickly Pear Cactus (*Opuntia*), 135, 491, 508, 519
Princeton (American Elm), 493
Propagation: age of cutting, 42; containers for, 53–54; cutting propagation, 37–43; and hardening off, 56–58, *57*; and hardwood cuttings, 43–44, 49, 52; and hardwood deciduous cuttings, 44–45; and narrow-leaved evergreen cuttings, 45; and plant selection, 49–50; and quick-dip solutions, 52–53; root cuttings, 46; and rooting hormones, 45, 51, 52–53; and rooting media, 54–55; rooting process, 38–39; and seed collection, 4; semihardwood (greenwood) cuttings, 43, 46–47, 49, 52, 53, 55; softwood cuttings, 43, 47–49, *48*, 53, 55; and technology, 1; and water loss, 55–56; and wounding, 51. *See also* Germination; Planting; Seed collection; *and specific plants*
Prosopis (Mesquite), 412–414
Prosopis glandulosa (Mesquite), 12, 383
Prosopis glandulosa var. glandulosa (Honey Mesquite), 414, 519
Prosopis glandulosa var. torreyana (Western Mesquite), 414
Prosopis pubescens (Screwbean Mesquite, Tornillo), 414
Prosopis reptans (Creeping Mesquite, Dwarf Screwbean), 414
Pruning: air pruning of roots, 2, 31, 32, *33*; and transplantation, 63–64
Prunus (Plum, Cherry), 10, 12–13, 21, 415–419
Prunus angustifolia (Chickasaw Plum, Sandhill Plum), 417
Prunus caroliniana (Cherry Laurel), 417–418, 439
Prunus havardii (Havard Plum), 418
Prunus mexicana (Mexican Plum), *8*, 415, 416, 418. *See also color plates*
Prunus minutiflora (Texas Almond, Peach-brush), 418
Prunus rivularis (Creek Plum), 416, 418
Prunus serotina var. eximia (Escarpment Choke-cherry), 416, 419
Prunus serotina var. rufula (Southwestern Black Cherry), 419
Prunus serotina var. serotina (Choke-cherry, Wild Black Cherry), 417, 418–419
Prunus texana (Sand Plum), 419
Prunus umbellata (Flatwoods Plum, Slow Cherry), 416, 419
Ptelea trifoliolata (Hop-tree, Wafer-ash, Cola de Zorillo, Pinacatillo), 420–421
Pulsing, 26
Purple Clematis (*Clematis pitcheri*), 213–214. *See also color plates*
Purple Sage (*Leucophyllum*), 6, 37, 154, 335–340, 391
Purple Sage (*Leucophyllum frutescens*), 37, 76, 129, 135, 147, 249, 336, 337, 338, 339–340, 383, 458, 515. *See also color plates*
Pyramid Magnolia (*Magnolia pyramidata*), 357–358, 359
Pyrus (Crabapple), 7, 10, 12–13
Pyrus angustifolia (Southern Crabapple), 423
Pyrus arbutifolia (Red Chokeberry), 423
Pyrus ioensis (Blanco Crabapple), 422–423
Pythium ultimum, 35

Quassia family (*Simaroubaceae*), 172–173
Quercus (Oak, Encino), 6, 10–11, 14, 30, 42, 424–436
Quercus alba (White Oak), 429, 430
Quercus buckleyi (Texas or Spanish Red Oak), 6, 427, 429, 431, 435
Quercus canbyi, 434
Quercus emoryi (Emory Oak), 429–430
Quercus falcata (Southern Red Oak), 430
Quercus fusiformis (Escarpment Live Oak, Encino Chaparro), 427, 430, 434, 436

Quercus gambelii (Gambel Oak), 430
Quercus glaucoides (Lacey Oak, Encino Roble), 430
Quercus graciliformis (Graceful Oak), 431
Quercus gravesii (Chisos Red Oak, Graves Oak, Encino Colorado), 431
Quercus grisea (Gray Oak, Encino Prieto), 431
Quercus hinckleyi (Hinckley Oak), 431
Quercus hypoleucoides (Silverleaf Oak), 431
Quercus incana (Sandjack Oak, Bluejack Oak), 431
Quercus intricata (Coahuila Scrub Oak), 432
Quercus laurifolia (Laurel Oak), 432
Quercus macrocarpa (Bur Oak), 5, 7, 427, 432. *See also color plates*
Quercus marilandica (Blackjack Oak), 427, 432
Quercus meuhlenbergii (Chinquapin Oak), 432–433
Quercus michauxii (Swamp Chestnut Oak), 432
Quercus mohriana (Mohr Oak, Shin Oak), 432
Quercus nigra (Water Oak), 433
Quercus oblongifolia (Mexican Blue Oak), 433
Quercus phellos (Willow Oak), 433
Quercus polymorpha (Mexican White Oak), 433–434
Quercus pungens var. vaseyana (Vasey Oak), 434
Quercus rhizophylla, 434
Quercus rugosa (Netleaf Oak), 434
Quercus shumardii (Shumard Red Oak), 4, 427, 431, 434–435
Quercus sinuata var. breviloba (Bigelow Oak, Shin Oak), 435
Quercus stellata (Post Oak), 427, 434, 435
Quercus velutina (Black Oak), 6, 435–436
Quercus virginiana (Coastal Live Oak, Encino), 32, 426, 427, 436
Quick-dip solutions, 52–53

Rabbit-eye Blueberry (*Vaccinium virgatum*), 499
Raincloud (Cenizo), 336, 340
Rainfall patterns, 2, 6, 17, 22
Ranunculaeceae (Crowfoot family), 212–214
Rare plants, 5–6, 59
Raspberry (Autumn Sage), 459
Read, Robert, 452
Red Barberry (*Berberis haematocarpa*), 138, 139
Red bay (*Persea borbonia var. borbonia*), 392–393
Red-berried Juniper (*Juniperus pinchotii*), 13, 319, 321
Red Buckeye (*Aesculus pavia var. pavia*), 93
Redbud (*Cercis*), 6, 10, 32, 192–196
Red Chokeberry (*Pyrus arbutifolia*), 423
Red Maple (*Acer rubrum var. rubrum*), 79, 84
Red Mulberry (*Morus rubra*), 371
Redroot (*Ceanothus*), 176–178
Redroot (*Ceanothus herbaceus*), 178
Red-tipped Photinia, 403
Red Velvet (Autumn Sage), 459
Remote Pinyon (*Pinus cembroides var. remota*), 399
Resin-bush (*Viguiera stenoloba*), *8*, 145, 147, 458, 491, 506–508. *See also color plates*
Retama (*Parkinsonia aculeata*), 191, 382–384
Retama China (*Cercidium texanum*), 189–191
Reverchon's Hawthorn (*Crataegus reverchonii*), 239
Rhamnaceae (Buckthorn family), 176–178, 217–220, 437–439
Rhamnus caroliniana (Carolina Buckthorn), 6, 10, 344, 437–439
Rhizoctonia solani, 35
Rhododendron (Azalea), 440–442
Rhododendron canescens (Hoary Azalea), 441
Rhododendron coryi (Azalea, Wild Honeysuckle), 441
Rhododendron oblongifolium (Texas Azalea), 441–442
Rhododendron prinophyllum (Texas Honeysuckle, Early Azalea), 441, 442
Rhus (Sumac), 11, 13, 19, 21, 438, 443–449, 462

Rhus aromatica (Fragrant Sumac), 27, 443, 446, 448
Rhus coppalina (Shining Sumac), 446–447, 448
Rhus glabra (Smooth Sumac, Scarlet Sumac), 447
Rhus lanceolata (Prairie Flame-leaf Sumac), 10, 32, 444, 445, 447–448. *See also color plates*
Rhus microphylla (Little-leaf or Desert Sumac, Agrito, Correosa), 273, 448, 491, 515
Rhus trilobata var. pilosissima (Squaw Bush, Polecat Bush), 448
Rhus virens (Evergreen Sumac, Lentisco), 34, 242, 444, 445, 448–449, 458
Rio Bravo ™ (*Leucophyllum langmaniae*), 336, 339
Rio Grande Cottonwood (*Populus fremontii var. wislizenii*), 411
Riverbank Grape (*Vitis riparia*), 511
River Birch (*Betula nigra*), 140–141
River Fern (*Dryopteris*), 157
River Walnut (*Juglans microcarpa*), 316–317. *See also color plates*
Rivinia humilis (Pigeon Berry), 92, 157, 364, 459
Rock Cedar (*Juniperus ashei*), 122, 319, 320
Rock-Rose (*Pavonia lasiopetala*), 29, 38, 390–391, 458. *See also color plates*
Romer Acacia (*Acacia roemeriana*), 73, 77
Roosevelt Weed (*Baccharis neglecta*), 131–132
Rooting: and bottom heat, 45; containers for, 53–54; environment for, 53; and native plants, 2; process of, 38–39; root cuttings, 46; rooting hormones, 45, 51, 52–53; rooting media, 54–55; stages of, 40. *See also specific plants*
Roots: adventitious roots, 39, 42, 46; air pruning of, 2, 31, 32, *33*; lateral and interior branching, 2, 32; and mycorrhizal fungi, 34; tap-roots, 2, 30, 31–32, 34; and transplantation, 59, 62–63, 64
Rosaceae (Rose family), 104–106, 197–199, 234–239, 272–274, 415–419, 422–423, 500–501
Rosa de Juan (*Cephalanthus occidentalis*), 184–185
Rosea (Autumn Sage), 458
Rose Mallow (*Hibiscus*), 302–305
Rose Mallow (*Hibiscus moscheutos*), 304, 305
Rose-mallow Pavonia (*Pavonia lasiopetala*), 29, 38, 390–391, 458. *See also color plates*
Rough-leaf Dogwood (*Cornus drummondii*), 27, 224, 225, 226, 227, 439
Rough Maguey (*Agave scabra*), 98
Rubiaceae (Madder family), 184–185
Rusty Black-haw Viburnum (*Viburnum rufidulum*), *9*, 26, 52–53, 482, 503–504, 505. *See also color plates*
Rutaceae (Citrus family), 112–114, 206–207, 260–261, 420–421, 519–520

Sabal (Sabal, Soyate, Palma Real, Palmetto), 30, 450–453
Sabal guatemalensis, 452
Sabal louisiana, 452
Sabal mexicana (Texas Palmetto, Palma Micharros, Palma Real, Soyate), 30, 451–452, 453
Sabal minor (Dwarf Palmetto), 451, 452, 453
Sabal x mexicana Read (Brazoria Palmetto), 452–453
Sabino (*Taxodium distichum var. distichum*), 4, *8*, *9*, 12, 32, 379, 483–485. *See also color plates*
Sacahuiste (*Nolina*), 92, 350, 375–377, 458, 517
Sage (*Salvia*), 38, 147, 456–459
Sage family (*Labiatae*), 456–459
Salicaceae (Willow family), 409–411, 454–455
Salix (Willow), 14, 39, 51
Salix amygdaloides (Peach-leaf Willow), 455
Salix nigra (Black Willow, Sauz, Sauz Serrano), 454–455
Salix taxifolia (Yew-leaf Willow), 455
Saltbush (*Atriplex*), 127–130
Salvia (Sage, Salvia), 38, 147, 456–459

Salvia ballotaeflora (Mejorana, Blue Shrub Sage, Crespa), 117, 458
Salvia coccinea (Tropical Sage), 161, 364, 459
Salvia greggii (Autumn Sage, Cherry Sage), 391, 457, 458–459. *See also color plates*
Salvia microphylla, 459
Salvia regla (Mountain Sage), 459
Salvia roemeriana (Cedar Sage), 161, 364, 517
Sambucus caerulea (Blue Elderberry), 462
Sambucus canadensis (Elderberry, American Elder), 460–462
Sambucus mexicana (Mexican Elderberry), 462
San Carlos Festival (Autumn Sage), 459
Sanderson (Texas Redbud), 196
Sandhill Plum (*Prunus angustifolia*), 417
Sand Holly (*Ilex ambigua*), 311
Sandjack Oak (*Quercus incana*), 431
Sand-Paper Tree (*Ehretia anacua*), 255–257
Sand Plum (*Prunus texana*), 419
Sand-weed (*Hypericum fasciculatum*), 307
San Jose Cenizo (Cenizo), 340
Sapindaceae (Soapberry family), 463–465, 495–496
Sapindus saponaria var. drummondii (Soapberry, Jaboncillo, Amole de Bolito), 463–465
Sapotaceae (Sapodilla family), 149–150
Sarsaparilla-vine (*Smilax pumila*), 472
Sassafras (*Sassafras albidum*), 466–468
Sauz (*Salix nigra*), 454–455
Sauz Serrano (*Salix nigra*), 454–455
Saw-briar (*Smilax glauca*), 472
Saxifragaceae (Saxifrage family), 275–276, 313–314, 394–396
Scarification: acid scarification, 18–20, 21, 22; active yeast method, 21; and hard seed coats, 17–18; hot water scarification, 18, 20–21; mechanical scarification, 18; and seed collection, 21–22; sodium hypochlorite treatment, 20; and stratification, 27
Scarlet Buckeye (*Aesculus pavia var. flavescens*), 93
Scarlet Clematis (*Clematis texensis*), 213, 214
Scarlet Sumac (*Rhus glabra*), 447
Schaefferia cuneifolia (Desert Yaupon, Capul, Panalero), 469–470
Schama, Simon, xxii
Scott's Red (Autumn Sage), 458
Screwbean Mesquite (*Prosopis pubescens*), 414
Scrophulariaceae (Snapdragon family), 335–340
Scuppernog (*Vitis rotundifolia*), 510, 512
Sedge (*Carex*), 459, 482
Seed cleaning, 12–13, 22, 25, 28
Seed collection: and cleaning, 12–13, 22, 25, 28; and hard seed coats, 21–22; and provenance, 4–5, 25; and seed ripening, 5–6, 10–11; and stock plants, 11; and storage, 13–14; tools and materials for, 11–12. *See also specific plants*
Seed dispersal, 5
Seedlings, 33, 35, 36
Seed provenance, 4–5, 25
Seed ripening, 5–6, 10–11, 23
Seed shapes, *8–9*
Seed storage, 13–14. *See also specific plants*
Seep-willow (*Baccharis neglecta*), 131–132
Semihardwood (greenwood) cuttings, *41*, 43, 46–47, 49, 52, 53, 55
Septoria hippocastani (leaf-spot disease), 92
Service-berry (*Amelanchier*), 104–106
Service-berry (*Amelanchier arborea*), 105
Seven-leaf Creeper (*Parthenocissus heptaphylla*), 389
Shadbush (*Amelanchier*), 104–106
Shade structures, *57*, 58, 63
Shadscale (*Atriplex confertifolia*), 129–130
Shagbark Hickory (*Carya ovata*), 166
Shining Sumac (*Rhus coppalina*), 446–447, 448
Shin Oak (*Quercus mohriana*), 432
Shin Oak (*Quercus sinuata var. breviloba*), 435
Shortleaf pine (*Pinus echinata*), 399
Shreve, Loy, 316
Shumard Red Oak (*Quercus shumardii*), 4, 427, 431, 434–435

Sierra Bouquet ™ (*Leucophyllum pruinosum*), 336, 338
Sierra Madre Torchwood (*Amyris madrensis*), 30, 112, 113, 114
Silk-tassel bush family (*Garryaceae*), 286–289
Silky Camellia (*Stewartia malacodendron*), 476–477
Silverado ™ (Cenizo), 340
Silverbell (*Styrax*), 14, 478–480
Silvercloud (Violet Silverleaf), 336, 337, 339
Silver Dalea (*Dalea bicolor var. argyraea*), 246–247
Silver-leaf Mountain Mahogany (*Cercocarpus montanus var. argenteus*), 12, 197–199
Silverleaf Oak (*Quercus hypoleucoides*), 431
Silver Smoke (Arizona Cypress), 242
Simaroubaceae (Quassia family), 172–173
Simpson, Benny, xxv, 81, 109, 182, 203, 276, 338, 339, 340, 419, 434, 459
Skelton-leaf Goldeneye Daisy (*Viguiera stenoloba*), *8*, 145, 147, 458, 491, 506–508. *See also color plates*
Slippery Elm (*Ulmus rubra*), 494
Slow Cherry (*Prunus umbellata*), 416, 419
Smilax (Green-briar, Cat-briar), 471–472
Smilax glauca (Saw-briar, Cat-briar), 472
Smilax laurifolia (Bamboo-vine), 472
Smilax pumila (Sarsaparilla-vine), 472
Smilax rotundifolia (Green-briar, Stretch-berry), 472
Smoke Tree (*Cotinus obovatus*), 6, 228–231
Smooth Alder (*Alnus serrulata*), 99–100
Smooth Sumac (*Rhus glabra*), 447
Snake Herb (*Dychoriste linearis*), 145
Snakewood (*Colubrina texensis*), 217–218
Snapdragon family (*Scrophulariaceae*), 335–340
Snowbell (*Styrax*), 14, 478–480
Snowberry (*Symphoricarpos orbiculatus*), 157, 481–482
Soapberry (*Sapindus saponaria var. drummondii*), 463–465
Soapberry family (*Sapindaceae*), 463–465, 495–496
Soap-bush (*Guaiacum angustifolium*), 261, 292–294. *See also color plates*
Soaptree Yucca (*Yucca elata*), 516
Sodium hypochlorite treatment, 20
Softwood cuttings, 43, 47–49, *48*, 53, 55
Soil: and cuttings, 53, 54–55; and field sowing, 35–36; and germination, 23–24, 33; microorganisms in, 2, 34; mixes of, 2, 33–34; and transplantation, 62, 63, 64, 65. *See also specific plants*
Solanaceae (Nightshade family), 160–161, 352–353
Sophora affinis (Eve's Necklace), 32, 475
Sophora gypsophila var. guadalupensis (Guadalupe Mountain Laurel), 475
Sophora secundiflora (Texas Mountain Laurel, Mescal Bean, Frijolito, Frijolillo), *9*, 21–22, 76, 129, 147, 242, 403, 473–475. *See also color plates*
Sophora tomentosa var. occidentalis (Yellow Sophora), 475
Sotol (*Dasylirion*), 248–250, 281
Sotol (*Dasylirion leiophyllum*), 250, 327
Sour-gum (*Nyssa*), 378–379
Southern Arrow-wood (*Viburnum dentatum*), 505
Southern Bay-berry (*Myrica cerifera*), 372–374
Southern Crabapple (*Pyrus angustifolia*), 423
Southern Magnolia (*Magnolia grandiflora*), 356, 358–359
Southern Red-Coat Juniper (*Juniperus silicicola*), 318, 319, 321
Southern Red Oak (*Quercus falcata*), 430
Southern Sugar Maple (*Acer barbatum*), 81, 85
Southwestern Black Cherry (*Prunus serotina var. rufula*), 419
Southwestern White Pine (*Pinus strobiformis*), 400
Soyate (*Sabal*), 30, 450–453
Soyate (*Sabal mexicana*), 30, 451–452, 453
Soyate (*Yucca rostrata*), 517
Spanish-Bayonet (*Yucca*), 135, 458, 513–518
Spanish Bayonet (*Yucca treculeana*), 518
Spanish Dagger (*Yucca faxoniana*), 516–517

Spanish Dagger (*Yucca treculeana*), 518
Spanish Grape (*Vitis berlandiera*), 511
Spanish Red Oak (*Quercus buckleyi*), 6, 427, 429, 431, 435
Spank (Chomonque), 291
Sparkleberry (*Vaccinium arboreum*), 498
Spicebush (*Lindera benzoin*), 343–344
Spiny Kidney-wood (*Eysenhardtia spinosa*), 269
Spiny Saltbush (*Atriplex confertifolia*), 129–130
Spoon-leaf Bouchea (*Bouchea spathulata*), 144, 145
Spring planting, 29
Spurge family (*Euphorbiaceae*), 88–89
Squaw Bush (*Rhus trilobata var. pilosissima*), 448
Stachys coccinea (Texas Betony), 157, 482
Staff-tree family (*Celestraceae*), 179–180, 262–263, 469–470
Stagger-bush (*Lyonia mariana*), 355
Sterculiaceae (Chocolate family), 365–366
Stewartia malacodendron (Silky Camellia), 476–477
Stock plants, 11, 50
St. John's Wort (*Hypericum*), 306–308
St. John's Wort family (*Hypercaceae*), 306–308
Stratification, 23–27
Strawberry Bush (*Euonymus americanus*), 262–263
Stretch-berry (*Smilax rotundifolia*), 472
Styracaceae (Styrax family), 295–296, 478–480
Styrax (Silverbell, Snowbell), 14, 478–480
Styrax americana (American Snowbell), 479, 480
Styrax family (*Styracaceae*), 295–296, 478–480
Styrax platanifolia (Sycamore-leaf Snowbell), 480. *See also color plates*
Styrax texana (Texas Snowbell), 480
Sugarberry (*Celtis*), 181–183, 462
Sugarberry (*Celtis laevigata*), 182
Sugar Maple (*Acer saccharum*), 81, 82, 84, 85, 86–87
Sulfuric acid, 18–20
Sumac (*Rhus*), 11, 13, 19, 21, 438, 443–449, 462
Sumac family (*Anacardiaceae*), 228–231, 401–403, 443–449
Summer-sweet (*Clethra alnifolia*), 215–216
Sunflower family (*Asteraceae*), 131–132, 208–209, 264–266, 290–291, 385–387, 506–508, 521–522
Super Bloomer ™ (Turk's Cap), 364
Swamp Chestnut Oak (*Quercus michauxii*), 432
Swamp Privet (*Forestiera acuminata*), 278–279
Swamp Tupelo, 379
Sweetbay (*Persea borbonia var. borbonia*), 392–393
Sweetbay Magnolia (*Magnolia virginiana*), 359
Sweetbells (*Leucothoe racemosa*), 341–342
Sweetbrush (*Aloysia macrostachya*), 103
Sweet Grape (*Vitis cinerea*), 511
Sweetgum (*Liquidambar styraciflua*), 345–346. *See also color plates*
Sweet Mountain Grape (*Vitis monticola*), 511
Sweet Pepper-bush (*Clethra alnifolia*), 215–216
Sycamore (*Platanus*), 434
Sycamore-leaf Snowbell (*Styrax platanifolia*), 480. *See also color plates*
Sycamore Plane Tree (*Platanus occidentalis*), 407–408
Symphoricarpos guadalupensis (Guadalupe Snowberry), 482
Symphoricarpos longiflorus (Fragrant Snowberry), 482
Symphoricarpos orbiculatus (Indian Currant, Snowberry, Coral-berry), 157, 481–482

Tabachín del Monte (*Caesalpinia mexicana*), 151–152
Tap-roots, 2, 30, 31–32, 34
Tasajillo (*Opuntia leptocaulis*), 103
Tassel-white (*Itea virginica*), 313–314
Taxodium distichum var. distichum (Bald Cypress, Sabino, Ahuehuete), 4, *8*, *9*, 12, 32, 379, 483–485. *See also color plates*

Taxodium mucronatum (Monteczuma Bald Cypress), 434, 484, 485
Tecoma stans (Yellow-bells), 145
Tecoma stans var. angustata (Esperanza, Yellow-bells), 334, 486–487
Tecoma stans var. stans, 487
Tenaza (*Pithecellobium pallens*), 406
Tepeguaje (*Leucaena pulverulenta*), 334
Tepozán (*Buddleia sessilflora*), 148
Texas, *xxxiv*, 5, 24, 28
Texas Adelia (*Forestiera acuminata*), 278–279
Texas Almond (*Prunus minutiflora*), 418
Texas Ash (*Fraxinus texensis*), 283, 285
Texas Azalea (*Rhododendron oblongifolium*), 441–442
Texas Barberry (*Berberis swayseii*), 137, 138, 139
Texas Betony (*Stachys coccinea*), 157, 482
Texas Buckeye (*Aesculus glabra var. arguta*), 22, 36, 93
Texas Clematis (*Clematis texensis*), 213, 214
Texas Ebony (*Pithecellobium flexicaule*), 30, 261, 404–406
Texas Elbow-bush (*Forestiera pubescens*), 278, 279
Texas Honeysuckle (*Rhododendron prinophyllum*), 441, 442
Texas Indigo Bush (*Amorpha roemeriana*), 109
Texas Kidney-wood (*Eysenhardtia texana*), 267–269
Texas Lantana (*Lantana horrida*), 117, 324–326
Texas Mahonia (*Berberis swayseii*), 137, 138, 139
Texas mock-orange (*Philadelphus texensis*), 396
Texas Mountain Laurel (*Sophora secundiflora*), 9, 21–22, 76, 129, 147, 242, 403, 473–475. *See also color plates*
Texas Palmetto (*Sabal mexicana*), 30, 451–452, 453
Texas Palo Verde (*Cercidium texanum*), 189–191
Texas Palo Verde (*Parkinsonia texana var. texanum*), 190
Texas Persimmon (*Diospyros texana*), 10, 30, 103, 251, 252–254
Texas Pistachio (*Pistacia texana*), 6, 58, 129, 401–403
Texas Ranger (*Leucophyllum*), 6, 37, 154, 335–340, 391
Texas Ranger (*Leucophyllum frutescens*), 37, 76, 129, 135, 147, 249, 336, 337, 338, 339–340, 383, 458, 515. *See also color plates*
Texas Redbud (*Cercis canadensis var. texensis*), 194, 196
Texas Red Oak (*Quercus buckleyi*), 6, 427, 429, 431, 435
Texas Sacahuiste (*Nolina texana*), 377. *See also color plates*
Texas Silver-leaf (*Leucophyllum frutescens*), 37, 76, 129, 135, 147, 249, 336, 337, 338, 339–340, 383, 458, 515. *See also color plates*
Texas Snowbell (*Styrax texana*), 480
Texas Sotol (*Dasylirion texanum*), 250
Texas Star Hibiscus (*Hibiscus coccineus*), 304
Texas Torchwood (*Amyris texana*), 112, 113, 114
Thompson Yucca (*Yucca thompsoniana*), 517
Thorn-crested Agave (*Agave lophantha*), 98
Threatened plants, 5–6, 59
Thundercloud (Violet Silverleaf), 336, 339
Tilia americana (American Basswood), 489
Tilia caroliniana (Carolina Basswood), 488–489
Tiliaceae (Basswood family), 488–489
Tipton, Jimmy, 194
Tipton Flame (Mexican Redbud), 194
Tiquilia greggii (Plume Tiquilia, Hierba del Cenizo, Oreja del Perro), 6, 490–491
Tissue culture, 1
Tomatillo (*Lycium*), 352–353
Tomatillo (*Lycium berlandieri var. berlandieri*), 352, 353, 519
Torchwood (*Amyris*), 112–114
Tornillo (*Prosopis pubescens*), 414

Torrey, John, 403
Torrey Yucca (*Yucca torreyi*), 518
Tracy, Sue, 276
Transplantation: of cuttings, 58; and plant choice, 59, 62; and roots, 59, 62–63, 64; of seedlings, 36; of shrubs from field, *60*; and site preparation, 64–65; tools and procedures for, 62–64; of trees in field, *61*. *See also specific plants*
Traveler ™ (Texas Redbud), 194
Trident Red Maple (*Acer rubrum var. trilobum*), 86
Tropical Sage (*Salvia coccinea*), 161, 364, 459
True Mountain Mahogany (*Cercocarpus montanus*), 199
Trumpet-creeper (*Campsis radicans*), 158–159. *See also color plates*
Trumpet-creeper family (*Bignoniaceae*), 142–143, 158–159, 174–175, 200–203, 486–487
Tubercled Saltbush (*Atriplex acanthocarpa*), 129
Tulipan del Monte (*Hibiscus cardiophyllus*), 303, 304, 391
Tulip Poplar (*Liriodendron tulipfera*), 347–348
Tulip-tree (*Liriodendron tulipfera*), 347–348
Tupelo (*Nyssa*), 378–379
Turk's Cap (*Malvaviscus arboreus var. drummondii*), 38, 92, 161, 362–364, 459, 517–518
Twisted Acacia (*Acacia schaffneri var. bravoensis*), 74, 77–78
Twisted-leaf Yucca (*Yucca rupicola*), 514, 517–518
Two-leaved Senna (*Cassia roemeriana*), 169
Two-winged Silverbell (*Halesia diptera*), 295–296

Ulmaceae (Elm family), 181–183, 492–494
Ulmus (Elm, Olmo), 14, 492–494
Ulmus alata (Winged Elm), 493
Ulmus americana (American Elm), 493–494
Ulmus crassifolia (Cedar Elm, Olmo), 493, 494
Ulmus rubra (Slippery Elm), 494
Uña de Gato (*Acacia greggii*), 73, 77, 78
Uña de Gato (*Acacia wrightii*), 32, 73, 77, 78
Uña de Gato (*Mimosa*), 367–369
Uña de Gato (*Mimosa biuncifera*), 368
Ungnadia speciosa (Mexican Buckeye, Mona, Monilla), 12, 22, 439, 495–496. *See also color plates*
Urban landscapes, and development, xxii–xxiii
Utah Service-berry (*Amelanchier utahensis*), 106
Uva (*Vitis*), 7, 12–13, 509–512

Vaccinium (Blueberry, Farkleberry), 497–499
Vaccinium arboreum (Farkleberry, Sparkleberry), 498
Vaccinium arkansanum (Highbush Blueberry), 498–499
Vaccinium virgatum (Rabbit-eye Blueberry), 499
Vara Dulce (*Aloysia macrostachya*), 103
Vara Dulce (*Eysenhardtia texana*), 267–269
Vasey Oak (*Quercus pungens var. vaseyana*), 434
Vasey's Adelia (*Adelia vaseyi*), 88–89
Vauquelinia angustifolia (Chisos Rosewood, Palo Prieto), 500–501
Veiny-leaf Lantana (*Lantana macropoda*), 326
Velvet Ash (*Fraxinus veluntina*), 285
Velvet-pod Mimosa (*Mimosa dysocarpa*), 369
Verbena (Verbena), 391
Verbena bipinatifida (Verbena), 458
Verbenaceae (Verbena family), 101–103, 144–145, 155–157, 210–211, 324–326
Verticillum, 192
Viburnum (Viburnum, Arrow-wood), 26, 502–505
Viburnum acerifolium (Maple-leaf Viburnum), 504–505
Viburnum dentatum (Southern Arrow-wood), 505

Viburnum Hawthorn (*Crataegus viburnifolia*), 239
Viburnum nudum (Possom-haw Viburnum), 505
Viburnum rufidulum (Rusty Black-haw Viburnum), *9*, 26, 52–53, 482, 503–504, 505. *See also color plates*
Viguiera stenoloba (Skelton-leaf Golden-eye Daisy, Resin-bush), *8*, 145, 147, 458, 491, 506–508. *See also color plates*
Vines, Robert, 452
Violet Silverleaf (*Leucophyllum candidum*), 336, 339
Virgin-bower (*Clematis*), 7, 212–214
Virgin-bower (*Clematis drummondii*), 212, 213
Virginia Creeper (*Parthenocissus quinquefolia*), 38, 388–389
Virginia Sweet-spire (*Itea virginica*), 313–314
Viscid Acacia (*Acacia neovernicosa*), 74, 76
Vitaceae (Grape family), 110–111, 388–389, 509–512
Vitis (Grape, Uva), 7, 12–13, 509–512
Vitis acerifolia (Panhandle Grape), 511
Vitis aestivalis (Pigeon Grape), 511
Vitis arizonica (Canyon Grape), 511
Vitis berlandiera (Spanish Grape), 511
Vitis cinerea (Sweet Grape), 511
Vitis cordifolia (Frost Grape), 511
Vitis monticola (Sweet Mountain Grape), 511
Vitis mustangensis (Mustang Grape), 511
Vitis palmata (Missouri Grape, Catbird Grape), 511
Vitis riparia (Riverbank Grape), 511
Vitis rotundifolia (Muscadine, Scuppernog), 510, 512
Vitis vulpina (Fox Grape), 512

Wafer-ash (*Ptelea trifoliolata*), 420–421
Walnut (*Juglans*), 6, 10–11, 14, 22, 315–317
Walnut family (*Juglandaceae*), 164–166, 314–317
Wand Butterfly-bush (*Buddleia racemosa*), 148
Warm stratification, 26–27
Warren Jones ™ (Desert Willow), 203
Washington (American Elm), 493
Water Ash (*Fraxinus caroliniana*), 284
Water Hickory (*Carya aquatica*), 166
Water loss, 55–56
Water Oak (*Quercus nigra*), 433
Water supply, xxii, xxv, 2, 22
Water Tupelo (*Nyssa aquatica*), 378, 379
Wax-myrtle (*Myrica cerifera*), 372–374
Wax-myrtle family (*Myricaceae*), 372–374
Weather trends, 2, 5, 6, 17, 22, 43
Weeping Juniper (*Juniperus flaccida*), 319, 321
Western Hop-hornbeam (*Ostrya knowltonii*), 381
Western Mesquite (*Prosopis glandulosa var. torreyana*), 414
Western Sycamore (*Platanus occidentalis var. glabrata*), 408
Western Yellow Pine (*Pinus ponderosa*), 398, 400
West Indian Lantana (*Lantana camara*), 325
Whitcomb "Root-maker" ™ pots, 32, 194, 201, 333
White Alder (*Clethra alnifolia*), 215–216
White Alder family (*Clethraceae*), 215–216
White American Beauty-berry (*Callicarpa americana var. lactea*), 157
White Ash (*Fraxinus americana*), 283–284, 285
White Brush (*Aloysia*), 101–103
White Brush (*Aloysia gratissima*), 102–103
White Bush Honeysuckle (*Lonicera albiflora var. albiflora*), 350
White Cloud (Cenizo), 336, 340
White Oak (*Quercus alba*), 429, 430
White Storm (Desert Willow), 203
Whitethorn Acacia (*Acacia constricta*), 74, 76
Wild Black Cherry (*Prunus serotina var. serotina*), 417, 418–419
Wild Honeysuckle (*Rhododendron*), 440–442
Wildlife, and seed collection, 5, 10
Wild Olive (*Cordia boisseri*), 30, 221–223. *See also color plates*

Wild Privet (*Forestiera*), 30, 42, 277–279
Will, Robbi, 193
Williams, Lisa, 222
Willow (*Salix*), 14, 39, 51
Willow family (*Salicaceae*), 409–411, 454–455
Willow Oak (*Quercus phellos*), 433
Willow Rooting Substance (WRS), 51
Winged Elm (*Ulmus alata*), 493
Winterfat (*Ceratoides lanata*), 186–188
Wislizeni Senna (*Cassia wislizenii*), 167–169
Witch-hazel (*Hamamelis virginiana*), 11, 297–299
Witch-hazel family (*Hamamelidaceae*), 297–299, 345–346
Witch's broom, 182
Wolfberry (*Lycium*), 352–353
Woolly Butterfly-bush (*Buddleia*), 146–148
Woolly Butterfly-bush (*Buddleia marrubifolia*), 147, 148. *See also color plates*
Woolly Pyramid Bush (*Melochia tomentosa*), 365–366
Worrell, Bill, 410
Wounding, 51
Wright's Acacia (*Acacia wrightii*), 32, 73, 77, 78
Wright's Mist Flower (*Eupatorium wrightii*), 266
Wright's Silk Tassel (*Garrya wrightii*), 242, 289
WRS (Willow Rooting Substance), 51

Yaupon Holly (*Ilex vomitoria*), 309, 312, 344, 439
Yellow-bells (*Tecoma stans*), 145
Yellow-bells (*Tecoma stans var. angustata*), 334, 486–487
Yellow Sophora (*Sophora tomentosa var. occidentalis*), 475
Yew-leaf Willow (*Salix taxifolia*), 455
Yucca (Yucca, Spanish-Bayonet), 135, 458, 513–518
Yucca angustifolia (Narrow-leaf Yucca), 515
Yucca arkansana (Arkansas Yucca), 514, 515
Yucca baccata (Datil Yucca, Banana Yucca), 515–516
Yucca carnerosana (Carneros Yucca), 516–517
Yucca constricta (Buckley Yucca), 516
Yucca elata (Soaptree Yucca, Palmilla), 516
Yucca faxoniana (Giant Dagger, Palma, Spanish Dagger, Palmilla, Palma Barreta, Palma Samandoca), 516–517
Yucca pallida (Pale-leaf Yucca), 514, 517
Yucca rostrata (Beaked Yucca, Big Bend Yucca, Palmita, Soyate), 517
Yucca rupicola (Twisted-leaf Yucca), 514, 517–518
Yucca thompsoniana (Thompson Yucca), 517
Yucca torreyi (Torrey Yucca), 518
Yucca treculeana (Old Shag, Spanish Bayonet, Spanish Dagger, Palma), 518

Zanthoxylum fagara (Lime Prickly-ash, Colima), 519–520
Zarza (*Mimosa pigra*), 369
Zexmenia hispida (Zexmenia Daisy), 147, 521–522
Zorillo (*Choisya dumosa*), 206–207
Zygophyllaceae (Caltrop family), 292–294, 327–329